CAUGHT IN THE MIDDLE EAST

CAUGHT IN THE MIDDLE EAST

U.S. Policy toward the Arab-Israeli Conflict, 1945–1961

PETER L. HAHN

The University of North Carolina Press
Chapel Hill and London

Set in Minion by Tseng Information Systems, Inc.
Manufactured in the United States of America

Some portions of this book appeared,
in slightly different form, in "The View from Jerusalem:
Revelations about U.S. Diplomacy from the Archives of Israel,"
Diplomatic History 22, no. 4 (Fall 1998): 509–32,
and in
"Alignment by Coincidence: Israel, the United States,
and the Partition of Jerusalem, 1949–1953,"
International History Review 21, no. 3 (Sept. 1999): 665–89.

☉ The paper in this book meets the guidelines for permanence
and durability of the Committee on Production Guidelines
for Book Longevity of the Council on Library Resources.

Library of Congress Cataloging-in-Publication Data
Hahn, Peter L.
Caught in the Middle East: U.S. policy toward the Arab-Israeli
conflict, 1945–1961 / Peter L. Hahn.
p. cm.
Includes bibliographical references and index.
ISBN 0-8078-2840-8 (cloth: alk. paper)
1. Arab-Israeli conflict—Diplomatic history.   2. Arab-Israeli
conflict—Peace.   3. United States—Foreign relations—
1945–1989.   I. Title.
DS119.7 .H335   2004
956.04—dc22
2003017454

08 07 06 05 04   5 4 3 2 1

For my father,

Alvin C. Hahn

and my mother,

Mary Jane Hahn

CONTENTS

MAPS

ACKNOWLEDGMENTS

I am grateful to several institutions that provided generous financial assistance for the research and writing of this book. The J. William Fulbright Foreign Scholarship Board underwrote a lengthy research experience in the Israeli archives. The National Endowment for the Humanities provided two summer stipends that enabled me to write several chapters of this study. Ohio State University supported this project on many levels. The College of Humanities and the Department of History granted research funds for travel to U.S. and British archives and sabbaticals for writing. The Melton Center for Jewish Studies, the Middle East Studies Center, and the Center for Labor Research underwrote several research ventures to Israel. The Mershon Center for the Study of International Security and Public Policy supported my study of Hebrew, an essential part of my research plan. The College of Humanities, the Department of History, and the Melton Center provided a subvention that facilitated the publication of this book. To those who provided and distributed these funds, I am thankful.

Archivists at several repositories eased the challenge of conducting research for this book. In the United States, I benefited from the kind assistance of Kathy Nicastro, J. Dane Hartgrove, and Wilbert B. Mahoney at the National Archives; Dennis Bilger at the Harry S. Truman Library; and Dr. James Leyerzapf at the Dwight D. Eisenhower Library. In Israel, I received notable help from Gilad Livne, Ronit Cohen, and Galia Baron at the Israel State Archive; from Dr. Tuvia Friling and Hana Pinshow at the David Ben-Gurion Library; and from the staff of the Central Zionist Archives. I appreciated the service of Dorit Sarig and Tammy Yannai as my research assistants in Sde Boqer and Jerusalem.

I owe a word of thanks to several Hebrew teachers who taught me the language skills I needed to find the treasures hidden in the Israeli archives. Shaula Gurari, Professor Roger Kaplan, and Professor Reuben Ahroni offered expert instruction in a series of elementary, intermediate, and advanced courses at Ohio State University. A battery of instructors at the Rothberg International School of the Hebrew University of Jerusalem diligently shepherded me through an intensive *ulpan*. As I sorted through the thousands of photocopies of Israeli records that I carried back from Jerusalem, Milly Meckaiten, an Ohio State

University undergraduate student, served meritoriously as my tutor-translator. These gifted experts in Hebrew equipped me to add an important dimension of inquiry to this project.

I have been fortunate during the years I worked on this book to have the support and encouragement of a number of professional colleagues. Carole Fink read the entire manuscript more than once and graciously offered wise counsel and insight. I have also been fortunate to work with the talented and resourceful staff of the University of North Carolina Press, including Charles Grench, Pamela Upton, Amanda McMillan, Kathleen Ketterman, and Ellen Goldlust-Gingrich. Robert J. McMahon and another, anonymous referee recruited by the press made countless helpful suggestions on improving this work. I benefited from formal and informal discussions of my research with such fellow scholars as Nathan J. Citino, Avner Cohen, Michael J. Cohen, Matthew Davis, Brian Etheridge, Zvi Ganin, Galia Golan, Mary Ann Heiss, Rashid Khalidi, David Lesch, Douglas Little, Michelle Mart, Benny Morris, Michael Oren, Zaki Shalom, Avi Shlaim, Amy Staples, David Tal, William O. Walker, and Salim Yaqub. In addition to sharing their scholarly expertise, Yaacov Bar-Siman-Tov, Uri Bialer, Shlomo Slonim, and Ronald Zweig offered professional support and warm hospitality to my family and me during my research fellowships in Jerusalem, for which I remain thankful. I am grateful to my current graduate students, Susan Dawson, Matthew Masur, Robert Robinson, Yuji Tosaka, John Tully, Dustin Walcher, and Jennifer Walton, whose research assistance and inquisitive minds fostered my work. I am indebted to my mentor, Melvyn P. Leffler, and my colleague, Michael J. Hogan, for their steadfast support of my professional development in the publication of this book and in many other ways.

I owe my greatest debt of gratitude to those individuals who mean the most to me. My wife and best friend, Cathy, has immeasurably contributed to the completion of this study by offering words of encouragement, patiently accepting my absences, and relocating our home to Jerusalem during my Fulbright fellowship. Our children—Anna Jane, Benjamin, Paul, and Mark—have grown up as this project has grown old. I am proud of their accomplishments, and I thrive on the joy they bring to life.

Finally, I acknowledge the love and support of my parents, Mary Jane Hahn and Alvin C. Hahn. All my life, they have taught me by exhortation and example, sacrificed for my security and education, provided me sustenance for body and soul. No one could ask for finer parents. In grateful recognition of their selflessness and guidance, I dedicate this book to them.

Columbus, Ohio
June 2003

ABBREVIATIONS

AACOI	Anglo-American Committee of Inquiry
CIA	Central Intelligence Agency
DMZ	Demilitarized Zone
ESM	Economic Survey Mission
FY	Fiscal Year
IDF	Israel Defense Forces
IO	Bureau of International Organization Affairs
IPC	Iraq Petroleum Company
JCS	Joint Chiefs of Staff
JVP	Jordan Valley Plan
MAC	Mixed Armistice Commission
MEC	Middle East Command
MEDO	Middle East Defense Organization
NATO	North Atlantic Treaty Organization
NE	Division of Near Eastern Affairs (1944–49); Office of Near Eastern Affairs (thereafter)
NEA	Division of Near Eastern Affairs (to 1944); Office of Near Eastern and African Affairs (1944–49); Bureau of Near Eastern, South Asian, and African Affairs (thereafter)
NSC	National Security Council
PCC	Palestine Conciliation Commission
TVA	Tennessee Valley Authority
UAR	United Arab Republic
UNEF	United Nations Emergency Force
UNRWA	United Nations Relief and Works Agency for Palestine Refugees in the Near East
UNSCOP	United Nations Special Committee on Palestine
UNTC	United Nations Trusteeship Council
UNTSO	United Nations Truce Supervisory Organization

CAUGHT IN THE MIDDLE EAST

INTRODUCTION

Because of the Cold War, the United States became deeply involved in the Middle East after 1945. Committed to containing communism around the globe, the Harry S. Truman and Dwight D. Eisenhower administrations strove to maintain access to petroleum resources, military bases, and lines of communication in the Middle East and to deny these assets to the Soviet Union. Under these two presidents, the United States also sought to promote peace in the region, to sustain governments supportive of Western political objectives, and to maintain a liberal economic system conducive to U.S. commercial interests. In short, U.S. officials sought stability in the Middle East on behalf of their objectives in the region and around the world. Stability in the region, these leaders assumed, would help them safeguard their vital interests and prevail in the Cold War. Conversely, they feared that instability would open the region to Soviet influence, ruin indigenous goodwill toward the West, and possibly spark another world war.

The Arab-Israeli conflict directly threatened Middle East stability in the late 1940s and 1950s. Unrelenting antagonism triggered two wars and numerous skirmishes. Peace proved elusive as leaders on both sides expressed a preference for conflict over compromise. Israel refused to repatriate Arab Palestinian refugees, who became a political cause for the leaders of Arab states. Restrictions on trade and shipping and disagreements about territorial boundaries and waterways embittered all of the protagonists. The conflict destabilized the Middle East and thereby imperiled U.S. vital interests.

This book analyzes U.S. policy toward the Arab-Israeli conflict from 1945 to 1961. To stabilize the Middle East, U.S. officials sought in principle to resolve the conflict. They worked to avert Arab-Israeli hostilities and to end the wars that erupted in 1948 and 1956. In the interim, the U.S. government tried to negotiate permanent peace settlements among the belligerents and resolved to settle specific controversies regarding borders, the treatment of Palestinian refugees, Israeli access to Arab waterways, the dispensation of Jordan River water, and the status of Jerusalem. In short, U.S. officials wished to end the Arab-Israeli conflict before it damaged American interests.

Despite the importance of Arab-Israeli peace to regional stability, however, U.S. officials subsumed their peacemaking to other Cold War interests. The U.S. government tempered its dedication to conflict resolution with a determination to deny the Soviets any opportunity to gain political influence in the Middle East. The United States refrained from imposing stringent peace terms on either side and eventually even tolerated the conflict in an effort to safeguard the country's relationships with Middle East states and to steer them away from Moscow. The United States prioritized anti-Soviet containment over Arab-Israeli settlement, preferring a region in conflict under U.S. hegemony to a region at peace under Soviet influence.

In the end, the United States failed to resolve the overall Arab-Israeli conflict or any of its specific disputes. Failure resulted in part from the deep reluctance of the Arab states and Israel to make concessions or compromises but also resulted from the United States' self-imposed restraints on peacemaking, which undermined its moral and political credibility in the eyes of local states. U.S. peace initiatives occasionally deepened the conflict by aggravating the passions of the principals and accentuating their disagreements. Despite U.S. efforts to resolve the conflict, peace remained elusive.

While confronting this peacemaking conundrum, the United States became inextricably involved in the Middle East. As they resisted communism worldwide, U.S. leaders assigned increasing strategic and political importance to the Middle East. They gradually assumed the duty of defending Western interests there, even at the risk of war against the Soviet Union or a local state. In short, the Cold War compelled the United States to make deep and enduring commitments to regional security. By 1961, the United States found itself caught in the Middle East, unable to escape the responsibilities that American leaders had assumed.

The United States also became caught in the middle of the Arab-Israeli conflict. U.S. officials felt compelled by their global containment policy to intercede in the Arab-Israeli conflict and to preserve sound relations with all sides of the dispute. Operating within the limits set by U.S. anti-Soviet policy, however, American officials proved unable to accomplish a peace settlement and in the process of trying strained relations with both sides. Snared in the middle of a nasty fight, the United States found it impossible to arbitrate a settlement or to avoid the combatants' resentment.

The United States remained trapped in the middle of the Arab-Israeli conflict because American policy emanated from two distinct and conflicting perspectives. One impulse took root in the State and Defense Departments. Driven by such national security concerns as containment, access to military bases, and preservation of oil sources, adherents to this approach advocated close relations with Arab states. The second impulse centered on the White House staff and Congress. Reflecting such domestic concerns as electoral politics, public opinion, and cultural values, proponents of this position favored close relations with Israel. As U.S. policy regarding the Arab-Israeli situation evolved, these competing impulses struggled for the president's mind.

Competition between the national security and domestic impulses significantly shaped U.S. policy toward the Arab-Israeli conflict. This competition frequently resulted in U.S. policies that were compromises between the pro-Israel and pro-Arab perspectives, a tendency that rendered the United States unable to side with one antagonist over the other or to find a solution to the conflict that both sides would accept.

Between 1945 and 1961, Presidents Truman and Eisenhower laid the foundations of a U.S. Middle Eastern policy that endured for decades. To apply anticommunist containment doctrine to the Middle East, these presidents accepted responsibilities for the stability and security of the region that lasted beyond the end of the Cold War. Truman's and Eisenhower's involvement in the Arab-Israeli conflict began an enduring U.S. effort to make peace in the region. By 1961, the United States had developed a policy of supporting conservative regimes and resisting radical revolutions in the Middle East, a policy that persisted —in that and other regions of the Third World—until the twenty-first century. This examination of the Truman-Eisenhower era thus clarifies the foundations of long-term U.S. policy in the Middle East.

This book analyzes U.S. policy toward the Arab-Israeli conflict, developing several important themes. First, distinctions exist between the policy making of Truman and that of Eisenhower. An unsteady president distracted by momentous developments around the world, Truman usually made decisions about the Middle East in reaction to events there. Consequently, his policy often appeared ambivalent and inconsistent. In contrast, Eisenhower, who became president when Cold War tensions had stabilized, devoted personal attention to the Middle East, proactively made policy, and showed more consistency. Despite such differences, these two presidents shared a determination to privilege Cold War security concerns over peacemaking ventures, and both dealt relatively evenly with Israel and the Arab states.

Second, this book examines the domestic political context in which U.S. officials made foreign policy, assessing the prodigious lobbying on behalf of Israel by U.S. citizens, members of Congress, and private interest groups and, where possible, measuring Israel's influence in mobilizing such support. Because the lobbying often conflicted with what officials in the State and Defense Departments defined as national interests, those officials resented and resisted the pressure. This study elucidates how the diplomats balanced their foreign policy aims with domestic political restraints.

The evolution of U.S.-Israeli relations forms a third theme of this study. Many scholars describe the U.S.-Israeli relationship as "special" because of instances of U.S. support for Israel and because of the deep sympathy for Israel in

U.S. public opinion.[1] While acknowledging such special ties, this book stresses that disagreements on security-related issues involving the Arab states generated friction and acrimony in the official relationship. In this sense, this work offers an important corrective to the special-relationship thesis.

Although not a work of Israeli history per se, my analysis speaks indirectly to a controversy among scholars of Israeli relations with the Arab states. For decades, the prevailing body of scholarship sympathetically portrayed Israel's foreign policy as defensive, justified, reasonable, and wise.[2] This "orthodox" school came under sharp attack in the late 1980s when a younger generation of Israeli scholars, called the revisionist or "new" historians, critically evaluated Israeli diplomacy as provocative if not aggressive, unjustified in its treatment of Palestinians, and regrettable.[3] Publication of revisionist scholarship provoked intense resistance from defenders of the orthodox school as well as an impassioned debate among scholars and citizens in Israel and elsewhere.[4] Although not intended to be revisionist history, this book does not refrain from discussing aspects of Israeli history that the orthodox school has either denied or glossed over.

A fourth theme of this book is U.S. relations with the Arab states that most directly challenged Israel—Egypt, Jordan, Syria, Lebanon, Iraq, and Saudi Arabia.[5] Conflict with Israel fueled the growth of Arab nationalism, which spawned revolutionary unrest in several states, radicalized significant Arab constituencies, threatened Western economic interests, and encouraged neutralism in the Cold War. The United States sought to preserve conservative Arab regimes and to stem the growth of Arab nationalism while avoiding what U.S. officials considered the unfathomable step of completely abandoning Israel. This volume assesses the U.S. effort to reach these goals in the Arab world.

U.S.-Arab relations evolved in a context of great dynamism in intra-Arab relationships. Between 1945 and 1961, tension developed as Arab powers expressed a desire for transnational unity but engaged in political conflicts. The Arab League, founded in 1944–45 to promote pan-Arab solidarity, declined in importance by the early 1950s. In its place, Bruce Maddy-Weitzman explains, Arab national leaders built a regional balance of power marked by "loosely structured, shifting coalitions derived from temporarily shared interests." Although the Arab states shared such ideologies as pan-Arab unity, revolutionary socialism, and anticolonialism, Malcolm Kerr suggests that by the late 1950s these countries engaged in "a dreary and inconclusive cold war" among themselves that overshadowed their relationships with the United States, the Soviet Union, and Israel. This book evaluates U.S.-Arab relations in the context of this intra-Arab cold war.[6]

Finally, this work analyzes the influence of the Anglo-U.S. relationship on U.S. policy toward the Arab-Israeli conflict. The United States considered Britain its closest ally in the Cold War, but U.S. and British views toward the Arab-Israeli controversy often conflicted. Moreover, the 1945–61 period witnessed the sharp decline of the British Empire and the rise of the United States as a global power. This book elucidates the manner in which U.S. officials resolved inconsistencies between the demands of the Atlantic alliance and American national objectives in the Middle East at a time when the relative power of the United States and Britain reversed.[7]

This book, in short, analyzes the evolution of U.S. policy toward the Arab-Israeli dispute during the first two presidential administrations after World War II. The volume assesses how U.S. officials approached the regional conflict and why they implemented certain policies toward it and explains the making of U.S. policy in its global, regional, and binational dimensions. While focused mainly on diplomatic and security issues, this work also addresses the domestic political and cultural dimensions of U.S. policy, explaining why the United States failed to resolve the Arab-Israeli conflict and assessing this failure's impact on American interests in the Middle East and elsewhere.

The book is organized in such a way as to draw attention to several facets of U.S. policy during this era. Part I summarizes the pre-1945 origins of the Arab-Zionist controversy and U.S. involvement in it (chapter 1) and examines the Truman administration's approach to Palestine through 1949 in the context of U.S. global concerns during the early Cold War (chapters 2–4). These chapters aim for brevity since much of the literature on U.S. policy toward Palestine has concentrated on the years preceding Israeli independence in 1948.

Part II examines Truman's policy in 1949–53, when the president made several momentous decisions regarding the Arab-Israeli conflict (and a period that has received much less scholarly attention than the preceding four years). Chapter 5 assesses regional and global concerns that shaped Truman's thinking about the Arab-Israeli conflict, and chapters 6–9 study the development of the president's policy regarding such points of controversy as borders, refugees, and Jerusalem, among others. Chapter 10 evaluates the impact of the conflict on U.S. relations with Israel and the Arab states.

Part III analyzes Eisenhower's policy during his first administration. Chapter 11 examines the regional context of U.S. policy in the mid-1950s, and chapters 12–14 evaluate Eisenhower's efforts to resolve specific Arab-Israeli disputes and to negotiate a comprehensive peace settlement. U.S. policy during and after the 1956–57 Suez-Sinai War forms the subject of chapters 15 and 16.

Part IV analyzes the late Eisenhower period. Chapters 17–19 establish the regional context of U.S. policy and evaluate the president's policy toward specific Arab-Israeli disputes and crises. Chapter 20 evaluates the evolution of U.S. relations with Israel and the Arab states during the Eisenhower years.

While preparing this book, I aspired to honor the noble ideal among diplomatic historians of conducting research in multiple archives and in multiple countries. Within the United States, I examined the papers of Truman and Eisenhower as well as the records of the State Department, the Pentagon, the National Security Council, the Central Intelligence Agency, and various individual diplomats. Consulting such a wide range of sources proved invaluable, revealing how key officials balanced domestic concerns against overseas goals, diplomatic objectives against security imperatives, and bureaucratic ambitions against the national interest. I also conducted extensive research in the archives of Israel (most of which are in Hebrew) and Britain. These records revealed the foreign wellsprings of U.S. diplomacy, the overseas impact of that diplomacy, and other features of U.S. policy that remain shrouded in U.S. archives. (No official records of the Arab states were available when I conducted research for this book.) I hope that such research gives this book distinctive breadth and depth.[8]

It is difficult to write about the Arab-Israeli conflict because the subject remains controversial. Not merely an academic, historical issue, it continues to generate passionate debate among citizens and scholars who identify with one side or the other in the current conflict. In writing this book, I have attempted to remain impartial, agreeing with Mark Tessler that the conflict "is not a struggle between good and evil but rather a controversy between two peoples who deserve recognition and respect, neither of whom has a monopoly on behavior that is either praiseworthy or condemnable."[9] In short, this book seeks to empathize with all sides to the Arab-Israeli dispute but to sympathize with none.

Part I

1

GENESIS
The Palestine Conflict to 1945

The Arab-Israeli conflict that emerged after World War II originated in ideological, political, and military developments of preceding decades. When Ottoman authority collapsed during World War I, Britain assumed control of Palestine as a mandate under the League of Nations. The Jews and Arabs of the
territory sought political independence, coming into conflict with each other
and with Britain. World War II undermined Britain's ability to govern the mandate and encouraged the Jews and Arabs to fulfill their aspirations through diplomacy and force. Traditionally isolated from the politics of the Middle East,
U.S. officials became involved in this dispute as President Franklin D. Roosevelt
balanced his personal and political interests against the demands of the Anglo-
U.S. wartime alliance.

A brief clarification of terms in is order. Britain called its mandate "Palestine," derived from the Roman name given the land in A.D. 135. During the mandate, the area's residents—Arab and Jewish—considered themselves "Palestinians." "Israel," the name adopted by the Jewish state in 1948, borrowed from the
ancient "Eretz Yisrael" (the Land of Israel), which Anita Shapira calls "a holy
term, vague as far as exact boundaries of the territory are concerned but clearly
defining ownership."[1] After declaring independence on 15 May 1948, Palestinian
Jews called themselves "Israelis." With the exception of a small number who
became citizens of Israel, most Arab Palestinians became refugees from Israel,
identified themselves as Palestinians, and called the land they aspired to control
"Palestine." For the sake of simplicity, this book refers to the Arab residents of
and refugees from Palestine as "Palestinians," the Jewish residents of mandatory
Palestine as "Jews," and the Jews of Israel as "Israelis."

The modern state of Jordan occupies territory that belonged to Britain's
original Palestine mandate. Britain established the territory of "Transjordan" on
the land east of the Jordan River, appointed Abdallah ibn-Hussein as its emir
in 1921, and granted Transjordan its independence in May 1946, when Abdal-

lah proclaimed the Hashemite Kingdom of Jordan. U.S. officials referred to the territory as "Transjordan" until June 1949, when the government in Amman convinced the Americans to use "Jordan." For convenience, this book refers to the territory as "Transjordan" before May 1946 and as "Jordan" thereafter.[2]

The Zionist-Arab Clash in Palestine to 1945

The modern Arab-Jewish conflict over Palestine originated as a clash of ideologies. Zionism, the dream of Jews to return to their ancient homeland, spawned waves of migration of European Jews to Palestine before World War I. Arab nationalism, by contrast, infused the indigenous inhabitants of Palestine with a burning desire to achieve political independence from foreign rule. To satisfy its imperial ambitions, Britain took responsibility for governing Palestine after World War I. Under Britain's watch, Zionists and Arab nationalists clashed, with intensifying violence, for control of Palestine.

Although its roots reached to antiquity, "Zionism" emerged as a term and as a political force in Europe in the late nineteenth century. Rising anti-Semitism in Europe, an emerging Jewish identity that transcended nation-state boundaries, and the political activism of Theodor Herzl and others gave birth to a political Zionism that aimed to reestablish a Jewish presence in Palestine. By 1914, some eighty-five thousand European Jews had migrated to Palestine and organized a *yishuv*, or Jewish community. Their Zionism, which Dan V. Segre defines as a "landless spiritual nationalism," contained the seeds of the state of Israel.[3]

The experience of settlement in Palestine transfigured the Jewish community. According to various scholars, the *yishuv* originally embraced the progressive ideals of social justice and human fraternity and eschewed political and military power. The environment confronting early settlers in Palestine, the spread of militant ideology among a generation of Jews born there, and the dramatic experience of the Holocaust, however, gave rise to an assertive ideology that rationalized political power, force, and domination over Palestinian Arabs.[4] Following the linguistic turn in Western academic writing, Nachman Ben-Yehuda and Yael Zerubavel suggest that Israel's founders exaggerated the heroic aspects of historical episodes to create a mythology that inspired Israelis to fight for their national existence.[5]

Chaim Weizmann and David Ben-Gurion emerged as the most important Zionist leaders of the pre-1945 period. Weizmann, a Russian-born chemist, served as president of the World Zionist Organization (1921–29) and of the Jewish Agency for Palestine (1929–31, 1935–46), in which positions he advanced Zionist goals through diplomacy in London. Ben-Gurion, a Polish-born Zionist who emigrated to Palestine in 1906, established the Labor Party of the Land of

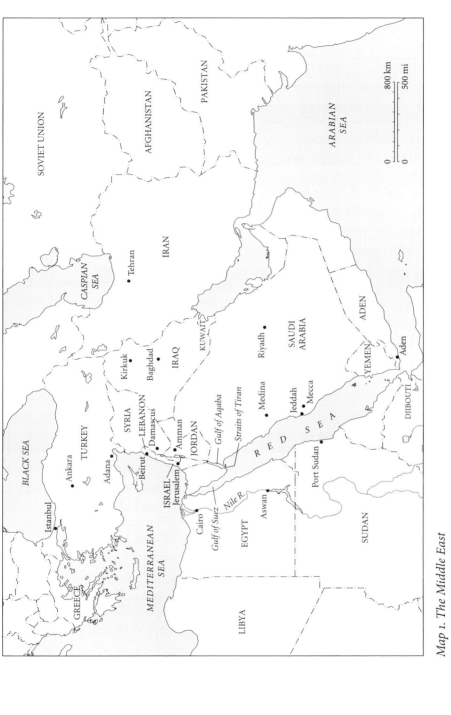

Map 1. The Middle East

Israel as the dominant political party among Palestinian Jews, served as chairman of the executive committee of the Jewish Agency, and otherwise laid the groundwork for Jewish statehood. The two men disagreed about the means to achieve statehood, and Ben-Gurion arranged Weizmann's 1946 ouster from the World Zionist Organization. But their parallel efforts proved complementary at advancing Zionist ambitions in Palestine.[6]

Modern Arab nationalism emerged after Napoleon's conquest of Egypt in 1798 shattered Arab people's complacency about their subject status under Ottoman rule. Nationalists promoted Islamic reform, territorial patriotism, and pan-Arab identification, Albert Hourani observes, to modernize their societies and escape foreign suppression. Communities in Egypt, Syria, and other Arabic-speaking areas developed a sense of common identity—what Benedict Anderson called "an imagined political community"—based on shared language, culture, and history. According to Rashid Khalidi, Palestinian nationalism blossomed in the early twentieth century as a result of an attachment to Jerusalem, cultural activities, local politics, the Arab Revolt of 1936–39, and opposition to Zionism.[7]

The seeds of the post–World War II clash between Zionism and Arab nationalism were planted before World War I. To a certain extent, the Zionist and Palestinian Arab communities established patterns of interaction in their daily lives, tried to align their political ambitions and intellectual outlooks, and even considered a partnership to advance their common aims in relation to European imperialism. Yet both communities gradually realized the incompatibility of their national aspirations. By 1914, members of each community predicted conflict between Palestine's 66,000 Jews and 570,000 Arabs.[8]

The Ottoman Empire's loss of control of Palestine and the British conquest of the region during World War I proved to be a catalyst for Arab-Zionist conflict because British statesmen made conflicting agreements and deals with the two sides. In the May 1916 Sykes-Picot agreement, Britain secured French recognition of a British sphere of influence in Palestine. In correspondence with the Hashemite Sharif Hussein of Mecca in 1915–16, the British high commissioner in Cairo, Henry McMahon, implicitly promised British support for Arab independence in Palestine and other areas in exchange for an Arab revolt against the Ottoman Empire. To serve certain domestic political and diplomatic objectives, Britain also pledged in the November 1917 Balfour Declaration to "view with favour the establishment in Palestine of a national home for the Jewish people." Preoccupied by the war in Europe, diplomats in London failed to reconcile these Middle East policies.[9]

Having issued these conflicting statements about the future of Palestine, Britain secured its hold on the land through war and diplomacy. The capture of Baghdad (March 1917) and that of Jerusalem (December 1917) put Britain in position to demand postwar control of Iraq and Palestine. In autumn 1918, Allied and Arab forces captured Damascus, where Britain allowed Hussein's son, Faisal, to establish a regime. In 1919–22, Britain secured mandates over Palestine and Iraq, established Transjordan as a separate territory, and recognized Abdallah (Faisal's brother) as its emir. Britain made Faisal, whom France deposed from Damascus, king of Iraq.[10]

Britain maintained a prominent position in several Arab states through the end of World War II. It signed a mutual-defense treaty with Iraq in 1930, established air bases in the country at Habbaniya and Shuaiba to protect oil fields and transit routes, officially recognized Iraqi independence in 1933, and bolstered the Iraqi monarchy against indigenous challengers. In Transjordan, Britain nurtured a close political relationship with Emir Abdallah, signed a series of mutual-defense treaties beginning in 1928, and appointed British officers to command the Arab Legion. After signing a mutual-defense treaty with Egypt in 1936, Britain developed a sprawling base complex in the Suez Canal Zone, which by 1945 contained extensive facilities and nearly eighty-four thousand British soldiers.[11]

In Palestine during the interwar years, British authorities presided over a situation of general stability punctuated by outbursts of violence. Britain preserved a rudimentary stability in the mandate by exercising political, police, and administrative powers. In 1922, it affirmed the right of Jews to reside in Palestine but limited Jewish immigration and pledged not to promote Jewish majority rule or statehood. In exchange for his cooperation, the British allowed the mufti of Jerusalem, Amin al-Husayni, to govern the Palestinian Arab community. Yet the stability of Palestine was repeatedly broken by Arab-Jewish violence. Hundreds of Jews and Palestinians died in hostilities in 1919–21, 1929, and 1933.[12]

Political tensions erupted in the Arab Revolt of 1936–39. A growing stream of Jewish immigrants to Palestine contributed to a large increase in the Jewish population, which numbered 66,000 (10 percent of the population) in 1920, 170,000 (17 percent) in 1929, and 400,000 (31 percent) in 1936. Convinced that such population changes challenged Palestinian political and economic interests, the Arabs resisted. In 1936, they organized a massive labor strike that triggered rioting and violence against Jews and British officials as well as reprisals by both groups against the Palestinians. British authorities forced al-Husayni into exile, arrested many Palestinian elites for insurrection, and considered partitioning Palestine into an Arab state and a Jewish state.[13]

In 1939, the threat of world war prompted Britain to formulate a Palestinian policy consistent with Arab interests. Despite the Arab revolt, Britain appeased Arab sensitivities to stabilize Palestine, redeploy its twenty thousand soldiers there, and protect its oil assets and military bases in Arab states. In the White Paper of 1939, Britain strictly limited Jewish immigration to seventy-five thousand persons over five years, scheduled such immigration to terminate in March 1944, and prohibited Jews from purchasing land outside Jewish settlements. Palestinian Arabs would gain gradual control of administrative offices and win statehood within ten years.[14]

A measure of wartime expediency, the White Paper of 1939 planted the seeds of serious postwar conflict. Jews denounced the document as an unethical and illegal sellout of their vital interests but also realized that they must support the British-led military coalition battling Nazi Germany for control of Europe. "We must help the [British] army as if there were no White Paper," Ben-Gurion aptly observed, "and we must fight the White Paper as if there were no war." The *yishuv* thus refrained from contesting British power in Palestine during the war and sent volunteers to fight in Europe under British command. Yet the Jewish community also routinely violated the White Paper by promoting illegal immigration, and the British responded by denying authorized immigration quotas.[15]

Britain's policy toward the Jews became untenable when the Middle East became secure from Nazi attack in 1943. Propartition sentiment revived within Prime Minister Winston Churchill's wartime cabinet, and increasing militancy among Palestine's Jews foreshadowed massive postwar resistance to the White Paper. Learning of the Holocaust, British officials realized that to terminate Jewish immigration in March 1944 would be impossible to justify to international public opinion. Churchill grew cold to the idea of helping the Jews, however, after Zionist extremists assassinated his friend, Minister of State Lord Moyne, in Cairo in 1944. Churchill did not change official policy toward Palestine before he departed the prime ministry in summer 1945.[16]

Despite the terms of the White Paper, the Arabs of Palestine did not thrive politically during World War II. The Palestinian elite remained divided, dispirited, and disorganized, and British bans on political activity before 1943 encouraged political passivity. The exiled Mufti al-Husayni arranged the assassination of his chief Palestinian rival, Fakhri Nashashibi, in Baghdad in 1941, met Adolf Hitler, and offered to collaborate with the Nazis to expel Britain from Palestine. British authorities tolerated al-Husayni but resolved to deny him power in Palestine.[17]

Surrounding Arab states also took an interest in Palestine. The Arab League devoted its founding conference in Alexandria in September–October 1944 to the issue and demanded that Britain honor the rights of Palestinians. In March 1945, the league called on Britain to fulfill its pledges to establish a Palestinian state. Saudi Arabia, Iraq, Syria, Lebanon, and Egypt warned of dire consequences to any power that helped establish a Jewish state in Palestine. By 1945, several Arab regimes based their popular support on vigilance in pushing for Palestinian interests. Britain's inability to broker an internal solution to the Palestine conflict set the stage for the emergence of international conflict after 1945.[18]

Origins of U.S. Involvement in Palestine

Before World War II, U.S. diplomats paid little attention to the Middle East in general and to Palestine in particular. By the 1930s, some U.S. citizens had begun to press President Roosevelt to endorse Zionism. During World War II, however, government officials identified national security reasons for endorsing Britain's anti-Zionist policy. As Roosevelt tried to balance domestic political and diplomatic interests, his policy toward Palestine became unclear and inconsistent.

Prior to 1940, U.S. officials counted few political interests in the Middle East. The American government took episodic interest in protecting the fortunes of U.S. merchants and missionaries and passively promoted anticolonialism but refrained from challenging Anglo-French hegemony in the region. U.S. presidents occasionally endorsed Zionism to serve their domestic political interests but never seriously challenged Britain's policy, especially after the start of World War II. Although "deeply concerned" by the White Paper of 1939, Roosevelt told the leader of the Zionist Organization of America, Rabbi Stephen S. Wise, that "in the present light of things it is terribly difficult" to protest the document. In June 1941, Roosevelt encouraged Jewish leaders to trust Britain to defend Palestine's Jews.[19]

Despite Roosevelt's detachment, many U.S. citizens embraced Zionism in the 1930s and early 1940s. The U.S. Jewish community initially was non-Zionist and passive on diplomatic issues. Counting only sixty-five thousand members in 1933, U.S. Zionist groups foresaw immigration to Palestine as a long-term quest under British direction and viewed statehood as a distant dream. Sharing Roosevelt's view that Zionism might damage security interests, Rabbi Wise promoted a moderate version of Zionism favoring polite lobbying and philanthropy. Militant Zionists, under the intellectual influence of Ze'ev Jabotinsky, made little headway in capturing U.S. Jewish opinion before World War II.[20]

Stimulated by the plight of European Jewry, however, a more activist Zionist lobby took shape during the war. Encouraged by Ben-Gurion, activists led by Rabbi Abba Hillel Silver secured a resolution from a Zionist convention in 1942 that demanded immediate termination of the British mandate and establishment of a Jewish state in Palestine between the Mediterranean and the Jordan River. Rejecting Wise's gradualism, Silver founded the American Zionist Emergency Council, which organized vigorous, grassroots lobbying campaigns to convince Congress and other public and civic institutions to endorse a Jewish state. The membership of American Zionist organizations soared to more than one million by 1947. Anti-Zionist groups such as the American Council for Judaism, formed in 1942 on the premise that Judaism was a religious rather than national identity, lost influence.[21]

Many non-Jewish U.S. citizens also sympathized with Zionism. They pitied the victims of Nazi persecution, identified with Jewish settlers seemingly repeating the U.S. frontier experience, predicted that Jews would make Palestine prosper, and looked down on Muslims and Arabs. Many evangelical Christians favored the establishment of a Jewish state as a fulfillment of biblical prophecy. Zionism also spread into Congress. When Britain discussed repudiating the Balfour Declaration in October 1938, for example, sixty-two representatives and nine senators advised Roosevelt to protest. In 1942, Senator James E. Murray (D-Montana) urged the president to organize a Jewish army in Palestine to defend Western security interests in the region.[22]

Despite such domestic pressures, Roosevelt privileged national security considerations during the war. He was determined to avoid any step in Palestine that would undermine the Anglo-U.S. alliance or the prospect of victory over the Axis. In July 1943, when Jewish leaders pressed Britain for a pledge of postwar statehood, U.S. and British officials jointly declared that the British presence in Palestine remained vital to wartime strategy and that discussions about the disposition of the land should be postponed until war's end. "Disorder in Palestine," Acting Secretary of War Robert P. Patterson cautioned, "would affect adversely the situation in the whole area and possibly even the course of the entire war." [23]

Intelligence officials reinforced the importance of Allied security interests in the Middle East. The director of the Office of Strategic Services, William Donovan, repeatedly advised Roosevelt that any hint of pro-Zionism would imperil Arab friendship, which was vital to the war effort. In 1944, when intelligence officers detected an initiative by Soviet agents in Cairo to spread communism in the region, Donovan advised that friendship with Arab powers seemed crucial for the postwar era as well. The Office of Strategic Services became concerned that "a vocal and influential segment of US public opinion" might stimulate Anglo-U.S. tensions, undermine U.S. interests in Arab states, and allow the Soviet Union to enter the region.[24]

To protect Allied wartime interests in the Arab states, U.S. leaders professed non-Zionism to Arab leaders. Abdul Aziz Ibn Saud, an Arabian desert warlord and charismatic religious figure who established the kingdom of Saudi Arabia in 1932, emerged as a staunch U.S. partner during World War II. Saudi oil, produced and marketed by the U.S.-owned Arabian-American Oil Company, fueled the Allied war effort. In 1943, Roosevelt declared the kingdom vital to U.S. national security, provided it with generous military and economic aid, and stationed U.S. soldiers there. Saudi Arabia possessed such political and strategic importance that Roosevelt seriously considered Ibn Saud's extremely anti-Zionist views. "The obvious rights of the Arabs, which are clear as the sun," Ibn Saud wrote in 1943, "may not be dimmed by historic fallacies or social and economic theories of the Zionists, which theories God has not ordained." Roosevelt soothed the monarch (as well as King Faisal of Iraq and Emir Abdallah of Transjordan) by pledging to consult Arab leaders before changing U.S. policy toward Palestine.[25]

Likewise, Roosevelt resisted pressure to endorse Zionist aspirations. In 1941–42 he rejected appeals from Zionist leaders that he encourage Churchill to create a fifty-thousand-man Jewish Brigade within the British Army on the grounds that such a step might trigger a mutiny in the Egyptian army at a critical moment in the war in Africa. Roosevelt also rejected Zionist pressure to endorse an independent Jewish state in Palestine. Weizmann funneled a steady stream of messages to Roosevelt through Treasury Secretary Henry Morgenthau and Special Counsel Samuel I. Rosenman, administration insiders who were Jewish and who quietly promoted the welfare of European Jewry. Weizmann implored the president in a personal meeting on 12 June 1943 that "the Arabs must be told that the Jews have a right to Palestine." Citing familiar security arguments, Roosevelt rejected the appeal. Even Morgenthau refrained in 1944 from pressuring the British because "they are scared to death of the Arab question." [26]

Roosevelt remained sensitive to Arab concerns even as Palestine became a domestic political issue in 1944. Zionists convinced numerous members of Congress to cosponsor a joint bipartisan resolution endorsing Jewish statehood in Palestine and asked Roosevelt to approve the measure. Saudi Arabia, Egypt, Iraq, Syria, and Yemen angrily protested the resolution, and Pentagon officers warned Roosevelt and members of Congress that its passage would damage military interests. Roosevelt convinced Speaker of the House Sam Rayburn (D-Texas) to kill the resolution. "The volume of protests which have come in from practically all the Arab and Moorish countries," he explained, "illustrates what happens if delicate international situations get into party politics." [27]

On the eve of the November 1944 election, by contrast, Roosevelt gave in slightly to Zionist pressures. The Democratic and Republican Parties endorsed unlimited Jewish immigration to Palestine and political independence for the *yishuv*. Representative Emanuel Celler, a New York Democrat and a Jew, asked Roosevelt to pressure Britain to revoke the White Paper of 1939, warning that Republican nominee Thomas Dewey "would steal the show right from under our noses" by issuing such a commitment. Rosenman advised Roosevelt that "you would be substituting action for the mere words of Dewey and the Republican platform." To win Zionist votes without angering Churchill, Roosevelt's campaign speeches called for land surveys that would facilitate eventual Jewish settlement.[28]

Once reelected, however, Roosevelt again resisted Zionist pressure. In December 1944, 399 members of Congress endorsed the pro-Zionist resolution shelved earlier in the year, and Zionists sought Roosevelt's support. But Roosevelt opposed the resolution, following the State Department's advice that the resolution would damage "the general international situation." "Give me an opportunity to talk with Stalin and Churchill," Roosevelt told Democratic legislators on the eve of the Yalta Conference. "Naturally I do not want to see a war between a million or two million people in Palestine against the whole Moslem world."[29]

Wartime and postwar security concerns reinforced Roosevelt's reluctance to endorse Zionist aspirations. The Office of Strategic Services discerned Palestinian amity toward Russia in newspaper editorials, cooperation between the Russian Orthodox Church and Palestinian Christians, pilgrimages by Soviet Muslims to Mecca, and an Arab appeal to Moscow for help in resisting Zionism. While Palestinian Arabs were pleased that Roosevelt killed the pro-Zionist resolution in Congress, the U.S. consul in Jerusalem, Lowell C. Pinkerton, warned, "their love—like their hate—is entirely superficial and will only last until they take offense at some little thing."[30]

Astounded by the fervor of Arab anti-Zionism, Roosevelt appeased Arab statesmen. Prince Abdul Ilah, regent to the throne of Iraq, argued that "Palestine is as Arab as Devonshire is English or Virginia is American." Leaders in Syria, Transjordan, Yemen, and Lebanon made similar statements. After King Ibn Saud spoke likewise during a personal meeting in February 1945, Roosevelt pledged not to make Palestinian policy that was hostile to Arab interests. "No decision altering the basic situation of Palestine," he assured Arab rulers, "should be reached without full consultation with both Arabs and Jews."[31]

Conclusion

Certain patterns in U.S. wartime policy regarding Palestine persisted after the war. Public and congressional opinion strongly influenced White House advisers to support Zionism, while a determination to promote national security interests in the Middle East during and after the war led State Department officials to oppose Zionism. A division emerged between the White House staff and the State Department, and both sides sought to influence presidential decision making. This tension between domestic politics and national security would persist through the 1945–61 period.

For his part, Roosevelt left an ambiguous legacy on Palestine. He consistently elevated national security imperatives over his political interests in satisfying Zionists. In the process he helped to avert an Arab-Jewish conflict that might have destabilized the Middle East and hampered the Allies' prosecution of World War II. However, Roosevelt also made certain concessions to the Zionist cause that did not infringe on security interests. For example, he hinted during the 1944 political campaign that he was not averse to accelerated Jewish immigration to Palestine, and he refused to rule out, as Arab leaders insisted, a prospective Jewish state in Palestine. Such concessions planted the seeds for trouble in the U.S. relationships with Britain and the Arab powers.

In view of Roosevelt's behavior, it is not surprising that scholars disagree about his legacy. Accentuating Roosevelt's wartime accomplishments, Zvi Ganin notes that Roosevelt "walked so skillfully on the Palestinian tightrope." Other authors, however, argue that Roosevelt burdened his successors by compromising security concerns with his own domestic political interests. "Roosevelt's conduct was riddled with deception," Kenneth Ray Bain observes. "The parade of fictions, half-truths, self-contradictions, and secrets left his successor an inconsistent legacy of advice that did more to confuse than to enlighten." [32] Roosevelt's successors would indeed face a complicated situation in Palestine.

2

SECURITY AND POLITICS
The Context of U.S. Policy toward Palestine after 1945

When he took office near the end of World War II, President Harry S. Truman inherited a messy situation in Palestine. Forced to confront the massive challenges of winning the war, adjusting to a new global order, and managing the home front, Truman found little time to study or understand the complexities of the Middle East. Consequently, his administration began to shape a policy toward Palestine that lacked the strong, sure hand of presidential leadership.

Global, regional, and domestic factors complicated Truman's task in Palestine. In light of the emerging Cold War, U.S. security experts assigned new importance to the protection of interests in the Arab states, resolved to become more involved in the region, and sympathized with Arab attitudes regarding Palestine. On the regional level, Britain's inability to contain mounting violence in Palestine destabilized the mandate and threatened to plunge neighboring states into war. On the home front, Truman's advisers contested the anti-Zionism of the State Department and Pentagon and urged the president to adopt a pro-Zionist policy for domestic political and other reasons. From the beginning of Truman's presidency, competition between the national security and domestic impulses caused tension in U.S. policy regarding Palestine.

The Importance of the Middle East to the United States

Because of the Cold War, the United States ascribed increased significance to the Middle East. U.S. leaders came to view the Middle East as critical to containing Soviet power in Europe and Asia. These American officials reasoned that military facilities and oil resources gave the Middle East Arab states enormous military value, and economic, cultural, and political reasons also seemed to make it crucial to align the region with the West. U.S. officials resolved to pursue an anti-Soviet policy in the Mideast by becoming involved as a partner of Britain.

U.S. security experts feared that the Soviet Union had postwar designs on the Middle East. In hindsight, Soviet Premier Joseph Stalin seems to have considered the Middle East less important than Europe or East Asia in his ideological quest to promote socialism and in his preparations for conflict with the capitalist world. Stalin tried to project his influence in Turkey and Iran in 1945–46, for example, but backed down when Western powers resisted. Yet U.S. officials assumed that Stalin had inherited Russia's traditional quest for warm-water ports and friendly regimes in states along its southern border. Thus, the American government interpreted Stalin's forays into Turkey and Iran as a portent of Soviet entrance into the Middle East.[1]

U.S. security planners deemed it essential to exclude Soviet influence from the Middle East. According to contingency war plans devised during the late 1940s by strategists in Washington and London, military bases in Arab states would prove essential to victory in any armed conflict with the Soviet Union. Possession of bases in Egypt would enable the Western allies to conduct a punishing aerial offensive against the Soviet industrial heartland, to concentrate armored forces for offensive ground action, and to position intelligence gathering, propaganda, and covert action operations close to the enemy's frontier. The Suez Canal, interregional air routes, and other communications facilities gave the Middle East additional security importance in peace and war. "If a hostile Power secured control of this area," U.S. and British officials agreed in 1947, "not only would we lose very important resources and facilities but it would acquire a position of such dominating strategic and economic power that it would be fatal to our security. It is therefore vital that we must retain a firm hold on the Middle East."[2]

Western strategists also assigned vast importance to the Middle East's petroleum resources. The region boasted the world's largest proven oil reserves, and U.S. and British officials considered that oil vital for the economic reconstruction of Western Europe; furthermore, the oil had to be denied to Soviet Russia in peace or war. "Access to the oil of the Persian Gulf area and the denial of control of the Mediterranean to a major, hostile, expansionist power," the Central Intelligence Agency (CIA) estimated in 1947, "are deemed to be essential to the security of the US."[3]

U.S. officials also recognized the commercial importance of the Arab states. In 1947, 2,813 U.S. ships transited the Suez Canal, and U.S. investors owned 23.75 percent of Iraq's oil industry. U.S. trade with Syria, Lebanon, Palestine, and Transjordan increased sixfold between 1939 and 1948. Although commercial assets in the Middle East were modest relative to those in other regions, U.S. officials saw Middle East commerce as important as part of the Atlantic Charter's vision of a global capitalist system of free trade. The "prosperity of the Western World," State Department officials summarized in 1950, seemed "closely linked with the fate of the Near Eastern countries."[4]

U.S. leaders also valued cultural and political factors in the Middle East. The region contained the holy sites of Islam, a religion with three hundred million believers in Africa and Asia. Officials in Washington believed that a century of philanthropic and missionary activity by U.S. citizens had created a reservoir of goodwill between the United States and Middle East Muslims. Such friendliness would quickly erode if the West followed policies that Muslim states deemed inimical. Any hostile power dominating the region, State Department officials reasoned, "would be in a position to extend cultural and political penetration to the remainder of the vast Moslem area, now generally friendly to us."[5]

The United States also developed extensive interests in Saudi Arabia. During and after World War II, the Pentagon leveraged rights to an air base at Dhahran by providing generous foreign aid. In 1946, King Ibn Saud hired Americans to engineer a ten-year plan to modernize the country's infrastructure. The Arabian-American Oil Company owned a concession to produce Saudi oil and controlled an underground reserve that contained more oil than was estimated to exist in the United States. By 1946, the company had invested $100 million in its operations, and by 1949 it produced 550,000 barrels of oil per day, claimed $350 million in investments, and employed five thousand Americans in the country. U.S. investors owned half of the Saudi Mining Syndicate. Trans World Airlines depended on servicing facilities at Dhahran for its flights between Cairo and India, making Saudi Arabia, in the words of one U.S. official, "an important way station on this great commercial international air route."[6]

Other Arab states also boasted important assets. Egypt's Suez Canal and network of military facilities, controlled by the British Empire in 1945, gave the country economic and strategic value. The State Department considered Iraq important because of its prestige in the Arab community, its emerging independence from Britain, and its promise as a future political partner. Jordan, by contrast, lacked political integrity and economic or security assets. The State Department considered its independence, formally granted in 1946, a sham in light of Britain's right to occupy the country and its command of the Arab Legion.[7]

To safeguard vital American interests in the Middle East, U.S. officials formulated several important policy principles. First, the leaders frequently clarified that stability in the Middle East would best serve U.S. security, political, and economic interests. In this estimation, achieving stability meant establishing a democratic, pro-Western, and anticommunist sociopolitical framework. "It is our policy," Joseph C. Satterthwaite, the director of the State Department's Office of Near Eastern and African Affairs (NEA), clarified in one typical statement, "to assist the Near Eastern countries in maintaining their independence, to strengthen their orientation towards the West, and to discourage any tendencies towards the development of authoritarian and unrepresentative forms of government." Stable political regimes would facilitate economic development, which would, in turn, further stabilize the region.[8]

Second, U.S. officials resolved to replace their prewar aloofness from the Middle East with involvement in the region. "It is extremely important that the influence of the United States should increase rather than decrease during the next few critical years in the Near and Middle East," the NEA's Loy Henderson advised in September 1945. U.S. officials must abandon "the comfortable old pre-war era when we felt it unnecessary to trouble ourselves with the trend of events in distant lands." Such thinking proved to be the first U.S. step toward an enduring commitment in the Middle East.[9]

Third, U.S. officials came to believe that they needed to cooperate with Britain. Before 1945, U.S. and British firms competed for oil concessions in the Middle East, and as World War II ended, U.S. officials viewed Britain as a rival for commercial opportunities in the region. State Department officials opposed Britain's preeminent position in Egypt and Iraq as exclusionary, outmoded, and prone to inflaming local opposition and regretted that President Franklin D. Roosevelt's wartime deference to Britain had undermined U.S. interests in the Arab states. In mid-1945, the State Department defined equality of commercial opportunity as an objective in the Middle East.[10]

The onset of the Cold War, however, compelled the United States and Britain to renew their World War II–era special relationship. As the two powers cooperatively bolstered West Germany; shored up Greece, Turkey, and Iran; implemented the Marshall Plan; challenged the Soviet blockade of Berlin; and signed the NATO alliance, U.S. officials eschewed competition with Britain regarding the Middle East. "If we fight one another" over oil, Deputy Director of the Office of European Affairs John D. Hickerson aptly commented, "the Russians will find it easier to throw us both out." Rather, U.S. and British officials made joint contingency war plans that relied on bases in the Middle East. "There is no question of attempting to replace British by U.S. influence, or vice versa," they agreed in 1947. The two powers would "strengthen and improve our mutual position by lending each other all possible influence and support."[11]

The Conflict in Palestine, 1945–1947

In the aftermath of World War II, British officials found the situation in Palestine unmanageable. They searched in vain for a political solution to the Arab-Zionist conflict that both sides would accept and realized that the strategic advantages of controlling Palestine did not justify the costs. Within the mandate, British authorities proved unable to stem unauthorized Jewish immigration, to halt Arab-Jewish violence, or to avoid becoming the targets of Jewish violence. By 1947, Britain considered abandoning its mandate.

As the war ended, British diplomats faced the daunting task of deciding Palestine's future. After debating a variety of potential solutions, the Colonial Office and the Foreign Office preferred a binational state but realized that both the Jews and Arabs would object. At the same time, Prime Minister Clement Attlee and Foreign Minister Ernest Bevin, leaders of the Labour government elected in July 1945, decided to dismantle Britain's colonial structure in the Middle East, India, and elsewhere. Determined to preserve the Anglo-U.S. alliance to resist Soviet encroachments in Europe, Bevin became willing to evacuate Palestine and became sensitive to U.S. interests there.[12]

A Ministry of Defence reassessment of Palestine dovetailed with Bevin's thinking. The security experts, who were determined to hold a base in Egypt, initially considered Palestine crucial as "the core of the natural defences of Egypt against an attack from the north." They also eyed Palestine as an alternative base site if Britain were forced to depart Egypt. By mid-1946, however, the experts saw Palestine as a strategic debit because of its modest base facilities and unfriendly local peoples, and legal advisers doubted that the United Nations would allow Britain to militarize the mandate. By bolstering its presence in Palestine, other officials realized, Britain would alienate Arab states in which it had extensive strategic interests.[13]

Furthermore, political and military circumstances within Palestine made it difficult for the British to administer the territory. The establishment of the United Nations and the independence of Syria and Lebanon from France in 1944–46 aroused Palestinian nationalists' hopes for political independence. But Mufti Amin al-Husayni had discredited himself in British eyes through his association with Adolf Hitler, and the Palestinian elite remained fragmented among six political parties. In December 1946, the mufti gained command of a thirty-five-thousand-man Palestinian militia known as the Arab Youth Movement. Together with such shadowy groups as the Arab Blood Society, which conducted reprisals against Palestinians who sold land to Jews, the militia aimed violence against the *yishuv*.[14]

Britain also faced the costly and awkward task of preventing illegal immigration of Jews without appearing insensitive to the survivors of Nazi genocide. Tens of thousands of European Jewish war refugees, unwilling or unable to return to their prewar homes, sought to emigrate to Palestine in defiance of British law. Between May 1945 and May 1948, some 70,000 Jews were smuggled into Palestine, helping to push its Jewish population to 720,000. From October 1946 to April 1947, the British Navy intercepted seven ships carrying 5,000 illegal immigrants. One of these vessels was the *Ben Hecht*, a ship sponsored by the American League for a Free Palestine, crewed by 20 U.S. citizens, and carrying 612 illegal immigrants, which was detained on 22 February 1947.[15]

The increasing militancy of Palestine's Jews also troubled the British. Three

Jewish militias had emerged in the early 1940s. The Haganah (Jewish Resistance Organization), a formal defense force linked to the Jewish Agency, numbered fifty thousand soldiers. Two shadowy extremist groups also took form: the Irgun Sva'i Leumi (National Military Organization), headed by Menachem Begin, and Lohama Herut Israel (Fighters for the Freedom of Israel, known as Lehi or the Stern Gang), headed by Abraham Stern. Together, the Irgun and the Stern Gang fielded some six thousand fighters. During World War II, the extremist groups engaged in terrorism and guerrilla warfare against British authority, including the assassination of Lord Moyne in 1944. The more mainstream Haganah co-operated with Britain in the formation of the Jewish Brigade and in the suppression of the extremists after Moyne's assassination. The Haganah followed David Ben-Gurion's dictum of fighting the war as if there were no White Paper of 1939 in the hope that Britain might provide Jewish statehood as a reward.[16]

In late 1945, however, even the moderate Haganah used violence for political purposes. When Ben-Gurion concluded that the British government would neither allow substantial immigration nor promote Jewish statehood, he ordered Haganah forces to sabotage British railroads and oil installations, and he encouraged ships carrying illegal immigrants to bear arms and resist British patrols. In response, Britain bolstered its military forces in Palestine from fifty thousand in September 1945 to one hundred thousand in late 1946. During Operation Agatha on 29 June 1946, seventeen thousand British soldiers swept through Jewish strongholds to arrest suspected militants and seize weapons. Fearing an even more thorough crackdown, Ben-Gurion elevated diplomacy over force and suspended Haganah operations against the British from July 1946 to November 1947.[17]

The Irgun and the Stern Gang offered a more deadly challenge to British personnel. Between May 1945 and May 1946, British forces in Palestine suffered 184 killed and 371 wounded in terror attacks. Severe countermeasures such as Operation Agatha failed to curb the extremists. On the contrary, on 22 July 1946, within a month of the operation, the Irgun bombed the King David Hotel in Jerusalem, the center of British military and political authority, killing 92 British, Jews, and Arabs. On 1 March 1947, a terrorist bomb at the British Officers Club in Jerusalem killed 22. The British declared martial law in West Jerusalem, Tel Aviv, and other Jewish enclaves as talk of revenge swept the ranks of the British army. According to Robert Macatee of the U.S. consulate in Jerusalem, Jewish leaders had good reason to worry that British troops would "start a pogrom."[18]

While many British officials demanded escalation and revenge, however, Attlee and Bevin entertained the possibility of withdrawal. They believed that Palestine lacked the strategic assets needed to justify military operations to pacify it. Terrorism eroded morale among British soldiers and exhausted the tolerance of the war-weary British public. British officials looked to escape the debilitating conflict in Palestine.[19]

The Internal Dynamics of the Truman Administration

The internal dynamics of the Truman administration significantly influenced the evolution of U.S. policy toward Palestine. Several of Truman's personal advisers encouraged him to endorse Zionist ambitions. In contrast, the State Department and Pentagon warned that supporting Zionism would undermine vital national interests in the Arab world. Truman had to make key policy decisions about Palestine while torn by the conflicting advice of his personal and professional advisers.

Truman became president on 12 April 1945 with little experience in national leadership. Roosevelt had selected the Missourian as vice president in 1944 more because of his political identity as a moderate, internationalist southerner than because of his natural abilities. During his eighty-three days as vice president, Truman privately met Roosevelt only twice and neither visited the White House Map Room nor received briefings on the Yalta Conference, the Manhattan Project, or Roosevelt's delicate diplomacy in the Middle East. As Truman faced the challenges of securing victories in Europe and Asia and managing the transition to peacetime at home and overseas, he displayed a degree of insecurity manifest in his mistrust of the bureaucracies in the State Department and Pentagon and his assertive if not brash style of making decisions.[20]

Before becoming president, Truman had shown a mixture of political opportunity and caution regarding Palestine. As a U.S. senator, he had maintained contacts with Zionists, endorsed individual Jews' petitions for immigration, and publicly condemned Nazi genocide. For security reasons, however, he remained reluctant to endorse a Jewish state in Palestine. Truman admired several American Zionists, including his friends Eddie Jacobson and Max Lowenthal, Rabbi Stephen Wise, and First Lady Eleanor Roosevelt, but he despised Rabbi Abba Hillel Silver of Cleveland, a Republican and more militant Zionist activist. (After Silver pounded on Truman's desk while making a point during a meeting in July 1946, Truman banned the rabbi from the White House and later remarked that "terror and Silver are the contributing causes of some, if not all, of our troubles.")[21]

Scholars generally agree that Truman facilitated the creation of Israel but disagree on his motives. John Snetsinger, Evan M. Wilson, Dan Tschirgi, and Bruce J. Evensen underscore evidence that Truman and his political advisers shaped foreign policy to gain financial contributions and the votes of U.S. Jews. Truman submitted to public and press pro-Zionism, they argue, because he lacked a sophisticated understanding of U.S. interests in the Middle East.[22]

Other scholars assert more favorably that Truman made policy on humanitarian and cultural grounds. News of the Holocaust, these authors argue, compelled him to facilitate the relocation to Palestine of the remnants of European Jewry. Clark Clifford attributes to Truman a "long history of sympathy for the underdog [and] sheer human concern for a people who had endured the torments of the damned." Such sentiments, Michael T. Benson observes, dovetailed with ideas rooted in Truman's evangelical Christian upbringing—namely, his appreciation for Bible prophecies about the restoration of a Jewish state, his sympathy for Jews as the chosen people of the Old Testament, and his basic moral sense of right and wrong, which compelled him to honor the promise implicit in the Balfour Declaration. Politics naturally mattered, Clifford maintains, but remained "a minor factor." Peter Grose adds that Truman angered Zionists on certain key issues and points out that he lost New York in the 1948 election.[23]

More nuanced interpretations argue that a combination of factors influenced Truman. Michael Cohen acknowledges the importance of electoral considerations but stresses that "no number of Jewish votes or sum of Jewish money could have persuaded Truman to adopt a policy that he believed ran counter to the national interest." Zvi Ganin, David McCullough, Alonzo Hamby, and Arnold Offner attribute Truman's policy to a mixture of political and humanitarian considerations, anti-Soviet calculations, personal integrity, and mistrust of the State Department.[24]

One reason for the ambiguity in Truman's legacy is that he was pulled in different directions by his personal and professional advisers. No personal aide was more influential than the pro-Zionist Clifford, Truman's special counsel from July 1946 to January 1950. Jacobson, Truman's former business partner and a Jewish Zionist, used friendship with the president to provide Zionist activists with access to the White House. In 1947, Truman appointed an avowed Zionist, General John Hilldring, to the U.S. delegation to the United Nations, where he could monitor State Department officials whom the president suspected of disloyalty. In 1948, Truman named a Christian Zionist, James B. McDonald, rather than a professional foreign service officer, to serve as the first U.S. representative to Israel.[25]

David K. Niles also seemed to wield influence over presidential policy. The son of Russian Jewish immigrants and a career civil servant, Niles served as Roosevelt's adviser on minority affairs and maintained that post under Truman. Niles kept in close contact with Zionist and Israeli envoys and strove to influence Truman to endorse Zionist goals. Clifford's assistant, George Elsey, remembered Niles as a "most secretive individual who slunk rather furtively round the corridors of the White House and the Executive Office Building." Loy Henderson, an anti-Zionist State Department official who competed with Niles for influence, considered him "the most powerful and diligent advocate of the Zionist cause" at the White House and a sinister figure who divulged classified infor-mation to Zionists. Rabbi Silver considered Niles a political asset who provided Zionist leaders access to the Oval Office. In 1951, Israeli Foreign Minister Moshe Sharett wrote to Niles, using his first name and commending him for his "in-estimable assistance during all these momentous years." Niles replied on White House stationery that "I shall continue to the end of my days to be grateful to our Heavenly Father, and to my own beloved country, for the opportunity that was given me to be one of the instruments through which President Truman" helped establish Israeli independence.[26]

Public opinion also encouraged Truman to support Zionism. Resolutions passed by state governments, rhetoric of members of Congress, political plat-forms, and speeches of leading politicians from both major parties revealed an enormous groundswell of support for Zionism. "There is a large and aggressive element in public opinion which not only wholeheartedly endorses the Zionist position, but even criticizes the Administration for not going far enough in fol-lowing a pro-Zionist line," State Department officials noted in 1946. By contrast, anti-Zionism, "if it exists, has not been articulate." In late 1947, the White House received 135,000 letters about Palestine, nearly all endorsing Zionist demands.[27]

In combination with the pro-Zionist public opinion, a powerful anti-Arab bias in U.S. culture created an anti-Arab frame of reference in the minds of some U.S. leaders. Inspired by Edward W. Said's suggestion that Western culture en-hanced imperialism by lacing a racial bias and a sense of exceptionalism into Western perceptions of Arab peoples, recent scholarship suggests that U.S. news media, Christian churches, and other cultural mediators cast Jews in a favorable light but spoke rarely and negatively about Arab peoples. Indeed, members of Congress who endorsed Zionism often disparaged the mufti as pro-Nazi and the leaders of Arab states as coldhearted.[28]

Anti-Zionist officials in the State Department and Pentagon offered a coun-tervailing force against the pro-Zionism of Truman, the White House staff, and public opinion. Undersecretary of State Robert A. Lovett, Policy Planning Staff Director George F. Kennan, and Secretary of Defense James Forrestal predicted that promoting Zionism would trigger war in the Middle East, undermine U.S. interests in the Arab world, and drive the Arab states into partnership with the Soviet Union. George C. Marshall, the five-star general who coordinated U.S. military operations during World War II and served as secretary of state in 1947–49, feared that supporting Zionism would strain the Anglo-U.S. alliance. Histo-rian Joseph W. Bendersky finds that widespread anti-Zionism among military officers grew from their long tradition of anti-Semitism. Indeed, Eliahu Epstein, director of the Washington-based Jewish Agency for Palestine, branded Tru-man's military aide, General Harry H. Vaughan, "a very bad influence . . . , an anti-Semite."[29]

Henderson, who became director of NEA in 1945, was perhaps the best-known anti-Zionist in the early Truman administration. Transferred from European affairs to the embassy in Baghdad in 1943 because his stalwart anticommunism countered the spirit of the wartime Grand Alliance, Henderson interpreted the emerging Arab-Zionist conflict from an anticommunist perspective. He calculated that establishing a Jewish state in Palestine would cause war in the Middle East and drive the Arab states into political partnership with the Soviet Union, to the detriment of vital U.S. interests. When Silver asked Henderson in June 1947 to give a personal assurance that he was "sympathetic to the Zionist point of view," Henderson demurred. His anti-Zionism made him a political liability to Truman, who, under pressure from Zionists, reassigned Henderson to the embassy in India in June 1948.[30]

Like Henderson, many State Department and Pentagon officials opposed Zionism because they feared that it would promote communism in the Middle East. They feared that Arab states would turn to Moscow to defeat Zionism and expressed concern about ties between Jewish immigrants and Eastern European governments. In 1945, British intelligence provided the State Department with a report, purportedly written by Poland's military intelligence service, that Soviet agents disguised as Polish Jewish immigrants were infiltrating Palestine. In 1947, British officials reported that the Irgun and the Stern Gang maintained contacts with the Polish vice consul in Jerusalem, Witold Senft-Liskowsky. These reports may have been fabricated or exaggerated by British officials to stimulate U.S. anti-Zionism. Even Colonel William Eddy, an ardent anti-Zionist who spent considerable time in Palestine, dismissed the reports of Soviet infiltration as "only talk." This evidence made an imprint on anti-Zionist State Department officials, however.[31]

State Department officials also opposed Zionism because they feared angering Arab leaders. On 16 January 1946, King Ibn Saud of Saudi Arabia and King Farouk of Egypt declared "that Palestine is an Arab country and that it is the right of its people and the right of Moslem Arabs everywhere to preserve it as an Arab country." At a summit meeting at Inschass, Egypt, on 28–29 May, Arab statesmen demanded an end to Jewish immigration, warned that pro-Zionism by the United States or Britain would be considered "a hostile policy . . . against the Arab countries," and pledged to support Palestinians "with every means possible."[32]

State Department officials initially balanced such declarations against evidence of Saudi moderation. In July 1945 conversations about Saudi Arabia's need for Western financial subsidies, Counselor for Economic Affairs Harold Hoskins noted that Ibn Saud had replaced his extreme rhetoric on Palestine with a simple statement that "the Arabs of Palestine wish only to be left alone and not to be overrun by Jews." In early 1946, Saudi officials claimed to fear aggression from Iraq and Jordan more than a Jewish presence in Palestine. "I am talking big because everyone else is," Ibn Saud told a U.S. military officer in September 1946, "but in the end Palestine will not affect my relations with the Americans."[33]

On balance, however, State Department officials accentuated the evidence that Zionism imperiled American interests in the Arab states. Despite evidence of Ibn Saud's moderation, most U.S. officials came to fear that his anger at U.S. Zionism would drive him to cancel U.S. air base rights at Dhahran, the Arabian-American Oil Company's oil concession, or Trans World's air transit privileges. State Department experts also worried that Egypt, Jordan, and Iraq would act on their threats to punish the West. Iraq's perception of U.S. Zionism, Henderson observed in August 1945, "handicaps our efforts to develop friendly and close relations."[34]

Pentagon officials also feared that Zionism threatened U.S. security interests. In early 1946, military intelligence officers predicted that a pro-Zionist outcome in Palestine would trigger Arab attacks on Western assets in the Middle East and that two hundred thousand soldiers and two years would be needed to suppress such attacks. Such a military encounter with the Arab states would weaken Western military forces in Europe and Asia and "throw the majority of Arabs of all classes into the arms of Soviet Russia." The Middle East, the Pentagon warned, "could well fall into anarchy and become a breeding ground for world war."[35]

Driven by such concerns, State Department officials tried to steer Truman away from his Zionist inclinations. "We should put President Truman on notice as soon as possible," NEA Chief Paul H. Alling warned Secretary of State Edward R. Stettinius Jr. on 13 April 1945, "that the Zionists will undoubtedly seize the first available opportunity to elicit from him a commitment on Palestine." Meeting with Truman on 26 May, Acting Secretary of State Joseph C. Grew stressed "the unfortunate and possible serious effect" of pro-Zionist action by the president. The State Department urged that "nothing be done to incur the hostility of the Arabs or the Moslem world."[36]

To their chagrin, State Department officials proved unable to exert satisfactory influence on Truman's policy decisions. Truman initially reiterated Roosevelt's assurances to Arab rulers, telling Emir Abdallah of Transjordan on 17 May 1945 that the new president would avoid decisions on Palestine "without full consultation with both Arabs and Jews." Gradually, however, Truman rejected the State Department's views as his populist distrust of eastern elites intensified. He privately derogated department officials as effeminate, snobbish, and disloyal "tea hounds" and "striped pants conspirators." As late as 1950, Truman reportedly remarked to Israeli Ambassador Abba Eban that the "striped-pants boys in the State Department are against my policy of supporting Israel" but that they would "soon find out who's the President of the United States."[37]

For their part, State Department officials resented what they considered unwise presidential policy making for domestic political interests. Harry N. Howard, who worked in the State Department research division in 1945–47, argued that Truman "made a fundamental mistake in his handling of the Palestine problem." Wilson noted that "our relations with the entire Arab world never recovered from the events of 1947–1948." Hamby more charitably concludes that "for Truman, caught in the middle, the result was an embarrassing no-win situation that threatened his control of foreign policy and left him a victim of something akin to political combat fatigue."[38]

Conclusion

At the dawn of the Cold War, foreign policy experts in the State and Defense Departments identified strategic, diplomatic, economic, and cultural interests in the Middle East and resolved to shield them from Soviet influence. To accomplish such a task, these officials aimed to pursue stability, become involved to an unprecedented degree, promote Anglo-U.S. collaboration, and preserve friendly relations with Arab states. As early as 1945, security officials made enduring commitments to prevent the spread of communism into the Middle East.

As U.S. officials took new interest in the Middle East as a region, they detected rampant instability in Palestine. The mandate's political deadlock, escalating violence, and declining strategic importance eroded British determination to maintain control. As the British searched for a feasible solution to the Palestine imbroglio, they would look to the United States for support and cooperation. The tendency to cooperate with Britain for strategic reasons formed one important foundation of U.S. policy toward Palestine in the late 1940s.

Dynamics within the Truman administration complicated the U.S. approach to the Middle East. In general, the president accepted the State Department's and Pentagon's views on the strategic importance of the Middle East and the Anglo-U.S. partnership. When the issue of Zionism surfaced, however, Truman felt pulled by competing unofficial interests based on domestic political, cultural, and humanitarian considerations. U.S. policy making regarding Palestine in the late 1940s thus involved a contest between official and unofficial interests. The clash produced a policy marked by ambiguity and inconsistency and strongly but not exclusively inclined toward Zionism.

3

AMBIVALENCE
Truman's Policy toward Palestine, 1945–1947

President Harry S. Truman profoundly affected the establishment of the state of Israel and the emergence of the Arab-Israeli conflict as a major international issue. Although he inherited the controversy from Franklin D. Roosevelt, Truman's decisions helped transform the dispute from a quarrel over immigration and landownership in a British mandate to a major contest over the right of the Jews of Palestine to form a sovereign state. Truman made fateful decisions that deeply invested the United States in the Arab-Israeli conflict.

In reaching his crucial decisions, Truman was buffeted by conflicting advice from opposing corners of his administration. Consistent with public opinion, most White House staff members urged the president to endorse the creation of a Jewish state. The State and Defense Departments, by contrast, advocated anti-Zionism to preserve security interests such as amity with Britain and military, transportation, and oil assets in Arab states. Torn by such conflicting pressures, Truman displayed a pattern of decision making marked by ambivalence and inconsistency.

Truman's Early Involvement in Palestine

A controversy regarding the immigration of Jews first drew Truman's attention to Palestine. In June 1945, Zionist groups demanded that Britain repudiate the White Paper of 1939 and immediately permit immigration of one hundred thousand Jews, but Britain offered to allow only fifteen hundred immigrants per month until the White Paper's quotas were exhausted. For a mixture of reasons, Truman endorsed the Zionist demand, and the British reaction led him to accept a new and risky degree of involvement in the controversy. As he became enmeshed, Truman demonstrated a measure of ambivalence that would become a trademark of his policy toward Palestine.

Truman endorsed the Zionist position on Jewish immigration to Palestine for domestic political and humanitarian reasons. He learned of the abysmal conditions in war refugee camps in Europe and of the high costs of maintaining such facilities. December 1945 and May 1946 opinion polls showed that between 78 and 80 percent of Americans who had followed the issue favored Jewish immigration to Palestine. Pro-Zionist adviser Samuel I. Rosenman argued that admission of one hundred thousand Jews would not change the "basic situation" in Palestine and that Roosevelt had pledged only to consult the Arabs, not "to obtain their consent before he took action." In August 1945, Truman recommended to British Prime Minister Clement Attlee that one hundred thousand Jewish refugees be admitted to Palestine to relieve suffering and ensure "future peace in Europe."[1]

Truman's advice bothered the State Department, the Arab states, and Britain. NEA Director Loy Henderson warned that endorsing large-scale Jewish immigration would subject the immigrants to housing and employment shortages and trigger Arab resistance. Arab leaders strongly protested Truman's position. British Foreign Secretary Ernest Bevin openly stated his suspicion that Truman wanted Jews to migrate to Palestine because he did not want them in America and demanded that the president send four divisions of soldiers to stabilize the mandate as the immigrants arrived. "We have the Arabs to consider as well as the Jews," Attlee added. Admitting a hundred thousand Jews would "set aflame the whole Middle East."[2]

Such countervailing pressures gave Truman pause, causing inconsistency in his policy. In light of Attlee's protests, Truman hesitated on the immigration issue. But a pending mayoral election in New York City, in which a Jewish Republican candidate vied for the traditionally Democratic Jewish vote, compelled Truman on 29 September publicly to endorse the demand for a hundred thousand immigrants. Then, after Saudi Arabia, Transjordan, and Syria charged that Truman had violated Roosevelt's pledge, Truman resisted calls from Zionists to reiterate his 29 September statement. Unless Zionists were "willing to furnish me with five hundred thousand men to carry on a war with the Arabs," he told Senator Joseph H. Ball (R-Minnesota) in November, "we will have to negotiate a while."[3]

In reaction to Truman's diplomacy, Bevin proposed an Anglo-American Committee of Inquiry into the Problems of European Jewry and Palestine (AACOI). Bevin sought to share the burden of solving the Palestine problem, delay Jewish immigration to Palestine, resolve the problem of Jewish refugees in Europe, and, above all, fortify the Anglo-U.S. security partnership. Perhaps he assumed that he could manipulate the United States to bolster British policy. Equally interested in preserving the partnership with Britain, Truman approved the AACOI on the condition that it would consider Jewish immigration to Palestine a viable option.[4]

The twelve-member AACOI was created in November 1945 and conducted its mission over the following six months. Among its U.S. members were Judge Joseph Hutcheson (the cochairman), Frank Aydelotte of Princeton University, James McDonald of Columbia University, and Bartley Crum, a pro-Zionist attorney from San Francisco. Despite hostile reactions from both Zionist and Palestinian leaders, who derogated the committee as a useless stalling ploy, the AACOI held hearings in Washington and London, toured refugee camps in Europe, and gathered data in Palestine. Its 20 April 1946 final report recommended that Britain admit one hundred thousand Jewish immigrants that year, abolish restrictions on land purchases by Jews, and establish an international trusteeship to govern Palestine. It advised against Jewish or Palestinian statehood.[5]

This report drew criticism from the Jewish and Arab sides. Zionists censured the prohibition of statehood and, with camps in western Germany recently swollen with 450,000 refugees from Eastern Europe, complained that the figure of 100,000 immigrants to Palestine no longer sufficed. Anti-U.S. protests erupted in Egypt, Syria, Lebanon, Iraq, and Palestine. Mobs torched the U.S. Information Center in Beirut and marched on the British embassy in Baghdad. Arab summit meetings at Inschass, Egypt, on 27–28 May 1946 and at Bludan, Syria, on 8–12 June declared that the AACOI lacked legal authority, that Britain must honor the White Paper's promise of a Palestinian state, and that the United States lacked grounds for intervention. In letters to Truman, Lebanese President Bechara Khalil El-Khoury, Iraqi Chamber of Deputies President Mohammed Hassan Kubba, Iraqi Regent Prince Abdul Ilah, Jordanian King Abdallah, Syrian President Shukry al-Quwatly, and Saudi King Ibn Saud charged that the report resulted from a conspiracy between Zionists and the committee and warned that mass immigration of Jews would provoke war in Palestine and undermine Arab-U.S. amity.[6]

Truman's advisers divided along familiar lines over the AACOI report: the NEA warned of the dire consequences of supporting massive Jewish immigration, while General John Hilldring, assistant secretary for occupied territories in Europe, favored liquidation of refugee camps for financial and humanitarian reasons. On 30 April 1946, Truman publicly endorsed the report and asked Britain to revoke the White Paper of 1939. He assured Arab leaders that Jewish immigration "would neither prejudice the rights and privileges of the Arabs now in Palestine, nor constitute a change in the basic situation."[7]

In summer 1946, U.S. and British officials worked to implement the AACOI recommendations. In July, the leaders jointly advanced the Morrison-Grady Plan, which proposed the division of Palestine into four districts (Palestinian, Jewish, Jerusalem, and the Negev). The Palestinian and Jewish districts would practice self-government on municipal, educational, development, landownership, and public health matters, while a central government headed by a British high commissioner and funded by U.S. aid would deal with defense, police, trade, and other national matters. Although AACOI Commissioner McDonald saw the scheme as a subtle reversal of Truman's endorsement of Jewish immigration, NEA officials endorsed it as realistic and fair and urged Britain to sell it to the Palestinian Arabs and Jews.[8]

Origins of Partition

Before Britain could implement the Morrison-Grady Plan, it was overtaken by a proposal to partition Palestine into a Jewish state and an Arab state. Zionist leaders promoted the idea as a means to statehood, while Arab states, practicing obstructionism, opposed the creation of a Jewish state. Stymied, Britain referred the problem to the United Nations, which formed a committee that eventually recommended partition. Although U.S. officials disagreed about the merits of partition, Truman ultimately supported the idea.

In August 1946, the Jewish Agency openly demanded partition. The emergence of assertive Zionist leader David Ben-Gurion over moderate Chaim Weizmann signaled a new determination to achieve statehood. U.S. Zionists and Jewish Agency officials, encouraged by Truman's support of immigration, urged him to endorse a Jewish state. They hoped that Truman's concern about the November 1946 midterm elections would compel him to consent.[9]

Predictably, U.S. officials had differing opinions regarding partition. White House adviser David Niles urged Truman to endorse it as a means of neutralizing an expected pro-Zionist pronouncement from Republican politician Thomas Dewey. In contrast, State Department officials explained to Truman that "we might do more harm than good by intervening at this time." Truman temporized, and on 4 October 1946, the eve of the Jewish Yom Kippur holy day, he implicitly endorsed a Jewish state. Partition "would command the support of public opinion in the United States," he declared. "To such a solution our Government could give its support."[10]

Truman's motives for issuing the Yom Kippur statement have been widely debated. The president claimed purely humanitarian concerns. "I am not interested in the politics of the situation, or what effect it will have on votes in the United States," he explained. "I am interested in relieving a half million people of the . . . distressful situation." Despite this protestation, most scholars agree with Kenneth Ray Bain's assessment that Truman's declaration was "a political statement designed for domestic consumption and promising little hope of winning immigration relief for the refugees." Ironically, the statement failed to achieve domestic gains, as Dewey called for immigration of hundreds of thousands of Jews and Republicans won control of Congress in the 1946 election.[11]

While Zionists celebrated Truman's Yom Kippur statement, Britain and the Arab states protested vehemently. Attlee frankly complained that Truman had eviscerated the British leader's patient diplomacy with both parties. Lebanon branded the statement "wholly antagonistic to the Arab[s'] legitimate right to their country," and Iraqi leaders discussed breaking diplomatic relations with the United States. Saudi leaders accused Truman of supporting "Zionist aggression" and warned that they would consider reprisals ranging from an economic boycott to "underground guerilla warfare against Americans throughout the Arab World." Officials of the Arabian-American Oil Company warned that they might recharter as a British corporation to avoid the anti-U.S. backlash.[12]

Britain faced an impossible situation. Two rounds of Anglo-Arab-Jewish talks between September 1946 and February 1947 produced an irreconcilable deadlock: the Jews demanded a state, but the Arabs refused to approve one. Bevin realized that to endorse partition would infuriate the Arabs, to oppose it would provoke the Jews, and to impose a settlement on both parties would require financial and military resources that his government lacked. Escalating violence in Palestine made Bevin's problem acute. The July 1947 kidnapping and murder of two British sergeants ignited a frenzy of retaliatory rampages by British soldiers in Palestine and a wave of anti-Semitic outbursts in Britain. Illegal Jewish immigration added to the tension, and Britain lost prestige when it callously seized such vessels as the *Exodus*.[13]

To escape its predicament, Britain referred the Palestine issue to the United Nations in February 1947. That move seemed an admission of inability to resolve the controversy, a gambit to gain U.S. support, and a sign that Labour leaders favored decolonization of the mandate. When the U.N. General Assembly convened in April 1947, the Jewish Agency initially feared the proceedings because it lacked the U.N. voting rights enjoyed by five Arab states that proposed Palestinian independence. But the assembly defeated that measure and instead created the U.N. Special Committee on Palestine (UNSCOP) to study the problem. Bevin's referral to the United Nations would prove to be, in Zvi Ganin's apt phrase, "providential to the Zionist cause."[14]

Surprised by the sudden turns in Palestine diplomacy, State Department officials privately debated the merits of partition during the UNSCOP mission. On the one hand, some officials observed that partition would fulfill the territorial aspirations of the Jewish and Arab communities, end the arguments about immigration and landownership, and sidestep problems such as ethnic disunity in a uninational state. Partition also seemed attractive because in terms of self-government, taxation, education, and police, the "Jewish community is virtually a state at the threshold of birth." Counselor Benjamin V. Cohen concluded that partition offered the "best practical chance of settlement."[15]

On the other hand, NEA officials identified problems with partition. Borders drawn to recognize population demographics would complicate transportation, communications, defense, and economic development in both states. The 40 percent Arab minority in the Jewish state might lose civil rights. Partition seemed likely to trigger a war of Arab resistance that would create an opportunity for Soviet meddling and disrupt oil supplies needed to fuel the Marshall Plan in Europe. Henderson advanced an alternative plan to create a multinational trusteeship and grant independence when Palestine seemed ready.[16]

In light of their uncertainty regarding the best way to handle the Palestine problem, U.S. officials resisted Zionist pressure to endorse partition. Secretary of State George C. Marshall and Henderson convinced Truman on 5 June to urge citizens to avoid action prejudicing UNSCOP's objectivity. Privately, Truman displayed irritation at the Zionists. "We could have settled this Palestine thing if U.S. politics had been kept out of it," he grumbled in May. When a Chicago attorney warned that Truman's support for Palestinians would cost him the 1948 election, Truman privately complained that "it is drivels [*sic*] such as this that makes Anti-Semites." The president also once remarked that he had received "35,000 pieces of mail and propaganda" from Zionists and that he had "piled it up and put a match to it."[17]

U.S. officials also expressed relief that subtle Zionist efforts to influence UNSCOP seemed to backfire. The U.S. consul in Jerusalem, Robert Macatee, noted that UNSCOP had been "feted *ad nauseam* by the Jewish Community" but that most committee members proved immune to the lavish treatment. The Zionists seemed to win over only Enrique Fabregat of Uruguay and Jorge García-Granados of Guatemala. The latter ardently defended Zionist interests after reportedly enjoying "'a beautiful friendship' with a Jewess named 'Emma,'" but his behavior alienated his colleagues. "Can't you do something about these Banana Republics?" the Australian delegate asked Macatee in disgust. "They're terrible."[18]

In contrast to the Zionist campaign for partition, Arab leaders refused to cooperate with UNSCOP. Syria, Saudi Arabia, Yemen, and the Arab League protested that UNSCOP was biased against Arab interests, and Palestinians boycotted its hearings. Various statesmen warned that they would forcefully resist partition. Terrorist attacks, such as the 6 May bombing of the U.S.-owned Metro Cinema in Cairo, suggested that Arab public opinion associated partition with the United States.[19]

In a final report on 31 August 1947, UNSCOP unanimously advised the termination of the British mandate and independence of Palestine. A minority of three members called for Palestine to become a single federal state after three years of U.N. governance. But a majority of eight endorsed partition, with independence to follow a two-year transition period during which the United Nations would negotiate an economic union, safeguard minority rights, and

Beirut

Damascus

MEDITERRANEAN
SEA

LEBANON

SYRIA

GALILEE

Migdal

Haifa

WEST
BANK

Tel Aviv
Jaffa

Jordan River

Amman

Latrun
Jerusalem

Gaza

Hebron

DEAD
SEA

El Arish

ISRAEL

JORDAN

Auja

EGYPT

NEGEV

SINAI

Partition of 1947

Areas made part of Israel
after the Arab War, 1949

0   100 km

0   50 mi

SAUDI ARABIA

Map 2. Israel and Its Arab Neighbors

establish an international regime in Jerusalem. UNSCOP had chosen partition as the best solution to the Palestine dispute.[20]

The Partition Vote at the United Nations

The United States became deeply involved in the Palestine dispute during General Assembly consideration of UNSCOP's recommendation for partition. Consistent with their thinking since the early 1940s, State Department and Pentagon policy makers strongly opposed partition because they feared that it would eviscerate U.S. interests in the Arab world. But Truman, in keeping with his action during the immigration debate, rejected this advice and fully supported partition on terms favorable to the prospective Jewish state. With U.S. backing, the General Assembly passed a partition resolution in November 1947. As the diplomats had anticipated, U.S. relations with Arab states experienced an immediate and deep decline.

The General Assembly convened in September 1947 to discuss the UNSCOP report amid growing awareness that partition had become a volatile issue. Britain made clear that it would not enforce partition and would depart Palestine no later than August 1948. Although some Zionists were displeased by certain aspects of the UNSCOP proposals, the Jewish Agency accepted partition because the plan would achieve statehood. By contrast, Iraqi Foreign Minister Fadhil Jamali called partition "ridiculous," the Syrian press derided it as a "mutilation," and King Farouk of Egypt protested vigorously. Shadowy terrorist groups bombed the U.S. consulate in Jerusalem on 13 October, threatened Americans in Iraq, and vowed to wage holy war to prevent partition.[21]

U.N. debates on the UNSCOP report forced U.S. officials to decide whether to support or oppose partition. Nearly all State Department officials opposed partition because it would trigger war, provoke Arab and Muslim retaliation against U.S. interests, and fail in the absence of British enforcement. "The Arab world is perilously close to the point at which governments no longer lead the people," the State Department observed, "but are dragged along in their wake." The NEA favored an international trusteeship, the UNSCOP minority plan, or immediate independence of a unified Palestine as the Arab states demanded. Only Robert McClintock of the State Department's Office of Special Political Affairs endorsed partition as the least objectionable alternative.[22]

Intelligence and military and experts also criticized partition. The Central Intelligence Group predicted that the plan would spawn violence, instability, xenophobia, and communist activity sponsored by Moscow. Partition "is capable of changing the development of the Arab World from one of evolution in cooperation with the West, to one of revolution with the support of the USSR."

The Joint Chiefs of Staff (JCS) declared that partition "would prejudice United States strategic interests" in oil-rich Iraq and Saudi Arabia. Joseph W. Bendersky suggests that the Pentagon's opposition to partition reflected a fear, nurtured by the military's anti-Semitic culture, that Zionism had planted the seeds of communism in the Middle East.[23]

Despite these concerns, Truman prevented such officials from blocking partition. When Marshall declared on 17 September that the United States "gives great weight" to the UNSCOP majority report, Zionists protested intensely that he had repudiated partition, and Truman directed the State Department explicitly to support it. At Niles's urging, the president appointed Hilldring to the U.S. mission to the United Nations to ensure that U.S. representatives obeyed the president's directive. State Department officials tried to appease Arabs by allocating the Negev Desert to the Arab state, but Truman quashed the idea after an emotional appeal from Weizmann. By November, the U.S. government indicated that it would vote for partition but would not pressure other states to do so.[24]

Truman's action was consistent with currents in U.S. public opinion. In 1947 and 1948, polls found that Americans supported partition by a two-to-one ratio. According to Eytan Gilboa, in 1948 the *New York Times* published thirty-one pro-Zionist/pro-Israeli editorials and zero pro-Arab ones, while the *Washington Post* ran eighteen pro-Zionist/pro-Israeli editorials and only one that was pro-Arab. Roman Catholics, who comprised nearly half of New England's population, remained anti-Zionist because their Church traditionally stressed that Jews had crucified Jesus Christ and opposed Jewish control of Christian shrines in Jerusalem. Nationally, however, such sentiment gave way to mounting sympathy for Holocaust survivors.[25]

As expected, Truman's decision to support partition alienated Arab governments. "This is the most dangerous step your country has ever taken in the Near Eastern political scene," Emir Faisal told U.S. Minister to Iraq George Wadsworth, echoing messages from other Arab quarters. Marshall clarified to Saudi, Syrian, Iraqi, Egyptian, and Lebanese envoys on 23 September that the United States aimed to support U.N. prestige more than endorse Zionism, but the Arab leaders warned that their citizens would not understand such subtleties.[26]

The General Assembly approved partition in November 1947 by a vote of thirty-three to thirteen, with ten abstentions. Consistent with Truman's directive, the U.S. voted in favor of the measure. In anticipation of an Arab backlash, Truman explained that he acted to support a majority recommendation of a U.N. committee and to reach a solution based on "reason, peace, and justice," not to perform a deliberately unfriendly act toward Arab states. "An apparently irresistible force is about to collide with a seemingly immovable object in Palestine," Clifton Daniel wrote in the *New York Times*, capturing the drama of the moment. "The force is Zionism and the object is Arab opposition to it."[27]

Unknown to Truman at the time, many U.S. citizens and members of Congress lobbied foreign states to support the partition resolution. Subsequent investigations by the State Department determined that Zionist individuals and groups—some claiming to speak for the U.S. government—had pressured delegations from Cuba, Honduras, Liberia, the Philippines, China, Haiti, and Ethiopia to support the measure. Pressures included cash bribes and threats to curtail business and U.S. foreign aid. Representative Sol Bloom (D–New York) telephoned the Liberian delegate to the United Nations, and thirty-one senators cabled the Greek legation. Filipino officials later admitted that they supported partition under pressure from ten senators.[28]

Rumors of such activities intensified the Arab anger ignited by the partition vote. Arab spokesmen amplified reports of the unofficial lobbying and levied accusations that Truman had personally phoned the presidents of Haiti and the Philippines, the State Department had pressured France, and the White House had ordered the delay in voting from 25 to 29 November solely to give Zionists time to line up votes. Such lobbying "made a mockery of the United Nations," Saudi officials charged. "I was myself there," Foreign Minister Faisal complained, "and saw the change in attitude of delegates before and after pressure was applied."[29]

Partition cast a pall over Arab-U.S. relations during the winter of 1947–48. Already strained by disputes over trade, military aid, and British imperialism, U.S. relations with Egypt suffered a major blow. The U.N. vote, U.S. Minister S. Pinckney Tuck reported from Cairo, was greeted "by widespread noisy demonstrations, by manifestoes and statements" against the United States. Egyptian Prime Minister Mahmoud Nokrashy Pasha revoked the Pentagon's privilege to overfly Egyptian territory and use Farouk Field in Cairo. The United States, embassy counselor Jefferson Patterson commented, "is certainly in bad odor at the moment."[30]

The situation in other countries looked no better. In Damascus on the day after the partition vote, a mob of two thousand people burned cars, smashed windows, and tore down the Stars and Stripes at the U.S. legation. Iraqi Defense Minister Shakir al-Wadi declared that "Americans had hopelessly lost Iraq's friendship." Camille Chamoun of Lebanon protested that "anything could have been [a] better solution" than partition. Saudi officials vowed to make "blood sacrifices" to prevent a Jewish state. "There are no assurances we can give nor any arguments we can use," U.S. Minister to Jidda J. Rives Childs cautioned, "to alter the King's attitude [of] implacable hostility and opposition" to partition.[31]

U.S. officials who assessed this situation took modest comfort in the absence of clear Soviet gains in Arab states. At first uninvolved in the Palestine dispute, the Soviet Union eventually backed a binational state solution and then approved partition, apparently to expedite the collapse of the British mandate and challenge the vestiges of British imperialism in neighboring Arab states. If nothing else, the Soviet move forestalled an immediate convergence of Soviet and Arab interests.[32]

Nonetheless, partition endangered Arab-U.S. relations and stability in the Arab world. The CIA predicted a winter of anti-U.S. violence, rising nationalism, and possible Soviet meddling followed by an Arab invasion of Palestine in the spring. "We are not only forfeiting the friendship of the Arab world," Henderson warned, "but we are incurring long-term Arab hostility towards us." The NEA's Gordon P. Merriam added that Arab states believed that a "Jewish beachhead in Palestine . . . would sooner or later be fatal to them."[33]

Conclusion

The United States became increasingly involved in the Palestine dispute in 1945–47. First drawn by a controversy over Jewish immigration to the British mandate, the Truman administration weighed in on the political status of the territory, served on the AACOI, and supported UNSCOP's majority proposal to partition Palestine. The increasing U.S. involvement resulted from the political activism of domestic Zionists and the official concern that declining British power and rising Arab-Jewish antagonism destabilized Palestine. The responsibilities that Truman incurred would prove difficult to relinquish.

During this formative period, a badly divided Truman administration gave crucial support to the Zionist cause. The State Department, Pentagon, and intelligence agencies opposed Zionism on security and diplomatic grounds, while Truman's personal advisers endorsed Zionism for political, cultural, and humanitarian reasons. At several crucial junctures, Truman ordered the implementation of pro-Zionist policy initiatives over the resistance of the security officials. His endorsement of Jewish immigration in 1945, his Yom Kippur statement in 1946, and his support of partition in 1947 revealed a pro-Zionist proclivity and a disregard for Arab sensitivities. His actions pleased Zionists, but U.S.-Arab relations soured, as the diplomats had anticipated.

By contrast, Truman refrained from unconditionally endorsing Zionism. He privately articulated disquiet over the situation in Palestine and regret that domestic political pressures influenced foreign policy (even as he submitted to such factors). After calling for immigration of a hundred thousand Jews, Truman refused Zionist entreaties to endorse a higher number. He declined to promote Zionist objectives during the UNSCOP mission and registered distaste for the assertive style of certain Zionist leaders. The unofficial meddling in the partition vote at the United Nations especially angered Truman. Although his actions appeared pro-Zionist, Truman also harbored anti-Zionist impulses. His indecisiveness caused inconsistency in his policy on Palestine and encouraged future conflict among his advisers.

4

DIPLOMACY AND CONFLICT
The Creation of Israel and the Arab-Israeli War
of 1948–1949

Although intended to resolve the Palestine conflict, the November 1947 U.N. partition resolution intensified the controversy. The May 1948 establishment of Israel and subsequent Arab-Israeli war caused U.S. leaders widespread political and military problems. In early 1948, the American government faced a dilemma about whether to support or rescind partition in the face of intense Arab opposition; in addition, the United States had to decide whether to recognize the state of Israel. When international hostilities erupted, issues such as Jewish immigration to Israel, arms supply to warring states, and economic aid to Israel aggravated the situation. The prospect of using U.S. soldiers to pacify Palestine lingered in the background. Israeli leaders attempted to exploit the 1948 U.S. presidential election to serve the new country's aims. In short, partition triggered developments that destabilized the Middle East and seriously challenged U.S. influence there.

Through this tumultuous period, the Harry S. Truman administration remained deeply divided into pro- and anti-Zionist camps. White House advisers favored policies that would facilitate the establishment of a Jewish state and please Zionist Americans; in contrast, officials in the State Department and Pentagon fretted about the decline in Arab amity toward the West, on which national security interests rested. In the months following partition, these two camps quarreled over partition, the recognition of Israel, Arab-Israeli disputes, and Israel's influence in U.S. domestic politics.

President Truman found it difficult to formulate a consistent policy toward the Palestine conflict. He was both distracted by momentous events in the Cold War and determined to privilege global considerations over Middle East interests whenever the two conflicted. He was buffeted by the conflicting advice of his personal and professional advisers and unable to reconcile his national and domestic political interests. Sudden and dramatic events in the Arab-Israeli conflict made it difficult for the president proactively to formulate policy. Truman's policy remained reactive and inconsistent in 1947–49 and contributed to the tension in U.S. relations with both Israel and the Arab community.

During the era of Israel's creation, U.S. officials and the leaders of Palestine's Jewish community faced the challenge of negotiating a major transition in their relationship. Accustomed to engaging in back-channel diplomacy among pro-Zionists inside and outside the U.S. government, poststatehood Israeli leaders found it difficult to limit themselves to formal diplomatic channels. The new country's government faced an "influence dilemma," an agonizing realization that unofficial diplomacy—however successful it seemed at shaping U.S. policy —alienated top U.S. officials and thus weakened the formal relationship between the two nations.

For their part, U.S. officials haltingly came to grips with the new circumstance of Israeli sovereignty. Israel achieved statehood infused with nationalism, ready boldly to pursue its national aims, and reluctant to honor U.N. decrees or foreign directives. U.S. officials, by contrast, expected Israel to adhere to U.S. pressure and U.N. resolutions as if Israeli territory were still a mandate. The American government faced a "firmness dilemma," thinking that firmness would compel Israel to submit to U.S. desires when in most cases that stance provoked Israeli defiance.[1] That most State Department officials referred in late 1949 to Israeli territory as "Palestine" and to Israelis as "Jews" reveals willful or subconscious reluctance to accept the reality of Israel. The influence and firmness dilemmas added layers of complexity to the evolution of U.S. policy in 1947–49.

Trusteeship, Pacification, and Israeli Statehood

U.S. policy toward Palestine passed through a tumultuous phase in early 1948. As mounting violence and Arab obstructionism made partition seem impractical, the State Department proposed replacing the partition plan with a U.N. trusteeship over Palestine. Truman approved this plan but also assured Zionists that he continued to support partition, an inconsistency that caused him political embarrassment. Yet in spring 1948, U.S. officials found trusteeship as unworkable as partition, belatedly seeking to enact a truce in Palestine as events there raced out of American control.

In the aftermath of partition, civil war erupted. Fighting intensified after 11 December 1947, when Britain announced that it would evacuate Palestine on 15 May 1948. Palestinian forces threatened Jewish settlements through March 1948, when the Haganah took the offensive, secured control of areas designated to the Jews by the partition plan, and opened a corridor to Jewish Jerusalem.

The Jewish Agency prepared to declare statehood, but Palestinian leaders and the Arab League failed to prepare an Arab state. Instead, Jordan fortified the West Bank, and other powers prepared to invade Jewish areas.[2]

Jewish immigration to Palestine also inflamed tensions. Arab states and Britain charged that Jewish immigrants took up arms against Palestinian Arabs. Concerned that many immigrants from Eastern Europe were communists, U.S. officials tried to block the landing in Palestine of the *Pan York* and *Pan Crescent*, ships that sailed from Bulgaria in December 1947 with twelve thousand passengers, including some two thousand reportedly "nominated" by Soviet authorities. Jewish Agency officials, however, disputed these charges and refused to halt the voyages.[3]

A controversy over arms control further destabilized the situation. The Truman administration imposed an embargo on arms supply to Palestine and neighboring Arab states in November 1947 and convinced the United Nations to follow suit in early 1948. Jewish Agency officials, U.S. Zionists, and White House advisers pressed Truman to abolish the embargo against the Jews, to no avail. At the same time, Zionists smuggled airplanes, explosives, and ammunition from the United States, while Britain secretly armed its Arab allies over low-key U.S. State Department protests.[4]

In this context, State and Defense Department officials renewed their opposition to partition. Evidence of Zionist meddling in the U.N. vote and Arab reactions to it reinforced these leaders' original resistance to the idea. The Arabian-American Oil Company suspended construction of the Trans-Arabian Pipeline—considered vital to Europe's oil supply—given unsettled conditions in Syria and Jordan. Above all, State and Defense officials feared that partition would lead to an Arab-Jewish war in which the Soviets would gain political influence. Britain refused to enforce the partition plan, the Pentagon opposed sending U.S. soldiers into the fray, and the long and overlapping territorial boundaries proposed in the U.N. resolution seemed a recipe for perpetual conflict. The State Department proposed asking the General Assembly to establish a trusteeship over Palestine under U.N. or Western supervision until the residents of Palestine formed a permanent government.[5]

Truman responded inconsistently to the trusteeship idea. He encouraged the State Department to pursue trusteeship by blaming the Palestine imbroglio on "British bullheadedness and the fanaticism of our New York Jews." More important, when Secretary of State George C. Marshall proposed asking the U.N. Security Council to reconsider partition, Truman approved "in principle," provided "that nothing should be presented . . . that could be interpreted as a recession on our part from the position we took in the General Assembly." At the request of U.S. officials, the Security Council voted on 5 March to reconsider partition.[6]

Truman affirmed this initial step toward trusteeship over the objections of personal advisers and Zionist activists. Special Counsel Clark Clifford warned that a policy shift would destroy U.S. and U.N. credibility and that the trusteeship idea "comes from those who never wanted partition to succeed and who have been determined to sabotage it." Zionist groups organized public rallies to pressure the administration to implement partition at once. On 8 March, however, Truman authorized Marshall to advance a trusteeship plan because partition seemed unworkable, and on 19 March, U.S. Ambassador to the United Nations Warren R. Austin asked the Security Council to approve such a plan. Distracted by mounting tensions caused by the 25 February Czech coup, Truman failed to clarify the timing of the State Department's action, consider the likely public reaction, or recognize the incompatibility of partition and trusteeship.[7]

Conversely, Truman also assured Zionists of U.S. support for partition. Exhausted by Zionist politicking, Truman had denied Jewish Agency leader Chaim Weizmann's request for an audience in February, but after Truman's longtime friend and former business partner, Eddie Jacobson, intervened, Truman agreed to meet Weizmann on 18 March. When Weizmann argued that "the choice for our people . . . is between statehood and extermination," Truman said that he remained committed to partition. Truman did not reconcile this pledge with the State Department initiative that he had approved on 8 March, and no one informed the State Department of Truman's new statement.[8]

Austin's U.N. announcement of the presidentially approved new policy on trusteeship occurred one day after Truman's pledge to Weizmann, igniting a major political controversy and a frenzy of angry accusations. The State Department expressed bewilderment about Truman's actions. Clifford accused the State Department of deliberately misleading the president by failing to disclose its ultimate intentions, while the pro-Zionist public pilloried the administration for double-crossing the Zionists. "Isn't that hell?" Truman fumed in his diary. "I'm now in the position of a liar and a double-crosser." Truman had not realized that he was following an inconsistent policy, Alonzo Hamby aptly observes, "until reality hit him like a sledgehammer."[9]

Despite the political firestorm, U.S. officials pursued the trusteeship initiative against great odds. Truman clarified publicly on 25 March that he sought a trusteeship as a temporary measure, designed to stabilize Palestine from the expiration of the mandate on 15 May until partition could be implemented. State Department officials took steps to establish a trusteeship regime. They convened the General Assembly on 17 April and circulated a trusteeship charter among U.N. members. Yet even if the United Nations approved trusteeship, Gordon P. Merriam of the NEA noted, "the difficulties in the way of working it out are colossal."[10]

The reluctance of any power to enforce trusteeship formed one major difficulty of the plan. The JCS estimated that enforcement would require between one hundred thousand and two hundred thousand U.S. soldiers, and Secretary of Defense James Forrestal warned that sending fifty thousand troops would drain defense spending, exhaust the entire U.S. Army and Marine reserves, and render "meaningless" the American commitments to Italy, Iran, Greece, Turkey, and China. Army officers stressed that one hundred thousand British troops had proved unable to stop terrorism and that U.S. forces would face comparative disadvantages based on their "lack of established intelligence channels and unfamiliarity with languages, customs, and terrain." The deputy director of army intelligence, Colonel Carter W. Clarke, concluded that "no US troops should be sent to Palestine."[11]

Domestic political pressure also undermined the prospect for trusteeship. On 23 March, Truman noted a Zionist "barrage" on the issue, and envoys from the American Jewish Committee, the American Jewish Labor Council, and various labor unions visited Foggy Bottom to denounce trusteeship. State Department officials detected "a new smear campaign" against NEA Director Loy Henderson, the main advocate of trusteeship, and in early May Truman appointed General John Hilldring as special assistant to Marshall, apparently to balance Henderson. David Ben-Gurion mobilized Nachum Goldmann, a Zionist long active in the Jewish Agency and the World Jewish Congress, to lobby U.S. officials to support partition as the best resolution of the civil war in Palestine.[12]

Nor did trusteeship win the support of Zionists in Palestine or their Arab opponents. "The Jews have no use for trusteeship," Eliahu Epstein of the Jewish Agency told Henderson. Agency leader Moshe Sharett informed Marshall on 8 May that the agency would declare statehood a week later. "The State was within our physical grasp," he argued. "We would not commit suicide to gain [the] friendship" of the United States. While Syria, Lebanon, Iraq, Jordan, and Egypt applauded the reconsideration of partition, they remained profoundly suspicious of trusteeship, especially after Truman's 25 March statement. According to the CIA, Arab countries viewed the trusteeship plan as "a device for the surreptitious imposition of partition."[13]

Escalating violence in Palestine further diminished the prospects for any diplomatic settlement of the Arab-Jewish controversy. On 9 April, Irgun and Stern Gang forces entered the Arab village of Deir Yasin and killed 250 persons, half of them women and children, stirring anger among Palestinians. The British withdrawal from Haifa on 21 April triggered a battle for that city. After the Haganah reopened the road from Tel Aviv to Jerusalem on 10 May, the fight for Jerusalem intensified.[14]

In fact, U.S. officials proved unable even to negotiate a truce in Palestine. Truman called for a cease-fire in his 25 March statement, and State Department officials pressed for the cessation of hostilities. The Security Council passed a cease-fire resolution on 17 April and established the Truce Commission, comprised of the U.S., French, and Belgian consuls in Jerusalem, on 23 April. But the Jewish Agency indicated that it would accept a truce only if it gained statehood, while the Arab Higher Committee and the Arab League demanded a revocation of partition and a moratorium on Jewish immigration as conditions for a truce. To widespread Arab public acclaim, Arab leaders meeting in Amman on 26 April decided to occupy Palestine on the termination of the mandate.[15]

Badly wounded by the violence and animosity in Palestine, the trusteeship plan was finished off by the declaration of Israeli statehood on 15 May 1948. As the British mandate expired, the National Council of Jewish Communities of Palestine declared the independence of Israel in the territory allotted to a Jewish state under the partition plan. "No one can question the courage or the high purpose of this act of self-assertion," the *New York Times* commented, capturing the significance of the deed, "or doubt that Partition, long discussed, long challenged, long postponed, is now a living fact."[16]

To make good their declaration of independence, Zionist leaders quickly formed a provisional government of Israel. Ben-Gurion became prime minister, and Chaim Weizmann, whose moderate diplomacy seemed ill-suited to the task of securing independence, occupied the largely ceremonial office of president. Moshe Sharett, for years a close adviser of Ben-Gurion in the Jewish Agency, became foreign minister. The provisional government established the Israel Defense Forces (IDF) on the foundation of the Haganah to defend the new state and quickly organized other departments to govern its people and land.[17]

Recognition of Israel

The declaration of Israeli statehood confronted U.S. officials with a stark choice. Since March, they had increasingly sensed the futility of trusteeship and anticipated a declaration of Jewish statehood. Deliberations on how to react to such an event intensified in early May as American leaders realized the imminence of the declaration. When confronted with a decision about recognizing the new Jewish state, Truman dropped his interest in trusteeship and made another important policy change.

Consistent with the established pattern, Truman heard conflicting advice from the State Department and the White House staff on the issue of recognition. At a crucial meeting on 12 May, Clifford urged Truman to indicate at once that he would recognize a Jewish state, both to affirm his support of partition and to steer the new state away from communism. Undersecretary of State Robert A. Lovett urged Truman to wait, warning that making such a move while the Security Council debated trusteeship would destroy the prestige of the U.S. government. Upset that Truman had even consulted domestic advisers, Marshall protested that recognition would comprise a "transparent dodge to win a few votes" and remarked that if Truman ordered it, Marshall would vote against the president in the upcoming election. That statement, Clifford later recalled, was Truman's "sharpest rebuke ever" and "brought the meeting to a grinding halt."[18]

To the deep regret of the State Department, however, Clifford found a way to facilitate Truman's early recognition of the Jewish state. After Truman told Clifford that the United States would recognize the Jewish state once it was established, Clifford encouraged Jewish Agency officials to declare statehood at once and to solicit U.S. recognition. Within eleven minutes of the proclamation of Israeli independence, Epstein requested and Truman approved U.S. recognition. To no avail, Lovett asked Clifford to delay recognition by a few days both to prepare Arab states for the news and to ensure the physical safety of U.S. envoys in the region.[19]

Truman's action dramatically affected the Palestine situation as well as U.S relations with Israel and Arab states. Recognition of Israel, Anne O'Hare McCormick wrote in the *New York Times*, "does more than anything to give it reality and to emphasize the difference between the Palestine problem of today and that of yesterday." Israelis were electrified by news of the deed. But Marshall told Truman that it made "a hell of a mess" at the United Nations, while Director of Navy Intelligence E. T. Wooldridge added that "our prestige and influence in the Middle East has suffered what may be irreparable damage."[20]

In the weeks that followed, the State Department tried to limit the impact of recognition. With Truman's approval, Lovett clarified that the United States would withhold de jure recognition because Israel's borders were in flux and because communists might gain control of the government. The department also announced that the U.S. envoy to Israel, Charles F. Knox Jr., would serve as special representative rather than minister or ambassador and that the United States did not recognize the new government as the legal guardian of the Jews of Jerusalem. The State Department also advised the Pentagon to verify that military attachés to the mission in Tel Aviv were neutral on the Arab-Israeli dispute.[21]

Although elated by U.S. recognition, some Israelis felt unsatisfied by U.S. policy. Prime Minister Ben-Gurion thanked Truman for helping to "end the agelong Jewish tragedy," but Epstein, who became Israel's first special representative in Washington, considered the absence of de jure recognition a rebuff. White House staff members worried that the Republican Party would exploit the limited recognition. Clifford's aide and foreign policy adviser, George M. Elsey, called the terms of Knox's appointment "a snub" that would boomerang on Truman.[22]

Recognition of Israel enraged the Arab states and Britain. Navy intelligence officials detected widespread dismay among Arab peoples and evidence that most governments were "profoundly shocked" and ready to blame the United States if Arab armies entering Palestine were repulsed. Recognition enraged Britain, Policy Planning Staff Chairman George F. Kennan noted, threatening to "disrupt the unity of the western world and to undermine our entire policy toward the Soviet Union." British Foreign Secretary Ernest Bevin wrote that Truman's action "left us bewildered and frustrated."[23]

U.S. officials who worried about the impact of Truman's move were somewhat relieved when the Soviet Union extended full, de jure recognition of Israel within days of its creation. The Soviets were motivated by an affinity for Israelis as fellow victims of Nazi depredations, an awareness that Israel allowed communists to function politically while Arab states repressed communists, and an identification with Israel's leaders, many of whom were socialists with East European or Russian roots.[24] Yet U.S. officials continued to worry that Arab rage, even without Soviet backing, would undermine vital interests in the region.

Truman's decision to recognize Israel at the moment of its birth has remained controversial among historians. Michael T. Benson, for example, sympathetically portrays the president as honoring his cultural values and keeping his word despite bureaucratic opposition. Michael Cohen more critically concludes that "Truman had made tyrannical use of his prerogative" and "rendered incalculable damage to American integrity, and to the prestige of the United Nations."[25] Such views are not mutually exclusive. Truman's recognition of Israel was a lineal descendent of his earlier pro-Zionist policies and support for partition. Coming on the heels of the trusteeship initiative, however, recognition also comprised a tactical reversal that aggravated Arab discontent regarding U.S. policy, sharpened the divide within the U.S. government, and stained the U.S. reputation.

U.S. Policy during the Arab-Israeli War

The simultaneous expiration of the British mandate, declaration of Israeli statehood, U.S. recognition of Israel, and invasion by Arab armies drastically changed the situation in Palestine. An undeclared civil war among inhabitants of a British mandate suddenly became an international war. The issues that had monopolized U.S. attention since 1946—partition and trusteeship—became moot points, replaced by a desire to support U.N. efforts to contain the fighting and to find terms for a permanent settlement of the Arab-Israeli conflict.

The Arab-Israeli war that began in May 1948 passed through a series of hostilities and uneasy cease-fires. Warfare raged from 15 May to 8 June, followed by a truce from 8 June to 8 July, followed by a burst of fighting from 8 to 18 July before a second cease-fire took effect. The early military situation was extremely fluid and confusing. Centered in Tel Aviv and Haifa, the IDF defended Israel's Jewish population and maintained access to Jerusalem. Two Egyptian columns moved northward, one along the coast and another toward Hebron and Jerusalem. Lebanese and Syrian troops fought Jewish forces in the north and northeast, and the Arab Legion crossed the West Bank and approached Jerusalem. Palestinians battled the IDF in the middle of the country. Sporadic consultations between Israeli and Arab statesmen did little to stem the war.[26] (See map 2.)

Israel clearly bested its adversaries during war and truce. In May, Israel repulsed Lebanon's foray into northern Palestine and conducted raids north of the border, and in early June the Jewish state destroyed two major Egyptian garrisons between Migdal and Gaza. In violation of the first truce, the IDF bolstered its defenses of Jerusalem, airlifted in two thousand British- and U.S.-trained soldiers, stole two Cromwell tanks from departing British forces, acquired Soviet weapons, and landed at Haifa a ship bearing men of military age and weapons. When Egyptian tanks broke the truce by attacking the IDF, Israel launched an offensive while blaming Cairo for resuming the war. As Israel gained territory and morale, Israeli Foreign Minister Sharett boasted in July that the Arab powers' decision to fight "has been their undoing."[27]

Arab forces, by contrast, suffered a string of setbacks. As they emerged from the yoke of European imperialism, Arab states tended to compete for regional influence. Suspicious of one another's territorial ambitions in Palestine, they refrained from coordinating military tactics. Michael Doran finds that Egypt entered the war as much to halt Jordan's move into Palestine and avert a Syrian-Iraqi union as to crush Israel. Moreover, the arms embargo forced Arab states to restrict operations, and morale plummeted among combat soldiers who faced an energized Israel. By July, Director of Central Intelligence R. H. Hillenkoetter reported, Arab leaders realized that they faced a hopeless military situation in Israel.[28]

The United States took a relatively passive posture during the early fighting. Truman focused on his reelection campaign and departed Washington for three weeks in June. The Soviet blockade of Berlin on 24 June absorbed the attention of top officials. Dispirited by the sudden widening of the conflict and by Truman's recognition of Israel, State Department officials merely endorsed the 20 May appointment of Count Folke Bernadotte of Sweden as U.N. mediator, encouraged the belligerents to honor the cease-fire resolutions passed by the Security Council on 22 May and 15 July, and maintained the arms embargo despite pressure from both sides to lift it. Foggy Bottom's frustration with the situation was revealed in foreign service officer Robert McClintock's private remark that he was leaving Washington on 2 July for a vacation at Martha's Vineyard, "where I intend to wash away the sins of the Chosen People—and their equally sinful adversaries—in clear salt water."[29]

Passivity also marked U.S. policy on the question of sending troops to enforce a U.N. settlement. In July–August, Bernadotte requested U.S. combat soldiers to guard his mission as it relocated from Rhodes to Jerusalem, to protect a crucial water pumping station at Latrun against sabotage, and to patrol the Israeli-Jordanian front near Jerusalem. But Pentagon officers doubted that U.S. forces would pacify the land, predicted that Arab states would criticize the arrival of American troops, and feared that terrorist attacks by the Irgun or the Stern Gang might even draw the United States into war against Israel. Compliance with Bernadotte's requests would generate other requests for U.S. police forces worldwide, the JCS feared, and, given the tensions over Berlin, trigger a Soviet response. Not even the 12 August demolition of the Latrun water station changed the Pentagon's thinking. It even refused State Department pleas for marines to guard U.S. diplomats in Jerusalem and Tel Aviv. Not until October, after U.S. envoys received death threats, did Forrestal send forty marines to the consulate in Jerusalem.[30]

In contrast to their unwillingness to send combat forces, U.S. officials acceded to Bernadotte's request for U.S. soldiers to serve as U.N. observers. The Pentagon reasoned that such observers might help Bernadotte implement a lasting cease-fire and diminish the danger of the Arab states turning to the Soviets. Officials in the Office of the Secretary of Defense considered the dispatch of observers the Pentagon's second-highest priority, after Berlin, in mid-1948. Truman approved on 1 June, and State Department officials arranged that only the United States, France, and Belgium—members of the Truce Commission— would supply such personnel. By August, 115 U.S. soldiers were assigned as U.N. observers in Israel/Palestine.[31]

War-related issues caused U.S.-Israeli relations to have a rocky beginning. Confronting the firmness dilemma, U.S. officials had difficulty accepting Israeli statehood. Affirming Bernadotte's decision that immigration of men of military age violated the cease-fires, for example, American leaders favored restrictions on Jewish immigration to Israel, slowed the departure of Jewish men from Germany, and reacted passively when Lebanon arrested sixty-nine Jewish men of military age aboard the *Marine Carp*, an American Export Lines passenger ship that called at Beirut en route to Haifa. Israeli officials, by contrast, insisted that they had a sovereign right to control immigration to their country.[32]

The United States and Israel also quarreled about the U.S. arms embargo. Backed by its domestic supporters, Israel pressed Truman for weapons during the first week of its independence, when Arab ground offensives and an Egyptian air raid on Tel Aviv made the new country anxious for warplanes and antiaircraft guns. Obtaining arms was "a matter of life or death," Sharett noted on 22 May. There "were no words [to] express [the] desperate urgent need of planes," he added weeks later. Israel's envoy to the United Nations, Abba Eban, argued that the U.N. embargo had expired with the mandate and should not apply to sovereign Israel.[33]

State Department and CIA officers, however, convinced Truman that the embargo enhanced the prospect of a negotiated settlement by limiting all powers' capacity to make war. Arab leaders would regard U.S. arming of Israel "as a virtual American alliance with the Jewish war effort and an American declaration of war" against the Arabs, the State Department cautioned. Arab states would sever relations with the West, curtail oil exports, and turn to Moscow for political assistance. Arab efforts to halt arms deliveries to Israel might trigger U.S.-Arab war, imperiling "the foundation-stone of US policy in Europe—partnership with a friendly and well-disposed Britain." With Truman's blessing, State Department officials rigidly enforced the embargo, protesting reported violations by Panama and Switzerland, blocking the export to Egypt of spare parts for civilian aircraft used by King Farouk, and monitoring Soviet arms supplied to both sides.[34]

The experience of the U.S. observers assigned to the United Nations also caused friction between the United States and Israel. An army attaché reported that the observers became "unanimous in disgust at Jewish actions," blamed the IDF for 90 percent of truce violations, and considered Israeli officials "cocky, arrogant, wise guys, liars" while Egyptians and Jordanians seemed "very cooperative." Because the Israelis defied Bernadotte, Marshall told Truman, the United States should withhold de jure recognition, oppose Israeli membership in the United Nations, and reject Israeli loan requests.[35]

Under the firmness dilemma, however, U.S. leaders had limited means to shape Israeli behavior. Indeed, Israeli officials chafed at the presence of U.N. officials in the country. "A large body of foreign people coming here to lay down the law on behalf of the U.N. went against the grain of the man in the street," Sharett told Bernadotte. "Why should Americans, Frenchmen, Belgians, and Swedes be coming here to boss us? . . . Why should we be treated as inferiors, when at long last we had achieved our independence?"[36]

The Bernadotte Plan

Reversing their passivity during the early months of war, U.S. officials became involved in a plan for a permanent settlement in Palestine formulated by U.N. mediator Bernadotte. Although the Arab states and Israel showed little enthusiasm for the plan, the State Department vigorously promoted it. But the department made little headway against Arab and Israeli opposition before Israeli extremists murdered Bernadotte in September 1948. U.S. efforts to promote the plan might even have stimulated additional Israeli military action.

Bernadotte sketched a framework for a final Arab-Israeli settlement in August 1948. He proposed that Arab states acquiesce in the existence of Israel, that Jordan annex the portions of Palestine not designated to Israel, and that both powers approve border alterations. In what was billed as a territorial compromise, Israel would retain the western Galilee, which had been designated to the Arabs but occupied by the IDF, and relinquish the Negev, which lay outside Israel's control although originally designated to it. An international regime would govern Jerusalem, and Israel would repatriate Palestinian refugees.[37]

Although Truman authorized Marshall to promote the Bernadotte Plan, Arab and Israeli leaders reacted coldly. Arab states refused to negotiate with Israel and complained about the absence of provisions for establishing a Palestinian state. Israeli officials declared no confidence in Bernadotte and insisted on direct Arab-Israeli negotiations rather than U.N. mediation. Sharett called the plan "a complete capitulation to Anglo-Arab pressure" and discarded the idea of relinquishing the Negev as "rubbish."[38]

To sell his proposal, Bernadotte made the fateful decision to move his headquarters from Rhodes to Jerusalem in late summer 1948. Israeli officials feared that Bernadotte's presence would raise the prospect of internationalizing Jerusalem, and rumors abounded in Israel that the mediator was a British agent. On 17 September, one day after Bernadotte formally submitted his plan to the United Nations, the Stern Gang assassinated him in Jerusalem.[39]

Israeli officials expressed deep remorse at Bernadotte's death. Sharett announced that he was "outraged by [the] abominable assassination . . . by desperadoes and outlaws who are execrated by [the] entire people of Israel." Foreign Ministry political adviser Leo Kohn felt chastened by Western allegations that extremist statements by government officials had encouraged the assassins. Israeli authorities promptly arrested two hundred Stern Gang members and pledged to ensure that no similar events occurred. (Cary David Stanger concludes, however, that Israel never brought the killers to justice.)[40]

U.S. officials and the media expressed profound anger at the assassination. Ralph Bunche, a U.S. diplomat in U.N. service, called the murder "an outrage against the international community." U.S. Consul John J. Macdonald charged the Israeli military governor in Jerusalem, Bernard Joseph, with personal responsibility for Bernadotte's death, and U.S. Navy Commander William R. Cox, a U.N. observer who had ridden in the automobile in which Bernadotte was killed, reported that Israel conducted a halfhearted investigation to find the gunmen. The *New York Times* condemned the "atrocious crime" as a blow to "the great experiment of substituting reason for force." At the extreme, U.S. Minister to Damascus James H. Keeley concluded that the murder provided "a good time to review the role that Jews have played in world affairs from the crucifixion of Christ, the Messiah, to the assassination of Bernadotte, the mediator, and to re-orient American policy accordingly."[41]

In the aftermath of Bernadotte's death, the State Department vigorously promoted his plan. Perhaps department officials were motivated by guilt over the Pentagon's refusal to supply the mediator with bodyguards; perhaps they calculated that they could exploit the worldwide remorse regarding the assassination to forge a consensus for a settlement. Bernadotte's death offered "a rare opportunity for settling this dispute if acted on decisively and promptly," Lovett told Truman. Marshall published and publicly endorsed the plan on 20–21 September. The assassination elevated the more ambitious and talented Bunche as the new mediator, Amitzur Ilan notes, and motivated several Western states to embrace the Bernadotte Plan.[42]

Unfortunately for the State Department, neither the Arab states nor Israel showed any inclination to approve the plan. Jordan agreed to consider it, but Lebanon, Iraq, Saudi Arabia, and Egypt charged that Bernadotte's murder revealed an Israeli expansionism that rendered peaceful coexistence impossible. The plan confirmed the "Zionist rape of Palestine," Syrian Foreign Minister Mushin Barazi noted. "If the United States . . . will give New York City to its Jewish inhabitants," Syrian President Shukry al-Quwatly chided, he would acquiesce "in the mutilation of Palestine and might even include a portion of Syria in the bargain."[43]

Israel remained equally hostile to the plan. Hoping that time would weaken the emotional effect of the assassination, the Foreign Ministry resolved to stall the plan at the United Nations, force Marshall to rescind his endorsement, and mobilize U.S. Zionists to win over Truman. Sharett attacked the territorial provisions of the plan, insisting that Israel must have both the Negev (which provided room for development, mineral wealth, and access to the Gulf of Aqaba) and the western Galilee (which the Arab states that invaded Israel did not deserve).[44]

In contesting these expansive Israeli claims, U.S. officials inadvertently encouraged Israel to resume warfare in late 1948. Some Israeli officials argued privately that bold action would ease U.S. pressure to yield Israeli claims to the Negev in exchange for control of the western Galilee, and the IDF touted its ability to rout Egyptian units in the southern desert. In this context, Deputy Undersecretary of State Dean Rusk commented to Eban on 1 October that Egypt's occupation of the Negev weakened Israel's claim to it. Five days later, the Israeli cabinet authorized Ben-Gurion to initiate military action in Negev.[45]

Ben-Gurion quickly used this authority to seize the northern Negev. Reports that Egypt fired on an Israeli convoy provided a pretext for a 15–21 October Israeli offensive that captured Beersheba, secured the northern Negev, and encircled a major contingent of Egyptian soldiers at Al Faluja. A 19 October Security Council cease-fire resolution urged both states to return to their pre–15 October borders. Israel accepted the cease-fire on 21 October but refused to surrender the land it had captured.[46]

U.S. Politics and the Decline of the Bernadotte Plan

Seriously wounded by Israeli and Arab opposition, the Bernadotte Plan also suffered damage during the 1948 U.S. presidential election campaign. Israeli officials were alarmed that Democratic and Republican leaders suspended campaigning on foreign policy issues because this silence enabled the State Department to promote the Bernadotte Plan. Thus, Israeli leaders encouraged the candidates of both parties to break their consensus and openly oppose the plan. Their efforts paid off in late October, when Truman pledged to reject key provisions of the plan, making it impossible for the State Department to sell it in the international realm.

To the despair of Israeli leaders, their country had declined as an issue in U.S. politics in summer 1948. The Republican Party platform called for recognition of and economic aid to Israel, and the Democrats pledged to recognize Israel, protect its borders, and provide it aid and arms. In light of the Berlin crisis, however, leaders of the two parties agreed not to campaign on foreign policy issues. Informed of this consensus by a "responsible source" in the U.S. government, Epstein reported in August that Truman was ready "to sacrifice Jewish interests if . . . greater stability can be assured." The bipartisan consensus made it hard for Israelis to counter Marshall's endorsement of the Bernadotte Plan.[47]

The rise in popularity of Bernadotte's plan in the aftermath of his murder galvanized Israeli officials to attack the bipartisan consensus as a means of undermining the plan. Epstein asked "friends in Government circles," such as White House adviser David Niles, Federal Security Administrator Oscar Ewing, and Hilldring, to urge Truman to denounce the plan. "Only intervention of your friend . . . can avert the worst dangers," Weizmann wrote to Eddie Jacobson. "Please go and see him without delay reminding him of [the] Democratic Party pledge." The American Zionist Emergency Council denounced the Bernadotte Plan in full-page advertisements in major newspapers.[48]

Truman's political advisers also crusaded against the Bernadotte Plan. The "Jewish situation in New York and large cities [has] turned against us terrifically by [the] Marshall and Bevin Bernadotte Plan," Democratic National Committee Chairman William M. Boyle Jr. advised Press Secretary Matt Connelly. Clifford warned, "We understand from our man on the Dewey train [*New York Star* reporter Bartley Crum] that Dewey is going to issue a very strong statement" criticizing the plan. On 29 September, Clifford phoned Lovett from the president's train in Tulsa to urge that Marshall repudiate the plan because "pressure from the Jewish groups on the President was mounting." Lovett replied, however, that reversing course would "label this country as . . . completely untrustworthy in international affairs."[49]

Israeli officials also pressed Republicans to renege on the consensus. The Israelis tasted success when Republican foreign policy expert John Foster Dulles wrote to Rabbi Abba Hillel Silver that Marshall's endorsement of the Bernadotte Plan was "in no sense a 'bipartisan' decision, but the decision of the Administration." In early October, however, Dulles disavowed this view in conversations with Israeli officials, and he and Rusk reaffirmed the agreement not to campaign on foreign policy. "Nothing could be more harmful to our cause," Epstein commented privately, "than this kind of a 'bipartisan' policy."[50]

Under Israeli and U.S. Jewish pressure, the bipartisan consensus finally collapsed in mid-October. Silver helped "mobilize our people all over the country . . . for an organized public expression of the Jewish position on the Bernadotte Plan," while Epstein pressured Dewey to issue a favorable statement that would force Truman, poised for a campaign swing through New York, to reply in kind. On 22 October, Dewey released a letter affirming his support of his party's platform on Israel. Two days later, Truman reiterated his support for the Democratic platform, notably the plank that Israel's borders must not be changed without its consent. Even Lovett conceded that Truman had to take this step, and Clifford called Dewey's action "the best thing that has happened to us to date."[51]

Israeli officials tried to cement their achievement by encouraging Truman to mistrust the State Department. Arthur Lourie of Israel's delegation to the United Nations launched "an energetic offensive" involving New York Mayor William O'Dwyer, labor leader Jacob S. Potofsky, and Senator Herbert H. Lehman (D–New York) to alert Truman that the State Department had betrayed him while he campaigned away from Washington. The Israelis also mobilized administration insiders such as Clifford, Niles, Ewing, and Agriculture Secretary Charles Brannan. One of these contacts reportedly got Truman "madder than hell," and, on 29 October, Truman ordered Marshall that "no statement be made or no action be taken on the subject of Palestine . . . without obtaining specific authority from me." Unaware of the Israeli-orchestrated pressure, Lovett attributed the president's message to Clifford's paranoia during the "silly season" of electoral campaigning, noting that "it has been absolute hell here."[52]

In a case of the influence dilemma, however, Israel's efforts to reach Truman caused problems. Epstein sensed that such efforts produced "undesirable complications" in his relations with the State Department. "Even loyal friends in Washington seem irritated," Israeli Foreign Ministry officer Michael Comay added. Indeed, Marshall complained to Sharett on 14 November that Israel nurtured "both direct official contacts as between governments and indirect internal influence through American circles." The United States would no longer tolerate back-channel intrigues, the secretary of state warned, but would protest by recalling its envoy to Tel Aviv. Truman would not overrule Marshall on this point, a White House source told Epstein, because Lovett had convinced the president that national security was at stake.[53]

In the aftermath of the presidential election, the State Department briefly tried to advance territorial provisions of the Bernadotte Plan on terms consistent with Truman's promise to gain Israel's consent to any border changes. After securing Truman's approval by stressing the strategic importance of linking British bases in Jordan and Egypt, Marshall asked Israel to relinquish the Negev in exchange for the western Galilee. Israeli retention of both territories, Lovett told Comay, was "morally and politically unsound." The State Department also supported a 4 November Security Council resolution calling on belligerent states to withdraw to their 15 October borders, a provision that would have required the Israeli departure from the northern Negev.[54]

The department found it impossible, however, to achieve such territorial changes under the conditions imposed by Truman. The Arab states and Israel made clear their enduring opposition to all aspects of the Bernadotte Plan, and Weizmann wrote to Truman that Israelis would not depart the Negev "unless they are bodily removed from it." Lovett proposed sanctions to compel Israel to honor the 4 November resolution, but Truman disapproved. The State Department settled for another Security Council resolution, dated 16 November, that urged the belligerents to negotiate armistices either directly or through the mediator.[55]

In December, the United Nations laid the Bernadotte Plan to rest. Because "events have overtaken many aspects" of the plan, Marshall rejected a proposed General Assembly resolution to affirm it. Instead, he supported an 11 December resolution that contained no mention of the Bernadotte Plan and established the Palestine Conciliation Commission (PCC)—with U.S., French, and Turkish members—to replace the mediator and pursue a settlement of the borders issue. Sharett was elated by what he called this "last and decisivest defeat" of the Bernadotte Plan. "We were on a good bicycle," G. Lewis Jones of the NEA noted, in what amounted to an obituary for the plan, "until somebody let the air out of the tires."[56]

War and Armistices, 1948–1949

As the Bernadotte Plan declined, Arab-Israeli hostilities resumed and threatened to escalate into wider conflict. During an offensive to conquer the southern Negev, Israeli forces crossed into Egypt and attacked British aircraft, thereby raising the prospect of British military action against Israel. To prevent such a development as well as to end the Israeli-Egyptian hostilities, U.S. diplomats actively searched for a permanent peace agreement. Stymied, they at least convinced the belligerents to sign armistice agreements.

Emboldened by the Bernadotte Plan's lack of success, Israeli leaders turned to hostilities to secure the southern Negev. Disputing U.N. authority to impose arbitration on his sovereign state, Ben-Gurion rejected Bunche's offer to negotiate an armistice as well as a similar offer from Major General William Riley, a U.S. officer serving as U.N. chief observer. Eliahu Sasson, director of the Israeli Foreign Ministry's Middle East Department, privately noted that the Israeli prime minister "has some military plans he wants to carry out prior [to] any serious official talks." On 22 December, the IDF attacked Egyptian units in the southern Negev using the rationale that Egypt refused to make peace.[57]

Israel's offensive provoked severe Western criticism. Britain proposed a stern U.N. resolution to force Israel to desist. But U.S. officials, arguing that the United States must remain impartial as a PCC member, shepherded a mere cease-fire resolution through the Security Council on 29 December. The same day, however, reported IDF crossings into Egypt aggravated the situation. Britain dispatched a battalion of combat soldiers to Aqaba and warned that if the reports proved true, the British treaty obligation to defend Egypt "would of course come into play." Truman warned Israel to withdraw at once from Egypt.[58]

Israeli officials tried to mitigate U.S. concerns. Sharett explained that the IDF crossed the border "in hot pursuit of an enemy driven out from a territory he had invaded in the course of a war of aggression." In a series of messages to Truman, Weizmann quoted the Psalms to explain Israel's military successes and hinted that the Soviets would back Israel in any fight with Britain. "I only pray" that Britain's "mischievous propaganda," he added, "may not succeed in misleading and embarrassing our friends."[59]

As the Israelis who sensed the influence dilemma might have anticipated, their appeals fell flat, and the United States persisted in pressuring Israel to evacuate Egypt. "Public and official Washington opinion [is] dangerously tense, almost hostile," toward Israel, Epstein reported. Even Truman considered Israel a "troublemaker, endangering [the] peace by flouting [the] U.N." In this context, Sharett assured the United States on 1 January 1949 that the IDF would retreat from Egypt. After Egypt agreed on 4 January to conduct armistice talks, Israel accepted the U.N. cease-fire on 7 January, ending the round of hostilities.[60]

Ironically, the moment of greatest drama in the battle occurred after the cease-fire took effect. When Egypt charged that IDF units remained in Egypt, British planes reconnoitered the battle zone, and five of them were shot down by Israeli jets. Israel charged that the British planes had invited the fire by over-flying Israeli combat forces, but Britain responded by putting its forces on alert, declaring all Israeli aircraft hostile, and issuing an ultimatum for Israel to withdraw from Egypt. Truman urged Britain to show restraint but warned Israel that in case of a showdown, he would protect his "vital common interests" with Britain rather than his friendship with Israel. Even though Prime Minister Clement Attlee relented under domestic criticism for risking war, Ben-Gurion withdrew his forces from Egypt on 10 January, bringing the crisis to a close.[61]

The 7 January cease-fire set the stage for Egyptian-Israeli armistice talks mediated by Bunche. U.S. officials endorsed the talks but generally allowed Bunche to take charge. They intervened only once, when Truman pressed Israel to allow Egyptian troops at Al Auja to withdraw unharmed. On another occasion, the State Department prepared to take Egypt's side in an argument about Beer-sheba. But after Eliahu Elath (formerly Epstein) "briefed Niles and Clifford" and left a "short paper for their Chief," the department remained silent. Egypt and Israel signed an armistice on 24 February 1949.[62]

In the months that followed, U.S. officials encouraged Bunche's mediation of armistice agreements between Israel and other Arab belligerents. Israeli negotiations with Lebanon, considered the Jewish state's least-hostile adversary, stalemated when the IDF refused to depart occupied territory in southern Lebanon. Although U.S. officials declined to become involved, Israel agreed to withdraw on the rationale that the security value of south Lebanon was not worth the risk of alienating the United States and France, PCC members that tended to look after Lebanon. Israel and Lebanon signed an armistice on 23 March.[63]

Israel and Jordan mediated a similar deal. Negotiations briefly stalled in March when the Arab Legion reported that IDF units threatened Aqaba and had entered Jordan at Gharandal. State Department officials discouraged both powers from hostilities, and Israeli officers who contemplated operations against Jordan reconsidered amid warnings that such operations would anger Truman and stimulate a British move into the Negev. "Our international position though seemingly impressive," Israeli Ambassador to the United Nations Eban cabled, "could be reversed overnight if Truman became alienated." Israel and Jordan signed an armistice on 3 April.[64]

U.S. officials also took maximum interest but minimal action in deescalating the Iraqi-Israeli confrontation. Iraq stubbornly refused to engage in armistice talks and announced that it would simply withdraw its twenty thousand soldiers from Palestine, turning over to Jordan control of the land the Iraqis occupied. When intelligence reports indicated that the IDF planned to occupy the territory in question, U.S. Secretary of State Dean G. Acheson cautioned Sharett on 22 March that departure of the Iraqis would contribute to stability. The Iraqi withdrawal took place without incident.[65]

The Israeli-Syrian armistice required the most time and effort by Bunche. Talks were delayed by Colonel Husni Zaim's coup in Damascus in March 1949 and by Ben-Gurion's refusal to consider Zaim's offer of an armistice in exchange for land inside the border of Palestine. In fact, Ben-Gurion ordered the IDF to enter Syria to defend a border kibbutz in the aftermath of Zaim's coup, and the Israeli prime minister later called Zaim "a little Mussolini" whose taunts made war likely. U.S. officials quietly encouraged Ben-Gurion to make peace and Zaim to withdraw to his side of the border. Israel and Syria signed an armistice on 20 July, bringing to a close the Arab-Israeli war of 1948–49.[66]

Conclusion

Israel clearly won the war of 1948–49. It secured national independence, suppressed its Palestinian population, rebuffed foreign invasion, and secured control of territory apportioned to it by the partition plan as well as additional land designated to others. The new nation also used politics, diplomacy, and war to derail the Bernadotte Plan, which called on Israel to concede territory in exchange for peace. Although its strategic position remained tenuous in 1949, Israel enjoyed a remarkable degree of security. The Arab states, by contrast, were defeated militarily and dispirited politically.

The Cold War, which had drawn the United States to the Middle East, shaped overall U.S. policy toward the Arab-Israeli conflict at this decisive moment. When the crisis over Berlin portended global war in the summer of 1948, for example, the United States refrained from sending soldiers to enforce the Bernadotte Plan, which promised to settle the conflict on compromise terms, and censured Israeli military moves against Egypt and Jordan, which might have resolved the conflict on terms favoring Israel. Privileging anticommunist containment over an Arab-Israeli settlement per se, U.S officials refrained from compelling either side in the dispute to make the concessions necessary to end the conflict.

Within the Cold War context, the United States found it necessary to adjust to the momentous changes in Palestine that followed the partition resolution. After Israel declared statehood, efforts to reconsider partition, establish a trusteeship, and formulate a truce gave way to attempts to achieve cease-fires and promote a permanent peace settlement of an international conflict. U.S. diplomats slowly came to grips with the new reality of Israeli statehood and the concomitant decline in U.N. and U.S. authority to shape developments in the former Palestine.

As U.S. officials faced the problems associated with the emergence of the new Israeli nation, the old division between pro-Zionists on the White House staff and anti-Zionists in the State Department and Pentagon persisted. These two camps engaged in heated debates over numerous issues ranging from recognition of the Jewish state to the Bernadotte Plan. Prodded into action by Israeli officials and animated by domestic political concerns, the pro-Zionists convinced Truman to recognize Israel, hamper the Bernadotte Plan, and take other steps in support of Israel. As in the months preceding the partition resolution, Truman offered critical support for Zionist aspirations in Palestine and Israel. Even the experts in the State Department and Pentagon who opposed the creation of a Jewish state eventually acknowledged that Israel was there to stay.

Yet U.S. support of Israel had limits. In early 1948, Truman authorized the State Department to consider trusteeship instead of partition, and he refused to deploy troops to defend the Jewish community of Palestine or the new state of Israel or to provide Israel with weapons, even when most observers predicted its doom. He declined to promise recognition of the Jewish state before it was established, and he allowed the State Department to dilute his 15 May 1948 action by withholding de jure recognition and by appointing a minor official as envoy to Tel Aviv. Truman occasionally expressed his disgust for certain U.S. Zionists and for the back-channel lobbying conducted by Israeli officials. He hesitated to defend Israeli territorial interests in August 1948 and, when safely reelected, he firmly discouraged Israeli military ventures against Egypt and Jordan.

As a result of this tension in Truman's policy, both Israel and the Arab states found reason to fault the United States. Arab leaders repeatedly protested U.S. support for Israel. Israeli officials complained about the limits of that support. U.S. officials found themselves unable to avoid the displeasure of either side.

U.S. officials hoped that the armistices of 1949 would enable the belligerent states to negotiate formal peace treaties soon thereafter. Negotiations that followed on war-related issues, however, proved that a wide gulf separated Israel from its Arab neighbors. The dream of a permanent peace would prove elusive.

Part II

5

SECURITY COMMITMENTS
U.S. Strategic Interests in the Middle East, 1949–1953

In the aftermath of the Arab-Israeli war of 1948–49, the United States faced new and troubling circumstances in the Middle East. Interpreting the outbreak of the Korean War in June 1950 as Soviet aggression, U.S. officials braced for a similar strike against Western interests in the Middle East. American leaders also came to fear that the Arab-Israeli conflict would facilitate Soviet expansionism in the Middle East by undermining the stability and pro-Western orientation of states there. Worse, the British ability to defend the region declined, as did the U.N.'s capability to pacify the situation.

Because these circumstances seemingly challenged American interests in the Middle East, U.S. officials became more involved in the region. They devoted weapons supply, security assurances, and military and economic aid to befriend states and prevent Soviet expansion. The U.S. government overcame its traditional reluctance to assume responsibility for regional security and proposed a security apparatus to shield the area from Soviet attack. To prevent Soviet exploitation of Arab-Israeli tensions, the United States also tried to pacify or contain the conflict. Taking action to defend vital interests against perceived Soviet threats, the United States became further enmeshed in the Middle East as a result of its worldwide strategy for containing communism.

After 1949, the traditional division within the Harry S. Truman administration between pro- and anti-Zionists faded slightly for two reasons. First, while President Truman remained responsive to domestic political pressures to back Israel, after his reelection he demonstrated an unprecedented degree of impartiality. Second, in January 1949 Truman appointed as secretary of state Dean G. Acheson, who had earned the president's trust and confidence while serving as undersecretary of state in 1945–47 and by negotiating the North Atlantic Treaty Organization (NATO), coordinating diplomacy regarding the Korean War, implementing rearmament under NSC-68, and developing other containment measures in 1949–53. Truman defended Acheson when conservative Republicans criticized his defense of Alger Hiss and distance from Nationalist China.[1] Under Acheson, State Department officials obtained Truman's explicit consent to their policies on Arab-Israeli issues, and Truman refrained from overturning their handiwork. Although ambiguities appeared, U.S. policies became more consistent after 1949.

U.S. Interests in the Middle East

The strategic importance that the United States attached to the Middle East increased in the late 1940s. The Arab states—especially Egypt, Saudi Arabia, and Iraq—possessed special importance because of their military facilities and oil resources. British influence among Arab states served as a bulwark against Soviet expansion and internal discord. Israel also assumed strategic importance because of its location at the center of the region and its internal political complexion.

Arab states retained vast importance as a source of petroleum. They supplied half the oil consumed by U.S. armed forces in 1947 and most of that fueling the European Recovery Program. Loss of such a commodity, the Central Intelligence Agency (CIA) noted, "might compel the US to utilize dwindling oil reserves which would otherwise be husbanded for periods of national emergency." U.S. capital investments in the oil industry, the State Department added, generated "substantial revenue" in federal taxes.[2]

The Arab states also seemed vital in military terms. The State Department, Pentagon, CIA, and National Security Council (NSC) repeatedly expressed their belief that military bases and proximity to the Soviet Union made the region "of critical importance to the security of the United States." The area's importance increased in 1950, when the Korean War raised global tensions and Pentagon officers began to consider Greece and Turkey integral to the defense of Western Europe. Should the Arab states "fall under the control of the Soviet Union" by war or subversion, State Department officials noted in 1952, "the immediate as well as the ultimate cost to the United States would be incalculable."[3]

U.S. officials identified strategic interests in specific Arab states. Egypt remained prominent in U.S. and British contingency plans for war against the Soviet Union. "There is *no substitute for Egypt* as a base," G. Lewis Jones of the NEA wrote in 1950. The JCS resolved to maintain the U.S. air base at Dhahran, Saudi Arabia in peacetime, occupy it in wartime, and deny it to "any potentially hostile Power." After discussions with U.S. Air Force officers, the American minister to Jidda, J. Rives Childs, likened Saudi Arabia to "an immense aircraft carrier lying athwart a number of the principal air traffic lanes of the world" as well as the sea lanes of the Indian Ocean, Persian Gulf, and Suez Canal. Iraq occupied a position near "major communications lines for three continents," State Department officials added in 1952, and provided "a base in close proximity to the Soviet border." Eytan Gilboa finds that U.S. public opinion also valued Arab states as strategic partners in the Cold War.[4]

U.S. officials might have taken comfort in the absence of explicit Soviet maneuvering in the Middle East between 1949 and 1953. Premier Joseph Stalin, lacking the strength to contest Anglo-American dominance in the region, focused his attention elsewhere. While gratified that Israel's emergence had drained British power from Palestine, Stalin came to see Israel as a bourgeois nationalist state, dependent on American Jews. He curtailed support of Israel, suspended arms supply and emigration of Jews, and adopted an anti-Semitic orientation at home that led to suspension of Soviet-Israeli diplomatic relations in February 1953. Stalin also remained cold to Arab leaders, whom he considered reactionary pawns of British imperialism. He denounced the Egyptian revolution of 1952 as a coup by nationalist military officers in collusion with the West.[5]

Yet U.S. officials identified several threats to Western interests in the Arab Middle East. Inequality of wealth and power caused revolutionary tendencies and resentment against Western nations. Decolonization generated a wave of nationalism conducive to Soviet exploitation and intraregional conflict. Rivalries among the Saudi monarchy, the Egyptian crown, and the Hashemite kingdoms of Iraq and Jordan added to the volatility. Although Stalin appeared uninterested, the CIA estimated that the Soviet Union "desires to achieve eventual control" of the region. Worse, NEA officials noted, Arab states believed "that our [U.S.] support of Israel is inimical to their interests."[6]

To protect American interests against such threats, U.S. officials sought to stabilize the Arab states. "It is our policy to assist the Near Eastern countries in maintaining their independence, to strengthen their orientation toward the West, and to discourage any tendencies towards the development of authoritarian and unrepresentative forms of government," NEA officials asserted in March 1949. U.S.-Arab relations should reflect "friendship, trust, and cooperation," Gordon P. Merriam of the Policy Planning Staff observed, or "our task of supporting . . . Greece, Turkey, and Iran will be that of holding up an arch which lacks foundation."[7]

Britain remained at the center of U.S. plans for stability among the Arab states. Jointly establishing the NATO alliance in 1949 and waging war in Korea in 1950, U.S. and British leaders naturally sought to align their security policies in the Middle East. They resolved to overcome the Palestine-related strain in their relationship, manifest in Ernest Bevin's February 1949 critique of U.S. policy as "let there be an Israel and to hell with the consequences." Security planners in Washington and London reaffirmed their shared war plans and other common strategic interests in the Middle East. The two powers, Acheson believed, had "no differences whatever in our main objective" of regional security and stability.[8]

Indeed, U.S. officials relied on Britain to secure the Middle East. Given budgetary factors and likely congressional reluctance, the State Department demurred when Egypt, Iraq, Lebanon, and Syria sought alliances with the United States and when Britain suggested extending NATO to the region. U.S. commitments to Western Europe and East Asia, the department asserted, necessitated that Britain maintain its traditional dominance in the Middle East.[9]

After 1949, the Pentagon also ascribed strategic potential to Israel. Across the Jewish state ran oil pipelines from Iraq to the Mediterranean and roads and railroads that had once linked Egypt with Lebanon, Syria, and Jordan. Israel's "excellent, although limited, system of well-developed airfields and air bases" would provide crucial tactical advantages to whatever power controlled them in a world war. In the event of global conflict, the JCS hoped that Israel would allow Western troops to contest a Soviet thrust along the Jordan rift, contribute troops to such operations, and open the Cairo-Alexandretta railroad to Western forces. The Joint Strategic Survey Committee advised in April 1949 that Israel "should be oriented towards the Western Democracies."[10]

U.S. officials were relieved to watch Israel develop along a temperate political path. David Ben-Gurion's moderate socialist party led the provisional government, displaced extremists on the right and left, and, according to the CIA, steered "a middle course between socialism and free enterprise." Ben-Gurion established the principle of civilian control of a unified national military by suppressing the Stern Gang and the Irgun. Most notably, he ordered the IDF to destroy the *Altalena*, an Irgun ship that arrived in Tel Aviv from France in June 1948 bearing weapons and discharging nine hundred men of military age. Foreign Minister Moshe Sharett, reputedly more inclined to settle with the Arab states, balanced Ben-Gurion's trademark hawkishness toward his neighbors. To the relief of U.S. officials, the moderate socialists dominated the coalition government established after democratic elections on 25 January 1949.[11]

U.S. officials also overcame fears of communism in Israel. In early 1949, some Pentagon officers continued to worry that many Soviet-bloc Jewish immigrants to Israel had "passed through Communist indoctrination courses." But intelligence officials observed that Israeli communist parties were small in number, divided by Arab-Jewish antagonism, and far removed from power and that Israel's reliance on private U.S. benefactors would brake any inclination to consider communism. Sharett reassured Acheson by declaring that "by their nature and heritage the Jews were individualists and the theory of Communism was abhorrent to them."[12]

U.S. officials remained deeply concerned, however, that Israel practiced neutrality in the Cold War. They disliked Israel's record of alternately voting with the East and the West in U.N. ballots, its recognition of Communist China in January 1950, and its eagerness to facilitate Jewish emigration from Eastern Europe and secure political recognition from communist and neutral countries. Indeed, Sharett and Ben-Gurion reasoned privately that neutrality would not only please the Israeli people and affirm Israeli independence but also enable the Israeli government to resist U.S. pressure to concede in the Arab-Israeli dispute.[13]

As East-West tensions mounted in 1949, U.S. officials viewed Israeli neutrality with deepening concern. The JCS worried that Israel was "not necessarily anti-Soviet" and "may become a danger or an asset" in a world crisis. U.S. intelligence officers suspected that the Jewish state's apparent tie to the United States "appears to be largely motivated by the tangible benefits which it has been able to obtain rather than by any basic alignment with the West." Acheson groused to Truman that Israel's voting record at the United Nations was "favorable to the Russians."[14]

Such U.S. criticism gave Israeli leaders pause. Officials in the Foreign Ministry's United States Division warned in early 1950 that the State Department would "punish us for neutrality" and urged their government to identify openly with the West. In response, Sharett personally assured Truman that Israel would never side with the Soviet Union because the new country relied on the political and economic support of five million U.S. Jews. Sharett also launched a January 1950 publicity campaign to reinforce this point in U.S. public discourse. Israeli neutrality remained intact, however, prior to the Korean War.[15]

Arms Supply and the Tripartite Declaration of 1950

After 1949, U.S. officials faced a dilemma regarding the arms supply to the Middle East. The State Department and Pentagon favored allowing Britain to arm Arab states on behalf of Western security objectives. By contrast, White House staff and members of Congress—in some cases mobilized by Israel—called such arms aid a threat to the Jewish state. Forced to decide between preserving security interests in Arab states and safeguarding Israel and his domestic political interests, President Truman shaped a new policy that further deepened U.S. involvement in the Middle East.

Arms supply to the Middle East belligerents had been curtailed by U.N. embargoes of May and July 1948. Having unilaterally suspended arms exports to the Middle East in November 1947, the U.S. government rigidly enforced these restrictions and encouraged other Western powers to do so. The United States even withheld from Saudi Arabia, Iraq, and Jordan arms designated to repulse Soviet expansionism. U.S. officials maintained this policy despite evidence that Israel as well as certain Arab states had acquired weapons from Czechoslovakia.[16]

The arms embargo became an issue as Arab-Israeli armistices were signed in 1949. In April, Britain asked the United States to help abolish the restrictions, citing the need to arm its treaty partners—Iraq, Egypt, and Jordan. These Arab states endorsed a repeal, and U.N. mediator Ralph Bunche posed no objection to such a step. Having benefited from the embargo, however, Israeli officials favored extending it. British rearmament, they argued, would encourage Arab reluctance to sign final peace treaties and trigger a debilitating arms race.[17]

In August, Truman approved a conditional repeal of the embargo. The State Department had advised him that prolonging the embargo would anger Britain, signal a lack of confidence in U.N. peacemaking, and lead Arab states to seek arms from Eastern Europe. Yet the United States clarified that it would authorize commercial sales to Middle East states of only those arms necessary for "maintaining internal law and order" and "providing reasonable requirements of self defense" and that it would coordinate supplies with Britain and France to avoid an arms race. The U.S. ambassador to the United Nations, Warren R. Austin, announced this policy to the Security Council on 4 August, and U.S. and British officials began coordinating arms sales to the Mideast. The U.N. Security Council formally abolished the embargo on 11 August.[18]

In keeping with Austin's announcement, the United States limited arms sales to Middle East states. In 1949–50, it allowed Egypt to purchase trainer warplanes and modest amounts of spare parts and authorized Britain to release to Egypt Lend-Lease guns valued at $350,000 and spare parts for Sherman tanks. Yet the United States rejected other Egyptian requests to purchase U.S. arms or to acquire title to U.S. weapons and ammunition previously supplied to Britain. U.S. officials also discouraged Syria from requesting arms. By January 1950, the United States had approved commercial sales to Israel of ammunition, aircraft, and vehicles but denied Israeli requests to purchase 75mm guns, tanks, jet planes, and advanced training aircraft because such items would not "constitute 'legitimate security requirement.'" The State Department also discouraged Canada from selling ammunition and artillery to Israel.[19]

Despite U.S. restraint, arms supply became a major issue when Israel contested British weapons deliveries to Egypt and Iraq. Israel protested that the arms would not enhance the Arab powers' standing against the Soviet threat but would enable them to attack Israel. "Never since the establishment of the State of Israel," Israeli Ambassador to the United States Eliahu Elath told Acheson in January 1950, "had the leaders . . . been so apprehensive for the security of the nation." But Acheson favored the British rearmament on security grounds and doubted that Egyptian leaders would again attack Israel. They would not be "so foolhardy as deliberately to unleash upon themselves," he told the Israelis, "the disaster which such a move would surely bring."[20]

Unable to stop the flow of British arms to the Arab states, Israel sought to gain access to the U.S. arsenal. Elath asked the United States to export jet fighters, tanks, armored cars, aircraft, howitzers, and radar and communications equipment. When the Pentagon's Munitions Board considered the request in March 1950, however, air force and army experts decided that Israel had "the preponderance of striking power" in the region and that additional arms acquisitions "would increase Israel's offensive capabilities and give incentive to offensive planning." In May, the Pentagon formally rejected the arms request.[21]

Consideration of the Israeli arms request strained U.S.-Israeli relations. The State Department expressed frustration that Israel seemed unrelenting in its pressure on the issue. Military attaché Colonel Benjamin Arzi repeatedly pressed Pentagon officials and received five negative replies in ten days. One answer, he reported on 1 March, "barely verges the border of common politeness and doesn't even take the trouble of softening the negative reply." Tensions increased when the Pentagon notified Israel that the new country would have to reveal information about its military capabilities to be considered for arms sales. Israel protested that such information would reveal its vulnerabilities and reach British and Arab hands.[22]

To overcome the Pentagon's reluctance to arm them, Israeli leaders orchestrated a sweeping public relations campaign. They enlisted numerous members of Congress, which had returned to Democratic control in 1949, to pressure Acheson to release arms to Israel. Israeli embassy staff secretly briefed American Federation of Labor President Philip Murray and Congress of Industrial Organizations President William Green to argue Israel's case in meetings with Acheson and Truman. In addition, the Israelis mobilized several U.S. Jewish leaders to argue the case for arms on Capitol Hill and in other venues and appealed for help from such high administration officials as Special Counsel Clark Clifford, Federal Security Administrator Oscar Ewing, Agriculture Secretary Charles Brannan, and Interior Secretary Oscar L. Chapman. To reach the public, embassy officers discreetly distributed position papers, lobbied prominent Republicans, and arranged favorable newspaper editorials.[23]

Despite some sensitivity to the influence dilemma, Israel pressed this campaign. For example, Abba Eban, who became Israel's ambassador to the United States in 1950, doubted that Acheson would change his policy under "the extremely hard attacks which are being made now against the State Department" and warned that the pressure risked the "irreplaceable asset" of U.S. sympathy. Sharett, however, remained confident that he could leverage U.S. arms and noted that he might lose the future support of U.S. Jews if he did not take advantage of their concern on the issue. A report from presidential adviser David Niles that the Israeli campaign was influencing Truman encouraged Sharett to proceed.[24]

As Niles reported, the Israeli political campaign turned Truman against the Pentagon and State Department. The NSC, meeting on 6 April without Truman in attendance, approved a policy of supporting British rearmament of Egypt and denying U.S. arms to Israel. Within two weeks, however, Truman reversed that policy because "it was much too one-sided and . . . it would cause trouble. . . . We were not doing what we should to arm the Jews appropriately." Clearly revealing domestic political motives, Truman ordered the State Department to formulate an arms supply policy that would satisfy the "many active sympathizers with Israel in this country."[25]

To affirm the Anglo-U.S. security partnership on terms acceptable to Truman, the State Department resourcefully conceived the Tripartite Declaration. In it, the United States, Britain, and France agreed to condition arms supply to any Middle East state on its willingness to pledge nonaggression. Issued in late May, the declaration authorized arms supply to Middle East states "for the purposes of assuring their internal security and their legitimate self-defense and to permit them to play their part in the defense of the area as a whole." If any state broke its nonaggression pledge, the three Western powers would "immediately take action, both within and outside the United Nations, to prevent such violation." The Pentagon objected to the declaration, fearing that a border incursion would force a U.S. troop deployment that might trigger a Soviet reaction. But Truman, cloaking his domestic political concerns, approved the document on the promise that it would "bring calm to the present uneasiness in the Near East."[26]

To Truman's delight, public opinion supported the Tripartite Declaration. Supporters of Israel were elated that the president had redressed the arms supply imbalance and opened U.S. arsenals to Israel. Internationalists were pleased that the United States had shared the responsibility for Middle Eastern security. "Now we have one more link," the *New York Times* commented, "in the strong chain binding the free nations together and holding them safely against the onslaughts of the totalitarian world."[27]

Israeli officials reacted positively but cautiously to the declaration. Informed of it early by a White House source, Sharett privately welcomed the statement as a check on arms supply to and aggression by the Arab powers. Ambassador Elath celebrated that it would help guarantee Israel's borders and leverage U.S. weapons. By contrast, Foreign Ministry Director-General Walter Eytan suspected that the declaration was designed to promote "Western guardianship" of the region and to undermine Israeli neutrality in the Cold War "by holding out arms bait." Foreign Ministry officials renewed their campaigning among members of Congress and other U.S. supporters to ensure that the declaration did not impinge on Israeli interests.[28]

Arab reactions to the declaration seemed generally positive. Saudi Arabia approved the measure as an anticommunist device, and Lebanese Minister to Washington Charles Malik called it "the most important contribution to peace in the Near East made by the three powers." Syria's political and military leaders welcomed the declaration as a safeguard against Israeli expansion. The Arab League signaled conditional acceptance in June. By August, U.S. officials considered the declaration a success because it "had a beneficial effect in reducing tension in the Near East."[29]

U.S. officials occasionally used the Tripartite Declaration to promote stability in the region. In July 1950, when the Syrian minister to Washington, Faiz el-Khouri, expressed fear of an Israeli attack, Assistant Secretary of State George C. McGhee encouraged el-Khouri to "place full confidence" in the declaration. Citing U.S. obligations to act as a signatory, the State Department monitored an Israeli-Jordanian border clash in September, deterred leaders of other Arab countries from interfering in Syrian politics in November, and reassured leaders of Saudi Arabia, Lebanon, and Syria who feared unification schemes by other Arab states. In early 1951, when Israeli officials expressed concern about Arab ambitions, McGhee encouraged the Israeli leaders "to depend on the three great powers' declaration." At a February 1951 meeting in Istanbul, U.S. chiefs of missions called the declaration "a useful stabilizing factor."[30]

Although the Tripartite Declaration allowed arms supply, the State and Defense Departments released only a small trickle of weapons to the region. In 1950, American officials discouraged Iraq from requesting arms, offered Lebanon modest military training that served U.S. intelligence-gathering aims, and denied Egyptian requests for weapons (except for the sale of eighteen AT-6 training aircraft). The two departments approved Israeli purchases of machine guns, aircraft, and a three-hundred-ton patrol boat but denied the Jewish state recoilless rifles, tanks, tank guns, and jets; opposed an Israeli effort to purchase 122 Sherman tanks from the Philippines; and blocked a shipment of mercury from Spain to Israel. In 1950–51, Israel purchased weapons worth $8.7 million; all the Arab states combined purchased arms valued at $4 million. The Tripartite Declaration initially limited arms supply to the belligerent powers.[31]

The Middle East Command

In addition to advancing the Tripartite Declaration, the United States embarked on another policy transformation in late 1950. Alarmed by the outbreak of war in Korea, U.S. officials assumed that the Soviet Union would try to expand into the Middle East. Empowered by the rearmament under NSC-68, the global anticommunist policy paper approved by Truman in mid-1950, and concerned by a perceptible decline in British capabilities, American leaders shed their traditional reluctance to incur security commitments in the region. But such officials found that the Arab-Israeli conflict and Arab-Western tensions frustrated the effort to establish a viable security apparatus.

The Korean War raised U.S. concerns about Middle East security. Suspecting that the Soviet Union had inspired North Korean aggression, officials in Washington feared similar and possibly simultaneous attacks in Europe, Asia, and the Middle East. "Soviet rulers have resolved to pursue aggressively their world-wide attack on the power position of the United States and its allies," the Intelligence Advisory Committee warned in December 1950, "regardless of the possibility that global war may result." If war erupted in Europe, a Soviet thrust into the Middle East seemed certain.[32]

Fear of a Soviet incursion into the Middle East dovetailed with concern about Arab anger at U.S. policy toward Israel. "Cool area reaction to the Korean situation stands as a warning signal" of Arab discontent, the State Department reasoned. Arab states would have to decide "whether to cast their lot irrevocably with the West, to remain neutral, or to drift into the Soviet orbit," NEA officials observed in December 1950, adding in 1951 that the West need not "lose the Middle East as it has lost China." Furthermore, "a more positive and aggressive policy . . . should keep the Middle East from going behind the Iron Curtain."[33]

To safeguard the Middle East against the Soviets and to assuage Arab anger about Israel, U.S. planners resolved to erect a security pact on an Arab foundation. Inspired by the NATO agreement, they conceived of an integrated command structure, called the Middle East Command (MEC), that would enlist Arab states as partners of the West. By basing MEC in Egypt, they also hoped to solve an Anglo-Egyptian dispute over military bases in the Suez Canal Zone and settle an Anglo-U.S. disagreement over allied naval commands. By October 1950, the United States and Britain enlisted France and Turkey jointly to invite Egypt to join MEC and base it in Cairo.[34]

Israel presented a delicate challenge to the establishment of MEC. The Pentagon gained a new appreciation for Israel during the Korean War, realizing that the IDF was the local force most capable of contesting a Soviet thrust into the Middle East. Moreover, fear of Soviet aggression seemed to attract Ben-Gurion to the United States, and Israel protested Soviet emigration restrictions and the political repression of Soviet and Czechoslovak Jews. (Israeli-Soviet tensions would rise steadily until the two powers broke diplomatic relations in February 1953.)[35]

U.S. officials also welcomed Israel's limited support of their policy in Korea. Israel censured North Korea for aggression, endorsed U.N. action to defend South Korea, sent a medical unit to Korea, and voted for U.N. sanctions against

China and North Korea. In addition, Sharett offered to commit Israel to fight against any Soviet attack on the Middle East if the United States provided weapons and a security guarantee. In early 1951, Ben-Gurion requested U.S. military aid and invited U.S. officials to base their regional defense plans on Israel.[36]

Yet U.S. security planners remained concerned by evidence of lingering Israeli neutralism. Israeli public opinion forced Ben-Gurion to affirm his policy of neutralism, and certain Foreign Ministry officials openly questioned the value of friendship with the West. With regard to Korea, Israel refused to send combat troops, criticized the U.S. advance into North Korea, voted to seat Communist China at the United Nations, and withheld support from U.S. cease-fire terms. Opposition parties prepared motions of no confidence against Ben-Gurion for merely receiving a British general in February 1951. Such episodes caused some State Department officials to suspect that Soviet agents had infiltrated Israel.[37]

In light of Israeli neutralism and Arab-Israeli dynamics, U.S. and British planners decided to exclude Israel from MEC. Because Israel and the Arab States would refuse to collaborate in a unified command, McGhee noted, if Israel were enlisted, "the whole concept will be stillborn." When assuring Ben-Gurion that MEC would protect Israel, the U.S. ambassador to Tel Aviv, Monnett B. Davis, attributed Egypt's inclusion to the "plain fact of geography . . . that the Suez Canal and the main Middle East base were situated on Egyptian territory." Mindful of a possible domestic backlash against this policy, Acheson explained to Truman the rationale for excluding Israel and stressed that MEC would give the Arab states "something more productive to think about than their feud with Israel."[38]

Despite the exclusion of Israel, Egypt inflicted a severe blow to MEC in October 1951. When approached by the four Western sponsors, Egyptian leaders not only rejected the MEC proposal but also abrogated their defense treaty with Britain and demanded that British forces withdraw from Egypt. The United States and Britain then invited other Arab governments to join the command, but they declined because of widespread public approval of Egypt's action. Only Syrian Prime Minister Hassan Abdel Razzak el Hakim openly endorsed MEC, provoking a crisis that led to his resignation. Although Israel was excluded from MEC, intra-Arab political dynamics undermined the U.S. initiative.[39]

Despite this outcome, Israeli officials criticized the Western intent to enlist Egypt in MEC. Membership would enhance Egypt's prestige, provide it leverage over Israel, and increase its military power, Sharett complained, yet Egypt remained technically at war with Israel. Egypt's rejection of MEC "would save the Western Powers from a fatal mistake," Ben-Gurion told Davis on 15 October, because the Egyptians were undemocratic, imperialist, reactionary, and corrupt and "simply did not belong to the 'free world.'"[40]

Yet Israel also feared that the United States would pressure it to join MEC. Even though MEC membership would enhance Israeli security, secure U.S. economic aid, and please U.S. Jews, Sharett reasoned, it would also imperil Soviet Jews, divide the Israeli public, and disclose Israeli military secrets to the Arab states. Israeli intelligence officials suspected that the United States designed MEC to enable "a preventive war . . . against Russia's 'soft belly'" or to empower the Sixth Fleet "to deliver atomic bombs on Russia" in wartime. Sharett advised Ben-Gurion to encourage "Western confidence in our ultimate intentions in the event of conflict" but to stress "our difficulties about openly joining the Western military camp in peacetime."[41]

Israeli leaders were surprised and relieved to find receptive minds in Washington when they conveyed this position in November. Ben-Gurion discouraged the Western powers from enlisting Israel in a regional pact that would provoke Moscow. Rather than collaboration with Arab powers under MEC, Sharett told Acheson, Israel "preferred a direct and practical connection, on a special footing, suited to our particular circumstances." State Department officials immediately approved Israel's request not to join MEC.[42]

Bruised by Arab and Israeli criticism, the MEC concept further suffered when U.S. officials realized in early 1952 that the West lacked the ability to defend the Middle East. The Pentagon calculated that Western powers would need fifteen divisions and 1,200 aircraft to hold the region, while Britain and Turkey had available only fourteen divisions and 375 aircraft. Stunned to realize such "wholly inadequate" capabilities, the Policy Planning Staff advised a war plan including "the use of atomic weapons against the mountain passes into the area." The JCS shared the despair over British incapabilities but doubted that atomic bombs would be "practicable or desirable."[43]

In a futile effort to overcome MEC's shortcomings, U.S. and British officials modified the plan in June 1952. To dilute Arab opposition, they renamed it the Middle East Defense Organization (MEDO), called it a planning board rather than a command, and tried to sell the idea to Arab military officers rather than to the politicians who seemed preoccupied by Israel. But Egypt remained hostile to any defense arrangement prior to British evacuation of the canal zone, and other Arab states remained reluctant to defy Egypt. Israel fervently opposed MEDO because, it believed, Western arms supplied to Arab states "will be used not against Russia but against Israel." Lacking any local support, the MEC-MEDO concept languished.[44]

The failure of MEC and MEDO led the State Department to reexamine its cardinal tenet of reliance on Britain to defend the Middle East. Given that Britain had departed India, Palestine, and Libya; lost influence in Greece, Turkey, Iran, Jordan, and Iraq; and seemed unable to defend the Middle East, State Department officers noted in August 1952, "it is no longer safe to assume, automatically, that Britain can and should be considered the principal protector of western interests in the Middle East." Even if Britain felt "great resentment," Acheson noted, "we had the responsibility in the Middle East and had to do something about it." Although the MEC-MEDO concept lay in shambles, the United States stood ready to take charge in the region.[45]

Debates over Economic and Military Aid

After 1949, Truman administration officials resolved to shore up the Western presence in the Middle East by dispensing economic and military aid to local states. As in the question of arms sales, they found that Arab-Israeli tensions complicated the task. Israel exerted powerful political pressures on the administration to grant massive sums of aid and weapons, to which the Arab powers and Britain vociferously objected. Israel also fought tenaciously against prospective U.S. aid to Arab states. Again, debates about such issues divided foreign policy experts in the State Department and Pentagon from political advisers in the White House and other voices sympathetic to Israel. Again, Truman faced the task of reconciling diplomatic and domestic political objectives.

The Arab-Israeli conflict complicated the task of dispensing economic aid to Middle East states. Approved by Truman in March 1951, NSC 47/5 authorized grants of economic and military aid "to strengthen the several Arab States and Israel, to improve their political and economic stability, and to increase their will and ability to resist penetration by the USSR." Hopeful that "an integrated and balanced" grant aid program would also promote Arab-Israeli harmony, the State Department planned, in fiscal year (FY) 1952, to grant $968,000 to Israel, $10.2 million to Syria, $3.2 million to Lebanon, $4.9 million to Jordan, $5 million to Iraq, $870,000 to Egypt, $384,000 to Saudi Arabia, and $393,000 to Yemen.[46]

Israel launched a bid to secure $150 million from the U.S. government to facilitate absorption of one million immigrants. In March 1951, the new state formally asked for such a grant in FY 1952 funds. Expecting the State Department to reject the request, Israeli officials promoted it in myriad circles. They enlisted eminent Republican Senator Robert A. Taft of Ohio and freshman Democratic Senator Paul H. Douglas of Illinois to cosponsor a bill endorsing the request. A former adviser to Ambassador Eban, I. L. Kenen of the American Zionist Council, lobbied White House advisers, members of Congress, and leaders of Jewish groups to pressure Truman to endorse the Taft-Douglas bill. Israeli President Chaim Weizmann followed up in correspondence to the president, and Ben-Gurion, touring the United States on a campaign to sell bonds, argued for the bill during a meeting with Truman. When Acheson protested such lobbying, Eban defended it as "strictly legitimate in a pluralistic democratic society."[47]

Arab states complained about the congressional backing of the Israeli aid request. The U.S. minister to Damascus, Cavendish W. Cannon, reported that the

Taft-Douglas bill sparked a "violently anti-American campaign" in the Syrian press, while Egyptian embassy counselor Mohamed El Kouny charged that passage would be "unfair and unjust." Lebanon, Jordan, and Saudi Arabia also protested. "I seriously doubt whether we can pull through in this area" if the United States approved the Israeli request, Gordon Mattison of the embassy in Cairo warned. "It won't be taken lying down."[48]

State Department officials urged Truman to oppose the Israeli gambit. They considered the $150 million sum exorbitant, resented Israel's lobbying of Congress, and anticipated catastrophic damage to U.S.-Arab relations. Burton Y. Berry of the NEA predicted that fulfilling the request would "have serious consequences on our special strategic interests in Greece, Turkey, Iran." U.S. prestige in Saudi Arabia "will go completely out of sight if we take this action to aid Israel," General Hoyt S. Vandenberg informed the State Department. "The Israeli program scares me."[49]

Truman formulated a compromise solution to the Israeli aid dispute. On the one hand, Acheson persuaded the president to oppose the Taft-Douglas bill even though it gained broad support on Capitol Hill. On 4 April, Truman summoned Abraham Feinberg, president of the Development Corporation for Israel, to demand that "political Jews be kept quiet for the time being." "I have never seen him so distraught," Feinberg commented after the meeting, "and his attitude was a complete contrast to his usual buoyancy and optimism."[50]

On the other hand, Truman avoided alienating supporters of Israel by increasing levels of aid to both sides in the Middle East. On 24 May, he recommended allocations of $23.5 million in economic aid for Israel, $23.5 million in economic aid for the Arab states, $50 million for Palestinian refugee relief, and $41.5 million for military grants to area states. In October 1951, after months of complicated negotiations and Israeli lobbying, Congress approved $65 million in aid for Palestinian refugees and the Arab states, $65 million for Israel, and $40 million in military aid.[51]

The reaction of Middle East states to this aid program revealed the difficulty of negotiating the politics of the region. Israel complained that the $65 million allocation was insufficient to meet its needs. Several Arab statesmen protested that Israel's allocation equaled the combined Arab allocation, while Syrian Minister el-Khouri considered "any aid to Israel . . . an unfriendly act." In response, McGhee told Arab leaders that the relief for refugees would redound to their advantage. Any country that criticized the aid package "with Communist-type clichés" might lose its funding, he added. The United States "is not forcing grant aid" on any power.[52]

Similar controversies beset subsequent discussions on aid. In late 1951, Israel requested $126 million in FY 1953 funds to enable it to absorb six hundred thousand Jewish immigrants. Arab leaders repeated their earlier protests and added a charge that immigration would lead to Israeli expansionism and thus create regional strife. Sensitive to Arab concerns but also cautious lest Israel attempt another gambit in Congress, Truman and Acheson proposed an $80 million aid package to Israel. In July 1952, Congress allocated $73 million to Israel in FY 1953.[53]

In addition, Israeli requests for emergency financial aid aggravated tensions within the Truman administration. Facing a financial crisis in mid-1952, Israel petitioned for $11.5 million from White House discretionary funds. The director of the Mutual Security Agency, W. Averell Harriman, who had recently announced his candidacy for the White House, awarded Israel $19 million—a sum in excess of what Israel had requested. Annoyed, the State Department opposed a subsequent Israeli request for $20 million in Mutual Security Program funds and secured Truman's approval of a "sterner attitude regarding our assistance to Israel." Ben-Gurion directed Eban, however, to pressure Truman, Harriman, and Democratic Party leaders on the hunch that they felt vulnerable on the eve of a national election. Indeed, in August Truman approved another emergency advance of $25 million to Israel.[54]

The State Department won over Truman, however, on an Israeli request for a $124 million debt-consolidation loan from the U.S. government or the Export-Import Bank. In summer 1952, Eban recruited Niles and other prominent U.S. Jews to press Truman and Harriman to approve the request, claiming that it would stabilize Israel's economy. But McGhee argued that the United States had been "beaten over the head" in Arab states with charges of "alleged US favoritism to Israel," and State Department economic experts advised rejection of the loan request on fiscal grounds. Truman followed this advice.[55]

In addition to economic aid, the question of grant military aid to Middle East states emerged as a major issue in 1951–52. The October 1951 Mutual Security Act made available $40 million for grant military aid to Middle East states, but the State Department and Pentagon froze allocations pending the outcome of the bid to establish MEC. Israel requested $15 million in grant military aid to finance construction of airfields, ports, and railways. When the State Department hinted that military aid would be reserved for MEDO members, Sharett protested that Israel must not be "pressed down [to the] Arab level and treated as another Lebanon." He spearheaded an effort among administration insiders, members of Congress, and U.S. Jewish leaders to gain Truman's approval of the request.[56]

The Pentagon and State Department firmly opposed Israel's bid for grant military aid. They feared that it would anger Arab leaders and exacerbate Arab-Israeli tension and again resented Israel's use of pressure tactics. Even Harriman reasoned that military aid to Israel "would be contrary to the security interests and political objectives of the United States" in light of "the complex and explosive political atmosphere" in the Middle East.[57]

Israeli determination to secure grant aid intensified after Britain sold fourteen military jets to Syria, Jordan, and Iraq and fifteen to Egypt, even though the British also sold fourteen jets to Israel and elicited nonaggression pledges mandated by the Tripartite Declaration. Israel was "convinced [that] its existence is in jeopardy," Davis observed. Ben-Gurion asked for U.S. F-84 jets to rectify the imbalance, and Sharett ordered an "all-out effort" to mobilize members of Congress and private citizens to secure Truman's compliance. Eban sent Feinberg and Eddie Jacobson, with an Israeli embassy memorandum in hand, to ask Truman to approve grant aid as a "valedictory benefit" to Israel. Truman, however, refused the jet request.[58]

U.S. officials also divided over grant military aid to the new government of Egypt, which was established in July 1952. In August, the State Department and Pentagon agreed that they should "scrape together a representative selection" of arms to orient the regime to the West, endear it to MEDO, and deter it from attacking Israel. With Truman's permission, State Department officials invited General Mohammed Naguib, nominal head of the new regime, to apply for a grant of $10 million. NEA officials considered such aid to Egypt "a matter of great urgency."[59]

But Israel launched a major initiative to block the proposed aid to Egypt. Adopting a principle that he called "both you and I shall not have," Sharett protested to Acheson that such aid "would make the prospects of a peaceful settlement more remote, heighten the already existing tension, promote an arms race and gravely affect Israel's security and economic problem." Eban appealed to members of Congress and administration insiders, organized a major letter- and editorial-writing campaign, and sought to "rally world opinion" to Israel's side. American Zionist Council Chairman Louis Lipsky warned Acheson on 30 December 1952 that discussion of arming Egypt "is alarming to Israel's many friends in this country."[60]

Israeli efforts blocked U.S. grant military aid to Egypt. On 29 December, Eban reported, Truman promised Feinberg that no such deal would take place. The president dispensed with the matter during a 7 January 1953 discussion with Acheson and Harriman at the White House. After a brief debate, Truman accepted Harriman's reasoning that the lame duck president should not bequeath to the incoming Dwight D. Eisenhower administration a legacy of grant military aid to Egypt. Instead, Truman authorized a $10 million economic aid grant to that country.[61]

The U.S. Approach to Arab-Israeli Problems

Becoming increasingly involved in the Middle East after 1950, U.S. officials also resolved to solve the Arab-Israeli conflict. Although the 1948–49 war had destabilized the region, pessimism about resolving the controversy initially deterred American leaders from involvement. In 1950, however, for reasons similar to those driving the U.S. quest for MEC, officials in Washington resolved to reduce Arab-Israeli tensions. Peace in the region would diminish the prospects for Soviet expansionism there.

In 1949, U.S. officials identified the Arab-Israeli conflict as a major source of Middle East instability. Together with problems such as economic dislocation, government incompetence, and intra-Arab rivalries, Office of Near Eastern Affairs (NE) officials estimated, the Arab-Israeli dispute threatened to render the Arab states "highly vulnerable to Soviet penetration and eventual overthrow." The existence of Israel "will be a disturbing factor in the Near East for many years." Conversely, NEA officials predicted in March 1949, a settlement would eliminate such threats to U.S. security interests. The Joint Strategic Survey Committee advised that Arab-Israeli conflicts "should be reconciled at least to the extent that Israel and the Arab states would act in concert to oppose Soviet aggression."[62]

Despite their desire for a settlement, U.S. officials initially doubted that it could be accomplished and refrained from trying. The CIA expected the conflict to persist "for a great many years," while U.S. diplomats in the Middle East, surveying political conditions in March 1950, detected "little likelihood of an early over-all settlement in Palestine." Through mid-1950, the State Department deferred to the United Nations to take the initiative to find an Arab-Israeli settlement. A major U.S. effort seemed likely only to aggravate relations with Israel and the Arab states.[63]

In late 1950, the State Department switched its tack, resolving to find a solution to the Arab-Israeli conflict because it threatened the stability of the Middle East from within. The United Nations proved unable to broker a comprehensive peace, NEA officials observed, and the conflict exacerbated "the power and violence of the Nationalist movements" in Arab states. The greatest peril to U.S. vital interests in the Middle East, the NSC summarized in April 1952, "arises not so much from the threat of direct Soviet military attack as from acute instability, anti-western nationalism, and Arab-Israeli antagonism which could lead to disorder and eventually to a situation in which regimes oriented toward the Soviet Union could come to power."[64]

U.S. officials identified certain principles on which to search for Arab-Israeli settlement. Truman approved an NEA strategy of distancing the United States from British and French imperialism, improving U.S. bilateral ties with each

Middle East country, and mitigating the Arab-Israeli conflict on "a framework of strict impartiality." To accomplish such ends, the NSC advised using "all feasible and appropriate means" to abate "Arab distrust of Israel and resulting animosity toward the United States," while the State Department resolved to pressure Israel to limit immigration and eschew expansionism. The United States would not abandon Israel but would instill in Arab minds "a more realistic appreciation of the fact that Israel is there and is likely to remain there for some time."[65]

Conclusion

U.S. policy toward the Middle East changed dramatically in 1949–53. Consistent with Cold War aims of containing Soviet power, U.S. officials reaffirmed the importance of security, economic, and political assets in the region. The global containment policy seemed to require stabilizing the area, aligning Israel and the Arab states with the West, and protecting them from Soviet expansionism. New circumstances in the region and elsewhere forced the United States to pursue such objectives more actively after 1949 than before.

In 1950–52, the United States became demonstrably more involved in the Middle East. U.S. security planners had previously relied on Britain to safeguard the region and on the United Nations to settle the Arab-Israeli conflict. After 1950, however, the Soviet Union displayed increasing interest in the Middle East, conditions within the region seemed conducive to such expansionism, and British capabilities to defend the region declined. The United States thus accepted enduring commitments to Middle East stability and security while affirming its reliance on Britain as a security partner.

The shift from reliance on Britain to direct involvement was manifest in the evolution of U.S. policy toward arms supply to Middle East states. Israeli protests against British armament of Arab states in early 1950 convinced Truman to implement the Tripartite Declaration, designed to ensure parity of Western arms supply to the Arab states and Israel and to deter intraregional aggression. On one level, the declaration represented a creative device for reconciling security interests with domestic political demands and establishing a modicum of Arab-Israeli stability. On a deeper level, the policy represented a major U.S. departure from reliance on Britain and the first explicit American commitment to Middle East security.

In addition to issuing the Tripartite Declaration, the United States took other initiatives to secure and stabilize the region. U.S. officials tried to erect MEC to protect the area from Soviet military aggression and dispensed economic and military aid to area states to stabilize them, bolster their ability to resist communism, and align them with the West. U.S. officials also explored a permanent settlement of the Arab-Israeli conflict that would contribute to peace and stability within the region.

A variety of circumstances frustrated these initiatives. Arab leaders torpedoed MEC because it smacked of imperialism and threatened their balance of power. Israel opposed Western reliance on Arab powers as military partners because this policy threatened Israel's security. Israel's ability to leverage substantial levels of U.S. economic aid provoked an Arab backlash, while U.S. efforts to provide grant military aid to Egypt collapsed under the weight of Israeli resistance. U.S. officials concluded that a comprehensive Arab-Israeli peace settlement was impossible to accomplish in the short term. The United States thus proved unable to reconcile its global ambitions with the security concerns of the local powers.

6

PRESIDENTIAL PASSIVITY
Truman and the Peace Process, 1949–1953

In 1949–53, the Harry S. Truman administration desired peace settlements that would officially end the Arab-Israeli war, establish permanent borders around Israel, and restore stability to the Middle East. To achieve that goal, U.S. officials initially worked through the United Nations, but it proved unable to elicit sufficient compromises or concessions from either side. American officials then encouraged Israeli-Jordanian and Israeli-Egyptian bilateral deals, but these efforts proved equally futile. When a 1951 Syrian-Israeli crisis stoked tensions, U.S. officials helped avert a full-scale war, but the Arab-Israeli conflict persisted.

Several factors complicated U.S. peacemaking. The Truman administration occasionally identified certain Cold War interests that conflicted with the desire for Middle East peace. Domestic political pressures made it difficult for officials to pressure Israel. White House advisers and the State Department disagreed on various facets of U.S. diplomacy and battled for the president's ear. Both Israel and the Arab states demanded U.S. endorsement of their positions on certain disputes. U.S. officials attempted to reconcile their global, regional, and domestic interests in a consistent and cogent policy toward Arab-Israeli peacemaking but proved unable to find a recipe for success.

Failure of the Arab-Israeli Peace Process

At the time of the armistice agreements in early 1949, the United States naturally favored a permanent Arab-Israeli peace agreement. U.S. officials initially supported U.N. peacemaking but found it difficult to square diplomatic objectives, such as convincing Israel to make concessions deemed necessary for peace, with political circumstances, such as domestic pressure on Truman to safeguard Israel's interests. While peacemaking in 1949–50 would have proven difficult in any case, inconsistencies in U.S. diplomacy hindered U.N. efforts to achieve a settlement.

The United Nations organized the first international effort to make Arab-Israeli peace following the war of 1948–49. In December 1948, the Security Council created the Palestine Conciliation Commission (PCC), comprised of U.S., French, and Turkish representatives, to mediate a settlement. Under the leadership of the U.S. delegate, Truman's personal friend Mark Ethridge, the PCC established a headquarters in Jerusalem in January 1949 and convinced Israel, Egypt, Jordan, Syria, and Lebanon to attend a peace conference at Lausanne, Switzerland, starting on 27 April. Iraq and Saudi Arabia refused to attend, but the latter agreed to abide by any settlement.[1]

Ethridge's hope of effecting an Arab-Israeli settlement at Lausanne quickly died. Arab representatives, he reported on 9 May, "are staying in their hotel rooms," refusing even to meet the Israelis. Arab envoys asked Ethridge to compose a treaty that they could sell to their peoples as a U.N.-imposed settlement, a responsibility Ethridge refused to incur. Israeli Foreign Minister Moshe Sharett directed envoy Abba Eban to issue conciliatory statements upon arriving at Lausanne but then to refuse to concede on any major issue. The director-general of the Israeli Foreign Ministry, Walter Eytan, visited Lausanne and spent "two hours talking and one hour drinking" with Ethridge "to get him into a more amiable frame of mind," but Ethridge refused to relax his pressure on Israel to concede. The Israelis were "arrogant [and] drunk with success," Ethridge reported. "It was open to doubt whether they were at all interested in peace."[2]

Given such attitudes, the conference quickly deadlocked. Ethridge convinced the Arab states and Israel to sign a protocol on 12 May that acknowledged the November 1947 partition resolution, approved peace negotiations, implied Arab recognition of Israel, and committed Israel to withdraw to partition-plan borders, but reservations attached by various powers stripped the protocol of value. Ethridge reported on 20 May that the conference had reached "a virtual stalemate," and on 15 June he adjourned the proceedings for three weeks in hope of inspiring fresh thinking. Ethridge's efforts, the CIA noted, "make abundantly clear that little basis for agreement between the Jews and Arabs exists."[3]

Despite subsequent U.S. efforts to broker a settlement, the Lausanne conference collapsed in August 1949. Paul A. Porter, who replaced Ethridge as U.S. delegate to the PCC, arrived at Lausanne on 16 July and presented a peace plan that included Israeli cession of the southern Negev. But Sharett rejected this plan as "garbage" from "the boys at the State Department." Frustrated, Porter recommended suspension of the Lausanne conference. Truman and Secretary of State Dean G. Acheson agreed, realizing that "no real basis for conciliation between the parties exists at the present time."[4]

During the Lausanne conference, U.S. and Israeli diplomats squared off on territorial issues. Israel indicated that it would retain Jaffa and the western Galilee, territories that it had occupied beyond the partition borders. Since no Arab

Palestine state had emerged, the Foreign Ministry argued, Israeli withdrawal would deliver such lands to Arab states, a result not intended by the United Nations. Prime Minister David Ben-Gurion also rejected Jordan's demand for a corridor to the Mediterranean by declaring that "Israel could not be cut in two."[5]

Truman initially authorized the State Department to contest Israeli retention of land beyond the partition borders. Even Special Counsel Clark Clifford conceded on 28 March that Israeli claims to additional lands must be secured "by friendly dealing and negotiation with the Arabs." Accordingly, Truman wrote to King Abdallah of Jordan that "Israel is entitled to the territory allotted to her" by partition, but "if Israel desires additions . . . it should offer territorial compensation." The State Department repeated this policy in numerous messages to Israel.[6]

The border issue became a sore point between the United States and Israel at Lausanne. The State Department rejected an Israeli proposal to retain the western Galilee and Jaffa without compensation. Israel's refusal to heed U.S. policy was "a slap in the face for the President," Ethridge commented, and "a declaration of intellectual warfare against the United States." State Department officials were also angered by evidence that "certain agents of the Israeli Government" had indirectly pressured Truman to relent. In June, the department suggested "immediate adoption of a generally negative attitude toward Israel."[7]

Truman approved the State Department's suggestion. Undersecretary of State James E. Webb presented the president with a choice between approving department policy on behalf of "our national interest" or overruling it in light of "strong opposition in American Jewish circles." Truman subsequently warned Ben-Gurion that his refusal to honor partition borders would force the United States to conclude "that a revision of its attitude toward Israel has become unavoidable." When Webb reported Israeli efforts to pressure Truman through back channels, moreover, the president decided "to stand completely firm." In August, Truman endorsed Porter's plan to remove the southern Negev from Israel and declared that Israel "sh[ou]ld be left under no illusion . . . that there is any difference of view" between the White House and the State Department.[8]

Rather than buckling, Israeli leaders responded to Truman's message with firm diplomacy. They argued that Arab aggression had invalidated the partition resolution and that Israeli security depended on occupation of territory beyond the partition lines. The Foreign Ministry also intensified its indirect pressure on Truman by "recruiting everybody we've got . . . , all the Baruchs, Crums, Frankfurters, Welles, young and old Roosevelts, etc., and making an all-out effort" to change Truman's mind. "No fair-minded man will deny us the right to retain that part of our ancient land," Israeli President Chaim Weizmann wrote to Truman, "which has become ours at a terrible cost of blood and treasure in the course of a war forced upon us by others."[9]

Despite his initial firmness toward Israel, Truman soon caved in under the pressure from Israel and its domestic supporters. Shortly after endorsing Porter's plan, Truman apparently authorized Clifford to tell Israeli officials that he would support their retention of the Negev. On 19 August, Truman pledged to Eddie Jacobson, who visited the White House at Ambassador Eliahu Elath's behest, that "no single foot of land will be taken from Israel in [the] Negev." Truman's change of heart forced Acheson to suspend pressure on Israel and adjourn the Lausanne conference.[10]

The PCC faded into obscurity after the Lausanne conference. The commission sponsored talks in New York in October 1949, in Geneva in January–July 1950, and in Jerusalem in June 1950, but all deadlocked amid familiar, mutual accusations of bad faith. Convinced that any effort to arbitrate a settlement would prove futile given both sides' reluctance to compromise, the State Department remained passive about these initiatives. Many U.S. officials agreed in mid-1950, in the words of the American ambassador to Tel Aviv, James G. McDonald, that the "PCC is condemned by its own record and . . . should be scrapped." Although the United Nations voted in late 1950 to preserve the commission, its importance declined.[11]

Meanwhile, Arab and Israeli attitudes toward comprehensive regional peacemaking hardened. U.S. diplomats monitored Arab peoples' persistent opposition to considering peace with or recognition of Israel. In June 1951, Abdallah told the PCC that he personally would defy the Arab League in peacemaking but that he could not "defy my own people." Political dynamics inside Israel also hindered peacemaking. Ben-Gurion claimed a victor's prerogative to dictate peace terms and vowed to rest Israel's security on its army rather than on Arab promises. So strongly did public opinion support this view that the moderate Sharett refused U.S. suggestions that he declare that he desired peace.[12]

Despite the obstacles, the State Department tried in 1951–52 to jump-start the peace process. Acheson directed Ely E. Palmer, a U.S. official serving as chairman of the PCC, to invite Israel, Egypt, Syria, Jordan, and Lebanon to a September 1951 conference in Paris to discuss terms for a general peace, but the conference foundered from the start. Palmer proposed a detailed plan for peace, including mutual economic concessions, extensive Israeli concessions on the refugees issue, and U.N.-supervised talks on other issues. The Arab states accepted these terms, but Israel firmly rejected them despite U.S. pressure to concede. Egypt, having defied the West over MEC, then also criticized the plan, and U.S. officials realized the pointlessness of their efforts and suspended the conference in November.[13]

In late 1952, the United States lost control of the moribund peace process. After the Arab states placed the Palestine issue on the General Assembly agenda, Israel upstaged them by pushing through a U.N. committee a resolution calling for direct negotiations leading to peace. Eban, the Israeli ambassador to Washington, dispatched Jacobson and the president of the Development Corporation for Israel, Abraham Feinberg, to the White House, where they convinced Truman to order the State Department "to muster all support you can" for the resolution. But Israel's motion lacked backing among other U.N. members, and the assembly defeated it on 19 December. To U.S. officials, this episode revealed how ineffectual the peace process had become.[14]

Failure of Bilateral Israeli-Arab Negotiations

As the PCC withered, U.S. officials encouraged prospective bilateral peace treaties between Israel and each of its Arab adversaries. Such treaties, the Americans believed, would further the quest to restore stability to the Middle East. But promoting bilateral peace treaties proved to be as difficult as achieving a regional settlement. On occasion, U.S. officials even hindered the peace process when it threatened to intrude on their Cold War security interests.

Peace prospects seemed nil in several cases. Lebanon would not negotiate directly with Israel, the Lebanese minister to Washington, Charles Malik, told Assistant Secretary of State George C. McGhee in February 1950, because "it did not trust the Jews" and because negotiations would imply recognition. Ben-Gurion bypassed a chance to meet Husni Zaim, who ruled Syria from 30 March to 14 August 1949, because the Israeli leader detected a Syrian conspiracy to assassinate him. In early 1950, Syrian Prime Minister Khalid al-Azm hinted that he would consider peace with Israel, but U.S. officials doubted that the Syrian public would consent. An Israeli-Iraqi settlement remained out of the question.[15]

In contrast, peace between Israel and Jordan appeared possible, and U.S. officials promoted it. "The cause of peace in the Near East would be greatly furthered," Truman wrote to Abdallah after Israeli-Jordanian negotiations opened in November 1949, "if the states most directly concerned in the Palestine dispute should find it possible to agree among themselves upon the basic elements for a just settlement." On 24 February 1950, Israel and Jordan initialed a peace treaty that established borders near the armistice lines, pledged nonaggression for five years, promoted commerce, and established joint control of Jerusalem.[16]

Although U.S. officials desired peace in principle, the draft treaty gave them pause. When Abdallah submitted the pact for approval, his cabinet, fearing a backlash among Palestinian residents of the kingdom, decided to await elections scheduled for 11 April. To avoid galvanizing nationalists in those elections, Truman refrained from pressuring Abdallah to ratify the deal. Opposition to the treaty among other Arab powers also deterred U.S. intervention. The Arab League voted to condemn, expel, and impose economic sanctions on any member that made peace with Israel, and Syria vowed to seal its border with Jordan if it ratified the treaty. Endorsing the pact would damage U.S. relations with other Arab powers.[17]

When the peace treaty became embroiled in a dispute over the West Bank remnant of Arab Palestine, moreover, U.S. officials privileged their security objectives over the treaty. Having occupied the West Bank during the 1948–49 war, Jordan annexed the territory in April 1950. When signing the armistice, however, Israel refused to recognize Jordan's control; Israel also refused to recognize the annexation. As a deterrent to Israeli expansion, Britain promptly extended the Anglo-Jordanian defense treaty to the West Bank. Although the annexation rekindled Jordanian-Israeli tension, the State Department approved the move on behalf of Britain's security interests.[18]

U.S. officials also remained aloof when Jordan torpedoed the draft peace treaty with Israel. After his cabinet refused to ratify the pact or renew negotiations, Abdallah announced that his kingdom must gain Eilat before it would make peace. Israel rejected that suggestion and asked U.S. officials to encourage Abdallah to approve the February treaty, but they refused. Jordan and Israel, McGhee told Jordanian counselor Abdul Monem Rifai, should "reach peace on a basis which was mutually satisfactory to them."[19]

In the face of U.S. passivity, the prospects of an Israel-Jordan peace treaty crashed under a wave of violence and regicide. After a series of border incidents in summer 1950, a Jordanian roadblock erected at Gharandal in December nearly provoked war as the IDF mobilized troops, issued an ultimatum, and buzzed King Abdallah's palace with a warplane. Although Abdallah dismantled the roadblock and fired the defense minister who had imposed it, the king also threatened to "organize terrorism and sabotage within Israel." The U.S. minister to Amman, Gerald A. Drew, noted that the Israelis "have lost their one sincere friend in [the] whole Arab world." The assassination of King Abdallah by a Palestinian gunman on 20 July 1951 virtually eliminated the chance of Israeli-Jordanian peace during the Truman presidency. Episodic negotiations between Jordan and Israel in 1951–52 quickly degraded into quarrels about trade and territory.[20]

U.S. officials intervened in the Israel-Jordan situation only when border violence peaked in 1952. After a series of terrorist infiltrations in January, Israel retaliated by killing three Palestinian villagers near the armistice line. Sharett justified the move by declaring that the "language of reprisals is [the] only one Arabs seem to understand," but the State Department called Israel's actions "extremely grave violations" of the armistice. Under such pressure, Israel submitted to a U.N.-brokered deal in which Israel and Jordan pledged to seal their own borders to stop exfiltration of persons from Jordan to Israel. That deal restored calm to the border, although the climate for peacemaking remained cold.[21]

U.S. officials also passively encouraged periodic peace talks between Israel and Egypt. In late 1949, the American ambassador to Cairo, Jefferson Caffery, and ambassador to Tel Aviv, McDonald, transported messages between the two governments. That kind of participation, however, only made U.S. officials aware of the deep disagreements between the two powers and the political constraints that hindered King Farouk from settling. "While certain elements in Egypt feel that a peace settlement with Israel is necessary," U.S. officials concluded in July 1950, "no government so far has had the courage to proceed."[22]

The outbreak of war in Korea in June 1950 created a brief burst of U.S. enthusiasm for Egyptian-Israeli peace. Feeling a degree of urgency because of the Korean situation, State Department officials conceived of a settlement in which British forces would evacuate the canal zone, as Egypt demanded; Egypt would make peace with Israel; and Britain would occupy military bases in the Gaza strip. Such a plan, McGhee hoped, would "achieve the dual objective of satisfying our defense considerations and breaking the Arab-Israeli impasse at an important point." But security experts in Washington and London rejected the plan because Gaza lacked sufficient military facilities, and the Israeli expulsion of two thousand Bedouin from the Negev into Egypt angered leaders in Cairo. Foreign Minister Mohammed Salaheddin told Acheson that peace with Israel was "out of the question." Soaring nationalism in Egypt, provoked by the rejection of MEC in October 1951, diminished the chance of peace with Israel.[23]

The July 1952 Free Officers' revolt against King Farouk created a window of opportunity for peacemaking late in the Truman presidency. Sensing that General Mohammed Naguib, who nominally headed the new regime in Cairo, desired a settlement, Ben-Gurion declared in the Knesset on 18 August that "there is . . . no reason or basis for a quarrel between Egypt and Israel." Israeli and Egyptian diplomats in Paris conducted secret, occasional peace talks from August to October. The two states also reconvened the Israeli-Egyptian Mixed Armistice Commission (MAC) after a ten-month hiatus and agreed to stop border exfiltrations.[24]

On behalf of Western security interests in Cairo, however, U.S. officials refrained from encouraging such promising developments. Hoping that Naguib would accommodate Western security interests in the canal zone military base, NEA officials feared that raising the sensitive issue of Israel given the volatile political situation in Cairo would undermine or alienate the new regime. They denied Sharett's requests to pressure Naguib to make peace and even urged Israel to make concessions on various issues, thereby bolstering Naguib's prestige.[25]

Acheson finally encouraged Israeli-Egyptian peacemaking in the twilight of the Truman presidency, but to no avail. As secret talks resumed in Paris, Naguib allowed an Israel-bound food ship to transit the Suez Canal, visited a Cairo synagogue, and blocked an Arab League resolution encouraging discrimination against Jews. Acheson encouraged Israel to interpret these gestures as sincere. When Naguib criticized an Israeli-German economic aid deal and demanded a corridor across the Negev, however, Israeli officials came to see his gestures as empty gimmicks designed to secure U.S. aid. They planned "concentrated anti-Naguib diplomacy and propaganda" to erode his stature in the United States. In the absence of U.S. activism, Egyptian-Israeli peace failed to materialize.[26]

The Huleh Dispute

In contrast to their passivity regarding bilateral peace talks, U.S. officials became immersed in the Huleh dispute of 1951–52, a crisis that threatened to plunge Israel and Syria into war. Because of the gravity of the situation, U.S. officials felt compelled to become more deeply involved in it than in peacemaking be-tween Israel and other Arab states. Perhaps because the stakes seemed so high, Truman remained evenhanded in the Huleh controversy despite pressure from Israel to endorse its case. Although U.S. officials helped to avert an escalation to war, they failed to achieve progress toward a final peace agreement and angered both Israel and Syria in the process.

The dispute involved property rights along the Israel-Syria border near Lake Huleh, which emptied to the south into the Jordan River. To improve public health and reclaim land, in October 1950 Israel launched a public works pro-gram to drain malarial marshes north of Lake Huleh by straightening four kilo-meters of riverbank south of the lake and lowering its water level. The work to the south centered in a demilitarized zone (DMZ) and required the flooding of land owned by Israelis and Palestinians. Promising to compensate landowners, Israel sent bulldozers into the DMZ in January 1951.[27]

Controversy ensued when Syria protested the reclamation project to the Israeli-Syrian MAC. The MAC chairman, General William E. Riley, found merit in Syria's complaint that the project disrupted the lives of Palestinians. Because Israel lacked the sovereign right to expropriate land in the DMZ, he ruled, the country must halt operations until Syria approved. Rather than stopping con-struction, however, Israel rejected Riley's ruling on legal grounds, boycotted the MAC, and sent armed patrols to protect its workers in the DMZ. On 15 and 25 March, violence flared between the patrols and local landowners, and Syrian Premier Adib al-Shishakli alerted his army for action.[28]

The Huleh dispute confronted U.S. officials with a difficult dilemma. On the one hand, the State Department questioned the legitimacy of Syria represent-ing the Palestinian landowners and saw merit in Israel's efforts to drain the Huleh marshes. Malarial mosquitoes, Burton Y. Berry of the NEA observed to Syrian envoys, "respected no boundary lines." On the other hand, the depart-ment blamed Israel for provoking tension by infringing on Palestinians' prop-

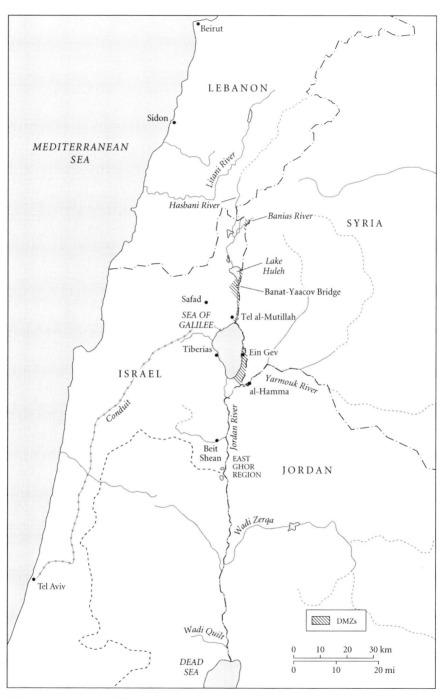

Map 3. The Jordan Valley Watershed

erty rights and for defying U.N. authority. The department pressed Israel to withdraw its troops from the DMZ and to honor MAC directives.[29]

Rather than comply with U.S. demands, Ben-Gurion escalated the situation in April by dispatching troops to expel eight hundred Palestinians from three villages in the DMZ. The "idea is [to] clear [the] Syrian frontier belt . . . once [and] for all of Arabs," Eytan privately explained to Eban, "thereby asserting our rule and possession beyond doubt." When an Israeli patrol reached al-Hamma on 4 April, Syrians opened fire, killing seven. To retaliate, the IDF demolished the three evacuated Arab villages and bombed nearby Syrian army positions.[30]

The Israeli government divided internally over Ben-Gurion's bold move. IDF officers strongly approved the action as a means to continue the reclamation project, dispute the MAC's authority, and challenge Syria. By contrast, the more dovish Sharett censured the IDF's "thoughtlessness and irresponsibility," while Eban warned that the move undermined Israeli prestige. To mitigate the diplomatic damage, Sharett suspended work at Huleh for the Passover holiday and convinced Ben-Gurion to apologize for the reprisal raid.[31]

To protect their interests, U.S. officials censured Israel. Acheson feared that the Israeli action might provoke full-scale war, and a request from Syria and Saudi Arabia to invoke the Tripartite Declaration against Israel, although denied by the State Department, underscored the prospect of being drawn into such hostilities. Harry N. Howard of the NEA warned that acquiescing to Israel's actions would confirm Arab charges of U.S. complicity in Israeli expansionism. Accordingly, Acheson urged Ben-Gurion to avoid the "slightest semblance [of] provocation." The State Department drafted a Security Council resolution that censured Israel's attack on Syria and demanded that Israel halt drainage operations and allow the villagers to return.[32]

U.S. officials also encouraged Syria to defuse the crisis. Acheson praised the "helpful and constructive attitude" of the Syrian prime minister, who pledged to abide by MAC rulings, and discouraged "further recourse to violence" by Syrian forces. Minister Faiz el-Khouri reported on 9 April that Syrian troops had departed the DMZ, and on 12 April the government in Damascus pledged its peaceful intent. Syria complained, however, that it received more stringent treatment than Israel did from the State Department; furthermore, Syria charged, 250 Israeli soldiers remained in the DMZ.[33]

Despite U.S. efforts to end the Huleh crisis, it escalated into large-scale violence. On 2 May, fighting between Israeli and Syrian forces near Tel al-Mutillah in Israeli territory near the DMZ and at Shamalneh in the DMZ triggered a four-day artillery duel. On 6 May, the IDF launched a massive strike that repelled the Syrians at a cost of forty Israeli lives. Fighting ended on 10 May, two days after the Security Council passed a cease-fire resolution. Israel blamed Syria for provoking the battle, Syria blamed Israel, and officials in Washington were unable to determine who fired first.[34]

Alarmed by the fighting, U.S. officials took action in the Security Council to end it. The State Department recruited Britain, France, and Turkey as cosponsors of a resolution that called on all powers to end the crisis. The resolution alluded to Syrian provocations but reproached Israel for its 5 April air strike on Syria, its defiance of the MAC, and its maltreatment of Palestinians. Suspicious that the resolution revealed the State Department's "accumulated irritation" at them, Israeli officials complained that the measure would strain U.S.-Israeli relations and reward Syrian aggression. The Israeli government mobilized Jacobson; White House adviser David Niles; Weizmann; the executive director of the American Zionist Council, Jerome Unger; and publicist Freda Kirchwey to pressure Truman to block the resolution.[35]

Truman resisted the Israeli pressure, and the Security Council passed the resolution on 18 May by a vote of ten to zero, with the Soviet Union abstaining. Available records fail to clarify why Truman resisted Israeli appeals or whether he noticed the campaign to influence him. When he received a cable from Weizmann, Truman told Acheson, "I know nothing about this situation." It is possible that the president, uninformed about the entire dispute, simply deferred to the State Department to make policy.[36]

U.S. officials deemed it prudent to rein in the Arab states' ecstasy regarding the U.N. resolution. According to U.S. Minister to Damascus Cavendish W. Cannon, Arab League officials meeting in the Syrian capital were "surprised and heartened by tangible proof that [the] West [was] seeking justice in this instance." Syrian minister el-Khouri thanked McGhee for the "concrete evidence" of U.S. impartiality. Lest Syria indefinitely obstruct the drainage project, the State Department endorsed the project as a benefit to the region and clarified that the department had not intended to "give veto power over drainage [of the] swamp to any party."[37]

Israel, by contrast, earned U.S. satisfaction by partially accepting the Security Council resolution. Sharett realized that defiance of the United States risked economic grants, military aid, and other advantages. The State Department "has many means of revenge," warned Moshe Keren, counselor at the Israeli embassy in Washington. Yet capitulation seemed likely to trigger criticism from Knesset members and the IDF. To balance his diplomatic and domestic interests, Sharett halted drainage work on Arab-owned land on 24 May but declared that the project would continue on Israeli-owned land. Once General Riley approved these terms, U.S. officials rejected Syrian protests and a British suggestion that the Security Council order Israel to halt all work.[38]

Although the Security Council resolution curtailed the violence at Huleh, tension persisted for months. Israel and Syria quarreled over the fate of some

eight hundred Palestinians dislocated from the DMZ by Israeli action. MAC officials' efforts to ascertain each family's desire to return to its land or receive compensation from Israel were hampered by Israeli demolition of homes, police
interference, and, reportedly, elimination of heads of families. Angry at Riley
for allowing Israel to resume its work, Syria discouraged the Palestinians from
accepting compensation. Acheson chastised both states for using the villagers
"as pawns of national policy," but neither Israel nor Syria relented.[39]

Despite U.S. efforts to settle it, the Huleh dispute persisted in 1951–52. The
State Department proposed that Israel and Syria partition the DMZ along the
Jordan River. Syria agreed, but Israel refused to negotiate anything other than
a peace treaty, refusing to budge even when al-Shishakli offered in late 1952 to
partition the DMZ ten meters east of the Huleh-Jordan-Galilee waterline and at-
tach the Ein Gev enclave to Israel, thus relinquishing Syria's access to the water.
The "high-level talks" that the United States arranged between the two states in
October 1952, Fred S. Waller of NEA observed, "turned out to be neither high
level nor much of a talk."[40]

U.S. officials were thus left with the task of containing the Huleh dispute.
In August 1952, al-Shishakli threatened to use force to stop the Huleh drainage operation, and Israel demanded that the State Department punish the
Syrian leader by cutting economic aid. Assistant Secretary of State Henry A.
Byroade admitted that he "called the Syrian boys in and gave them hell about
al-Shishakli's statements," but the department refused to punish him, preferring
al-Shishakli to the alternatives. Al-Shishakli's threats, Parker T. Hart of the NEA
told the Israelis, were "just politicians' bark for internal needs."[41]

Conclusion

After the United Nations negotiated the Arab-Israeli armistices of 1949, the
task of reaching final peace treaties remained. The protagonists in the conflict
claimed to desire peace on certain conditions. U.S. officials favored peace in
principle on behalf of their interests in the Middle East. The United Nations attempted peacemaking with a variety of diplomatic initiatives. Yet peace did not
materialize in 1949–53.

Several reasons account for the failure of peacemaking. Political conditions
in the Middle East were simply not conducive. Emboldened by victory, Israeli
leaders rested their security on their military prowess rather than on compromises with the Arab states and categorically refused to yield any territory occupied in the war. Embittered by defeat, most Arab leaders and peoples sought
to disable Israel, prevent it from expanding, and gain territory at its expense.
Intra-Arab rivalries encouraged firmness toward Israel, as signified by the assassination of Jordan's moderate King Abdallah by a disaffected Palestinian. The

PCC, erected by the United Nations to achieve a settlement, could not overcome such obstacles.

The United States offered limited and ineffective leadership in peacemaking. To be sure, U.S. officials supported the peace process by endorsing the U.N. conference at Lausanne, backing arbitration efforts by the PCC, encouraging Israeli-Jordanian and Israeli-Egyptian bilateral negotiations, and advising the major protagonists to make concessions. In the face of intense Arab-Israeli animosity, however, U.S. leaders refrained from taking major initiatives. Moreover, the American government privileged Cold War interests over Arab-Israeli settlement when the two conflicted. Thus, U.S. officials endorsed Jordan's annexation of the West Bank despite the displeasure that the action caused Israel and discouraged Egyptian-Israeli negotiations that might have undermined the Naguib regime, on which Western security seemed to rest.

The Truman administration's deep internal divisions with respect to Israel also compromised U.S. peacemaking capabilities. Perhaps still regretting the creation of Israel over their objections, State Department officials advised Truman that Israel must make substantial concessions to accomplish a peace treaty. Mobilized by the Israeli embassy, however, certain officials and private citizens encouraged Truman to reject such advice. This battle for Truman's mind ended in a draw. Political advisers convinced Truman to prohibit the State Department from compelling Israel to surrender territory beyond the partition borders but failed to convince the president to block a Security Council resolution critical of Israel's behavior in the Huleh crisis. In any case, such internal divisions neutralized the administration's ability to lead.

Passive toward peacemaking in general, the Truman administration became actively involved in Arab-Israeli diplomacy only when tensions triggered hostilities. When the Huleh crisis portended war, U.S. officials worked rapidly and effectively to cap the violence and restore the status quo. But in most cases, the administration did not throw its full support behind peacemaking, encouraging the principals to negotiate settlements but refraining from vigorous action. U.S. officials saw no easy path to achieving a settlement.

7

REPATRIATION VERSUS RESETTLEMENT
The Palestinian Refugee Crisis, 1949–1953

One of the most troublesome issues to emerge from the Palestine War was the displacement of hundreds of thousands of Palestinians from Israeli-controlled territory. For humanitarian, strategic, and political reasons, U.S. officials tried both to mitigate the suffering of these refugees and to find some means to integrate them into the region's societies and states. This effort foundered, however, against Israel's rock-solid refusal to repatriate substantial numbers of refugees and the Arab states' equally firm refusal to resettle the Palestinians. Failure to resolve this vexing situation accentuated Arab-Israeli animosity.

Several factors shaped U.S. diplomacy regarding the refugee crisis. First, U.S. officials took action because they expected that the Soviet Union would use the situation to gain political influence in the Middle East. Second, the State Department and White House staff disagreed on the concessions they expected from Israel and competed to influence President Harry S. Truman. Third, U.S. officials aimed for a compromise settlement that would preserve good relations with all involved powers. These factors stimulated U.S. action in the dispute but also limited the American ability to achieve a settlement.

The Refugee Crisis

The exodus of Palestinian refugees from Israel became a major issue during the Palestine War because of the scale and complexity of the displacement. Nearly one million Palestinians took refuge in camps in Arab states. This situation inflamed passions among the Palestinians and other Arab peoples, reducing the prospect of peace. In U.S. thinking, the refugees appeared to represent both tragic victims of war and fertile ground for communism. Yet U.S. officials who sought to resolve the crisis found the governments of the region reluctant to cooperate, concede, or compromise.

The refugee crisis originated in the dynamics of war. In April 1949, the State

Department estimated that 700,000 Palestinians had fled Israeli-controlled territory. The Palestine Conciliation Commission (PCC) counted 950,000 "Palestine refugees and destitute persons" residing in the West Bank (630,000), Lebanon (131,000), Jordan (99,000), Syria (85,000), and Iraq (5,000). Food and water shortages made the situation "critical," Secretary of State George C. Marshall noted at the onset of the exodus. "Disease is rampant and [the] sanitation situation unspeakable." In November 1948, the General Assembly asked states to contribute thirty-two million dollars for emergency relief, and on 11 December, the assembly authorized the PCC to "facilitate the repatriation, resettlement and economic and social rehabilitation of refugees and payment of compensation" for lost property.[1]

Israeli responsibility for the flight of the refugees has been a subject of intense debate. Many chroniclers have echoed the Israeli government's claim that the refugees left of their own volition, enticed by Arab leaders to relocate to Arab-controlled areas on the promise of help in liberating their homeland. The "Arab exodus [is a] direct result [of] aggression organised by Arab States," Israeli Foreign Minister Moshe Sharett claimed. However, revisionist scholars such as Benny Morris, Erskine Childers, and Nur Masalha cite evidence that the Israel Defense Forces (IDF) compelled Palestinians to flee. Israel must explore "all possibilities of getting rid, once and for all, of the huge Arab minority which originally threatened us," Sharett commented in August 1948. "What can be achieved in this period of storm and stress will be quite unattainable once conditions stabilize."[2]

Whatever caused the departure of the refugees, Israel categorically refused to allow them to return to its territory. Repatriates would form a "source [of] imminent danger," Sharett repeatedly asserted. Israeli Ambassador to the United States Eliahu Elath argued that returnees would "not feel comfortable as a racial or religious minority group." Israeli leaders insisted that the Arab states that attacked must resolve the problem. Government seizures of Palestinian property under the absentee-property ordinance of 12 December 1948 signaled Israel's intent to transfer Palestinian property to Jewish immigrants.[3]

Arab leaders, by contrast, charged that Israel had fomented the exodus of refugees and insisted that Israel repatriate all who desired to return. Most Arab states "insist upon the repatriation of all the Palestinian refugees," the State Department noted. In the Arab view, "Israel, and to a lesser extent the United Nations and the United States, created the problem and are responsible for its solution."[4]

For humanitarian and security reasons, the United States promoted relief for refugees. Hundreds of thousands of destitute people living with inadequate shelter and food and facing the approach of winter, the State Department observed in October 1948, portended "a tragic disaster" of "catastrophic proportions." The Pentagon regretted that the refugees' suffering made them susceptible to communism, angered Arab peoples, and aggravated the Palestine dispute. The State Department encouraged the Red Cross, churches, and oil companies to contribute one million dollars in relief, and the Pentagon and the Public Health Service dispatched physicians, sanitary engineers, and epidemiologists to refugee camps. Even the Central Intelligence Agency (CIA) rendered assistance "on an informal basis." The State Department named foreign service officer Stanton Griffis as the director of U.N. Relief for Palestine Refugees and convinced Congress to fund half of the U.N.'s thirty-two-million-dollar relief program.[5]

When contemplating a long-term solution to the crisis, Truman initially took the view that Israel must repatriate the refugees. The refugees "should be permitted to return to their homes," U.S. Ambassador Warren R. Austin declared to the United Nations on 20 November 1948, and "adequate compensation should be arranged for the property of those who choose not to return." Truman affirmed this statement in January 1949 and reassured Jordan's King Abdallah in April that repatriation "is a matter of deep personal concern to me." U.S. officials were confident that U.N. supervision of repatriation would safeguard Israel against infiltration by terrorists and saboteurs.[6]

Truman and other U.S. officials embraced this position for several reasons. First, many leaders were bothered by the physical suffering of the refugees and by Israel's seizures of their property. In a statement typical of State Department thinking in late 1948, Minister to Damascus James H. Keeley regretted that "Arab refugees from Israeli terror" were "dying of starvation and exposure while their ancestral homes are given to Jewish DP's [displaced persons] from Europe." Repatriation promised to end the suffering.[7]

State Department officials also identified political reasons to support repatriation. Israel should accept repatriation as "evidence of its desire to establish amicable relations with the Arab world." Resolution of the crisis, Gordon Mattison of the NEA added, "would lay a firm basis for Israeli-Arab friendship and mutual confidence." Israel's absorption of Jewish immigrants, officials in Washington added, invalidated its claim that it lacked the fiscal means to repatriate Palestinians.[8]

Security concerns provided a third motive for supporting repatriation. The State Department observed that the refugee problem "is directly related to our national interests." Secretary of Defense Louis A. Johnson agreed that the crisis would "aggravate conditions of insecurity, unrest, and political instability, with attendant opportunity for Soviet penetration." "If winter comes with no help," PCC Chairman Mark Ethridge warned in June 1949, "there will be an explosive situation."[9]

U.S. officials gradually tempered their quest for repatriation with a recognition that some refugees must resettle in Arab states. State Department officials reasoned that circumstances in Israel would prevent every refugee from returning. Substantial U.S. economic aid, American officials hoped, would convince the refugees to surrender their "very natural desire to return to their . . . fig tree and vine" in favor of "some other fig tree and vine elsewhere." In March 1949, the department concluded that Israel should repatriate a fixed number of refugees and compensate others whom Arab states would absorb.[10]

Even as U.S. policy moderated, however, American and Israeli officials clashed over the U.S. expectation that Israel should repatriate some refugees. To U.S. chagrin, Israel frustrated PCC attempts to implement the U.N. resolution of 11 December 1948. In February 1949, Ethridge and Sharett argued to a standstill about the suggestion that Israel affirm repatriation in principle. In March, Prime Minister David Ben-Gurion clarified that Israel would compensate refugees for expropriated lands only if the Arab states paid Israel war damages. Israel "has prejudiced [the] whole cause of peaceful settlement," Ethridge reported to Truman, by the "cold-bloodedness of her attitude toward refugees." At a PCC meeting in Beirut in April, Ben-Gurion consented to repatriate a tiny number of refugees seeking reunion with their families, but he refused to approve repatriation in principle on grounds of "self-preservation."[11]

With Truman's endorsement, the State Department exerted considerable pressure on Israel to make additional concessions. Secretary of State Dean G. Acheson urged Sharett and Ben-Gurion to show "magnanimity and humanity" and to "make a real contribution" that "would make it possible for the President to continue his strong and warm support for Israel." When Israeli officials refused to bend, Truman spoke bluntly to Israeli President Chaim Weizmann on 23 April. "I am rather disgusted with the manner in which the Jews are approaching the refugee problem," Truman later confided to Ethridge.[12]

The pressure from Truman softened the thinking of several Israeli officials but failed to change their policy. Ambassador to the United Nations Abba Eban advised Sharett to make concessions because the issue had become a "point of honour with [the] U.S.A. closely affecting [the] whole relationship." To appease Truman, Weizmann pledged to consider "all the possibilities of resettlement and repatriation in the Near East." Ben-Gurion and Sharett, however, refused to buckle in the face of U.S. demands.[13]

Early U.S. Initiatives to Solve the Crisis, 1949

Given the PCC's inability to settle the refugee problem, the United States promoted a solution that blended repatriation of some refugees by Israel and resettlement of others by the Arab states. Neither the Arab states nor Israel, however, would make any concessions, and the effort to sell the U.S. plan strained

American relations with both sides. Israel tried to settle the matter by driving a wedge between the State Department and the White House with a diplomatic ruse, but the scheme backfired, provoking the first crisis in U.S.-Israeli relations. The United States proved unable to negotiate a settlement or to avoid residual damage to its own interests.

The State Department's Arab Refugee Working Panel conceived of a plan for refugee settlement in April 1949. Because mass repatriation "is manifestly impossible from the political, economic, and geographical point of view," the panel envisioned a long-range program in which the United States, Britain, the World Bank, and oil corporations would finance public-works and economic-development programs in Arab states that would enable them to absorb large numbers of refugees. The panel hoped that Israel would repatriate two hundred thousand refugees and the Arab states (especially Iraq and Syria) would resettle five hundred thousand, and the panel wanted Congress to allocate half of the three hundred million dollars needed over three years to finance the scheme.[14]

Truman approved the State Department plan, authorizing Undersecretary of State James Webb to implement it despite fiscal concerns raised by the Bureau of the Budget and political doubts expressed by the Senate Foreign Relations Committee. Recently named a special assistant to the secretary with rank of minister to handle the refugee problem, George McGhee promoted the plan among World Bank and British officials. Acheson directed U.S. diplomats to launch the "strongest diplomatic approach" to Israel and the Arab states "to soften their respective attitudes."[15]

Two Arab states reacted positively to the U.S. initiative. Syrian Prime Minister Husni Zaim pledged to resettle 250,000 refugees provided that foreign investment developed his country before he revealed his concession to his people. Otherwise, he told Keeley, the "powerful opposition would attack him for selling out to [the] Jews and their backers." Jordan offered to resettle nearly 600,000 refugees in the West Bank in exchange for financial aid. But U.S. officials believed that the country's eagerness exceeded its abilities, and in summer 1949, the government in Amman reconsidered its enthusiasm for the plan.[16]

Other Arab powers expressed reluctance about the U.S. plan from the beginning. Lebanon's prime minister argued that admitting refugees would upset his country's delicate confessional balance between Christians and Muslims. Iraqi Foreign Minister Muhammed Fadil Jamali declared that his country "has no moral, legal, or logical reason" to resettle refugees. Saudi Arabia agreed to endorse resettlement only after Israel repatriated most refugees and compensated the remainder. Egypt declared that it lacked room for immigrants. The U.S. consul in Jerusalem, William C. Burdett, reported that the refugees themselves wished to return to their homes.[17]

U.S. officials pressed the Arab states to cooperate with the plan, but to no avail. In June, the State Department told Jordan, Saudi Arabia, Syria, Iraq, Lebanon, and Egypt that the United States was "deeply disappointed" by the deadlock on the issue and expected them, together with Israel, to implement a solution bankrolled by the United States. In the absence of a settlement, the United States might end its funding of U.N. relief programs, which would impose major financial burdens on the Arab states. The Arab countries refused, however, to approve the U.S. plan.[18]

Israel also rejected the State Department's plan on security and political grounds. Citing "moral considerations," Israeli officials conceded on 4 May that they would repatriate a handful of refugees, compensate owners of abandoned property, contribute humanitarian relief, and safeguard the rights of minorities within their borders. But leaders of the Jewish state refused additional concessions on the grounds that the Arab states were "entirely responsible" for the crisis. The refugees were "members of an aggressor group defeated in a war of its own making," Ben-Gurion told Truman on 8 June. "Israel cannot in the name of humanitarianism be driven to commit suicide."[19]

To deflect U.S. pressure, Israel briefly floated its own scheme. Ben-Gurion proposed that Israel annex the Gaza Strip and absorb its 230,000 refugees and 80,000 permanent residents. The State Department initially considered this idea "perhaps the key that would unlock the whole problem" and recommended it to Egypt. But Egypt responded that the plan would give Israel land as a reward for fulfilling an obligation mandated by the U.N. resolution of 11 December 1948. The plan smacked of "cheap barter," Ambassador Kamil Abdul Rahim added, because it "exchang[ed] human lives for territory." Given Egypt's resistance, U.S. officials allowed the Gaza plan to wither.[20]

Israel also resisted the State Department plan by appealing through various channels to the White House. Elath reported that the president of the Development Corporation for Israel, Abraham Feinberg, personally urged Truman, Special Counsel Clark Clifford, and presidential secretary Matt Connelly to accept Israel's position and to replace Ethridge with an appointee sympathetic to Israel. The Israeli Foreign Ministry mobilized lobbyist I. L. Kenen, General John Hilldring, and U.S. Jewish journalists to promote Israel's position. U.S. Ambassador to Tel Aviv James B. McDonald argued Israel's case in a direct communication to Clifford, as did Weizmann in an impassioned letter to Truman.[21]

In this instance, the State Department neutralized Israel's indirect appeals to the White House by alerting Truman to the pressure. "Israeli officials have in fact informed our representatives in Palestine," Webb warned the president, "that they intend to bring about a change" in U.S. policy "through means available to them in the United States." Bothered by this allegation, Truman told Webb "that he has no doubt as to the wisdom of the course being followed" by the State Department. Truman informed several visiting Jewish leaders that "unless they were prepared to play the game properly and conform to the rules they were probably going to lose one of their best friends."[22]

Annoyed by the Israeli pressure, in fact, Truman authorized a series of severely worded messages intended to pressure Israel to concede. The United States "is seriously disturbed by the attitude of Israel," a late May message from Truman to Ben-Gurion stated. If Israel remained inflexible, the administration "will regretfully be forced to the conclusion that a revision of its attitude toward Israel has become unavoidable." Because Ben-Gurion's response merely "repeats the familiar arguments," State Department officials advised Truman to adopt "a generally negative attitude toward Israel." Truman authorized an aide-mémoire to Israel on 24 June that called the refugee problem "a common responsibility of Israel and the Arab States, which neither side should be permitted to shirk."[23]

The pressure from Truman weakened Israeli leaders' resolve. Israel risked "the profound alienation of President Truman," Eban warned. Public opinion favored the Arab view, Uriel Heyd of the Israeli embassy in Washington added, "from Justices on the Supreme Court . . . down to the man in the street." To ease U.S. pressure, Sharett proposed to the Israeli cabinet on 5 July that Israel repatriate one hundred thousand refugees in exchange for a peace treaty. The cabinet authorized him to explore informally whether Truman would endorse such terms.[24]

While scoping out Truman's thinking, Sharett triggered a diplomatic brouhaha that snowballed into a U.S.-Israeli crisis. Acting through the general counsel of the Israeli Embassy in New York, Eban recruited Hilldring to visit Truman and discern his views on Sharett's settlement scheme. Unaware of this arrangement, Truman admitted that he might approve the scheme if it promised to break the deadlock. Although Truman admonished Hilldring not to repeat the details of their meeting, Hilldring conveyed the president's position to David Niles, who informed Israeli embassy officials, who relayed the news to Sharett. Encouraged, Sharett formally proposed to Truman on 28 July that Israel would absorb one hundred thousand refugees if the Arab states made peace and agreed to resettle all other refugees.[25]

Unaware of Truman's conversation with Hilldring, the State Department considered Israel's offer insufficient. McGhee told Elath that Israel should accept 230,000 refugees, the number it would have absorbed under Ben-Gurion's Gaza plan. Burdett interpreted Israel's offer as a hollow gesture to evade U.S. pressure and one from which Israel would wiggle away in the end. Acheson criticized the " 'take it or leave it' attitude" of Israel's offer. On 9 August, the State Department formally rejected Israel's offer.[26]

In what proved to be a major misstep, Sharett tried to overcome the State Department's opposition by cashing in Truman's assurance to Hilldring. Israeli

Foreign Ministry political adviser Reuven Shiloah told a department official that Truman had approved the 100,000 figure in his meeting with Hilldring. But State Department officials replied by strictly warning against any attempt to divide the White House from them, by resecuring Truman's support for a demand that Israel repatriate 250,000 refugees, and by notifying the CIA that a source in the White House had divulged classified information to Israel. Stuart Rockwell of the NEA bluntly warned Israeli envoys that their country's gambit would spawn anti-Semitism in the United States.[27]

Truman reacted angrily to the Israeli effort to turn him against the State Department. He promptly suspended the $49 million balance of Israel's $100 million Export-Import Bank loan and approved other such measures against Israel. "I would be less than frank," he wrote to Weizmann, "if I did not tell you that I was disappointed." The United States "wishes no harm" on Israel, Rockwell told Zalman Liff, an Israeli official at Lausanne, "but cannot go on pampering it."[28]

The suspension of the bank loan deeply irritated Israel. The State Department portrayed the move as a decision by bank officials based on a lack of progress toward peace that undermined Israel's ability to repay. But Elath did not buy this explanation. He asserted that the suspension "cut across the type of relationship . . . which should exist between Israel and the United States" and that it would weaken Israel and undermine its ability to make peace. The clash over the refugee issue shook U.S.-Israeli relations to the core.[29]

The Economic Survey Mission, 1949–1951

Facing Israeli and Arab rigidity on the refugee dispute, the United States tried to settle the problem by a new path. The State Department launched an initiative under U.N. auspices to foster economic development that would meet the refugees' physical and economic needs. U.S. officials hoped that such a technical approach would enable Middle East states to sidestep the deadlock between repatriation and resettlement. By 1951, the initiative had modestly achieved its economic objectives but had neither reassured the principals in the dispute nor resolved their political stalemate.

Several factors compelled the State Department to try the economic development plan. U.S. officials continued to worry about the refugees' physical suffering and susceptibility to political extremism. The intense Arab and Israeli resistance to political compromise made a political settlement seem impossible. Moreover, the emergency relief funds provided by the United Nations in late 1948 were expected to run out in December 1949, and Congress seemed unlikely to renew indefinitely such funding. The State Department reasoned that it could not remain inactive regarding the refugee crisis.[30]

With Truman's approval, the State Department initiated its plan in late 1949.

At the U.S. behest, on 1 September 1949 the PCC created an Economic Survey Mission (ESM) and directed it to study Middle East economic conditions and write a technical plan "to overcome economic dislocations created by the hostilities" and "to facilitate the repatriation, resettlement, and economic and social rehabilitation of the refugees." U.S., British, French, and Turkish officials would staff the mission under the leadership of Gordon R. Clapp, chairman of the board of the Tennessee Valley Authority (TVA). Like many experts in the 1940s, Clapp believed that technical assistance could stabilize the Third World.[31]

U.S. officials worked hard to overcome Arab resistance to the ESM. Lebanon and Saudi Arabia complained that the mission would delay repatriation and channel U.S. economic aid to Israel, and Syria threatened to mobilize the Arab League to oppose the mission. The State Department responded that the ESM would compose an economic master plan to reverse the PCC's string of failures in peacemaking. Describing himself as "an engineer and not concerned with politics," Clapp added that the ESM would determine the value of abandoned Arab property in Israel and Israel's ability to compensate refugees. This campaign convinced Arab leaders to consult with Clapp, who visited Lebanon, Egypt, Jordan, and Syria by 1 October.[32]

Israel also viewed the ESM with skepticism. Privately, the Foreign Ministry feared that Clapp's plans for public works in Arab states would enrich the refugees, solidify their sense of community, and increase pressure for repatriation. Israel pledged to work with the mission but also indicated that it would not raise its offer to repatriate one hundred thousand refugees. When he visited Israel in October, Clapp noted that Sharett provided a "long lecture on Arab responsibility for Arab-Jewish war and Israeli history from Moses to date."[33]

After touring the Middle East, the ESM issued a report to the United Nations in December 1949, proposing relief and public works projects to benefit the refugees. Silent on the issue of repatriation versus resettlement, the report proposed various programs at a price of $54.9 million for the period January 1950 to June 1951. Priority would be given to construction of dams and irrigation works at Wadi Zerqa and Wadi Quilt, Jordan, projects that would employ seventy thousand workers and indirectly support four hundred thousand refugees. (See map 3.) The report also urged Lebanon to begin a works program in the Litani River Valley and Syria to launch a reclamation project in the Ghab Swamps of the Orontes Valley. The full program would be administered by a permanent U.N. agency that would work with each state to ensure that the initial programs evolved into long-term development. After June 1951, local states would be expected to provide for the needs of the refugees within their borders.[34]

State Department officials identified merits in the ESM report. At a cost comparable to relief operations, Arthur Gardiner noted, the proposed works "were not simply 'make-work' schemes with no permanent value but were actually developmental in nature." The Clapp report conformed to the State Department's growing realization that massive repatriation was impossible. According to the deputy director of the Office of United Nations Affairs, Durward Sandifer, and the deputy assistant secretary of the NEA, Raymond A. Hare, the plan would lead to the resettlement of most refugees in Arab states, an outcome the report downplayed "for reasons associated with Arab sensibilities."[35]

U.S. officials strongly supported the Clapp report. On 8 December, they pushed through the General Assembly a resolution that created the United Nations Relief and Works Agency for Palestine Refugees in the Near East (UNRWA) to administer the program. Comprised of U.S., British, French, and Turkish representatives, the UNRWA established itself in Beirut in April 1950 and assumed responsibility for refugee relief on 1 May. On 5 June, Truman signed the Foreign Economic Assistance Act, which allocated $27.5 million for the UNRWA, and Britain and France agreed to contribute most of other funds needed.[36]

Israel and the Arab states, however, showed little enthusiasm for the Clapp report. Israeli officials privately criticized its "vagueness [and] superficiality" about aid to their state. Although King Abdallah signaled his support, Egypt and Lebanon were more restrained, and Syria declared that its acceptance of aid for public works would not imply that it would settle politically with Israel. In May 1950, refugees at camps in Sidon and Damascus declared a labor strike, refused rations and medical care, and closed schools in protest against the thrust toward resettlement. In response, Clapp noted that "I for one expected no quick and overwhelmingly successful result."[37]

U.S. Failure to Settle the Crisis, 1950–1952

Because the Clapp report proposed only stopgap measures, U.S. officials continued to seek a political settlement of the refugee dispute in 1950–52. Convinced that the problem destabilized the Middle East politically and economically, they pursued four parallel initiatives—under U.N. and U.S. auspices—to achieve a compromise settlement. Israel and the Arab states refused to make any concessions, however, and the U.S. quest to solve the refugee problem fell short.

One of the four U.S. initiatives involved remobilizing the PCC. At U.S. urging, the PCC visited Jerusalem in August 1950 to stimulate negotiations on the refugee issue, and the commission organized a September–November 1951 meeting in Paris to promote a deal based on repatriation and resettlement. Arab and Israeli leaders remained unresponsive, however, and both conferences deadlocked. Chairman Ely Palmer reported that a "sense of futility" overwhelmed the PCC.[38]

Second, U.S. officials endorsed a proposal by UNRWA Chairman John Blandford to resolve the issue by resettling the refugees in Arab states at Israeli and

U.N. expense. Blandford proposed that Israel and the United Nations each contribute $100 million to fund development schemes in Arab states that absorbed
refugees. The United States cosponsored a resolution, passed by the General
Assembly on 30 November 1950, to implement the Blandford plan and pressed
Israel to contribute $5 million as a first installment. In 1952, Israel paid $2.8 million to the Blandford scheme (and released the frozen assets of Palestinian bank
accounts worth $14.5 million) but announced that such payments fulfilled the
Jewish state's duty to repatriate refugees.[39]

Even while promoting the Blandford plan, Truman launched a third U.S.
mission to solve the refugee problem. In December 1951 he dispatched Edward
Locke as a special representative of the State Department to explore U.S. aid
programs in Arab states. "There are too many plans and too much talk and not
enough action," Truman instructed Locke. "I want you to try to get action." In
April 1952, Locke proposed a major program to develop railroads, highways,
rivers and harbors, and oil pipelines in the Middle East. The United States would
invest one hundred million dollars, and the World Bank, United Nations, and
other powers would add four hundred million dollars over three to five years.[40]

The Locke proposal had a mixed reception in Washington but ultimately
died there. Although the NEA favored the plan as promoting regional stability,
Truman shelved the proposal because Congress seemed unlikely to fund it. In
September 1952, Locke tried to revive his idea in the White House but badly
fumbled his presentation and insulted the president. Truman recalled Locke and
abolished his office, telling an aide that he had "known Mr. Locke for many
years and was surprised by the attitude which . . . he had displayed."[41]

In late 1952, the Truman administration made one final push to settle the
refugee problem by pressing Israel to repatriate between fifty thousand and one
hundred thousand refugees and compensate the remainder. U.S. officials argued to Israel that it might benefit from the return of certain refugees and that
a concession might mollify the Arab states and thereby contribute to peace. The
American government also told Arab leaders that refusal to resettle refugees
seemed "cruel" since "the chances of repatriation were exceedingly slight and
the existence of false hope could only end in increased bitterness."[42]

The U.S. initiative failed immediately. Sharett gave it a "sharp categorical
negative." Concessions by Israel, Eban added, would appear to be a "sign [of]
weakness and provoke further hostile measures by Arabs." Nor were Arab leaders cooperative. Resettlement would violate the refugees' "ever present desire
to return . . . home," Syrian Foreign Minister Zafar Rifai warned. "No amount
of compensation can ever make them forget their attachment to their place
of birth."[43]

At the end of the Truman presidency, the U.S. quest to end the refugee crisis
remained unrealized. U.N. programs had reduced the number of refugees on

relief from 1,019,000 in 1949 to 850,000 in 1952, but State Department officials remained frustrated and perplexed by their inability to facilitate a permanent solution to the problem. Despite the United States' best efforts to conceive a practical and equitable solution, neither side to the dispute would concede or compromise.[44]

Conclusion

The Palestinian refugee crisis posed great difficulty for U.S. officials during the second Truman administration. The existence of hundreds of thousands of Palestinian refugees threatened the U.S. objective of Middle East stability. While Western officials scrambled to provide basic necessities to the refugees, a complicated political dispute erupted between the Arab states, which insisted that Israel offer the refugees a choice between repatriation to Israel or compensation for their lost property, and Israel, which refused this demand and insisted that Arab governments resettle the refugees.

Both Israel and the Arab states identified compelling reasons to refuse concessions on the issue. Each side blamed the other for the crisis and assigned the other responsibility to solve it. Both sides cited security and economic concerns that precluded their absorption of Palestinians. Leaders in all states felt unable to capitulate in light of their national aspirations and domestic public opinion, and rivalries among Arab states further reduced the prospect of concession. The mutual mistrust and fear that pervaded Arab-Israeli relationships in the shadow of the Palestine War discouraged compromise.

For a variety of reasons, U.S. officials sought to solve the refugee crisis. Humanitarian concern drove them to provide funds needed to care for the refugees, as did fear that the Soviet Union would exploit the refugees' suffering and anger to spread communism. U.S. officials sought to solve the dispute before it alienated the Arab states from the West or triggered a war that would destabilize the region; furthermore, American leaders hoped that progress in solving the refugee issue might create a spirit of conciliation leading to solutions of other Arab-Israeli disputes.

U.S. officials conceived several tactical plans to advance American objectives. The U.S. government helped establish the PCC to provide relief and to search for a long-term solution. American officials founded the ESM to formulate a regional development scheme that would facilitate refugee repatriation and resettlement. The United States endorsed various plans conceived by U.N. officials and by the U.S. envoy to the region, Locke. American leaders applied political pressure on Israel to repatriate a sizable number of refugees and on the Arab states to resettle vast numbers of Palestinians under various schemes.

Unfortunately for the United States, none of these diplomatic initiatives solved the problem. When the Truman presidency ended, U.S. officials had arranged international relief to mitigate the physical hardships facing the refugees but had failed to solve the political question of the refugees' permanent disposition. The United States lacked the means to force Israeli or Arab concessions, and available financial incentives proved insufficient to secure Arab or Israeli compliance with U.S. wishes.

U.S. policy toward the refugees experienced a palpable shift in 1949–53. Echoing the position of Arab states, the Truman administration initially expressed a determination to force Israel to accept the principle that every refugee had the right to choose between repatriation to or compensation by Israel. U.S. policy gradually evolved toward the more balanced view that a final settlement must be based on a combination of repatriation and resettlement. By 1951, officials in Washington concluded that large-scale repatriation would prove impossible in light of Israeli resistance, thus essentially embracing the Israeli view that resettlement on a grand scale offered the only realistic solution.

The evolution of U.S. policy from the Arab side to the Israeli view did not reflect an innate favoritism toward Israel among officials in Washington. On the contrary, for much of the period U.S. officials were profoundly angry at Israel for its stubborn refusal to accept their counsel. Truman approved extraordinary measures to punish Israel in 1949 for its categorical rejection of his advice and its indirect efforts to force his hand. Even Israel's supporters in Congress and on the White House staff criticized the country's attitude toward the refugees on humanitarian grounds. The shift in U.S. policy also revealed a realistic understanding of the firmness dilemma. U.S. officials originally assumed that they could force Israel to meet U.N. resolutions that mandated repatriation and compensation but gradually realized that Israel had the means to resist. American policy was modified to take into account this new reality.

Israel also gained a deeper understanding of the influence dilemma. Israeli officials initially assumed that they could change unfriendly State Department policy by appealing through back channels to Truman, as had repeatedly been the case in the past. On the issue of the refugees, however, Israel found that Truman resisted and resented the informal approach. Consequently, Sharett eased the pressure on Truman and modified Israeli policy toward the refugees by offering more substantial repatriation and some compensation. Such steps placated the United States until its policy aligned with Israel's position.

8

HOLY PLACES
The Question of Jerusalem, 1949–1953

In addition to the refugee issue, the fate of Jerusalem also posed an intractable problem after the Palestine War. During the hostilities, Israel and Jordan had militarily occupied the city. After their armistice, the two powers agreed to divide the city and plotted to fend off foreign challenges to their control. In contrast, the United Nations, the United States, and other powers aimed to establish international control of the city as mandated by U.N. resolutions of 1947–48. In ensuing negotiations, a coalition of Arab and Catholic states sought to force Israel and Jordan to relinquish their claims.

In a major difference from the refugee issue, U.S. involvement in the Jerusalem dispute declined over time. U.S. officials initially resisted the Israeli-Jordanian division of the city and sought to settle the issue on terms consistent with U.N. resolutions. As the international deadlock over the city deepened, however, the United States calculated that it lacked vital national interests in the issue. Contemplating the high costs of imposing a settlement over Israeli and Jordanian resistance, President Harry S. Truman and Secretary of State Dean G. Acheson shifted to passive tolerance of the partition of the city.

Jerusalem has been a subject of contention among scholars. Shlomo Slonim emphasizes the legitimacy of Israel's sovereignty over the city. Henry Cattan mounts a legalistic challenge to Israel's claims, while Edward W. Said and Ian W. Lustick suggest that Israel artificially projected the idea of Jewish sovereignty over a united city to undergird its territorial acquisition. Meron Benvenisti aptly observes that "the chronicles of Jerusalem are a gigantic quarry, from which each side has mined stones for the construction of its myths—and for throwing at each other."[1]

The Status of Jerusalem in 1949

The political fate of Jerusalem emerged as a complex issue in 1947–49. The partition resolution of November 1947 declared the principle of *corpus separatum*—that Jerusalem should be established as an international zone under U.N. control. On 11 December 1948, the General Assembly reaffirmed this principle and directed the Palestine Conciliation Commission (PCC) to compose a plan to internationalize the city under U.N. auspices. Having occupied Jerusalem during the war, Israel and Jordan jointly resisted the idea. U.S. officials faced a dilemma between upholding U.N. resolutions or recognizing the reality of binational control. By spring 1949, the United States resolved this dilemma with a compromise that left the United States at odds with Israel.

The Israeli-Jordanian division of Jerusalem was fraught with tension. During the war, Israel had taken control of western Jerusalem (called the New City), where the Jewish population was concentrated, while Jordan had occupied the Old City and Arab neighborhoods to the east, north, and south. In May 1949, the two states agreed to make permanent their de facto division of the city in defiance of U.N. resolutions. But they remained on the verge of violence, as Jordan denied Israel's demand for a corridor to Mount Scopus and Israel threatened to open a route by force. Firefights flared in June as soldiers maneuvered along the border. Israel mobilized troops and canceled military leaves, and Jordan pledged to fight in defense of its interests.[2]

Israeli leaders made clear that they would never accept international control over Jewish Jerusalem as prescribed by the U.N. resolutions. The Israeli Constituent Assembly met in the New City as the provisional government enforced abandoned-property laws, scheduled municipal elections, and established its Supreme Court and various ministries there. Given the U.N.'s failure to defend the New City against Arab attack, Foreign Minister Moshe Sharett told the PCC in February 1949, Israel "could not now entrust [the] security of Jews in Jerusalem to any outside agency." The Jerusalem issue was settled "3,000 years ago when Bel Yishai (King David) made Jerusalem the Jewish centre," Prime Minister David Ben-Gurion announced, linking his policy to the ancient Jewish cultural attachment to the city. "The living Jerusalem will not again accept any rule but that of its own people, Israel."[3]

Monitoring the situation in Jerusalem, Truman and Acheson sought first to prevent violence. With the president's blessing, Acheson warned Sharett that "any government which attempts to effect a particular settlement by the renewal of hostilities or the threat of hostilities would incur a grave responsibility before the community of nations." U.S. officials convinced Israel and Jordan to join a Mixed Armistice Commission, which arranged a truce among border troops in late June.[4]

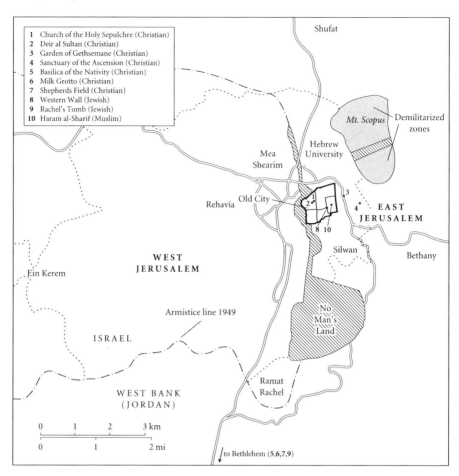

1 Church of the Holy Sepulchre (Christian)
2 Deir al Sultan (Christian)
3 Garden of Gethsemane (Christian)
4 Sanctuary of the Ascension (Christian)
5 Basilica of the Nativity (Christian)
6 Milk Grotto (Christian)
7 Shepherds Field (Christian)
8 Western Wall (Jewish)
9 Rachel's Tomb (Jewish)
10 Haram al-Sharif (Muslim)

Shufat

Mt. Scopus   Demilitarized zones

Mea Shearim   Hebrew University

Rehavia   Old City   EAST JERUSALEM

Silwan   Bethany

WEST JERUSALEM

Ein Kerem

Armistice line 1949   No Man's Land

ISRAEL

Ramat Rachel

WEST BANK (JORDAN)

0   1   2   3 km
0   1   2 mi

to Bethlehem (5,6,7,9)

Map 4. Jerusalem

When violence had been averted, Truman delegated Acheson to sort out the city's political future. Many U.S. officials naturally wished to honor the U.N. resolutions calling for a *corpus separatum* and to deny local states any rewards for military action. U.S. Christian churches also encouraged the State Department to ensure international control of various holy places in the Jerusalem area.[5] But Deputy Undersecretary of State Dean Rusk worried that promoting a *corpus separatum* would "cause a very strong unfavorable reaction in Israel and in American Zionist circles." A *corpus separatum* would prove economically unviable, the NEA projected, and would require a four-thousand-man U.N. police force costing thirty million dollars per year. The U.S. consul in Jerusalem, William C. Burdett, observed that despite its cultural affiliation for the holy places, the United States lacked any strategic interests in Jerusalem and therefore should welcome the stability inherent in an Israeli-Jordanian binational division.[6]

Acheson resolved this dilemma by compromising between practicality and the principle of international control. The United States would aim for a settlement in which Israel and Jordan would administer portions of the city under a U.N. commissioner empowered to supervise local administration and to guarantee free access to the holy places. While committed to upholding U.N. resolutions, Acheson recognized "considerable flexibility in what might constitute an international regime."[7]

Israeli officials were pleased by Acheson's flexibility but remained troubled by his refusal to recognize their sovereignty in Jerusalem. The question reached a flashpoint in February, when Sharett asked Ambassador James G. McDonald to attend the opening ceremony of the Constituent Assembly in Jerusalem. McDonald wanted to accept the invitation as a gesture to Israel, but Burdett and PCC Chairman Mark Ethridge countered that McDonald's attendance would undermine efforts to establish international control of the city. With American patience frayed by Israel's offensive against Egypt in the Negev, Truman approved Acheson's decision to order McDonald to decline the invitation.[8]

In the months that followed, U.S. insistence on international control produced additional tension with Israel. With Truman's explicit approval, Acheson pressed Israeli leaders to "recognize international . . . authority for the Holy Places." In reply, Ben-Gurion told the PCC that Israel would accept "international supervision of holy places" but not U.N. sovereignty. "Jerusalem is to Jews," he argued, "what Rome and Paris are to Italians and French respectively." Tension between U.S. and Israeli leaders began to mount.[9]

U.N. Approaches to the Jerusalem Issue, 1949

As Truman and Acheson formulated a policy on Jerusalem, the United Nations began to debate the city's future. Unable to resolve the issue, the PCC recommended to the General Assembly a plan that blended international control and local governance of Jerusalem. U.S. leaders supported the plan despite Israeli and Jordanian opposition, but the General Assembly voted instead to reaffirm the concept of a *corpus separatum*. This outcome outraged Israel and left Acheson and Truman frustrated and despondent about the quarrel.

In March 1949, when the PCC addressed the question of Jerusalem, the commission became bogged down in controversy. Ethridge, the U.S. delegate, advocated the State Department's principle of local administration by Jordan and Israel under international control. France proposed complete internationalization, including a U.N. police force, court system, citizenship, and currency, a plan that Ethridge considered "impossible and fantastic." Jordan and Israel rejected both the U.S. and the French plans and suggested that the PCC recognize their bilateral division of the city.[10]

After months of deliberation, on 1 September 1949 the PCC submitted to the General Assembly a "Draft Instrument Establishing a Permanent International Regime for the Jerusalem Area." Under the plan, Israel and Jordan would provide civil governance in their respective zones. The United Nations would appoint a non-Arab, non-Israeli administrator who would be advised by a mixed council of nine Jerusalem residents and protected by U.N. guards. The administrator would protect the holy places, guarantee human rights, and ensure demilitarization. Mixed and international tribunals would deal with civil law.[11]

Israeli officials firmly rejected the instrument. Because it blended irreconcilable U.S. and French ideas, Foreign Ministry official Michael Comay compared the plan to "one of the gargoyles on the medieval cathedrals, with the head of one animal and the body of another." Because the plan would violate the security of Jerusalem's Jews, the Foreign Ministry concluded, it "clearly and definitely exposes the principle of internationalization as impractical and unjust." As extremists in Israel vowed to resist the instrument with violence, Sharett told Acheson that the plan had "fanned into new flame" a Jewish affinity for Jerusalem that had existed "some thousands of years."[12]

Although skeptical of the instrument, Acheson endorsed it. His advisers worried that the plan might prove impractical in the face of Israeli and Jordanian resistance but also feared that France might revert to the *corpus separatum* if the instrument were rejected. Acheson decided to support the instrument as "the best chance of achieving an international regime and in the hope that the parties will acquiesce in a United Nations decision." He endorsed the measure in an address to the General Assembly on 21 September and urged Sharett to seek a solution "by calm and constructive means."[13]

As in the past, Israel sought to overturn Acheson's policy by appealing to Truman. If the United Nations imposed an administrator on Israel, McDonald wrote to Truman's special counsel, Clark Clifford, "a repetition of the Bernadotte tragedy would not be improbable." As Israeli Ambassador to the United States Eliahu Elath took credit for mobilizing "White House friends," presidential adviser David Niles encouraged Truman to postpone a U.N. vote on the instrument and Agriculture Secretary Charles F. Brannan confided that he "constantly consulted" Truman on the issue. Such pressure continued even as Israeli intelligence detected the State Department's mounting resentment of the tactic.[14]

Having anticipated such an Israeli effort to reach Truman, Acheson was ready to counter it. On 21 November, he secured the president's explicit approval of the State Department policy. Truman authorized Acheson to support the instrument as a practical plan to establish international safeguards of the holy places, restore peace to Jerusalem, and demilitarize the city. The United States would support the PCC plan despite Israeli and Jordanian protests.[15]

Although Acheson defeated Israel in the battle for Truman's support, the secretary of state lost control of the General Assembly debate on the instrument. Under the sway of its Catholic citizens, Australia introduced a resolution directing the United Nations Trusteeship Council (UNTC) to establish a *corpus separatum* by spring 1950. The State Department opposed this resolution as impractical, but several U.N. delegations, lobbied by Archbishop of New York Francis Cardinal Spellman, endorsed it. On 9 December, Catholic states, Arab states except Jordan, and the Soviet bloc passed the resolution by a vote of thirty-nine to fourteen, with five abstentions.[16]

Passage of the 9 December resolution frustrated most U.S. officials. Acheson seemed to throw up his hands in despair. He informed Truman that he would "say to the Vatican and the Jews that they should get together and talk to each other, but that we are not going to coerce them." According to Israeli intelligence, by contrast, Edwin Wright of the NEA admitted that the vote pleased the State Department's Arabists because it would encourage Arab powers to "raise a lot of hell against Israel."[17]

The 9 December resolution also divided U.S. public opinion. The measure was popular among Catholics, who viewed Israel with suspicion regarding allegations of Israeli violence against Christian shrines, mistreatment of Palestinians, and refusal to internationalize Jerusalem. But other voices criticized the resolution because it failed to safeguard Israel's interests. The *New York Times* dismissed the U.N. document as "ill-advised" and "unrealistic" because it defied Israeli and Jordanian policies.[18]

As was to be expected, Israeli leaders staunchly opposed the 9 December resolution. Sharett instructed his subordinates to protest the measure and seek its reversal at the United Nations, and he planned to delay implementation until the resolution "fall[s] of its own weight and [the] U.N. itself admit[s] unfeasibility." "It would take an army to get [the] Jews out of Jerusalem," Ben-Gurion warned McDonald, "and the only army I see willing to occupy Jerusalem is Russia's." More ominously, the prime minister declared to the Knesset on 13 December that Israel would resist the resolution by transferring government offices and the Knesset to Jerusalem and seeking access to the Old City.[19]

The Transfer of Israeli Government Offices to Jerusalem

As pledged, Ben-Gurion moved the prime minister's office to Jerusalem on 14 December, adding a layer of contention to the Jerusalem dispute. Having previously indicated its opposition to such a move, the United States refused to recognize Jerusalem as Israel's capital, relocate the American embassy to the city, or even conduct official business there. Aware of their limited capabilities, however, U.S. leaders eventually softened this policy. Discerning the limits of U.S. power, Israeli officials strengthened their resolve to exercise power in Jerusalem.

Ben-Gurion's decision to transfer government offices to Jerusalem capped months of debate about such a move. In August 1949, the prime minister urged his cabinet to declare Jerusalem the capital as a means of presenting the world with a fait accompli while the PCC deliberated. When Sharett cautioned against antagonizing the United States or Catholic countries, the cabinet approved the principle of transfer but delayed implementation. Aware of these deliberations, Acheson indicated his disapproval of any transfer because it would prejudice U.N. debates and, by angering Arab states, undermine Arab-Israeli negotiations on other issues. Sharett gave assurances that Israel would not "force the hand of the General Assembly."[20]

Ben-Gurion's move to Jerusalem in violation of such assurances produced a sharp reaction in Washington. He regretted having to flout the United Nations, the prime minister confided to his diary, but the move was necessary to safeguard the Jews of Jerusalem and to demonstrate Israeli resolve after the passage of the 9 December resolution. NEA officials, by contrast, construed the move "as open opposition by Israel to the United Nations" and refused to rule out some punitive measure by the Security Council. When Israeli embassy counselor Moshe Keren explained that Israeli public opinion had forced Ben-Gurion's hand, Raymond Hare of the NEA countered that on Jerusalem issues, "Israel had to reckon as well with world opinion."[21]

To the end of the Truman presidency, Acheson consistently refused to recognize Jerusalem as Israel's capital but found it impossible to reverse the move. He repeatedly denied Israeli requests for recognition because the Jewish state had acted "in clear violation" of U.N. resolutions. Yet Acheson refrained from compelling Israel to return its government to Tel Aviv. When Iraqi chargé Abdullah Ibrahim Bakr suggested punitive measures by the United States in early 1950, Assistant Secretary of State George McGhee replied that pressure on Israel would only "strengthen the Government in its present policy."[22]

The United States also showed some ambivalence in its conduct of official business in Israel. To put some teeth into his nonrecognition policy, Acheson refused to locate the U.S. embassy in Jerusalem and required U.S. diplomats in Israel to conduct business in Tel Aviv. Only the consul in Jerusalem could make "non-official courtesy and social contacts" in the city. But these regulations caused U.S. diplomats hardship and embarrassment, so in February 1951 Acheson authorized embassy officials to conduct ad hoc visits to Jerusalem provided that they clarified on each occasion that their government favored internationalization of the city.[23]

Even as he came to terms with Ben-Gurion's transfer to Jerusalem, Acheson protested Israel's plans to relocate its Foreign Ministry there. In May 1952, Sharett announced that he would move his ministry to Jerusalem in six to eight months, "not [as] a political demonstration but [as] a domestic and organizational necessity." This announcement disturbed Acheson. "There should be a special international regime for Jerusalem," the State Department declared in July. The United States "would not view favorably the transfer of the Foreign Office" to Jerusalem and would not locate its embassy there.[24]

The U.S. protests did not greatly concern Israeli officials. Foreign Ministry legal adviser Shabtai Rosenne downplayed the gravity of the U.S. protest because it neither contested the transfer of other government offices to Jerusalem nor demanded a reversal of the decision to transfer the Foreign Ministry. U.S. officials seemed most angry at Israel's "tactical mistake" of not informing the United States of the decision before announcing it. One U.S. official corroborated this observation by complaining to Ambassador to Washington Abba Eban that news of the transfer had "brought [a] flood of Arab representations to State Dep[artmen]t [officials] when they [were] not ready."[25]

In light of such assessments, Sharett remained determined to move his ministry but avoided rushing the action. Together with similar reactions by Britain, France, Turkey, Australia, and Italy, U.S. protests convinced him to postpone the transfer until the autumn 1952 General Assembly session adjourned. After the U.S. presidential election, Eban urged Sharett to complete the move by the end of December, on the hunch that Truman would relocate the U.S. embassy to Jerusalem but President-elect Dwight D. Eisenhower would not. But Sharett decided that logistical impediments prevented relocation before March 1953.[26]

The Convergence of U.S. and Israeli Policy, 1950–1952

As Israel established its presence in Jerusalem, the United Nations pursued its 9 December 1949 resolution to establish a *corpus separatum*. Truman and Acheson faced a difficult decision about whether to support a U.N. resolution that most Arab and Catholic states favored, Israel opposed, and the U.S. leaders deemed impractical. Careful not to embrace openly Israel's position for fear of international backlash, the American government worked subtly to derail the U.N. initiative and then adopted a passive posture toward the Jerusalem issue. Although they disapproved of its policy, Acheson and Truman allowed Israel to achieve its goals.

Action by the UNTC in the aftermath of the 9 December 1949 resolution confronted U.S. officials with a dilemma. To fulfill the resolution, the UNTC urged Israel to suspend its transfer of government offices to Jerusalem and, on 4 April 1950, voted to establish a *corpus separatum* in the city. Truman and Acheson did not wish to defy the United Nations or anger the Vatican or Arab states, but the American government had opposed the 9 December resolution, deeming a *corpus separatum* impractical. Thus, U.S. leaders decided to cooperate officially with the UNTC but to derail the *corpus separatum* through indirect means.[27]

Acheson implemented this decision through public and private action. As a member of the UNTC, he announced, the United States would "participate constructively when the Council undertakes the task concerning Jerusalem." But he also told Niles, who told Elath, that the secretary of state preferred a deal among Israel, Jordan, and the Vatican. Moreover, the United States abstained on the UNTC statute of 4 April and convinced the council to delay implementation until Jordan and Israel commented on the measure. The State Department also encouraged King Abdallah of Jordan to defy an Arab League resolution favoring internationalization. At U.S. urging, the UNTC reported to the General Assembly in June that it was unable to establish a *corpus separatum*.[28]

Thereafter, Truman and Acheson adopted a passive approach to the Jerusalem issue. On "orders from the White House," Stuart Rockwell of the NEA noted, the State Department would "let someone else take the lead" since it "got its knuckles rapped" in December 1949. The department had "nothing to sponsor, support, or suggest," McGhee told Eban. "Our present intention is not to play an active role on this issue," noted Burton Y. Berry of the NEA.[29]

Truman and Acheson apparently based their passivity toward international control on rational consideration of political factors. No security imperatives dictated any immediate settlement terms, they reasoned, and the viability of international control had declined. A *corpus separatum*, Rockwell advised, was "no longer practicable" because the deadlocks among Israel, Jordan, and the Vatican were irresolvable.[30]

It is harder to discern the extent to which Israeli pressure on the White House and U.S. public opinion shaped Truman's policy. Israeli records reveal that Ben-Gurion recruited Zionist activist Bartley Crum to urge Truman to resist a *corpus separatum*. To stress the "Biblical promise" of a Jewish Jerusalem, the Foreign Ministry declared, in a letter sent to Truman over Weizmann's signature, that "Jerusalem has been our capital since the days of David and Solomon." Eban recruited Federal Security Administrator Oscar Ewing to deliver this letter to Truman in person.[31]

Israel also influenced U.S. public opinion on the subject. In information (or *hasbara*) operations, the Jewish state presented its case to the U.S. people through rhetoric, propaganda, and other activities. Israeli officials also mobilized Protestants to neutralize Catholic political power, noting that Protestant opinion had turned favorable in 1950. Israeli officials concluded that such *hasbara* operations generated broad U.S. public support that Truman had to respect during an election year. Given the timing of the operations, however, it appears that Truman had decided his policy before *hasbara* would have had any impact on him.[32]

Even though their policy aligned with Israel's, Truman and Acheson refrained from openly endorsing Israel's position lest they offend the Arab states. Lebanon's minister in Washington, Charles Malik, complained to McGhee on 1 August of the "curve of deterioration" in U.S. support for U.N. resolutions regarding Jerusalem. Syrian Minister Faiz el-Khouri likened Israel's position to "that of a thief who has robbed you of all your furniture and compromises by offering to give you back a chair." Iraqi and Egyptian officials revealed similar views. While failing to trigger any reconsideration of *corpus separatum*, such protests restrained U.S. leaders from explicitly approving Israel's policy.[33]

In 1950–52, the Jerusalem issue receded from the United Nations' attention. In late 1950, the General Assembly debated the issue but failed to pass a resolution. Sensing that deadlock facilitated Israel's objectives, the Jewish state discouraged U.N. discussion in 1951 by arguing that arrangements worked out in 1950 by Israel, Jordan, and local Christian communities adequately safeguarded the sanctity of the holy places. When the General Assembly failed to pass any resolution on Jerusalem in 1952, U.S. Ambassador Warren R. Austin noted that the Israelis reacted with "satisfaction bordering on enthusiasm."[34]

Some State Department officials remained reluctant to see the issue disappear. A U.N. presence in Jerusalem, NEA officials asserted in October 1952, would ensure Arab security, help resolve the refugee problem, and undergird armistices. Even a token presence "would serve as a steadying influence in the area" and "furnish the world with a listening post." Others believed that backing internationalization would give "dramatic evidence to the Arab world that we can say 'no' to Zionism."[35]

Yet Truman and Acheson allowed the Jerusalem issue to recede as Israel wished. "We see no point in supporting any schemes for the internationalization," the NEA reasoned in October 1951. Acheson opposed a debate on Jerusalem during the November 1951–February 1952 General Assembly meeting, and in November 1952 he resolved to take no initiative on Jerusalem at the General Assembly and to offer no support if some other power raised the issue. On 17 December 1952, Truman directed Acheson to "take sides with the Israeli Delegation against the Arabs" on the issue.[36]

Conclusion

International diplomacy on the subject of Jerusalem produced winners and losers. Israel and Jordan obtained what they wanted—bipolar control of the city in defiance of U.N. resolutions. Jordan firmed up its occupation of the Old City, while Israel not only planted its government in the New City but affirmed in the minds and hearts of its citizens an indelible attachment to the city. Other Arab states were denied their objective of resisting Israeli and Jordanian encroachments, and the Vatican and the United Nations failed to establish a *corpus separatum*.

For the United States, the results of the debate were mixed. Denied their original goal of an international city, Truman and Acheson gradually realized that they lacked vital interests there and could not afford the financial or strategic costs of enforcing internationalization. Thus they abandoned their commitment to a *corpus separatum* and passively tolerated Israeli and Jordanian control. The debate over Jerusalem witnessed a gradual convergence of U.S. and Israeli views. Such an outcome, although not what U.S. officials initially desired, proved acceptable to them.

The Jerusalem issue generated substantial tension between the United States and Middle East powers. Arab states other than Jordan complained that the United States failed to honor U.N. decisions to establish an international regime in the city. Many Arab leaders saw U.S. acceptance of Israel's transfer of government offices to Jerusalem as favoritism. Truman's refusal to recognize Jerusalem as Israel's capital, to relocate his embassy there, or to oppose openly the UNTC's internationalization initiatives revealed his desire to limit the damage that his policy caused U.S.-Arab relations.

Although U.S. and Israeli policies regarding Jerusalem eventually converged, the debates on the issue also generated some tension between the United States and Israel. Even when the United States abandoned *corpus separatum*, Israeli leaders criticized the American refusal to recognize their sovereignty in Jerusalem. For its part, the United States regretted Israel's defiance of U.N. authority and refused to recognize Jerusalem as Israel's capital. Israeli efforts to influence Truman, however effective, generated resentment among U.S. officials.

9

TANGLED WEB
The U.S. Failure to Solve Multiple Controversies, 1949–1953

In addition to the major controversies over peace terms, borders, refugees, and Jerusalem, several other issues generated Arab-Israeli conflict in 1949–53. Disputes arose regarding Israeli access to the Suez Canal, the availability of Arab oil for the refinery at Haifa, the status of Jewish citizens of Arab states, the rate of Jewish immigration to Israel, and the repercussions of German monetary reparations to Israel. The Harry S. Truman administration tried to resolve these controversies in hope of laying a foundation for a more stable and peaceful region. Success proved elusive.

U.S. policy toward these Arab-Israeli disputes reflected three basic tendencies. First, in contrast to his personal decision making on the border, refugee, and Jerusalem issues, President Truman deferred to Secretary of State Dean G. Acheson to decide U.S. policies on the other disputes. Second, Acheson balanced his desire for Arab-Israeli peace with U.S. security interests. In addition, he sought to maintain a balance between the Arab states and Israel as a means of preserving sound relations with both sides. However, U.S. leaders again found themselves unable to effect settlements or to avoid a backlash from either side.

The Haifa Refinery Closure and Suez Canal Blockade

The Arab-Israeli war of 1948–49 generated two related disputes over the shipment of commodities, especially oil, to Israel. During the war, Iraq closed pipelines that had carried oil to a refinery at Haifa, Palestine, and Egypt closed the Suez Canal to any ship bound to or from Israel. These restrictions clearly violated the U.S. principles of free trade and free seas, upset the British, and stimulated vigorous Israeli protests. But the restrictions did not directly threaten U.S. interests, and the State Department anticipated that its intercession on Israel's behalf in Baghdad or Cairo would tarnish U.S.-Arab relations. Although U.S.

officials occasionally endorsed British diplomacy on the issue for the sake of the Atlantic alliance, they refrained from advocating Israel's interests.

The dispute over the Haifa oil refinery originated during the Palestine War. Before 1948, the British-owned refinery acquired crude oil from Iraq through pipelines owned by the Iraq Petroleum Company (IPC), a joint venture between the Anglo-Iranian Oil Company (whose principal owner was the British government), the Compagnie Française des Pétroles (whose principal owner was the French government), and the private U.S. firms Socony Vacuum and Standard Oil of New Jersey. The refinery had a production capacity of ninety thousand barrels per day and added fifty million dollars per year to the British economy and five million dollars per year to British tax revenues. In April 1948, labor unrest and violence prompted British managers at Haifa to close the facility. After occupying Haifa, Israel refined forty thousand tons of crude oil that remained in IPC tanks, but Iraq categorically refused to reopen the IPC pipelines to the city, thereby depriving a military adversary of energy.[1]

During the war, U.S. officials showed little sympathy for Israel's situation. Israel argued that reopening the refinery would benefit Arab and European consumers, Western transport firms, and all powers that desired regional peace. "Israel has a refinery and the Arab states have crude petroleum," the Israeli ambassador to the United States, Eliahu Elath, asserted. "These things must be knit together." Upset by Israeli rejection of the Bernadotte Plan, however, Acheson showed no interest in Israel's argument.[2]

A controversy regarding Israeli shipping rights on the Suez Canal also originated during the Arab-Israeli war. On 15 May 1948, Egypt closed the canal to any ships traveling to or from Palestine and seized Palestine-bound goods from ships in Egyptian ports. Together with Iraq's closure of pipelines, these restrictions pinched Britain, the principal owner of the Suez Canal Company. With U.S. shipping companies forced to adjust routes, the State Department protested that the measures violated the Suez Canal Convention of 1888, and the U.S. government discouraged Egypt from imposing other restrictions. But Egypt remained firm on the issue for months after signing the armistice.[3]

The canal restrictions became a major Egyptian-Israeli dispute in 1949. In September, Egypt eased the restrictions but left in place a ban on Israeli ships and on any other vessels carrying arms, ammunition, or oil to Israel. Israeli officials called the blockade a "warlike action" and "a severe economic handicap," justified their conquest of the Negev as a countermeasure, and protested to the United Nations and the Israeli-Egyptian Mixed Armistice Commission that the blockade contradicted Egypt's assurances of peacefulness. Citing the absence of a formal peace treaty with Israel, authorities in Cairo defended the restrictions on security grounds.[4]

Although generally unsympathetic to Israel's plight, Acheson modestly supported a British initiative to reopen the Haifa refinery in summer 1949. Britain proposed that Iraq reopen IPC pipelines if Israel would establish a free port in Haifa and guarantee that finished oil products would be sold abroad. Britain also shipped crude oil from the Caribbean to prime the Haifa refinery, loaded several tankers in the Persian Gulf with Iranian crude, and asked King Farouk to allow the tankers to transit the Suez Canal. As a gesture to Britain, the State Department endorsed the British gambit in Baghdad and Cairo despite the realization that reopening the Haifa refinery might "make it impossible for American companies producing oil in the Middle East to sell their output." In any case, Iraq and Egypt rejected the initiative.[5]

U.S. officials withheld support from a French scheme to lift the oil blockade in late 1949. Citing cumulative losses of twenty-five million dollars from the IPC pipeline closure, France proposed that the IPC construct a new pipeline to Sidon, Lebanon, to resume the flow of Iraqi oil to Europe. But the State Department feared that Israel might retaliate by nationalizing the Haifa refinery, and the U.S. firms involved in the IPC advised that submission to Iraq would set a dangerous precedent. Without U.S. support, the French plan collapsed.[6]

During the remainder of the Truman presidency, U.S. officials declined to pursue the reopening of the IPC pipeline to Haifa. "The Iraqi politician who would agree to opening the pipelines while Haifa was still in Jewish hands," NEA officials reasoned, "had not yet been born." To press Baghdad to resume the flow of oil to Haifa would prove futile and damage U.S.-Iraqi relations. Thus, the United States tolerated the oil blockade, and the Haifa refinery remained closed.[7]

The United States also tolerated the Suez Canal closure in 1949–51. Acheson limited himself to occasional protests to Egypt about procedural obstacles imposed on ship captains. He reasoned that the United States, a nonsignatory to the 1888 convention, lacked a mandate to enforce that covenant, that intrusion might encourage other powers to challenge U.S. regulation of the Panama Canal, and that Egypt was legally entitled to impose the blockade. In spring 1951, Acheson denied a British request to protest Egypt's policy because such a move would aggravate tensions over the Huleh dispute, stir Egyptian resentment, and fail to change Egyptian policy.[8]

Acheson openly opposed the canal blockade only when Britain contemplated forceful remedies. In 1949 and again in 1951, British officials considered sending destroyers to escort tankers through the canal en route to Haifa. Such a move, Assistant U.S. Secretary of State George C. McGhee warned Acheson, would trigger an Anglo-Egyptian armed clash that would have "extremely serious" consequences for Western interests throughout the Arab world. Thus, in both instances Acheson urged Egypt and Iraq to reopen the canal and the IPC pipelines. U.S. intervention failed to change Egypt's or Iraq's policy but helped to convince British officials to refrain from naval action.[9]

Despite U.S. expressions of concern, Egypt not only refused to rescind the canal restrictions but also imposed a blockade on the Gulf of Aqaba. After Israel occupied the Negev, the Egyptian military, with Saudi approval, occupied Tiran and Sanafir, uninhabited islands dominating the shipping routes into the gulf, in January 1950. (See map 5.) A month later, Egypt pledged to U.S. officials that the islands would not be used to halt shipping in the gulf. In February 1951, however, Egypt announced that it would stop at the entrance to the gulf any ships flying the Star of David and would seize contraband from them.[10]

The Canal Question at the United Nations

The controversy over the Suez Canal intensified in 1951 when Israel protested Egypt's restrictions to the United Nations. Together with Britain, Israel pressed the United States to support a Security Council resolution critical of Egypt, while Egypt pressed the United States to resist such a move. With his advisers divided over the best course of action, Acheson temporized and eventually tried to take a moderate stance in the U.N. debates. But moderation proved impractical.

Several factors led Israel to appeal the canal blockade to the Security Council in 1951. Israeli Foreign Ministry officials calculated that the blockade had cost the country $152 million in lost commerce since 1948. U.N. consideration of the issue, moreover, would embarrass Egypt and distract attention from Israeli activities in the Huleh dispute. "We have nothing to lose," the Israeli ambassador to Washington, Abba Eban, reasoned. "At best [the] Canal would be opened while at worst Egypt and [the] Western Powers would be embroiled in open conflict on [the] highest international stage while our own position is one of immaculate virtue." Foreign Minister Moshe Sharett asked the Security Council to pass a resolution declaring that the blockade impeded free trade, destabilized the Middle East, and violated the armistice, the U.N. charter, and the convention of 1888.[11]

Israel sought U.S. support for this move. Sharett argued to the American ambassador to Tel Aviv, Monnett B. Davis, that because the United States had sponsored the Huleh resolution that censured Israel, the United States must also sponsor a canal resolution that censured Egypt. Refusal would level a "smashing blow" to the armistice by affirming the "pernicious Egyptian doctrine that [a] state of war exists." Eban mobilized U.S. "Jews, press, and friends" to lobby the State Department. Some officials there acknowledged the validity of Israel's

legal case "but hope not to be forced [to] plunge into icy waters," Eban cabled
Sharett. "Therefore we must push."[12]

Britain endorsed Israel's appeal to the Security Council and urged the United
States to cosponsor an appropriate resolution. Such action would quell British
parliamentary pressure to use force against Egypt, which spiked in July after the
Egyptian navy stopped and searched a British ship, the *Empire Roach*, that was
sailing in the Gulf of Aqaba and bearing arms for Jordan. As a mounting Anglo-
Iranian crisis cast doubt on the security of Britain's refinery at Abadan, moreover, reopening the Haifa refinery seemed increasingly critical. With Anglo-
Egyptian base talks stalemated, British officials further reasoned, there seemed
to be nothing to lose. Middle East states would interpret inaction, Foreign Minister Herbert Morrison observed to Acheson, "as a sign of doubt and hesitation
on the part of the maritime powers."[13]

Egypt, however, asked the United States to reject the Israeli initiative. Egyptian leaders maintained that their canal closure was legal. The Anglo-Egyptian
and Anglo-Iranian quarrels, Mohamed Kamil Abdul Rahim, the Egyptian ambassador to Washington, argued, made the present moment the "worst possible
time [to] debate such [an] explosive question." Arab League Director-General
Azzam Pasha warned that Security Council hearings "will cause another flare-
up of Arab countries against the UK and US."[14]

These conflicting pressures divided U.S. officials. NEA officials advocated cosponsoring a resolution, as Israel and Britain wished, to affirm the Anglo-U.S.
partnership, defend freedom of navigation, and maintain impartiality between
the Arab states and Israel. "In the Huleh dispute we started calling the shots
as we saw them (in that instance against Israel)," G. L. Jones of the NEA noted.
"We must not flinch from the same course when the blame lies largely on Egypt.
There is a moral issue here."[15]

Other U.S. officials advised against supporting Israel. U.S. Ambassador to the
United Nations Warren R. Austin warned that Israel's initiative would harden
Egyptian resolve, intensify Arab-Israeli bitterness, and strain U.S.-Egyptian relations. Ambassador to Cairo Jefferson Caffery predicted that Egypt would defy
the resolution, rendering it meaningless. The assassinations of former Lebanese
Prime Minister Riad el-Solh on 16 July and Jordan's King Abdallah on 20 July,
the acting U.S. representative to the United Nations, Ernest A. Gross, observed,
illustrated the "wide-spread Arab hostility to [the] West stemming from past
history and creation of Israel." Supporting a resolution favorable to Israel would
"further stimulate this nationalist reaction."[16]

Acheson initially resolved this dilemma by temporizing. He argued in U.N.
debates that the canal restrictions were "unreasonable, impracticable, and unjust." The United States would not take the lead in debates, however, and would

consider cosponsorship only if the resolution aimed solely to lift the restrictions and only if it needed U.S. cosponsorship to pass. Acheson also tried to avoid a Security Council debate by encouraging Egypt to abolish the restrictions.[17]

After 26 July, when the Security Council opened debate on Israel's petition, Acheson shifted his policy. Britain proposed a resolution critical of Egypt, and an acrimonious debate ensued. To wrest control of the situation, Acheson agreed to cosponsor the British resolution as a means of delaying its passage. Then he used his prerogative as cosponsor to delay proceedings for several weeks while seeking an "out-of-court" settlement with Cairo. Egypt remained stubborn, however, and by the end of August, Acheson had decided against additional delays.[18]

Acheson's support of the anti-Egypt resolution proved crucial to its ultimate success. In late August he directed his advisers to overcome a series of procedural obstacles imposed by Turkey, France, and the Soviet Union as each power weighed the repercussions of voting on its standing in the Arab world. On 1 September, the Security Council passed a resolution calling on Egypt to abolish all restrictions on canal transit. The Soviets, consistent with their relative aloofness from the Middle East, abstained.[19]

The United States immediately recognized that the resolution would prove ineffective. Egypt would indefinitely delay compliance, and any effort "to badger the Egyptian Government" on the matter would undermine the Palestine Conciliation Commission peace conference in Paris or wreck Anglo-Egyptian negotiations on the base issue. Worse, from Caffery's point of view, the passage of the resolution exacerbated Egyptian nationalism, undermined U.S. prestige in Cairo, and triggered Egypt's October decision to reject the Middle East Command and abrogate the Anglo-Egyptian treaties.[20]

Wary of further provoking Egyptian nationalism, Acheson refrained from enforcing the Security Council resolution. In February 1952, he asked Egyptian Prime Minister Ali Maher Pasha to make the restrictions "quietly disappear" but backed off when Maher demurred. Acheson also discouraged Israel from raising the matter at the United Nations, especially after the July 1952 Egyptian revolution seemed to create conditions in Cairo more conducive to an Anglo-Egyptian base settlement. On 2 September, he told Israeli leaders that "the present moment is not opportune" for pursuing the issue.[21]

Israeli officials remained dissatisfied with such U.S. passivity. In late 1951, they considered sending a tanker into the canal to "establish free transit as a fact," declining to act only because of expected U.S., British, and French opposition. As restrictions persisted in 1952, Israel frequently demanded that the United States enforce the resolution, criticized the United States for subordinating a U.N. resolution to American national interests in Cairo, and threatened to reappeal to the Security Council. But Acheson proved immune to such appeals, and at the close of the Truman presidency, Israeli aims remained unfulfilled.[22]

U.S. Involvement in Other Arab-Israeli Disputes

In the aftermath of the Palestine War, Acheson became involved in several additional quarrels that exacerbated the Arab-Israeli conflict. These disputes centered on the comparatively minor issues of the welfare of Jews in Arab states, Jewish immigration to Israel, and German financial reparations to Israel. None of these clashes had the capacity to spark a second round of warfare or to gain the attention of the United Nations, but each one diminished the prospect for Middle East peace and stability. Thus, Acheson searched for a solution to each dispute.

Acheson became enmeshed in a controversy centering on Israel's fundamental belief that the Jews of the Diaspora should "return" to Israel. In addition to the thousands of European Jews who had reached Palestine before Israeli independence, Israel absorbed 250,000 immigrants in 1948–49 and announced plans to absorb 200,000 per year indefinitely. By 1951, Israel had absorbed tens of thousands of Jews from Poland, Bulgaria, Czechoslovakia, Yemen, and Iraq and was encouraging the immigration of Iran's 70,000 Jews and the 1.75 million in the Soviet Union. The ingathering would eliminate minority problems and anti-Semitism in many countries, Sharett stressed to Acheson, and siphon "manpower . . . from the Soviet reservoir into the Western reservoir."[23]

The migration concerned Acheson because it added to Arab-Israeli tension. Arab states charged that substantial immigration of Jews would inevitably lead to Israeli territorial expansionism. The Arabs also complained that the new Jewish arrivals occupied the vacant homes of Palestinian refugees, reducing the likelihood of repatriation. Sensitive to these concerns, Acheson also attributed Israel's financial instability to its immigration rate. To stem the tide, he advised Israel to limit its immigration to its "economic capacity" to absorb new citizens.[24]

In 1950, Acheson denied Israel's requests for large-scale economic aid to settle immigrants because he disliked the Jewish state's immigration policy. With Truman under domestic pressure to aid Israel, however, Acheson approved eighty million dollars in economic aid for Israel in FY 1953, in part to help "absorb into the productive economy of Israel refugees already arrived and to permit a moderate rate of immigration." He offered this aid although he recognized "a measure of validity" in the Arabs' fear that immigration would trigger Israeli expansion.[25]

Acheson also reluctantly mediated a dispute over the well-being of Iraqi Jews. In 1949, Sharett asked the State Department to investigate evidence that Iraq had persecuted two thousand Iraqi Jews. When McGhee replied evasively, Sharett ordered Ambassador Elath to "make things unpleasant" for Baghdad by organizing demonstrations outside the Iraqi embassy in New York and to recruit U.S. journalists to "kick up [a] row." After the American Zionist Emergency Council pressured him on the issue, Truman ordered Acheson to investigate.[26]

The State Department examined but rejected the Israeli allegations against Iraq. The report found that although Iraqi Jews experienced "certain difficulties," they were not subjected to "a campaign of genocide or of general persecution." Privately, U.S. officials suspected that Israel had raised the matter primarily to facilitate Jewish emigration from Iraq. Conversely, on the basis of a "completely reliable" source in the Truman administration, Israeli leaders concluded that the State Department had declined to defend Iraqi Jews as a result of its interests in the IPC pipeline.[27]

To mollify Israel, Acheson endorsed Israel's quest to relocate Iraqi Jews to Israel, but tensions rose over that issue. In March 1950, Iraq granted its Jewish citizens the right to emigrate but required them to register their intent to do so and deprived registrants of their citizenship and financial assets. Acheson rejected an Israeli request to protest such actions on the grounds that Iraq would reply by protesting Israel's maltreatment of Palestinians. By July 1951, 106,662 Jews had left Iraq for Israel, but Israel charged that those who remained suffered persecution.[28]

The Arab-Israeli conflict also complicated an international dispute regarding West Germany's obligation to compensate Israel for the Nazi regime's persecution of Jews. In negotiations in 1950–52, West German Chancellor Konrad Adenauer agreed to compensate Israel because a majority of Germans shared the guilt of Nazism. For legal and political reasons, U.S. officials remained aloof from these talks, although they quietly encouraged West Germany to make concessions when the talks deadlocked in early 1952. In an agreement signed in September 1952 and ratified in March 1953, West Germany pledged to provide Israel with commodities valued at $715 million over a twelve-year period.[29]

The Arab-Israeli dispute intruded into the German-Israeli negotiations from the beginning. In 1951, Sharett sought U.S. support for his negotiating position by hinting that German restitution would enable Israel to compensate Arab refugees. In early 1952, Syria and Lebanon pressured the State Department to ensure that German reparations were sequestered for such purposes. When the reparations deal was signed, the Arab states threatened a trade embargo against West Germany if it made payments to Israel. Members of the German cabinet and Bundestag hesitated to ratify the deal in the face of such threats. Declaring that he had "no desire whatsoever to become embroiled in Arab-Israeli troubles," Adenauer pressed for ratification but asked the United States to head off an Arab embargo.[30]

In response to Adenauer's concerns, Acheson discouraged Arab states from exacting retribution on West Germany. He suggested to Arab governments that the principle of German reparations would strengthen the legal ground of refugees seeking compensation from Israel. He also encouraged Israel urgently to consider compensation to Palestinian refugees for lost property. Assistant Secretary of State Henry A. Byroade assured West German officials that the Arab states were unlikely to impose an embargo even if reparations were approved.[31]

Yet the Arab states censured West Germany and the United States for the reparations deal. Speaking for the Arab League Political Committee, the Egyptian premier, General Mohammed Naguib, charged that the accord would make Israel "a menace to [the] very existence of [the] Arab States" by increasing its military capabilities. Lebanon charged that the United States had "coerced" West Germany into approving the deal, while Syria alleged that only U.S. aid to West Germany enabled it to compensate Israel. In Beirut, Chargé James C. Lobenstine reported, the United States received the "brunt of adverse criticism." The State Department denied having pressured Germany and explained the deal as solely a German-Israeli matter, but few Arab leaders were persuaded.[32]

Conclusion

In 1949–53, the Arab states and Israel quarreled over a variety of issues. Iraq's closure of oil pipelines that supplied the Haifa refinery became a point of contention. Egypt's restrictions of transit on the Suez Canal provoked Israeli anger and triggered a diplomatic showdown at the United Nations. The immigration of Jews to Israel, the status of Jews in Arab states, and the West German–Israeli reparations agreement exacerbated hostile feelings. These issues contributed to the ill will and mistrust in Arab-Israeli relations after the Palestine War.

Acheson approached these controversies intent on acting impartially and containing conflict. He opposed British and Israeli schemes to break the Suez Canal blockade with force and diplomatically pressed Egypt to ease the blockade. He discouraged massive Jewish immigration to Israel but refused Arab demands to block it, and he resisted Israeli pressures to accentuate the hardships facing Jewish citizens of Arab states. Acheson declined to interfere in the West German–Israeli reparations accord, as Arab leaders urged, and he encouraged Arab leaders to accept the deal. Domestic political concerns interfered in Acheson's diplomacy only when Truman directed the secretary of state to provide Israel with aid for immigrant absorption and to investigate Israeli charges that Iraq persecuted its Jewish citizens.

Despite such relative immunity to domestic concerns, Acheson found it impossible to protect U.S. interests while remaining impartial between Israel and the Arab states. On the Suez Canal issue, he endorsed a Security Council resolution to serve the U.S. interests of placating Britain and affirming legal and free trade principles, but he refrained from enforcing that resolution because it undermined U.S. security interests by stoking Egyptian nationalism. While he helped avert violence over the canal, Acheson made no progress toward solving the dispute and in the process strained U.S. relations with both Israel and Egypt. Similarly, his efforts to mediate the disputes over the Haifa refinery, Jewish immigration, Arab Jews, and German reparations fell short and frustrated one or both sides of the controversies. Try as he might, Acheson proved unable to contain or resolve any of these disputes, which would create discord for years to come. Given the resulting tension in U.S. relations with Israel and the Arab states, it is evident that he paid a price for trying.

10

THE IMPACT OF CONFLICT
U.S. Relations with Israel and the Arab States, 1949-1953

The Arab-Israeli conflict deeply influenced U.S. relations with Israel and its Arab adversaries during Harry S. Truman's second administration. Israel continued to divide the makers of U.S. foreign policy along the same fault lines that formed in 1947–48. The new state enjoyed strong support among several influential U.S. officials and citizens with access to President Truman, who remained outwardly friendly. Israel also cultivated its favorable image among members of Congress and in U.S. public opinion. Wary that the domestic pressure to side with Israel undermined security and diplomatic interests, the State and Defense Departments resented such efforts.

The Arab-Israeli situation affected the quality of U.S.-Israeli relations by shaping American handling of several issues pertaining to the Jewish state. Truman and Secretary of State Dean G. Acheson faced decisions about whether to extend de jure recognition to Israel, support its application for membership in the United Nations, and provide it with economic aid. Given the tensions within the Truman administration, such issues simultaneously caused amity and discord in U.S.-Israeli relations.

Although inconsistent, U.S. support of Israel negatively affected U.S. relations with the Arab states in 1949–53. In particular, relations with Syria and Egypt experienced severe tension. Even those Arab states that remained on friendly terms with the West—Jordan, Lebanon, Iraq, and Saudi Arabia—registered deep reservations about U.S. policy. Israel was not the only reason for conflict between Western powers and the Arab states, but the Jewish state did constitute a major source of discord.

The Enigma of U.S.-Israeli Relations

In 1949–53, the United States and Israel developed a complex and ambiguous relationship. On the surface, the relationship appeared warm and friendly, as

Israel garnered support and sympathy among key members of the Truman administration, both Democratic and Republican members of Congress, and the U.S. public. At a deeper level, however, tension developed between the United States and Israel as the makers of foreign policy in both states clashed over several principles and issues. Although U.S. and Israeli policy occasionally converged on such matters, the policy-making process caused friction between the two states.

Contemporary observers of the U.S.-Israeli relationship recorded evidence of warmth and friendliness. James G. McDonald, Truman's special representative (1948–49) and ambassador (1949–51) to Israel, considered the Israeli people "markedly friendly," while British Ambassador to Washington Oliver Franks reported that Israel "enjoys in the United States an unusual measure of Christian as well as Jewish goodwill." On a 1951 visit to the United States, Israeli Prime Minister David Ben-Gurion gained audiences with Truman, Acheson, Secretary of Defense George C. Marshall, and Truman's special assistant, W. Averell Harriman; in addition, Ben-Gurion enjoyed enthusiastic receptions at numerous public appearances across the country. U.S. Jews and non-Jews, the first secretary of the Israeli embassy, Esther Herlitz, observed, "stand steadfastly at the right hand of Israel."[1]

Israeli officials carefully cultivated U.S. goodwill. Cognizant of the importance of Truman's friendship, they encouraged him to assert his authority in U.S. policy making. They appealed to his pride with such gestures as naming a recreation room at a disabled soldiers' hospital near Tel Aviv for his mother, Martha Truman. "It seemed providential that Israel should have arisen" when Truman was president, Foreign Minister Moshe Sharett told the U.S. leader in person in July 1952. "We in Israel had felt all along that he was our true friend."[2]

Israeli officials also nurtured ties with certain presidential advisers whom the Israeli leaders called their "friends in the White House." David Niles, Truman's adviser on minority affairs, continued to brief Israeli envoys about policy developments within the White House and to lobby Truman on Israel's behalf. Ambassador McDonald divulged the internal dynamics of U.S. policy to Israeli officials and pressed Britain, France, Italy, and Greece to recognize Israel. "No better man could have been chosen by President Truman," Ambassador Eliahu Elath observed of McDonald. Harriman and Eddie Jacobson, a friend of Truman, also advocated Israel's interests in the White House.[3]

Israeli officials also sought close relations with members of Congress. In February 1949, for example, Elath hosted a dinner party for eight of the ten Jewish members of Congress, including such powerful representatives as House Judiciary Committee Chairman Emanuel Celler (D–New York), House Foreign Affairs Committee Chairman and fourteen-term representative Sol Bloom (D–New York), and committee members Jacob K. Javits (R–New York) and Abraham A. Ribicoff (D-Connecticut). Israeli envoys also secured the support of non-Jewish members of Congress by encouraging their pro-Zionist constituents to express their opinions. When Senator Theodore F. Green (D–Rhode Island) criticized Israel in April 1952, the Israeli ambassador to the United States, Abba Eban, arranged a "flood of protests from Rhode Island" in response.[4]

Israeli officials also encouraged admiration of Israel in U.S. public opinion. The Foreign Ministry conceptualized a comprehensive information (*hasbara*) program in late 1949 to bolster Israel's image amid criticisms of its policies on the refugees and Jerusalem issues. By 1950, Abraham Harman, the *hasbara* chief stationed in New York, organized visits of American notables to Israel, maintained close ties with U.S. labor leaders, and established posts in Israeli studies at U.S. universities. His staff claimed to influence editorials in U.S. newspapers, win the support of U.S. Christians, and shape film and television productions. Pro-Israel media pressure on the State Department during the Huleh controversy of 1951, Herlitz summarized, "shows you that it pays to have a press campaign."[5]

While sympathy for Israel in the White House, Congress, and public opinion created a veneer of friendship toward Israel, a reservoir of resentment in the State and Defense Departments added a frosty edge to the relationship. The State Department remained alarmed that domestic pressure on Truman to support Israel threatened vital security interests in the Arab states. By June 1949, the department monitored an "Israeli smear campaign" against State Department officials who resisted the pressure. In contrast to favorable public perceptions of Ben-Gurion, U.S. Navy Intelligence labeled him "a militant Zionist" who cavorted with Irgun and Stern Gang terrorists. U.S. military attachés in Tel Aviv reportedly mistrusted their Israeli contacts. Irritated by Israel's various conduits to the White House, officials in the Bureau of Near Eastern, South Asian, and African Affairs (NEA) provided Truman in June 1949 with "a CIA report from Damascus relating to certain activities of Ambassador McDonald." Within months, Truman authorized Acheson to recall McDonald.[6]

Acheson also resented the pro-Israel rhetoric of members of Truman's cabinet. In a typical speech in 1950, for example, Vice President Alben Barkley called Israel "an oasis of liberty in the desert of despotism." Acheson's advisers concluded that such rhetoric stoked anger in the Arab states, as was manifest in bombings of U.S. legations in Beirut and Damascus, anti-U.S. statements by Arab leaders, and abstentions on U.N. resolutions regarding Korea. The secretary of state persuaded Truman to curtail his pro-Israel rhetoric but considered cabinet members' speeches to be a continuing problem.[7]

Israeli officials reciprocated the ill feelings in the State and Defense Departments but felt ensnared by the influence dilemma. The director-general of the Foreign Ministry, Walter Eytan, accused William J. Porter of the U.S. delegation at Lausanne of "abominable conduct," and Ben-Gurion found Acheson "rather stiff" at a May 1951 meeting. Worse, Truman became more deferential to the State Department after his reelection in 1948. "We cannot easily expect a repetition of events like the recognition of Israel by the fist of the President without his even consulting the Department of State," embassy counselor Moshe Keren observed in 1950. Although the NEA posed a "bottleneck" for pro-Israel policy, Israeli officials realized that asking Truman to overrule the bureau would inflame the situation.[8]

The tension between Israeli and U.S. diplomats stemmed not only from personal and political rivalry but also from a divergence in thinking about security issues. U.S. defense experts considered Israel an obstacle to the regional stability on which Western interests rested, and the National Security Council (NSC) grumbled about Israel's neutralism and "intensely nationalistic" character. For its part, the Israeli Foreign Ministry's United States Division resented "American interference and pressure in matters between us and our neighbors." Because the United States aimed for "stability and peace" in the Middle East, the division noted, "we are seen as a disruptive factor. . . . Israel is a 'bone in the throat'" of the United States.[9]

This divergence of thinking, aggravated by tensions over the Arab-Israeli conflict, strained U.S.-Israeli relations on several issues. In late 1948, for example, Israel sought U.S. de jure recognition, and Special Counsel Clark Clifford, McDonald, and various members of Congress endorsed the request. After Marshall emphasized that the May 1948 U.S. de facto recognition had alienated the Arab states, however, Truman hesitated. He recognized Israel only after a permanent government was elected in January 1949; to Israel's displeasure, he simultaneously recognized Jordan.[10]

U.S. and Israeli officials also sparred briefly on the question of Israeli membership in the United Nations. Truman accepted Clifford's reasoning that Israel deserved a U.N. seat, like several Arab states, and he directed Acheson to support the Jewish state's request for membership. With U.S. support, in March 1949 the Security Council approved a resolution affirming Israeli membership. But Acheson, angry at Israel's "liberal use of big stick in armistice talks," then sought to delay the new country's U.N. admission to demonstrate that Israel "cannot continue to ignore with impunity [the] opinion [of the] world community." Truman agreed and authorized Acheson to bury the Israeli petition in a General Assembly committee.[11]

Israel, however, again waged a triumphant battle for Truman's mind. Elath mobilized certain "White House friends" to argue to the president that Israel was more likely to cooperate with U.N. peacemaking initiatives as a member. Truman also reasoned, Acheson noted, that a reversal of the U.S. endorsement of December 1948 would cause "confusion and irritation" with the administration and that supporting Israel's admission might result in American leverage over the country. On 11 May, the General Assembly passed a U.S.-cosponsored resolution to admit Israel.[12]

U.S. and Israeli officials also squabbled over an Export-Import Bank loan to Israel. When Israel held elections and signed armistice agreements in early 1949, the State Department approved a $100 million bank loan to Israel. With Truman's approval, however, Acheson ordered bank officials to sequester the loan's $49 million balance in August 1949 because of Israel's policy toward Palestinian refugees. Israel used Niles as a conduit to complain to Truman about the State Department's "coercion and blackmail," and Acheson, feeling pressured by the White House, capitulated. He approved allocations of $2.4 million in late August and $20 million in October even though Israel remained unyielding on the refugee issue.[13]

The United States and the Arab World

The Arab-Israeli conflict severely strained U.S. relations with the Arab world. The war of 1948–49 and the disputes that followed stimulated a wave of Arab nationalism and passion, much of it aimed against the United States. The State Department monitored the decline in Arab-U.S. amity and worried about its impact on vital American interests in the Arab states. Although the degree of tension between the United States and each Arab country varied and stemmed from multiple causes, U.S. experts concluded that U.S. standing among Arab powers declined because of Israel.

Various U.S. officials concluded that the Palestine conflict destabilized Arab governments and threatened U.S. status in the Arab world. The Central Intelligence Agency (CIA) predicted that anti-Western nationalists would exploit popular discontent with the Arab defeats in Palestine to overthrow moderate, pro-Western Arab governments. Worse, Arab nationalists considered the creation of Israel a case of "Western Zionist aggression." The chairman of the Palestine Conciliation Commission (PCC), Mark Ethridge, told Truman that the Arab states "have great bitterness toward the UN and the United States." During a 1950 tour of Arab states, NEA intelligence adviser W. Wendell Cleland found that "the Palestine problem overshadows all problems." Arab League General Secretary Azzam Pasha told Assistant Secretary of State George C. McGhee that U.S. policy "caused great bitterness in the Arab world which cannot be dispelled in a moment."[14]

Many U.S. officials feared that the instability caused by the Palestine conflict might open the Arab states to Soviet power. Communism in Arab states seemed limited by such factors as Islam, traditional social mores, the absence of large labor forces, Soviet support of partition in 1947, and severe government repression. "If you could find a Communist in Saudi Arabia," King Ibn Saud tellingly mentioned to Air Force Brigadier General Edwin M. Day, "I will hand you his head." Yet U.S. officials noted that nascent communist movements had existed in many Arab states since 1941 and that Soviet propaganda exploited Arab anticolonialism. The CIA doubted that Arab leaders would openly embrace communism but feared that as Arab nationalists attempted to overthrow pro-Western regimes, "the ensuing chaos would provide suitable conditions for Soviet exploitation."[15]

Arab ambivalence regarding the Korean War accentuated U.S. concerns about the orientation and stability of Arab powers. In late 1950, Lebanon, Iraq, Saudi Arabia, Syria, and Jordan quietly endorsed the U.S. action in Korea, but Egypt, the lone Arab power able to send troops to Korea, refused to do so. Worse, Arab leaders expressed resentment that the United States enforced U.N. resolutions in Korea but not in Israel as well as a preference for a negotiated Korean settlement short of complete U.S. victory.[16]

U.S. relationships with individual Arab states varied widely, but all experienced tension over the Palestine issue. Jordan remained on comparatively sound terms with the United States. To reward Abdallah's moderation toward Israel, Truman received a personal envoy from the king and recognized his government in January 1949. When counselor Abdul Monem Bey Rifai affirmed in August 1950 that Jordan was "solidly behind the West" in Korea, Acheson raised the status of the U.S. legation in Amman to an embassy. In 1951, McGhee and King Abdallah enjoyed a warm and friendly meeting in Amman and the NSC exempted Jordan from U.S. laws that denied aid to states trading with the Soviet Union.[17]

The assassination of King Abdallah on 20 July 1951 tested the U.S. reliance on Jordan. Uncertain of the assassin's motives, the CIA feared that neighboring states or anti-Western elements within Jordan might take advantage of Abdallah's successor, his son, Talal, who lacked Abdallah's stature and had a history of mental illness, and of Talal's fifteen-year-old son, Crown Prince Hussein. But the Arab Legion proved able to maintain internal order and deter foreign encroachment. A modicum of stability returned in August 1952, when Talal was deposed and Hussein was named king. (A regency council ruled until Hussein reached age eighteen in 1953.)[18]

The turmoil of 1948–49 also challenged U.S. amity with Lebanon. Alluding to the decades of U.S. philanthropy in their country and to U.S. support for their national independence in 1943, Lebanese officials expressed a desire to align with the West in the Cold War. But they also criticized U.S. support of Israel, which they considered a danger to their security. After the State Department encouraged Lebanon to make peace with Israel in April 1950, someone tossed a small bomb over the wall of the U.S. embassy in Beirut, a deed that the U.S. minister to the country, Lowell C. Pinkerton, took as Lebanon's response. In August, the Lebanese minister to Washington, Charles Malik, complained to McGhee that "the US does not give a damn about the Arabs."[19]

With little success, U.S. officials adopted a policy of "friendly firmness" toward Lebanese leaders in 1951. "We cannot expect them to forget Palestine," minister to Beirut Harold B. Minor noted, "but we can ask them to turn their backs on the past and face the future resolutely and confidently with us." The State Department withheld economic aid until Lebanon shifted its focus from Israel to the Middle East Command concept. Yet tension persisted, as is evident in the collapse of negotiations on a treaty of friendship, commerce, and navigation in 1951. "It is hard to exaggerate [the] intensity of Leb[anon's] anti-Israel feelings," John H. Bruins observed from the Beirut embassy, "which are [the] number one deterrent to our aims here since we are labelled as [the] number one Israel friend."[20]

U.S.-Lebanese relations improved only after Camille Chamoun was elected president of Lebanon on 23 September 1952. Chamoun pledged to side with the West in any world war, requested U.S. arms, and offered military bases to the United States. Acting Lebanese Foreign Minister Fouad Ammoun committed the new government to collaborating "to the fullest extent possible with the West and particularly with the United States." Chamoun pledged to support U.S. efforts to deescalate the Arab-Israeli conflict. "There were no problems between the United States and Lebanon," he declared, "that could not be settled right away."[21]

The Palestine War also strained U.S.-Saudi relations. According to the first secretary of the Saudi embassy, Ahmed Abdul Jabbar, U.S. support of partition in spite of Foreign Minister Prince Faisal's strong objections comprised "a personal defeat for the Prince . . . as he had prided himself upon his grasp of American affairs." Saudi friendship "cooled considerably" when the United States recognized Israel, State Department officials noted in May 1949, because King Ibn Saud feared that Israel would expand at Arab expense and perhaps import communism to the region. Citing "the painful events in Palestine," Ibn Saud only temporarily extended the 1945 Dhahran base pact when it expired in 1949.[22]

Despite these tensions, the U.S.-Saudi relationship stabilized in late 1949. As the armistices diminished tensions, the State Department noted that "our relations with Saudi Arabia are definitely improving." Ibn Saud recognized "that there was too great a community of interest between the United States and Saudi Arabia," the U.S. minister to Jidda, J. Rives Childs, told Truman in September, "for him to be deflected from his course of friendship with us." Even Prince Faisal decided that "the deed is done," State Department officials noted in December. The Saudis would stop "feeding rancor with a dead issue."[23]

Economic and security ties provided incentives to heal the breach. Ibn Saud never canceled U.S. oil concessions and even allowed oil companies to expand operations in late 1949. When the king proposed a U.S.-Saudi military alliance in March 1950, McGhee offered an assurance that the United States "will take most immediate action at any time that the integrity and independence of Saudi Arabia is threatened." After the Pentagon provided military aid, Ibn Saud signed a five-year renewable Dhahran base agreement in June 1951. Truman added to the rapprochement by dispatching his personal physician to treat the ailing king on four occasions in 1950–52.[24]

Through the Truman presidency, however, Arab-Israeli tensions threatened U.S.-Saudi cordiality. To the chagrin of the Pentagon, Ibn Saud expressed more concern about Israeli expansionism than about Soviet expansionism. Prince Faisal complained about U.S. economic aid to Israel and about pro-Israeli statements by members of Truman's cabinet. State Department officials unsuccessfully protested Saudi embargoes on imports from U.S. firms owned by Jews, discrimination against U.S. officials who were Jewish, and denial of overflight rights to airplanes with Jewish passengers. Saudi leaders remained "critical and cynical upon occasion" about U.S. policy toward Israel, U.S. officials noted in 1951, thereby testing the foundation of U.S.-Saudi friendship.[25]

U.S. relations with Iraq also suffered because of Palestine-related issues. Negotiations on a friendship, commerce, and navigation treaty deadlocked in part because Iraq refused to lift its trade embargo on Israel. Iraqi leaders resented U.S. requests to reopen Iraq Petroleum Company pipelines to Israel and complained that Israel received extensive U.S. financial aid while "the Arab states receive promises." U.S. efforts to sell the MEC-MEDO concept in Baghdad fell flat as Iraqi leaders claimed to fear Israel more than they feared communism. State Department officials repeatedly observed that U.S.-Iraqi antagonism resulted from "one factor, namely, the support to Israel given by the United States."[26]

The Arab-Israeli conflict also contributed to tension between the United States and Egypt. The long history of U.S.-Egyptian amity, the State Department observed in 1950, had collapsed as a result of U.S. support of partition, recognition of Israel, and policy on the refugee and border issues. Egypt refused to endorse U.S. policy in Korea, Wells Stabler of the NEA concluded, because of "the bitterness which still exists over the Palestine question." Israel would galvanize Egyptian nationalism against the United States for some time because the topic possessed "a deep-seated hold on public opinion" in Egypt.[27]

Anger about Israel exacerbated Egypt's discontent with U.S. policy regarding the Anglo-Egyptian base dispute. Having tried in vain for years to expel British troops from their country, Egyptian officials criticized U.S. reluctance to endorse this quest. Acheson concluded that Egypt's mounting anticolonial fervor blinded the country to the value of the MEC-MEDO concept and threatened to trigger a radical revolution in Cairo. The Anglo-Egyptian conflict, he noted to the NSC in 1952, "was made the more complicated . . . by the violent Arab hatred against us because of our sympathy for the Israelis."[28]

The July 1952 Egyptian revolution pushed Arab-Israeli issues to the back burner, but only briefly. The new regime, led by General Mohammed Naguib and Colonel Gamal Abdel Nasser, implemented domestic reform and discussed security cooperation with the United States. Naguib downplayed the conflict with Israel and even attended services in the Synagogue of the Grand Rabbi in Cairo. But State Department suggestions that Egypt consider peace with Israel and open the Suez Canal to Israeli shipping had no effect. The Egyptian-Israeli conflict remained unresolved, a looming impediment to U.S.-Egyptian amity.[29]

In 1949–52, the United States sought to maintain good relations with Syria as it experienced recurrent instability. Colonel Husni Zaim took power in a bloodless coup on 30 March 1949 but was ousted and executed by fellow army officers on 14 August. A third coup in December opened a period of instability that lasted until Colonel Adib al-Shishakli seized power on 29 November 1951. Despite their distaste for military takeovers, U.S. officials recognized each new regime both to deter neighboring states from encroaching on Syria and to preserve diplomatic influence in Damascus. The CIA worried that Syria might drift toward Moscow until al-Shishakli crushed the Muslim Brotherhood and the Communist Party and firmly entrenched himself in 1952.[30]

During the period of instability, Arab-Israeli tensions aggravated U.S.-Syrian relations. Syria repeatedly demanded that the United States compel Israel to repatriate Palestinian refugees. U.S. officials blamed anger over Israel for a bomb explosion in the garden of the U.S. legation in Damascus in April 1950 and for Syrian indifference to the Tripartite Declaration of May. Negotiations on economic aid, which the State Department hoped would improve relations, collapsed amid what McGhee called "a considerable growth of anti-American sentiment" resulting from U.S. support of Israel. Syria seemed more likely "to complain of the Ex[port]-Im[port] Bank loan to Israel," one U.S. official lamented, "than to prepare an application for a bank loan."[31]

The tension persisted after al-Shishakli stabilized Syria. Al-Shishakli told U.S. officials that only the threat of Israeli expansion prevented him from joining MEDO. Negotiations on an arms deal collapsed when U.S. officials realized that Syria wanted weapons to defend against Israeli rather than Soviet attack. U.S.-Syrian relations, NEA officials noted in November 1952, were friendly but "not at the optimum, primarily because of the Syrians' concept of how we stand toward Israel."[32]

The State Department concluded that Israel-related issues formed the prime cause of Arab-U.S. tensions. Intelligence officials estimated that Arab resentment of U.S. policy toward Israel surpassed anticolonialism, Anglophobia, and economic maladjustments as the largest factor behind anti-Western Arab nationalism. The Soviets sought a "high position in [the] Arab world which is already full of neutralism," Minor, the U.S. ambassador in Beirut, warned when U.N. debates on Arab-Israeli peace ended inconclusively in late 1952. The Arab world might "drift into chaos and ultimately go [the] way of China."[33]

Conclusion

The Arab-Israeli conflict influenced U.S. relations with Israel and the Arab states in 1949–53. The U.S. relationship with Israel displayed both accord and discord. Israel enjoyed the friendly support of President Truman, the White House staff, Congress, and influential private citizens in the United States. Much of this support derived from the traditional pro-Zionism of the White House and public opinion, while some of it resulted from the conscious efforts by Israeli officials to mobilize "friends" in the United States. By contrast, professionals in the State and Defense Departments remained suspicious of Israel, which they viewed as an impediment to their goal of a stable and pro-Western Arab world.

Such tensions within the administration shaped the resolution of such diplomatic issues as U.S. recognition of Israel, Israeli membership in the United Nations, and economic aid to Israel. In each case, State Department professionals preferred to extract certain concessions as the price of favorable U.S. policy. But Truman, sensitive to domestic pressures, ultimately ordered enactment of policies that provided Israel what it wanted. As in the disputes over borders, refugees, and Jerusalem, Israel's lobbying of Truman stoked anger among State Department officials, revealing the risks to Israel inherent in the influence dilemma.

The Arab-Israeli conflict profoundly altered U.S. relations with the Arab states. Embittered by defeat in the Palestine War, Arab leaders deeply resented U.S. support of Israel and reinforced one another's defiant refusals to make peace. To be sure, factors such as decolonization, nationalism, economic underdevelopment, and inter-Arab rivalries contributed to the discord between the Arab community and the United States, but U.S. policy toward Israel seriously aggravated the tensions.

Relationships between the United States and individual Arab countries declined markedly in 1949–53, although variations occurred. Relations with Jordan remained fairly warm, although the 1951 assassination of King Abdallah destabilized the state. Lebanon, Iraq, and Saudi Arabia remained stable and disposed toward the West but strongly disliked U.S. policies deemed favorable to Israel. Disagreements over Israel-related issues inflamed U.S. relations with Egypt and Syria.

In 1953, Truman and Acheson might have felt a small measure of optimism regarding the Arab states. Despite the deterioration since 1947, U.S. relations with the Arab states had avoided complete collapse. Some Arab leaders seemed supportive of U.S. security ambitions and responsive to requests for cooperation. The rise of Hussein in Jordan, Chamoun in Lebanon, Naguib and Nasser in Egypt, and al-Shishakli in Syria, together with the persistence of the Saudi monarchy, offered a ray of hope for stability in the Arab world. If the Arab states could be stabilized and the Arab-Israeli conflict mitigated or contained, then the United States might achieve its goal of a Middle East free of Soviet control. Such hopes would be tested repeatedly in the years to come.

Part III

11

COLD WAR FRAMEWORK
U.S. Perspectives on the Middle East, 1953–1957

Determined to prevail in the Cold War, President Dwight D. Eisenhower maintained key provisions of Harry S. Truman's global strategy of containing the Soviet Union. Like his predecessor, Eisenhower considered the Middle East vital to U.S. security and resolved to defend the region against Soviet political and military expansion. Perceiving an increasingly acute Soviet threat to the region, Eisenhower took more immediate action than Truman had to protect U.S. interests. In so doing, the new president significantly deepened the long-term U.S. commitment to Middle East security.

Eisenhower also modified Truman's policy toward the Arab-Israeli conflict. Convinced that Truman had favored Israel over its Arab neighbors to the detriment of U.S. interests, Eisenhower resolved to practice impartiality in the dispute. Whereas Truman had made policy in reaction to sudden, tumultuous changes in the region, Eisenhower shaped a proactive policy that sought in principle to solve the Arab-Israeli conflict. Despite his impartial and proactive disposition, however, Eisenhower found himself, like Truman, unable to solve the controversy and remain on amicable terms with both sides.

Eisenhower brought to office substantial experience in international and military affairs. A 1915 graduate of West Point, he earned a reputation as the army's most capable staff officer in a variety of training and command assignments in the 1920s and 1930s, and he commanded the Allied invasions of North Africa, Italy, and France during World War II. Although he had avoided domestic politics while a professional soldier, Eisenhower courted financial backers and polished his public image while holding a variety of official and private positions during the Truman presidency. Both major parties courted him in 1948, but Eisenhower waited until 1952 to accept the Republican nomination. He won the White House after campaigning on the principles of anticommunism, integrity, and internationalism. Eisenhower's enormous popularity among voters contributed to the Republican Party's capture of both houses of Congress.[1]

Secretary of State John Foster Dulles served as Eisenhower's chief foreign policy adviser. The grandson and nephew of former secretaries of state, Dulles was educated at Princeton, served as counsel to the U.S. delegation to the Paris Peace Conference of 1919, and emerged as a prominent international lawyer in the 1920s and 1930s. Dulles gained experience in Truman's administration as delegate to the San Francisco Conference in 1945, delegate to the U.N. General Assembly in 1945–49, and ambassador-at-large in 1950–51. Diagnosed with cancer in 1956, Dulles remained influential as secretary of state until shortly before his death in 1959.[2]

Eisenhower implemented policy in the Middle East in close consultation with Dulles. Despite the prevailing 1950s image of a passive president routinely deferring to his cabinet secretaries, revisionist historians have emphasized that Eisenhower understood foreign policy problems and made crucial policy decisions. The conception of an in-charge chief executive weakened Dulles's early reputation as the administration's leading diplomat, although Dulles revisionists have stressed that the secretary of state acted as Eisenhower's policy adviser and executor. "Eisenhower always made the decision," Richard H. Immerman notes in a centrist perspective, "but always after consulting Dulles."[3] As this and subsequent chapters will reveal, Eisenhower and Dulles closely collaborated in shaping U.S. policy in the Middle East, thereby avoiding some of the internal divisions that bedeviled Truman's policy making.

The Strategic Importance of the Middle East

In 1953–56, the Eisenhower administration affirmed the doctrine of containment and applied it anew to the Middle East. U.S. officials remained concerned with the orientation of the region, whose strategic and oil assets remained critical to U.S. security. Sensing a Soviet campaign to expand into the Third World, Eisenhower became determined to erect a Middle East security pact as a shield against Soviet advance. In short, the Cold War continued to provide the basic framework for U.S. Middle East policy.

While upholding the doctrine of containment, Eisenhower engineered important changes in U.S. global strategy. Whereas Truman tended to make Cold War policy in reaction to sudden events and crises overseas, Robert R. Bowie and Immerman observe, Eisenhower drew on his considerable strategic and diplomatic experience to formulate a comprehensive grand strategy for the Cold War. After establishing a rational system for formulating security doctrine, Eisenhower developed an approach based on avoidance of nuclear war through deterrence, toleration of Soviet power within the country's current borders, balance between military preparations and fiscal economy, reliance on

European allies to share defense burdens, and cultivation of partnerships with Third World countries.[4]

Eisenhower generally continued the global partnership with Britain that had persisted during the Truman years. The new U.S. president had earned honorary British citizenship for his military exploits in World War II, and he deeply admired Winston Churchill, the British wartime statesman who had returned to the prime ministry in 1951. The two leaders affirmed anti-Soviet containment as the fundamental Western policy in Europe and Asia. In August 1953, they launched a joint covert operation to remove Iranian Premier Mohammed Mossadegh, a nationalist who had expropriated British oil facilities, and restore the pro-Western Shah Mohammad Reza Pahlavi. As some scholars have pointed out, Anglo-U.S. disagreements arose over China, Indochina, and competing oil claims in the Buraimi Oasis along the Saudi border with Oman. But Eisenhower and Churchill honored their friendship forged in the war. A summit meeting with Churchill in late 1953, Eisenhower wrote, "was for me a sort of homecoming, a renewal of an old and close relationship."[5]

With the situation in Europe stabilized and the Korean War at a standstill, the Third World assumed increasing importance in U.S. thinking during the early Eisenhower presidency. World War II had unleashed the forces of decolonization against European empires in the Middle East, Asia, and Africa, where revolutionary leaders, animated by nationalism and anti-Western passions, aspired to establish nation-states endowed with independence and self-rule. Critical scholars argue that Eisenhower occasionally misread Third World nationalism as a Soviet-orchestrated phenomenon, subverted his anticolonial ideals, and squandered opportunities to build healthy relationships with nationalist leaders. Most notoriously, the president ordered covert operations in Iran in 1953 and in Guatemala in 1954 to replace popular nationalist leaders with undemocratic but U.S.-oriented regimes. Revisionist scholars counter that Eisenhower opposed European imperialism in principle, understood the vitality of nationalism, and distinguished it from communism but nonetheless considered accommodation with nationalists less important than promoting security interests.[6]

The Middle East in particular continued to loom large in U.S. strategic thinking after 1953. The region's military bases, lines of communication, and Suez Canal, all in close proximity to the Soviet Union, held tremendous military importance. The Joint Strategic Plans Group considered control of the Middle East vital to the defense of NATO's right flank and to the successful prosecution of war against the Soviet heartland if global hostilities should occur. State Department officials noted that Christian, Muslim, and Jewish holy places throughout the region added cultural importance. Soviet capture of the Middle East, the

National Security Council (NSC) resolved, would leave U.S. security "critically endangered." By 1954, the Pentagon drafted plans to use U.S. rather than British forces to defend the region against Soviet attack.[7]

Access to Middle East oil remained a vital U.S. interest. By 1955, proven oil reserves in Middle East states totaled between 100 billion and 150 billion barrels, three to five times more than U.S. reserves. Middle East states produced some 3 million barrels per day—including 1 million each from Saudi Arabia and Kuwait and 600,000 from Iraq—and supplied 90 percent of the oil consumed in Western Europe. "The uninterrupted supply of oil from the Middle East is so vital," the Pentagon's Joint Middle East Planning Committee observed in early 1956, "that nothing should be allowed to threaten its continuance." If oil deliveries were disrupted, the Operations Coordinating Board added, Western Europe's "will to resist communist collaboration would be greatly weakened."[8]

To protect such vital interests, Eisenhower furthered the quest to stabilize the Middle East. In a series of 1953–55 policy papers, State Department officials resolved to pursue intraregional peace, promote economic development, encourage local powers to help defend against Soviet incursion, and improve bilateral relations with local states. The United States, Bromley K. Smith of the NSC special staff summarized in 1955, needed "stable, viable, friendly governments in the area capable of withstanding Communist-inspired subversion from within and willing to resist Communist aggression."[9]

U.S. officials perceived numerous obstacles to Middle East stability. The peoples of the region provided "tinder for Communist conflagrations," Edmund A. Gullion of the Office of Near Eastern Affairs (NE) noted in early 1953, because they were "poverty-stricken, suspicious of the West, animated by a fierce nationalism, [and] divided by political disputes and religious and racial differences." While touring the region in early 1953, Dulles observed that Britain and France had become "more a factor of instability rather than stability." The emergent nations of the Middle East, the NSC added, also disliked the United States because it associated with the European imperialists and with Israel.[10]

After 1953, U.S. officials had reason to fear growing Soviet influence in the Middle East. Nikita Khrushchev, who emerged as Soviet leader after a brief power struggle following Stalin's death, promoted peaceful coexistence with the West on European issues but welcomed political competition in the Third World. In 1954–55, the Soviet Union sought political and economic ties with Third World leaders and promoted nonalignment of their states to undermine Western imperial assets. Elevating pragmatism over ideology, Khrushchev nurtured closer relations with Egypt, which Stalin had eschewed, on the reasoning that Premier Gamal Abdel Nasser's nationalism might provide a vehicle for contesting Anglo-American hegemony in the region.[11]

U.S. officials monitored the increasing Soviet interest in the Middle East. They interpreted Soviet broadcasts in Middle East media in 1953 about the arrests of prominent Jews in Prague and Moscow as a bid to impress Arab audiences. In 1954 the NSC recognized that through trade agreements, industrial fairs, public declarations, and U.N. diplomacy, the Soviet Union "is striving to create chaos and to nullify the influence of the Western Powers." Operations Coordinating Board officials observed in 1956 that Soviet behavior had shifted from "encouraging local parties and engaging in small covert operations" to "an extensive economic and diplomatic effort which seriously threatens the British and American position in the area."[12]

U.S. officials were especially sensitive about apparent Soviet bids to gain influence over Middle East oil. In 1954, U.S. officials monitored evidence of Soviet support of a labor strike among oil workers in Dhahran. Khrushchev declared in 1955 that the Western imperialists used Israel to gain control over Arab natural resources and offered in 1956 to build an oil refinery in Syria. The Pentagon, State Department, and NSC discerned a Soviet conspiracy to undermine Western oil assets in Arab states and disrupt the flow of oil to Western Europe.[13]

U.S. officials were also bothered by Soviet political offensives in Egypt and Syria. Soviet leaders launched a "vigorous diplomatic offensive" to dispense aid to Middle East regimes, State Department intelligence officials noted in 1955. Nasser's emergence as a neutralist leader—signified by his attendance at the Asia-Africa Conference at Bandung, Indonesia, in April 1954—disturbed U.S. officials. The Soviet-Egyptian arms deal of September 1955 seemed doubly troubling because it signaled new departures both in Soviet assertiveness in the region and in an Arab state's receptivity to Soviet aid. The Soviets encouraged neutralism in Syria to weaken Western influence in the northern tier of the Middle East. The United States feared not a "dramatic Communist move within Syria," intelligence officials advised Dulles, but "a Soviet-sponsored Syrian drift into a firmly anti-Western position."[14]

To advance stability against internal hindrances and external threats, the Eisenhower administration resolved to become more involved in the Middle East. Unless the United States promoted security and economic development, NEA officials advised, "the possibilities for forward-looking and progressive leadership will be lost, and the Arab world placed in grave danger of Soviet subversion." Dulles returned from a tour of the region in early 1953 convinced that the United States must "increase its influence in the Middle East at the earliest possible moment" and convey to Arab states that it had "sympathy for the legitimate aspirations of the people." In 1953–54, the NSC resolved to take bold new initiatives to stabilize the Middle East, deny it to the Soviets, win over its peoples, and prevent war in the region.[15]

To secure its interests, the Eisenhower administration refined Truman's defense planning for the region. Eisenhower and Dulles concluded that Truman's concept of the Middle East Defense Organization (MEDO) based in Egypt was impossible to establish. Egyptian Ambassador-designate to Washington Ahmed Hussein told Assistant Secretary of State Henry A. Byroade on 4 May 1953 that MEDO was "completely unacceptable" because it infringed on Egyptian sovereignty. Israeli opposition further weakened the idea's appeal. After detecting widespread resistance to MEDO during his tour of the region, Dulles informed his advisers that the scheme was "on the shelf."[16]

After abandoning MEDO, U.S. officials gravitated toward a security pact based on the northern tier states of Turkey, Iraq, Iran, and Pakistan. Iraq and Turkey seemed more receptive than Egypt did to Western defense schemes, Dulles told the NSC in spring 1953, because these countries felt "the hot breath of the Soviet Union on their necks." Restoration of the pro-Western Shah of Iran in August 1953 made the northern tier scheme viable. The Joint Chiefs of Staff (JCS) envisioned "an association of indigenous forces under indigenous command" located close to the Soviet Union and immune to the Anglo-Egyptian and Arab-Israeli conflicts.[17]

U.S. officials breathed life into the northern tier concept by encouraging area states and Britain to form a defense alliance. The United States extended military aid to induce Turkey and Pakistan to sign an agreement on 2 April 1954 pledging cooperation and consultation in defense matters. After months of painstaking diplomacy, Iraq and Turkey signed a more formal mutual-defense pact in Baghdad on 24 February 1955. Britain joined the pact in April, Pakistan in September, and Iran in October. The pact was governed by a Ministerial Council that met semiannually, a sitting Council of Deputies based in Baghdad, and committees responsible for military plans, economic cooperation, countersubversion strategies, and other matters. The United States refrained from joining the Baghdad Pact to avoid Soviet retaliation, Egyptian criticism, or Israeli demands for a compensatory defense commitment. Nonetheless, U.S. support was crucial to the pact's formulation.[18]

From the beginning, U.S. officials recognized several flaws in the northern tier concept. The combat forces of Baghdad Pact members, including British forces in the region, seemed incapable of even slowing a Soviet invasion. The plan among pact members to launch "tactical atomic attacks on the fighting value and speed of advance of the Russian forces" would fail, the Joint Strategic Plans Committee noted, because the participants lacked delivery capabilities. Soviet air atomic attacks in the early stages of a war, by contrast, would destroy most military bases, supply depots, and oil fields in the northern tier states. Soviet ground forces would easily move south in eastern Iran and outflank pact forces defending along the Zagros Mountains. Access to the ports, roads, and railroads needed to provide Western reinforcements from the south, Major General Alfred Johnson, deputy director of logistics on the Joint Staff, noted, would require "the wholehearted cooperation and participation" of Syria, Lebanon, Saudi Arabia, Kuwait, and Egypt. The lack of such cooperation, of course, had redirected U.S. thinking to the northern tier.[19]

U.S. officials also identified problems with a prospective U.S. commitment to defend pact states in the event of war. In 1955, the JCS considered establishing "a small U.S. nuclear delivery capability in the Middle East" to stymie any Soviet attack but found local base and weapons storage facilities insufficient for the task. Moreover, any hint of a U.S. atomic umbrella, Pentagon planners speculated, would discourage pact members from working out collective self-defense measures. To bolster the pact would accentuate its weaknesses and incur a responsibility that the United States wished to avoid.[20]

Further complicating the situation, Arab states other than Iraq criticized the Baghdad Pact. Viewing Iraq as its rival for leadership in the Arab world, Egypt charged that the pact divided the Arab community, undermined the Arab League Collective Security Pact, and served European colonial and Israeli interests. Egypt, Syria, and Saudi Arabia formed a partnership in October 1955 to deter other Arab states from joining the pact. In exchange for offers of Anglo-U.S. financial aid to build the Aswân Dam in late 1955, Nasser suspended active opposition to the pact provided that no other states were recruited to join it. But when Britain tried unsuccessfully to enlist Jordan in early 1956, Nasser reemerged as a sharp critic. The Baghdad Pact "was the most significant turning point in Arab politics since the 1948 war," Elie Podeh notes. "It shattered the Arab system, leading to new political groupings and new patterns."[21]

The Israeli attitude toward the Baghdad Pact also complicated the situation. As in the case of MEDO, U.S. officials excluded Israel from the northern tier scheme to avoid a categorical Arab rejection of it. Israel did not contest that decision but profoundly opposed the pact because it would funnel weapons to Iraq and encourage Turkey to mollify Arab states at the expense of Turkish-Israeli amity. Dulles's retort that the pact would benefit Israel by dividing the Arab states and preventing Iraqi aggression did not ease Israeli concerns.[22]

Despite the weaknesses in the Baghdad Pact, the Pentagon gradually embraced the idea of U.S. adherence to it. As late as June 1955, Defense and State Department planners agreed that Turkey and Pakistan should carry the burden of defense. By October, however, the chairman of the JCS, Admiral Arthur Radford, found this approach "unsatisfactory" in view of Egyptian-Israeli tensions and "increased Soviet interest in the Arab States." During Radford's December visit to Baghdad, Iraqi officials complained that Nasser, despite his opposition to the pact, had gained Soviet arms and an Anglo-U.S. offer to fund the Aswân Dam. Other member states grumbled that U.S. absence aggravated the pact's military impotence and the political difficulty of dealing with Britain. In early 1956, the JCS recommended that the United States join the pact "without delay."[23]

Eisenhower declined to accept formal membership in the Baghdad Pact, but he wove the United States into the agreement's structure both to bolster it and to deflect allied and Pentagon pressure to join. In September 1955, he named the U.S. Army attaché in Baghdad as U.S. military observer to the pact. In early 1956, he authorized State Department observers to attend the first meeting of the pact's Economic Council, paid one-sixth of the pact's annual budget, appointed eight staff to its secretariat, and authorized the U.S. military observer to participate in military planning. In April, the United States joined the Economic and Countersubversion Committees, and in November it established the Baghdad Pact Military Liaison Group in the Iraqi capital.[24]

Eisenhower's policy of supporting the Baghdad Pact from a distance has provoked a range of scholarly judgments. William Stivers and Magnus Persson argue that the pact served U.S. interests by containing communism in the Middle East and securing Europe's right flank. Robert W. Stookey observes that Eisenhower drew Arab nationalist and Soviet backlash by supporting the pact but weakened the alliance by refusing to join. Ritchie Ovendale, Steven Z. Freiberger, G. Wyn Rees, Elie Podeh, and Nigel John Ashton emphasize that disagreements about the timing of the pact's creation, U.S. membership, and Jordan's role in it strained the Atlantic alliance. In any case, U.S. support of the pact, which aggravated Arab-Israeli as well as intra-Arab tensions, revealed that Eisenhower privileged his anti-Soviet containment objectives over his desire to make Arab-Israeli peace.[25]

The U.S. Approach to the Arab-Israeli Conflict, 1953–1954

Intent on stabilizing the Middle East against perceived Soviet activism, the Eisenhower administration could not avoid the Arab-Israeli conflict. Because that dispute provoked anti-Western sentiment in Arab states, hindered the establishment of a regional defense scheme, and limited economic and social development, Eisenhower and Dulles concluded that solving the problem would serve their ambitions in the region and affirmed their intent to act as peacemakers in 1953–54. Hindered by several obstacles, however, U.S. officials initially remained inactive on the issue.

Eisenhower and Dulles applied three basic principles to the Arab-Israeli conflict. First, in light of apparent Soviet activism in the Middle East, the U.S. leaders reiterated the importance of settling the conflict. Any Israeli attack on an Arab state, the NSC noted in 1954, would cause "a decisive movement of the area away from the West and possibly into the Soviet sphere of influence." Rear

Admiral Edwin T. Layton, the Joint Staff's deputy director for intelligence, observed that Arab-Israeli tension "offers the Communist Bloc a troubled water in which to fish." Arab-Israeli peace seemed conducive to containment.[26]

Second, Eisenhower and Dulles impartially approached the Arab-Israeli situation. While the United States must not "turn back the clock on the existence of Israel," the State Department noted in 1953, it must correct Truman's "lopsided" favoritism of Israel. Dulles aimed "to convince the Arab World that the United States is operating upon a policy of *true* impartiality," while Eisenhower resolved to be "as tough with the Israelis as with any other nation." The NSC restated this view in 1954.[27]

Third, U.S. officials expressed a general desire to become directly involved in making Arab-Israeli peace. The United States, State Department counselor Douglas MacArthur II told Israeli Minister to Washington Reuven Shiloah in May 1953, aspired "to cultivate an atmosphere of mutual trust and convince both sides that an agreement is in their interest." State Department officials aimed to provide economic aid to Arab states and Israel as an incentive to settle their disputes. Rejecting Britain's desire to delay peacemaking until it achieved a base settlement with Egypt, Eisenhower approved an NSC plan to promote settlements of major Arab-Israeli controversies and seek full and final peace treaties.[28]

Hope for an early Arab-Israeli peace, however, foundered on the animosity between the two sides and Arab-Arab political dynamics. Lebanese Minister to Washington Charles Malik observed in April 1953 that Israel's immigration, expansionism, and support in Western states had convinced most Arab statesmen that current Israeli territory "is but a bridgehead from which the Zionists . . . will sweep over and conquer the entire Arab Near East." A meeting of Arab foreign ministers in Cairo resolved that peace depended on Israel's willingness to relinquish land beyond the original partition lines. Each foreign minister supported this extreme position, U.S. Ambassador to Amman Joseph C. Green reported, "lest he appear less patriotic and less anti-Israel than the others."[29]

Such sentiments solidified in 1954. Arab leaders seemed willing to tolerate Israel's existence and unlikely to provoke a second round of fighting, but they hoped that Israel would collapse if they isolated it and pressed for the return of Palestinian refugees. Arab statesmen strove for "eventual liquidation of Israel as a political entity," the State Department observed. "The Jewish state is regarded as a cancer on the body of the Arab Middle East. Quite frankly, the Arabs want it removed."[30]

The Israelis also did not seem eager to settle. Prime Minister David Ben-Gurion claimed to desire peace only if it did not require cession of land, international control of Jerusalem, or repatriation of refugees. "The stability of the Middle East does not depend on 'arrangements,'" he commented in April 1953, "but on cultural uplifting of the Arabs, and this requires a long-term plan." Foreign Minister Moshe Sharett favored the status quo because a U.S. "peace offensive" might make Israel appear weak or force it to concede on vital issues. Given Israeli resistance to compromise with Arab states and its policy of reprisals against border provocations, the State Department sensed by 1954 that Israel had lost faith in the armistices and was contemplating assertive action on the calculation that the situation would have to deteriorate into violence before improving.[31]

In light of such obstacles, the Eisenhower administration initially refrained from promoting Arab-Israeli peace. During his spring 1953 tour of the Middle East, Dulles showed little interest in peacemaking. "The U.S. has no God-given right to settle the problems of the whole world," he told Sharett and Ben-Gurion. U.S. officials "did not want to butt in where they were not wanted or where they could not be helpful." In meetings with Egyptian leader Mohammed Naguib in Cairo, Dulles refrained from promoting peace and instead deliberated the Anglo-Egyptian base problem and Egypt's position in Western defense schemes.[32]

Such passivity regarding the Arab-Israeli situation persisted in mid-1954. State Department experts deemed the Arab-Israeli problem insurmountable in the short term and hoped only that regional economic development might eventually create political stability, generate resources needed to care for refugees, and provide incentives for Arab-Israeli cooperation. In addition to deterring aggression, U.S. diplomats in the Middle East concluded in May that they should explore solutions to the controversies over refugees, Jerusalem, borders, and water usage. But the time for such solutions had not yet arrived in light of "presently irreconcilable basic attitudes."[33]

Conclusion

Because of the Cold War, Eisenhower deepened the U.S. commitment to the security of the Middle East. U.S. national security rested in part on the West's assured access to the Middle East's oil, military bases, and other assets. Given the importance assigned to the region, American officials worried that political instability, economic underdevelopment, and Arab-Israeli conflict destabilized the Middle East from within and were alarmed by mounting evidence that Soviet leaders sought to exploit such factors to erode Western interests and enhance the Soviet position in the region. To provide military security in the Middle East, Eisenhower abandoned the Truman-era MEDO concept and created the Baghdad Pact along the region's northern tier. When that agreement proved insufficient to its task as a result of tactical military inadequacies and opposition from the Soviet Union, Israel, and most Arab states, the United

States bolstered the pact with a variety of steps short of formal membership. In the process, the United States became further enmeshed in the region.

Concerns about regional security also influenced the new administration's approach to the Arab-Israeli conflict. Evidence that the Soviet Union sought to gain influence in the Middle East by exploiting the Arab-Israeli dispute convinced U.S. officials to favor Arab-Israeli peace in principle. In view of the deep mutual animosities of the parties to the dispute, however, the administration remained inactive as a peacemaker through mid-1954 as Eisenhower doubted his ability to negotiate peace. As the following chapters reveal, however, the Cold War subsequently made the Arab-Israeli conflict seem more dangerous to U.S. interests and prodded Eisenhower and Dulles into action.

12

BORDER WARS
Eisenhower, Dulles, and Arab-Israeli Frontiers, 1953–1955

President Dwight D. Eisenhower and Secretary of State John Foster Dulles confronted a complex situation along Arab-Israeli borders in 1953–55. The 1948–49 war had left a delicate status quo resting on fragile armistices rather than peace treaties. Although relatively static in the late Truman era, this status quo was challenged in 1953–55 by a rising tide of border violence, as Arab infiltrators waged low-intensity warfare against Israel and Israel responded with force. Numerous incidents along Israel's borders with Jordan, Egypt, and Syria stoked tensions, diminished peace prospects, and threatened to lead to the resumption of hostilities that would destabilize the entire Middle East.

Eisenhower's and Dulles's reactions to this situation had two striking features. First, the leaders felt that security interests compelled the United States to shed its initial reluctance to become involved in the controversy and to devise diplomatic tools to pacify the borders. Second, although the United States failed to solve the border conflicts, in the process of trying Eisenhower and Dulles angered the principals to the dispute and perhaps even aggravated underlying Arab-Israeli tensions, resulting in a difficult political controversy.

Problems on Israel's Border with Jordan

As Eisenhower took office, mounting tension along the Jordanian-Israeli border threatened to trigger hostilities between the two countries. Drawn to the controversy by a series of violent episodes, Dulles initially blamed Israel for aggravating the situation by enacting an aggressive border security policy, but his firm criticism of that policy had little effect. Over time, Dulles sought a more evenhanded solution to the border turmoil. In another case of the firmness dilemma, however, he found Israel unwilling to accept any foreign scheme that challenged the Jewish state's sovereignty.

Tensions on the Israeli-Jordanian border escalated in early 1953. Israel refused to renew a "local commanders" agreement under which military officers from both states had pledged cooperatively to stop illegal border crossings. Instead, the Jewish state declared that it would engage in "active defense" of its borders by ambushing infiltrators and pursuing them into Arab states if necessary. Foreign Minister Moshe Sharett conceded to the Israel Defense Forces (IDF) the authority to conduct reprisals without consulting him. By February, IDF forces had made five reprisal raids into Jordan.[1]

Israel cited several reasons for adopting the reprisal policy. In 1952, infiltrators from Jordan had stolen goods worth one million Israeli pounds, killed thirteen civilians, and left fifty-three soldiers dead and fifty-six wounded. Reprisals against Jordanian targets promised to achieve revenge, deter future infiltrations, and boost the morale of border-area soldiers and civilians. The absence of progress toward peace agreements, frustration at Western armament of Arab states, and discomfort caused by the Arab economic boycott also encouraged a more bellicose posture.[2]

Jordanian and U.N. officials criticized Israel's new policy and disputed the rationale behind it. Jordan denied responsibility for border infiltrations and accused Israel of aggression. Jordan portrayed the infiltrators as uneducated persons crossing artificially drawn borders to harvest crops or visit relatives, as had been done for years. U.N. officials in the area attributed most illegal crossings to traditional patterns of smuggling and disputed Israel's contention that the incursions threatened Israel's vital interests. Many U.N. observers even suspected that Israeli kibbutzim, facing economic problems, pilfered from each other and blamed nearby Arabs.[3]

Dulles accepted Jordan's view of the situation but appealed to Jordan and Israel to defuse the tension. U.S. Army intelligence officers considered most border crossings harmless acts of commerce and suspected that Israel engaged in reprisals to satisfy its public opinion or provoke a second round of war that would enable it to gain territory. Dulles placed "considerable responsibility" on Israel and urged Israeli diplomats to "act with maturity." However, he also asked Jordan to prevent exfiltrations and thereby reduce tensions.[4]

Despite his initial evenhandedness, Dulles sharply criticized Israeli reprisals during a series of 1953 incidents. In February, IDF forces attacked Jordanian soldiers at Falama to retaliate for a guerrilla attack on an Israeli railway. Calling Israel's action "a grave danger to the security and stability of the area," Dulles threatened to invoke the Tripartite Declaration of 1950 if Israel continued "to flout friendly counsel and take matters into [its] own hands." Prime Minister David Ben-Gurion told Dulles that the Israeli leader was "astonished and hurt" by this reproach and refused to suspend reprisals.[5]

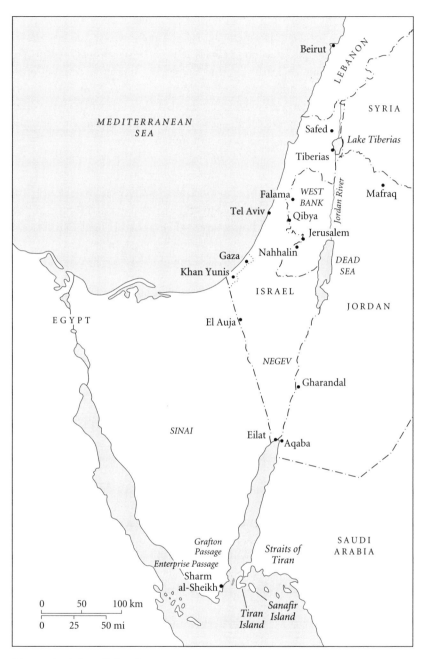

Map 5. Arab-Israeli Borders

U.S. concern with the border deepened in April, when a gun battle erupted between IDF and Jordanian forces in Jerusalem. The U.S. consul at Jerusalem, S. Roger Tyler Jr., considered the incident the "most grimly serious threat to peace between [the] two countries" since 1949. Although Dulles reproached both sides for the episode, he concluded that Israel's reprisals policy earned it "circumstantial responsibility." Under pressure from the American secretary of state, Israeli leaders agreed to renew the local commanders agreement on 8 June, but violence flared in the following months.[6]

Dulles more severely criticized Israeli behavior in the October Qibya incident. After Arab infiltrators murdered an Israeli woman and two children on 13 October, four hundred IDF soldiers retaliated during the night of 14–15 October by attacking the Arab village of Qibya, killing forty-five civilians, demolishing thirty-nine homes, and shelling neighboring villages to prevent interdiction by the Arab Legion. Despite his personal misgivings about the raid, Sharett publicly justified it as a step to protect border residents. He asked how the United States would react if Mexican bandits crossed the border and murdered American citizens.[7]

The Qibya raid provoked criticism in many countries. Echoing other Arab states, Jordan denounced Israel's "acts of butchery" and demanded that Western powers "do something drastic" to punish the Jewish state. U.S. embassy counselor Francis H. Russell told Sharett that the raid "created revulsion among American people [and] was [a] violation of every moral standard." Even U.S. Jewish leaders criticized the raid, and some members of the Israeli Knesset called it a "murderous frenzy" and "Nazi actions." Sharett told the Israeli cabinet that the operation "exposed us in front of the whole world as a gang of bloodsuckers."[8]

To deal with the Qibya situation, Dulles used the United Nations to censure Israel and, in the spirit of evenhandedness, to encourage Jordan and Israel to prevent such incidents in the future. After publicly reproaching Israel, he pushed a 24 November resolution through the Security Council that expressed "the strongest censure" of the raid, called on Israel to avoid such action in the future, and urged Jordan to reduce exfiltrations. Dulles promoted the resolution despite Israeli objections that it "will make peace impossible for a long time to come."[9]

During the Qibya episode, a split developed in State Department thinking about the border controversy. Outraged by the Qibya raid, some of Dulles's advisers criticized his decision to target Jordan, however slightly, in the U.N. resolution. During one debate, Israeli Ambassador to the United States Abba Eban learned, Dulles "vented his wrath" at Assistant Secretary of State Henry A. Byroade for being too firm toward Israel. Thereafter, NEA officials reportedly derided Dulles and spread "nasty rumors" about leading U.S. Jews.[10]

This split within the State Department deepened after a major border incident in March 1954. Israel declared Jordan responsible for an ambush of an Israeli bus in the Negev and retaliated by attacking Nahhalin, killing nine and wounding fourteen civilians. Jordan asked the United States to invoke the Tripartite Declaration against Israel, and Lebanon asked the United States to secure another U.N. resolution. Taking a hard line, Byroade warned the Israeli Minister to Washington, Reuven Shiloah, that "neither side would be allowed [to] involve [the] area in war without having their heads knocked about." Byroade then urged Dulles "to make it abundantly clear to Israel our conviction that her policy of force will not pay, and . . . may force us into a position of open opposition." But Dulles rejected this advice on the reasoning that Jordan contributed to the tension by refusing to make peace. "To read the riot act to the Israeli Ambassador at this stage would produce no useful results," he decided. "We may and should protest. But not deliver any ultimatum."[11]

Rather than censure Israel, Dulles promoted an initiative to arbitrate an Israeli-Jordanian border stabilization deal. British, French, and U.S. officials conceived a plan to increase the personnel and mobility of U.N. observers, demarcate borders and erect physical barriers along them, and regularize innocent transit of Palestinians between the Gaza Strip and Jordan, although Britain and France rejected a U.S. suggestion that Western soldiers guarantee border security. On 22 May 1954 the three Western powers floated the plan in Amman.[12]

Despite a promising beginning, the tripartite border plan faded quickly. In June, Jordan partially approved the plan, and the sponsors submitted it to Israel. Within days, however, tensions flared when a firefight erupted between Israeli and Jordanian soldiers in Jerusalem. Israel then rejected the plan on 29 July, asserting that the armistice contained sufficient provisions to ensure peace, that the proposed strengthening of U.N. machinery would infringe on Israeli sovereignty, that Israel and Jordan alone could demarcate their border, and that Israel would not allow Arab transit across its territory under U.N. management. Israel, the NEA grumbled, had "tripped up" the effort to stabilize the Middle East. The State Department learned anew the firmness dilemma: Israel would not condone any international initiative that treated the country like a mandate.[13]

By 1955, a tenuous calm settled on the Israel-Jordan border. Jordan suppressed exfiltration, and the Anglo-Jordanian treaty seemed to deter major Israeli strikes. Yet Jordanian nationalism mounted against both Britain and Israel, and in early 1956 King Hussein felt compelled to remove British General John Bagot Glubb as commander of the Arab Legion. As Israeli-Egyptian tensions increased, several Jordanian leaders indicated that if Israel attacked Egypt, they would invade Israel. U.S. efforts to pacify the Israel-Jordan border had failed.[14]

Problems on Israel's Border with Egypt

The United States was also drawn into an emerging conflict between Israel and Egypt. At odds over a variety of issues, the two powers engaged in a border war that increased in intensity in 1953–55. As the violence mounted, Dulles took a series of steps to arrest the tension before it escalated into full-scale war. As in the case of Jordan, he initially criticized Israel's reprisals policy but gradually demonstrated some sympathy for the Jewish state's resort to arms. Also as in the case of Jordan, Dulles found it extremely difficult to end the border clashes.

Egyptian-Israeli relations soured in 1953–54 for several reasons. Israeli leaders worried about Egyptian leader Gamal Abdel Nasser's ambitions as he forced Mohammed Naguib to resign, consolidated power in Cairo, and espoused pan-Arab nationalism. As Britain and Egypt moved toward settling their base dispute, Ben-Gurion feared that Egypt's assumption of Britain's military bases, together with promised U.S. military aid to Cairo, would threaten Israeli security. Egypt crushed a conspiracy between Israeli covert agents and Egyptian Jewish saboteurs to disrupt the Anglo-Egyptian base negotiations by conducting terrorist attacks against Western facilities in Cairo and leaving evidence that Egyptians had perpetrated the acts. Tension mounted as Egyptian authorities arrested and hanged two of the conspirators. As chapter 13 will reveal, Egypt's closure of the Suez Canal to Israeli shipping also generated animosity.[15]

As tension mounted over these issues, border violence inflamed the Egyptian-Israeli situation. In 1953–54, Israel charged that Palestinian infiltrators from Egypt had committed murder, theft, and other crimes against Israelis. A military incident occurred at al-Auja in late 1953, and in September 1954, U.N. inspectors found that a recent sapper operation in Israel had originated in Egypt. Despite Nasser's public disavowals, Israeli intelligence concluded that he had organized the raids. The IDF planned a major reprisal against him.[16]

Dulles became involved in this border conflict in the hope of preventing hostilities. He urged Nasser to remove a Palestinian battalion of the Egyptian army from the front, to monitor the movement of explosives, and to cooperate with Israel to seal the border. Dulles also encouraged Sharett, who replaced a retiring Ben-Gurion as prime minister on 9 December 1953, to show restraint toward the border incidents. Nasser pledged to comply with U.S. requests to stop exfiltrations into Israel, but Sharett warned that he could not practice moderation indefinitely in the face of Arab assaults along all of his borders.[17]

The Egyptian-Israeli border situation exploded on 28 February 1955 when IDF units raided an Egyptian army outpost at Gaza in the first planned assault on soldiers by soldiers since the armistices of 1949. Thirty-eight Egyptians, all but one of them soldiers, died in the attack. U.S. diplomats saw the raid as the culmination of Israel's frustrations with border incursions and Western arms aid to Iraq. Egypt was targeted because it boasted the most powerful Arab army, refused to make peace, maintained the canal blockade, and executed the two Jewish saboteurs. To add to the crisis, the raid triggered two days of rioting by Palestinian refugees in Gaza that overwhelmed local police and destroyed U.N. buildings and vehicles.[18]

Dulles rebuked Israel for the raid. His advisers blamed Ben-Gurion's 17 February return to government as minister of defense for triggering the attack. Israel's behavior "works clearly and progressively against her own interests," Dulles intoned to Sharett. Israel must shed its "mistaken belief that she can shoot her way . . . into a peace treaty with her neighbors." Under U.S., British, and French direction, the Security Council passed a resolution on 29 March that criticized Israel and omitted any reference to Egyptian misdeeds.[19]

Dulles also censured the broader Israeli reprisals policy manifest in the raid. Privately, his advisers warned that retaliation such as the Gaza raid would undermine Arab cooperation with the Baghdad Pact, kindle Arab extremism, and diminish prospects of a peace deal. For their part, Israeli intelligence officers interpreted Dulles's "severe denunciation of Israel" as an effort "to appease Egypt" for U.S. security reasons. Thus, Eban asserted to the State Department that Israel's reprisals were justified because the Arab states were waging a war of attrition via cross-border attacks.[20]

Despite Dulles's diplomacy, the border grew more tumultuous. Even before the Security Council passed the 29 March resolution, sabotage and sniping incidents continued in Israel, with deadly results. Nasser gave his word to U.S. officials that he was not involved in these attacks and blamed Palestinian irregulars under command of the mufti, Amin al-Husayni, living in exile in Egypt. As Israelis increasingly began to demand reprisals, Sharett warned that Nasser was "playing with fire." Byroade, who became the U.S. ambassador to Egypt on 10 March, warned Dulles that Israel or Egypt "may pull the temple down." Nasser "cannot take another Gaza-like attack by Israelis lying down."[21]

Hoping to avert another massive military raid, Dulles more actively interceded in the confrontation. He decided to use the 29 March U.N. resolution as a "point of departure for [a] determined effort [to] arrest [the] growing chain [of] incidents" along Israel's borders, especially Gaza. He conveyed to Israel, Egypt, Jordan, Lebanon, and Syria that the "events flowing from Gaza" proved conclusively that border violence would strain, not improve, Arab-Israeli relations.[22]

Over subsequent months, Dulles followed several diplomatic avenues to head off Egyptian-Israeli border violence. First, he encouraged Egypt and Israel to pacify their border under U.N. auspices. General Eedon L. M. Burns, a Canadian who headed the U.N. Truce Supervision Organization in Palestine, proposed that the two powers arrange regular consultations between local commanders, erect barriers along the border, ban irregular troops from the frontier, and establish joint patrols on both sides of the border. Egypt accepted only the joint patrols idea, while Israel accepted all the proposals except that one, on the grounds that such patrols would infringe on its sovereignty. To no avail, Dulles's advisers urged Israel to approve joint patrols by noting that U.S. soldiers had patrolled with communist troops in places like Vienna. State Department officials also could not convince Nasser to agree to a meeting between top-level Israeli and Egyptian officials to jump-start the process.[23]

Second, Dulles opposed an Israeli move to seek redress at the United Nations. Smarting from the Security Council's censure of the Gaza raid, Israel sought a U.N. resolution condemning Egypt for provocative behavior along the border. But Dulles discouraged Israel from raising the issue and refused to endorse a complaint the Jewish state filed over U.S. objections. During debates on 19 April, he blocked a resolution on the reasoning that the Security Council should not weaken the effect of the Gaza resolution. That outcome, U.S. Ambassador to the United Nations Henry Cabot Lodge Jr. estimated, comprised a "severe diplomatic defeat" for Israel.[24]

Third, Dulles reproached both Israel and Egypt when violence flared. In May, for example, an IDF reprisal raid in Gaza provoked a gun battle that resulted in six Egyptian and nine Israeli casualties. U.S. officials admonished both states for their behavior, urged Israel to reconsider the joint patrols idea, and pressed Nasser to agree to high-level negotiations. Such diplomacy not only failed to curb the violence but also drew criticism from both Sharett and Nasser, who demanded complete U.S. backing of their policies.[25]

Fourth, Dulles discouraged other powers from becoming involved in the Israeli-Egyptian dispute. Saudi Arabia pledged "solidarity with Egypt" as it resisted "repeated perfidious aggressions by Israel," and Syria and Iraq vowed to fight with Egypt in a general war against Israel. Britain warned that treaties obliged it to defend Egypt against invasion and recommended reaffirmation of the Tripartite Declaration. Dulles, however, discouraged the Arab states from joining the fray and distanced the United States from the pledges inherent in the Tripartite Declaration.[26]

Unfortunately for the United States, a final push to end the border crisis through U.N. diplomacy sputtered in summer 1955. After intricate negotiations, Egyptian and Israeli military officers agreed in principle to meet jointly with General Burns to discuss border pacification. But after several weeks of delay, the meeting on 29 June immediately mired down in squabbles over the agenda and the ranks of the attending officers. With U.S. backing, sporadic talks followed in July and August, but those meetings were marked by discord, prone to frequent suspensions, and canceled by Nasser after three Egyptian soldiers died in a firefight on 22 August.[27]

The persistent border confrontations escalated into a crisis in late August. To avenge the Egyptian deaths of 22 August, Nasser dispatched twenty-four commandos to infiltrate Israel. At the risk of compromising sources, a U.S. intelligence officer in Cairo appealed to Nasser to cancel the operation. He pledged compliance, but ten commandos, reportedly out of radio contact, committed acts of terrorism that left seventeen Israelis dead over six days. Sharett rejected a cease-fire suggested by the State Department as long as "Egyptian gangs running wild" perpetrated "beastly and inhuman acts" on his people. On 31 August, he ordered the IDF to conduct a major reprisal against Egyptian facilities at Khan Yunis. One Israeli soldier and at least twenty-five Egyptian soldiers and twenty-five civilians perished in the fighting, and Israeli war jets shot down two Egyptian Vampires flying over Israel on 1 September.[28]

Although he had censured Israel's earlier reprisal in Gaza, Dulles conspicuously refrained from collaring Israel on this occasion. Apparently aware of Israel's intentions, Byroade took the extraordinary step of telephoning from Cairo hours before the assault to urge Dulles to telephone Sharett and advise restraint. But Dulles opted merely to phone the U.S. ambassador to Tel Aviv, Edward B. Lawson, asking him to see Sharett. Dulles presumably recognized that the circumstances warranted Israel's impending retaliation.[29]

In any event, U.S. officials tried to contain the violence at Khan Yunis. On 1–3 September, Jordan and Syria announced that they would fight beside Egypt if general hostilities erupted, Syria advanced troops to its border, and Israel ordered a general mobilization as an artillery duel raged along the Egyptian-Israeli frontier. U.S. officials endorsed a cease-fire brokered by General Burns on 4 September and pushed a supporting resolution through the Security Council four days later. The causes of the crisis remained unresolved, however, and the violence spoiled the climate for peacemaking.[30]

Problems on Israel's Northern Borders

While distracted by the border wars involving Jordan and Egypt, Dulles experienced mixed results in trying to contain violence along Israel's borders with Lebanon and Syria. In the case of Lebanon, minimal diplomatic intercession by U.S. officials helped prevent the outbreak of violence. In the case of Syria, however, tensions simmered despite U.S. restraints, boiling over during a major military engagement in 1955.

The State Department intervened to preserve tranquillity along the Israel-Lebanon border when incidents threatened to disrupt it. In April 1955, for example, the Lebanese army arrested three Israelis who had crossed the border equipped with weapons, military maps, and rations. Arguing that the three men were private citizens, Israel sent forces into south Lebanon, seized nine Lebanese civilians, and offered to swap captives. The State Department convinced Israel to release the Lebanese without condition and then persuaded Lebanon to release the Israelis.[31]

U.S. officials also became involved in a more complicated dispute in September. After infiltrators from Lebanon attacked an Israeli bus near Safed, Israel asked Lebanon for permission to retaliate against Palestinian refugees in south Lebanon. Lebanese authorities criticized the attack on the bus and ordered all Palestinians to evacuate land within ten kilometers of Israel but refused to permit an Israeli reprisal. The State Department urged the Israelis to show restraint, and they held back. The department was able to prevent hostilities in a dispute in which neither protagonist felt that war would advance its interests.[32]

The Syrian-Israeli border proved a more intractable problem for U.S. diplomats. In June 1953, tensions flared over three demilitarized zones (DMZs) established by the United Nations in 1949. Israeli forces occupied large sectors of the zones, and understaffed U.N. inspection teams proved unable to investigate such developments or to enforce rulings. In bilateral and U.N.-sponsored talks, Israel and Syria discussed liquidating the DMZs by drawing a permanent border, but disputes over water rights, security of settlements, and landownership prevented agreement. In early 1954, Syria argued that pronouncements by Israeli leaders, IDF troop concentrations in northern Israel, and two Israeli gunboat attacks on Syrian targets near Tiberias revealed Israeli aggressive intent. U.S. officials tried to contain this animosity and prevent war.[33]

The difficulties of negotiating a resolution to this situation increased during an Israeli-Syrian confrontation over the fate of five Israeli soldiers captured by Syria after crossing the border with sabotage equipment in December 1954. In January 1955, the Israeli-Syrian Mixed Armistice Commission (MAC) censured Israel for sending the soldiers and directed Syria to return them, but Syria kept the men in detention, and one committed suicide. To no avail, the State Department asked Syria to comply with the MAC ruling and release the soldiers. As the men remained in captivity, bellicosity soared among the Israeli people, and the IDF conducted a small October raid into Syria.[34]

The border situation exploded in violence when Israel conducted a massive raid against Syria on 11 December 1955. Advancing by land and sea, six hundred Israeli soldiers attacked Syrian positions to the east and north of Lake Tiberias. Fifty-two Syrians were killed, and thirty-two were captured or declared missing. Israel claimed that the attack was provoked by Syrian firing on an Israeli police boat on the lake on 10 December, but U.S. officials found this charge "unimpressive and unconvincing" since an operation of such scale would have required at least a week of planning. They concluded that Ben-Gurion had ordered the attack to demonstrate his resolve, avenge Syria's detention of the captured soldiers, and counter an October Egyptian-Syrian defense agreement.[35]

Reacting to the raid, Dulles imposed a measured punishment on Israel. Eisenhower authorized the secretary of state to criticize the operation and to suspend an impending deal to provide Israel with weapons. Dulles also supported a U.N. Security Council resolution, passed on 19 January 1956, censuring Israel for the attack. To assuage Syria, he expressed "deep regrets" over the violence and indicated that he "deeply deplore[d] the recurrence of retaliatory action."[36]

However, Dulles refused to take additional steps to punish Israel, as Arab states demanded. He refused requests from Syrian Prime Minister Said el-Ghazzi to invoke the Tripartite Declaration against Israel, cancel economic aid to Israel, and expel Israel from the United Nations. In a 19 January 1956 resolution, in fact, the Security Council mentioned Syrian cease-fire infractions that preceded the Tiberias raid. Chief of Intelligence Major Abdel Hamid Sarraj, a notable figure in the Syrian army, told U.S. envoys that Syria remained dissatisfied with the resolution and "would be satisfied only with [the] disappearance of Israel."[37]

Conclusion

As the Arab-Israeli border situation deteriorated in 1953–55, Eisenhower and Dulles became deeply involved. Dulles tried to persuade the various parties to eschew violence, to negotiate border pacification arrangements, and to consider U.N. schemes for reducing tension. As hostilities mounted, he pressured Arab statesmen to prevent exfiltrations into Israel, criticized Israel for certain reprisals, and supported U.N. resolutions that censured perpetrators of violence. By 1955, Dulles found himself more involved in the Arab-Israeli border controversy than he had intended or desired, and he remained unable to resolve the conflict or to avoid the anger of the states involved.

U.S. diplomacy in the border controversy revealed an important transition in State Department views on Israel. Consistent with the department's traditional disposition to view Israel critically, many officials initially censured Israel's reprisal policy as unjustified and provocative. By 1955, however, Dulles tempered this feeling with a begrudging recognition that Israel deserved to retaliate against certain perpetrators of violence. This recognition reflected Dulles's personal disposition to deal evenhandedly with Arab-Israeli matters and marked a milestone in the State Department's institutional acceptance of Israel as a state.

As Eisenhower and Dulles became more involved in the border situation, they unintentionally contributed to the mounting Arab-Israeli tensions by advancing U.S. security interests in the Middle East. For example, the decision to arm Arab states as a means of bolstering the Baghdad Pact increased Israeli insecurity, which became manifest in its reprisal policy. U.S. efforts to facilitate

British withdrawal from Egypt and to groom revolutionary Egypt as a security partner had a similar effect.[38] Determination to remain on friendly terms with both Israel and the Arab states for Cold War reasons restrained the United States from compelling either side to submit to the other.

U.S. involvement in the border conflicts was marked mostly by failure. Dulles made a positive difference in only one situation, by deterring Israel and Lebanon from allowing minor incidents to escalate into serious conflict. His involvement helped avert outbreaks of major hostilities between Israel and Jordan, Egypt, and Syria, but the tension in those relationships intensified over time. As American diplomacy proved insufficient to arrest—let alone reverse—the region's march to war, Eisenhower and Dulles concluded that they must adopt a more interventionist approach to the region by attempting to initiate a peace process focused on certain Arab-Israeli disputes.

13

CORNUCOPIA OF CONFLICT
Water, Jerusalem, Refugees, and Trade, 1953–1955

As violence flared along Israel's borders, several other disputes with origins in the 1940s also destabilized the Arab-Israeli situation in the early years of the Dwight D. Eisenhower administration. Conflicts simmered over the proper disposition of the Jordan Valley water, the status of Jerusalem, the rights of Palestinian refugees, and Arab economic warfare against Israel. President Eisenhower and Secretary of State John Foster Dulles sought impartially to resolve these conflicts and thereby promote Arab-Israeli amity, improve relations with all Middle East states, and stabilize the region against Soviet meddling.

The U.S. quest to mitigate the Arab-Israeli disputes, however, was laden with difficulty and complexity. First, Eisenhower and Dulles found it extremely difficult to resolve Arab-Israeli disputes without favoring one side or the other. American leaders were unable to make progress toward a settlement or to avoid tensions with both sides. Second, the quest to defuse the Arab-Israeli conflict occasionally clashed with the larger ambition of Soviet containment, and Eisenhower and Dulles deemed it necessary to privilege containment over Arab-Israeli accord. Moreover, detecting evidence of rising Soviet activism in the Middle East, the U.S. leaders deepened their role in the region but found it hard to achieve their objectives.

Jordan River Water

At the dawn of the Eisenhower presidency, one Arab-Israeli quarrel concerned control of and access to the Middle East's precious freshwater. Eisenhower saw in the water controversy both a threat to the stability of the region and an opportunity to achieve an Arab-Israeli agreement that would promote regional development and provide a foundation for peace. He launched a major diplomatic initiative to persuade the Arab states and Israel to approve an impartial technical development plan that would benefit all parties. His aides made remarkable progress in selling the scheme but ultimately proved unable to secure a formal agreement.

Debates over freshwater in the Palestine-Israel area centered on two rivers. The Jordan River, the most prized waterway, flowed from springs and precipitation runoff in northern Israel, southern Lebanon, and southern Syria, formed Lake Huleh in northern Israel, and ran south to Lake Tiberias (also known as the Sea of Galilee or the Kinneret) and then the Dead Sea. After 1948, the Israeli-Syrian and the northern Israeli-Jordanian borders roughly followed the river, while the kingdom of Jordan, once it occupied the West Bank, controlled the southern stretch of the river and the Dead Sea. The Yarmouk River flowed westward along the Syrian-Jordanian border to the Jordan River south of Lake Tiberias.[1] (See map 3.)

The Harry S. Truman administration took notice when the Arab states and Israel began quarreling over these waterways in 1949–52. The State Department advised Israel, Jordan, Syria, and Lebanon to coordinate their water usage under a regional development scheme, but conflicts such as the Huleh episode prevented progress. In 1951, the department encouraged Jordan and Israel to negotiate a bilateral deal for shared usage of the Jordan River, but no settlement materialized. Instead, Israel began drawing irrigation water from the Jordan River north of Tiberias, while Jordan planned an irrigation dam on the Yarmouk.[2]

Eisenhower and Dulles moved at once to solve the water controversy. On the negative side, they feared that the riparian states, if left to themselves, would pursue uncoordinated and inefficient development plans and even come to blows. On the positive side, the U.S. leaders saw a unique opportunity to promote Arab-Israeli cooperation and economic development for local peoples. A regional water scheme, Dulles observed, would "provide [the] greatest good to [the] greatest number" of people.[3]

In summer 1953, NEA officials promoted a cooperative venture between Jordan and Israel based on a technical study conducted by engineers from the Tennessee Valley Authority (TVA). The study concluded that Jordan's plan for the Yarmouk River would cost sixty-six million dollars and take seven years of construction time but would result in a reservoir with insufficient capacity to meet the kingdom's needs. For a mere three million dollars over two years, by contrast, engineers could construct a canal from the Yarmouk River to Lake Tiberias and a retention dam on the lake that would serve the water needs of both Israel and Jordan and enable the resettlement of more than four hundred thousand Palestinian refugees in Jordan. The scheme assumed that Israel would grant Jordan access to water in Lake Tiberias.[4]

Dulles stressed to Jordan and Israel the economic and political advantages of bilateral water development, but the two countries rejected the idea. Intent on guarding its sovereignty, Israel refused to grant Jordan access to Lake Tiberias.

After speaking to Jordanian leaders, the U.S. chargé in Amman, Andrew G. Lynch, reported that "economic sense is not the criterion by which they reach decisions." The Jordanian shared the Arab axiom, as voiced by a Lebanese official, that any leader who made a deal with Israel "would fall before sunset. King Abdullah, [the] last man who tried it, was riddled with bullets."[5]

As the NEA had feared, conflict ensued in the absence of a regional development plan. In September 1953, Israel started excavating a canal at Banat Yaacov to divert Jordan River water for electricity production and economic development. Syria charged that the canal project violated the 1949 armistice, treaded on the rights of Palestinian landowners, and gained Israel a military advantage. On 23 September, the United Nations Truce Supervision Organization (UNTSO) chairman, Major General Vagn Bennike of Denmark, directed Israel to suspend its work. Suspicious that the State Department had influenced Bennike, however, Israeli Prime Minister David Ben-Gurion defied the ruling and accelerated the excavation at Banat Yaacov. Because Israel's move threatened the goal of regional development, Dulles endorsed Bennike's finding and quietly suspended economic aid to Israel.[6]

Israel relented on the Banat Yaacov project only after the Qibya raid earned the country international reproach. Angered by the raid, Dulles publicized his earlier suspension of aid to Israel. Bothered by the episode, Foreign Minister Moshe Sharett convinced the Israeli cabinet, over Ben-Gurion's opposition, to stop work at Banat Yaacov if ordered by the United Nations. When the Security Council resolved on 27 October that Israel should suspend work on the canal, Israel pledged to comply, and Dulles resumed economic aid.[7]

The Banat Yaacov canal issue festered, however, and Dulles became tangled in it. Israel asked the Security Council to approve its project, while Syria requested a resolution declaring the project a violation of the armistice. To solve the controversy evenhandedly, Dulles advanced a resolution that simply urged both parties to honor UNTSO decisions. When the Security Council voted in January 1954, however, the Soviets vetoed this resolution because Syria disapproved it. Impartiality "only incurs the wrath of both sides," Dulles fumed. "We could only win the friendship of either side if we deliberately devised policies to 'hurt' the other side."[8]

To escape this predicament, Eisenhower and Dulles launched an ambitious initiative to achieve a regional water usage agreement. They based their program on an impartial, technical study, known as the Jordan Valley Plan (JVP), composed by TVA engineers under a UNRWA contract. Unlike the first TVA plan for Israel and Jordan, the JVP provided a blueprint for maximizing usage of water resources by all Middle East states and for devoting those resources to refugee relief projects.[9]

To lead such an initiative, Eisenhower appointed Eric Johnston, chairman of the Advisory Board for International Development, as a personal representative, with the rank of ambassador and a military plane at his disposal. In October 1953, the president tasked Johnston with promoting the JVP to Jordan, Syria, Lebanon, and Israel by indicating that U.S. economic and military aid hinged on their cooperation. Johnston saw the JVP not merely as an engineering project but as "a means of constructing the foundation on which peace in the area may ultimately be built."[10]

Despite such optimism, Johnston faced enormous difficulties. Israel had recently refused Jordanian access to Lake Tiberias. The Qibya raid, the U.S. chargé in Amman, Talcott Seelye, noted, "dashed to smithereens" any chance that Jordan would talk with Israel about the water issue. Egyptian officials said that Israel's reprisals made it hard to negotiate. Envoys from Lebanon, Iraq, and Egypt told Dulles that Johnston "should be recalled gracefully" because of his membership in the pro-Zionist American Christian Palestine Committee.[11]

Despite such handicaps, Johnston made remarkable progress toward a compromise settlement of the water issue during a series of visits to the Middle East. By November 1953, he had elicited pledges from Lebanon, Jordan, Syria, Egypt, and Israel not to reject out of hand the JVP. In spring 1954, Arab and Israeli leaders affirmed the principle of unified water development under international supervision. In late 1954, Johnston convinced both sides to agree to storage of water from the Yarmouk and Jordan Rivers in Lake Tiberias.[12]

Johnston reached an even bigger milestone in early 1955. He persuaded the foreign ministers of Lebanon, Syria, and Jordan to approve a "tentative memorandum of agreement," a good-faith but nonbinding accord that allocated one-third of the available water of the Jordan and Yarmouk Rivers to the Arab states and the balance to Israel. The Arab states also conceded that Israel would be permitted to use its water outside the Jordan Basin, that the water would be stored in Lake Tiberias under a neutral water master, and that Israel could resume work on the diversion canal at Banat Yaacov. As incentives, Johnston offered Jordan twenty-one million dollars in U.S. aid to build a storage dam on the Yarmouk River and Dulles offered Lebanon a five-million-dollar loan.[13]

Israel initially rejected the memorandum of agreement, however. Ben-Gurion, who retired from the prime ministry on 9 December 1953, confided to his diary that Johnston sought "to impose some kind of American mandate on Israel. . . . I support keeping Israeli sovereignty at any price." Sharett, who succeeded Ben-Gurion as the Israeli leader, refused to grant Arab states access to Lake Tiberias, submit to international supervision, or yield control of Jordan River water. Through seven intense meetings in early 1955, Johnston pled with Sharett to concede, but he remained firm. "It would be a sad day if Ambassador Johnston and I had to part company," he commented, "but Israel cannot give away its vital resources."[14]

The JVP quickly faded after Israel hesitated to accept the plan. Furious at Israel's February 1955 Gaza raid, Jordan, Syria, and Lebanon retracted their approvals of the JVP. Syria and Lebanon also recanted because they realized that the plan would provide Jordan commercial gains, to the detriment of the other Arab countries. Johnston persuaded Sharett to approve the JVP in July, but this agreement came too late to assuage the Arab states. Border clashes in August and the Soviet-Egyptian arms deal in September inflamed passions on both sides. In October, the Arab League voted to postpone discussion of the JVP.[15]

Once the JVP collapsed, U.S. officials found themselves in the midst of another conflict over water. Israel announced that on 1 March 1956 it would begin diverting water from the Jordan River within the limits proposed by the JVP. Still smarting from the December 1955 Lake Tiberias raid, Syria vowed to resist such action with military force, and Egypt, Saudi Arabia, Jordan, Iraq, and Lebanon pledged to back Syria militarily. "There might well be a war for the Jordan waters," special assistant to the U.S. president Harold Stassen feared. To head off such a calamity, U.S. officials warned Israel that they would hold it accountable for hostilities related to Banat Yaacov and told the Arab states that the United States would oppose an attack on Israel.[16]

U.S. officials used the war scare to make one final push for the JVP, encouraging Middle East states to approve the plan not only to end the present showdown but also to resolve the underlying dispute and secure economic benefits through cooperation. Ben-Gurion, who had returned to the prime ministry in November 1955, eased the threat of war by suspending operations at Banat Yaacov but asserted the right to resume work at any time and showed little interest in the JVP. Echoing other Arab leaders, Egyptian Premier Gamal Abdel Nasser declared the plan "completely dead and abandoned." The U.S. effort to solve the water issue foundered.[17]

Jerusalem

The Eisenhower administration also inherited a controversy regarding Jerusalem. Before 1953, Christian churches and most Arab states had promoted internationalization of the city as provided in U.N. resolutions, while Israel and Jordan sought recognition of their de facto partition of the city. In 1953–55, Dulles was forced to decide whether to promote the U.N. ideal of international control of Jerusalem, whether to endorse the transfer of the Israeli Foreign Ministry to the city, and whether to allow U.S. diplomats to conduct business there. Despite his best efforts to avoid controversy, he became enmeshed in the conflict over the city.

Dulles quickly grasped the Jerusalem dilemma. On the one hand, he opposed Israeli-Jordanian annexation on the reasoning that "the world religious community has claims in Jerusalem which take precedence over the political claims of any particular nation." On the other hand, to internationalize the city would require foreign military forces, a burden the Pentagon wished neither to bear nor to entrust to the Soviets. To resolve this dilemma, Dulles proposed recognizing Israeli-Jordanian political control of Jerusalem but establishing "functional internationalization" of the city's holy places.[18] (See map 4.)

Dulles's approach failed to resolve the controversy over the city's status. The Vatican and the Arab states firmly rejected the concept of "functional internationalization." Jordan and Israel resolutely opposed a Vatican proposal to demilitarize Jerusalem. To no avail, Arab states protested U.N. inaction to enforce its resolutions. When the debate stalemated in 1955, internationalization of any variety was a dead idea.[19]

Dulles also faced the delicate issue of Israel's claim of Jerusalem as its capital. In early 1953, Sharett told the American secretary of state that Israel would move its Foreign Ministry to Jerusalem by June because the ministry needed quarters near other ministries. Sharett asked Dulles "to discontinue urging Israel not to move." Worried that the transfer would antagonize the Arab states, however, Dulles advised indefinite delay. In a meeting with Sharett during a May 1953 visit to Israel, Dulles repeated his opposition to the transfer.[20]

Despite such statements, Israeli officials wishfully concluded that Dulles would accept a transfer in fact. In a social encounter in Israel, Dulles expressed to an Israeli official his desire that if the Israelis "did move the Ministry to Jerusalem, we would not do it while he was around; it would embarrass him greatly." Sharett interpreted this remark as a hint that Dulles would approve a transfer if it occurred after his visit. Sharett's conclusion was reinforced by Dulles's June remark that he most highly valued international control specifically of the holy places.[21]

Confident that Dulles would not protest, Sharett announced on 10 July that the Foreign Ministry would relocate to Jerusalem three days later. He declared that geographic distance had "impaired the Ministry's effective discharge of its primary function," that U.N. resolutions had proven "inherently unimplementable," and that Israel would not object to international control of the holy places. Sharett hoped that this concession, together with the interval of time since Dulles's tour, would forestall a strong U.S. reaction.[22]

Sharett's announcement, however, annoyed Dulles and caused U.S.-Israeli discord. Fearing that the transfer would exacerbate regional tensions, Dulles protested that it would "prejudice the United Nations' freedom of choice in considering the future of this historic and venerated area." When Sharett alluded to Dulles's May remarks, the U.S. secretary of state explained that Sharett had badly misconstrued them. The United States, Dulles declared, would not recognize Jerusalem as Israel's capital or move its embassy there. To indicate his resolve, Dulles instructed the embassy in Tel Aviv to conduct business with Israel only at a Foreign Ministry liaison office in Tel Aviv, to decline invitations to official functions in Jerusalem, and to encourage other embassies to act likewise. Sharett delicately protested that U.S. envoys must not "treat the capital as an area 'out of bounds.'" U.S. policy "is blasphemy," Ben-Gurion more bluntly declared. "Christ himself came to Jerusalem. So did Dulles, a religious man."[23]

Despite Dulles's initial reaction, U.S. opposition to the transfer remained measured. When Saudi Arabia, Iraq, Lebanon, Egypt, Syria, and Yemen demanded a more vigorous U.S. reaction, Acting U.S. Secretary of State Walter Bedell Smith deplored the move but added that internationalization as envisioned in 1947 was dead. The State Department also confessed that it lacked the ambition to pursue the issue and even discouraged Israel from raising international control of the holy places during the current U.N. session because doing so might disrupt deliberations on Korea. Despite Dulles's protests, Sharett realized, the United States would tolerate his move.[24]

Dulles also amended the restrictions on U.S. diplomats when U.S. interests demanded such action. When the boycott of Jerusalem hampered his mid-1954 initiatives to pacify the Jordanian-Israeli border, Dulles authorized embassy staff to conduct business in Jerusalem if they informed the Foreign Ministry that U.S. policy toward Jerusalem remained unchanged. He also permitted U.S. envoys to call on the prime minister but not the foreign minister in Jerusalem, a somewhat puzzling directive given that Sharett held both offices from 9 December 1953 to 2 November 1955. Counselor in Tel Aviv Francis H. Russell first met Sharett, wearing the hat of prime minister, in Jerusalem on 10 August 1954.[25]

The 26 July 1955 Israeli elections further jolted Dulles's restrictions. The polling compelled Sharett to resign as prime minister on 15 August 1955, although the Knesset directed him to remain in office until November while Ben-Gurion formed a cabinet. Dulles anticipated that prohibiting visits to Sharett in Jerusalem once he became only foreign minister would divert influence to Ben-Gurion at a time when the U.S. secretary of state preferred Sharett's moderation to Ben-Gurion's hawkishness. Dulles therefore authorized the U.S. ambassador to call in secret on the foreign minister in Jerusalem provided that he reciprocated with visits to Tel Aviv. The principled U.S. refusal to recognize Jerusalem as Israel's capital broke down at the practical level.[26]

Palestinian Refugees

Eisenhower and Dulles also faced a difficult situation regarding Palestinian refugees. On the humanitarian issue of satisfying the physical needs of the refugees, the U.S. leaders succeeded in extending U.N. relief operations. But trouble arose in the larger political dispute when the United States shifted in favor of resettlement of refugees in Arab countries rather than repatriation to Israel. Dulles tried to wrest concessions from Israel to soothe Arab resentment at this policy, but Israel refused to yield, and the Arab states remained upset.

The refugee problem remained deadlocked in early 1953. The United Nations Relief and Works Agency for Palestine Refugees in the Near East (UNRWA) counted 868,133 refugees, including 475,000 in Jordan, 206,000 in Gaza, 103,000 in Lebanon, and 86,000 in Syria. Arab leaders repeated their shopworn demands that Israel repatriate the refugees, while Israel stubbornly insisted that the Arab states resettle the people. The State Department noted that the refugees were languishing in squalor, "an embittered group, subject to subversion."[27]

Eisenhower and Dulles turned first to the issue of ensuring subsistence relief to the refugees. The UNRWA was scheduled to expire on 30 June 1954, and members of Congress threatened to withhold U.S. funds from the agency unless it reduced relief rolls. A solution, Representative Frances P. Bolton (R-Ohio), chairwoman of the House Foreign Affairs Committee subcommittee on the Near East and Africa, declared, "can and must be found." While the State Department worked on that task, Dulles resolved to extend the UNRWA's mandate for humanitarian and security reasons. With tenuous congressional backing, he convinced the General Assembly to extend the UNRWA's mandate until June 1955 (and subsequently until June 1960).[28]

When contemplating the political aspects of the refugee problem, Eisenhower and Dulles deemed resettlement of refugees in Arab states to be the only practical solution. Dulles recognized that Israel would never allow massive repatriation and suspected that Arab leaders kept "the problem alive as a political weapon against Israel and against the West." Thus, he concluded, "a great majority of the refugee population must find its future in Syria or Iraq." Accordingly, the State Department planned economic development schemes to facilitate refugee resettlement in Arab states, blocked an Arab quest for a U.N. censure of Israel's refusal to repatriate refugees, and even suggested that the UNRWA curtail relief to force Arab states to absorb Palestinians. Scholar Mohammed K. Shadid observes that Dulles failed to appreciate the refugees' intense devotion to their native land; however, U.S. officials probably understood this devotion but simply could not accommodate it.[29]

To make resettlement seem more acceptable to the Arab states, Dulles sought to force Israel to compensate the refugees in some way. Although Israel had accepted compensation in principle in 1949, deep disagreements remained in 1953 over the amounts, methods, and conditions of payment, and Israel made clear that it could not afford compensation unless the United States provided substantial financial aid. NEA officials conceived a scheme, vaguely reminiscent of the G.I. Bill, to create a national corporation that would collect payments from Israel, borrow capital from the U.S. Treasury, and compensate refugees by issuing credits or loans to build homes, buy land, or begin businesses in Arab states. But U.S. officials predicted that such a program would exhaust U.S. foreign aid resources and dissatisfy Arab leaders who demanded Israeli sacrifice.[30]

State Department officials explored several options to facilitate Israeli compensation. They proposed, as "the moral equivalent" of repatriation, that Israel earmark for refugee compensation all funds saved from any future reopening of the Suez Canal to Israeli shipping or that Israel yield its share of Jordan River water for the welfare of refugees. The department also considered the prospect of linking West Germany's promised reparations to Israel to Israel's promised compensation to refugees. Israel resisted these ideas, however, and the State Department dropped them.[31]

U.S. officials made modest progress only in a scheme to compel Israel to release blocked bank accounts of Palestinians. After months of negotiations, the Palestine Conciliation Commission and the UNRWA arbitrated an agreement in which Israel would release the blocked accounts at a rate of one pound sterling ($2.80) per Israeli pound to those qualified Palestinians who submitted applications by 31 May 1953. Israel agreed to pay some $14 million under the scheme. U.S. officials noted, however, that Arab extremists discouraged eligible refugees from applying for reimbursements and that banks in Jordan refused to cooperate in the transfer of funds.[32]

Economic Warfare

In consultation with Eisenhower, Dulles also confronted tensions regarding Arab economic warfare against Israel. In 1953, the Arab League maintained a boycott against Israel, Egypt closed the Suez Canal and the Gulf of Aqaba to Israel-bound ships, and other Arab states interfered with potential Israeli trade. Israel charged that these restrictions were illegal and belligerent and demanded U.S. action to abolish them. But Dulles remained inactive on the reasoning that intercession would not change Arab policy but would only alienate Arab leaders.

The boycott represented the clearest manifestation of Arab economic warfare against Israel. What had begun as haphazard efforts by individual Arab states to isolate Israel economically took on an air of design and permanence in 1952, when the Arab League established a Boycott Office in Damascus to punish foreign firms doing business with Israel. The Boycott Office identified firms that maintained branches in Israel, distributed Israeli exports, or employed Israeli agents to import goods to the Middle East, and the office denied those firms permission to conduct any business in Arab states. As an incentive to cooperate, the Boycott Office allowed firms accused of wrongdoing to escape punishment by halting their offensive actions.³³

The boycott incensed Israel. Combined with Iraq and Jordan's closure of the Haifa pipeline and various states' denial of port rights to ships and planes that called in Israel, the boycott cost Israel more than sixty million dollars in lost revenues. Israeli officials repeatedly appealed to the United States, Britain, and France to move against the boycotts and blacklists as violations of the armistice agreements.³⁴

Although the boycott troubled Dulles, he declined to act against it. On the one hand, the boycott contradicted free trade ideals, retarded regional economic development, and diminished the chance of a political settlement. On the other hand, Dulles's advisers deemed the boycott "legally excusable" because some Arab states remained at war with Israel. Furthermore, American officials realized that the United States had imposed similar restrictions against the Soviet bloc and predicted that outside interference seemed likely to alienate Arab leaders without changing the situation. As a result, the State Department took only the occasional mild step of protesting the blacklisting of certain U.S. firms as "unwarranted." As anticipated, such efforts had little effect.³⁵

Egypt's closure of the Suez Canal to Israel-bound ships also caused tension. Israel charged that the closure violated rulings by the U.N. mediator, the Mixed Armistice Commission, and the Security Council and caused intolerable losses in trade. After Israel signed a 1954 oil deal with Iran, denial of the canal cost the Jewish state an estimated ten million dollars per year in lost revenue. Anticipating that Egypt would impose additional obstacles after Britain agreed to withdraw from the Suez Canal Zone in 1954, Israeli leaders launched a firestorm of protests at Western states and at the United Nations.³⁶

Dulles remained reluctant to take up Israel's case, continuing to believe that criticism of the restrictions would only alienate Egyptian leaders. Thus, he repeatedly discouraged Israel from raising the controversy at the United Nations on the grounds that debates would complicate the delicate Anglo-Egyptian base negotiations or aggravate the Banat Yaacov controversy. Although he disapproved of Egypt's restrictions in principle, Assistant Secretary of State Henry A. Byroade told Israeli Ambassador Abba Eban in December 1953 that "this was a poor time to summon Egypt before the bar of world opinion."³⁷

Against their wishes, U.S. officials were forced into action on the canal in 1954. After Egypt detained a number of ships, Israel formally complained to the Security Council that Egypt continued to defy the council's September 1951 resolution. Egypt countered with a complaint that Israel had violated other council resolutions, and both powers sought U.S. backing. Unable to prevent council action, Dulles supported a resolution critical of Egypt, but the Soviet Union, consonant with Nikita Khrushchev's strategy of impressing Arab nationalists, vetoed the measure. Dulles worried that Cairo felt indebted to Moscow and consequently refused Israeli entreaties to freeze economic aid to Egypt until it opened the canal.[38]

Israel provoked a confrontation over the canal in September 1954. The five-hundred-ton *Bat Galim*, flying the Star of David, entered the canal en route from Eritrea to Haifa, carrying meat, hides, and plywood. Eban admitted to U.S. officials that Israel had dispatched the ship to force a U.N. debate on the issue. The Egyptian navy seized the *Bat Galim* and arrested the crew. Israel protested to the Security Council in September and October 1954, February and August 1955, and September 1956, charging Egypt with "piracy" and "lawless conduct" in violation of the Suez Canal Convention of 1888 and the Security Council resolution of 1951.[39]

U.S. officials regretted Israel's recourse to such action. They suspected that Israel had dispatched the ship to disrupt the pending Anglo-Egyptian base deal and to pressure Eisenhower during the U.S. midterm elections. American leaders doubted that Egypt would concede under pressure and predicted another Soviet veto of any resolution critical of Egypt. Thus, the State Department urged Egypt to release the ship and crew but also criticized Israel's move as provocative, delayed Security Council hearings, and urged Israel to negotiate directly with Cairo. Egypt released the *Bat Galim* crew in January 1955 but kept the cargo and pressed the ship into its navy in August 1956.[40]

Another confrontation emerged in the early 1950s over Israeli transit rights in the Gulf of Aqaba. The gulf offered a potential trade route between Israel's southern coast and the Red Sea, bypassing the Suez Canal. But ships could enter the gulf only through the Grafton or Enterprise Passages, both of which flowed between the Egyptian Sinai and Tiran Island, less than four miles to the east. Sovereignty over Tiran was unclear, but most experts considered it Egyptian or Saudi. In 1950–51, Egypt had occupied the island with Saudi approval, positioned coastal artillery batteries along the straits, and closed the straits to Israeli warships and to any Israel-bound vessel bearing weapons, automobiles, metals, oil products, or foodstuffs. Cumbersome application procedures discouraged shipping companies from plying the straits with any goods. The State Department considered Egypt's blockade legal since both channels lay within three miles of Egypt or the Egyptian-occupied Tiran Island.[41]

A row developed over the Aqaba blockade during the August 1955 Egyptian-Israeli border crisis. Israel hinted that it would use force to break the blockade, and France proposed that the Western powers jointly press Cairo to open the gulf. Because such a démarche would damage relations with Nasser, however, Dulles rejected it. Foreshadowing the Suez-Sinai War of 1956, Sharett declared that Israel would defend its right of "free passage through this international channel, at whatever time and by whatever method it will see fit."[42]

Conclusion

From its inception, the Eisenhower administration faced Arab-Israeli disputes regarding Jordan River water, Jerusalem, Palestinian refugees, and Arab economic restrictions against Israel. These conflicts threatened to undermine the U.S. objective of a stable and peaceful Middle East integrated into the Western orbit. If unresolved, Arab-Israeli disputes might turn the Arab world against the West or provide an opening for Soviet power to enter the region. Indeed, the Soviet Union's vetoes of U.N. resolutions critical of Egypt and Syria and the Soviet arms deal with Egypt seemed to validate U.S. fears regarding Soviet political expansion into the Middle East. Dulles sought to settle or contain these disputes, thereby mitigating the Arab-Israeli conflict and finding some basis for promoting permanent peace.

Eisenhower and Dulles initially centered their attention on the conflict over water. They formulated the JVP to avert hostilities, promote Arab-Israeli cooperation, and perhaps facilitate a general peace. In short, the United States hoped that an impartial, technical solution to an economic development puzzle would prove acceptable to the adversaries and provide residual political benefits. Despite making progress in promoting the JVP, however, Johnston proved unable to finalize a deal before his momentum stalled. In the end, he failed to promote either unified water development or peace.

On other issues, Eisenhower and Dulles remained more passive. Dulles abandoned the campaign to internationalize Jerusalem, although he contested Israel's claim to the city as the country's capital both to protect cultural interests there and to soothe Arab anger. Although Eisenhower and Dulles took steps to prevent wholesale human suffering among Palestinian refugees, the U.S. leaders realized that Israel would never repatriate the refugees and therefore favored resettlement as the only solution to the problem. They tolerated Arab economic restrictions against Israel despite intense Israeli pressure to overturn them.

In these issues, Eisenhower and Dulles displayed a tendency to act impartially by favoring Israel on some issues and the Arab states on others. The U.S. acceptance of the status quo in Jerusalem and abandonment of refugee repatriation resembled Israel's positions on those issues. The JVP, by contrast, expected Israel to concede in the areas of water claims and acceptance of an international authority. U.S. toleration of Arab economic restrictions favored the Arab states.

Eisenhower and Dulles learned that passivity and evenhandedness caused problems. Arab-Israeli disputes remained unsolved and continued to generate tension. In each quarrel, either the Arab states or Israel faulted the United States for failing to take its side. This continuing state of affairs made Eisenhower and Dulles ready to consider a greater U.S. role in the Arab-Israeli conflict.

14

STILLBORN
The U.S. Peace Process and the Resumption of War, 1955–1956

In 1955–56, the Dwight D. Eisenhower administration launched the first U.S. initiative to negotiate a comprehensive Arab-Israeli peace settlement. Consonant with their declared national security aims, President Eisenhower and Secretary of State John Foster Dulles formulated an elaborate peace plan and encouraged Egypt and Israel to accept it as a first step toward a multilateral settlement. A series of events in 1955, however, aggravated Arab-Israeli tensions and dashed hopes for an end to the conflict. In fact, a war scare swept the region and led Eisenhower to prepare for military action if necessary to halt aggression. The president became more personally involved in Middle East diplomacy, intensifying his search for a peace settlement in early 1956, but his effort foundered on both sides' refusal to compromise.

The diplomacy of peacemaking was complicated. Having earlier resolved to resist Soviet influence in the region, Eisenhower actively promoted Arab-Israeli peace to head off a nascent Soviet-Arab rapprochement. When Arab-Israeli animosity increased, he felt compelled to deploy military forces to the region and even to prepare to intervene in hostilities. Determined to stabilize the Middle East on behalf of U.S. global interests, Eisenhower found it difficult to avoid the assumption of responsibilities that created the risk of involvement in armed conflict in the region. The comprehensive peace plan devised in 1955 appeared strikingly balanced on paper, but all powers to the conflict rejected it as unfair. Ironically, Eisenhower's peacemaking exacerbated Arab-Israeli tensions and strained U.S. relations with all parties to the dispute.

The Alpha Plan

Eisenhower and Dulles became deeply involved in Arab-Israeli peacemaking in 1955. Together with Britain, the U.S. leaders formulated a comprehensive plan, code-named Alpha, to settle the major disputes using permanent peace treaties.

Even though Arab-Israeli tensions escalated as 1955 unfolded, Dulles publicized the terms of the peace plan and urged Israel, Egypt, and other Arab states to accept it. But the local states, unenthused about the plan, became even less willing to approve it as the prospects for peace dimmed.

The Alpha plan originated in conversations between U.S. and British leaders in 1954. Because the Soviets seemed likely to exploit Arab-Israeli disputes that the United Nations could not solve, the National Security Council (NSC) resolved in July to "assume responsibility in developing solutions and ensuring their implementation." Encouraged by the Anglo-American collaboration in solving the Italian-Yugoslav Trieste controversy in October, Dulles and British Foreign Minister Anthony Eden agreed to consider composing a comprehensive Arab-Israeli peace plan. To secretly formulate peace terms in early 1955, Eden appointed Foreign Office Assistant Undersecretary of State Evelyn Shuckburgh, and Dulles named Francis Russell of the Bureau of Near Eastern, South Asian, and African Affairs (NEA).[1]

Dulles realized that major obstacles blocked the path to peace but remained determined to try. Given the intensity of the conflict, Ambassador to Jidda George Wadsworth observed, "surely it is expecting too much that the Arabs and Jews will be able truly to bury the hatchet." Conversely, NEA officials saw "a glimmer of hope here and there" in improved U.S. relations with certain Arab leaders, Egyptian Premier Gamal Abdel Nasser's pledge to consider peacemaking once he settled the base issue with Britain, and relative tranquillity along Israel's borders in late 1954–January 1955. American leaders hoped that if they could nudge Egypt and Israel to make peace, other Arab states would follow. "Whilst we are not over-optimistic about our chances of success," Shuckburgh noted in February 1955, "we agree that the attempt should be made."[2]

Eisenhower and Dulles also resolved to promote peacemaking before domestic politics hindered them from acting impartially. "We should make an all-out effort to get a settlement," they agreed in February 1955, "before the elections of '56." "If the Republicans failed to offer measures acceptable to American Jewry" in an election year, Dulles told the British, "the Democrats would surely promise them." Dulles even used politics as a diplomatic lever, advising Lebanese Ambassador to the United States Charles Malik to support a peace plan in 1955 because "both political parties . . . will be under strong pressure to support Israel" in 1956.[3]

In early 1955, Shuckburgh and Russell outlined the Alpha plan. It proposed that Israel would repatriate seventy-five thousand refugees over five years and pay $280 million to compensate others for lost property. Arab states would absorb the remaining eight hundred thousand refugees and terminate the Suez Canal blockade and the economic boycott. All parties would accept the Jordan Valley Plan (JVP). Israel would give Jordan free access to a port at Haifa, and both sides would allow mutual civil air and telecommunications access. A U.N. entity would oversee and guarantee free access to the holy places of Jerusalem. To sweeten the deal, the United States would dispense more than $1 billion over five years, including $120 million for the JVP, $100 million for the Aswân Dam as an incentive to Nasser, $150 million to help Israel compensate refugees, and $250 million in military aid.[4]

The Alpha plan paid special attention to territory. It proposed a "converging triangles" scheme in which Israel would yield to Egypt and Jordan triangular pieces of land in the Negev, positioned point to point so that the Arab states would control an east-west corridor that bridged a similarly shaped Israeli corridor running north-south. Dulles rejected Britain's wish for large converging triangles in the northern Negev because "it would look on a map like a serious dismemberment of Israel," and the Alpha plan contained a more modest triangles scheme in the southern Negev. The plan also called for minor border adjustments and mutual division of demilitarized zones and no-man's-lands between armistice lines. Prepared to accept major new responsibilities, the United States and Britain would guarantee the borders "against change by armed force."[5]

Despite high U.S. and British hopes for Alpha, Egypt reacted unenthusiastically to the plan. Nasser showed interest when Eden presented the plan during a visit to Cairo on 20 February. But the signing of the Baghdad Pact on 24 February made Nasser angry at the West, and the Gaza raid on 28 February made him bitter and vengeful toward Israel. After returning from the Bandung Conference in May, Nasser accused the United States of plotting to overthrow him and demanded Israeli evacuation of the Negev rather than the converging triangles scheme. Promoting Alpha in this context would be "unwise and useless," U.S. Ambassador to Cairo Henry A. Byroade advised. The plan seemed "clearly impossible for the time being."[6]

Israel also indicated opposition to Alpha, even before officially being informed of the plan. The Gaza raid, U.S. Ambassador to Tel Aviv Edward B. Lawson noted, indicated that the "sands of time ran out on Israel[i] moderation policy." Israelis possessed "the deepest and most emotional feelings" on land, he added, and "any back-down, even involving relatively small areas and areas of little value, such as sand and rock, would be difficult." Having heard rumors of Alpha, Israeli envoys reportedly applied the technique of "wine goes in and secrets come out," getting two State Department officials "very drunk," in which state they disclosed key provisions of the plan. Armed with such knowledge, Israeli Prime Minister Moshe Sharett pressed Dulles to issue a security guarantee to Israel instead of floating a peace plan.[7]

Despite the tepid reactions from Egypt and Israel, Dulles resolved to advance the Alpha plan in summer 1955. However bleak the prospects, Undersecretary of State Herbert Hoover Jr. reasoned, "we might wait in vain for a better time."

Inaction, Dulles added, would promote insecurity and leave the Middle East vulnerable "to aggression from without." Dulles also attributed some of the distance between Israel and Egypt to negotiating tactics, portraying Nasser's "greatly exaggerated" claims in the Negev as merely "an initial statement of trading position."[8]

In August, Dulles decided to publicize the Alpha plan. Over the objections of NEA experts who predicted negative Israeli and Egyptian reactions, Dulles reasoned that publicizing the plan seemed more likely than secret negotiations "to avoid outbursts and to attract inquiries into our proposals." The approach of the 1956 election and intelligence reports of an impending Soviet-Arab rapprochement also convinced him, in different ways, to declare U.S. peace terms "while we can speak as the friend of both" sides. Dulles publicly announced the Alpha plan on 26 August, expressing his hope that it would instill in the Arab states and Israel "a sense of urgency in seeking a settlement."[9]

Israel and the Arab states reacted to Dulles's speech, however, with varying degrees of skepticism. The Israeli ambassador to Washington, Abba Eban, called the proposed Israeli cessions of territory a "built-in deadlock," and Sharett ordered *hasbara* activities to challenge these provisions. Lebanon, Jordan, and Iraq expressed sympathy for Alpha's purposes but insisted that Israel would need to make major concessions. Nasser echoed that demand and added that the United States must sell him arms and dissolve the Baghdad Pact. Saudi Foreign Minister Prince Faisal deemed it "impossible" for Arab states to "forgive or accept" the creation of Israel, and Syrian and Palestinian spokesmen were equally critical.[10]

Although Dulles remained enthused about Alpha, most NEA officials realized that it had fallen flat. Dulles called the reactions of Middle East states "gratifyingly thoughtful, sober, and responsible" and stressed that no power had summarily rejected the plan. Arab reactions were "not as violently against as was feared," he told Eisenhower, while Israeli thinking "seems more favorable than anticipated." The NEA, by contrast, found little reason to hope that Alpha would work. Egypt and Israel voiced irreconcilable positions on the major issues and showed no inclination to compromise. "The situation resembled an oriental bazaar bargain," Russell and Shuckburgh agreed, "in which neither vendor nor purchaser would name the starting price."[11]

The NEA's pessimism was reinforced by developments in the Middle East. The Israel-Egypt border crisis of late August erupted days after Dulles's address, and other episodes of violence along Israel's borders with Egypt and Syria stoked passions between September and November. The Soviet-Egyptian arms deal, finalized within a month of Dulles's speech, boded ill for Alpha by alarming Israel. "If Nasser were going to bring the Communist conspiracy to Israel's doorstep," Eban argued, "if behind him there should arise a hinterland of Soviet support, this was a menace to Israel's survival. . . . Nasser could no longer be believed."[12]

By November, even Dulles realized that Alpha faced perilous times. Because the Soviet-Egyptian arms deal indicated new Soviet involvement in the Middle East, U.S. officials became even more determined to promote Arab-Israeli peace, but they also realized, as the CIA put it, that the arms deal "will complicate if not block" Alpha. Eisenhower lamented that he had "begged to be allowed to be friends of both sides—but that there has been that flaming antagonism." Desperate to rescue Alpha, Dulles authorized Eden publicly to endorse the plan on 9 November and to demand that Israel cede a corridor linking Jordan and Egypt in the Negev. "It was probably good," Dulles told Eisenhower, "to administer some shock treatment to Israelis about territory."[13]

Despite such "shock treatment" of Israel, the territorial issue mortally wounded Alpha by December 1955. Israeli officials approved Alpha's terms on Jerusalem, water, trade, refugees, and communications but categorically refused to cede any land. "The people of Israel . . . were 100% opposed to any cession" of territory, Eban summarized. "The whole proposal smacks of Munich." With the backing of Iraq, Jordan, and Lebanon, by contrast, Nasser offered to concede on the Jerusalem and refugee issues if Israel affirmed the principle of territorial contiguity between Egypt and Jordan. Alpha clearly had failed.[14]

Preparing for War in the Middle East, 1955–1956

As Dulles promoted the Alpha plan in late 1955, a war scare swept the Middle East and triggered a momentous shift in U.S. policy in the region. Fearful that hostilities would gravely destabilize the Middle East, Eisenhower decided to use military force if necessary to deter or thwart Arab or Israeli aggression. After the usual consultation with Britain, the Pentagon planned for various contingencies, including the use of U.S. ground combat forces to stop an Arab-Israeli war. Because the prospect of sending soldiers into harm's way seemed so undesirable, U.S. officials also implemented certain military and diplomatic maneuvers designed to avert an Arab-Israeli clash. Still, Eisenhower brought the United States the closest it had ever been to armed conflict in the Middle East.

The Middle East war scare followed the Soviet-Egyptian arms deal of September 1955. As Defense Minister David Ben-Gurion replaced Sharett as prime minister on 2 November 1955, Israeli officials alerted the State Department that they were contemplating a "preventive war" to destroy Egypt's power before it could absorb promised Soviet arms. Evidence that Israel mobilized troops in November prompted a Pentagon alert that a war might erupt suddenly. In early 1956, Arab states charged that Israel intended to attack Jordan and Gaza and to drop atomic bombs on Iraqi and Saudi oil fields. Israeli intelligence anticipated that the Arab states would provoke a war by forcing masses of refugees to march into Israel, and Ben-Gurion considered war "inevitable" by summer.[15]

U.S. officials doubted that either side in the dispute sought war but sensed that hostilities might nonetheless erupt. In light of economic problems in Israel and Egypt, NEA officials concluded in February, "neither side seems in very good shape for war." Both sides repeatedly denied any intent to provoke hostilities; however, U.S. intelligence officials observed that "the proximity of large forces, heightened tensions in the area, the weakening of restraining factors, growing Arab self-confidence, and Israeli fears" raised the chances that "an incident or a miscalculation might develop into a major conflict."[16]

Alarmed by such reports, Eisenhower's staff initially resolved to respond to any hostilities with economic and limited military means. If war erupted, the NSC planning board (comprised of officials from State, Defense, Treasury, and the Bureau of the Budget) advised Eisenhower to "compel the withdrawal of the aggressor's forces" by imposing a maritime and aerial blockade of trade with and aid to the aggressor state. If necessary, U.S. air and naval forces in the Middle East could attack the ground forces of an aggressor state, with profound consequences.[17]

Officials in Washington sharply debated the potential use of U.S. ground forces to reverse Arab or Israeli aggression. In principle, Dulles's advisers favored ground military intervention if economic measures failed to end a war. The Pentagon and the Bureau of the Budget, however, strongly opposed such a move because it would require five hundred thousand soldiers, deplete NATO combat reserves, encourage the Soviets to make mischief, and either provoke pro-Israel U.S. citizens or undermine relations with Arab and Muslim states. After a vigorous discussion of this issue on 20 and 27 October, the NSC resolved to consider—without obligation—additional military options if necessary.[18]

As Arab-Israeli tensions mounted in early 1956, Eisenhower shed the initial reluctance regarding ground intervention. When Eden asked the president to plan joint armed operations to counter Arab or Israeli aggression, Eisenhower replied that he could not engage in ground warfare without explicit congressional authorization. Shortly thereafter, however, Eisenhower ordered the Pentagon and State Department to coordinate with Britain contingency plans for ground military action. Eisenhower made this momentous policy shift to address concerns about the prospect of Arab-Israeli war and to please an ally.[19]

Consonant with Eisenhower's directive, the Pentagon planned for war in the Middle East. To establish a range of options, officers drafted plans to evacuate U.S. nationals, deter Arab-Israeli war, impose a maritime blockade on Israel or Egypt, and intervene with air or ground forces to defeat aggression. To prepare for ground operations, the Joint Chiefs of Staff (JCS) alerted two army divisions for deployment to a base at Adana, Turkey; deployed the Second Marine Division to ships in the eastern Mediterranean; dispatched one tactical air force wing to the region; and enhanced the Sixth Fleet. The Pentagon ordered local commanders to be ready to "deter, localize, minimize, and terminate difficulties" caused by Israel or any Arab state. On 6 July, Arthur Radford, chairman of the JCS, notified Secretary of Defense Charles E. Wilson that U.S. forces in the Middle East theater were sufficiently armed with munitions, including atomic weapons, to conduct a range of operations as ordered by the president.[20]

The State Department also prepared for hostilities in the Middle East. In the event of war, NEA officials planned to determine which state had perpetrated aggression, seek a Security Council cease-fire resolution, and notify the belligerents of the range of steps the United States might take. The department also worked quietly to obtain the permission of Morocco, Libya, Italy, Greece, and Turkey for U.S. forces to use American military bases in those countries for action in an Arab-Israeli clash.[21]

Even while devising these plans, Pentagon officers firmly opposed ground operations in an Arab-Israeli conflict. Army Brigadier General Forrest Caraway, chairman of the Joint Middle East Planning Committee of the JCS, urged that the Pentagon try to avoid such action. A prolonged occupation on the scale of Korea would be "too wasteful to tolerate," he advised, and even a token show of force would risk Soviet intervention, with grave consequences. The JCS realized that military operations against Israel would provoke a firestorm of domestic protest. Arab peoples, by contrast, would be "easily swayed by fanatical leaders" to resist invading U.S. soldiers, and Arab governments "may close the Suez Canal, revoke existing base rights, expropriate oil fields, cut pipe lines, and seize other Tripartite interests in the area."[22]

Given such reluctance to fight in the Middle East, the Pentagon organized naval patrols designed to prevent Arab-Israeli war. Eisenhower authorized such "show the flag" patrols on 2 February in hope that "awareness and interest in what the U.S. and British might do" would deter Arab or Israeli aggression. The patrols would also signal U.S. resolve to stabilize the region and facilitate any military action that became necessary. Accordingly, four U.S. destroyers sailed the eastern Mediterranean and made their presence known by radioing passing ships, conducting training drills, and visiting ports in Israel and Egypt. Two other destroyers patrolled the Red Sea and called at Port Said, Port Sudan, Jidda, Djibouti, and Aden. British ships engaged in similar voyages. When the patrols were discontinued in June, Chief of Naval Operations Arleigh Burke deemed them a success at fulfilling their purposes.[23]

On 1 May, Eisenhower also approved a State Department plan called Operation Stockpile (or "arms in escrow") to deter Arab-Israeli war. The plan called for the United States to stockpile weapons in the Mediterranean region and pledge to deliver them to any victim of aggression in the Middle East. The navy dispatched to the Mediterranean the USS *Oglethorpe*, loaded with weapons and ammunition earmarked for any Arab state attacked by Israel. The air force stockpiled in Europe twenty-four F-86 jets, spare parts, and ammunition, earmarked for Israel in the event of an Arab attack. Dulles intended to publicize the operation when the *Oglethorpe* reached the Mediterranean in July, but Eisenhower canceled Operation Stockpile after the onset of the Suez Canal crisis.[24]

U.S. officials also modified their policy toward arms sales to Israel when doing so seemed likely to prevent war. Israel made a series of increasingly desperate pleas for U.S. weapons after the Soviet-Egyptian arms deal of 1955. Eisenhower incurred "a very grave moral responsibility," Ben-Gurion declared, by denying Israel a means of self-defense. But U.S. intelligence officials calculated that arming Israel would trigger "a strong shift in Arab attitudes away from the West and toward the Bloc." U.S. interests would not be served, Dulles told Sharett, by "putting primary reliance upon the capacity of Israel to defend itself by force of arms."[25]

In spring 1956, Eisenhower's reluctance to arm Israel wavered. The Pentagon feared that unmatched Soviet arms supply to Arab states would trigger Arab bellicosity or provoke Israel to initiate a preventive war before summer, while the Jewish state retained superior strength. After three Israelis died in a firefight with Syria, Eisenhower commented that he preferred arming Israel to sending U.S. soldiers to defend it. Selling weapons to Israel would also serve the Omega initiative, a plan to confront Egypt with firm diplomacy that Eisenhower approved in March.[26]

U.S. domestic concerns also encouraged Eisenhower to provide arms to Israel. Israeli lobbyists persuaded more than 150 members of the House of Representatives to petition the administration to sell Israel arms worth fifty million dollars. The *Washington Post* editorialized that such a deal would "check the war hawks on both sides" and "cool down the immediate danger of war." Just before announcing his intent to run for a second term as president on 1 March, Eisenhower observed that "we were being too tough with the Israelis with respect to arms."[27]

By contrast, Dulles's reluctance to provide arms to Israel deepened in the face of Israeli efforts to press the issue through U.S. domestic channels. Dulles complained to Eban about Israel's "political warfare" against Eisenhower on the issue. Alluding to U.S. citizens who lobbied for Israel, Russell complained about "ill-informed attacks from well-intentioned people who took their lead from the Israel[i] Government." Such pressure made Dulles less inclined to arm Israel because "we did not want our policy to seem to be made by the Zionists."[28]

In spring 1956, Eisenhower and Dulles conceived of a way to funnel arms to Israel without risking a backlash in the Arab states. The U.S. government would persuade France and Canada to sell military jets to Israel and to deny that they acted under U.S. pressure. In late April, Eisenhower formally refused Israel's weapons requests, explaining to Ben-Gurion that U.S. arms sales would not "serve the cause of peace and stability in the world." French and Canadian jets, the president hinted, would give Israel enough security to resist a preventive war.[29]

The Failure of the Peace Process

Faced with the prospect of war in the Middle East, Eisenhower and Dulles tried not only to deter hostilities but also to achieve a permanent peace. They dispatched a special emissary to arbitrate an Egyptian-Israeli settlement, endorsed a similar mission by the U.N. secretary-general, and searched for other means to bring the adversaries to the peace table. All such efforts were stymied by the unwillingness of Middle East states to make concessions on the major issues, however, and the tensions gripping the region increased. By mid-1956, the U.S. peace process had stalled.

In early 1956, Eisenhower resolved to make another all-out bid for peace between Egypt and Israel. "We are ready to do anything within reason to bring them closer together," he wrote in January. The president appointed former Undersecretary of Defense Robert Anderson as a special emissary to arbitrate a bilateral peace treaty. Eisenhower hoped that the recent Anglo-U.S. offer to fund construction of the Aswân Dam might win Nasser's cooperation and that Israel's insecurity stemming from the Soviet-Egyptian arms deal would force the Jewish state to negotiate. Between January and March, Anderson conducted a series of clandestine meetings with Nasser and Ben-Gurion.[30]

Unfortunately for Eisenhower, Anderson failed to broker agreements on the major issues. Nasser stood by the traditional demand for repatriation of refugees, Ben-Gurion demanded resettlement, and both leaders refused to compromise. Nor could Anderson resolve the deep differences over the Negev. Ben-Gurion offered air and railroad transit privileges to Egypt, Jordan, and Lebanon but categorically refused Nasser's bid for "substantial territory connecting Egypt and Jordan and forming a part of one or the other of these two countries." Other ideas, such as arranging a swap of the Negev for Gaza, establishing U.N. control of the Negev, and constructing a causeway across the Gulf of Aqaba, were also discarded.[31]

Anderson also failed to build a positive relationship between Ben-Gurion and Nasser or to secure either leader's commitment to make peace. Ben-Gurion requested a personal meeting with Nasser and insisted that any peace deal should take effect at once, before Egypt could absorb Soviet arms. Citing domestic and inter-Arab politics, Nasser rejected both demands and refused Anderson's suggested compromises of a top secret encounter with Ben-Gurion aboard a U.S. Navy vessel and an immediate settlement with delayed publicity. Eisenhower realized in March that the Anderson mission had failed and blamed both Egypt and Israel. "The chances of a peaceful settlement seem remote," he noted. "It is a very sorry situation."[32]

When the Anderson mission deadlocked, Dulles turned to the United Nations to promote Arab-Israeli peacemaking. He proposed that the United Nations dispatch a new mediator endowed with substantial authority to arrange peace talks on the basis of the armistice agreements or the Lausanne protocol of 1949. The Security Council passed a resolution on 5 April, appointing Secretary-General Dag Hammarskjöld to the task. Eisenhower promptly encouraged Ben-Gurion and Nasser to cooperate with the secretary-general.[33]

As Hammarskjöld ventured to the Middle East to negotiate peace treaties, however, Egypt and Israel nearly started a war. After an Egyptian attack on an Israeli patrol left three Israelis dead, the IDF retaliated by shelling the town of Gaza, killing fifty-six people. Telling Byroade that he could not sit "idly by in face of slaughter of civilians under his protection," Nasser sent into Israel hundreds of fedayeen commandos, who killed ten Israelis and wounded thirty-eight. The IDF became "wild with rage," Lawson reported, and determined to retaliate with a massive strike against Egypt. Eisenhower urged restraint on both states. Hammarskjöld scrambled to secure a cease-fire and troop withdrawal agreement on 19 April, only hours before the IDF planned to launch a major military operation against Egypt.[34]

In such a context, Hammarskjöld's mission to promote peace collapsed. Nasser flatly refused to work with the U.N. secretary-general. When Hammarskjöld suggested Israeli concessions at the height of fedayeen violence, Lawson reported, Ben-Gurion became "so upset and his speech . . . so incoherent that I feared he would have a stroke." "This is a mission of bad will," Ben-Gurion roared. "Is he Ambassador of Nasser?" Stymied, the secretary-general advised the Western powers to consider working with the Soviets to promote an Arab-Israeli settlement. The Security Council ended his mission with a 4 June resolution urging all parties to honor cease-fires, respect armistices, and seek peace.[35]

In the aftermath of the Hammarskjöld mission, U.S. officials searched fruitlessly for some means to revive the peace process. Russell conceived such schemes as advancing Alpha on a piecemeal basis, redirecting UNRWA funding to Arab states willing to absorb refugees, and recruiting Lebanon to sell the Johnston Plan (renamed for Lebanese Foreign Minister Salim Lahoud) to other Arab states. Alarmed by Egypt and Israel's near war of April, the Policy Planning Staff even approved the unprecedented step of inviting the Soviet Union to help arbitrate a Middle East settlement. U.S. officials found, however, that political conditions simply were not conducive to any such diplomacy.[36]

As peacemaking stalled, Eisenhower fretted that the threat of war persisted.

Dulles feared that Israel might initiate hostilities after Ben-Gurion, on 18–19 June, replaced Foreign Minister Sharett with the more hawkish Golda Meir and declared to the Knesset that the government would disregard the armistices if provoked. After a series of border incidents in July, the Israeli cabinet authorized Ben-Gurion to conduct reprisals against Jordan, and Jordan mobilized its armed forces. Hammarskjöld returned to the Middle East to press Israel, Jordan, and Egypt to pacify their borders, but within days, firefights erupted near Jerusalem. Eisenhower braced for war.[37]

Conclusion

On behalf of American regional interests, U.S. officials strenuously attempted through a variety of diplomatic and military initiatives to promote Arab-Israeli peace in 1955–56. These leaders formulated the Alpha plan as a blueprint for a settlement and tried to convince Israel and Egypt to accept the plan through diplomacy capped by Robert Anderson's mission to the region. After the Alpha initiative stalled, the United States supported Hammarskjöld's peace mission; failing that, the U.S. government even contemplated peacemaking in collaboration with the Soviets. U.S. officials sought to deter war by stationing combat troops in the region, dispatching navy vessels to show the flag in the region, and stockpiling arms earmarked for any victim of attack.

The harder U.S. officials tried to make peace, ironically, the more hostile the Arab-Israeli situation became. The Alpha plan fell victim to unfortunate and ill-timed occurrences in the Middle East. Days after Eden presented the Alpha plan to Nasser in February 1955, the Gaza raid aggravated the Egyptian leader's anger at Israel. Days after Dulles publicly outlined the plan in August 1955, violence along the Egyptian-Israeli border nearly erupted into full-scale war. Hammarskjöld's April 1956 mission to make peace floundered as yet another border crisis between Egypt and Israel intensified both sides' ardor for war. The deterioration of Egyptian-Israeli relations in 1955, which U.S. officials had no way of anticipating, proved deadly to Alpha.

U.S. peacemaking was undermined not only by Arab-Israeli tensions but also by other developments in the Middle East, including some initiated by the United States. Nasser's anger at the West for establishing the Baghdad Pact contributed to his reluctance to approve Alpha. U.S. concern with Nasser's drift toward neutralism embittered U.S. officials, who feared that the Soviets would gain entry to the region through Cairo. The U.S. refusal to arm Israel, based on a desire to avoid risking interests in the Arab states, helped turn the Jewish state against the Alpha plan. In short, U.S. Cold War policies and priorities often conflicted with the quest to make Arab-Israeli peace, which suffered as a result.

Scholars have reached a range of conclusions about the Alpha peace plan. Mordechai Bar-On considers it a "pathetic, . . . naive, [and] more than slightly ridiculous" plan that not only failed but aggravated Arab-Israeli passions in the process. By contrast, Neil Caplan portrays Alpha as a reasonable and fair proposal that failed largely because of the unfortunate timing of events, unforeseeable Soviet interference in regional politics, and uncontrollable Arab and Israeli attitudes.[38]

The Alpha plan earned a mixed legacy. On the positive side, it represented a comprehensive effort by the Western states to resolve the Arab-Israeli conflict, the first attempt of its kind. U.S. officials maintained their policy of impartiality by promoting Alpha in 1955, before the electoral dynamics of 1956 pressured them to adopt a stance favoring Israel. In early 1956, Eisenhower became sympathetic to Israeli requests for arms supply for U.S. domestic political as well as diplomatic reasons. Yet his decision to rely on allies to supply weapons to Israel, rather than to supply U.S. arms and reap the domestic political rewards, reveals a determination to maintain impartiality as a peacemaker.

Conversely, certain features of the Alpha plan doomed it to failure. No matter how fair and impartial, it proved unable to overcome the deep-seated intransigence of local powers. Promotion of Alpha increased tensions by focusing local leaders' attention on the points of contention and by raising fears on both sides that the West would force them to make concessions that they considered inimical to their vital interests. Because Alpha demanded territorial concessions, for example, Israel firmly resisted the plan, criticized it as unfair, mobilized U.S. sympathizers against it, and demanded arms and a security guarantee in its stead. The State Department's suspicion that Israel conducted the Gaza raid to abort the emerging Alpha plan, while impossible to prove, is plausible.

In 1955–56, Eisenhower involved the United States in the Arab-Israeli situation to an unprecedented extent. The Alpha plan placed the United States at the center of the peace process and included a momentous offer to guarantee Arab-Israeli borders if the Middle East states made peace. Anderson was the first U.S. emissary to become deeply and intimately involved in the peace process. Eisenhower directed the Pentagon to bolster the U.S. Navy presence in the theater and to prepare to fight in the region both as a deterrent against aggression and as a corrective if war erupted. Eisenhower and Dulles conducted an operation to supply weapons to any victim of aggression and funneled weapons from allied powers to Israel. Britain's role as junior partner in and France's exclusion from the U.S. endeavors of 1955–56 signaled a major shift from the international collaboration manifest in the Tripartite Declaration of 1950. Even after the burst of Alpha-era peacemaking faded, the increased U.S. involvement in the Arab-Israeli situation would endure for years.

15

DESPERATION DIPLOMACY
U.S. Policy during the Suez-Sinai War of 1956

The Arab-Israeli conflict took a new and unexpected turn after Egyptian Premier Gamal Abdel Nasser nationalized the Suez Canal Company in July 1956. Nasser took over the British- and French-owned firm to demonstrate his independence from the European colonial powers, to avenge an Anglo-U.S. denial of economic aid, and to garner the profits the company earned in his country. Britain and France responded by threatening to use force to recover ownership of the waterway. U.S. President Dwight D. Eisenhower sought to resolve the dispute before it triggered hostilities, but the Suez-Sinai War nonetheless erupted in October when Israel, in secret partnership with Britain and France, attacked Egypt.

Cold War interests shaped Eisenhower's policy toward the crisis. He opposed the use of force against Egypt because it seemed likely to enhance Soviet prestige in the Arab world. Assessing the Soviet Union's intentions in the Middle East on the basis of Soviet behavior in Eastern Europe, the president feared an advance in the Middle East or a direct attack on Britain and France. Eisenhower moved quickly to end the Suez-Sinai War, both to deny the Soviet Union political advantages in the Arab states and to remove the risk of Soviet military action that would have grave consequences for world peace.

Arab-Israeli factors complicated Eisenhower's diplomacy during the crisis. Israel pressed him to guarantee its transit rights on the canal in any settlement of the dispute. By autumn 1956, instability in Jordan portended an Israeli incursion into that country or an Arab-Israeli war for control of it. The collusion among Britain, France, and Israel to attack Egypt completely melded the canal controversy and the Arab-Israeli conflict, adding a new dimension of complexity to the situation.

The Suez-Sinai imbroglio confronted Eisenhower with several challenges. He found it necessary to react hastily to confusing and quickly unfolding developments. He incurred Israel's anger by denying its objectives but also felt the heat of the Arab backlash against Anglo-French imperialism. The turmoil corroded the foundations of the Anglo-U.S. strategic partnership even as Eisenhower prepared to fight the Soviets if they militarily attacked his ally. Because U.S. involvement in the Middle East had deepened on Eisenhower's watch, he confronted a perilous situation, one of the most serious of the Cold War.

U.S. Policy in the Suez Crisis

Nasser's nationalization of the Suez Canal Company touched off a four-month international crisis during which Britain and France prepared to use military force against Egypt unless Nasser relented. Consonant with the goal of stabilizing the Middle East, Eisenhower approached the canal crisis on three basic and interrelated premises. First, he sought to avert a military clash and settle the canal dispute with diplomacy before the Soviet Union exploited the situation for political gain. Second, he aimed to avoid alienating Arab nationalism and included Arab statesmen in his diplomacy to end the crisis. Third, he sought to isolate Israel from the canal controversy. Mixture of the volatile Arab-Israeli and Anglo-French-Egyptian conflicts, Eisenhower feared, would ignite the Middle East.

From the dawn of the crisis, Eisenhower promoted diplomacy over violence as the best means to address the canal dispute. He sympathized with Britain's and France's desire to recover the canal company but feared that an attack on Egypt would destabilize the Middle East and play to the Soviets' advantage. Eisenhower directed Secretary of State John Foster Dulles to defuse the crisis on terms acceptable to Britain and France, through public statements, negotiations, two international conferences in London, establishment of a Suez Canal Users Association, and U.N. deliberations. By late October, these efforts proved fruitless, and Anglo-French preparations for war continued.[1]

In refusing to endorse Anglo-French force against Egypt, Eisenhower displayed sensitivity to Arab nationalism. Nasser's seizure of the canal company was widely popular among his own and other Arab peoples. Even though the other Arab countries feared Nasser's expansionism, Iraq, Jordan, Saudi Arabia, and Lebanon declared that they would back Egypt if it were attacked by Western armies. "Our problem in the long run was how to guide the new nations from colonialism to independence in an orderly way," Dulles commented. "We must have evolution, not revolution."[2]

The surge in Nasser's popularity among Arab peoples, however, short-circuited Eisenhower's efforts to settle the canal crisis in partnership with Arab leaders. The president dispatched Robert Anderson on a secret mission to ask

King Saud, who had ruled Saudi Arabia since the 1953 death of his father, Ibn Saud, to pressure Nasser to retreat on the canal issue. Saud convinced Nasser to curtail propaganda broadcasts on Radio Cairo and to meet a Western delegation from the first London conference, but the king refused to press Egypt for additional concessions and criticized the U.S. suspension of economic aid to Egypt. Dulles also tried unsuccessfully to turn Iraqi officials against Egypt by emphasizing that Nasser had destabilized the region.[3]

Eisenhower also tried to separate the canal crisis from the Arab-Israeli conflict. Early in the crisis, the Intelligence Advisory Committee warned that Israel might join a Western attack or initiate its own assault on Egypt during the canal showdown. Dulles abhorred such a prospect because, he told the National Security Council (NSC), "any action which would put the Israelis out in front in the Suez situation would solidify the Arab world." The Arab-Israeli conflict "should not be allowed to intrude itself into the present matter," the Bureau of Near Eastern, South Asian, and African Affairs (NEA) advised. Israel was told "to keep quiet during the coming period."[4]

To serve this aim, Dulles marginalized Israel's interests during the London conferences. Having for years resisted Egypt's canal restrictions, Israel demanded a seat at the conferences and warned against "decisions that ignore Israel's rights." But Dulles denied Israel's request to attend and blocked discussion of its grievances against Egypt. "Reports from London indicate that Dulles was king of the conference," Walter Eytan of the Israeli Foreign Ministry noted, "and, as such, made sure that Israel should not be mentioned there."[5]

Dulles also blocked several Israeli gambits to exploit the canal crisis for its own gain. Israel proposed, for example, to build an oil pipeline from Eilat to Haifa as a bypass to the canal for Persian Gulf oil destined for Europe. But Dulles declined Israeli Ambassador to the United States Abba Eban's repeated requests to discuss the idea on the grounds that Arab states would easily render such a pipeline inoperable and that mere discussion of it might appear as acquiescence in Nasser's seizure of the canal company. Dulles also rejected Eban's request to send a U.S. oil tanker bound for Israel into the canal to test Nasser's reaction before the canal issue was settled. Dulles also did not show any sympathy for Israeli complaints in September that Egypt had closed the canal to a Greek ship carrying cement from Haifa to Eilat and had formally impounded the *Bat Galim*, the Israeli ship seized in 1954.[6]

Dulles also marginalized Israel during the Security Council's October hearings on the canal crisis. Israeli Foreign Minister Golda Meir demanded "energetic American action" to ensure Israel a voice in the hearings, and Eban asked for an opportunity to explain that the blockade violated the 1951 Security Council resolution and had cost Israel untold millions of dollars. But Dulles replied that if Eban addressed the council, the Arab states would demand a voice and the proceedings "would become a mockery." The Security Council denied Israel's request to speak, and Dulles, in his own speech to the council, failed even to mention the 1951 resolution that directed Egypt to open the canal to Israeli shipping.[7]

Meanwhile, U.S. officials sensed a spike in Israeli bellicosity toward Egypt. In August, fedayeen raids from Gaza raised Israeli insecurity and provoked reprisal raids. Because the first London conference had failed to reverse Nasser's seizure of the canal company, Eban feared that Nasser would "look for new worlds to conquer" and asked the United States to guarantee Israel's security. "Strong elements in Israel" sought to use the Suez crisis to launch a war on Egypt or Jordan, the Israeli minister to Washington, Reuven Shiloah, warned on 20 September. Feelings were "extremely high."[8]

Wary of such Israeli sentiments, Eisenhower and Dulles supported modest arms supply to Israel. To avoid provoking Nasser early in the canal crisis, Dulles delayed a planned release of helicopters, half-tracks, and machine guns to Israel and discouraged Canada from announcing its planned sale of F-86 jets. In August, however, he quietly released the U.S. weapons, reasoning that such a move would balance Nasser's acquisition of Soviet arms, disprove Anglo-French accusations that Eisenhower favored Nasser, and please pro-Israel voters on the eve of the 1956 election.[9]

Dulles also discreetly supported the previously arranged Canadian sale of warplanes to Israel. In late September, Canada announced that it would sell Israel twenty-four F-86 jets and released twelve planes for immediate shipment. Dulles privately endorsed the sale, although he publicly portrayed it as a purely Canadian decision, and he refused a suggestion from his former law partner, Arthur H. Dean, who occasionally delivered messages from Israeli officials, that Dulles maximize domestic political gain by openly supporting the deal. (The Canadian arms deal never came to fruition. Canada suspended delivery of the jets when Israeli-Jordanian border tensions rose in October, and Israel canceled the deal in November.)[10]

Dulles also tolerated France's covert supply of Mystère military jets to Israel. France had asked the Near East Arms Coordinating Committee, the top secret Anglo-U.S.-French body established under the Tripartite Declaration of 1950 to coordinate arms supply to Middle East states, to approve a sale of twenty-four Mystères to Israel. After the Suez crisis broke, France officially postponed the sale at Eisenhower's request, but in September, U.S. intelligence detected that France had covertly sent between forty-eight and sixty Mystères to Israel. Pentagon intelligence officers stressed that Israel lacked the personnel and facilities to deploy all the Mystères and that France unloaded the planes because it was unhappy with their performance. Eisenhower and Dulles quietly tolerated the deal.[11]

U.S. Policy toward the Israeli-Jordanian Border

Eisenhower's quest to resolve peacefully the Suez Crisis was seriously compli-cated by a series of hostile incidents along the Israeli-Jordanian border that threatened to trigger a full-scale war. To defend his kingdom and to insulate it from internal turmoil, King Hussein invited Iraq to station troops in his coun-try, a step that Israel vowed to contest. U.S. officials suddenly realized that Jor-dan might fall victim to internal discord or foreign conquest. An Israeli invasion of Jordan seemed possible.

The Israeli-Jordanian border crisis escalated sharply in mid-September. When infiltrators from Jordan killed six soldiers and seven civilians in Israel, the Israel Defense Forces (IDF) retaliated by killing sixty-nine soldiers while demol-ishing three Jordanian army posts. Israeli officials justified the reprisals as acts of self-defense against facilities used to raid their territory. But General Richard Collins, deputy director for intelligence on the Joint Staff, detected Israeli "con-tempt for the capability of the Jordan Army and . . . an open invitation for them to 'come out and fight.'" King Hussein deployed his entire army to the West Bank, raising the Pentagon's concern that public pressure would force him to assault Israel or that the IDF would attack and destroy his army while it sat in such an exposed position.[12]

Dulles tried to contain the Israeli-Jordanian tensions. He complained to Israel that its reprisals only aggravated Arab animosity. The first secretary of the U.S. embassy in Tel Aviv, William L. Hamilton, told Pinhas Eliav of the Israeli Foreign Ministry's U.S. Division that the "U.S. will do everything to prevent a messy little war." Dulles pressed Jordan's ambassador to the United States, Abdul Monem Rifai, to admit that "hot-headed" Jordanian military officers de-served some blame for the border violence and declined to endorse a Jordanian appeal to the Security Council to impose sanctions on Israel. Instead, the U.S. secretary of state sought subtly to turn Jordan against Egypt by charging that Nasser's stubbornness on the canal issue gave the Israelis "a protective shield behind which they can take strong measures."[13]

King Hussein complicated the border situation in late September by asking King Faisal of Iraq to station a division of fifteen thousand Iraqi troops in Jor-dan to deter Israeli attack. King Faisal denied the request, Pentagon intelligence learned from sources in Baghdad, because he feared that such a move might trigger rather than prevent Israeli preemption and because he wanted his sol-diers at home to suppress expected disturbances orchestrated by Nasser. But Faisal agreed to stockpile weapons at Mafraq and send a company or a battalion to guard them. (See map 5.) Iraqi Prime Minister Nuri Said asked the United States to endorse this move and to send Jordan a few thousand rifles and machine guns.[14]

In principle, Dulles conditionally approved an Iraqi deployment to Jordan. Provided that Iraq sent a small force without armor and kept it east of the Jordan River, he reasoned, the stability provided by such a force would reduce the risk of Jordan collapsing under internal, Egyptian, Israeli, or Soviet pressure. The troop deployment would also enhance Iraq's prestige and lessen Egypt's standing among the Arab masses. Britain also endorsed the Iraqi move as a safeguard against Israeli attack and Egyptian subterfuge.[15]

In early October, Dulles convinced Israeli Prime Minister David Ben-Gurion to accept a limited Iraqi deployment in Jordan. Ben-Gurion initially resolved to occupy the West Bank if Iraqi troops entered Jordan because, as he wrote in his diary, "we do not want an enemy at our country's gates." When Dulles stressed, however, that lightly armed Iraqi soldiers at an outpost east of the Jordan River would stabilize Jordan to Israel's advantage, Ben-Gurion relented. "If Iraq sends troops to [the] other side of [the] Jordan River, we will do nothing," he said. "If they send troops to our borders, that is different." If Jordan were dismembered by other Arab states, Israel would not sit idle, Eban added. "Everybody, not only Arabs, would dream dreams."[16]

As Israeli-Jordanian tensions escalated in mid-October, however, Ben-Gurion rescinded his concession regarding Iraqi troops. After forty Jordanians and fifteen Israelis died in a border clash on 10–11 October, Britain sent Hunter aircraft to Jordan and announced the British intention to provide air defense of the kingdom. This action, together with Britain's recent endorsement of a political union among Iraq, Jordan, and Syria, provoked Ben-Gurion to contest an Iraqi entry into Jordan. Such a move, Ben-Gurion told Eisenhower, would "acutely aggravate the threat to Israel's security."[17]

This reversal of Israeli policy dismayed Eisenhower and Dulles. They believed that Israel exaggerated British intentions, and intelligence officials detected in Israeli behavior a determination to expand at Jordan's expense. Dulles reasoned that Israel might be tempted to annex Jordan because it tottered on the verge of collapse, because the canal crisis would preclude Egyptian intervention, and because domestic political pressures would prevent a vigorous U.S. response. Eisenhower warned Israel that he would not tolerate an attack on Jordan.[18]

Dulles's calculation that Israel might try to exploit the U.S. presidential election prompted Eisenhower to declare that he would not make policy toward Israel on the basis of electoral concerns. The president's position "should not be influenced by domestic political considerations," he told Dulles, but by "what was right and what was in our overall national interest." Eisenhower would rather lose votes than adopt a position that "would not permit us to live with our conscience." He added that "no considerations of partisan politics will keep this government from pursuing a course dictated by justice and international decency."[19]

Political dynamics within the Arab community ultimately blocked the deployment of Iraqi troops in Jordan. Iraq postponed at the last minute a border crossing planned for 15 October after disagreements developed over command arrangements. Iraq hesitated a second time, according to Pentagon intelligence reports, when Syria and Egypt discussed sending their forces to Jordan to counter an Iraqi deployment. When Egypt, Jordan, and Syria signed a mutual-defense pact on 24 October, the prospect of Iraqi units moving into Jordan evaporated.[20]

Although the tension over an Iraqi deployment faded, Eisenhower continued to worry that Jordan remained vulnerable to internal collapse or external conquest. On 21 October, Jordanian voters elected as prime minister Suleiman al-Nabulsi, a rival to King Hussein, and a Chamber of Deputies consisting of nineteen anti-Western, nine neutralist, and twelve pro-Western members. Dulles expected Egyptian intrigue to gain influence in Amman, while the Joint Chiefs of Staff (JCS) expected "serious internal disorder, military intervention by neighboring states, or both." Nervousness swept the NSC on 26 October when Director of Central Intelligence Allen Dulles relayed an unconfirmed (and false) report that King Hussein had been assassinated. Bracing for trouble, Eisenhower predicted that "we are going to have a donnybrook in this area."[21]

The Suez-Sinai War

As Eisenhower anticipated, a donnybrook quickly enveloped the Middle East. The melee erupted after Israel conspired with Britain and France to wage war on Egypt. Although Eisenhower and Dulles saw evidence of the collusion, they were caught off guard when Israel invaded the Sinai on 29 October. With Dulles hospitalized at the height of the crisis, Eisenhower imposed sanctions on the colluding powers and achieved a cease-fire, but not before Britain and France joined the fighting and the Soviet Union threatened to widen the conflict into a world war. Despite Eisenhower's efforts to segregate the Arab-Israeli conflict from the canal crisis, the two problems intersected, with nearly catastrophic results.

France, Israel, and Britain began coordinating plans to attack Egypt in early October. French army officers suggested to Ben-Gurion on 3 October a plan in which France would bomb Alexandria while Israel invaded the Sinai. At a 16 October meeting in Paris, French Premier Guy Mollet and British Prime Minister Anthony Eden agreed that if Israel attacked Egypt, France and Britain would defend the move and use their veto powers to protect Israel from Security Council reproach. Angry at having "been double-crossed by Mr. Dulles" in his promotion of the Suez Canal Users Association, Mollet and Eden calculated that Eisenhower would decline to stop such an assault before the U.S. election. U.S. efforts to stop Britain and France from attacking Egypt, ironically, led the two European powers to enlist Israel as a partner in a scheme that broadened the scope of the conflict.[22]

These consultations set the stage for secret meetings on 22–25 October at Sèvres, near Paris, at which British, French, and Israeli officials colluded to make war on Nasser under an elaborate ruse. They agreed that Israel would initiate war with Egypt on 29 October, that Britain and France would issue ultimatums on 30 October ordering Egyptian and Israeli troops to withdraw from the canal zone, and that if, as expected, Nasser rejected the ultimatums, Britain and France would bomb Egyptian airfields within forty-eight hours, occupy the canal zone, and depose Nasser. These terms were written in a protocol signed on 24 October by Ben-Gurion, French Foreign Minister Christian Pineau, and British Foreign Office Undersecretary Patrick Dean. Eden ratified the deal the next day.[23]

Ben-Gurion agonized over the collusion before approving it. He felt isolated and insecure because of the U.S. refusal to provide substantial weapons or to approve his reprisal raids as Arab military capabilities increased. The collusion plan, if enacted before the U.S. election, offered a means to stop Nasser from launching an Arab crusade against Israel. Conversely, Ben-Gurion worried that Nasser might survive the onslaught and that the United States or Soviet Union might intervene. After France offered to shield Israel from Security Council censure and to defend the Jewish state against Egyptian air strikes, Ben-Gurion signed the protocol. On 25 October, he ordered the IDF to mobilize for an attack on the Sinai.[24]

The Israeli military mobilization alarmed and perplexed U.S. observers. Since August, top U.S. officials had downplayed the prospect of Israeli involvement in an Anglo-French assault on Egypt on the logic that Israel would gladly allow other powers to demolish its biggest military foe. Unsure of the purpose of Israel's mobilization, Eisenhower sent messages to Ben-Gurion on 27–28 October that recalled Israeli pledges not to provoke war, noted that no threat against Israel justified its mobilization, and warned against an attack on any power. Dulles warned U.S. embassies in the Middle East, especially those in Cairo and Amman, to exercise vigilance, and the Pentagon ordered an immediate evacuation of U.S. citizens from Jordan.[25]

Some U.S. officials suspected that Israel intended to attack Egypt, perhaps with Anglo-French complicity. When Ben-Gurion declared the mobilization a reaction to the imminent arrival of Iraqi forces in Jordan, U.S. Ambassador to

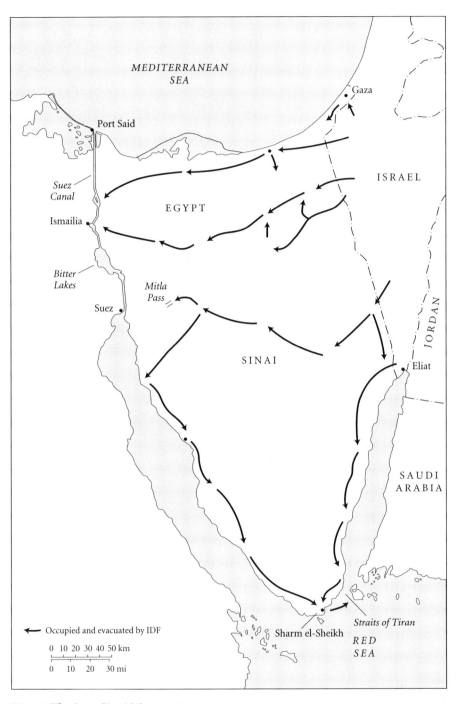

MEDITERRANEAN
SEA

Gaza

Port Said

Suez
Canal

ISRAEL

EGYPT

Ismailia

Bitter
Lakes

Mitla
Pass

Suez

SINAI

JORDAN

Eliat

SAUDI
ARABIA

Occupied and evacuated by IDF

0 10 20 30 40 50 km

0   10   20   30 mi

Sharm el-Sheikh

Straits of Tiran

RED
SEA

Map 6. The Suez-Sinai War, 1956

Tel Aviv Edward B. Lawson reported that the Israeli prime minister spoke "with considerable and deliberate caution and was not very effective." The Central Intelligence Agency (CIA) and the interdepartmental Watch Committee concluded that the movement of Israeli troops and vehicles to the south portended a military strike against Egypt. Allen Dulles later claimed that the CIA suspected Anglo-French complicity after detecting the secret Eden-Mollet meeting in Paris on 16 October, a meeting "that we were not otherwise informed about."[26]

Despite such intelligence, Eisenhower and Dulles found reason to doubt that Israel would attack Egypt or that Britain and France would become involved. Dulles learned that Israel had not withdrawn funds from its accounts in U.S. banks, suggesting that it intended a brief strike on Jordan rather than a prolonged war in Egypt. When Dulles inquired, the British and French embassies denied knowledge of Israel's intent and claimed also to be worried about it. When Dulles suggested that Britain and France might be involved in Israel's move, Eisenhower commented that "he just cannot believe Britain would be dragged into this."[27]

Eisenhower and Dulles were also distracted from the Middle East by foreign and domestic developments. On 23 October, Hungary erupted in rebellion against Soviet rule. On 26 October, the NSC discussed at length an impending coup in Syria, which, according to historians Douglas Little and David W. Lesch, the CIA had organized. Eisenhower spent most of 26–27 October strategizing with advisers about the election on 6 November, and he departed on a campaign trip to Florida and Virginia on 29 October. Dulles ventured to Dallas on 27–28 October to lecture on diplomacy.[28]

Dulles discerned Anglo-French-Israeli collusion on 29 October but even then failed to realize the magnitude of the plot. He anticipated that Israel would occupy the West Bank and, if Egypt responded, invade the Sinai as well or that Israel would send a tanker into the canal: when Egypt stopped the vessel, Britain and France would have a cause for war. Dulles apparently did not consider a three-power invasion of Egypt. He resolved to use a 30 October Security Council hearing, slated to consider the Israeli-Jordanian border situation, to press Israel to explain its mobilization. But Israel struck before Dulles could take such action.[29]

Israel's 29 October invasion of Egypt instantly clarified Eisenhower's understanding of the situation and impelled him to take action to restore peace. As the president hastened back to Washington, Dulles predicted that Israel's action would provoke Nasser to close the canal, Syria to sever its oil pipelines, and the Soviet Union to rally to Egypt's side. Thus, Eisenhower resolved to fulfill his pledge to oppose aggression in the Middle East, to avert intervention by Britain and France, and to deny the Soviets a chance to intrude into the situation. He ordered immediate U.N. action to halt the Israeli assault. When Britain declined jointly to protest Israeli action at the United Nations on 30 October, Eisenhower proceeded alone.[30]

Domestic political circumstances complicated Eisenhower's decision to oppose the Israeli attack. Israel asked sympathetic members of the administration and Congress to advocate its interests to the president, and Ben-Gurion recorded that White House speechwriter Eli Ginsberg toned down the criticisms of Israel in Eisenhower's 31 October speech. Perhaps thinking of Israel and the impending U.S. election, the president cautioned his staffers on 1 November that they "must *not* single out and condemn *any one nation*."[31]

Eisenhower resisted the domestic pressures, however. The *New York Times* and the *Washington Post* editorialized that although Nasser had provoked the trouble, the United States should nonetheless compel Israel to halt its offensive. Gallup poll data revealed that 10 percent of Americans approved of Israel's attack, but 47 percent disapproved. Perhaps aware of such trends in public opinion, Eisenhower claimed that he "gave strict orders . . . that we would handle our affairs exactly as though we didn't have a Jew in America."[32]

Meanwhile, Britain's refusal to cooperate at the United Nations confirmed Eisenhower's growing suspicion that Britain and France were deeply involved in the Israeli attack. Indeed, as IDF units advanced across the Sinai, the European allies vetoed two cease-fire resolutions in the Security Council, issued their contrived ultimatums to Egypt and Israel, and bombed military targets in Egypt in preparation for an invasion. Shocked that his closest allies were committing what he viewed as a grave error, Eisenhower secured a resolution in the General Assembly, where Britain and France lacked veto power, that demanded a cease-fire, an arms embargo, and a withdrawal of foreign forces from Egypt. Because war with Britain or France was "unthinkable," he cautioned the NSC, he would "do what was decent and right, but still not condemn more furiously than we had to."[33]

Yet Eisenhower's diplomacy failed to prevent the widening of the war. On 4 November, three days after securing the cease-fire resolution, the State Department secured another General Assembly resolution establishing a United Nations Emergency Force (UNEF). Comprised of soldiers from Canada and other states, UNEF would intervene between the belligerents and thereby prevent Anglo-French troop landings. With strong public backing, Eisenhower ordered U.S. transport planes to rush Canadian soldiers from West Germany to Egypt, but Canada delayed the operation until its parliament approved. On 5 November, British and French forces landed in Egypt.[34]

Unable to stop the tripartite attack, Eisenhower moved to preserve amity with Egypt by distancing himself from the offensive. Assistant Secretary of

State William M. Rountree assured Egyptian Ambassador to the United States Ahmed Hussein that the president had lacked foreknowledge of the Anglo-French ultimatums and had tried to block Anglo-French military intervention. U.S. diplomacy at the United Nations, Nasser confessed, convinced him of U.S. sincerity. The United States "has won [the] area without firing a shot," he told CIA officials in Cairo, who found his praise of their government "so effusive . . . as to be almost embarrassing."[35]

Eisenhower and Dulles also discerned that the tripartite assault had rallied Arab opinion to Nasser's side. In Baghdad, the collusion triggered massive anti-British rioting and public demands that Iraq leave the Baghdad Pact. King Saud asked Eisenhower "to check this treacherous aggression . . . by the Zionist group." Jordan threatened to attack Israel; invited Iraqi, Syrian, and Saudi troops to occupy the East Bank; denied Britain the use of its air bases at Mafraq and Amman; severed relations with France; and demolished an Iraq Petroleum Company oil pipeline near Irbid. Syria invoked its defense pact with Egypt and placed its forces under Egyptian command. The "whole Arab world was boiling," Iraqi Ambassador to Washington Moussa al-Shabandar observed.[36]

U.S. leaders took a measured view of this Arab backlash. To soothe it and avert a Soviet-Arab rapprochement, Dulles emphasized to Arab leaders that Eisenhower sought to end the hostilities with diplomacy. But the U.S. secretary of state also rejected Arab demands for American military action to stop Britain and France on the grounds that such a move, in Rountree's words, would destroy "the world structure as it now existed." The CIA doubted, moreover, that Arab leaders would start a war against Israel that they were likely to lose. "They talk big," Allen Dulles told the NSC, "but they have few military capabilities."[37]

Eisenhower and Dulles also sought to isolate the Soviet Union from the Suez-Sinai War. On 31 October, Dulles assured Soviet leaders that he was trying to stop the Israeli attack and urged them to refrain from intervention. The CIA dismissed French reports of an impending Soviet intervention in Syria in view of the logistical difficulties of such a move, the unlikelihood that the Soviets would risk general war, and the suspicion that France sought to divert attention from Suez. Indeed, wary of their military inferiority in the region, Soviet leaders cautiously avoided involvement in the hostilities, even removing from Egypt Soviet advisers, tanks, and bombers that had recently arrived under the terms of the 1955 arms deal.[38]

Yet the prospect of Soviet intervention intensified on 5 November, sending the 1956 war into its most dangerous phase. When British and French paratroopers landed along the Suez Canal one day after Soviet forces crushed the revolution in Hungary, Soviet Premier Nikolai Bulganin proposed joint U.S.-Soviet military steps to halt the Anglo-French attack and vaguely threatened to use "atom and hydrogen weapons" against London and Paris. On the basis of the timing and wording of these threats, historian Galia Golan concludes that the Soviets lacked the intention or capability to enter the war and sought only to score political points in neutralist Middle East states. U.S. Ambassador to Moscow Charles E. Bohlen, however, called the Soviet threats "as close to [an] ultimatum as possible without so stating," and a plausible source at the United Nations reported that Soviet envoys had offered to send troops to Arab states. Within days, the CIA had gathered reports of Soviet military planes and soldiers arriving in Syria and had intercepted a message indicating that the Soviets would "do something" for Egypt.[39]

The Soviet threats and actions alarmed Eisenhower. "The Soviets are scared and furious" because of Hungary, he observed, and ready "to take any wild adventure." The CIA suspected that Soviet troops might engage in "small-scale attacks by air or submarine" against Western forces in the Mediterranean or fire guided missiles at Israel. If "the Soviets attacked the French and British directly, we would be in war," Eisenhower resolved, and if Soviet forces were detected in Syria "then there would be reason for the British and French to destroy them." Tensions escalated days later when a high-altitude Western military plane was shot down over Syria. "Such a feat would be impossible for the Syrian air force," the chairman of the JCS, Admiral Arthur W. Radford, warned. "The Russians may have much more air[power] in Syria than we currently estimate."[40]

Alarmed by these developments, the Pentagon prepared for a world war against the Soviet Union. Between 29 October and 4 November, the JCS ordered an aircraft carrier and an antisubmarine hunter-killer group to sail from the Atlantic to the Mediterranean, alerted other forces for action, and braced for attack by Egyptian, Israeli, or even British and French forces. After Soviet leaders threatened intervention, the JCS placed the Strategic Air Command and the Continental Air Defense Command on "increased readiness stage," redeployed naval vessels to monitor Soviet submarines and to reconnoiter the Distant Early Warning line, canceled leaves and training missions, and ordered commanders worldwide to increase "general vigilance." By 11 November, the Sixth Fleet was positioned between Crete and Malta, poised to launch air strikes in Egypt or the Levant and vigilant against attacks by Soviet jets from Eastern Europe or Syria. Other naval forces stood by in the Atlantic and Pacific for rapid transfer to the Middle East if needed.[41]

Shaken by the sudden prospect of global war, Eisenhower moved quickly to head it off. He applied political and financial pressures on the four belligerents to accept on 6 November a U.N. cease-fire deal that took effect the next day. State Department officials endorsed U.N. Secretary-General Dag Hammarskjöld's efforts to deploy UNEF to Egypt at once. They persuaded Nasser to authorize UNEF to patrol his territory despite his fear that its Canadian soldiers

would appear to his people as British troops in disguise. To secure Nasser's cooperation, Hammarskjöld made a concession, which would prove decisive on
the eve of the 1967 Arab-Israeli war, that Egypt would retain the right to order
UNEF to leave.[42]

As the cease-fire took effect, Eisenhower took some comfort in evidence that
the Soviet threats against Britain and France had redounded to U.S. advantage.
Nasser told CIA officers that he neither wanted nor invited Soviet intervention,
and he urged that the U.S. Sixth Fleet check any Soviet move into the region. Despite the Soviet ultimatum, U.S. Ambassador to Amman Lester D. Mallory observed, the Jordanian public appreciated U.S. diplomacy to end the crisis. Israeli
leaders denounced the Soviet threats. "Except for his signature, I would have
thought this note was written by Hitler," Ben-Gurion commented on a missive
from Bulganin. Soviet threats and action in Budapest "testify what these communist Nazis are capable of doing."[43]

Yet Eisenhower remained uneasy about Soviet intentions in the Middle East
even after the Suez-Sinai War ended. The CIA and the Joint Intelligence Staff
doubted that the Soviets desired or sought war with the West or another major
Arab-Israeli clash that would result in the defeat of Soviet-supplied Arab armies.
But American intelligence officials suspected that the Soviets would risk war to
hinder resolution of the canal controversy, promote leftist radicalism in Syria,
perpetuate Arab-Israeli tension, or improve Soviet-Arab relations. The Pentagon continued to fear Soviet meddling in Syria and predicted in late November
that war between Syria and one or more of its neighbors "could occur with little
warning." U.S. forces worldwide remained on alert until late December.[44]

Conclusion

The 1956 Suez-Sinai episode was the most serious situation the United States
had ever faced in the Middle East. Despite U.S. efforts, an international crisis
over the Suez Canal persisted for several months and triggered a tripartite military assault on Egypt. The United States halted the attack even though two of its
closest allies were instigators but did not do so before the Soviet Union threatened to intervene. Eisenhower's preparations for world war against the Soviet
Union revealed the gravity of the crisis at its peak.

Because of its various dimensions, the Suez-Sinai crisis was also one of the
most complex situations Eisenhower ever faced. On an intraregional plane, it
had origins as part of the Arab-Israeli conflict. Egypt and Israel had sparred over
Israeli access to the canal since 1948, and Arab-Israeli tensions regarding borders, security, and other issues had increased sharply since 1955. Opportunisti-
cally assertive toward the seemingly moribund kingdom of Jordan, Israel initially remained passive toward the canal dispute on the hope that Britain and

France would deflate the Jewish state's nemesis, Nasser, with diplomacy or force. But Israel eventually embraced the collusion scheme and trained its firepower on Egypt. A surge in Arab solidarity behind Nasser united the Arab world at the height of the crisis and threatened to unhinge Eisenhower's reliance on certain Arab leaders.

At the interregional level, the crisis pitted Britain and France against Egypt in a decolonization flashpoint. The European powers resolved to wage war against Egypt to recover their property, restore their imperial images, and check Nasser's power. Eisenhower sympathized with his allies' objectives but rejected the propriety of military means. Thus, Britain and France colluded with Israel to undermine Nasser, a deed that linked the Arab-Israeli conflict to the European-Egyptian controversy and created a crisis of complex magnitude.

The crisis also took on a global dimension when the Soviet Union threatened to intervene in the fighting and to carry the war to France and Britain and encouraged Arab states to resist a Western-Israeli conspiracy to expand. Eisenhower briefly sensed that world war loomed, and even after the threat of Soviet aggression waned, he feared that war might nonetheless result from error, miscalculation, or some act of desperation by the Soviets. Collusion triggered a Soviet reaction that raised the specter of global war.

Eisenhower addressed the Suez-Sinai episode on all three levels. Giving first priority to his Cold War interests, he foiled Soviet ambitions in the Middle East and vowed to protect Britain and France from Soviet attack. Amid the tensions over Soviet threats to fire missiles at London and Paris, he showed no interest in Bulganin's suggestion of joint U.S.-Soviet action to halt the Suez-Sinai War. With the Soviets excluded, Eisenhower sought to end the Anglo-French and Israeli assaults on Egypt and in so doing to restore the stability on which U.S. regional interests rested.

Although Eisenhower ended the Suez-Sinai War without Soviet involvement, the imbroglio marked the nadir of U.S.-British postwar relations. Eisenhower's refusal to endorse British military operations against Egypt impelled Eden to hatch the collusion scheme as a means of deceiving the U.S. president. Feeling betrayed and calculating that the collusion undermined Western security interests throughout the Third World, Eisenhower used political and economic leverage to force the attackers to desist. So humiliated were Britain and France that a deterioration in the Western alliance loomed.

The Suez-Sinai War constituted a major setback in the U.S. quest to stabilize the Middle East. The episode caused turmoil, war, Soviet meddling, additional Arab-Israeli animosity, and the decline of Allied power in the region. By ending the hostilities and avoiding military conflict with the Soviets, Eisenhower escaped a complete disaster. He even restored a modicum of stability by arranging a cease-fire, averting Soviet military intervention, avoiding an irreparable breach with Britain and France, and preserving some respect in Cairo. But the task of curing the regional instability caused by the crisis remained daunting. Success would depend on Eisenhower's ability to extend the cease-fire, compel the belligerents to withdraw from Egypt, and settle the controversy over the Suez Canal that had initially sparked the crisis.

16

PERSISTENT CONFLICT
The Aftermath of the Suez-Sinai War

At the cease-fire of the Suez-Sinai War, Israel occupied the Gaza Strip and the Sinai, while Britain and France controlled corridors along the Suez Canal. Having stopped the military advance of the colluding powers, the Dwight D. Eisenhower administration demanded that they withdraw unconditionally from Egyptian territory. Facing U.S. economic and oil sanctions, Britain and France complied in December 1956.[1] But Israel declined to pull back unless it gained border security, freedom of transit on the Suez Canal and the Gulf of Aqaba, and assurances that Egyptian Premier Gamal Abdel Nasser would not restore the status quo antebellum in the Sinai or Gaza. The Arab-Israeli component of the Suez-Sinai War persisted long after the European and global dimensions faded.

President Eisenhower and Secretary of State John Foster Dulles engaged in months of painstaking diplomacy to achieve Israeli withdrawal and restore a modicum of stability to the Middle East. Cold War interests deterred them from seeking Soviet assistance to achieve such goals, and congressional and public opinion prevented them from using sanctions to force an Israeli departure. In the end, Eisenhower found a way to avert a recurrence of Egyptian-Israeli war and to mitigate tensions over borders, Israeli transit, and Egyptian governance of Gaza. In the process, however, tensions developed between the United States and both Israel and Egypt.

The Debate on the Israeli Occupation of Egypt

In the months following the cease-fire, U.S. and Israeli officials debated the legitimacy and longevity of Israel's occupation of Egypt. They initially addressed the legitimacy of Israel's attack and the necessity of its withdrawal from occupied territory. As time passed, the debate centered on the terms of Israeli evacuation of the Sinai, Sharm al-Sheikh, and Gaza. Israel also challenged a U.N. decision regarding the duration of the deployment of the United Nations Emergency Force (UNEF) between the Israeli and Egyptian armies. Although Eisenhower and Dulles decided to make concessions to Israel, they pressured Israel first to agree to withdraw unconditionally from all occupied territory. But Israel proved reluctant to pull back without ironclad guarantees of its interests.

The earliest U.S.-Israeli debate focused on the legitimacy of Israel's attack on Egypt. Israel claimed that the Israel Defense Forces (IDF) had captured enough Soviet-made weapons in the Sinai to have armed eighty thousand Egyptian soldiers, battle plans for an impending Egyptian-Jordanian-Syrian invasion, "very deadly poison" intended for Israeli drinking water, and "copies of 'Mein Kampf' in Arabic everywhere." Israel's incursion into Egypt, Prime Minister David Ben-Gurion wrote to Eisenhower's friend Walter Bedell Smith, was justified by "the nightmare of continuous aggression and the threat of extinction" the Jewish state faced.[2]

But Eisenhower considered Israel's attack unjustified. Doubtful of Egypt's capability to invade Israel, Pentagon officers noted that the captured supplies included neither unconventional weapons nor stockpiles earmarked for Soviet troops. State Department officials observed to Israeli envoys that preventive war in principle threatened international order, that the Soviets would have stopped the collusion scheme by severe means had Eisenhower not halted it, and that Israel must learn to deal with Arab provocations through the United Nations.[3]

U.S. and Israeli officials also disagreed in principle about Israel's occupation of Egyptian territory. The State Department warned Israel that unless it evacuated Egypt, the Arab states would turn to Moscow, opening the Middle East to Soviet influence that would cause Israel's demise. Eisenhower expressed to Ben-Gurion his "deep concern" that an Israeli refusal to withdraw might "impair the friendly cooperation between our two countries." Ben-Gurion resolved in late 1956, however, that he would withdraw only if Egypt restrained the fedayeen, ended the canal blockade, and negotiated a formal peace treaty. Israel "never planned to annex the Sinai Desert," Ben-Gurion assured Eisenhower, and would "willingly withdraw" if these conditions were met.[4]

To bolster Ben-Gurion's message to Eisenhower, Israeli officials in Washington conducted "comprehensive *hasbara*" activities on the Suez crisis and mobilized sympathetic Americans to pressure the White House. The American Jewish Committee urged Dulles to seek a comprehensive Arab-Israeli peace on terms consistent with Israeli security, while Zionist activist Rabbi Abba Hillel Silver pressed the secretary of state to secure for Israel transit rights on the Gulf of Aqaba and permission to annex Gaza. Leaders of seventeen major U.S. Jewish groups, meeting on 27 November, passed resolutions endorsing Israel's action and urging Eisenhower to support it.[5]

Israeli officials discerned sympathy for their position in certain corners of the Eisenhower administration. Ben-Gurion sensed that Director of Central Intelligence Allen Dulles, Chairman of the Joint Chiefs of Staff (JCS) Admiral Arthur Radford, and presidential confidante Walter Bedell Smith supported the Israeli prime minister's objective of ousting Nasser. The Israeli minister to Washington, Reuven Shiloah, noted that John Foster Dulles became more anti-Nasser once the Soviets interceded in the crisis. As Dulles's health declined beginning in 1956, however, control of State Department policy seemingly passed to Undersecretary Herbert Hoover Jr. and Ambassador to the United Nations Henry Cabot Lodge Jr., who unalterably opposed Israel's attack on Egypt. Eisenhower, reelected president on 6 November, seemed immune to the domestic pressures to support Israel. In November, he declined Ben-Gurion's request for a private audience to discuss the Sinai situation.[6]

Israeli occupation of the Sinai formed the first specific territorial issue debated by U.S. and Israeli leaders. On 21 November, Israel withdrew its troops several miles along the entire battle frontier and offered to evacuate most of the remaining Sinai if UNEF occupied three Egyptian military bases that had supported fedayeen operations. The State Department, however, insisted that Israel withdraw its forces from the Sinai "without conditions and without delay" and pushed a resolution with such terms through the General Assembly on 24 November. Israel yielded in hope of winning concessions on other disputes. In a staged withdrawal, the IDF evacuated the entire Sinai except Sharm al-Sheikh by 22 January 1957.[7] (See map 6.)

In contrast to its concessions on the Sinai, Israel remained firm on Sharm al-Sheikh. Since the IDF had occupied the city, Israel had enjoyed maritime access to the Gulf of Aqaba and made plans to develop Eilat as a major seaport. The Israeli ambassador to Washington, Abba Eban, stressed that an interoceanic transit line through Israel, paralleling the Suez Canal, would provide Europe "two lungs rather than one to breathe with." Israel would retain Sharm al-Sheikh until the Jewish state obtained international assurances of its transit rights on the gulf, Ben-Gurion declared. "No more will we be subject to Nasser's whims or charity."[8]

Ben-Gurion also took a firm position on Gaza. He decided not to annex it because Israel could not "digest" its 250,000 Palestinian refugees, but he refused to accept a restoration of the status quo antebellum. "In no event and in no manner will Israel agree to [the] return of [the] Egyptian invader" to Gaza, he declared. Israel must have some guarantee against "fedayeen murder units" based there. Ben-Gurion offered to withdraw from Gaza only if Israeli police forces remained to govern the strip in cooperation with UNEF and local civil authorities.[9]

Eisenhower made limited concessions to Israel on the Sharm al-Sheikh and Gaza issues. Dulles conceded that UNEF units rather than Egyptian troops should occupy Sharm al-Sheikh and that the international character of the Gulf of Aqaba should be guaranteed. But he also insisted that Israel first withdraw its forces unconditionally and submit to U.N. decisions on the deployment of UNEF. He also decided that Israel should transfer control of Gaza to UNEF, which should allow Egypt to restore civil but not military authority in the territory.[10]

Israel also quarreled with U.N. officials about the duration of UNEF's mission in the Sinai. Israeli leaders criticized U.N. Secretary-General Dag Hammarskjöld's concession to Nasser that UNEF's presence in Egypt depended on Egypt's consent, demanding safeguards to ensure that the General Assembly would decide whether and when to terminate the mission. Hammarskjöld reassured Israel that his deal with Nasser had "calculated ambiguity" and that when UNEF proved functional, he would ask Egypt to recognize the General Assembly's prerogative over it. But Israel remained unconvinced.[11]

The Debate on Sanctions and Israeli Withdrawal from Egypt

U.S.-Israeli debates on the terms of Israeli withdrawal from Egypt were overtaken in early 1957 by U.N. consideration of a resolution to impose economic sanctions on Israel. Third World states clamored for sanctions on the grounds that Israel refused to heed resolutions demanding its unconditional withdrawal. Eisenhower and Dulles reluctantly endorsed sanctions and even took the lead in formulating an appropriate resolution, both to force Israel to make concessions and to deflect a more severe resolution promoted by other powers. Public and congressional sympathy for Israel, however, sharply limited American leaders' options and, in the end, forced them to compromise with Israel.

The drive for sanctions emerged from U.N. action on the Israeli occupation of Egypt. On 19 January, the General Assembly passed a resolution demanding Israeli withdrawal to the armistice lines, and on 2 February the assembly passed two resolutions, one deploring Israel's refusal to comply and the other reaffirming the Egyptian-Israeli armistice and authorizing UNEF to occupy Sharm al-Sheikh and Gaza. On 22 February, Iraq, Lebanon, and four other states submitted a resolution condemning Israeli defiance of these U.N. directives and urging all states "to deny all military, economic or financial assistance" to Israel.[12]

Both the Arab states and Israel sought U.S. support for their positions on sanctions. Saudi Deputy Foreign Minister Yusuf Yasin advised the State Department that imposing sanctions would earn the United States "great prestige" among Arab states. Iraq, Jordan, Syria, Lebanon, and Egypt made similar approaches. In contrast, Ben-Gurion argued to Eisenhower the injustice of punishing Israel alone when Egypt also had violated U.N. resolutions. Because sanctions would not change Israeli policy, he added, enacting them would tarnish U.N. prestige.[13]

The sanctions debate confronted Eisenhower with a difficult dilemma. Several State Department officials argued that sanctions formed a proper response to Israel's refusal to heed the United Nations. The United States had endorsed sanctions on Israel by cosponsoring the 30 October 1956 Security Council resolution vetoed by Britain and France, Lodge argued. To reverse course in February 1957 would deal the United Nations "a body blow" and convince Arab states that the administration lacked the will to impose fair punishments on Israel.[14]

But Dulles remained leery of sanctions. If enforced broadly, he noted, sanctions would comprise Israel's "death sentence." He hesitated to punish Israel alone in light of Egypt's noncompliance with other U.N. resolutions or to set an undesirable precedent for similar measures against other countries. The *New York Times* found it "illogical to the point of nonsense" to force Israel to withdraw without first providing reasonable assurances of its future security. Mobilized by lobbyist I. L. Kenen, numerous members of Congress communicated to the White House their opposition to sanctions. Senate Majority Leader Lyndon B. Johnson (D-Texas) threatened to hold up Senate approval of the Eisenhower Doctrine, the administration's new regional policy (explained in chapter 17), if sanctions were imposed. Dulles recognized that the modest increase in the Democratic Party's majorities in the House and Senate in the 1956 election limited the president's options. In light of public and congressional attitudes, he told Lodge on 10 February, "we would have a terrible time on sanctions."[15]

To resolve the dilemma, Eisenhower approved a compromise proposal that avoided sanctions. In an aide-mémoire dated 11 February, Dulles demanded that Israel execute a "prompt and unconditional" withdrawal from Gaza, yield the strip to UNEF, and abandon the goal of stationing civil police there. Yet he also recognized the Gulf of Aqaba as "international waters" in which Israel had the right to "free and innocent passage." Once Israel yielded Sharm al-Sheikh to UNEF, the United States would "join with others to secure general recognition of this right." Using the carrot and the stick, Dulles described these terms as more valuable to Israel "than red ribbon and seals on paper treaties" and warned that Israeli noncooperation would lead to U.S. enforcement of U.N. sanctions.[16]

Neither the Arab states nor Israel approved the aide-mémoire. The concession to Israel on Sharm al-Sheikh left "the Arabs . . . terribly upset," Allen Dulles reported on 13 February. Because the United States had recognized Aqaba as international waters since 1950, Eisenhower and Dulles explained to Arab leaders, the aide-mémoire provided Israel no gains. But the American leaders' words fell on deaf ears. On the other side, Ben-Gurion rejected the aide-mémoire because it would not satisfy Israeli security imperatives.[17]

In the face of Israeli stubbornness, Eisenhower and Dulles embraced sanctions in principle. Israel's position was "unacceptable" and unlikely to improve given Ben-Gurion's "strongly emotional attitude," they reasoned. "Either we get the Israelis out, or the Russians will get the Israelis out," Dulles added, "and their influence will thus come into the Middle East to stay." Eisenhower decided to impose sanctions on governmental and private aid to Israel, including donations and Israeli bond purchases by U.S. citizens, a charity stream worth some one hundred million dollars per year.[18]

In contrast to Eisenhower's thinking, congressional opinion turned sharply critical of sanctions. Led by Lyndon Johnson, senators delayed Christian A. Herter's confirmation as undersecretary of state, blocked foreign aid programs, and vowed to remove the president's legal authority to enforce sanctions. Senate Minority Leader William F. Knowland (R-California) threatened to resign from the U.S. delegation to the United Nations if Eisenhower endorsed the move. "Israel is so right in its position," Representative Edith N. Rogers (R-Massachusetts) declared, that Eisenhower's proposal "is nothing less than a ludicrous fiasco." Representative Daniel J. Flood (D-Pennsylvania) added that sanctions would comprise "another cheap triumph for the little Hitler of the Middle East, Egypt's Nasser." The "pressure of the Jews," Dulles fumed privately, created "a very nasty situation on the Hill."[19]

To overcome such criticism, on 20 February Eisenhower invited to the White House Johnson, Knowland, Speaker of the House Sam Rayburn (D-Texas), and other leading legislators of both parties. Because Israeli defiance of U.N. resolutions would ruin U.N. prestige, open the Middle East to Soviet influence, and foment war, the president contended, sanctions were necessary. "Countries which depend on [the] US for help," Dulles added, "should follow us instead of us following them." After voicing reservations, most of the legislators deferred to the president on the issue. "America has either one voice or none," Rayburn conceded, "and the one voice was the voice of the President even though not everyone agreed with him."[20]

Despite Rayburn's concession, public opinion remained sharply critical of sanctions. "The terrific control the Jews had over the news media," Dulles observed, caused "very serious trouble" in the public realm. Eisenhower presented the case for sanctions in a nationally televised address on 20 February, but public opinion remained critical. Desperate, Dulles phoned an acquaintance at the National Council of Churches to ask Protestant clergy to support Eisenhower in their 24 February sermons. "It was impossible to hold the line because we got no support from the Protestant elements of the country," he intoned. "All we get is a battering from the Jews."[21]

The public criticism convinced Eisenhower to ease his pressure on Israel. On 20 February, he warned Ben-Gurion that the congressional leadership had approved sanctions, and he refused to delay the General Assembly debate scheduled to start in two days. Hours before the debate opened, however, Eisenhower decided that "a simple condemnation of Israel and vote of sanctions would be wrong." He directed Dulles to postpone the proceedings until 25 February and to find a "face-saving" formula that would provide Israel proper assurances while remaining sufficiently coercive to mollify the Arab states and compel Israeli compliance.[22]

Eisenhower's flinch set the stage for a convergence of U.S. and Israeli policy. At a climactic 24 February meeting with Dulles, Eban outlined a plan for Israeli withdrawal. Israel would withdraw from Sharm al-Sheikh if UNEF occupied the area and if the United States and other maritime powers would publicly endorse Israel's free transit rights on the gulf. Israel would yield Gaza to UNEF control if the United Nations would decide the strip's government and prevent restoration of the status quo antebellum. Cautioning only that Egypt must consent to any change in the Gaza government, Dulles endorsed Eban's proposal. The U.S. secretary of state told Eisenhower and Lodge that "he felt better tonight than he had for a long time. . . . Israel had gone so far that he did not think we could ever vote sanctions."[23]

The 24 February Israeli proposal constituted a major breakthrough that set the stage for Israeli withdrawal from Egypt. For several days, Israeli and U.N. officials quarreled over the details of Israel's proposal. When Eisenhower refused to rule out sanctions, however, Ben-Gurion conceded. On 1 March, Foreign Minister Golda Meir informed the General Assembly that Israel would withdraw from Gaza and Sharm al-Sheikh in accordance with the 2 February resolutions. Israeli military officers transferred their authority to UNEF units on 6–8 March. Eisenhower achieved his objective of Israeli withdrawal without imposing sanctions.[24]

While gratified by this outcome, Eisenhower and Dulles were concerned by Arab disappointment. Arab leaders seemed frustrated that Israel had avoided sanctions and a split with the United States, circulating rumors that the United States had offered Israel some secret incentive to withdraw. Saudi officials warned the United States not to support Israel's quest for navigation rights in the Gulf of Aqaba. So deep was Arab discontent that Dulles feared that Egypt would "kick [the settlement] over" by moving military forces into Gaza. He denied the rumors about secret assurances to Israel and stressed that Eisenhower had forced Israel to withdraw without gaining any new rights.[25]

The Debate on Gaza, the Gulf of Aqaba, and the Suez Canal

After Israel withdrew from Gaza and the Sinai, Egyptian-Israeli conflict persisted on three issues. Two of these disputes—Israel's resistance to Egyptian authority in Gaza and Arab opposition to Israeli shipping on the Gulf of Aqaba—briefly threatened to trigger renewed war. The third issue, Israel's demand for transit rights on the Suez Canal, complicated a larger international debate over the control and management of the waterway. Anxious to restore stability to the Middle East, Eisenhower and Dulles worked to resolve all three disputes.

Days after Israel's departure from Gaza, a controversy developed over the restoration of Egyptian authority there. Between 11 and 19 March, Nasser dispatched a civil governor into the territory and advanced troops to El Arish to assert his legal rights under the armistice and to restore Egyptian prestige damaged by his acceptance of UNEF. Israel protested that these moves revealed Nasser's intent to incapacitate UNEF and resume fedayeen operations. Nasser had "rekindled a dangerous tension in the Gaza Strip," Ben-Gurion wrote to Eisenhower. Israel might "have to make use of her right of self-defense."[26]

Eisenhower and Dulles restrained both sides in this dispute, urging Nasser to delay the governor's arrival until the United Nations arranged a border settlement and warning that the Egyptian leader would earn international reproach if his actions sparked a war. Fearing that Ben-Gurion might be "trigger-happy," Eisenhower also urged him to avoid "any precipitate action which might result in a deterioration of the situation." Meir visited Washington on 18 March to press Dulles in person for approval of an Israeli reoccupation of Gaza, but Dulles ruled such a move unjustified. Eisenhower also asked Britain and France to dissuade Ben-Gurion from taking action.[27]

To Eisenhower's relief, the situation in Gaza stabilized. Nasser refrained from sending troops into Gaza and suppressed the fedayeen. In negotiations with Hammarskjöld, Nasser recognized UNEF's right to transit Gaza, stockpile supplies, maintain an airfield, patrol the border, provide internal security in joint operations with Palestinian police, and use arrest and deadly force to stop exfiltration to Israel. Nasser also conceded, U.S. officials noted, that UNEF would remain in Gaza "until its task is completed—a determination which cannot be made by Egypt alone." Israeli leaders doubted the validity of Nasser's concessions and suspected that he would resume covert warfare once the attention of the United Nations waned. But Israel refrained from reoccupying Gaza with military force.[28]

The situation in the Gulf of Aqaba also generated tension in the weeks following Israel's withdrawal from Sharm al-Sheikh. UNEF's occupation of the area denied Egypt the ability to fire on ships entering the gulf, and Nasser agreed that UNEF could remain until U.N. officials withdrew it. Saudi Arabia, however, claimed sovereignty over Tiran and Sanafir Islands and the channels between them and vowed to "take all the necessary measures" to deny Israel access to the gulf.[29] (See map 5.)

Eisenhower and Dulles struck an ambiguous position on the issue. On the one hand, State Department lawyers considered the straits leading into the gulf international waters, and Dulles maintained that Israel was entitled to send ships through them. As he had pledged before Israel withdrew from Sharm al-

Sheikh, Eisenhower consulted other Western maritime states about taking joint action to affirm the international status of the waterway. Wary of Arab anger, however, he refrained from action to open the waterway. When Meir asked Dulles to arrange a voyage to Eilat of a ship flying the U.S. flag in order to affirm free access in principle, Dulles refused on flimsy grounds that he could not become involved in the private matter of ship schedules.[30]

Despite their efforts to avoid a fray, U.S. leaders became involved in a dispute involving the *Kern Hill*, a U.S.-flag tanker that Israel chartered from a Swiss firm and that passed through the channel and reached Eilat on 7 April. Egypt and Jordan protested the voyage as a threat to peace, and Saudi Arabia threatened to shell the next such ship to enter the straits. To deflect such anger, Dulles denied foreknowledge of the *Kern Hill*'s voyage, which U.S. leaders attributed to private shipping firms acting beyond government control. To create an impression of U.S. endorsement, however, Israel then publicized the fact that a U.S. destroyer in the Red Sea had sent a routine good luck message to the tanker, and Arab leaders bitterly protested. Astonished that a "simple act of seaman's courtesy" had provoked such anger, the JCS withdrew U.S. Navy ships from the Red Sea.[31]

Fortunately for Eisenhower, the situation in the Gulf of Aqaba stabilized after the *Kern Hill* episode. Egypt pledged to refrain from hostile action in the gulf. The State Department asserted to the Saudis that Israel had the legal right to innocent passage through the straits and warned that Saudi Arabia would probably lose if it asked the International Court of Justice to rule on the legal issues. Dulles also encouraged Israel to pursue its rights through quiet and nonconfrontational means, especially during a Jordanian political crisis in April. Ben-Gurion agreed to aim for an "air of routine normality" around Israeli shipping in the gulf.[32]

In addition to the problems of Gaza and Aqaba, Eisenhower and Dulles grappled with difficulties concerning the Suez Canal. The Americans first desired to reopen the waterway, which Egypt had blocked with sunken ships, cranes, and dry docks at the onset of hostilities. Closure of the canal disrupted international commerce, including oil deliveries to the West, reducing Saudi oil exports by one-third. When Israel evacuated the Sinai in January 1957, Nasser authorized the United Nations to conduct a canal clearance operation involving more than forty salvage vessels and bankrolled by the United States. The canal reopened in April 1957.[33]

Eisenhower also faced a deadlock over Nasser's nationalization of the Suez Canal Company. Dulles encouraged Hammarskjöld to broker a settlement, based on the Six Principles of October 1956, that ensured the principle of free transit for all powers. If Nasser proved uncooperative, U.S. Secretary of the Treasury George M. Humphrey advised, Eisenhower should "station battleships at both ends of the canal and prevent the transit of any ships." But Dulles countered that he "was not anxious to get into a war in the Middle East in place of the British and French." Dulles could only protest when Nasser announced in March that Egypt's Suez Canal Authority would operate the canal and collect all tolls in accordance with the 1888 convention and the U.N. Charter.[34]

To the chagrin of U.S. leaders, Israel intruded as a factor in the effort to re-open the canal. In early 1957, Israel had delayed its evacuation of the Sinai until Egypt recognized its transit rights on the canal, while Egypt refused to reopen the canal until Israel evacuated its territory. Even after Israel withdrew from Gaza and the Sinai, the Jewish state demanded suspension of the canal clearance operations until Egypt granted Israel the right to use the waterway. Ben-Gurion also contemplated sending a ship into the canal to test Egyptian policy.[35]

To secure Western rights on the canal, Eisenhower and Dulles distanced themselves from Israel's transit interests and dispatched private banker John McCloy to Cairo to offer economic incentives if Nasser accepted the Six Principles. When Nasser charged that those principles were "cleverly drafted to cover Israel's case," however, Eisenhower and Dulles revealed that they valued favorable arrangements for Western ships on the canal more than they cared about Israeli transit rights.[36]

In April–May 1957, Eisenhower accepted Egyptian control of the canal and pressed other powers to do likewise. The president scotched British plans to depose Nasser if he remained recalcitrant and urged British Prime Minister Harold Macmillan to accept Egyptian control. Dulles denied Israel the privilege of addressing the Security Council on the issue and discouraged the Jewish state from challenging Nasser's resolve with a test case. In May, the State Department authorized U.S. shipping companies and the U.S. Navy to transit the canal and pay tolls to Egypt.[37]

Conclusion

The Suez-Sinai War caused sharp territorial disputes between Egypt and Israel. Backed by other Arab states, Egypt demanded that Israel withdraw unconditionally from Gaza and the Sinai. While willing to depart from most of the Sinai, Israel remained in Sharm al-Sheikh in hope of securing transit rights on the Gulf of Aqaba. Israel also refused to withdraw from Gaza before securing guarantees against the resumption of fedayeen activity there.

In principle, Eisenhower and Dulles agreed with the Arab view that Israel, one of the aggressor states in the Suez-Sinai conflict, should withdraw unconditionally from the occupied territories. When diplomacy seemed unable to achieve such an outcome, the U.S. leaders endorsed the Arab view that the United Nations should impose sanctions on Israel. Conversely, the president and secretary of state also saw merit in Israel's position on the Gulf of Aqaba.

Public and congressional opinion, moreover, sharply limited Eisenhower and Dulles's ability to compel Israeli withdrawal.

Within the limits established by domestic circumstances, Eisenhower and Dulles used diplomacy to arrange an Israeli withdrawal. They applied a mixture of pressures (such as support of U.N. resolutions ordering Israel to depart the territories) and inducements (such as a clarification of the traditional U.S. support of Israeli transit rights on the Gulf of Aqaba) to convince Israel to evacuate occupied territory as quickly and unconditionally as possible. Dulles made clear to Arab leaders that he had issued to Israel no special promises that met its original conditions. Eisenhower advanced a U.N. sanctions resolution even as he realized that domestic circumstances would prevent him from enforcing it.

U.S. leaders worked hard to ease the tense situation along the Egyptian-Israeli frontier after the Israeli withdrawal in early March. For several weeks, potentially explosive conflicts persisted over Egyptian governance of the Sinai and Gaza and Israeli rights on the Gulf of Aqaba and the Suez Canal. In view of the antebellum tensions over transit rights and border security issues, it would not have seemed surprising if fighting had resumed in early 1957. Yet war was averted, at least in part because U.S. officials dissuaded each state from initiating hostilities or provoking the other side to do so.

By spring 1957, a tenuous calm had returned to the Egyptian-Israeli frontier. Egypt had gained control of the Suez Canal from Britain and France and implicitly reasserted its ability to deny Israel access to the waterway. Israel had achieved access to the Gulf of Aqaba, which lessened the economic importance of the canal blockade. A stalemate formed on Gaza, as Egypt reasserted its sovereignty but refrained from remilitarizing the area. The United States was relieved to see a shadow of stability restored in the region.

Yet serious questions remained about the duration of UNEF's occupation of Sharm al-Sheikh and Israel's right of access to the Gulf of Aqaba. With regard to Gaza, Egypt and Israel held conflicting views about UNEF's rights to patrol the border, Egypt's right to restore its mode of governance, and Israel's right to defend proactively against fedayeen raids. These disputes would keep the Israeli-Egyptian conflict at the forefront of policy makers' thinking for years to come.

Part IV

17

SECURITY AFFIRMED
U.S. Regional Considerations in the Middle East after the Suez-Sinai War

From the point of view of the United States, the Suez-Sinai War destabilized the Middle East. In its wake, the Dwight D. Eisenhower administration identified new factors, notably fervent Arab nationalism serving the objectives of the Soviet Union, that challenged the traditional quest to maintain Western primacy in the region. Because security experts continued to consider the Middle East vital for security, political, and economic reasons, the Suez-Sinai War forced the United States to reconfigure its long-term approach to the region. In the late 1950s, President Eisenhower brought his fundamental policy toward the Middle East into line with the new circumstances.

To protect vital U.S. interests in the Middle East in the late 1950s, Eisenhower blended new approaches with old ones. Most notably, he instituted the Eisenhower Doctrine, a declaration that the United States would use economic aid, military aid, and armed forces to stop the spread of communism in the region. The president also revived the U.S. friendship with Britain, reaffirmed the Baghdad Pact, and modified his arms supply policy. To a degree, these security enhancements were determined by Eisenhower's earlier identification of security imperatives in the Middle East. When British influence waned and Soviet assertiveness increased during the Suez-Sinai War, the U.S. president saw no choice but to raise his commitment to the region.

While affirming the importance of regional security, Eisenhower and Secretary of State John Foster Dulles curtailed their efforts to make Arab-Israeli peace. They endorsed conflict resolution in principle but calculated that a comprehensive peace initiative would fail and perhaps even stoke tensions by accentuating differences. To their dismay, the U.S. leaders came to realize that even when they refrained from peacemaking, their relations with Israel and the Arab states were strained by American support of or security collaboration with the other side.

The Eisenhower Doctrine

At the end of the Suez-Sinai War, Eisenhower worried that the demise of Anglo-French influence and the rise of Soviet interest in the Middle East boded ill for the preservation of U.S. objectives in the region. Consequently, he assumed explicit responsibility, under a new security concept called the Eisenhower Doctrine, for stopping communist expansion in the region by fiscal and military means. The president secured congressional approval of this doctrine but found it difficult to convince the Arab states or Israel of the doctrine's purpose or usefulness. Nonetheless, the Pentagon prepared to enforce the doctrine against threats external or indigenous to the region. By assuming new responsibilities in the Middle East, Eisenhower raised the prospect that the United States would fight in the region or even on a global scale.

Eisenhower conceived the doctrine as an adjustment to the consequences of the Suez-Sinai War. Given the collapse of British prestige and the rise of Soviet interest, he decided to establish a new mechanism for U.S. intervention to stabilize the region against Soviet threats or internal turmoil or revolution. "We have no intention of standing idly by," the president declared in December 1956, "to see the southern flank of NATO completely collapse through Communist penetration and success in the Mid East." Dulles told Britain, France, and Turkey that "we intend to make our presence more strongly felt in the Middle East."[1]

Even as he conceived the doctrine to replace British power, Eisenhower renewed his friendship with Britain. Anglo-U.S. discord over Suez was "something of a sad blow," he commented, "because, quite naturally, Britain has not only been, but must be, our best friend in the world." During a March 1957 meeting with British Prime Minister Harold Macmillan, the president happily noted that the Anglo-U.S. partnership had healed quickly. "Macmillan is . . . one of my intimate wartime friends," he observed, "so it is very easy to talk to him on a very frank, even blunt, basis." Hoping "to restore our old relationships with Washington," Macmillan welcomed the Eisenhower Doctrine.[2]

Eisenhower also clearly revealed the doctrine's anti-Soviet purposes. Soviet leaders charged that the doctrine "protects and covers up colonialism," and Foreign Minister Dmitri Shepilov proposed that the United States, Soviet Union, Britain, and France jointly negotiate an Arab-Israeli peace treaty, pledge noninterference in Middle East states, curtail arms supply to the region, and evacuate military bases and abolish security pacts there. With Eisenhower's blessing, the National Security Council (NSC) rejected this proposal as a ruse to demolish Western influence in the region and a betrayal of those Middle East states that had resisted Soviet power.[3]

Eisenhower considered the doctrine superior to other schemes to stabilize the Middle East. He rejected a proposal from a member of Congress to break with the Arab powers and bolster Israel as a U.S. bastion. The president also dismissed the idea of building a U.S. security apparatus on an Arab foundation because moral and domestic political factors made it impossible to break with Israel and because Arab nationalists seemed vulnerable to becoming unwitting agents of Soviet expansionism. While Dulles acknowledged that "there may be nationalist and patriotic trends which are wholly free from communist inspiration," he also believed that "International Communism seeks to infiltrate its agents into all movements within non-Communist countries which tend[s] to create discord as between the free nations or to weaken non-Communist governments."[4]

Eisenhower asked Congress to approve the doctrine in early 1957. He requested authority to dispense two hundred million dollars in economic and military aid and to commit armed forces to defend any country seeking assistance against international communism. He pledged to avoid intraregional quarrels and to concentrate on defending the area against communist aggression, and he portrayed the authority to dispatch troops as a deterrent that would reduce the chance of war. Pointing to "the existing vacuum that must be filled by the United States before it is filled by Russia," the president told members of Congress that the doctrine was "important . . . to the peace of the world."[5]

Skeptical of Eisenhower's proposal, however, some members of Congress dragged their feet. Various senators openly criticized the doctrine on the grounds that it would dangerously inflate presidential authority, expose the country to unnecessary military risks, and waste financial resources. Senator Allen J. Ellender (D-Louisiana) called the doctrine "unnecessary, super-superfluous, even impolitic, doubtless unwise, and wholly unjustified." "Future historians," Senator Wayne L. Morse (D-Oregon) added, "may have to record it as a chapter written in blood."[6]

In the end, Eisenhower prevailed in the domestic debate. He mobilized allies on Capitol Hill to promote his rationale for the doctrine. The *New York Times* urged lawmakers to endorse the idea as a bulwark against Soviet aggrandizement. Congress passed a resolution approving the doctrine on 7 March, and Eisenhower signed the measure into law two days later. Former Congressman James P. Richards, appointed by Eisenhower as special assistant with the rank of ambassador, visited Middle East leaders between March and May to seek their endorsements of the doctrine by offering them economic and military aid.[7]

Arab reactions to the Eisenhower Doctrine varied widely. Lebanon and Libya (like Turkey, Iran, and Pakistan) endorsed the doctrine even before Congress approved it and warmly welcomed Ambassador Richards, who dispensed $12.7 million in economic and military aid in Beirut and $4.5 million in Tripoli. King Hussein of Jordan approved the doctrine but asked Richards to stay away from the country while the king engaged in a power struggle with Prime Minister

Suleiman al-Nabulsi, who denounced the doctrine and led demonstrations cele-brating the termination of the Anglo-Jordanian treaty on 15 March. Richards allocated $16 million to Iraq (plus $12.5 million for regional projects of the Bagh-dad Pact) and $20 million to Saudi Arabia, although the leaders of both coun-tries warned that U.S. support of Israel would erode the prestige of both the United States and pro-Western Arab leaders in the minds of the Arab masses.[8]

Syria and Egypt, by contrast, showed no support for the Eisenhower Doc-trine. Officials in the Bureau of Near Eastern, South Asian, and African Affairs (NEA) directed Richardson to avoid Syria because of its regime's unfriendliness toward the United States. Preoccupied with achieving Israeli withdrawal from his territory, Egyptian Premier Gamal Abdel Nasser declined to invite Richards to visit Cairo to discuss the doctrine. Eisenhower feared that Nasser might tar-nish the doctrine by rejecting it and consequently refrained from pressing the matter. Years later, Nasser told a member of Congress that the doctrine seemed "a device to re-establish imperial control by non-military means" and that he would "have nothing to do with it and felt it was directed at Egypt as much as at any communist threat."[9]

Eisenhower intended to isolate the doctrine from Israel, which suited Israeli leaders. The State Department opposed special aid for Israel in light of its rela-tive security against communism and the likely reaction among Arab states to such aid. For his part, Israeli Prime Minister David Ben-Gurion disliked the doctrine because it promised to strengthen Western-Arab ties and reward Arab states that remained hostile to his country. He also feared that U.S. pressure to affirm the doctrine would imperil Israel's budding rapprochement with the Soviet Union and endanger "*aliyah* [immigration to Israel] from Poland and three million [Jews] in Russia." Israeli officials were pleased that Nasser's criti-cism of the doctrine damaged its prospects at no cost to their own interests.[10]

Richards failed to reach an accord with Israeli leaders about the doctrine. In fact, in light of Arab passions, he wished to avoid Israel and visited the coun-try only after being ordered to do so by Dulles, who cited "very strong feeling on the Hill." Given their mutual lack of enthusiasm for any Israeli association with the doctrine, Richards and Israeli leaders debated the doctrine to a stand-still. On the grounds that Israel was not threatened by communism, Richards rejected Foreign Minister Golda Meir's requests for a pledge to defend Israel against Arab as well as Soviet attack and for economic aid to construct housing for recent East European immigrants. Meir and Ben-Gurion refused publicly to affirm the doctrine for fear of endangering the welfare of Russian and East European Jews.[11]

The Pentagon prepared to implement the Eisenhower Doctrine even at risk of triggering a third world war. In the event of U.S.-Soviet hostilities, the Joint

Chiefs of Staff (JCS) planned to provide "a strategic defense of the Middle East area, with the U.S. and other allied strategic air offensives making a major contribution to this defense." Such a war would likely become worldwide in scope and involve an "intensive exchange of atomic weapons during a short initial phase" followed by a Western offensive, bolstered by atomic weapons, against the Soviet Union. Military bases in the Middle East would prove crucial to both the aerial campaign and the ground offensive.[12]

The JCS also planned to enforce the doctrine in a regional context. In the event of an Arab-Israeli crisis, the Pentagon would position forces to deter hostilities and to isolate and terminate any fighting that occurred. The Pentagon also conceived various schemes for intervention in any state that became an agent of communist expansion. While Egypt and Syria appeared the most likely targets, by December 1957 the JCS composed plans to protect U.S. nationals or to intervene in several countries. U.S. military officers seemed confident that they would prevail in any such limited engagement with air and naval power augmented by small, mobile, nuclear-capable ground troops.[13]

The Pentagon calculated that it could enforce the Eisenhower Doctrine with its forces as then arrayed. The Sixth Fleet maintained a sizable presence of aircraft carriers, support ships, and a marine battalion in the Mediterranean, and during the Jordan crisis of April 1957 the fleet moved from ports in France to battle stations in the Eastern Mediterranean in fifty hours. A smaller Middle East task force routinely patrolled the Persian Gulf, the Arabian Sea, and the Red Sea. The Air Force had the capability to send a combat fleet to Adana, Turkey, within six hours of notification; to commence operations within another six hours; and to launch atomic strikes within seventy-two hours of arrival. The army earmarked a regimental combat team of eleven thousand soldiers in Europe and two divisions in the United States for action in the Middle East. Once alerted, an advance party of six hundred soldiers would be airlifted to the region, with the remainder airlifted immediately or brought by sea within twenty-five days. With such combat-ready, atomic-capable, and mobile forces, the JCS expressed confidence that the Eisenhower Doctrine had teeth.[14]

In 1958, the Pentagon reaffirmed its readiness to fight in the Middle East even as regional political conditions complicated the U.S. military's tasks. As instability mounted in Lebanon and Jordan, American officers drafted contingency plans for intervention in either state and stockpiled supplies at forward bases in Turkey, Cyprus, and Libya. In June, the JCS affirmed its plans to intervene in Arab-Israeli hostilities, which might erupt "with little or no warning." By issuing the Eisenhower Doctrine, the United States assumed the risks of involvement in a war in the Middle East or even against the Soviet Union.[15]

Regional Security and Arms Supply

While formulating the Eisenhower Doctrine, Eisenhower had to reconsider two cornerstones of his policy in the Middle East. Erected as an anti-Soviet containment barrier along the northern tier of the region, the Baghdad Pact was shaken by Britain's strike on Egypt in 1956. Eisenhower had to decide whether to abandon, revive, or formally join the scheme. In addition, the September 1955 Soviet-Egyptian arms deal and the insecurity it caused in Israel had undermined the arms control provisions of the Tripartite Declaration of 1950. Flooded with arms requests by Israel and various Arab states, Eisenhower deliberated the consequences of weapons supplies on his quest for regional stability.

Because Britain's attack on Egypt endangered the Baghdad Pact, Eisenhower clarified his support of the alliance. Meeting in Tehran in November 1956, Shah Mohammad Reza Pahlavi of Iran, President Iskander Mirza of Pakistan, Prime Minister Adnan Menderes of Turkey, and Prime Minister Nuri Said of Iraq criticized Britain's resort to arms against Egypt. The U.S. State Department feared that the pact might collapse, affirmed it, and declared that "a threat to the territorial integrity or political independence of the members would be viewed by the United States with the utmost gravity."[16]

Yet Eisenhower proved more cautious on the issue of whether to adhere formally to the pact. The northern tier states pressed him to join to redress the loss in British prestige and to bolster the pact against Soviet threats and Arab nationalist criticism. Without the United States, Iraqi Crown Prince Abdul Ilah told Dulles, "we are four zeroes and those only add up to zero." The Pentagon strongly supported U.S. adherence as a means to bolster the Iraqi government against internal insurgency, gain access to military bases in Iraq, and counter the alliance recently signed by Egypt, Syria, and Jordan. "The very life of the Baghdad Pact is at stake," the JCS argued.[17]

Most Arab states and Israel opposed U.S. membership in the Baghdad Pact. Syrian Prime Minister Sabri al-Asali called U.S. adherence unnecessary and provocative. At a February 1957 meeting in Cairo, several Arab leaders declared that the pact had fostered British aggression in Egypt, alienated Iraq from other Arab states, and brought the Cold War to the Middle East. If the United States joined the pact, these officials implied, they would embrace neutralism. Long opposed to the alliance because it funneled weapons to Iraq and stimulated Soviet arms supply to Egypt and Syria, Israeli leaders protested in late 1956 that U.S. adherence might invite a Soviet attack on their state. Branding the pact forever "hostile to Israel," *hasbara* officials portrayed the treaty to the U.S. public as a pro-Egypt venture that had lost sight of its anti-Soviet purpose.[18]

Eisenhower and Dulles identified several reasons to decline membership. Joining the pact, Dulles believed, would undermine U.N. efforts to solve the

Suez controversy and intensify the Soviet effort at "hopping over the 'northern tier' line" through covert, economic, and psychological measures. Membership would identify the United States with "Iraq's violently anti-Israel attitude and also Iraq's ambitions vis-à-vis Syria, Jordan, and Saudi Arabia." Joining would also cause "irresistible pressure" in Congress to issue Israel a security guarantee, which the State and Defense Departments opposed. Eisenhower endorsed but refused to join the pact, confident that informal participation would serve U.S. interests without the risks of formal adherence.[19]

Moreover, Eisenhower and Dulles increasingly considered the Baghdad Pact obsolete. Beset by various weaknesses from the outset, the pact declined in importance as U.S. officials rested their security on the Eisenhower Doctrine, and Iraq withdrew from the agreement eight months after the country's July 1958 revolution. "We should welcome and encourage" Iraqi departure from the Baghdad Pact, Dulles subsequently told British officials. Lacking Arab members was "a healthier position, particularly in relation to Israel." When Iraq departed, the pact's remaining members renamed it the Central Treaty Organization and relocated its headquarters to Ankara. But the organization never mustered real strength as an anti-Soviet defense mechanism.[20]

Eisenhower also reconsidered the issue of arms supply to the Arab states and Israel. He approved arms supply to Jordan and Saudi Arabia after they endorsed the Eisenhower Doctrine. In early 1958, the United States earmarked fifteen F-86 jets for Iraq, while Britain provided six Hawker Hunter jets to Lebanon and twelve to Jordan. The United States declared officially that it armed the Arab powers to help defend the region against Soviet attack; in reality, however, the United States also acted to neutralize the political fallout from Egypt's recent acquisition of Soviet military jets.[21]

By the same token, Eisenhower denied arms to Syria and Egypt. In early 1957, Nasser arranged an Arab conference in Cairo that declared that Arab states would seek Soviet arms unless the West supplied these needs, but Eisenhower resolved not to compete with the Soviet Union for Egypt's loyalty. It also did not seem prudent to arm Egypt in light of its disputes with Israel or to arm Syria, given its political orientation. When King Saud questioned whether such a policy actually drove Egypt and Syria into Soviet arms, Eisenhower explained that they had foolishly chosen to align with Soviet "materialistic atheism." By 1958, Egypt had accepted Soviet aid worth hundreds of millions of dollars.[22]

Eisenhower also faced a 1957–58 Israeli campaign to acquire new weapons. Israeli officials protested that the Arab states, divided in loyalties to East and West, collectively received large quantities of arms that posed a serious danger to the Jewish state. In October 1957, the country's leaders requested weapons to balance the submarines and MiG-19 aircraft that had recently arrived in Egypt and Syria. Because Nasser would soon deploy one thousand Soviet tanks, Meir argued in late 1958, Israel needed U.S. funds to increase its arsenal to two hundred tanks.[23]

The president declined the Israeli requests, however. Dulles downplayed Arab rhetoric about destroying Israel, telling the country's ambassador to Washington, Abba Eban, that "Israel was just a good thing for politicians to talk about." Although the Arab states possessed more weapons than Israel, CIA and State Department officials concluded, Israel's superiority in airpower, logistics, and skill would enable it to defeat an attack by any combination of its Arab enemies. Eisenhower refused to supply Israel with bombers or tanks because they had offensive applications. Dulles told Eban in 1957 to strive for "a respectable defensive posture" rather than a preponderance of arms.[24]

The Decline of the Peace Process

In principle, Eisenhower and Dulles considered Arab-Israeli peace a foundation of a stable and noncommunist Middle East. After the Suez-Sinai War, however, the American officials found the Arab states and Israel unprepared to make the concessions required by a comprehensive, Alpha-style peace plan. Thus, the president and secretary of state decided, over the objections of the Pentagon, to suspend such peacemaking initiatives until the local states became more prepared to cooperate. Convinced that peace initiatives doomed to failure would only aggravate Arab-Israeli tensions, Dulles even hindered such initiatives by other countries. In 1957–61, the United States put comprehensive peacemaking to rest.

The Suez-Sinai War initially rekindled Eisenhower's interest in promoting Arab-Israeli peace. He confided privately that he lost sleep trying to solve such a conflict "with no limit either in intensity or scope." He even offered to collaborate with neutralist Indian Prime Minister Jawaharlal Nehru to formulate Arab-Israeli settlement terms. The Suez-Sinai War demonstrated, State Department officials noted, that Arab-Israeli peace "is prerequisite to political stability and economic and social progress in [the] Near East." In early 1957, Eisenhower and Dulles realized that a permanent settlement of the Arab-Israeli conflict would serve the Eisenhower Doctrine's purposes.[25]

Yet U.S. efforts to facilitate an Arab-Israeli settlement in late 1956 met strong opposition. In November, Dulles proposed a General Assembly resolution to create a five-nation committee to formulate a comprehensive peace plan. Ben-Gurion demanded direct Arab-Israeli peace talks, however, while Nasser refused to consider peace terms while foreign armies occupied his country. U.N. Secretary-General Dag Hammarskjöld advised that the resolution might undermine his efforts to achieve troop withdrawal and canal clearance. Dulles shelved the resolution in December. "We had tried our best," he explained, "but there was not much else we could do at this time."[26]

In 1957, Dulles discerned serious obstacles to peacemaking in the Arab states. Egyptian Foreign Minister Mahmoud Fawzi asserted that "peace was out of the question." Iraq, Lebanon, and Saudi Arabia jointly demanded that any peace plan must be based on the 1947 U.N. resolutions on Palestine, which would strip Israel of vast parcels of land on which it had settled some five hundred thousand Jews. The Arab countries argued that the 1947 resolutions were legally binding, that removing land from Israel would help liquidate the Palestinian refugee crisis, and that promotion of such terms would inflate the prestige of conservative Arab states and undermine that of radical ones. Dulles rejected this Arab demand on the rationale that "the clock could not be turned back."[27]

Israel also resisted peacemaking on U.S. terms in 1957. U.S. Ambassador to Tel Aviv Edward B. Lawson reported that official and public opinion in Israel preferred peacemaking while the country remained militarily superior. But Israeli officials denigrated the terms of the 1955 Alpha plan, and Ben-Gurion demanded to negotiate peace directly with his Arab counterparts rather than through an intermediary, a position that U.S. officials considered a roadblock to settlement. "This was the worst possible moment," Eban told Dulles in the autumn, "to raise the question of the totality of an Arab-Israel settlement."[28]

The new factor of Soviet involvement further reduced U.S. hopes for promoting a comprehensive peace plan. In spring 1957, Soviet officials asked to participate in any great power initiative to pacify the Middle East, and French Ambassador to Washington Hervé Alphand conceded that the "door should be left open a little" to East-West cooperation. In November, Soviet leader Nikita Khrushchev proposed a U.S.-British-French-Soviet guarantee of Middle East borders as a basis for peace. Sensing that the Soviets had instigated the Arab push to revive the 1947 resolutions, however, Eisenhower and Dulles suspected that the Soviets aimed to split the Western alliance. The State Department told the French that it "strongly opposed" Soviet participation "in any way in the formulation of policy in Middle East matters." Eisenhower added that he had "no confidence in the Soviet Union."[29]

In light of the Arab, Israeli, and Soviet positions, Eisenhower and Dulles decided not to resume any peacemaking initiative on the scale of the Alpha plan. While peace remained his objective, Eisenhower commented on 6 February, "the moment was not propitious" to promote it. He and Prime Minister Macmillan agreed at the Bermuda summit in March that they would seek only "piecemeal settlement of various particular problems as they arise." Dulles rejected an elaborate proposal by Assistant Secretary of Defense Mansfield D. Sprague to head up a vast road-rail-pipeline development scheme along the

Egyptian-Israeli border as a means of promoting cooperation between the two powers. The secretary of state also turned down a June recommendation from U.N. Ambassador Henry Cabot Lodge Jr. to revive the Alpha plan.[30]

In late 1957, the Pentagon challenged Dulles's passivity regarding peacemaking. Suspecting that the State Department refrained from compelling Israel to settle with the Arab states for domestic political reasons, the JCS observed that Arab-Israeli tensions had opened Egypt and Syria to Soviet influence. "The threat to U.S. security inherent in failing to take the initiative," the JCS advised, "is so great as to transcend the interests of any minority group within the United States." Assistant Secretary of State William M. Rountree countered to Chief of Naval Operations Admiral Arleigh A. Burke that promotion of a peace settlement would only arouse nationalist Arab leaders and undermine conservative ones.[31]

Dissatisfied with such reasoning, Pentagon officials debated Dulles on peacemaking during a January 1958 NSC meeting. Because "World War III could very well commence" in the Middle East, Deputy Secretary of Defense Donald A. Quarles argued, "a strong initiative by the United States was required." Dulles conceded that the Arab-Israeli deadlock was "tragic and disturbing" because "we are confronted with a clear threat to the security of the United States." But he found the Pentagon's prescription "simply not realistic." Because Israel was "the darling of Jewry throughout the world," he explained, "there were certain courses of action which simply could not be followed." The United States, he concluded, could engage only in "muddling through."[32]

In the final draft of NSC policy paper 5801, the council essentially approved Dulles's "muddling through" approach. Despite the attraction of an Alpha-style settlement, U.S. officials were prepared to accept "a settlement short of formal peace and addressed to some rather than all of the outstanding issues, and with only some rather than all of the Arab states." Under the Eisenhower Doctrine umbrella, the United States would deter and thwart aggression within the Middle East, prepare politically and militarily to defend victims of attack, and endorse U.N. initiatives to settle any outstanding issues. But the United States would suspend the comprehensive peace process.[33]

Consistent with this policy, Dulles resisted other countries' appeals to make peace. Britain proposed that the two Western allies issue a joint declaration of terms for compromise settlement of the refugee, security, and border issues. But Dulles rejected the proposal as "inopportune," predicting that it would fall flat and in the process undermine his effort to convince the Arab states that international communism posed a greater menace than Israel did. In late 1957, he also declined a request from Canada, Norway, Australia, and Lebanon to lead a comprehensive peacemaking venture.[34]

Until the end of the Eisenhower administration, U.S. officials refrained from

launching a major peace initiative. In November 1958, the NSC ranked settlement of the Arab-Israeli conflict as a national objective in the Middle East lower
in importance only than containment of communism and preservation of oil.
Because Israel and its Arab neighbors were not prepared to make peace, however, Eisenhower and Dulles remained convinced that "we simply could not bull
our way through to a settlement of the problem by our efforts alone." Dulles's declining health—he retired from the State Department in April 1959, one month
before cancer claimed his life—also stymied peacemaking. His successor, Christian A. Herter, lacked the prestige and presidential confidence needed to launch
a major initiative. "Any early Arab-Israeli peace settlement," Armin Meyer of
the NEA observed in July 1959, "is out of the question."[35]

State Department officials remained unmoved even when the major 1960
presidential candidates endorsed peacemaking. In an address to the American Zionist Organization on 25 August, Democratic nominee John F. Kennedy pledged that as president he would host an Arab-Israeli peace conference
at the White House. Two days later, Vice President and Republican nominee
Richard M. Nixon told the same group that he would assign Ambassador Lodge
as a special emissary to settle the conflict. State Department officials viewed both
pledges as sheer politicking. After Kennedy's victory in the general election,
Meyer confided to M. S. Weir of the British embassy that Kennedy's planned
summit seemed "an unrealistic approach which stood little chance of acceptance by the Arabs." Meyer preferred to "see the present comparative calm continue."[36]

Conclusion

After the Suez-Sinai War, special challenges confronted Eisenhower and Dulles
as they sought to secure the Middle East. Turmoil in the region, the collapse
of British influence, and growing Soviet influence posed formidable hindrances
to U.S. aspirations. Through the Eisenhower Doctrine, and to a lesser degree
through the Baghdad Pact and arms supply, the United States sought to preserve its vital interests in the Middle East in the late 1950s.

The Arab-Israeli conflict complicated this task by challenging the Eisenhower Doctrine. U.S. officials intended the doctrine to shield the Middle East
from the external influence of the Soviet Union. Arab states, however, disliked
the doctrine in large part because of their mounting anti-Western anger stemming from frustrations regarding Israel. Israel feared that the doctrine would
augment the power of its adversaries and disadvantage Soviet Jews. The Arab-
Israeli conflict weakened the foundation of the Eisenhower Doctrine, in other
words, and the doctrine in turn further aggravated that conflict.

The Arab-Israeli conflict also affected U.S. policy toward the Baghdad Pact.

Certain Arab states opposed the pact for many reasons, among them the perception that the pact eroded the unity the Arabs needed to deal with Israel. Israel criticized the pact because it channeled arms to Iraq. Israeli opposition to U.S. membership in the pact in the absence of a security guarantee to Israel struck a chord in U.S. public and congressional opinion and thereby reinforced Eisenhower's decision to maintain distance from the agreement.

U.S. arms supply policy faced similar obstacles. Certain Arab states' animosity toward the West and acceptance of Soviet weapons undermined the U.S. aim of avoiding a regional arms race. U.S. arming of those states with proper political dispositions—Iraq, Jordan, Saudi Arabia, and Lebanon—added little to regional security. Because of Israel and Egypt's mutual animosity, the United States withheld from those countries the arms that might have contributed to regional security against Soviet attack. The absence of arms supply to Israel intensified its feeling of insecurity, and Egypt's growing dependence on Soviet arms aggravated its tense relationship with Israel.

During the late 1950s, Eisenhower and Dulles sought in principle to pacify the Arab-Israeli conflict. In light of the Suez-Sinai War, the Arab-Israeli dispute posed the single greatest internal threat to regional stability. In practice, however, U.S. leaders sensed that circumstances were simply not propitious for a comprehensive settlement. Beginning in 1957, the United States grew passive on the matter and even opposed initiatives by other powers, using the rationale that efforts to make peace would not only fail but also backfire by consolidating negotiating positions, stoking passions, and otherwise increasing rather than decreasing the intensity of the conflict. Grand schemes such as the Alpha plan of 1954–56 remained on the shelf during Eisenhower's second term as president.

In the late 1950s, Eisenhower privileged his objective of containing the Soviet Union over his quest to resolve the Arab-Israeli conflict. He consciously declined a Soviet proposal to establish spheres of influence in the Middle East and instead erected a containment system based on the Eisenhower Doctrine, the Baghdad Pact, and arms supply to local states, even though such security measures stimulated local resistance and aggravated Arab-Israeli tensions. In short, Eisenhower desired Arab-Israeli peace less than he worried about Soviet ambitions to seize the Middle East from the West. Peacemaking became a casualty of the Cold War.

18

CONTAINING CONFLICT
U.S. Efforts to Avert Arab-Israeli Clashes, 1957–1961

In the late 1950s, the Arab-Israeli situation remained rife with controversy. Israel considered intervention in Jordan during a 1957 political crisis in Amman, and thereafter Israeli-Jordanian relations remained tense, with war a distinct possibility. Israel also confronted hostile regimes in Cairo and Damascus, which joined to form the United Arab Republic (UAR) in early 1958. A political crisis in Lebanon, coupled with a sudden revolution in Iraq, aggravated tensions across the region in mid-1958 and prompted the United States and Britain to intervene militarily in Lebanon and Jordan. Israel repeatedly figured in Western political calculations in the region.

Although the Dwight D. Eisenhower administration refrained from seeking a comprehensive Arab-Israeli peace settlement in the late 1950s, U.S. leaders tried evenhandedly to head off potential military conflicts between Israel and its Arab neighbors. The United States worked impartially to reduce Israeli-Jordanian and Israeli-Syrian tensions by cautioning all sides peacefully to settle their conflicts. President Eisenhower intervened in Lebanon and supported the British occupation of Jordan to deny expansionist targets to both Israel and the UAR. In essence, Eisenhower practiced dual containment, seeking to avert Israeli and Arab expansion. Yet, as in the past, his evenhandedness provoked criticism from all parties in the conflict.

The Cold War loomed large in Eisenhower's policy toward these disputes. His decisions to bolster the monarchy of Jordan, to tolerate the UAR, and to send soldiers into Lebanon were driven by a determination to deny the Soviets opportunities to spread political influence. Having defined anticommunist containment in the Middle East as a vital objective, Eisenhower felt compelled to undertake risky political ventures, to place U.S. troops in harm's way, and to accept a limited level of Arab-Israeli conflict.

The Jordan Crisis and Jordanian-Israeli Relations

In early 1957, Jordan experienced a political crisis that involved both an internal revolt and a threat of external meddling that portended Arab-Israeli war. On behalf of their ambition to stabilize the Middle East, Eisenhower and Secretary of State John Foster Dulles took steps both to save King Hussein and to deter an international clash over his country. After the crisis, Jordan experienced border-related controversies with Israel that were aggravated by the larger Arab-Israeli rivalry. With Eisenhower and Dulles distracted by other issues, State Department officials contained these disputes.

The Jordanian crisis of 1957 originated as an internal struggle for power. Suleiman al-Nabulsi, appointed prime minister after the elections of October 1956, encouraged a nationalist movement to overthrow King Hussein and enter a federation with Syria and Egypt. After months of political skirmishes, Hussein asserted his authority in April. Bolstered by thousands of Bedouin warriors who entered Amman, he dismissed al-Nabulsi and Army Chief of Staff General Ali Abu Nuwar on charges of conspiring with communists to undermine the king's authority. Having feared the collapse of the monarchy, U.S. officials promptly stabilized Hussein with tens of millions of dollars in aid.[1]

The crisis in Jordan also triggered an international showdown. Pronouncements and troop movements indicated that Syria might intervene in Jordan to help the rebels and that Iraq or Saudi Arabia might enter to defend the monarchy, while a reported partial mobilization by Israel revealed that it might seize the West Bank if Jordan disintegrated. Syria branded Israeli mobilization a threat, while Israel charged that Egypt and Syria had instigated fedayeen attacks to provoke an Israeli reaction that would justify an Arab military incursion into Jordan. Nervous U.S. officials feared that any spark—such as the death of King Hussein—would set off a chain reaction leading to a war over Jordan. U.S. intelligence officers could only hope that "the neighboring states will work to preserve the Kingdom lest each . . . lose out in the division of the spoils."[2]

While stabilizing Jordan internally, Eisenhower also took steps to protect it from external encroachment. He publicly reaffirmed the Tripartite Declaration as a deterrent to foreign intervention, a measure of dual containment. The Pentagon ordered the Sixth Fleet to sail to the eastern Mediterranean, stationed the Sixth Fleet Amphibious Task Group in Beirut, positioned two destroyers near Massawa-Aden, and alerted ground and air units in Europe for possible deployment to air and land bases in Turkey and Lebanon.[3]

Although war was averted, the Jordanian episode caused tension between the United States and Egypt. Egyptian Premier Gamal Abdel Nasser deftly denied that he had interfered in Jordan, but U.S. officials disputed his claim and concluded that Egyptian and Syrian expansionism imperiled the pro-Western states of the Middle East. The State Department noted that the outcome of the Jordan crisis spelled a political defeat for Nasser, and the department braced for him to retaliate on the canal or some other matter.[4]

The Jordanian crisis also added to tensions between the United States and Israel. Foreign Minister Golda Meir pledged to remain "sensible and quiet" while U.S. leaders saved King Hussein, but she complained that they underestimated the danger of an Arab attack on Israel and demanded that they issue a security guarantee against Iraqi or Saudi military forces that might move into Jordan. Undersecretary of State Christian A. Herter denied the request and emphasized Iraq's recent assurance of peacefulness as well as Saudi military inferiority. When Israeli officials complained about infiltrations from Jordan, the State Department cautioned the Jewish state to avoid provocation on the border.[5]

After the April crisis, U.S. officials became involved in a series of border controversies between Israel and Jordan. The first clash started in July 1957, when Israeli workers escorted by soldiers entered the Israeli side of a neutral zone south of Jerusalem to plant trees as an erosion control measure. (See map 4.) Goaded by Egyptian and Syrian accusations that he had made a secret deal with Israel to divide the zone, King Hussein asked the U.N. Security Council to order Israel to cease the operation on grounds that it violated the armistice. Israel countered that Jordan had earlier violated the armistice by building military trenches and a highway in the zone.[6]

U.S. officials initially restrained both Israel and Jordan but eventually pressed Israel to relent in the face of Egyptian subversion of Jordan. At first, the State Department advised Israel to halt the tree planting because its benefits did not justify provoking Jordan; furthermore, the department warned Jordan that a Security Council debate might result in a censure of Jordan. When the Security Council considered the matter on 4 September, the United States voted for a vague resolution affirming the armistice and calling on the United Nations Truce Supervision Organization (UNTSO) to report on the situation. When Radio Cairo called for King Hussein's assassination because he was soft on Israel, however, Dulles demanded that Israel halt its project to the ease pressure on the king.[7]

Israel relented slightly as a result of the U.S. effort. Although Prime Minister David Ben-Gurion privately regretted that Dulles "whined" about the issue and called him an accessory to Arab blackmail, the Israeli leader agreed on 30 October to suspend the tree planting for eight weeks "to help King Hussein." Israeli officials also offered to furnish King Hussein with intelligence about rebel movements within Jordan (and Dulles suggested the CIA as a delivery channel). While grateful, Dulles remained concerned that Israel had suspended rather than canceled the work. He rejected Israeli pleas to dismiss Jordan's complaint to the Security Council even as he pressed Jordan to retract it.[8]

U.S. officials also intervened in a series of Israeli-Jordanian clashes regarding the status of Jerusalem's Mount Scopus. Under a 7 July 1948 agreement, Israeli civilians had occupied a demilitarized enclave on Mount Scopus, with Jordan permitting fortnightly convoys to supply the residents. But showdowns developed in November 1957, when Jordan prevented passage of a regular convoy, and in May 1958, when Jordan blocked another convoy and Israeli patrols halted Palestinian civilian traffic on a roadway through the enclave. U.N. efforts to arbitrate a permanent access agreement failed, and tensions rose amid reports of Israeli troop concentrations in the area. During these episodes, the State Department urged restraint on both sides, cautioned Israel that any setback suffered by King Hussein would boost Arab radicals, and arbitrated deals to defuse tensions.[9]

The State Department also became involved in a war scare over the West Bank. Ben-Gurion declared in October 1958 that Israel would demand demilitarization of that area if its political status changed. Citing this statement and reports of Israeli mobilization, UAR officials charged that Israel planned to attack Jordan. The State Department encouraged Israel to clear the air with a statement of peaceful intentions and reminded Nasser of the U.S. policy of opposing aggression. Ben-Gurion denounced reports of Israeli mobilization as "stupid falsehoods" and gave assurances that Israel harbored no expansionist ambitions.[10]

Although pleased that war was averted, State Department officials realized that a general settlement between the two states remained unachievable. In early 1960, King Hussein floated a peace plan including his own recognition of Israel and temporary limits on Jewish immigration to Israel. But Armin Meyer of the Bureau of Near Eastern, South Asian, and African Affairs (NEA) reasoned that Jordan's leaders had taken a grave risk since Nasser would "make mincemeat out of them" if he learned of the plan. "There would not be an Arab-Palestine settlement for a generation," Meyer estimated, so it seemed unwise to back a plan "with so small a chance of success, at risk of bringing on King Hussein's death by assassination."[11]

Israeli Problems with Egypt and Syria

While working to preserve Jordan, the United States also wrestled with persistent tensions between Israel and its more powerful neighbors, Egypt and Syria. American efforts to nudge Egypt and Israel to consider peacemaking made no progress before Egypt and Syria merged in February 1958 into the UAR, a development that accentuated Israel's insecurity by unifying the militaries of two adversaries. Both before and after the merger, moreover, a series of incidents along the Israeli-Syrian border raised the prospect of war. U.S. officials adopted a position of strict neutrality in these disputes, aiming above all to deter either side from any action that might provoke general hostilities.

In 1957, the United States tried with little success to stabilize the Egyptian-Israeli relationship. Neither Nasser nor Ben-Gurion responded affirmatively to U.S. suggestions to consider peacemaking. Nasser "is in the mood to make extreme statements," CIA officials noted in 1957, including "a call for holy war against Israel." Although Nasser assured U.S. Ambassador to Cairo Raymond A. Hare in late 1957 that an "Egyptian attack on Israel can be ruled out," Israeli officials remained alarmed by evidence of Egyptian covert actions in other Arab states and fedayeen training along the Israeli-Egyptian border. "There was no hope of doing business with Nasser," Israeli Embassy First Secretary Shimshon Arad declared in January 1958.[12]

U.S. officials worked to stem Egyptian-Israeli tensions, which increased in early 1958 as a result of intra-Arab rivalries. When Egypt and Syria formed the UAR, Jordan and Iraq countered the move with a federation. In such a context, Arab powers competed in broadcasting hostile propaganda against Israel, which again asked for U.S. security assurances against such threats. James M. Ludlow of the NEA advised, however, that the division of the Arab world into two blocs improved Israeli security. The anti-Israel rhetoric served domestic political interests in the Arab states, Dulles told Israeli Ambassador to Washington Abba Eban, and was "not . . . a cause for Israel to be frightened."[13]

U.S. officials also became involved as a neutral arbiter in a series of disputes between Israel and Syria as an independent state and UAR member. In early 1957, Syria massed troops along its border with Israel and seized an Israeli fishing boat on Lake Tiberias. Israel fortified trenches and constructed a bridge in the northern demilitarized zone (DMZ), causing Syria to complain to the Security Council that such work violated the armistice. Suspicious that domestic and intra-Arab politics fueled this complaint, the State Department remained reticent during the Security Council debates, which resulted in the acquittal of Israel, but warned Israel to desist from provocative actions in or near the DMZ.[14]

U.S. officials adhered to this sort of neutral position when a firefight erupted along the Israeli-Syrian border in July. Allen Dulles blamed the violence on "the young and militant group in Syria" that "wanted a foreign adventure as an excuse for taking over the government." Israel complained to UNTSO about Syrian behavior, Arad told NEA officials, "to let the Syrians know that they were playing with fire." Although Syria seemed at fault, the State Department urged restraint on both powers. Dulles told Israel that Syria made empty threats for intra-Arab consumption and rejected Israel's request to invoke the Eisenhower Doctrine against Damascus.[15]

In 1958, U.S. officials found it increasingly difficult to remain neutral in such controversies. When Israel resumed work on the Huleh canal in March, Syrian soldiers fired on the workers, and a tank and artillery duel followed. A series of violent border incidents over subsequent months culminated in a major artillery battle in December. Despite UNTSO findings that the UAR provoked the battle, U.S. officials urged both sides to show restraint. U.S. neutrality in a clearcut case of Syrian attack made Israeli officials so angry, Eban warned, that a "crisis" existed in U.S.-Israeli relations.[16]

Through the end of the Eisenhower presidency, the State Department performed a balancing act between Israeli and Syrian claims. Tension peaked in January 1959, when Syrian and Israeli forces scuffled over control of Lake Tiberias, and again in early 1960, when a series of border fights erupted. In such episodes, Israel pressured the United States to sponsor Security Council hearings condemning the UAR for provocation and vowed to fight if necessary to preserve Israeli national security. U.S. officials, however, attributed partial blame for the incidents to Israel's actions in the DMZ, recognized that Syria had legitimate claims to Lake Tiberias, urged both sides to maintain the peace, and opposed Security Council hearings because they would raise rather than diminish tensions.[17]

Israel and the Crises in Lebanon and Jordan, 1958

In 1958, revolutionary unrest in three pro-Western Arab states profoundly alarmed Eisenhower and Dulles. In Lebanon, a Nasser-inspired revolt threatened the government. In Jordan, nationalists continued plotting to oust King Hussein. In July, a sudden revolution in Iraq caused U.S. leaders to worry that similar coups might occur in Beirut and Amman. Generally reluctant to intervene militarily in any of these situations, Eisenhower decided during the Iraq crisis to dispatch U.S. Marines to Lebanon and to support the British occupation of Jordan. He acted because he calculated that a collapse of either state would provoke a clash between the UAR and Israel that would become violent or open the door to Soviet intrigue. Eisenhower practiced dual containment of Israel and the UAR to serve his containment of the Soviet Union.

The Lebanon crisis originated in the country's sectarian divisions between Christians and Muslims. Since the country had obtained independence from France during World War II, Lebanon's government had been based on a "national pact" that divided power between the two confessional communities. President Camille Chamoun, a Christian elected in 1952 to serve until 23 September 1958, practiced a pro-Western foreign policy and endorsed the Eisenhower Doctrine. Attracted to Nasser's pan-Arab nationalism, however, many of Lebanon's Muslims grew increasingly critical of their government. When Chamoun sought in early 1958 to amend the constitution to permit himself to serve a second six-year term, Muslims firmly resisted him.[18]

Eisenhower and Dulles took a deep interest in Lebanon when violence wracked the country in May 1958. The assassination of a rival Christian leader, Nasib Matni, on 8 May touched off three days of anti-Chamoun rioting. Mobs burned United States Information Service libraries in Tripoli and Beirut, and saboteurs severed Iraq Petroleum Company pipelines. U.S. officials rushed weapons to Chamoun, including eighteen tanks that arrived on 29 May, enabling government troops to end the rioting. But the Lebanese chief of staff, General Fuad Chehab, a moderate Christian who opposed Chamoun's bid for extended power, refused to crush the rebellion for fear of fragmenting his army along confessional lines. Instability lingered, and Chamoun asked the United States to intervene militarily to save his presidency.[19]

Chamoun's request presented Eisenhower with a dilemma. On the one hand, he sensed that intervention to prolong Chamoun's presidency would diminish U.S. prestige in many Third World states. On the other hand, intelligence officers blamed Nasser for instigating the rebellion by broadcasting radio propaganda and infiltrating hundreds of armed Syrians into Lebanon. At best, Eisenhower feared, Chamoun's fall would vault into power an anti-Western, pro-Nasser successor. At worst, it would trigger a UAR-Israeli war for control of Lebanon.[20]

To resolve this dilemma, Eisenhower informed Chamoun that the United States would contemplate intervention only if three conditions were met, and Chamoun quickly complied. Specifically, Lebanon must appeal to the United Nations for assistance against infiltration from the UAR, other Arab states must endorse U.S. intervention, and Chamoun must cancel his bid to remain in office. On 22 May, Chamoun appealed to the Security Council, which in June formed the U.N. Observer Group in Lebanon to investigate foreign involvement in Lebanon. He also persuaded Iraq and Jordan to endorse U.S. intervention and suspended his quest to remain president.[21]

As Chamoun met the U.S. conditions, Eisenhower faced intensifying pressure to intervene. The rebellion widened in June, and Chamoun told U.S. envoys that it was time to "pull the 'panic switch.'" Dulles warned that "the situation is slipping down the drain" and, with an explicit reference to Munich, ruled out a compromise between Chamoun and Nasser because "Lebanon would be taken in two bites instead of one." Britain signaled that it would consider U.S. intervention in Lebanon justified, and the *New York Times* warned that a "Lebanese Anschluss" by Nasser would gravely destabilize the Middle East.[22]

Despite such pressures, Eisenhower remained reluctant to take action in Lebanon. He doubted that intervention "would either solve the present crisis or enhance Lebanon's long term position in the area." Lebanon "has the capacity to solve this crisis without the use of foreign military forces," Dulles explained to Chamoun on 18 June. Although intervention might be the "lesser of two evils" when compared to Nasserite revolution, he elaborated to Eban, "it was a great evil." Lebanon might become, U.S. Navy officers observed, "a western supported island surrounded by a sea of Arab hate—almost a second Israel."[23]

The Iraqi coup of 14 July finally prompted Eisenhower, still with great reluctance, to send soldiers into Lebanon. "This is probably our last chance to do something in the area," he told his advisers. Dulles agreed that "the losses from doing nothing would be worse than the losses from action." Eisenhower ordered the marines to occupy strategic sites in Beirut and to preserve the independence and integrity of Lebanon, and he dispatched Deputy Undersecretary of State Robert D. Murphy to Beirut to find a political settlement that would enable an early withdrawal of U.S. troops. "We must get Lebanon into condition where it can take care of itself," Eisenhower told Dulles, "because we cannot keep troops there indefinitely."[24]

Eisenhower's notion of dual containment prompted him to intervene despite his earlier reluctance. On the one hand, the president wished to deny Nasser political control of Beirut and to make him feel vulnerable elsewhere. The "basic reason for our Mid East trouble, is Nasser's capture of Arab loyalty and enthusiasm throughout the region," Eisenhower observed. On the other hand, U.S. action would deter Israel from seizing territory in Lebanon on grounds of denying it to Nasser. Eisenhower and Dulles also reasoned that intervention would preserve their credibility in states relying on U.S. assurances and demonstrate that the United States was firmly resolved to prevent Soviet interference. Public support, evident in Gallup poll data showing 59 percent approval for the operation among residents of New York, Chicago, and Washington, eased Eisenhower's decision.[25]

Military intervention in Lebanon produced acceptable short-term results for the United States. General Chehab won election to the presidency on 31 July, accommodated the nationalists and Muslim rebels by distancing himself from the United States, and restored stability to Lebanon. His election, Allen Dulles told the National Security Council, was "probably the most favorable result under the complicated circumstances existing in Lebanon." U.S. forces withdrew from the country in late October.[26]

While U.S. forces occupied Lebanon, Eisenhower endorsed a British operation to prevent a revolution in Jordan. Hours after the coup in Baghdad, Britain suggested joint intervention to save King Hussein from a copycat rebellion. Dulles told Eisenhower that the secretary of state had "no enthusiasm" for the idea because King Hussein was an unpopular leader of an artificial state and intervention would inflame Arab nationalism and likely fail. The Joint Chiefs of Staff (JCS) endorsed intervention, however, and Allen Dulles warned that a power vacuum in Jordan would trigger an Israeli-Iraqi clash. In another act of dual containment, Eisenhower endorsed British action in Jordan but declined to send U.S. troops.[27]

Beyond Lebanon and Jordan, however, Eisenhower remained opposed to Western military action to contain intraregional conflict. Britain proposed joint military operations against Arab radicals in Iraq and Syria, and Allen Dulles warned that the Iraqi coup, if allowed to stand, would imperil not only Lebanon and Jordan but also Saudi Arabia, Turkey, and Iran. Yet Eisenhower refused to sanction "a big operation" in Iraq or Syria because doing so would run "far, far beyond anything which I have the power to do constitutionally." Moreover, Soviet leader Nikita Khrushchev warned that U.S. intervention in Iraq would cause "most dangerous and unforeseen consequences." Whereas the United States could manage an intervention in Lebanon, Dulles noted, "in the other countries, the thing might blow up."[28]

Indeed, despite U.S. moderation, the Western interventions in Lebanon and Jordan provoked tension between the superpowers. The Soviets publicly attributed the operations to "the yearning of the oil monopolies of the USA and other western powers to preserve their colonialist rule . . . and the failure of the Baghdad Pact and the notorious [Eisenhower] doctrine." In the Security Council, the United States and Britain vetoed Soviet resolutions demanding an immediate end to the occupations, and the Soviets vetoed U.S. resolutions approving them. After Khrushchev warned that Eisenhower was "playing with fire in a powder keg," the Pentagon prudently monitored Soviet maneuvers in Turkistan, Transcaucasia, and Bulgaria; sent five air squadrons to Adana, Turkey; placed forces worldwide on a general alert; and ordered North American Defense Command fighter interceptors, armed with MB-1 atomic rockets, to five-minute alert status.[29]

The British intervention in Jordan also involved the United States in a complicated Anglo-Israeli conflict. On 16 July, Ben-Gurion informed U.S. Ambassador to Tel Aviv Edward B. Lawson that the Israeli government would approve overflights of its territory by British planes headed for Jordan if the United States accepted "responsibility for the consequences." Before Washington could reply, Britain dispatched a paratrooper brigade from Cyprus to Amman in the predawn hours of 17 July. Israeli fighters fired on the British transport planes as they entered Israeli airspace, forcing most of them to return to Cyprus. At the urgent request of Britain, State Department officials asked Ben-Gurion's aides to awaken him at 4:00 A.M. and secure his approval for the British flights. The U.S. government also asked permission for its planes carrying oil needed by British forces in Amman to fly over Israel.[30]

The U.S. request confronted Ben-Gurion with a dilemma. On the one hand, he favored the Western interventions, fearing that if Chamoun and King Hussein fell from power, Soviet or Egyptian influence would surge against Israel. On the other hand, Ben-Gurion feared that collaboration would tarnish Israel's image in the eyes of Afro-Asian states, trigger massive domestic criticism, and, as Ben-Gurion told the British, provoke Soviet retaliation that "could wipe out Israel in 20 minutes." Ben-Gurion decided to tolerate but not formally approve the overflights. Britain and the United States, he noted, "will do what they must do, and if they pass through our country, we will protest." Israel denied "official permission for overflights," Herter noted, "but told us to go ahead."[31]

Ben-Gurion's concession stabilized the situation in Jordan for only a few days. By 24 July, British planes had airlifted eighteen hundred soldiers and various supplies to Amman, but the reliability of the aerial supply route was weakened by Israel's occasional protests and delays of flights. British forces in Amman remained critically short of manpower and supplies, and their efforts to establish a sea-rail supply line through Aqaba encountered logistical problems. In contrast to the rapid improvement in Beirut, the situation in Amman remained perilous well after British forces arrived. "Jordan stands on one man," Ben-Gurion aptly noted, in reference to King Hussein, "and if a bullet removes him then the British military will be of no use."[32]

In addition to endorsing Britain's petition to Ben-Gurion, U.S. officials provided psychological and logistical support for British operations in Jordan. The JCS ordered navy jets to overfly the West Bank at low altitudes, concentrating over refugee camps and along the Syrian border, with an intent, as Dulles noted, of "heartening [the British] up and showing our presence." The Pentagon also filled the gaps in Britain's tenuous supply lines. By 24 July, the U.S. Air Force had flown fifteen hundred drums of oil products from Beirut to Amman to tide over British forces until a tanker reached Aqaba on 26 July.[33]

This initial U.S. support prompted British officials to seek deeper U.S. military intervention in Jordan. Because King Hussein remained vulnerable, Prime Minister Harold Macmillan asked Eisenhower on 22 July to send combat troops or at least assume responsibility for all supply flights over Israel. Ben-Gurion "would raise much less political objection" to overflights by U.S. planes, the British leader reasoned. "The really vital thing is to ensure the arrival in Amman of an American force, however small," Macmillan noted privately. "Once the Americans are involved in Jordan, they will never allow the safety of their forces to be prejudiced by difficulties of overflying."[34]

Eisenhower immediately ruled out intervention by U.S. ground forces but approved U.S. aerial supply of British forces in Jordan if Israel approved. Top U.S. officials advised the president that properly supplied British troops would likely save King Hussein. But if King Hussein fell and British forces departed the country, Dulles warned, Israel would occupy the West Bank and the Arab states would resist, triggering "a dangerous chain reaction in the international field." As yet another measure of dual containment, Eisenhower asked Israel to authorize overflights of U.S. airplanes flying British supplies from Cyprus to Jordan.[35]

Ben-Gurion approved U.S. overflights but extracted a modest reward from Eisenhower. The Israeli leader authorized the overflights "for a number of days" but also requested a U.S. security guarantee to protect his state from retaliation for its acquiescence. The United States, he reasoned, must not "ask us to risk our existence to permit the survival of Hussein's regime for a few weeks." As U.S. airplanes began ferrying supplies to Amman, Eisenhower reminded Ben-Gurion of the Eisenhower Doctrine and added that "since the Middle East comprehends Israel, you can be confident of United States interest in the integrity and independence of Israel."[36]

Despite this assurance, the overflight arrangement collapsed in early August. Trouble started when the Soviet Union threatened to punish Israel for assisting the Western operations. Then British and U.S. officers asked for permission to use U.S. aircraft to shuttle an additional British battalion through Israeli airspace. Ben-Gurion decided that he could not approve the airlift of British soldiers in the face of the Soviet threats. To do so would constitute "a criminal act against his people," he told British Ambassador to Tel Aviv Francis Rundall. The Israeli air force would intercept flights beginning on 3 August.[37]

U.S. and British officials reacted angrily to Ben-Gurion's warning. Dulles expressed shock that Israel had capitulated to Soviet threats. "There were wide political implications in giving the USSR a sense of power in the Middle East by such subservient actions," he explained to Ambassador Eban. Israel must rely on the Eisenhower Doctrine rather than "do whatever the Soviet Union requested." On 4 August, Ambassadors Lawson and Rundall delivered similar messages directly to Ben-Gurion. By his own account, Rundall spoke "harshly" to the prime minister. By Ben-Gurion's account, Rundall "made my life miserable. A few times I wanted to get up and throw him out of the room."[38]

Yet Ben-Gurion relented in the face of Anglo-U.S. appeals. He convinced his cabinet to give him "a free hand" on the issue by arguing that those ministers who wished to prohibit overflights "do not understand the value of U.S. friendship." Ben-Gurion reported to the United States that he would allow the resumption of flights on 5 August, provided, in deference to domestic political concerns, that they occur only at night and carry only supplies rather than soldiers. Ben-Gurion "did not want to leave the impression," Eban explained, "that Israel had bowed to Soviet pressure." Thereafter, U.S. overflights of Israel proceeded relatively smoothly.[39]

Eisenhower and Dulles established the supply line to Jordan and backed ongoing British efforts there as a measure of dual containment. In short, the U.S. leaders continued to fear that if King Hussein fell, Israel would occupy the West

Bank, which the UAR would resist. The Soviets would support the UAR and the West would back Israel, Dulles noted, producing a situation "something like the Spanish Civil War." To avoid that outcome, Dulles cautioned Soviet Foreign Minister Andrey Gromyko not to force a British withdrawal from Jordan "until we see that the result will not be the reopening of the Arab-Israeli armistice." The American secretary of state rejected Gromyko's suggestion of a joint U.S.-Soviet guarantee of Jordan's borders as an alternative to British occupation on the grounds that Jordan needed British financial assistance.[40]

Dulles also used the prospect of Israeli expansion to contain the UAR. He occasionally cautioned Ben-Gurion not to move into Jordan but refrained from disclosing such messages to Nasser. There were "some advantages in the existence of an Israeli threat," Dulles told the British minister to Washington, Lord Hood, such as deterring Nasser from inciting antigovernment forces in Jordan. When UAR Foreign Minister Mahmoud Fawzi demanded that Britain depart Jordan, Dulles warned that such a move might provoke Israeli expansionism.[41]

From Eisenhower's vantage point, British intervention in Jordan was a success. The infusion of British troops and financial subsidies internally stabilized the kingdom, while U.S. diplomacy shielded it from external pressures. When British forces departed in late 1958, King Hussein's throne was secure. In addition, the Anglo-U.S. collaboration revealed that the breach of 1956 had fully healed. The two allies should "take complete satisfaction in the complete understanding and splendid co-operation which was evident between our two governments in these undertakings," Macmillan wrote to Eisenhower. If the two powers "continue to act together in spirit and in deed . . . I am sure we can deal successfully with any eventuality."[42]

Conclusion

The U.S. quest to stabilize the Middle East in the late 1950s was hobbled by outbreaks of unrest and instability. Jordan's spring 1957 political crisis portended the rise of anti-Western influence in that country. The persistent tension between Egypt and Israel and Syria and Israel, especially as the two Arab states formed the UAR in early 1958, threatened to trigger hostilities. Crises in Lebanon and Jordan in 1958 raised the possibility of an Israeli-UAR clash and opened the door to Soviet influence.

Intent on securing the Middle East, Eisenhower considered Jordan a special challenge. At the geographic center of the region and ruled by a weak monarchy, Jordan became the focal point of conflict between Israel and more powerful Arab states, notably Egypt. In 1957–58, insurgents loyal to Egypt or Syria seemed poised to overthrow King Hussein. Because Israel seemed unlikely to tolerate radical Arabs on the West Bank, King Hussein's collapse threatened to trigger a regional war over his land. To prevent such a calamity, Eisenhower aimed to preserve Jordan as a buffer zone separating powerful antagonists and thus prolonging peace in the region. In essence, he practiced a policy of dual containment designed to limit and isolate both Israeli and radical Arab power.

With regard to Israel's direct relations with Egypt and Syria, Eisenhower and Dulles sought fundamentally to preserve the tenuous status quo that had emerged after the Suez-Sinai War. As Israeli disputes with these Arab powers surged in 1958–59 — over border incidents, demilitarized zones, trade restrictions, and other issues — U.S. leaders sought to avert an escalation to violence through direct appeals to each power as well as a judicious deployment of U.N. machinery to dispel tensions. Such actions advanced the U.S. quest to stabilize the region by preventing an escalation of tensions.

The summer 1958 crisis in Lebanon posed a severe challenge to Eisenhower's objectives in the Middle East. When Chamoun's bid to extend his presidency provoked a rebellion by nationalists with ties to the UAR, Eisenhower hesitated to intervene on the calculation that he would stimulate anti-Western nationalism in Lebanon and elsewhere. He sent in marines only after a sudden and violent revolution in Baghdad raised the fear of a similar episode in Beirut, and in the process he facilitated Chamoun's removal from office. As in the case of Jordan, Eisenhower intervened in Lebanon at least in part to prevent a clash between the UAR and Israel vying to fill a vacuum of power.

During the late 1950s, Eisenhower accepted great responsibility for the Middle East's peace and stability. His involvement in Israeli disputes with Jordan, Syria, and Egypt revealed a determination to achieve stability as an antidote to anti-Western influence. Military intervention in Lebanon demonstrated a commitment to act forcefully in defense of vital interests that seemed imperiled. Support of British operations in Jordan revealed a resolve to bolster its pro-Western king. By practicing dual containment, Eisenhower sought to stabilize the Middle East and thereby to stanch Soviet influence there.

Eisenhower and Dulles aimed to take an impartial, neutral position in Arab-Israeli matters, adopting measured positions on various border questions. Even when Syria seemed clearly blameworthy for a spike in border tensions, Dulles urged both Israel and Syria to show restraint. In the absence of Arab-Israeli peace, however, such a neutral disposition strained U.S. relations with both sides.

19

SELECTIVE ACTIVISM
U.S. Efforts to Solve Arab-Israeli Disputes, 1957–1961

In principle, President Dwight D. Eisenhower and Secretary of State John Foster Dulles desired a comprehensive peace between Israel and the Arab states as a means of stabilizing the Middle East against Soviet influence in the aftermath of the Suez-Sinai War. So adversarial were the local powers, however, that a general peace seemed unattainable. Therefore, Eisenhower and Dulles made a concerted effort to alleviate certain points of contention and remained inactive regarding other disputes. Compared to the activism in peacemaking in 1953–56, this passivity in 1957–61 was striking.

The U.S. leaders displayed varying degrees of concern about the issues that caused Arab-Israeli tensions. The American government earnestly sought to settle the Palestinian refugee crisis for political, financial, and humanitarian reasons but initially intended to remain uninvolved on three other points of conflict—the controversies over Jordan Valley water, the Gulf of Aqaba, and the Suez Canal. The actions and initiatives of various protagonists, however, compelled the United States to become involved in those issues and to remain in the shadows of controversies regarding the status of Jerusalem, the Arab boycott against Israel, and Israeli immigration. U.S. involvement in all these disputes confirmed the idea that peacemaking might aggravate the Arab-Israeli conflict and strain U.S. relations with the principals.

Palestinian Refugees

In the late 1950s, the United States devoted serious attention to solving the Palestinian refugee issue. The Suez-Sinai War hardened the deadlock between the Arab states, which insisted that the refugees had the right to repatriation in accordance with the December 1948 U.N. resolution, and Israel, which insisted that Arab states must absorb the refugees. Despite the legacy of U.S. failures to solve the problem (the Clapp report, the Johnston plan, the Alpha plan), the State Department took renewed interest in the refugee problem in 1957.

State Department officials were drawn to the refugee problem by its scope and persistence. The number of refugees increased from 861,000 in 1951 to 922,000 in 1956 and to 1 million in 1959. Jordan's 500,000 refugees accounted for 36 percent of its population, while the 217,000 refugees in the Gaza Strip comprised 69 percent of its residents. Other sizable populations dwelled in Lebanon (103,000 in 1956) and Syria (90,000). More than half of the refugees were children under age fifteen. The United Nations Relief and Works Agency for Palestine Refugees in the Near East (UNRWA) provided shelter in camps for 39 percent of refugees plus food and clothing relief, medical care, education, and recreation services. The United States funded 70 percent of UNRWA's budget, about $23 million per year during the late 1950s.[1]

U.S. observers feared that the UNRWA relief system might break down. Caring for the growing refugee population drained the UNRWA's resources and left it with operating deficits of thirteen million dollars in 1957 and fifteen million dollars in 1958. In addition, the relief system was prone to corruption, such as "cream skimming" by refugees who retained their ration cards after they had abandoned UNRWA camps and become absorbed in Arab states. The Suez-Sinai War created logistical nightmares in Gaza by dislocating UNRWA personnel and sparking looting of supplies. Finally, UNRWA's mandate was set to expire on 30 June 1960. Many people feared, although no one could precisely articulate, what would happen if the relief agency disbanded in the absence of a political settlement.[2]

Several other factors kindled State Department determination to solve the refugee problem. The presence of the refugees in the West Bank aggravated Jordan's April 1957 political crisis. Members of Congress again expressed concern about the cost of providing indefinite relief, and Senator Jacob K. Javits (R–New York) actively promoted a solution based on resettlement in Arab states. On a more positive side, the UNRWA discerned a new moderation on the issue in Jordan and Israel, raising hope that a settlement might be within reach. After conducting a detailed study, the Palestine Conciliation Commission (PCC) estimated that the refugees had lost $460 million in property, which provided at least a starting point for negotiating Israeli compensation.[3]

Motivated to action, the State Department's Bureau of International Organization Affairs (IO) fashioned a blueprint for a settlement of the refugee issue in July 1957. The bureau proposed that the UNRWA's relief duties and U.N. funding would transfer to Arab governments by 1960. The State Department would encourage Israel to accept repatriation in principle while capping actual repatriation at one hundred thousand persons. The United States would allocate one hundred million dollars and Israel would earmark additional monies to compensate refugees who had lost property. On 6 August, Dulles's special assistant, Henry S. Villard, appointed a special State Department working group to consider the 10 plan.[4]

Department officials quickly discerned obstacles to the 10 plan. Jordan seemed the most willing but least able to resettle refugees, with a capacity to absorb only 175,000 of its 500,000 refugees. Lebanon had the capacity to absorb its 102,000 refugees but professed reluctance to upset its delicate confessional balance. Iraq and Egypt seemed able to resettle more than 500,000 refugees but demanded that Israel accept repatriation. Syria had in fact economically absorbed most of its 90,000 refugees, but tense political relations with the West, especially after the September 1957 U.S.-Syrian crisis, blocked any formal settlement. Israel adhered to the timeworn position that it would repatriate a strictly limited number of refugees and compensate others, but only if the Arab states accepted the major burden of resettlement.[5]

Such obstacles torpedoed the 10 plan. In late 1957, 10 officials urged Dulles to launch the initiative with appeals to Egypt, Saudi Arabia, and Israel. In light of regional political conditions, however, Villard advised Dulles instead to approve an "economic approach . . . designed not to *solve* the problem but to *eliminate* it over a period of time by raising living standards and creating job opportunities in the area." Dulles agreed to shelve the 10 plan and explore Villard's scheme, but it too proved unworkable. State Department experts estimated that Villard's plan would cost some eight hundred million dollars over ten years (compared to three hundred million dollars to continue relief under the UNRWA), and doubted that Congress would appropriate such funds.[6]

State Department officials, although frustrated by the situation, reverted to inaction. Middle East leaders "are utterly callous to the fate of these wretched human beings," U.S. Ambassador to Beirut Robert A. McClintock fumed. Eisenhower should do something to "galvanize our Israeli friends into serious thought" about the issue, McClintock advised, and ensure that "some of the galvanizing action was applied to the seat of the Arab trousers." But Undersecretary of State Christian A. Herter declined to act. The refugee problem "does not leave my mind during any part of my conscious hours," he explained, but "the moment seems inopportune to grasp the nettle firmly."[7]

Although unable to solve the refugee dispute, the State Department took action to extend the UNRWA's mandate. After coming under the control of a large Democratic Party majority in the 1958 election, Congress indicated its reluctance to renew funding of the UNRWA beyond its scheduled termination date of 30 June 1960, which in essence constituted a threat to disband the agency. The Arab states, by contrast, believed that they held a trump card—confidence that the United States would not dare to terminate the UNRWA before a settlement.

Anticipating a clash of wills between Congress and Arab leaders, the State Department asked Congress to extend funding beyond June 1960 and urged Arab statesmen to settle the refugee issue by then.[8]

At first, neither Arab states nor Congress accepted the department's requests. Arab leaders accused the United States of unjustly pressuring them to capitulate while allowing Israel to escape its responsibilities for repatriation. According to the Saudi ambassador to the United States, Abdullah al-Khayyal, the United States had earned the "moral and material responsibility" for refugee care by supporting Israel. Congress, meanwhile, learned that the UNRWA's eleven-year-old official roster of refugees included between one hundred thousand and two hundred thousand individuals who were not entitled to receive benefits and excluded thousands of children who were. Senators Albert Gore Sr. (D-Tennessee) and Gale McGee (D-Wyoming) called the rosters "immoral, dishonest, and unfair" and demanded revisions before Congress even considered extending assistance.[9]

Given this congressional attitude, State Department officials searched for some alternative to the extension of the UNRWA but had no success. In March 1959, they proposed that the United Nations transfer responsibility for the welfare and property of the refugees to the Arab states and replace the UNRWA with a new agency called the U.N. Arab Refugee Commission, "a budgeting and auditing operation" that would manage international relief funds. In May, Deputy Undersecretary of State C. Douglas Dillon urged the UNRWA to transfer responsibility for education to the Arab states. U.N. Secretary-General Dag Hammarskjöld told Dillon, however, that abolition of the UNRWA would "raise all Arabs in arms" and would "introduce a charge of dynamite into the whole Middle Eastern picture."[10]

U.S. officials found it prudent in late 1959 to relent under international pressure to extend the UNRWA. Pakistan and Indonesia proposed a General Assembly resolution to extend the UNRWA, and Arab envoys strongly endorsed the measure. While initially passive in light of Congress's attitude, State Department officials eventually supported the resolution, both to mollify the Arab states and to avoid terminating relief operations. On 9 December, by a vote of eighty to zero, with Israel abstaining, the General Assembly passed a resolution that extended the UNRWA for three years, empowered the PCC to seek a permanent solution, required updating of refugee rosters, and transferred to the Arab states responsibility for educating refugees. When the State Department reported some progress revising the UNRWA's refugee rosters in 1960, Congress begrudgingly renewed U.S. funding.[11]

While wrestling with the UNRWA problem in 1959–60, some U.S. officials quietly pressed Israel to accept repatriation in principle as a means to break the deadlock. The United States would not allow "a stampede of refugees across

Israeli boundaries," James M. Ludlow of the Bureau of Near Eastern, South Asian, and African Affairs (NEA) assured Israeli counselor Moshe Erell. Prime Minister David Ben-Gurion, however, categorically refused the request on the reasoning that "we will not agree to suicide." Accepting even a few repatriates, he told U.S. officials, "would be like an injection of poison.... They would enter Israel with a mission of destroying Israel."[12]

Unknown to U.S. officials, Israel's reading of U.S. policy encouraged the Jewish state's stubborn insistence on resettlement. Israeli Foreign Ministry officials sensed that U.S. leaders accepted the primacy of resettlement but were blocked from openly endorsing it by domestic opinion, European allies, U.N. officials, and Arab states. Thus, Israeli officials encouraged the State Department to affirm resettlement in principle and launched "a sweeping *hasbara* project among politicians, churchmen, reporters and public figures" to argue its advantages. In December 1959, presumably acting under Israel's lead, the leaders of various U.S. Jewish groups called on Herter, who had become secretary of state in April, to endorse the Israeli position.[13]

The State Department made one final push for a refugee settlement in the twilight of Eisenhower's presidency. NEA officials conceived a plan, approved by Eisenhower in June 1960, in which Israel would repatriate twenty-four thousand refugees per year for several years and the Arab states would resettle the remainder. The NEA hoped to recruit a Turkish emissary, acting as a member of the PCC, to conduct secret negotiations with Israel and the Arab states and to arrange a September 1960 international conference to approve the plan. Concern about congressional parsimony regarding the UNRWA motivated the NEA to action. "One of these years Congress will not come through" on allocations to the UNRWA, Senator J. William Fulbright (D-Arkansas) warned the department, "and then we will be confronted with a dangerous situation of unknown dimensions."[14]

Launched on 22 June, the State Department initiative fell flat. Turkey refused to risk its budding rapprochement with Egyptian Premier Gamal Abdel Nasser by associating with the plan. Meanwhile, Israeli and Arab leaders reminded U.S. officials that positions remained unchanged as the two sides quarreled over an Arab proposal to establish a U.N. custodian of Palestinian property in Israel. "There seemed to be no cure" for the problem, Eisenhower told Lebanese officials on 22 September, "and this was disturbing." The refugees, he told Nasser four days later, "lie heavily on the conscience of the world."[15]

Jordan River Water, the Gulf of Aqaba, and the Suez Canal

Although the United States refrained from proposing solutions to most Arab-Israeli disputes in 1957–60, it became involved in controversies over the disposition of Jordan River water and Israeli transit rights on the Gulf of Aqaba and the Suez Canal. With only cursory involvement by Eisenhower, State Department officials consciously declined to solve the Jordan waters issue on a comprehensive basis but considered the matter when Jordan and Israel advanced unilateral water development plans. The department also found it prudent to intercede in an Israeli-Saudi quarrel over Israeli shipping rights on the Gulf of Aqaba and became enmeshed in Egyptian-Israeli quarrels about the Suez Canal. Although U.S. diplomats believed it impossible to achieve an overall Arab-Israeli peace settlement, they found it necessary to manage specific aspects of the conflict.

The Jordan waters controversy posed a dilemma for State Department officials in the late 1950s. In principle, they favored unified water development as enunciated in the 1953 Jordan Valley Plan (JVP). However, they also recalled Eric Johnston's failure to implement the plan in 1953–56 because of Arab-Israeli disagreements regarding refugees and water allocation. In 1957–59, Johnston repeatedly pressed the State Department to resume his mission as a means to promote Middle East peace and stability. Convinced that political conditions in the region would render his labor futile, however, the department declined Johnston's offers.[16]

In the absence of a settlement, the waters controversy simmered in late 1957. Jordan announced plans to build a diversion canal from the Yarmouk River to East Ghor that would enable irrigation of twenty-five thousand acres of farmland, create four thousand jobs, and enable refugee resettlement. (See map 3.) U.S. engineers found the plan technically sound and consistent with the JVP, and officials of the United Nations Truce Supervisory Organization (UNTSO) ruled it consistent with the armistice. Israel, however, protested that the plan would double the salinity of the lower Jordan and deprive it of water during dry seasons. Israel also feared political and legal consequences if Jordan became the first state to use Jordan Valley waters.[17]

The State Department endorsed the East Ghor canal despite Israeli protests. In February 1958, Herter approved $2 million in U.S. aid to fund the $11 million project. Having failed to prevent such a move, Israel requested reciprocal U.S. aid to resume work on the diversion canal at Banat Yaacov, which would be relocated outside the demilitarized zone to avoid political problems. But Herter rejected this request, pointing out that the United States had already provided Israel a FY 1958 aid package worth some $80 million, including an Export-Import Bank loan of $24.4 million for development of water resources outside the Jordan basin.[18]

The water controversy shifted in 1959 to an Israeli plan to divert water from the Jordan River. Israel sought U.S. funds to build a 108-inch central conduit to Tel Aviv and a smaller pipeline to Beit Shean to stimulate agricultural and economic development. Israel would adhere to the water volume limits set in the

JVP and, at significant expense, avoid the political problems of Banat Yaacov by transferring the site of diversion to Lake Tiberias. The United Arab Republic (UAR), Lebanon, and Jordan, however, threatened to use force to stop the project and discussed the possibility of diverting Jordan River headwaters in Lebanon and Syria. "The Jordan is our river," Lebanese Foreign Minister Hussein Oueini declared. "We cannot tolerate that it be taken away."[19]

State Department officials tried to dampen this controversy by adopting a moderate pose. Concerned by the Arab outcry, they refused to endorse the Israeli conduit to Tel Aviv on the grounds that it would draw water in excess of JVP allocations and increase the salinity of the lower Jordan to unacceptable levels. But the department approved the smaller pipeline to Beit Shean, which respected JVP limits, and encouraged the Arab states to cooperate with Israel under the terms of the JVP. "Israel was in a position to take most of the waters," Assistant Secretary of State G. Lewis Jones told Jordanian Ambassador Yusuf Haikal, "if the Arabs did not come forward to claim their share."[20]

In 1959–60, the State Department became more supportive of Israel's diversion plan for several reasons. First, Israeli officials declared that the absence of U.S. assistance would force them to divert water from the politically volatile Banat Yaacov site. Second, Arab leaders categorically refused to cooperate in any unified development scheme. Third, the State Department deemed it prudent to mitigate anticipated congressional anger about an impending World Bank loan to the UAR by making some concession to Israel. Acting in secret to avoid Arab backlash, the State Department approved the conduit in January 1960 and endorsed Israel's application for a fifteen-million-dollar Export-Import Bank loan needed to build the project.[21]

The State Department also became involved in a dispute over the Gulf of Aqaba. Eleven Arab states jointly declared to the department that the gulf and the straits entering it were "Arab territorial waters," and King Saud told Eisenhower that an Israeli presence on the gulf would reward Israeli aggression and threaten the security of Muslim shrines under his guardianship. Dulles declared, however, that unless the International Court of Justice ruled otherwise, the United States would hold that "no nation has the right to prevent free and innocent passage in the Gulf and through the Straits giving access thereto." Because Israel had the same legal rights before the Suez-Sinai War, he added, this view did not reward Israeli aggression.[22]

To the consternation of American officials, the Aqaba dispute strained U.S.-Saudi relations. When King Saud sent an envoy to the State Department to contest U.S. declarations, Assistant Secretary of State William M. Rountree countered that the Security Council and the International Court of Justice would rule in favor of U.S. policy if Saudi Arabia appealed the matter. So tense was the mood of the talks, Rountree alerted Dulles, that the Aqaba issue "could well threaten our present effective relations with King Saud." Suspecting that Nasser had encouraged the king to defend Arab interests on the gulf to drive a wedge between Eisenhower and Saud, U.S. officials fretted that the ploy was working.[23]

Because of Saud's importance as an anticommunist leader, Eisenhower took action to soothe the Saudi monarch with modest concessions. "I am truly getting a bit uneasy," Eisenhower commented after reading a Saudi note, "about the increasing stiffness of King Saud's attitude." The president therefore assured Saud that the United States supported free transit on anticommunist rather than pro-Israel grounds, opposed Israeli warships using Arab waters in the gulf, pledged to honor any International Court of Justice ruling in Saudi Arabia's favor, and encouraged the Saudis to seek a Security Council resolution recognizing Saud as "Keeper of the Holy Places of Islam" and affirming the right of Muslim pilgrims to transit the gulf. Dulles told the National Security Council (NSC) on 18 July that Saud seemed "reasonably well satisfied" by Eisenhower's assurances, but U.S. and Saudi officials quarreled about the issue for months.[24]

In addition to reassuring Saud, U.S. officials restrained Israel when tensions spiked over rumored Israeli naval moves in the gulf. In May 1957, Saudi Arabia charged that an Israeli destroyer had passed through Saudi waters at the entrance to the gulf. To add to the tension, British intelligence officials warned that Israel was preparing to send a ship through the straits on about 1 June and to initiate a war if Egypt or Saudi Arabia interfered, and Iraq reported Israeli troops concentrated near Aqaba. Alarmed, Dulles asked Israel to refrain from sailing warships on the gulf or otherwise provoking Saud, a political counterweight to Nasser. Eban assured Dulles that Israeli warships in the gulf were "tied up at Eilat" and "virtually mothballed."[25]

In the late 1950s, the State Department settled on a policy of supporting Israeli commerce on the gulf but cautioning Israel against naval deployments there. With U.S. endorsement, more than twenty Israeli-flag vessels reached Eilat between June 1957 and January 1958, and Israel completed an oil pipeline from Eilat to the Mediterranean. On the eve of the April 1958 Islamic pilgrimage, by contrast, the State Department asked Israel to remove from the gulf two frigates and three patrol-torpedo boats stationed at Eilat. But Foreign Minister Golda Meir refused to "appease" any Arab state and denied that the warships would hinder Muslim pilgrims. Dissatisfied by this response, NEA officials periodically reminded Israel of their concern.[26]

In 1957–59, the United States tried to avoid involvement in the Israeli-Egyptian dispute over the Suez Canal. In May 1957, Dulles encouraged Egypt to open the canal to Israeli and Israel-bound ships but relented when several Arab states protested. He also counseled Israel to show "prudence and caution" in its quest to gain transit rights, and he refused Israel's request that he encourage U.S. merchant ships to call at Israeli ports and then sail into the canal to test Egypt's restrictions. Even without U.S. backing, however, Israel established a pattern of canal usage. By March 1959, forty foreign-flag vessels chartered by Israeli companies and bearing Israeli cargoes had plied the waterway.[27]

U.S. officials felt obliged to become involved in the canal issue when Nasser clamped down on Israeli transit privileges in May 1959. Egypt detained the Danish-flag *Inge Toft*, which had been chartered by Israel, but the ship's captain refused to relinquish his Israeli-owned cargo, Nasser declined to seize the cargo by force, and a prolonged standoff ensued. Israeli leaders condemned Nasser's action and threatened to appeal the case to the U.N. Security Council. To curtail the mounting tension, U.S. officials encouraged Hammarskjöld to resolve the issue and counseled Israel to maintain faith in such "quiet diplomacy" rather than in provocative action. As a result of U.N. diplomacy, Nasser released the *Inge Toft* in February 1960.[28]

U.S. officials became more deeply involved in the canal issue when they endorsed a one-hundred-million-dollar World Bank loan to Egypt for physical improvements to the waterway. The NEA supported the loan as a means to nurture a U.S.-UAR rapprochement, benefit Western maritime states, preempt prospective Soviet aid, and enhance the World Bank's reputation. Despite the restrictions on Israel, the NEA considered the UAR's operation of the canal "relatively satisfactory" and urged the bank to issue the funds when Nasser yielded on the *Inge Toft* case. The World Bank board unanimously approved the loan in December 1959.[29]

Israel strongly contested the World Bank loan and urged the United States to block it. Israeli envoys argued that the loan would reward Nasser while he unlawfully denied Israeli transit rights. As the State Department braced for "trouble . . . at the other end of Pennsylvania Avenue" on the issue, leaders of several U.S. Jewish groups demanded that the department block the loan on the grounds of free seas doctrine and "international morality." Hoping to torpedo the loan by provoking an incident, Israel chartered and sent into the canal the Greek-flag *Astypalea*, which Egypt detained.[30]

The State Department resisted such Israeli pressure, refusing to cancel the loan for domestic political reasons and criticizing Israel for dispatching the *Astypalea*. The United States could not serve, Jones told Israeli Minister to Washington Yaacov Herzog, as "the righter of wrongs in the Middle East." Frustrated at the inability to block the loan, Israeli leaders resolved in January 1960 to keep Suez transit "an active political issue" and to use *hasbara* to mobilize U.S. public opinion on the matter. The State Department pledged to protest canal restrictions whenever "such action would have a beneficial effect," but the restrictions remained in place at the end of the Eisenhower presidency.[31]

Jerusalem, the Arab Boycott, and Jewish Immigration

The State Department resisted involvement in three other Arab-Israeli controversies in the late 1950s. Even as U.S. diplomats realized that they could not dislodge Israel from its occupation of Jerusalem, they declined to recognize Israel's claim to the city as the Jewish state's capital in part because of Arab sentiment. In addition, the United States protested the Arab economic boycott of Israel as a restraint of free trade but refrained from vigorous action to end it. Furthermore, U.S. officials posed no objection to Jewish immigration to Israel, although they distanced themselves from it in light of Arab protests. The State Department avoided entanglement in all three issues. When forced to act, it walked a fine line between the two sides.

Through the late 1950s, State Department officials advocated the principle of international control of Jerusalem despite Israel's claims. (See map 4.) U.S. leaders discouraged foreign governments from opening diplomatic missions in Jerusalem to ensure that "attrition and *fait accompli*" did not undermine past U.N. decisions. Rountree instructed the U.S. ambassador-designate to Tel Aviv, Ogden Reid, to avoid any indication "that we are resigned to Israel's conduct of government in Jerusalem." When Israel questioned this policy, Rountree replied that the department had a "moral obligation" to uphold U.N. interests.[32]

Concern about Arab sentiment motivated the U.S. policy. Eisenhower declined an Israeli request to send a special emissary to Israel's tenth-anniversary celebrations in Jerusalem in April 1958, for example, on Dulles's advice that such a move would "foster antagonism toward us in the Arab world." The State Department also voiced concern at Israel's plan to hold a military parade featuring tanks and artillery as part of the celebration after Arab states protested that such a display of firepower would violate the armistice agreements.[33]

By 1959, the State Department's policy regarding Jerusalem was difficult to sustain but also difficult to modify. Armin Meyer of the NEA considered internationalization of Jerusalem "out of the question" because dislodging Israel or Jordan from the city would exceed "the realistic capability of the United Nations." Moreover, the isolation of U.S. diplomats in Tel Aviv rendered them unable to understand the Israeli government, while U.S. consular officials in Jerusalem "find themselves in a virtual cold war" with Israel over armistice-related issues. Meyer recommended a U.S. settlement with Jordan and Israel that recognized their de facto control of the city and established international control only of the holy places, but he realized that such an aim might prove impossible in the face of Arab resistance.[34]

The Arab economic boycott against Israel also confronted U.S. officials with a dilemma in the late 1950s. On the one hand, the boycott infringed on U.S. business practices; by 1960, twenty-three U.S. merchant ships had been denied permission to visit Arab states after calling at Israeli ports. Members of Congress sympathetic to Israel demanded suspension of U.S. economic aid to Arab states participating in the boycott. On the other hand, the State Department reasoned that firm action against the boycott would antagonize Arab states and encourage them to seek Soviet support. Therefore, the department occasionally criticized the boycott as a restraint of free trade but refrained from assertive action to end it. NEA officials also showed "impatience bordering on anger" when Israeli envoys repeatedly protested the embargo in early 1960.[35]

The boycott triggered a brouhaha in April 1960. Members of the Seafarers International Union protested the restrictions by picketing the *Cleopatra*, a UAR ship that docked in New York City. The U.S. Senate, mobilized by I. L. Kenen's American Israel Public Affairs Committee, passed the Douglas Amendment authorizing the president to suspend aid to any country that interfered with free transit in international waters. In retaliation, picketing against U.S. ships occurred in several Arab ports, and Bahrain delayed loading a U.S. Navy tanker and denied port rights to other navy ships. Eisenhower worried that the episode would erode his rapprochement with Nasser, provide the Soviet Union an opportunity for propaganda, and hobble the navy's petroleum distribution system. The controversy passed only after the State Department persuaded labor leaders to end the picketing in New York on grounds that it endangered U.S. national security.[36]

The State Department also monitored rising Arab-Israeli tensions caused by Jewish immigration to Israel. Meir justified a plan to absorb 2.5 million Soviet and Eastern European Jews by explaining that "the whole purpose in the creation of the State of Israel was to find a homeland for the Jewish peoples who were not happily settled elsewhere." Arab states protested, however, that such immigration would reduce the prospect of refugee repatriation and create expansionist pressures inside Israel. U.S. officials were torn between a recognition of the right of Jews to flee communism and take up residence in Israel and a fear that massive immigration would aggravate Arab-Israeli tensions. NSC staff members explored various means to reduce tensions, including encouraging Western countries to absorb Soviet Jewish émigrés.[37]

Immigration became a major issue in 1959, when Israel launched an effort to absorb Jews with funding by U.S. citizens. In March, three Israeli cabinet ministers toured the United States to raise some one hundred million dollars in private donations and twenty-five million dollars in bond sales to finance the immigration of hundreds of thousands of Soviet-bloc Jews. Arab protests centered on the provision in U.S. law granting tax deductions for such contributions by U.S. citizens. State Department officials regretted the link between immigration and U.S. funding but also realized that Congress was unlikely to change the tax law. They asked Israel to reduce publicity about fund-raising in the United

States and informed Arab leaders that the U.S. government had nothing to do with Israeli immigration.[38]

Conclusion

In the late 1950s, Arab-Israeli disputes threatened U.S. objectives in the Middle East. The Palestinian refugee problem festered, provoked bitterness between the Arab states and Israel, and, according to some observers, provided a fertile breeding ground for communism. Conflict over the usage of the waters of the Jordan Valley threatened to burst into hostilities. Israel quarreled with Saudi Arabia about the Gulf of Aqaba and with Egypt about the Suez Canal. Controversies regarding Jerusalem, the Arab economic boycott, and Israeli immigration policies provoked anger and animosity that destabilized the region.

Having decided that a permanent Arab-Israeli peace was unattainable, Eisenhower administration officials aimed selectively to contain or reduce Arab-Israeli tensions on these issues. The U.S. government tried to resolve the Palestinian refugee crisis before some factor—for example, the dismantling of the UNRWA or congressional parsimony—triggered a cataclysm. American officials became involved in the disputes over the Jordan Valley waters, the Gulf of Aqaba, and the Suez Canal when those controversies threatened to erupt into violence or cause political turmoil. In the ongoing quarrels about Jerusalem, the Arab boycott, and Israeli immigration policy, U.S. officials enacted passive policies designed to contain political conflict. While Arab-Israeli war did not erupt, U.S. officials measured virtually no progress in reducing Arab-Israeli tensions.

The administration's positions on these various matters placed it alternatively on the side of Israel or on the side of the Arab states. On the refugee issue, the United States embraced a moderate position that blended repatriation and resettlement, although by emphasizing the latter the United States leaned toward Israel. On maritime-access issues, U.S. officials endorsed Israel's right to sail into the Gulf of Aqaba but refrained from contesting Egypt's restrictions on Suez Canal transit. By tolerating the Arab boycott and rejecting Israeli policy on Jerusalem, U.S. officials implicitly sided with the Arab community (with the exception of Jordan on the matter of Jerusalem). Only in its balanced approaches to the Jordan Valley problem and the Jewish immigration controversy did the United States remain neutral.

Sincere efforts to achieve a compromise on the refugee issue earned the United States the reproach of both sides. On the canal and gulf access issues, Israel invariably accused the United States of insufficiently endorsing the Jewish state's legal rights, while Egypt and Saudi Arabia repeatedly questioned why the United States failed to appreciate their security interests. U.S. handling of the water usage dispute left each side suspicious. U.S. policy on Jerusalem alienated Israel and Jordan, which controlled the city, as well as other Arab states that sought to deny Israel a political presence there. Arab states accused the United States of subsidizing Israeli immigration through tax law provisions, while Israel criticized the U.S. tolerance of the Arab boycott.

Security concerns dictated that the U.S. government remain committed to defending the Middle East against Soviet encroachments, yet domestic political and diplomatic restraints prevented the United States from forcing a settlement either by imposing U.S. domination of the region or by completely taking the side of either Israel or the Arab community. For Cold War reasons, the United States remained determined to exclude Soviet power from the Middle East and to maintain working relationships with the Arab states and Israel. Such self-imposed restraints prevented the United States from actively seeking an Arab-Israeli peace agreement.

20

COST OF CONFLICT
U.S. Relations with Israel and the Arab States, 1953–1961

The Arab-Israeli conflict influenced U.S. relations with Israel and the Arab states in 1953–61. To correct what was perceived as the pro-Israel disposition of the Harry S. Truman government, the Dwight D. Eisenhower administration sought to practice impartiality on all Arab-Israeli questions. Israeli officials naturally resisted this shift; discord resulted from U.S. policy on specific Arab-Israeli conflicts, initiatives to promote Arab-Israeli peace, and other issues; and U.S.-Israeli relations hit bottom in 1956–58. Although Israel retained deep reservoirs of sympathy in U.S. public opinion, Arab-related disputes opened fissures in U.S.-Israeli official relations.

To a lesser degree, Israel-related issues affected U.S. relations with the Arab states. Relations with Egypt and Syria were strained by many factors, such as nationalistic challenges to Western interests in the Middle East, apparent communist inroads in Cairo and Damascus, and Egyptian intrigues against pro-Western Arab states. But the issue of Israel complicated policy initiatives in both states. The United States nurtured a rapprochement with Egyptian Premier Gamal Abdel Nasser in 1958–59; Israeli leaders detected this effort and opposed it, with some success. Compared to the late 1940s, U.S. relations with Jordan, Lebanon, Saudi Arabia, and Iraq remained relatively insulated from the influence of Israel during the Eisenhower years.

Complications in U.S.-Israeli Relations

The Arab-Israeli conflict strained U.S. relations with Israel in 1953–61. President Eisenhower's impartiality policy troubled Israeli leaders. The two states disagreed on a variety of Arab-related issues, such as peace terms, Israeli security, U.S. arms supply policy, and the Israeli nuclear program. Official relations declined dramatically during the Suez-Sinai War of 1956–57 and the Lebanon-

Jordan crisis of 1958. Although the relationship stabilized in 1959–60, the United States adhered to its policy of impartiality.

U.S.-Israeli relations were shaken in 1953 by Eisenhower's evenhandedness. While Truman had made policy "under direct political pressure by Jewish groups," Secretary of State John Foster Dulles told Israeli Prime Minister David Ben-Gurion that "Eisenhower did not owe that kind of political debt." Indeed, Eisenhower and Dulles agreed to practice "a policy of *true* impartiality" between Israel and Arab states. This shift in U.S. policy caused "great confusion . . . , nervousness and agitation," Israeli diplomats noted. "The Administration is not particularly responsive to Israel's position and there is no longer a Mr. Truman to pick up the telephone and order something done regardless of the consequences."[1]

Israel softened the impartiality policy by recruiting U.S. politicians to challenge it, but the tension remained. In 1953, Israeli envoys mobilized U.S. Jews to lobby members of Congress to pressure Eisenhower, and Israeli Ambassador to Washington Abba Eban persuaded prominent Democrat Adlai Stevenson to reject the president's request to affirm impartiality in the spirit of bipartisanship. Bowing to such political pressures, Dulles assured Eban on 8 October 1953 that the U.S. government and people "ascribed to their friendship with Israel a special importance." But Ben-Gurion suspected that "America wants in fact a mandate on Israel" and resolved that "we must keep our sovereignty, which is a condition of our existence."[2]

A relative decline in the influence of the Israel lobby added to Israel's frustration. State Department officials questioned the American Zionist Committee's tax-exempt status because of I. L. Kenen's lobbying. In 1954, Kenen created the American Zionist Committee for Public Affairs (renamed the American Israel Public Affairs Committee in 1959), which, lacking tax-exempt status, remained underfunded for years. Moreover, because U.S. officials complained that meeting individual Jewish leaders demanded too much time, in 1954 various Jewish groups formed the Conference of Presidents of Major American Jewish Organizations. Conference members collectively met Eisenhower on occasion but found their effectiveness limited by the need to arrive at a consensus before each visit. Ambivalence among members of the group about Israel's raids at Qibya and Gaza and invasion of Egypt also limited the conference's effectiveness as a pro-Israel lobby.[3]

Israeli leaders also regretted a slight decline in support for Israel among the U.S. people. In early 1957, the Gallup poll found that 33 percent of Americans held a favorable view of Israel, 53 percent were neutral, and 14 percent held unfavorable views. While popular attitudes toward Egypt were much less friendly, only 10 percent of Americans approved of Israel's October 1956 attack on Egypt, and 47 percent disapproved. Fifty percent expressed satisfaction with Eisenhower's handling of the Israeli-Egyptian clash—which included pressure on Israel to withdraw from the Sinai and Gaza—and only 23 percent voiced dissatisfaction.[4]

Relations between the United States and Israel were strained by their conflicting views of the Arab states. In the interest of anti-Soviet containment, U.S. officials sought to maintain influence among Arab powers, downplayed the seriousness of Arab threats to eliminate Israel, and called on Israel to seek peace by making certain concessions. Israel, in contrast, interpreted Arab propaganda and arms acquisitions as serious threats to Israeli security, used force to secure its borders, and demanded U.S. political support and arms supply. As a measure of the gulf between the two powers, Prime Minister Moshe Sharett justified Israel's February 1955 Gaza raid as "an act of self-defense of a beleaguered nation surrounded by enemies," while the Bureau of Near Eastern, South Asian, and African Affairs (NEA) argued that "such raids make the whole border situation worse and not better." When the State Department pressed Ben-Gurion to make peace by conceding territory to Arab states, he replied that "as long as we live we will not permit anyone to rob us of a single inch of our land."[5]

Disagreement over a prospective U.S. guarantee of Israeli security further strained U.S.-Israeli relations. Disturbed that American security schemes such as the Middle East Defense Organization, the Baghdad Pact, and the Eisenhower Doctrine enhanced Arab military capabilities, Israeli leaders sought an explicit U.S. security guarantee. But Eisenhower refused these requests on the grounds that such a provision would anger Arab leaders, distract them from the Soviet menace, and thereby undermine vital Western interests.[6]

Eisenhower's initiative in the late 1950s to mend his relationship with Nasser (discussed later in this chapter) also strained the U.S. relationship with Israel. Israeli officials relentlessly pressed the State Department to abandon rapprochement with the United Arab Republic (UAR) on the grounds that Nasser's political adventurism in neighboring states destabilized the region. Israeli Minister to Washington Yaacov Herzog expressed concern "lest improved U.S.-U.A.R. relations should be at the expense of Israel," and *hasbara* officials made plans to "raise hell" in U.S. public opinion on the issue. But State Department officials rejected the argument that improvement in U.S.-UAR relations would hurt Israel.[7]

The Arab factor also caused U.S.-Israeli discord on arms supply. Israel repeatedly requested U.S. weapons supply in 1953–56, especially during what Eban called the "solemn hour of national emergency" following the 1955 Soviet-Egyptian arms deal. Convinced that Israel had the capability to defeat its adversaries, however, the State Department calculated that arming Israel would alienate Arab states and ruin prospects for a permanent peace settlement. Arming Israel "would be fatal to our position in the Middle East," William M. Rountree of the NEA observed, because "the result would be a tiny Israel armed by the U.S. opposed to the Arab world supported by the Soviet bloc."[8]

U.S. arms supply policy continued to generate discord as the Soviets supplied weapons to Arab powers in the late 1950s. Citing the need to deter or thwart Arab attack, Israeli officials demanded substantial quantities of U.S. weapons, including tanks, aircraft, and antiaircraft missiles. The U.S. reply, Ben-Gurion told Eisenhower, would determine whether the Israelis "were to remain a free, independent nation or whether they were going to be exterminated." Except for token arms sales in 1958 and 1960, however, Eisenhower refused Israeli requests on the grounds that providing arms would trigger a Middle East arms race and encourage deeper Soviet-Arab ties.[9]

In the twilight of Eisenhower's presidency, U.S.-Israeli relations were further strained by Israel's nuclear program. U.S. intelligence confirmed in September 1960 that Israel had secretly constructed at Dimona a nuclear reactor capable of producing weapons-grade plutonium. Eisenhower's fears of a nuclear arms race in the Middle East were confirmed when Nasser declared in December that if Israel built an atomic bomb, the "UAR would get one, too, at any price." U.S. officials expressed to Israel that they "unequivocally opposed" nuclear proliferation in the Middle East and that Israel should allow international inspections to confirm Israel's claim that the Dimona reactor was devoted to peaceful purposes. Eisenhower remained troubled by Ben-Gurion's equivocal answer.[10]

While such security issues generated a climate of tension, U.S.-Israeli relations hit bottom twice during the Eisenhower years. During the Suez-Sinai War, Eisenhower called Israel "an aggressor," endorsed U.N. resolutions censuring Israel, and threatened to impose sanctions. The United States had "no moral reason to condemn our action . . . of self-defence," Ben-Gurion retorted, since the United States "has not experienced the nightmare of continuous aggression and the threat of extinction as we have." Eisenhower delayed sanctions because congressional and public opinion supported Israel, but only Ben-Gurion's decision to withdraw his forces from Gaza and Sinai enabled U.S.-Israeli relations to avoid further decline.[11]

During the crises in Lebanon and Jordan in 1958, even deeper disharmony gripped U.S.-Israeli relations as officials in Washington sensed that Israel had become a liability to their anti-Soviet containment policy. As U.S. Marines occupied Beirut, Dulles lamented that "Israel is a hostage held against us" by Soviet-supported Arab nationalists. He and Eisenhower justified intervention in Lebanon and Jordan as applications of dual containment, to deny those countries to Nasserite radicals and to Israel. Eisenhower agreed that "except for Israel we could form a viable policy in the area," although he wondered "how to take a sympathetic position regarding the Arabs without agreeing to the destruction of Israel." In August, by contrast, when the National Security Council (NSC) identified U.S. "bedrock objectives" (interests worth fighting to protect) in the Middle East, Eisenhower clarified that "preserving the independence of Israel should not be added to our bedrock objectives at this time."[12]

The NSC seriously reconsidered relations with Israel in November 1958, identifying Soviet expansionism "using Arab nationalism as its instrument" as the chief danger in the Middle East. To counteract this threat, the United States would need to build bridges to estranged Arab states, seek an Arab-Israeli compromise peace settlement, and discourage extraregional arms supply. To deter Israel from upsetting their plans, U.S. officials should "make clear as appropriate that, while U.S. policy embraces the preservation of the State of Israel in its essentials, we believe that Israel's continued existence as a sovereign state depends on its willingness to become a finite and accepted part of the Near East nation-state system."[13]

Israeli officials sensed the shift in U.S. thinking. The Foreign Ministry extensively discussed what it called the "crisis with the U.S.," which, overlooking the deeper U.S. uncertainties about the value of Israel, the Israeli government attributed to U.S. anger at Israel for suspending the overflights to Jordan. Some officials believed that "the anger was worthwhile; . . . it shook up the Americans a little bit and reminded them that it is not so simple to deal with us." But most Israeli leaders worried that U.S. irritation would persist indefinitely and permeate even Congress and the public. "We gained nothing from the crisis," Herzog noted, "and it would be better if it had not happened at all."[14]

In the aftermath of the 1958 crises, U.S.-Israeli relations stabilized as U.S. officials reaffirmed the impartiality policy. "We seek to treat Israel like any other friendly state," NEA officials resolved. "The interests of special groups in this country in Israel must be taken into account, but our policy must be based primarily on our national interests in the area, where there are other states with which we desire firm and friendly relations." Israel "occupies a very special place in U.S. international relations," Rountree instructed the U.S. ambassador-designate to Tel Aviv, Ogden Reid, in June 1959, but the "very close relationship with Israel has to be carefully balanced by our attention to the Arab states."[15]

The tension in official U.S. policy toward Israel was reflected in U.S. officials' private expressions about Israeli leaders. Michelle Mart has suggested that the United States revealed a preference for Israel by casting its people in favorable, masculine terms and the Arab people in unfavorable, feminine terms. U.S. officials, however, routinely feminized Israeli leaders. Ambassador to Tel Aviv Edward B. Lawson reported, for example, that Ben-Gurion was "emotionally upset and . . . near to tears" on a particular issue and in general "subject more to emotional than intellectual influences." For the same derisive effect, U.S. officials described Foreign Minister Golda Meir in masculine terminology. "She can out-Arab the Arabs," Donald C. Bergus of the NEA noted, "when it comes to the almost irresponsible use of strong language."[16] U.S.-Israeli official relations clearly remained less than special through the 1950s.

U.S. Relations with Egypt, Syria, and the United Arab Republic

U.S. relationships with Egypt and Syria experienced turmoil and tension during the Eisenhower presidency. The United States identified Nasser as a chief threat to its objectives in the Middle East because his neutralist foreign policy opened the region to Soviet influence. Syria experienced revolutionary change that portended a rise of communist influence there. U.S. officials adopted a firm, confrontational policy toward both states before they merged into the United Arab Republic in early 1958. Thereafter, Eisenhower tried to improve his relationship with Nasser as a means to contain communism in the region. Although many factors shaped U.S. relations with Egypt and Syria, Israel continually factored in as a point of contention.

In 1953–56, a measured friendliness in U.S.-Egyptian relations gave way to tension generated by several issues. Eisenhower and Dulles initially viewed Egypt as a potential partner in stabilizing the Middle East. They convinced Britain to end its military occupation of Egypt by 1956 and offered Egypt military and economic aid as an incentive to cooperate with U.S. policy. Tension developed in 1955, however, when Nasser demonstrated an independent ambition and refused to submit to U.S. dictates and desires. He vocalized pan-Arab aspirations, resisted the Baghdad Pact and the Alpha peace plan, accepted Soviet arms, and failed to respond suitably to U.S. offers to build the Aswân Dam. Under the Omega initiative of early 1956, Eisenhower canceled economic aid offers to Egypt, challenged Nasser's prestige, and contemplated covert operations to unseat him. By mid-1956, U.S.-Egyptian relations were strained.[17]

The Suez Crisis further damaged the relationship. While grateful that Eisenhower had halted the tripartite attack, Nasser demanded that the United States cut its ties with Britain, France, and Israel and accommodate Arab concerns. NEA officials, by contrast, urged Nasser to desist from past practices, such as fedayeen operations and the canal blockade, that had triggered the Israeli attack. U.S. leaders also pressed him to facilitate the deployment of the United Nations Emergency Force, negotiate a final settlement with Israel, halt covert operations in other Arab states, and cooperate with canal clearance. Nasser rejected such suggestions, however, reviving in U.S. minds the contempt that had fueled the Omega initiative.[18]

Nasser's reputation also declined in U.S. public opinion. "One man's angry will cannot be allowed to destroy a whole economic fabric in which half the world is vitally concerned," the *New York Times* commented in response to the nationalization of the Suez Canal Company. The United Nations must "rescue

Egypt from the folly of her dictator." By April 1957, 40 percent of U.S. citizens held Egypt more responsible for Arab-Israeli tension (compared to 12 percent who faulted Israel). A Gallup poll found that only 17 percent of Americans held a favorable view of Egypt, 52 percent were neutral, and 31 percent viewed the country with disfavor.[19]

Many factors deepened the tension in the U.S.-Egyptian relationship after the Suez Crisis. Profoundly mistrustful of the West, Nasser delayed canal clearance, rejected Western solutions to the question of canal ownership, attacked the prestige of pro-Western leaders in Lebanon and Iraq, criticized the Eisenhower Doctrine, and accepted Soviet military and economic aid. He was "literally engaged in a cold war against the West," U.S. Navy intelligence estimated. In response, Dulles maintained economic restrictions imposed during the canal crisis and pressed Turkey, Sudan, and several Arab states to isolate Nasser. On one occasion, he composed a harsh critique of Egyptian foreign policy that "hit under his guard," reported Ambassador to Egypt Raymond G. Hare after delivering Dulles's assessment to Nasser.[20]

U.S.-Syrian relations also deteriorated during Eisenhower's presidency. A basic friendship initially remained intact despite tensions regarding Israel-related issues, and the government of Colonel Adib al-Shishakli pledged to discuss peace terms with Israel and to cooperate with the West on security matters in exchange for U.S. aid. In February 1954, however, al-Shishakli fell in a military coup that opened a period of deep divisions among Syrian political and military officers. Most Syrian leaders criticized the Baghdad Pact, and Shukry al-Quwatly, who emerged as president in August 1955, accepted Soviet arms supply in 1956. U.S. and British officials planned a covert operation to overthrow al-Quwatly in October 1956, but during the Suez-Sinai War Syria exposed the plan, accepted Soviet arms and political support, and reportedly offered to provide a staging area for Soviet troops destined to intervene in Egypt.[21]

U.S.-Syrian relations reached a crisis in 1957. As U.S. observers detected rising communist influence in Syria, the government in Damascus denounced the Eisenhower Doctrine, accepted additional Soviet weapons, suppressed conservative opposition, and apparently fomented the revolt in Jordan. In May, the U.S. ambassador to Syria, James S. Moose Jr., reported "malicious Syrian criticism" of the United States. U.S. officials apparently launched a second covert operation in Damascus in August, but Syria infiltrated the conspiracy, expelled three U.S. diplomats (who were likely undercover Central Intelligence Agency [CIA] officers), and surrounded the U.S. embassy with tanks. In response, Eisenhower expelled two Syrian envoys from Washington.[22]

This diplomatic crisis prompted Western military maneuvers against Syria. CIA reports that communists had gained prominent government positions in Damascus during the showdown with Washington left Eisenhower concerned that the Soviet Union might annex Syria or subvert neighboring pro-Western regimes. He thus encouraged Turkey, Iraq, Lebanon, and Jordan to "band together, and using such excuses as necessary, move to eliminate the Syrian government." Eisenhower ordered the Pentagon to move the Sixth Fleet to the eastern Mediterranean, station NATO planes in Turkey, and alert military commands worldwide to prepare for war. Combined with signs that the Soviets sought to escalate the Cold War, Dulles considered events in Syria "the greatest peril for us since the Korean War." Soviet leader Nikita Khrushchev seemed "extremely dangerous . . . , crude and impulsive."[23]

Contrary to Eisenhower's wishes, only Turkey moved firmly against Syria. Jordan, Iraq, and Lebanon remained passive, and Saudi Arabia blamed the trouble in Syria on U.S. policies. Eisenhower realized that any attack on Syria would endanger the pipelines through which vast quantities of Iraqi and Saudi oil reached European markets, while members of Congress questioned the wisdom of U.S. military intervention. In contrast, Turkish leaders told U.S. officials that Syria represented "a cancer on the Middle East," and by September, Turkey had concentrated fifty thousand soldiers near the Syrian border. Dulles hoped that the Turkish move would "'cool off' Syrian hotheads."[24]

Eisenhower and Dulles feared that Israel would complicate the Syrian situation. Dulles urged Ben-Gurion to avoid any involvement, and to encourage Israel to remain passive, the CIA informed the prime minister of Eisenhower's plan for multinational action. But Dulles worried that Israel "may not stand by permanently," and the Pentagon monitored Israeli paratrooper maneuvers near Huleh. Dulles also feared that Syria, which kept most of its army on its border with Israel even as Turkey massed its troops, might attack Israel to rally other Arab states to the Syrian side. When Eisenhower suggested encouraging Arab states to wage a holy war on communism in Syria, Dulles replied that "if the Arabs have a 'holy war' they would want it to be against Israel." To mitigate such dangers, Eisenhower assured Arab leaders that "should Israel attempt to conquer any Arab state," he would "take action to prevent this."[25]

By late 1957, Eisenhower and Dulles faced a bind in Syria. To urge Turkey to relent from its military mobilization would comprise a retreat under Soviet pressure. But Dulles feared that unilateral Turkish military action "would have almost as bad an effect . . . as if the Israelis took military action on their own against Syria." Worse, Egyptian pilots and soldiers trickled into Syria, and on 13 October Cairo and Damascus formed a joint command to defend against Turkey, making it more difficult for U.S. officials to press Turkey into action.[26]

Eisenhower's escape from the bind in Syria materialized because of the merger of Egypt and Syria into the UAR on 1 February 1958. Fearing a communist victory in early 1958 elections, leaders of Syria's Arab Resurrection (Ba'athist) Party asked Nasser for a merger. Nasser agreed provided that Cairo would hold a dominant political position over Damascus. "It was sure that Nasser was to be the boss of the new Arab state," Director of Central Intelligence Allen Dulles observed.[27]

The rapid formation of the UAR surprised and concerned U.S. officials. The State Department predicted that the UAR would challenge Israel militarily, bolster Nasser's political and economic stature, and press Iraq, Saudi Arabia, and Jordan to join. Dulles considered stifling the UAR by "developing opposition in Syria among those who object to being denied their national existence," and he notified Iraq that Eisenhower would provide political support and military equipment "if the neighbors of Syria should feel compelled, in the face of provocations from Syria, to take action justifiable as self-defensive." But Dulles distanced the United States from such activity and, for political and logistical reasons, rejected a covert operations plan involving some "Syrian tribes."[28]

Despite their initial concerns about the merger, Eisenhower and Dulles soon identified its advantages. The UAR, they reasoned, would arrest the spread of communism in Damascus, absorb Nasser's political ambitions, and perhaps stoke tension between Cairo and Moscow. Moreover, U.S. opposition to the plan would prove "a sterile gesture" that galvanized Arab resentment, while prompt recognition would mollify Nasser. On such reasoning, the State Department announced that it would endorse any unification scheme approved by the Arab peoples involved, formally recognizing the UAR on 25 February.[29]

Recognition of the UAR came in the context of Eisenhower's initiative to improve his relationship with Nasser. After sensing that Nasser was worried about growing Soviet influence in the Middle East, Eisenhower had authorized Dulles in November 1957 "to attempt to bring Nasser back to our side" while avoiding "the position of 'bootlicking a dictator.'" A month later, Egyptian Foreign Minister Mahmoud Fawzi recognized "a need and grounds for cooperation." After recognizing the UAR, Dulles proposed to Nasser a series of deals, beginning with U.S. military equipment sales and economic aid, to build better relations. Relations improved modestly before tensions resurfaced in summer 1958 over the revolution in Iraq and the U.S. intervention in Lebanon.[30]

UAR concerns with Israel complicated the U.S. initiative. The UAR's ambassador to Washington, Ahmed Hussein, complained that the State Department gave Israel "a privileged position," while Nasser observed that Israel formed the "core of US difficulties with the Arab world." To alleviate Nasser's fear that the United States favored Israel, Eisenhower told Mostafa Kamel, who became UAR ambassador to Washington in August 1958, that their two governments must "work together cooperatively and intelligently to find an equitable solution" to the problems between them. But Nasser complained that the United States always treated "Israel as friendly and [the] UAR as hostile," and he openly suspected that Dulles would eventually "stab him in the back."[31]

Despite such initial attitudes, U.S. and UAR officials reached a rapprochement in 1958–59. After Nasser revealed that he was troubled by Soviet influence in Iraq and thus ready to make amends with the West, the State Department signed a December 1958 deal to provide the UAR with wheat. Compared to communism in the Arab states, Dulles explained to the NSC in January 1959, "certainly Nasser was the lesser of two evils." By December, U.S. food aid to the UAR surpassed $110 million, in exchange for which the UAR promoted anticommunist political initiatives in Iraq and toned down its anti-Western propaganda.[32]

U.S. and UAR officials sought to shelter their rapprochement from Israel. Eisenhower tried to downplay the food aid because Israel "would unquestionably be restive in a situation in which we rendered *open* support to Nasser." The State Department distanced itself from private U.S. charity to Israel and from a "malicious and harmful" public statement by Golda Meir about U.S.-UAR relations. For his part, Nasser reported that he refrained from seizing the cargo of the *Inge Toft* and blocked Arab League plans to form a Palestinian army in order to avoid antagonizing Eisenhower.[33]

Nevertheless, Israeli officials detected and challenged the rapprochement. Foreign Ministry officials warned the State Department that Nasser represented "fascist imperialism, which is actually supported and maintained by international communism." Israeli officials also launched a *hasbara* campaign in the U.S. media, arguing that Nasser would continue to attack his pro-Western neighbors. Nasser "is no less a liar now than he was in the past and there is no doubt he will cheat them again," Meir told *hasbara* officials. Americans "see only the communist danger," Ben-Gurion noted privately. "We see the Nasser danger."[34]

By 1960, the UAR-U.S. rapprochement had cooled in large part because of Israel. As his stature lagged in Damascus, Nasser accused Israel and U.S. Zionists of arranging anti-UAR newspaper editorials, labor activism in the *Cleopatra* case, and passage of the Douglas Amendment to disrupt U.S.-UAR relations. He also expressed resentment that many U.S. leaders voiced pro-Israel sentiments during the 1960 U.S. election campaigns. Nasser saw "no real problem in US-UAR relations," he told U.S. Ambassador to the UAR G. Frederick Reinhardt, "other than the problem of Israel."[35]

Israel also factored into U.S. officials' discussions about reviving the rapprochement by arranging a meeting between Eisenhower and Nasser in late 1960. Eisenhower accepted the State Department's advice not to receive Nasser at the White House because such a step would anger Israel and provoke a backlash among pro-Israel citizens and members of Congress. Instead, he agreed to meet Nasser at the United Nations on 25 September, securing the acquiescence of U.S. Jewish leaders by pledging to explain to Nasser in "plain language" that many U.S. citizens disliked UAR hostility toward Israel. But the State Department canceled Nasser's planned eight-day cross-country tour because of secu-rity and protocol concerns "during the heat of a presidential campaign."[36]

For their part, Israeli officials secretly orchestrated a publicity campaign to shape the Eisenhower-Nasser meeting. The Israeli embassy anonymously published and distributed several pamphlets containing excerpts from various newspaper stories and editorials critical of Nasser. Care was taken to ensure anonymity to avoid angering Eisenhower or appearing to be meddling. *Hasbara* officials took credit for a demonstrable increase in U.S. public scorn for neutralism.[37]

The Eisenhower-Nasser meeting in New York signaled renewed tension in U.S.-UAR relations. Eisenhower told Nasser that the United States wanted better relations with the UAR and that "we should take a good hard look at what can be done now" to settle the Arab-Israeli conflict. The president encouraged Nas-ser to accept that "Israel is." But Nasser countered that "Israel is the barrier to good U.S.-Arab relations." He complained that both Democrats and Republi-cans endorsed Israel's but not Egypt's interests while campaigning for office and that Israel but not Egypt received U.S. arms. "To accept Israel as a fact," Nasser declared, "would be to permit a thief to keep what he has stolen."[38]

U.S. Relations with Other Arab States

In contrast to its centrality in U.S. relations with Syria and Egypt, Israel dimin-ished as a factor in U.S. relations with Lebanon, Saudi Arabia, Jordan, and Iraq during the Eisenhower presidency. The United States enjoyed stable relations with Lebanon and Saudi Arabia and forged a close relationship with Jordan after 1956 in large part because these states, worried by the rise of Arab radicalism, tacitly acknowledged the existence of Israel and cooperated with U.S. security schemes. U.S.-Iraqi relations soured after the revolution in Baghdad in 1958, but Israel played only a minor role in that development.

Relations with Lebanon remained extremely friendly in the 1950s. Leban-ese leaders refrained from criticizing U.S. policy toward Israel. After Lebanon eagerly embraced the Eisenhower Doctrine, the United States provided the country with $3.8 million in military equipment and $10 million in economic aid. Anti-U.S. passion drove only a fraction of the popular unrest of 1957–58, and resentment of the U.S. military intervention vanished soon after the marines withdrew. "This is an era in Lebanon of good feeling toward the United States," Armin Meyer of the NEA noted after visiting Beirut in mid-1959. Saeb Salaam, who had criticized the United States in 1958, expressed friendship when he be-came prime minister in September 1960.[39]

The United States and Saudi Arabia also preserved a close friendship de-spite differences regarding Israel. King Saud routinely complained about Israeli policy on such issues as borders and refugees and bitterly protested Israeli aggression during the Suez-Sinai War. But he continued to cooperate with the United States on oil and defense matters, even as Eisenhower advised him to make compromises with Israel to resolve regional problems. On 31 January 1957, Eisenhower elicited from King Saud recognition that Israel "is now an historical fact and must be accepted as such."[40]

With limited effect, Israeli *hasbara* officials worked to reduce U.S.-Saudi accord. To counter the State Department's portrait of Saud as a heroic defender of oil and bases, Y. Harry Levin of the Israeli embassy distributed to the U.S. media negative information about the king during his 1957 visit to Washington. Levin sought to prove that Saud "is politically unreliable and to emphasize those sides of his life and his regime, his position toward the West, other religions, etc., that may sour his image in the eyes of the American public." Levin supplied information on Saudi monarchism and slave-labor practices to the AFL-CIO and other trade unions, civil rights leader A. Philip Randolph, and human rights groups. Levin took credit for arranging the widespread public protests that accompanied the king's arrival in the United States.[41]

U.S. officials also proved able to insulate Jordan from Israel-related trouble. In the early 1950s, Jordan remained a British protectorate. The kingdom's Anglophilia declined in 1955, when nationalist protests against the Baghdad Pact forced King Hussein to dismiss the British commanders of the Arab Legion, and collapsed in 1957, when backlash against the Suez War forced the king to repudiate the Anglo-Jordanian defense treaty. U.S. officials attributed Jordan's instability to several factors, among them a latent anti-Zionism among its Palestinian population and widespread anger at Israel's 1956 attack on Egypt.[42]

As British influence waned, the United States assumed responsibility for Jordan because it comprised a crucial buffer zone in a volatile region. The State Department and Pentagon noted evidence that Nasser covertly encouraged popular resistance movements within Jordan and anticipated that the fall of King Hussein would lead to invasion by Israel, Egypt, or Syria. Eisenhower thus invoked the Eisenhower Doctrine and provided Hussein thirty million dollars in economic and military aid between April and June 1957. In this way, the president used Jordan to implement dual containment of both Israeli and Egyptian-Syrian influence.[43]

Eisenhower and Dulles extended the dual containment policy twice in 1958. At the height of the July crisis, they worried that Baghdad's revolutionary regime might try to occupy Jordan, thereby prompting Israel to occupy the West Bank. Then, in October, Israel charged that Nasser was trying to unseat King Hussein and warned that it would not tolerate UAR control of East Jerusalem. Nasser denied that he meddled in Jordan and accused Israel of mobilizing soldiers to invade the kingdom. U.S. officials warned both Israel and the UAR against covert or overt incursions into Jordan.[44]

In 1959–60, U.S. officials were relieved to note that King Hussein had consolidated his position in Amman and stabilized his relationship with Israel. With Nasser preoccupied in Syria and Iraq, the State Department observed, King Hussein had crushed the pro-Nasser dissidents in his kingdom and built popularity through his personal charisma. At a March 1959 meeting in Washington, Eisenhower and Hussein affirmed their mutual friendship, and the president urged the king to make peace with Israel on the rationale that communism posed a greater danger than Israel did. (Eisenhower later commented to Dulles that the youthful Hussein was a "nice boy.") King Hussein was "the 'glue' which holds Jordan together," Meyer noted after visiting the kingdom in July. Furthermore, according to Meyer, Jordanian leaders and common people appreciated U.S. economic aid and recognized that "Israel is here to stay."[45]

The greatest U.S. worry about Jordan remained UAR intrigue. Nasser claimed that he preferred to keep Hussein in power to avoid the rise of a more powerful rival in Amman or Israeli expansion into the West Bank. Yet U.S. officials suspected that Nasser dispatched agents into Jordan to undermine Hussein's authority. Indeed, King Hussein blamed Nasser for the assassination of Jordanian Prime Minister Hazza al-Majali on 29 August 1960. U.S. officials discouraged Nasser from covert operations against Jordan, and Eisenhower bolstered King Hussein by inviting him to visit Washington. But the United States and Jordan remained suspicious of Nasser.[46]

Israel had little influence on U.S.-Iraqi relations, which remained friendly from 1953 to 1958. In exchange for U.S. military aid, Iraq became a charter member of the Baghdad Pact in 1955 because King Faisal desired security against Soviet and radical Arab expansionism. Dulles removed Israel as an issue by clarifying Eisenhower's impartiality policy to Iraqi Ambassador and Foreign Minister–designate Moussa al-Shabandar. By 1956, U.S. intelligence officers stressed that Iraq had suppressed communism, achieved financial stability, and passively tolerated Israel. In 1957, Eisenhower and Crown Prince Abdul Ilah affirmed the U.S.-Iraqi strategic partnership. When Iraq and Jordan formed a federation after the creation of the UAR in 1958, the State Department discouraged Israel from protesting.[47]

U.S.-Iraqi relations soured after the violent Iraqi revolution of July 1958. Latent anti-Western nationalism erupted during the revolution, in which the pro-Western monarchy fell, three Americans were killed, a mob seized United States Information Agency property, and U.S. diplomats were roughed up and charged with counterrevolutionary conspiracy. U.S. officials canceled deliveries of military jets and armored cars sold to the deposed regime (although deliveries of small arms and spare parts valued at one million dollars were continued as a counter to Soviet arms supply). The new regime of General Abdul Karim Qassim adopted an anti-U.S. disposition, canceled U.S. military aid deals, and withdrew Iraq from the Baghdad Pact. When Rountree visited Baghdad in December 1958, a violent mob pelted his motorcade with garbage and briefly threatened his personal safety before Iraqi soldiers intervened.[48]

The State Department adopted a policy of indirect opposition to Qassim. Although uncertain about whether he was a communist, the NEA detected communist influence in his "inner circle of advisors, the government propaganda apparatus, the Baghdad press, the 'street,' and the Peoples Resistance Forces." The NSC decided, however, that U.S. intervention, whether covert or overt, would backfire. While remaining outwardly friendly to Qassim, therefore, U.S. diplomats encouraged Nasser to mobilize Arab nationalism as a counterweight to Iraqi communism in the hope that the Iraqi army would oust Qassim. Israeli officials protested that this strategy inflated Nasser, whom they considered a greater danger than Qassim, but Dulles once again declared Nasser the "lesser evil."[49]

Despite setbacks, U.S. officials were pleased that their policy in Iraq achieved satisfactory results. In early 1959, a reported UAR covert operation in Baghdad failed, resulting in the political strengthening of the communists. In October 1959, an assassination attempt on Qassim also failed. The prestige of Iraqi communists declined, however, after communist army soldiers massacred Turkomans in Kirkuk in July 1959, and by early 1960, U.S. officials were relieved to notice that Qassim had seemed to gain the upper hand over the communists. While Qassim remained anti-Western, the danger of communists capturing Iraq seemed to have passed. Qassim was overthrown and killed in 1963.[50]

Conclusion

Differences regarding Arab-related issues strained U.S.-Israeli relations through the 1950s. Israeli leaders disliked the Eisenhower administration's impartiality, its mediation of Arab-Israeli disputes, and its deliberate efforts to mollify Nasser and King Saud. The Israeli government calculated that it should pursue arms supply, security assurances, and other strategic concessions from the United States to neutralize the mortal danger posed by the Arab states. By contrast, U.S. officials found Israel's security demands incompatible with America's Cold War interests in the Arab world. U.S. leaders disputed Israel's views on arms supply, security commitments, and Arab-Israeli conflicts.

Israeli officials perceived this dichotomy in the relationship. At the bilateral level, the deputy directory of the Foreign Ministry's U.S. Division, Pinhas Eliav, observed in September 1959, "everything is usually all right because there are many factors, spiritual, public, and even political that work for this friendship." At the multilateral level, however, U.S.-Arab and Israeli-Arab dynamics strained U.S.-Israeli relations because the United States took a position of "neutrality" toward Israel. "It is clear that there is a gap between these two levels, and the American attempts to bridge them are impossible." Although U.S.-Israeli bilateral relations were sound and the U.S. public liked Israel, Ben-Gurion noted in 1960, trouble occurred whenever the United States thought of Israel in its Middle East context because Arab interests weighed in.[51]

By contrast, Israel influenced U.S. relations with Egypt, Syria, and the UAR. These relationships were strained by disagreements about Cold War strategy and inter-Arab rivalries, but Israel remained a bone of contention. The Israeli attack on Egypt in 1956 galvanized Nasserist nationalism and aggravated U.S.-Egyptian tensions, and Israel challenged the U.S. rapprochement with the UAR in the late 1950s. The existence of Israel stimulated the anti-U.S. nationalism that strained U.S. relations with Syria, and the prospect of Israeli involvement in the 1957 crisis in Damascus complicated the situation from the U.S. perspective.

U.S. relations with other Arab powers became less susceptible to the Israel factor during the 1950s. As Eisenhower proclaimed impartiality between Israel and the Arab states, Lebanon, Saudi Arabia, and royalist Iraq constrained their anger at past U.S. support for Israel and supported U.S. security objectives in the region. After escaping its traditional dependence on Britain, Jordan accepted the support and protection of the United States, which treated the kingdom as a buffer against Israeli or Arab nationalist expansion. The revolutionary regime that took over Iraq in 1958 adopted an anti-U.S. disposition not because of Israel but because of U.S. support of conservative Arab states.

Despite efforts to follow an impartial policy, the United States found that its relations with Israel and the Arab powers were tainted by U.S. policy toward each side's adversary. Just as the United States eyed with suspicion powers that practiced neutralism in the Cold War, so too did Israel and the Arab states—which were engaged in a conflict at least as contentious as the Cold War—view with dismay U.S. impartiality. From the U.S. point of view, the costs of the Arab-Israeli conflict included strained relationships with Israel and certain Arab states.

CONCLUSION
Caught in the Middle East

For the first time in its history, the United States became deeply involved in the Middle East in 1945–61. Because of the Cold War, U.S. leaders defined vital interests in the region and took action to protect those interests as British power in the region waned and Soviet interest rose. The Arab-Israeli conflict, which brought war and turmoil to the Middle East, threatened to undermine U.S. interests by providing opportunities for Soviet inroads, aggravating anti-Western Arab nationalism, and destabilizing the region's political and economic foundations. Presidents Harry S. Truman and Dwight D. Eisenhower considered the conflict a problem demanding a solution.

From 1945 to 1961, Truman and Eisenhower acted to mitigate the tensions and disputes between Israel and its Arab neighbors. The presidents and their advisers worked diligently to avert hostilities and to end the wars of 1948–49 and 1956–57 as well as the intermittent border skirmishes. They formulated diplomatic initiatives to resolve the Arab-Israeli conflict in its entirety and to settle specific controversies piecemeal. Truman and Eisenhower started the enduring U.S. involvement in the Arab-Israeli peace process.

Yet the U.S. quest for Arab-Israeli peace fell short in 1945–61 in part because of limits U.S. leaders imposed on their peacemaking. While the antagonism among local powers generated the conflict, the United States frequently compromised its peacemaking objectives when they conflicted with its broader aims in the Cold War. Truman and Eisenhower rejected, for example, potential solutions to the Arab-Israeli dispute—such as collaboration with the Soviet Union or abandonment of Arab interests on behalf of Israel—that might have extended Soviet influence in the region. U.S. leaders also refrained from a strictly pro-Arab settlement of the conflict that would violate their domestic political interests and cultural values. The United States preferred to tolerate the Arab-Israeli conflict, despite its destabilizing tendencies, rather than to solve it at a cost to other interests.

By privileging Cold War interests over peacemaking ambitions, the United States even contributed to the Arab-Israeli conflict. To be sure, U.S. leaders helped contain the conflict by achieving cease-fires, ending border skirmishes, and curtailing escalations to general hostilities. By refraining from taking steps that might have led to peace, however, the U.S. government left in place a volatile formula for a perpetual conflict punctuated by explosive wars.

Caught in the Middle East: The United States and the Cold War

Because of the Cold War, the United States assigned increasing strategic and political importance to the Middle East. As the British ability to defend the area declined and Soviet ambitions increased, Truman and Eisenhower collectively made deep and enduring commitments to the security of the region. These leaders also sought to solve the Arab-Israeli conflict because it threatened Middle East stability. Although such commitments carried serious risks, the U.S. government found it difficult to relinquish them. By 1961, the United States was caught in the Middle East.

The Middle East contained several assets that U.S. officials deemed valuable. Western governments prized the oil extracted from Saudi Arabia, Iraq, and other Arab states and delivered through the networks of pipelines and sea routes branching across Syria, Lebanon, and Egypt. Several Arab states—notably Egypt and Iraq—boasted military facilities that figured in various Western schemes for containing Soviet power in peace and defeating the Soviet Union in war. The political loyalty of Arab Muslims—especially those who controlled Islam's holy sites in Arabia—seemed crucial to appeasing other Muslims from North Africa to South Asia. When it shed its original neutralist disposition, Israel also gained importance in the minds of U.S. strategists because of its central location, efficient military, strategic facilities, and democratic government.

U.S. security experts detected several threats to these Middle East assets. These officials assumed that the Soviet Union would seek to expand its power and influence into the region, to the exclusion of Western interests. Truman administration officials feared such Soviet expansionism even in the absence of hard evidence of it. Soviet overtures to Arab states in the 1950s—including vetoes of U.N. resolutions, economic and military aid, cultural gestures, and threats against Britain and France in 1956 and Israel in 1958—convinced Eisenhower and his advisers that the earlier fears remained valid. In addition to the external problem of Soviet expansionism, U.S. officials also feared that intraregional instability, resulting from decolonization, Arab-Arab rivalry, or Arab-Israeli conflict, would facilitate Soviet penetration.

To protect Middle East assets against the Soviet threat, Truman made the first U.S. commitments to Middle East security. In response to State Department warnings of Soviet expansionism, he approved the 1950 Tripartite Declaration, which implicitly committed the United States to guaranteeing Arab and Israeli borders. The outbreak of the Korean War raised the specter of a sudden Soviet intrusion into the region at a moment when emerging nationalism was eroding the Arab world's historic ties to the West, Britain's ability to defend the Middle East was declining, and NSC-68 was enabling the United States to assume new responsibilities. In 1951, Truman approved the proposed Middle East Command, which, if accepted by Egypt, would have committed the United States to defending the heart of the Middle East against Soviet attack.

Because containment of communism seemed to depend on Middle Eastern stability, the Truman administration also tried in principle to limit the Arab-Israeli conflict. The State and Defense Departments opposed the partition of Palestine and the recognition of Israel as a way of preventing a controversy that would alienate the Arab states from the West and provide an opportunity for the Soviet Union to gain political influence. After Truman helped establish Israel over such departmental opposition, such U.S. officials sought ways to end the Arab-Israeli hostilities and to solve the disputes left in its wake.

Eisenhower substantially deepened U.S. involvement in the Middle East to stem direct and indirect Soviet challenges to U.S. interests. To defend the region, he established the Baghdad Pact and informally integrated his military into it. Under the 1957 Eisenhower Doctrine, Congress authorized economic aid, military aid, and military force to stop the spread of communism in the Middle East, and the president interpreted the mandate as justifying involvement in complicated Jordanian, Syrian, and Lebanese disputes that were only remotely related to communism. He apparently authorized covert operations to change a government in Syria, and he positioned military forces to defend Turkey during a Turkish-Syrian confrontation that portended Soviet involvement. The military interventions in Lebanon and Jordan in 1958 represented unprecedented U.S. action in the Middle East.

Eisenhower also promoted Arab-Israeli reconciliation in 1953–56 on behalf of his Cold War aims. Competing with the West for influence in Third World countries, the Soviet Union gained political sway in Egypt, Syria, and other Arab states by vetoing Security Council resolutions, providing economic and military aid, and otherwise meeting Arab desires regarding Israel. Egyptian Premier Gamal Abdel Nasser emerged as a neutralist and dealt openly with nonaligned and communist governments around the world. Eisenhower tried to stymie the rise of Soviet influence by promoting the Alpha peace plan, and he quietly resolved to use military force to halt Arab-Israeli hostilities, thereby denying the Soviets the opportunity to intervene.

The Cold War continued to shape the U.S. approach to the Arab-Israeli conflict in the late 1950s. Eisenhower halted the tripartite attack on Egypt in 1956 because he feared that it would lead Nasser and other Third World leaders into dependency on the Soviet Union. The U.S. president pressed Israel to withdraw from the Sinai and Gaza in 1957 because he sensed that the Soviets would champion Egypt's cause. U.S. leaders maintained their impartiality on Arab-Israeli matters in large part to avoid giving the Soviets opportunities to gain political influence.

Although Truman and Eisenhower in principle desired Arab-Israeli peace, they gave higher priority to preserving Cold War interests when the two aims conflicted. Although the Pentagon considered the 1948 Arab-Israeli war a grave development, for example, commitments in Europe and Asia prevented the United States from sending soldiers to end the fighting. Because Truman's advisers hoped to erect an anti-Soviet defense agreement on the regime that took power in Egypt in 1952, they declined to pressure that regime to make peace with Israel, fearing that doing so would undermine the government's prestige in Cairo. U.S. officials refused to contemplate any resolution of the Jerusalem issue that risked the introduction of Soviet influence.

Eisenhower also privileged Cold War interests over Arab-Israeli peace. He established the Baghdad Pact and issued the Eisenhower Doctrine to prevent the spread of communism even though both measures aggravated Israeli insecurity. After the Suez-Sinai War, the administration suspended its original quest to make Arab-Israeli peace in favor of covert operations in Syria and military intervention in Lebanon and Jordan. In 1958–60, Eisenhower encouraged a rapprochement with Nasser, over vigorous Israeli objections, to deny the Soviets additional inroads in Cairo. To the president, global concerns were more important than the regional situation.

Cold War interests also prevented the United States from implementing alternative schemes to end the Arab-Israeli conflict. Truman and Eisenhower ruled out the use of military power to force a settlement on the belligerents because such action would have diminished the United States' worldwide ability to resist communism. The two presidents refused to collaborate with the Soviets to achieve a multilateral settlement because such a step would have enhanced Soviet political prestige. They refrained from favoring one side to the dispute to avoid driving the other into Soviet hands. The United States favored containment of the Soviet Union at the cost of Arab-Israeli conflict over Arab-Israeli peace at the cost of Soviet political gain. In this sense, the Cold War erected roadblocks on several prospective avenues to Arab-Israeli settlement.

The United States was drawn into dangerous situations as a result of Truman's and Eisenhower's commitments to Middle East security. Truman's Tripartite Declaration risked involvement in Arab-Israeli hostilities. Eisenhower became entangled in the Suez-Sinai conflict, which portended world war, and he placed U.S. soldiers in harm's way in Lebanon in 1958, risking some type of Soviet retaliation. His maneuvers in the Middle East on several occasions prompted the Pentagon to prepare for war there and elsewhere around the world. In short, Eisenhower's involvement in the Middle East was fraught with peril.

Caught in the Middle:
The United States and the Arab-Israeli Conflict

In 1945–61, Truman and Eisenhower generally sought to pacify the Arab-Israeli conflict and maintain good relations with all parties in it. On both counts, the presidents failed. They and their advisers proved unable to accomplish a peace settlement in light of the deep animosity between the Arab states and Israel and both sides' reluctance to make concessions or compromises. By trying to make peace, U.S. leaders strained relations with both sides. The United States was caught in the middle of the Arab-Israeli conflict.

Truman's initial policies toward Palestine satisfied neither side in the dispute. As Britain relinquished its mandate, the president promoted partition as a compromise between competing Zionist and Arab demands regarding the territory. But partition only partially pleased the Zionists and deeply angered the Arab states. The State Department thus tried in early 1948 to replace partition with trusteeship, but the Arabs remained unimpressed, the Zionists resented the move, and the initiative failed. Truman's decision to extend de facto recognition to Israel enraged the Arab states, but his decisions to delay de jure recognition and to contest Israeli territorial gains irritated the Israelis. In trying to accommodate the interests of both parties in the dispute, the Truman administration pleased neither.

Nor did Truman make headway in solving Arab-Israeli disputes after 1949. Despite U.S. backing, the Lausanne conference deadlocked. The State Department failed to find compromise solutions to the refugee crisis, the Suez Canal dispute, and border controversies. The U.S. government angered Israel by not recognizing its capture of Jerusalem and alienated the Arab states by not reversing that move. Truman and his advisers desired Arab-Israeli peace but could not conceive terms acceptable to the belligerent powers. American leaders repeatedly experienced the helplessness and misfortune of being caught between Israel and its Arab neighbors.

Eisenhower also quickly became ensnared in the Arab-Israeli conflict. In 1953–55, the local powers rejected his Jordan Valley Plan and Alpha peace plan. Violence persisted along Israel's borders with Egypt, Jordan, and Syria despite U.S. efforts to end it. Israel and the Arab states rejected Secretary of State John

Foster Dulles's moderate positions on the refugees, Jerusalem, and Banat Yaacov issues. Egypt and Syria criticized the measured terms of U.S.-backed U.N. resolutions on Israeli raids at Gaza and Lake Tiberias. Eisenhower and Dulles tried impartially to settle various disputes but reached no settlements and in the process strained relations with both parties.

The failure of the Alpha plan and the simultaneous rise of violence along Israel's borders in 1955–56 signified the shortcomings of Eisenhower's early peacemaking. His administration inadvertently damaged Alpha's prospects by establishing the Baghdad Pact, which angered Nasser, and by denying weapons to Israel, thereby sapping Israeli security and confidence in the West. Pressure from Eisenhower and Dulles to make peace actually galvanized both sides to resist concessions and remain confrontational. As the U.S. government promoted Alpha, violence swept along Israel's borders with Egypt, Syria, and Jordan, culminating in the Suez-Sinai War. The sorry legacy of Alpha confirmed that peace terms—no matter how impartial and fair from a Western perspective—could not be thrust upon hostile powers so mistrustful of each other and confident in their own abilities that they shunned compromise.

When the Suez-Sinai War erupted in October 1956, Eisenhower and Dulles were caught in a three-dimensional maelstrom. They confronted the challenges of ending hostilities between Egypt and Israel, curtailing a violent Egyptian-European decolonization struggle, and averting a Soviet attack on NATO allies. U.S. officials used firm diplomacy to halt the Egyptian-Israeli fighting, compel Britain and France to withdraw from Egypt, and defuse a superpower showdown. Eisenhower's pressure on Israel to withdraw from Egypt angered the Jewish state, however, while his acceptance of Israeli conditions for withdrawal and his withholding of sanctions on Israel earned Arab denunciation as a sellout to aggression. U.S. relations with both parties in the Israeli-Arab dispute were strained, and nothing was accomplished to resolve underlying Arab-Israeli grievances.

By the late 1950s, Eisenhower became passive toward peacemaking. The State Department helped contain border violence between Israel and Jordan, Egypt, and Syria but refrained from promoting a general settlement. And despite its interest in solving the refugee crisis and promoting water development, the department did not actively seek to solve either issue. U.S. diplomats passively tolerated the status quo regarding canal transit, the Gulf of Aqaba, Jerusalem, Jewish immigration, and the Arab boycott because chances of settlement seemed remote. American leaders concluded that because the Arab states and Israel were simply unprepared to settle, peacemaking would prove futile.

Even when avoiding the role of peacemaker, U.S. leaders found themselves the target of anger from and reproach by the parties in the Arab-Israeli conflict. To please Nasser, the State Department downplayed Israeli transit rights on the

Suez Canal, but the Egyptian leader remained recalcitrant and Israel became angry. Arab states criticized the implicit U.S. acceptance of Israel's positions on refugee resettlement, Jerusalem, and Gulf of Aqaba transit rights. Israel complained of U.S. arms supply to Arab states and its rapprochement with Nasser. Eisenhower tried to be friends with all countries, as he mused to Nasser in September 1960, but he could not avoid either side's backlash against his amity with the other.

The Leadership of Truman and Eisenhower

Although Truman and Eisenhower displayed different leadership styles, the two presidents ultimately adopted similar approaches to the Arab-Israeli situation. Comparisons of the two leaders' personal involvement in the Arab-Israeli situation, the consistency of their policy decisions, and the importance they ascribed to domestic political concerns show that Truman's and Eisenhower's policies during their first terms in office differed strikingly, while their policies during their second terms held more in common.

Truman displayed limited involvement in Arab-Israeli matters in 1945–49. He intervened episodically in Britain's handling of the Palestine issue and deferred to U.N. initiatives to determine what would follow the British mandate. His government remained aloof during the 1948–49 Arab-Israeli war and encouraged the United Nations to broker cease-fires and armistices. High-ranking U.S. officials intervened directly only in late 1948 and early 1949 to prevent the Israeli incursion into Egypt from embroiling Britain and to nudge the belligerent powers to sign U.N.-negotiated armistices. Lacking experience in Middle East diplomacy and distracted by momentous developments elsewhere in the world, Truman kept his distance from the Arab-Israeli conflict through 1948.

Given his interest in principle in resolving Arab-Israeli tensions, Truman showed less passivity after 1949. His advisers endorsed British plans to reopen the Haifa refinery but did not press the matter when the Arab states resisted, and U.S. officials aimed to contain tensions on such issues as the welfare of Jews in Arab states, Jewish immigration to Israel, and German reparations to Israel. On the Jerusalem issue, Truman and Secretary of State Dean G. Acheson affirmed the principle of *corpus separatum* but tolerated the Israeli-Jordanian division of the city. American officials averted war on the Huleh dispute but did nothing to solve underlying tensions and opposed 1952 Israeli-Egyptian peace talks that conflicted with U.S. security ambitions.

Eisenhower, by contrast, immediately became involved in the Arab-Israeli situation. He dispatched Eric Johnston to settle the Jordan water issue and vigorously promoted the Alpha plan. In addressing clashes along Israel's borders with Jordan, Syria, and Egypt, Eisenhower and Dulles moved from inactivity to promotion of U.N. action to direct arbitration and deterrence aimed at all sides. In 1955–56, Eisenhower positioned U.S. military forces in the Middle East to deter or reverse aggression. Such deployments comprised a remarkable difference from the 1940s, when the Pentagon balked at sending marines to protect U.S. diplomats in Jerusalem.

Eisenhower became deeply involved in the Suez-Sinai War. Before the outbreak of hostilities, he tried to settle the dispute over canal ownership, prevent Israel-related issues from complicating the situation, and head off Israeli-Jordanian and Israeli-Iraqi clashes. When war erupted, the president took center stage to halt the attack on Egypt, fend off Soviet political and military intervention, and force the attacking powers to relinquish their gains. He and Dulles also dominated U.N. debates on sanctions against Israel, the canal, and the deployment of U.N. troops in Gaza and Sharm al-Sheikh. Unlike Truman's limited role in the 1948–49 war, Eisenhower extensively intervened in the 1956–57 conflict.

Eisenhower became less active in Arab-Israeli peacemaking in the late 1950s. Convinced that peace would not materialize until the principals' attitudes softened, he declined to make an Alpha-style frontal assault to solve the overall conflict and relied on the State Department to contain the disputes regarding refugees, the Gulf of Aqaba, water, and border security. Eisenhower aimed to preserve the basic stability of the situation and prevent it from escalating to warfare while awaiting the distant day on which the antagonists became ready to make peace on their own volition. When crises erupted in Lebanon, Jordan, and Iraq in 1958, he took personal charge of U.S. policy. But as a whole, his diminished role during his second term approximated Truman's increased role in 1949–53.

Second, Truman displayed much less consistency than did Eisenhower in decision making on Arab-Israeli issues. Before 1947, Truman endorsed Jewish immigration to Palestine, paused when British Prime Minister Clement Attlee protested, reiterated the endorsement, and then paused again when Britain and Arab states complained. Truman supported partition but then approved and rejected trusteeship before reaffirming partition. He authorized Secretary of State George C. Marshall to promote the Bernadotte Plan, then retracted this decision after domestic advisers complained. Truman directed Acheson to adopt certain positions on the issues of Israeli membership in the United Nations and an Export-Import Bank loan to Israel but then reversed these decisions. The president sent firm messages to Israel, urging modification of its policy on the refugee and Jerusalem issues but ultimately refrained from forcing either matter.

Truman's inconsistency on Arab-Israeli issues had several causes. Thrust into the Oval Office at a time of enormous change in international affairs, the president lacked the experience and resources needed to manage foreign policy in the Middle East. Even when he issued momentous pronouncements on Palestine between 1945 and 1948, he did not follow through but deferred to Britain to conceive solutions consistent with his principles. Truman was absent from Washington for three weeks in June 1948, when the Arab-Israeli war passed through crucial phases. His ambivalence on Arab-Israeli matters revealed that he lacked understanding of his own objectives or of the impact of his tactics and that he made decisions spontaneously and sporadically.

Truman's waffling also stemmed from the deep divisions within his administration between pro- and anti-Zionists. Truman tried without success to walk a tightrope between the humanitarian concerns and political interests promoted by his political advisers and the diplomatic and strategic interests advocated by the State Department and the Pentagon. Suspicious that State Department professionals plotted to embarrass or betray him, the president frequently rejected their advice and pushed policy into a more pro-Zionist or pro-Israel orientation. The State Department refrained from subverting the seemingly distasteful presidential decisions on partition, recognition, and other issues but did push for alternative policies less favorable to Israel.

Once Acheson took over the State Department in 1949, the gap between the department and White House narrowed. Under the new secretary, the department learned to explain fully its recommendations, alert Truman to potential domestic political backlash, and secure his clear assent before proceeding with policy initiatives. Such practices brought more consistency to U.S. policy by reducing the president's earlier tendency suddenly to reverse department policy. Tensions between the White House staff and the State Department continued to simmer through 1953, however, as is evident in the battles for Truman's mind on such issues as arms supply to the Arab states and economic aid to Israel.

Compared to Truman, Eisenhower approached the Arab-Israeli conflict more consistently and impartially. On occupying the Oval Office, he consciously decided to become involved in Arab-Israeli matters in an impartial manner. He actively promoted the Jordan Valley Plan and the Alpha peace plan as balanced initiatives to promote regional reconciliation and crafted evenhanded stabilization schemes such as arms in escrow. Eisenhower repeatedly acted on his conviction that the United States must maintain friendly relations with both the Arab states and Israel.

To be sure, the Eisenhower administration did not consistently display unanimity on Middle East policies. Eisenhower's commitment to impartiality occasionally collided with lingering anti-Zionism in the Bureau of Near Eastern, South Asian, and African Affairs, which pressed Dulles more firmly to criticize Israel during the 1954 Israeli-Jordanian crisis and after the 1955 Khan Yunis and Lake Tiberias raids. The Pentagon also repeatedly pushed for more assertive policies than the president allowed on the questions of whether to join the Baghdad Pact, whether to approve Anglo-French force against Egypt in 1956, and whether to send U.S. troops into Iraq and Jordan in 1958. Because Eisenhower was a more proactive and in-charge executive than Truman was, however, these internal policy divisions did not cause the policy reversals and inconsistencies that marked the Truman years.

Third, Truman more than Eisenhower made decisions favoring Israel for domestic political reasons. In the late 1940s, U.S. Zionists frequently pressed Truman to make favorable policy, and he bowed in part to political considerations when he facilitated Israel's birth, recognized the new state, and abandoned the Bernadotte Plan. Truman also gave in to domestic pressure in 1949 when he prohibited the State Department from blocking Israeli admission to the United Nations or compelling Israel to relinquish the Negev, the western Galilee, or Jerusalem. Public pressure compelled the State Department unwillingly to provide aid for Israel to absorb Jewish immigrants and led Truman to order a State Department investigation into Iraq's treatment of its Jewish citizens. Israeli *hasbara* activities encouraged such favorable public thinking.

Truman's submission to domestic politics, however, had limits. The president refused to lift the arms embargo against Israel in 1948–49 despite protests from U.S. Zionists that refusing arms to the new state might result in its destruction. He refused to dispatch U.S. troops to rescue Israel when its fate looked precarious, and he withheld de jure recognition, contrary to public demand. In 1950–51, in contradiction to his domestic political interests, Truman approved the Middle East Command, endorsed a Security Council resolution critical of Israel's behavior in the Huleh crisis, and refrained from endorsing Israeli access to the Suez Canal. Confronted with the persistent advice of the State and Defense Departments about the risks of a pro-Zionist policy, Truman occasionally displayed elements of anti-Zionism.

In contrast, Eisenhower frequently acted on his claim of immunity to pro-Israeli domestic pressures. He proposed the Alpha peace plan in 1955 in full awareness that domestic supporters of Israel would sharply criticize the scheme. He resisted the temptation to reap domestic political rewards by providing arms to Israel in 1956. During the Suez-Sinai War, he disproved the assumption of the colluding powers that on the eve of a presidential election, he would not dare oppose an Israeli attack on Egypt. Eisenhower quickly halted the aggression despite the potential domestic repercussions.

On several occasions, however, Eisenhower modified his policy for domestic political reasons. Pro-Israel public opinion factored in his decisions to decline membership in the Baghdad Pact, to refrain from imposing sanctions on Israel in early 1957, and to consult Israel about the Eisenhower Doctrine. In 1958, political considerations helped convince Eisenhower not to break fully with Israel, as the Pentagon advised. Domestic criticism of a canal improvements loan to Egypt pressured him to back Israel's water conduit project. In

1960, domestic political calculations forced the State Department to withhold an invitation to Nasser to visit the White House and to cancel his tour of the country.

The similarities between Truman and Eisenhower seem as striking as the differences. Truman became increasingly active in Arab-Israeli affairs, while Eisenhower retreated from an initial burst of activism to an acceptance of the status quo. Although Truman at first displayed reactive and inconsistent policy making, he eventually overcame this tendency, while Eisenhower appeared more proactive and consistent from the start. Truman submitted to domestic concerns openly but within limits, while his successor vowed to resist domestic political pressures but frequently submitted to them. There was as much continuity as change in U.S. policy regarding the Arab-Israeli conflict after Eisenhower replaced Truman as president.

U.S. Relations with Israel, the Arab States, and Britain

Truman's and Eisenhower's tacit acceptance of the Arab-Israeli conflict had profound consequences for U.S. relations with Israel and the Arab states and a significant impact on American relations with Britain. Because of differences over aspects of the Arab-Israeli situation, the United States and Israel experienced a demonstrable degree of tension in their official relationship. The conflict inflicted more substantial damage on U.S. relations with many Arab states and spawned a general reorientation of the Arab world away from its earlier affiliation with the West. U.S. relations with Britain experienced moments of trial, but in general the Atlantic allies cooperated in preserving their basic vital interests in the Middle East.

U.S.-Israeli relations appeared very warm during the Truman presidency. Israel developed close ties to the White House, Congress, and the U.S. public that frequently resulted in favorable policy decisions. Truman provided crucial assistance to the establishment of Israel and never considered withdrawing support for its national integrity and sovereignty. Israel fared well in the United States on issues such as diplomatic recognition, admission to the United Nations, and economic aid. U.S. backing contributed immeasurably to Israel's survival.

Israel experienced much less friendly relations with the State and Defense Departments, however. To protect vital interests in Arab states, these departments worked to block Israel's establishment by resisting partition and promoting trusteeship. Even after Israel was created with Truman's blessing, State and Defense tried to maintain a certain distance from the Jewish state, especially when it seemed to be neutralist and susceptible to communist influence, and they convinced Truman to delay de jure recognition until Israel met certain conditions. Although the U.S.-Israeli relationship appeared outwardly warm, substantial tension existed at the working level.

The fundamental dichotomy in the U.S.-Israeli relationship during the Truman presidency was evident in the positions of the two powers on various Arab-Israeli issues. On the one hand, the Truman administration firmly rejected the Arab charge that Israel lacked political or moral legitimacy. On the other hand, the United States refused to issue the arms and security assurances that Israel desired, attempted to establish the Middle East Command in Egypt despite fervent Israeli protests, and refused to enforce U.N. resolutions that affirmed Israel's position on the Suez Canal transit issue.

U.S. and Israeli perspectives on several Arab-Israeli issues remained at wide variance even as the two countries' policies converged toward a common position. For example, the State Department eventually acceded to the Israeli view that massive repatriation of Palestinian refugees could never occur but nonetheless remained angry at Israeli stubbornness on the issue. The United States suspended its strong opposition to Israel's occupation of West Jerusalem but continued to criticize Israel's defiance of the United Nations and refused to recognize Jerusalem as Israel's capital. U.S. officials did not confirm Israel's positions on such issues but simply acceded to a status quo that favored Israel because American leaders lacked the will or ability to change the situation in the face of Israeli opposition. Given the relative lack of alignment on policy issues, anger and resentment remained in the relationship.

U.S.-Israeli relations were complicated by certain situations facing each government. U.S. officials confronted a "firmness dilemma" in which they calculated that treating the new state of Israel with firmness would force it to heed their demands; in reality, however, such firmness provoked defiance. For example, in late 1948 the State Department demanded that Israel accept the territorial provisions of the Bernadotte Plan on the assumption that the United Nations retained some influence in Israel, as purportedly had been the case under the mandate. U.S. officials soon learned, however, that Israel vigorously defended its control of territories that it deemed vital and in fact Israel resented the presumption that it must bend to U.N. dictates. In addition, the U.S. refusal to recognize Israeli sovereignty over Jewish Jerusalem struck Israeli officials and citizens as undue foreign meddling in their state's internal affairs. Only gradually would U.S. officials escape the firmness dilemma by treating Israel as a sovereign state rather than some semistate under U.N. auspices.

For their part, Israeli leaders faced an "influence dilemma" in the United States. Well aware of the anti-Zionism in the State and Defense Departments, the Israeli government routinely appealed to Truman through a circle of advisers and sympathetic private citizens with access to the Oval Office. Such advocates proved instrumental in convincing Truman to support partition, oppose trusteeship, recognize Israel, and block the State Department from compelling Israel to concede territory. During a quarrel with the State Department and Pentagon over economic and military aid, Israel mobilized sympathetic members of Congress to ensure its interests. Israeli officials formulated subtle *hasbara* initiatives to shape U.S. public opinion as another check on the State Department's power.

Israel exerted profound and significant influence on U.S. policy, but not without cost or risk. As Israeli officials realized, their back-channel contacts with the White House, as effective and necessary as they seemed, deeply angered the State and Defense Departments and thereby aggravated the original predicament facing Israel. To make matters worse for Israel, after his reelection Truman showed less favoritism, expressed regret at the politicking by Israel's U.S. supporters, and gave the State Department more latitude to make policy. The department registered its displeasure with Israeli *hasbara* operations that encouraged the public to contest U.S. government policy. Especially after 1949, these developments exacerbated Israel's agony over the influence dilemma.

Further tension developed during the Eisenhower years, when U.S. and Israeli officials took fundamentally different views on the correct Israeli disposition toward the Arab states. On behalf of the goal of regional stability, U.S. officials advised Israel to live quietly alongside the Arab states and concede on territorial and other issues to achieve a permanent peace. But Israeli leaders complained that U.S. prescriptions would only encourage Arab bellicosity and thus threaten the Jewish state's existence. Israel confronted its Arab adversaries, used military power to weaken them, and demanded U.S. arms and security guarantees. But U.S. officials refused to meet Israeli demands, criticized Israel's belligerence, and resented Israeli *hasbara* operations against U.S. impartiality.

This basic conflict remained unresolved through the end of the Eisenhower period and was clear in divergent policies toward security-related issues. Israel resisted U.S. security plans that augmented Arab states' military power. It criticized the Baghdad Pact because it channeled arms to Iraq and resisted U.S. plans to provide arms to other Arab states. Israeli leaders questioned whether the Eisenhower Doctrine would protect the Jewish state from Arab assault and worried that U.S. backing of Arab states would increase the dangers the country faced.

U.S.-Israeli official relations declined sharply during the 1956 Suez-Sinai War. Eisenhower was extremely displeased with Israel for attacking Egypt, a move that deceived and defied the United States, aggrieved Arab nationalism, spoiled a U.S. covert operation in Syria, raised the specter of Soviet military attack in the Middle East and Europe, and opened the door to Soviet influence in Arab states. Israel complained bitterly when Eisenhower forced the cessation of the attack and the relinquishment of territorial gains. Eisenhower threatened to impose sanctions on Israel to force it to withdraw and resented its success in mobilizing public and congressional supporters to block this move.

The U.S.-Israeli official relationship remained cold in 1957–58. During conversations on the Eisenhower Doctrine, Israel revealed reluctance to declare publicly that it would fight with the West against Soviet aggression, fearing to imperil three million Soviet-bloc Jews. At the same time, the United States expressed reluctance to enroll Israel in any anti-Soviet security scheme, fearing to alienate Arab powers. In 1958, as rebels toppled the Iraqi regime and threatened the Lebanese and Jordanian governments, U.S. officials seriously reconsidered the traditional U.S. policy toward Israel. Eisenhower removed Israel from a list of interests that the United States would fight to defend, and the Pentagon advised that the United States break all ties with Israel to preserve the waning American influence among Arab powers. Although he ultimately decided not to pull the plug on U.S.-Israeli relations, the president did not express deep admiration for Israel or its friendship.

Several other Arab-related issues also strained U.S.-Israeli relations. Eisenhower remained silent on Israeli transit rights on the Suez Canal, criticized Israel for sending ships into the canal, protested its stubbornness regarding Palestinian refugees, and contested its right to deploy naval vessels on the Gulf of Aqaba. During an Israeli-Syrian border dispute, the United States earned Israeli reproach for not siding with Israel even when the United Nations Truce Supervisory Organization ruled in Israel's favor. U.S. support of Israel's water conduit scheme came slowly and reluctantly. Israeli officials resented the U.S.–United Arab Republic (UAR) rapprochement and attacked it through diplomacy and *hasbara* that cast Nasser in unfavorable terms.

U.S. amity with Arab states, which had been built over decades of cultural and commercial involvement, collapsed quickly after World War II because of deep disagreements about Palestine. In making a series of decisions that boosted Zionism, Truman wiggled away from Franklin D. Roosevelt's pledge to consult Arab leaders before supporting political changes in Palestine. Enraged Arab leaders magnified evidence of U.S. pressure on other states to support partition, rejected the trusteeship plan, fought militarily against Israel despite U.S. discouragement, and blamed the United States for allowing Israel to retain territory in violation of the Bernadotte Plan. The widespread conviction that U.S. support was crucial to the creation of Israel and the bitter military defeat suffered at Israeli hands in 1948–49 left Arab peoples deeply resentful of the United States.

U.S.-Arab differences regarding Israel were aggravated by other factors. Decolonization, emerging anti-Western nationalism, economic underdevelopment, and inter-Arab conflicts caused a general discord between the United States and the Arab world. In contrast to the situation involving Israel, U.S. public opinion lacked a friendly predisposition toward Arab states or peoples, perhaps as a result of popular ignorance about Arab peoples and indifference if not opposition to Islam. Dismissive and derogatory remarks by U.S. officials about Arab leaders revealed an anti-Arab bias at the elite level that shaped the context of U.S.-Arab relations.

Arab-U.S. tensions created by Israel deepened in 1949–53. Arab leaders expressed anger at what they considered Truman's pro-Israel policies—awarding Israel as much economic aid as all Arab states combined, supporting a U.N. resolution favorable to Israel on the canal transit issue, facilitating Jewish immigration to Israel, and endorsing German reparations to Israel. Arab governments also condemned the United States for refusing to force Israel to repatriate Palestinian refugees or relinquish West Jerusalem. In 1951–52, the State Department made no progress in an effort to build better relations with Arab states on the condition that Israel would continue to exist. By 1953, U.S. officials measured steep deterioration in their relations with the Arab states.

The Eisenhower administration attempted to restore good relations with Arab states by practicing impartiality in the Arab-Israeli situation. U.S. officials refrained from approving Israel's water-diversion scheme at Banat Yaacov, recognizing Jerusalem as Israel's capital, or advocating Israel's interests in disputes about the Suez Canal, the Gulf of Aqaba, and the Arab boycott. Eisenhower opposed the prospective and actual use of force against Egypt in the Suez-Sinai crisis and pressured Israel to withdraw from the Sinai and Gaza. In the late 1950s, the U.S. president nurtured a rapprochement with Nasser to deter him from looking to the Soviet Union.

U.S.-Arab relations remained tense, however, through the 1950s. In early 1956, after losing patience with Nasser as a result of the Soviet-Egyptian arms deal, the collapse of the Anderson mission, and the negotiations about the Aswân Dam, Eisenhower and Dulles adopted the Omega policy to reduce Nasser's prestige. They later actively contained Egyptian influence in Jordan and groomed King Saud as an alternative to Nasser as a pan-Arab leader. Arab statesmen assigned little credit to the United States for ending the Suez-Sinai War, noted that Eisenhower flinched at imposing sanctions on Israel, and criticized his reluctance to break with Israel over its policies on Palestinian refugees, the Gulf of Aqaba, and water development. Nasser remained assertive, expansionist, and neutralist, and, despite the rapprochement of 1959–60, U.S.-UAR relations remained strained when the Eisenhower presidency ended.

In 1945–61, U.S. officials witnessed a disturbing division in the Arab world. At the end of World War II, the Arab states appeared to be tied loosely to the West through commercial and security arrangements with Britain and cultural and business ties to the United States. But Western observers viewed with alarm the overthrow of pro-Western regimes in Syria in 1949, Egypt in 1952, and Iraq in 1958, the near collapse of Lebanon in 1958, and the repeated challenges to the Jordanian throne. This transformation of the Arab world concerned the United States because the revolutionary movements and governments tended to espouse anti-Western nationalism and neutralism in the Cold War.

The Eisenhower administration became acutely concerned by the radicalization of Arab states, bolstering conservative governments against apparent radical intrigues by issuing arms supply and political support; avoiding formal membership in the Baghdad Pact to avoid angering radicals; and engaging in covert operations to unseat a radical regime in Damascus. The Eisenhower Doctrine offered protection to the conservative rulers of Saudi Arabia, Lebanon, Iraq, and Jordan and, as implemented, seemed more a weapon against Arab radicalism than communism. The U.S.-UAR rapprochement of the late 1950s originated in a realization that Egyptian influence might slow the rise of communism in Syria and Iraq. During the late 1950s, U.S. officials avoided Arab-Israeli peacemaking because it promised to encourage Arab radicalism.

While U.S. officials realized that the Arab-U.S. estrangement stemmed from many causes, these leaders sensed that the presence of Israel aggravated the fissure. Arab nationalism, galvanized by Israel's presence, targeted the United States because it had supported Israel. Moreover, although U.S. officials differentiated between nationalism and communism and recognized that anticommunism permeated Arab culture, they feared that anti-Israelism exceeded anticommunism in Arab states and that Arab governments might accept Soviet assistance in attacking Israel. The United States also feared that the Soviet Union would promote anti-Israeli and anti-Western extremist leaders in Arab states as a means of eradicating Western influence and projecting Soviet influence in the Arab community. The existence of Israel remained a source of contention in U.S. relations with Arab states, especially those that seemed most likely to open the door of the Middle East to the Soviet Union.

U.S. policy toward the Arab-Israeli conflict also influenced Anglo-U.S. relations after World War II. To defeat the Axis during the war, the United States and Britain had forged a global alliance that proved strong enough to survive minor quarrels, such as a commercial rivalry in the Middle East. Indeed, to avoid unnecessary risks to the alliance, U.S. officials deferred to Britain on major wartime policy decisions about Palestine. Pentagon strategists who collaborated with British officers to engineer the victory of 1945 emerged after the war as ardent advocates of continued partnership.

During the early Truman presidency, however, differences regarding Palestine tested the Anglo-U.S. partnership. Truman faulted Britain for producing the Palestine imbroglio, for refusing to enforce partition, and for arming Arab powers in violation of the U.N. embargo. British leaders were dismayed that Truman's pronouncements on Palestine complicated efforts to build a security

sphere in the Arab world. U.S. recognition of Israel so angered Britain that the
Atlantic alliance seemed imperiled. As the Palestine War raged in late 1948, Tru-
man blocked British efforts to revive the Bernadotte Plan, weakened the anti-
Israeli terms of a British draft U.N. resolution on the Negev, and urged Britain
to deescalate its military showdown with Israel along the Egyptian-Jordanian-
Israeli border.

Both the United States and Britain deemed it essential to maintain an alliance
for global security purposes, however, and after 1949 the two countries healed
their breach over Palestine. Britain deferred to U.S. leadership at the Lausanne
conference and supported U.S. initiatives at the United Nations. The Truman
administration reciprocated by endorsing Britain's efforts to reopen the Haifa
refinery and to abolish Suez Canal restrictions. In 1950–51, the two powers co-
operated in issuing the Tripartite Declaration and promoting the Middle East
Command.

The Suez-Sinai crisis notwithstanding, the tone of Anglo-U.S. cooperation in
the Middle East improved during the Eisenhower presidency. In 1954–55, U.S.
and British officials jointly conceived the Alpha peace plan and promoted the
Baghdad Pact. The Suez-Sinai imbroglio revealed fundamental disagreement
between the two powers over the means to recover control of the canal and the
wisdom of deposing Nasser, and the conflict included British deception of the
United States and resort to war despite U.S. objections. But the alliance survived
at the global level, and cooperation in the Middle East quickly resumed. The
two powers coordinated their policies on issues such as the Baghdad Pact, the
Suez Canal, and the revolution in Iraq; in 1958, the United States and Britain coordinated military operations in Lebanon and Jordan. The Suez-Sinai episode
marked the twilight of Britain's pretense to power in the Middle East and the
dawn of U.S. hegemony in the region, but the events of 1958 indicated that Britain remained an important U.S. ally.

Conclusion

Between 1945 and 1961, Truman and Eisenhower set the foundation of U.S.
policy toward the Arab-Israeli conflict in subsequent decades. The two presidents gradually assumed the responsibility of protecting Western interests in
the Middle East, and subsequent American leaders did not relinquish those responsibilities during the remainder of the Cold War. Later presidents also did
not relent in the quest to achieve stability within the Middle East by preserving
governments friendly to the West and favoring, at least in principle, resolution
of the Arab-Israeli conflict. Security and stability remained the watchwords of
U.S. policy in the Middle East for the duration of the Cold War.

Truman and Eisenhower amassed a mixed record in achieving regional security and stability. To an extent, they achieved their containment objectives in the Middle East. No government became communist or openly pro-Soviet, and several pro-Western regimes remained U.S. strategic partners. Yet the Soviet Union made inroads into the region by forming political and arms supply relationships with Cairo and Damascus, and the prospect loomed that the Soviets might exploit anti-Israel passions to turn the entire Arab world against the West. For decades, the region would remain vulnerable to a destabilizing U.S.-Soviet rivalry.

Truman's and Eisenhower's quest to manage rather than resolve the Arab-Israeli conflict entailed certain risks and ultimately faltered. In the short term, their efforts led to a deepening U.S. intervention in the Middle East, including the commitment of military forces and the prospect of hostilities against Soviet or Soviet-backed forces. Nonetheless, by the late 1950s, the strategy proved untenable as certain Arab powers drifted into anti-Western dispositions that left these countries vulnerable to Soviet influence. U.S. leaders found themselves caught in the Middle East, unable to relinquish the responsibilities that they had accepted even as those responsibilities became increasingly difficult to fulfill. And they were caught in the middle of the Arab-Israeli conflict, unable to resolve a dispute that would generate instability for years to come.

NOTES

Abbreviations Used in Notes

Acheson Papers	Dean G. Acheson Papers, Truman Library
Allen Dulles Papers	Allen W. Dulles Papers, Princeton University
Ayers Papers	Eben A. Ayers Papers, Truman Library
Ben-Gurion Papers	David Ben-Gurion Papers, David Ben-Gurion Library
CAB 128, 129	Records of the Cabinet Office, Public Record Office
CAB 134	Records of Cabinet Committees, General Series, Public Record Office
CINCNELM	Commander in Chief, U.S. Naval Forces, Eastern Atlantic and Mediterranean
CINCSPECOMME	Commander in Chief, U.S. Specified Command, Middle East
CJCS	Chairman, Joint Chiefs of Staff
Clapp Papers	Gordon R. Clapp Papers, Truman Library
Clifford Papers	Clark M. Clifford Papers, Truman Library
CNO	Chief of Naval Operations
Cohen Papers	Benjamin V. Cohen Papers, Library of Congress
Connelly Papers	Matthew J. Connelly Papers, Truman Library
COS	Chief of Staff
Dennison Papers	Robert L. Dennison Papers, Truman Library
DFPI	Israel State Archive, *Documents on the Foreign Policy of Israel* (Jerusalem: Government Printer, 1981–97)
Dulles Papers	John Foster Dulles Papers, Eisenhower Library
Dulles-Princeton Papers	John Foster Dulles Papers, Princeton University
Elsey Papers	George M. Elsey Papers, Truman Library
FO 371	Political Correspondence of the Foreign Office, Public Record Office
FO 800	Records of the Foreign Secretary's Office, Public Record Office
FRUS	U.S. Department of State, *Papers Relating to the Foreign Relations of the United States* (Washington, D.C.: U.S. Government Printing Office, 1969–92)
Goldmann Papers	Nachum Goldmann Papers, Central Zionist Archives
Harriman Papers	Averell Harriman Papers, Library of Congress
Herter Papers	Christian A. Herter Papers, Eisenhower Library

Howard Papers	Harry N. Howard Papers, Truman Library
Jackson Papers	C. D. Jackson Papers, Eisenhower Library
Jewish Agency Papers	Jewish Agency Papers, Central Zionist Archives
Johnson Papers	Lyndon B. Johnson Papers, Johnson Library
JSPC	Joint Strategic Plans Committee
Lloyd Papers	David Lloyd Papers, Truman Library
Locke Papers	Edwin A. Locke Papers, Truman Library
McGhee Papers	George C. McGhee Papers, Truman Library
Morgenthau Diary	Henry Morgenthau Jr. Diary, Roosevelt Library
Naval Aide Files	Naval Aide to the President Office Files, Truman Library
NIE	National Intelligence Estimate
Niles Papers	David K. Niles Papers, Truman Library
NSC Records	National Security Council Records, Truman Library
OCB	Operations Coordinating Board
OF	Franklin D. Roosevelt Papers (Official File), Roosevelt Library
ORIS	Officially Released Information System, Central Intelligence Agency
OSANSA	Office of the Special Assistant for National Security Affairs
PPF	Franklin D. Roosevelt Papers (President's Personal File), Roosevelt Library
PPS	Policy Planning Staff
PREM 8, 11	Records of the Prime Minister's Office, Public Record Office
Protocols-PGI	Protocols of the Provisional Government of Israel, Israel State Archive
PSB Records	Psychological Strategy Board Records, Truman Library
PSF	Harry S. Truman Papers (President's Secretary's File), Truman Library
PSF-FDR	Franklin D. Roosevelt Papers (President's Secretary's File), Roosevelt Library
Randall Journals	Clarence Randall Journals, Eisenhower Library
RG 43 (US)	Records of the Anglo-American Committee of Inquiry, National Archives
RG 59	General Records of the Department of State, National Archives
RG 93.08	Records of the Israeli Embassy in Washington, Israel State Archive
RG 130.02	Records of the Foreign Minister and Director-General of the Foreign Ministry, Israel State Archive
RG 130.20	Records of the U.S. Division, Foreign Ministry, Israel State Archive
RG 130.23	Records of the Foreign Ministry, Central Registry, Political Files, Israel State Archive
RG 218	Records of the Joint Chiefs of Staff, National Archives
RG 263	Records of the Central Intelligence Agency, National Archives

RG 273	Records of the National Security Council, National Archives
RG 319	Records of the Army Staff, Plans and Operations Division, National Archives
RG 330	Records of the Office of the Secretary of Defense, National Archives
Rosenman Papers	Samuel Rosenman Papers, Roosevelt Library
Silver Papers	Abba Hillel Silver Papers, The Temple, Cleveland, Ohio
SNIE	Special National Intelligence Estimate
Snyder Papers	John W. Snyder Papers, Truman Library
USD	United States Division, Israeli Foreign Ministry
Weizmann Papers	Chaim Weizmann Papers, Truman Library
WHCF-DDE	Dwight D. Eisenhower Papers (White House Central File), Eisenhower Library
WHCF-HST	Harry S. Truman Papers (White House Central File), Truman Library
Whitman File	Dwight D. Eisenhower Papers (Ann Whitman File), Eisenhower Library
WHO Files	White House Office Files, Eisenhower Library

Introduction

1. Some proponents of the special-relationship thesis (such as Reich, *Quest*; Raviv and Melman, *Friends*; and Safran, *Israel*) implicitly applaud such a relationship, while others (such as Hussein, *United States and Israel*; Ball and Ball, *Passionate Attachment*; and Rubenberg, *Israel*) criticize close U.S.-Israeli relations. Scholars who dispute aspects of the special-relationship thesis include Bar-Siman-Tov, *Israel*; Ben-Zvi, *United States and Israel*; Levey, *Israel*; Klieman, *Israel*; Quandt, *Peace Process*.

2. See, for example, Sachar, *History*; Halpern, *Idea*. For a critical survey of the literature in English and Hebrew, see Morris, *1948*, 1–34.

3. See Flapan, *Birth*; Morris, *1948*; Morris, *Birth*; Morris, *Israel's Border Wars*; Pappé, *Britain*; Shlaim, *Collusion*; Silberstein, *New Perspectives*; Sheffer, *Moshe Sharett*.

4. See Karsh, *Fabricating*; Shlaim, *Iron Wall*, 598; Teveth, "Charging"; Teveth, "Palestine Arab Refugee Problem"; Shlaim, "Debate"; Walzer, "History."

5. Recent scholarship that treats U.S.-Egyptian relations in great detail includes Alterman, *Egypt*; Ashton, *Eisenhower*; Holland, *America*; Hahn, *United States*; Wahab Sayed-Ahmed, *Nasser*. Studies of U.S.-Syrian relations include Lesch, *Syria*; Saunders, *United States*. Gendzier, *Notes*, examines U.S. policy in Lebanon; Citino, *Arab Nationalism*, probes U.S. policy in Saudi Arabia; and Little, *American Orientalism* and B. I. Kaufman, *Arab Middle East*, survey U.S. diplomacy across the region. On balance, however, scholars have paid relatively little attention to Israel's influence on U.S.-Arab diplomatic relations.

6. Maddy-Weitzman, *Crystallization*, 176–77; Kerr, *Arab Cold War*, 17. See also Podeh, *Quest*; Doran, *Pan-Arabism*.

7. Historians who stress the close friendship in U.S.-British relations include Dobson, *Anglo-American Relations*; Bartlett, *"Special Relationship"*; Louis and Bull, *"Special Relationship"*. Revisionists who stress rivalries and disagreements include Freiberger, *Dawn*; Thorne, *Allies*. Postrevisionist historians who acknowledge disagreements on certain is-

sues but emphasize the depth of alliance include Petersen, *Middle East*; Persson, *Great Britain*.

8. For a discussion of the value of conducting multinational research in diplomatic history, see Hahn, "View."

9. Tessler, *History*, xii.

Chapter 1

1. Shapira, *Land*, ix–x.

2. Editorial note, *FRUS, 1949*, 6:1080.

3. Segre, *Crisis*, vi. See also Penkower, *Emergence*; Gellner, *Nations*; A. D. Smith, *Ethnic Origins*; Tessler, *History*, 7–68.

4. Shapira, *Land*; Sternhell, *Founding Myths*; Silberstein, *Postzionism Debates*; Evron, *Jewish State*; Sofer, *Zionism*.

5. Ben-Yehuda, *Masada Myth*; Zerubavel, *Recovered Roots*.

6. Bar-Zohar, *Ben-Gurion*; Reinharz, *Chaim Weizmann*.

7. B. Anderson, *Imagined Communities*, 6. See also Hourani, *History*; Hourani, *Arabic Thought*; R. Khalidi, *Palestinian Identity*; Mattar, *Mufti*; Kimmerling and Migdal, *Palestinians*. Most scholars now reject Joan Peters's "empty land" thesis that Palestine was generally uninhabited before Jews immigrated there. See Peters, *From Time Immemorial*; McCarthy, *Population*.

8. C. D. Smith, *Palestine*, 29–36; Shlaim, *Iron Wall*, 1–5; Michael J. Cohen, *Palestine and the Arab-Israeli Conflict*, 3.

9. Balfour quoted in Reinharz, *Chaim Weizmann*, 204. See also C. D. Smith, *Palestine*, 42–65. For a competing view that the Balfour Declaration did not contradict the terms of the Sykes-Picot accord or the Husayn-McMahon correspondence, see Friedman, *Palestine*.

10. Stokesbury, *Short History*, 254–56; C. D. Smith, *Palestine*, 59–65.

11. Eppel, "Decline," 185–93; Pappé, "British Rule," 198–206; Hahn, *United States*, 2.

12. Caplan, *Palestine Jewry*; Kolinsky, *Law*; Michael J. Cohen, *Palestine to Israel*, 1–38.

13. Tessler, *History*, 238–41; Michael J. Cohen, *Palestine, Retreat from the Mandate*, 10–31.

14. Michael J. Cohen, *Palestine, Retreat from the Mandate*, 32–49, 66–87; unsigned memorandum, n.d., OF 700 (Palestine).

15. Ben-Gurion quoted in Gal, *David Ben-Gurion*, 68.

16. Zweig, *Britain and Palestine*, 148–76; Michael J. Cohen, *Churchill*, 185–260.

17. Howard to Henderson, 8 Nov. 1946, Howard Papers, box 2; Michael J. Cohen, *Palestine and the Great Powers*, 5–8, 184–91.

18. Michael J. Cohen, *Palestine and the Great Powers*, 184–97.

19. Roosevelt to Wise, 17 May 1939, OF 700. See also Roosevelt to Green, 2 May 1939, OF 700 (Palestine); Roosevelt to Lehman, 10 Oct. 1938, PPF, box 600; Neumann to Morgenthau, 3 Sept. 1941, Morgenthau Diary, vol. 437; Bryson, *Seeds*; F. W. Brecher, *Reluctant Ally*.

20. Berkowitz, *Western Jewry*; Berman, *Nazism*; Medoff, *Militant Zionism*.

21. Shpiro, *From Philanthropy to Activism*; Raphael, *Abba Hillel Silver*; Kolsky, *Jews*; Tivnan, *The Lobby*, 16–24.

22. Memorandums to the file, 21, 25, 27 Oct. 1938, PPF, box 601; memorandum to the file, 27 June 1942, OF 283 (Egypt); Ariel, *On Behalf*; Vogel, *To See*; Bain, *March*.

23. Patterson to Hull, 27 July 1943, Rosenman Papers, box 13. See also draft statement, n.d. [July 1943], Rosenman Papers, box 13; memorandums to the file, 5, 19 July 1943, OF 700 (Palestine).

24. OSS Research and Analysis Paper #2263, 20 July 1944, RG 43 (US), box 2. See also memorandum by Hoskins, 31 Aug. 1943, PSF-FDR, Diplomatic File, box 50; Donovan to Roosevelt with attachment, 5 July 1944, Donovan to Roosevelt, 19 Oct. 1944, PSF-FDR, OSS File, boxes 149–50.

25. Aide-mémoire by Ibn Saud, 20 Aug. 1943, PSF-FDR, Safe File, boxes 46, 50. See also Faisal to Roosevelt, [29 Nov. 1938], PSF-FDR, Safe File, box 46; Roosevelt to Ibn Saud, 9 Jan. 1939, OF 3500 (Saudi Arabia); memorandum to the file, 7 June 1943, OF 700 (Palestine); Roosevelt to Hull, 15 Aug. 1943, PSF-FDR, Diplomatic File, box 50; memorandum to Stettinius, 6 Mar. 1944, OF 3560 (Saudi Arabia); memorandum by Jones, 15 May 1946, RG 59, lot 57 D 298, box 10.

26. Memorandum of conversation by Weizmann, 12 June 1943, memorandum of conversation, 17 Aug. 1944, Morgenthau Diary, vols. 649, 763. See also diary entry, 14 May 1941, memorandums of conversations by Morgenthau, 7 July, 1 Dec. 1942, Weizmann to Morgenthau, 9 Dec. 1942, Morgenthau Diary, vols. 397, 547, 592, 595; Wise to Rosenman, 24 Aug. 1943, Rosenman Papers; Hull to Roosevelt, 30 July 1943, Weizmann to Rosenman, 4 Jan. 1944, Rosenman Papers, box 13.

27. Memorandum to the file, 7 Mar. 1944, OF 713 (Iraq). See also Rosenman to Roosevelt, 7 Feb. 1944, Rosenman Papers, box 13; memorandums to the file, 4, 14, 22 Mar. 1944, OF 283 (Egypt); Hull to legation in Jidda, 13 Mar. 1944, PSF-FDR, Safe File, box 50.

28. Celler to McIntyre, n.d. [1944], OF 700 (Palestine); Rosenman to Roosevelt, 16 Sept. 1944, Rosenman Papers, box 13. See also Wise to Rosenman, 26 Sept. 1944, Rosenman Papers, box 4.

29. State Department quoted in Henderson to Byrnes, 30 Aug. 1945, RG 59, 711.67N; Roosevelt to Celler, 16 Jan. 1945, PSF-FDR, Safe File, box 46. See also Murray to Stettinius, 6 Jan. 1945, RG 59, lot 54 D 403, box 8; Grew to Roosevelt, 12 Jan. 1945, Wagner to Roosevelt, 15 Jan. 1945, PSF-FDR, Safe File, box 46; memorandum to the file, 24 Jan. 1945, OF 3500 (Saudi Arabia).

30. Pinkerton to Merriam, 6 Mar. 1945, RG 59, lot 54 D 403, box 9. See also Murray to Grew, 29 Jan. 1945, RG 59, lot 54 D 403, box 8.

31. Abdul Ilah to Roosevelt, 10 Mar. 1945, Grew to legation in Baghdad, 24 Mar. 1945, PSF-FDR, Safe File, boxes 40, 46. See also Murray to Dunn and Grew, 22 Jan., 23, 29 Mar. 1945, RG 59, lot 54 D 403, box 8; Grew to Roosevelt with attachment, 10 Mar. 1945, PSF-FDR, Safe File, box 50; memorandum to the file, 11 Mar. 1945, OF 2418 (Syria); memorandum by Howard, 7 Apr. 1945, Howard Papers, box 3.

32. Ganin, *Truman*, 1–19; Bain, *March*, 28–30.

Chapter 2

1. Golan, *Soviet Policies*, 1–10, 29–34; Kuniholm, *Origins*, 303–431.

2. U.S.-U.K. agreed minute, 17 Oct. 1947, FO 800/476. See also Defence Committee paper, DO(47)23, 7 Mar. 1947, CAB 131/4; CIA, ORE 52, 17 Oct. 1947, PSF, Intelli-

gence File, box 254; Hahn, *United States*, 23–28, 49–56, 58–62; Devereux, *Formulation*; Michael J. Cohen, *Fighting*, 1–94.

3. CIA, ORE 52, 17 Oct. 1947, PSF, Intelligence File, box 254. See also Yergin, *The Prize*.

4. State Department briefing book, 10 Jan. 1950, Lloyd Papers.

5. Ibid. See also Kaplan, *Arabists*.

6. Memorandum by Sanger, 14 Nov. 1949, RG 59, lot 484, box 1. See also Truman to Ibn Saud, 12 Sept. 1945, WHCF-HST (Confidential), box 37; Sanger to Henderson, 6 Nov. 1946, RG 59, lot 57 D 298, box 10; Childs to Marshall, 27 Dec. 1948, RG 330, CD 6-3-3.

7. Henderson to Byrnes, 29 Aug. 1945, RG 59, 711.90G; Pinkerton to Byrnes, 29 May 1946, RG 59, 711.90I.

8. Satterthwaite to Humelsine, 4 Feb. 1949, RG 59, lot 54 D 43, box 9. See also policy manual, 16 Apr. 1945, PSF, Subject File: Cabinet.

9. Henderson to Acheson, 28 Sept. 1945, RG 59, 711.90.

10. Policy manual, 16 Apr. 1945, PSF, Subject File: Cabinet; Villard to Dunn, 29 May 1945, RG 59, lot 54 D 403, box 8; Hamilton to DC/R, 23 June 1945, RG 59, 611.41; Painter, *Oil*, 59–74, 160–65.

11. Hickerson to Achilles, n.d. [ca. 3 Aug. 1945], RG 59, 711.90; U.S.-U.K. agreed minute, 17 Oct. 1947, FO 800/476. See also Hogan, *Marshall Plan*; Leffler, *Preponderance*; Silverfarb, *Twilight*.

12. Michael J. Cohen, *Palestine and the Great Powers*, 16–28; Louis, *British Empire*.

13. Memorandum by Chiefs of Staff, 25 May 1946, DO(46)67, CAB 131/2. See also memorandum by Bevin, 13 Mar. 1946, DO(46)40, CAB 131/2; Michael J. Cohen, *Palestine and the Great Powers*, 29–42.

14. State Department policy statement, "Palestine," 3 Apr. 1947, RG 59, 711.67N; Tessler, *History*, 253–55.

15. State Department policy statement, "Palestine," 3 Apr. 1947, RG 59, 711.67N; Nachmani, *Great Power Discord*, 6–18; Kochavi, *Post-Holocaust Politics*.

16. State Department policy statement, "Palestine," 3 Apr. 1947, RG 59, 711.67N; Nachmani, *Great Power Discord*, 18–21; Michael J. Cohen, *Palestine and the Great Powers*, 68–74.

17. Michael J. Cohen, *Palestine and the Great Powers*, 68–90.

18. Macatee to Merriam, 2 May 1947, RG 59, lot 54 D 403, box 10. See also State Department policy statement, "Palestine," 3 Apr. 1947, RG 59, 711.67N; Michael J. Cohen, *Palestine and the Great Powers*, 68–74, 90–95; Nachmani, *Great Power Discord*, 18–21.

19. Michael J. Cohen, *Palestine and the Great Powers*, 90–95; McIntyre, *British Decolonization*, 31–33.

20. McCullough, *Truman*; Ferrell, *Harry S. Truman*; Donovan, *Conflict*.

21. Truman quoted in Grose, *Israel*, 228–30. See also Hamby, *Man*, 269–70, 410.

22. Snetsinger, *Truman*; Wilson, *Decision*; Tschirgi, *Politics*; Evensen, *Truman*. For a summary of debates in earlier generations of scholarship, see Bain, *March*, ix–xiv.

23. Clifford, "Recognizing," 4, 11. See also Benson, *Harry S. Truman*; Grose, "President."

24. Michael J. Cohen, *Truman*, 279. See also Michael J. Cohen, *Palestine and the Great Powers*, 45–48; Ganin, *Truman*, 99–109, 187–89; McCullough, *Truman*, 596; Hamby, *Man*, 404–5; Offner, *Another Such Victory*, 274–306.

25. Niles to Truman, 29 July 1947, Niles Papers, box 30; McCullough, *Truman*, 599; Hamby, *Man*, 409; McDonald, *My Mission*.

26. Elsey quoted in Michael J. Cohen, *Palestine and the Great Powers*, 46; Henderson quoted in Podet, "Anti-Zionism," 181–84; Sharett to Niles, 18 Mar. 1951, Niles to Sharett, 3 Apr. 1951, RG 130.02, 2414/27. See also memorandum by Sack, 21 May 1946, Silver Papers, Manson File; Epstein to Silver, 3 Oct. 1946, Epstein to Niles, 3 Oct. 1946, Silver Papers, Jewish Agency File.

27. Memorandum of conversation by Sanger, 4 Nov. 1946, RG 59, lot 57 D 298, box 10. See also Hamby, *Man*, 409–10.

28. Said, *Orientalism*; Said, *Culture*; Terry, *Mistaken Identity*; Suleiman, *Arabs*; Christison, *Perceptions*; Sha'ban, *Islam*; Obenzinger, *American Palestine*; Jansen, *United States*; Said and Hitchens, *Blaming*; Suleiman, "Palestine"; Celler to Truman, 20 Mar. 1946, PSF, Subject File, box 184.

29. Epstein to Silver, 15 July 1947, Silver Papers, Correspondence 7-1 File. See also Bendersky, *"Jewish Threat"*, 349–77; Louis, *British Empire*, 478–81; Miscamble, *George F. Kennan*.

30. Memorandum of conversation by Henderson, 19 June 1947, RG 59, lot 54 D 444, box 11. See also Kuniholm, *Origins*, 237–40; Brands, *Inside*, 115–28, 165–92; Podet, "Anti-Zionism."

31. Minutes of meeting, 10 Dec. 1947, RG 218, CJCS Leahy, box 10, 056 Palestine. See also C. P. English to Lyon and Neal, 15 Nov. 1945, RG 59, lot 56 D 359, box 1; consulate in Jerusalem to Marshall, 26 Nov. 1947, RG 263, Murphy Collection, box 92.

32. Arab declarations quoted in W. Khalidi, "Arab Perspective," 110. See also Grew to Truman, 14 May 1945, WHCF-HST (Official), box 771; Grew to Truman, 25 May 1945, RG 59, lot 54 D 403, box 8.

33. Memorandum of conversation by Hoskins, 2 July 1945, RG 59, lot 54 D 403, box 10; Grant to Byrnes, 30 Sept. 1946, RG 59, 711.90F. See also Byrnes to Eddy, 19 Jan. 1946, RG 59, 711.90F.

34. Henderson to Byrnes, 29 Aug. 1945, RG 59, 711.90G. See also memorandum of conversation by Hoskins, 2 July 1945, RG 59, lot 54 D 403, box 10; Byrnes to Eddy, 19 Jan. 1946, RG 59, 711.90F; Pinkerton to Byrnes, 29 May 1946, RG 59, 711.90I.

35. Paper by Military Intelligence Service, n.d. [ca. 15 Apr. 1946], RG 43 (US), lot 8, box 13; McFarland to State War Navy Coordinating Committee, 21 June 1946, PSF, Subject File, box 184. See also Reid to Lyons, 19 Sept. 1945, RG 43 (US), lot 8, box 13.

36. Alling to secretary, 13 Apr. 1945, RG 59, lot 54 D 403, box 8; memorandum of conversation by Grew, 26 May 1945, RG 59, lot 54 D 403, box 8; Henderson to Acheson, 28 Sept. 1945, RG 59, 711.90. See also State Department policy manual, 1 Apr. 1945, Stettinius to Truman, 18 Apr. 1945, PSF, Subject File, boxes 159, 184.

37. Truman to Abdallah, 17 May 1945, WHCF-HST (Official), box 771; Truman quoted in Hamby, *Man*, 409; Truman quoted in Eban, *Autobiography*, 156.

38. Howard quoted in Michael J. Cohen, *Palestine and the Great Powers*, 52; Wilson, *Decision*, 154; Hamby, *Man*, 404.

Chapter 3

1. Rosenman to Truman, 17 Oct. 1945, Truman to Attlee, 31 Aug. 1945, PSF, Subject File, boxes 184, 182. See also Gallup, *Gallup Poll*, 554, 584; Gilboa, *American Public Opinion*, 15–17; Bain, *March*, 61–80; Zweig, "Restitution."

2. Attlee to Truman, 14, 16 Sept. 1945, PSF, Subject File, box 182. See also Henderson to Byrnes, 31 Aug. 1945, PSF, Subject File, box 184; Kochavi, "Anglo-American Discord"; R. Khalidi, "United States Policy"; Louis, "British Imperialism," 11.

3. Truman to Ball, 24 Nov. 1945, PSF, Subject File, box 184. See also Truman to Attlee, 17 Sept. 1945, PSF, Subject File, boxes 182, 184; Henderson to Acheson, 4 Oct. 1945, RG 59, lot 54 D 403; Henderson to Byrnes, 9 Oct. 1945, RG 59, lot 56 D 359, box 1; Porter to Byrnes, 21 Nov. 1945, RG 59, 711.90D; Abdallah to Truman, 29 Sept. 1945, Truman to Abdallah, 17 Nov. 1945, WHCF-HST (Official), box 771.

4. British aide-mémoire, 19 Oct. 1945, British memorandum of conversation, n.d. [ca. 19 Oct. 1945], PSF, Subject File, box 184; Henderson to Truman, 11 Dec. 1945, WHCF-HST (Official), box 775; Nachmani, *Great Power Discord*, 26–57.

5. State Department policy statement, "Palestine," 3 Apr. 1947, RG 59, 711.67N; AACOI final report, 20 Apr. 1946, PSF, Subject File, box 184; Nachmani, *Great Power Discord*, 60–200; Bain, *March*, 93–113.

6. State Department intelligence paper, 9 Apr. 1946, RG 43 (US), lot 8, box 13; memorandum by Evan Wilson, 15 May 1946, RG 59, lot 54 D 403, box 9; Kubba to Truman, 7 May 1946, Abdul Ilah to Truman, 9 May 1946, Abdallah to Truman, 11 May 1946, El-Khoury to Truman, 14 May 1946, Kuwalti to Truman, 16 May 1946, Ibn Saud to Truman, 24 May 1946, WHCF-HST (Official), box 775.

7. Truman to Ibn Saud, 8 July 1946, WHCF-HST (Official), box 775. See also Truman to Byrnes, 30 Apr. 1946, Truman to Abdallah, 22 May 1946, Truman to Abdul Ilah, 22 May 1946, Truman to El-Khoury, 22 May 1946, Byrnes to legation in Baghdad, 22 May 1946, WHCF-HST (Official), boxes 771, 775; Henderson to Acheson, 15 May 1946, RG 59, lot 54 D 403, box 9.

8. Attlee to Truman, 10, 13, 27 May 1946, Truman to Attlee, 16 May, 5 June 1946, PSF, Subject File, box 184; McDonald to Snyder, 22 July 1946, Snyder Papers, box 22; Wilson to Pinkerton, 26 Aug. 1946, RG 59, lot 54 D 403, box 9.

9. Epstein to Goldmann, 9 Oct. 1946, Weizmann Papers, box 1; Michael J. Cohen, *Palestine and the Great Powers*, 135–62, 171–83; Ganin, *Truman*, 99–109.

10. Clayton to Truman, 12 Sept. 1946, PSF, Subject File, box 84; Truman to Attlee with attachment, 3 Oct. 1946, *FRUS, 1946*, 7:701–3. See also Truman to Clayton, 14 Sept. 1946, PSF, Subject File, box 84; Crum to Hannegan, 1 Oct. 1946, Silver Papers, Correspondence 1-3 File.

11. Truman to George, 8 Oct. 1946, PSF, General File, box 138; Bain, *March*, 136. See also Michael J. Cohen, *Palestine and the Great Powers*, 162–70.

12. Kuniholm to Byrnes, 16 Oct. 1946, RG 59, 711.90E; Ibn Saud to Truman, 15 Oct. 1946, WHCF-HST (Official), box 771; memorandum of conversation by Sanger, 6 Nov. 1946, RG 59, lot 57 D 298, box 10. See also Attlee to Truman, 4 Oct. 1946, *FRUS, 1946*, 7: 704–5; Moose to Byrnes, [29 Nov. 1946], RG 59, 711.90G; Brownell to Truman, 4 Dec. 1946, WHCF-HST (Confidential), box 38; memorandum of conversation by Sanger, 4 Nov. 1946, RG 59, lot 57 D 298, box 10.

13. Acheson to Truman, 12, 13 Dec. 1946, PSF, Subject File, box 170; memorandum of conversation by Acheson, 28 Jan. 1947, RG 59, lot 54 D 403, box 9; State Department policy statement, "Palestine," 3 Apr. 1947, RG 59, 711.67N; Jones, *Failure*.

14. Ganin, *Truman*, 120–21. See also State Department policy statement, "Palestine," 3 Apr. 1947, RG 59, 711.67N; memorandum of conversation by Carter, 3 May 1947, Shertok

to Marshall, 3 May 1947, RG 59, lot 53 D 444, box 11; Marshall to Truman, 16 May 1947, WHCF-HST (Official), box 771; McIntyre, *British Decolonization*, 31–33.

15. Gallman to Marshall, 16 June 1947, RG 59, 501.BB PALESTINE; Cohen to Lovett, 30 July 1947, Cohen Papers, box 12. See also NEA position paper, 7 July 1947, RG 59, lot 56 D 359, box 2.

16. Henderson to Marshall, 7 July 1947, *FRUS, 1947*, 5:1120–23; Kennan, *Memoirs*, 1: 380–81; Condit, *History*, 86–96.

17. Truman to Niles, 12 May, 23 Aug. 1947, PSF, Subject File, box 184; Truman quoted in Tivnan, *The Lobby*, 24. See also memorandum of conversation by Henderson, 19 June 1947, Henderson to Marshall, 30 June 1947, RG 59, lot 53 D 444, box 11; Marshall to Truman, 10 July 1947, RG 59, lot 54 D 403, box 9; Abbell to Truman, 19 Aug. 1947, Truman to Jacobson, 18 Oct. 1947, PSF, Subject File, box 184.

18. Macatee to Merriam, 21 July 1947, RG 59, 501.BB PALESTINE. See also Macatee to Marshall, 20 June 1947, RG 59, 501.BB PALESTINE.

19. Patterson to Jenkins, 8 May 1947, RG 59, lot 55 D 5, box 6; memorandums of conversations by Marshall, 7, 17 July 1947, memorandum of conversation by Henderson, 17 June 1947, RG 59, lot 53 D 444, box 11; Bailey to Marshall, 22 Sept. 1947, RG 59, 711.90F.

20. Luard, *History*, 160–67; Michael J. Cohen, *Palestine and the Great Powers*, 260–68.

21. Douglas to Marshall, 3 Sept. 1947, Memminger to Marshall, 7 Sept. 1947, RG 59, 501.BB PALESTINE. See also unsigned memorandum, 6 Nov. 1947, Merriam to Henderson, 20 Nov. 1947, RG 59, lot 54 D 403, boxes 9–10; Wilkins to Henderson, 13 Nov. 1947, RG 59, 501.BB PALESTINE; CIA, ORE 55, 28 Nov. 1947, PSF, Intelligence, box 254.

22. State Department memorandum, 20 Sept. 1947, RG 59, lot 54 D 403, box 9. See also memorandum by Notter, 6 Oct. 1947, RG 59, lot 53 D 444, boxes 9, 11; Cleland to Eddy, 12 Sept. 1947, memorandum by Eddy, 13 Sept. 1947, Merriam to McClintock, 17 Oct. 1947, RG 59, lot 54 D 403, boxes 8–9; McClintock to Lovett, 20 Oct. 1947, RG 59, 501.BB PALESTINE.

23. Central Intelligence Group paper, 11 Sept. 1947, RG 59, 501.BB PALESTINE; JCS to secretary of defense, n.d. [ca. 10 Oct. 1947], RG 218, CJCS Leahy, box 10, 056 Palestine. See also Norstad to chief of staff, 1 July 1947, paper by Royall, 24 Nov. 1947, RG 319, P&O 091 Palestine; Leahy to JCS, 10 Oct. 1947, RG 218, CJCS Leahy, box 10, 056 Palestine; CIA, ORE 49, 20 Oct. 1947, CIA, ORE 52, 17 Oct. 1947, CIA, ORE 55, 28 Nov. 1947, PSF, Intelligence, box 254; Bendersky, *"Jewish Threat"*, 377–87.

24. Statement by Marshall, *FRUS, 1947*, 5:1151. See also Mattison to Wilkins, 7 Nov. 1947, RG 59, lot 54 D 403, box 9; Wilkins to Henderson, 13 Nov. 1947, circular cable by Lovett, 25 Nov. 1947, Marshall to Lovett, 28 Nov. 1947, RG 59, 501.BB PALESTINE; memorandum of conversation by Henderson, 25 Nov. 1947, RG 59, lot 53 D 444, box 11.

25. Gallup, *Gallup Poll*, 686–87; Gilboa, *American Public Opinion*, 18–25; Feldblum, *American Catholic Press*, 1–15, 55–70.

26. Wadsworth to Johnson, 18 Sept. 1947, PSF, Subject File, box 184. See also memorandum of conversation by Boardman, 22 Sept. 1947, Wilkins to Merriam, 1 Nov. 1947, RG 59, 501.BB PALESTINE; memorandum of conversation by Alling, 26 Sept. 1947, RG 59, lot 53 D 444, box 11.

27. Truman to Ibn Saud, 21 Nov. 1947, *FRUS, 1947*, 5:1277–78; Clifton Daniel, "Zionists in Holy Land Ready to Set Up State," *New York Times*, 19 Oct. 1947, sec. 4, p. 4. See also memorandum of conversation by Kopper, 29 Nov. 1947, RG 59, 501.BB PALESTINE.

28. PPS/19 with attachments, RG 59, lot 64 D 563, box 30; memorandum of conversation by Armour, 26 Nov. 1947, RG 59, lot 53 D 444, box 9; Senator Brewster et al. to embassy of Greece, 27 Nov. 1947, RG 59, lot 64 D 563, box 30; Merriam to Henderson, 28 Nov. 1947, RG 59, 501.BB PALESTINE; Truman to Lovett, 11 Dec. 1947, *FRUS, 1947*, 5: 1309.

29. Memorandum of conversation by Henderson, 1 Dec. 1947, Childs to Marshall, 7 Feb. 1948, RG 59, 501.BB PALESTINE. See also Memminger to Marshall, 10 Nov. 1947, RG 59, 711.90D; memorandum of conversation by Villard, 27 Jan. 1948, RG 59, lot 64 D 563, box 30.

30. Tuck to Marshall, 1 Dec. 1947, RG 59, 501.BB PALESTINE; Patterson to Jenkins, 6 Dec. 1947, RG 59, lot 55 D 5, box 6. See also Tuck to Marshall, 3 Oct. 1947, RG 59, lot 64 D 5663, box 30.

31. Memminger to Marshall, 29 Nov. 1947, RG 59, 501.BB PALESTINE; memorandum of conversation by Colquitt, 3 Dec. 1947, RG 59, lot 53 D 444, box 11; Childs to Marshall, 2 Dec. 1947, 10 Feb. 1948, RG 59, 501.BB PALESTINE. See also memorandum of conversation by Marshall, 9 Oct. 1947, RG 59, lot 53 D 444, box 11; memorandum of conversation by Sanger, 29 Oct., 18 Nov. 1947, RG 59, 711.90F; memorandum of conversation by von Lossberg, 22 Nov. 1947, RG 59, 711.90G.

32. Golan, *Soviet Policies*, 35–40; Behbehani, *Soviet Union*, 56–63.

33. Henderson to Lovett, 24 Nov. 1947, *FRUS, 1947*, 5:1281–82; Merriam to Jones, 29 Jan. 1948, RG 59, lot 54 D 403, box 10. See also memorandum by Eddy, 10 Dec. 1947, Naval Aide Files, Subject File, Arabian Relations folder; CIA, CIA 3, 17 Dec. 1947, PSF, Subject File, box 203; CIA, ORE 69, 9 Feb. 1948, PSF, Intelligence, box 256.

Chapter 4

1. This observation is consistent with various scholars' argument that states with limited power have effectively resisted great powers' efforts at dominance or influence. See Gerges, *Superpowers*; Sayigh and Shlaim, *Cold War*.

2. Michael J. Cohen, *Palestine and the Great Powers*, 301–44.

3. Memorandum by McCown and Mattison, 2 Jan. 1948, RG 59, lot 54 D 403, box 8. See also Merriam to Jones, 29 Jan. 1948, RG 59, lot 54 D 403, box 10; memorandum of conversation by Jones, 27 Jan. 1948, RG 59, lot 53 D 444, box 11; record of conversation, 28 Apr. 1948, PREM, 8/859.

4. Minutes of meeting, 10 Dec. 1947, RG 218, CJCS Leahy, box 10, 056 Palestine; Henderson to Lovett, 27 Jan. 1948, Lovett to Henderson, 27 Jan. 1948, RG 59, lot 54 D 403, boxes 8–9; Hoover to Forrestal, 25 Feb. 1948, RG 330, Office of the Secretary of Defense Records, CD 2-1-21; Ordway to director of intelligence, 20 Feb. 1948, RG 319, P&O 474; memorandum by Inglis, 19 Mar. 1948, RG 218, CJCS Leahy, box 10, 057 Palestine; memorandum of conversation by Clifford, 24 Apr. 1948, Clifford Papers, Miscellaneous Memos File; Gass to Kollek, 14 June 1948, RG 93.08, 365/1; memorandum by USD (Hebrew), 15 Apr. 1949, RG 130.20, 2467/7.

5. JCS to Forrestal, n.d. [ca. 10 Oct. 1947], RG 218, CJCS Leahy, box 10, 056 Palestine; Merriam to Henderson, 11 Dec. 1947, RG 59, lot 56 D 359, box 1; memorandum by McCown and Mattison, 2 Jan. 1948, RG 59, lot 54 D 403, box 8; PPS/19, 19 Jan. 1948, RG 59, lot 64 D 563, box 30; Henderson to Rusk, 6 Feb. 1948, Rusk to Lovett, 11 Feb. 1948,

FRUS, 1948, 5:600–603, 617–18; Wedemeyer to Bradley, 13 Feb. 1948, RG 319, Army COS Files, 091 Palestine.

6. Wadsworth to Henderson, 4 Feb. 1948, RG 59, 711.90G; Truman to Marshall, 22 Feb. 1948, *FRUS, 1948*, 5:645. See also PPS/21, 11 Feb. 1948, report by NSC staff, 17 Feb. 1948, Marshall to Lovett, 19 Feb. 1948, Marshall to Truman, [21 Feb. 1948], State Department paper, [23 Feb. 1948], statement by Austin, 24 Feb. 1948, *FRUS, 1948*, 5:619–25, 631–33, 637–40, 648–49, 651–54.

7. Clifford to Truman, 8 Mar. 1948, *FRUS, 1948*, 5:690–96. See also Goldmann to Rosenbluth, 6 Feb. 1948, Goldmann Papers, Z6/269; memorandum of conversation by Henderson, 12 Feb. 1948, RG 59, lot 53 D 444, box 11; minutes of meeting, 17 Feb. 1948, Jewish Agency Papers, Z5/306; memorandum of conversation by Mattison, 2 Mar. 1948, RG 59, lot 53 D 444, box 11; Marshall to Austin, 8 Mar. 1948, *FRUS, 1948*, 5:697.

8. McCullough, *Truman*, 607–12; Weizmann, *Trial*, 472–74. See also Hamby, *Man*, 410–13; Rose, *Chaim Weizmann*, 436–39; memorandum of conversation by Satterthwaite, 13 Feb. 1948, RG 59, lot 53 D 444, box 11.

9. Truman quoted in McCullough, *Truman*, 610–11; Hamby, *Man*, 413. See also Humelsine to Marshall, 22 Mar. 1948, Marshall to Bohlen, 22 Mar. 1948, *FRUS, 1948*, 5:749–50; Michael J. Cohen, *Palestine and the Great Powers*, 347–60.

10. Merriam to Kohler, 29 Mar. 1949, RG 59, lot 54 D 403, box 10. See also Bevin to Cadogan, 16 Apr. 1948, PREM 8/859; memorandum to the file by McClintock, 19 Apr. 1948, Marshall to Austin, 10 May 1948, RG 59, 501.BB PALESTINE.

11. Forrestal to Marshall, 19 Apr. 1948, RG 330, CD 6-2-47; Clarke to director of P&O with attachment, 23 Apr. 1948, RG 319, 091 Palestine. See also Ohly to secretary of defense, 25 Mar. 1948, Leahy to Truman, 4 Apr. 1948, memorandum by Inglis, 19 Apr. 1948, Lovett to Forrestal, 23 Apr. 1948, Forrestal to Lovett, 23 Apr. 1948, memorandum to the file by Ohly, 14 May 1948, RG 330, CD 6-2-47; Douglas to Marshall, 22 Apr. 1948, RG 59, 501.BB PALESTINE.

12. Ayers Diary, 23 Mar. 1948, Ayers Papers, box 26; Merriam to Kohler, 29 Mar. 1949, RG 59, lot 54 D 403, box 10. See also memorandum of conversation by Mattison, 30 Mar. 1948, RG 59, lot 53 D 444, box 11; Henderson to Lovett, 14 Apr. 1948, RG 59, lot 54 D 403, box 8; Hadow to Mason, 2 May 1948, FO 371/68649; Tivnan, *The Lobby*, 25–28.

13. Memorandum of conversation by Mattison, 29 Apr. 1948, RG 59, lot 53 D 444, box 11; memorandum of conversation by Shertok, 8 May 1948, Goldmann Papers, Z6/59; CIA, CIA 4-48, 8 Apr. 1948, PSF, Subject, box 203. See also Pinkerton to Marshall, 27 Feb. 1948, Memminger to Marshall, 18 Mar. 1948, Dorsz to Marshall, 22 Mar. 1948, Macatee to Marshall, 6 Mar. 1948, Tuck to Marshall, 22 Apr. 1948, RG 59, 501.BB PALESTINE.

14. Wasson to Marshall, 13 Apr., 10 May 1948, *FRUS, 1948*, 5:817, 956–57.

15. Rusk to Lovett, 12 Apr. 1948, Lovett to Douglas, 3 May 1948, Ross to Marshall, 4 May 1948, RG 59, 501.BB PALESTINE; memorandum of conversation by Marshall, 12 May 1948, *FRUS, 1948*, 5:972–76; Shertok to Marshall, 29 Apr. 1948, RG 130.02, 2414/26; memorandum of conversation by Shertok, 8 May 1948, Goldmann Papers, Z6/59; record of conversation, 28 Apr. 1948, PREM, 8/859; CIA, CIA 5-48, 12 May 1948, PSF, Subject, box 203.

16. "The State of Israel," *New York Times*, 15 May 1948, p. 14.

17. Heller, *Birth*.

18. Memorandum of conversation by Marshall, 12 May 1948, *FRUS, 1948*, 5:972–76; Clifford quoted in McCullough, *Truman*, 612–20. See also Clifford and Holbrooke, *Counsel*, 3–25; Donovan, *Conflict*, 379–86.

19. Epstein to Shertok, 14 May 1948, *DFPI,* 1:3–4; Epstein to Truman, 14 May 1948, Austin to Marshall, 19 May 1948, *FRUS, 1948,* 5:989, 1013–15; Marshall to Epstein, 14 May 1948, RG 130.02, 2391/42.

20. Anne O'Hare McCormick, "Recognizing the Realities in the New Palestine," *New York Times,* 15 May 1948, p. 14; Marshall to Lovett, 17 May 1948, *FRUS, 1948,* 5:1007–8; Wooldridge to CNO, 27 May 1948, RG 330, 6-3-5.

21. Henderson to Lovett, 7 June 1948, RG 59, lot 54 D 403, box 8; Marshall to Douglas, 3 July 1948, Marshall to Memminger, 10 July 1948, RG 59, 501.BB PALESTINE; Lovett to Forrestal, 8 July 1948, RG 330, CD 18-1-44.

22. Ben-Gurion to Truman, 16 May 1948, *DFPI,* 1:11; Elsey to Clifford, 16 June 1948, Elsey Papers, box 60. See also Shertok to Marshall, 19 May 1948, Epstein to Shertok, 29 May 1948, *DFPI,* 1:31–32, 94–96.

23. Memorandum by Inglis, 19 May 1948, RG 330, 6-2-47; Kennan to Marshall, 21 May 1948, RG 59, 711.67N; Bevin to Inverchapel, 22 May 1948, FO 371/68649.

24. Behbehani, *Soviet Union,* 69–86.

25. Benson, *Harry S. Truman,* 133–73; Michael J. Cohen, *Palestine and the Great Powers,* 387. See also Ganin, *Truman,* 187.

26. Wooldridge to Forrestal, n.d. [late May 1948], RG 330, 6-2-47; memorandum of conversation by McClintock, 2 June 1948, RG 59, lot 53 D 444, box 12. For details of direct Arab-Israeli talks, see Caplan, *Futile Diplomacy,* 2:149–64; Shlaim, *Collusion*; Gelber, "Jewish-Arab Talks."

27. Shertok to Weizmann, 20 July 1948, *DFPI,* 1:363–69. See also Pinkerton to Marshall, 25 May 1948, MacDonald to Marshall, 9 July 1948, Kuniholm to Marshall, 9 July 1948, Lippincott to Marshall, 13 July 1948, RG 59, 501.BB PALESTINE; Wooldridge to CNO, 27 May 1948, RG 330, CD 6-3-5; Bolling to secretary of defense, 9 July 1948, RG 330, CD 6-2-47.

28. Doran, *Pan-Arabism*; Maddy-Weitzman, *Crystallization*; Podeh, *Quest*; Hillenkoetter to Truman, 19 July 1948, PSF, Intelligence, CIA folder; CIA, CIA 6-48, 17 June 1948, CIA 7-48, 14 July 1948, PSF, Subject, boxes 203–4.

29. McClintock to Rusk, 1 July 1948, RG 59, 501.BB PALESTINE. See also Wooldridge to secretary of navy, 24 May 1948, RG 330, CD 6-2-47; Ireland to Henderson, 7 July 1948, RG 59, lot 54 D 403, box 8; Marshall to Patterson, 7 July 1948, *FRUS, 1948,* 5:1195; Stabler to Marshall, 14 July 1948, MacDonald to Marshall, 19, 22 July 1948, RG 59, 501.BB PALESTINE.

30. Schuyler to Wedemeyer, 19 May 1948, RG 319, P&O 091 Palestine; Leahy to Forrestal, 7 July 1948, memorandum by Ohly, 22 July 1948, Halaby to Ohly, 6 Aug. 1948, RG 330, CD 6-2-47; CINCNELM to Marshall, 25 July 1948, RG 59, 501.BB PALESTINE; Marshall to MacDonald, 3 Aug. 1948, Forrestal to National Security Council, 19 Aug. 1948, Forrestal to Truman, 7 Oct. 1948, *FRUS, 1948,* 5:1275–76, 1307, 1462–63.

31. McClintock to Clifford, 1 June 1948, RG 59, 501.BB PALESTINE; Ohly to secretary of defense, 7 July 1948, Halaby to Ohly, 6 Aug. 1948, RG 330, CD 6-2-47; Marshall to Forrestal, 28 July 1948, RG 319, P&O 091 Palestine; Marshall to Bernadotte, 19 July 1948, *FRUS, 1948,* 5:1230.

32. Marshall to Pinkerton, 26 May 1948, *FRUS, 1948,* 5:1057; Patterson to Marshall, 8, 13 July 1948, RG 59, 501.BB PALESTINE; Shertok to Weizmann, 20 July 1948, *DFPI,* 1: 363–69.

33. Shertok to Epstein, 22 May, 13 July 1948, *DFPI,* 1:59, 328. See also Weizmann to Truman, 25 May 1948, *FRUS, 1948,* 5:1042–43; Eban to Weizmann, 10 July 1948, *DFPI,* 1: 312–17; Ilan, *Origin.*

34. NE paper, 27 May 1948, *FRUS, 1948,* 5:1060–61; paper by Merriam, 28 May 1948, RG 59, lot 54 D 403, box 8. See also memorandums for the president, 14, 26 May 1948, Marshall to embassy in Bern, 4 June 1948, Marshall to embassy in Panama City, 10 June 1948, RG 59, 501.BB PALESTINE; memorandum of conversation by Henderson, 17 May 1948, RG 59, lot 53 D 444, box 11; paper by Satterthwaite, 14 July 1948, *FRUS, 1948,* 5:1217–18; CIA, ORE 48-48, 5 Aug. 1948, PSF, Subject, box 255.

35. Sanderson to Marshall, 27 Aug. 1948, RG 59, 501.BB PALESTINE. See also Marshall to Truman, 16 Aug. 1948, PSF, Subject, box 184; Sullivan to Forrestal, 4 Nov. 1948, RG 330, CD 6-2-47.

36. Memorandum of conversation by Shertok, 10 Aug. 1948, RG 130.02, 2443/2.

37. Marshall to Douglas, 1 July 1948, draft telegram, 3 Sept. 1948, RG 59, 501.BB PALESTINE.

38. Shertok to Eban, 1 July, 15 June 1948, *DFPI,* 1:246, 158. See also memorandum of conversation by McClintock, 9 Aug. 1948, RG 59, lot 54 D 403, box 8; Marshall to Truman, 16 Aug. 1948, Marshall to McDonald, 1 Sept. 1948, *FRUS, 1948,* 5:1313–15, 1366–69; McDonald to Clifford, 24 Aug. 1948, Clifford Papers, box 13; CIA, addendum to ORE 38-48, 31 Aug. 1948, PSF, Intelligence, box 249; Caplan, *Futile Diplomacy,* 3:18–30.

39. MacDonald to Marshall, 16, 17 Sept. 1948, unsigned memorandum to Truman, 25 Sept. 1948, RG 59, 501.BB PALESTINE.

40. Sharett to Lie, 17 Sept. 1948, *DFPI,* 1:605. See also Shertok to McDonald, 18 Sept. 1948, Bunche to Shertok, 17 Sept. 1948, Shertok to Bunche, 19 Sept. 1948, Kohn to Shertok, 20 Sept. 1948, RG 130.02, 2427/10; Stanger, "Haunting Legacy."

41. Bunche to Shertok, 17 Sept. 1948, RG 130.02, 2427/10; "U.N.'s First Martyr," *New York Times,* 18 Sept. 1948, p. 16; Keeley to Marshall, 19 Sept. 1948, RG 59, 501.BB PALESTINE. See also Macdonald to Joseph, 1 Oct. 1948, RG 130.02, 2443/2; Cox to chief of naval personnel, 29 Oct. 1949, RG 59, lot 54 D 403, box 11.

42. Lovett to Truman, 18 Sept. 1948, Dennison Papers, box 3. See also circular cable by Lovett, 19 Sept. 1948, RG 59, 501.BB PALESTINE; Ilan, *Bernadotte.*

43. Keeley to Marshall, 26 Sept., 5 Oct. 1948, RG 59, 501.BB PALESTINE. See also Stabler to Marshall, 21 Sept., 3 Oct. 1948, Dorsz to Marshall, 21 Sept. 1948, Kuniholm to Marshall, 23, 26 Sept. 1948, Griffis to Marshall, 24 Sept. 1948, RG 59, 501.BB PALESTINE.

44. Memorandum of discussion, 27 Sept. 1948, *DFPI,* 1:640–44; Marshall to Satterthwaite, 10 Oct. 1948, RG 59, 501.BB PALESTINE; Shertok to Marshall, 29 Oct. 1948, RG 130.02, 2414/26.

45. Eban to Eytan, 1 Oct. 1948, minutes of meeting, 3 Oct. 1948, *DFPI,* 2:1–2, 6–13; cabinet minutes (Hebrew), 6 Oct. 1948, Protocols-PGI, vol. 11; Lovett to McDonald, 13 Oct. 1948, McDonald to Lovett, 14 Oct. 1948, *FRUS, 1948,* 5:1472–74, 1476–77.

46. Sharett to Ben-Gurion, 20 Oct. 1948, Shiloah to Sharett, 21 Oct. 1948, Eban to Sharett, 28 Oct. 1949, Eytan to Eban, 28 Oct. 1949, *DFPI,* 1:76, 82, 2:106–8.

47. Epstein to Silver, 3 Aug. 1948, RG 93.08, 376/9; Epstein to Shertok, 24 Aug. 1948, *DFPI,* 1:549–51. See also Eban to Goldmann, 22 June 1948, Epstein to Shertok, 27 Sept. 1948, *DFPI,* 1:199–203, 644–45; Ginsburg to Weizmann, 1 July 1948, RG 130.02, 2414/26; Dunne to Vaughan, 28 July 1948, PSF, Political, box 59; Niles to Clifford, 3 Aug. 1948, Clifford Papers, box 13.

48. Epstein to Shertok, 27 Sept. 1948, *DFPI,* 1:644–45; Weizmann to Jacobson, n.d. [Oct. 1948], Clifford Papers, box 13. See also Truman to Wise, 1 Oct. 1948, Dennison Papers, box 3; Marshall to Lovett, 1 Oct. 1948, *FRUS, 1948,* 5:1446; Epstein to Silver, 8 Oct. 1948, RG 93.08, 376/9.

49. Boyle to Connelly, 1 Oct. 1948, Barrows to Connelly, 1 Oct. 1948, Dennison Papers, box 3; memorandum of conversation by Lovett, 29 Sept. 1948, *FRUS, 1948,* 5:1430–31. See also Siskind to Boyle, 23 Sept. 1948, Lovett to Clifford, 24 Sept. 1948, Crum to Clifford, 28, 30 Sept., 3 Oct. 1948, Crum to Truman, 30 Sept. 1948, Clifford Papers, boxes 13–14.

50. Dulles to Silver, 30 Sept. 1948, Epstein to Silver, 8 Oct. 1948, RG 93.08, 376/9. See also Silver to Epstein, 5 Oct. 1948, RG 93.08, 376/9; Rusk to Marshall, 19 Oct. 1948, RG 59, 501.BB PALESTINE.

51. Epstein to Silver, 14 Oct. 1948, RG 93.08, 376/9; Clifford to Truman, 23 Oct. 1948, *FRUS, 1948,* 5:1509. See also Epstein to Sharett, 20–21, 25–26 Oct. 1948, *DFPI,* 2:74, 83, 95–97; Lovett to Marshall, 23–24 Oct. 1948, *FRUS, 1948,* 5:1507–8, 1512–14; Silver to Dewey, 26 Oct. 1948, Silver Papers, Correspondence 6-1 File.

52. Lourie to Eban, 28, 29 Oct. 1948, *DFPI,* 2:106–7, 113–14; Truman to Marshall, 29 Oct. 1948, PSF, Subject, box 159, Lovett to Marshall, 30 Oct. 1948, *FRUS, 1948,* 5:1527–28, 1533–34. See also Eban to Elath, 25 Oct. 1948, Eban to Sharett, 29 Oct. 1948, Epstein to Eban, 5 Nov. 1948, *DFPI,* 2:88, 111–13, 143–46; Jacobson to Weizmann, 29 Nov. 1948, Weizmann Papers, box 1.

53. Epstein to Eban, 5 Nov. 1948, note by Comay, 15 Nov. 1948, *DFPI,* 2:146–47, 181–83. See also Sharett to Elath, 19 Nov. 1948, Epstein to Sharett, 9 Dec. 1948, *DFPI,* 2:204–5, 281.

54. Minutes of meeting, 10 Nov. 1948, *DFPI,* 2:165–67. See also notes by Comay, 21 Oct. 1948, RG 130.02, 2414/26; McClintock to Lovett, 5 Nov. 1948, *FRUS, 1948,* 5:1551–53; Rusk to Marshall, 13 Nov. 1948, RG 59, lot 54 D 403, box 8.

55. Weizmann to Truman, 5 Nov. 1948, *DFPI,* 2:143–46. See also memorandum of conversation by Lovett, 10 Nov. 1948, Marshall to Lovett, 12–16 Nov. 1948, Lovett to Marshall, 14 Nov. 1948, *FRUS, 1948,* 5:1562–63, 1582–89, 1595–97, 1610–12; Epstein to Eban, 6 Nov. 1948, *DFPI,* 2:148–49; McDonald to Clifford, 26 Nov. 1948, Clifford Papers, box 14.

56. Circular cable by Marshall, 24 Nov. 1948, RG 59, 501.BB PALESTINE; Shertok to Eytan, 4 Dec. 1948, *DFPI,* 2:261–62; Jones to Satterthwaite, 8 Dec. 1948, *FRUS, 1948,* 5: 1650–51. See also Douglas to Marshall, 14 Dec. 1948, RG 59, 501.BB PALESTINE.

57. Sasson to Sharett, 19 Dec. 1948, *DFPI,* 2:306–7. See also Sharett to Meyerson, 5 Nov. 1948, Sharett to Eytan, 10 Nov. 1948, memorandum of conversation by Ben-Gurion (Hebrew), 27 Dec. 1948, *DFPI,* 2:141–43, 157–58, 315–16; Riley to Forrestal, 11 Dec. 1948, RG 218, CJCS Leahy, box 10, 057 Palestine; Rabinovich, *Road,* 47–54.

58. Franks to Lovett, 29 Dec. 1948, RG 59, 767N.83. See also Lovett to Jessup, 26 Dec. 1948, Holmes to Lovett, 28 Dec. 1948, Lovett to McDonald, 30 Dec. 1948, *FRUS, 1948,* 5: 1691–92, 1695–96, 1704; Lovett to Griffis, 3 Jan. 1949, *FRUS, 1949,* 6:602–3.

59. Sharett to McDonald, 3 Jan. 1949, *DFPI,* 2:335–37; Weizmann to Truman, 9 Jan. 1949, WHCF-HST (Confidential). See also Weizmann to Truman, 3 Jan. 1949, *FRUS, 1949,* 6:600–601; McDonald to Marshall, 11 Jan. 1949, PSF, Subject, box 181.

60. Epstein to Sharett, 6 Jan. 1949, *DFPI,* 2:347. See also McDonald to Marshall, 5 Jan. 1949, Rusk to Lovett, 5 Jan. 1949, Patterson to Marshall, 7 Jan. 1949, RG 59, 501.BB PALESTINE.

61. Epstein to Sharett, 10 Jan. 1949, *DFPI,* 2:349–50. See also Rusk to Ross, 7 Jan. 1949,

RG 59, 501.BB PALESTINE; British memorandum, 8 Jan. 1949, Elath to Sharett, 11, 12, 21 Jan. 1949, *DFPI*, 2:354–55, 358–59, 366–67, 389–90; minutes of meeting, 17 Jan. 1949, CAB 128, CM 3(49).

62. Eban to Sharett, 8 Feb. 1949, *DFPI*, 3:220. See also Marshall to Patterson, 11 Jan. 1949, Acheson to McDonald and Patterson, 24 Feb. 1949, RG 59, 501.BB PALESTINE; memorandums of conversations by Satterthwaite, 5, 21 Feb. 1949, RG 59, lot 55 D 5, box 5; memorandum of conversation by Acheson, 5 Feb. 1949, Acheson Papers; Eban to Sharett, 5 Feb. 1949, Elath to Sharett, 25 Feb. 1949, *DFPI*, 3:201–2, 275.

63. Pinkerton to Marshall, 8 Dec. 1948, Satterthwaite to Acheson, 18 Mar. 1949, RG 59, 501.BB PALESTINE; Eban to Eytan, 18 Mar. 1949, *DFPI*, 3:318–19.

64. Eban to Eytan, 15 Mar. 1949, *DFPI*, 2:500–501. See also Stabler to Acheson, 17, 27 Feb., 9 Mar. 1949, RG 59, 501.BB PALESTINE; minutes of meeting of Defence Committee, 9 Mar. 1949, PREM 8/1251; Elath to Sharett, 10 Mar. 1949, *DFPI*, 2:404; memorandum of conversation by Acheson, 10 Mar. 1949, Acheson Papers, memcons folder; Satterthwaite to Acheson, 16 Mar. 1949, RG 59, 767N.90.

65. Dorsz to Acheson, 7 Feb. 1949, Crocker to Acheson, 18, 21 Mar. 1949, Satterthwaite to Acheson, 16 Mar. 1949, RG 59, 501.BB PALESTINE; memorandum of conversation by Acheson, 22 Mar. 1949, RG 59, lot 53 D 444, box 12.

66. McDonald to Acheson, 17 May 1949, RG 59, 501.BB PALESTINE. See also Acheson to McDonald, 2 May 1949, McDonald to Acheson, 15 July 1949, RG 59, 501.BB PALESTINE; Keeley to McGhee, 30 Apr. 1949, RG 59, lot 441, box 3; Keeley to Acheson, 11 May, 24 June 1949, Acheson to Keeley, 20 July 1949, Acheson to McDonald, 20 July 1949, RG 59, 767N.90D; Sasson to Eytan, 22 Mar. 1949, Eban to Elath, 29 Apr. 1949, *DFPI*, 3:464–67, 543; Urquhart, *Ralph Bunche.*

Chapter 5

1. Chace, *Acheson.*

2. CIA, SR-13, 27 Sept. 1949, PSF, Intelligence File, box 260; State Department briefing book, 10 Jan. 1950, Lloyd Papers. See also NIE 14, 8 Jan. 1951, PSF, Subject, box 253; Investigative Branch intelligence summary (Hebrew), 1 June 1952, RG 130.02, 2445/11.

3. CIA, SR-13, 27 Sept. 1949, PSF, Intelligence File, box 260; State Department paper, n.d. [Oct. 1952], RG 59, lot 57 D 298, box 3. See also memorandum by Robertson, 14 Nov. 1949, RG 59, 711.9011; briefing book for secretary of defense, 24 Mar. 1950, RG 319, OPS 092 (top secret); JCS 2105/6, 7 Apr. 1950, RG 218, CCS 337 (3-20-50), box 50; NSC 129/1, [24 Apr. 1952], *FRUS, 1952–1954,* 9:222–26.

4. Jones to Nitze, 13 Sept. 1950, RG 59, lot 64 D 563, box 14; JCS 1881/1, 20 Oct. 1948, RG 218, box 31, CCS 381 Saudi Arabia (2-7-45); Childs to Marshall, 27 Dec. 1948, RG 330, CD 6-3-3; Bruce to Truman, 15 Aug. 1952, PSF, Subject File, box 181. See also unsigned paper, "The U.K. Base in Egypt," n.d. [ca. 8 Sept. 1951], steering group paper, 20 May 1952, RG 59, lot 55 D 5, box 6; CIA, NIE-44, 15 Oct. 1951, PSF, Intelligence, box 253; Gilboa, *American Public Opinion,* 25–27.

5. Golan, *Soviet Policies,* 40–43; Behbehani, *Soviet Union,* 104–14.

6. CIA, ORE 69-49, 12 Sept. 1949, PSF, Subject, box 256; NEA paper, n.d. [early Mar. 1950], *FRUS, 1950,* 5:239–44. See also memorandum by Merriam, 13 June 1949, NSC 47/2, 17 Oct. 1949, *FRUS, 1949,* 6:31–45, 1430–40; State Department briefing book, 10 Jan. 1950,

Lloyd Papers; CIA, CIA 5-50, 17 May 1950, PSF, Subject, box 208; paper by H. Morrison, 29 Mar. 1951, CP (51)94, CAB 129.

7. McGhee to Acheson, 15 Mar. 1949, memorandum by Merriam, 13 June 1949, *FRUS, 1949,* 6:827–42, 31–45.

8. Bevin quoted in Louis, "British Imperialism," 27; statement by Acheson, 24 Dec. 1949, Acheson Papers, box 64. See also Baylis, *Diplomacy*; Foot, "Anglo-American Relations"; Hahn, *United States,* 74–77.

9. Mattison to Merriam, 18 Apr. 1949, RG 59, lot 64 D 563, box 30; Satterthwaite to Jones, 27 Apr. 1949, RG 59, lot 54 D 403, box 9; memorandum by Wright, 19 Dec. 1949, FO 371/75056, E15252/1026/65; JSPC 877/73, 20 Sept. 1949, RG 218, JCS Subjective File CCS 686 (9-27-48), box 163; steering group paper, 21 Dec. 1951, RG 59, lot 55 D 5, box 5.

10. JCS 1684/28, 6 May 1949, Maddocks to army COS, 8 Apr. 1949, RG 319, P&O 091 Israel. See also NSC 47, 16 May 1949, *FRUS, 1949,* 6:1009–12; Jacobson to Eban, 25 Sept. 1950, RG 130.20, 2479/8.

11. CIA, SR 61, 24 July 1950, PSF, Intelligence, box 261. See also memorandum of conversation by Marshall, 26 July 1948, RG 59, lot 53 D 444, box 12; CIA, Intelligence Memorandum 108, 28 Dec. 1948, NSC Records, box 2; Pappé, "Moshe Sharett"; Shlaim, "Conflicting Approaches."

12. JCS 1684/28, 6 May 1949, RG 319, P&O 091 Israel; memorandum of conversation by Acheson, 22 Mar. 1949, RG 59, lot 53 D 444, box 12. See also Maddocks to army COS, 14 Jan., 8 Apr. 1949, RG 319, P&O 091 Israel; Ingersoll to Rockwell, 15 July 1949, RG 59, lot 54 D 403, box 10; Kohler to secretary of state, 13 Jan. 1949, McDonald to Acheson, 5 Dec. 1949, *FRUS, 1949,* 6:656–58, 1521–22; Schow to DeLoach, 19 Feb. 1951, CIA Records, ORIS.

13. Memorandum of conversation by Acheson, 22 Mar. 1949, RG 59, lot 53 D 444, box 12. See also Elath to Sharett, 9 Feb. 1949, *DFPI,* 2:424–45; Eytan to Shiloah, 11 Aug. 1949, Ben-Gurion to Sharett, 15 Sept. 1949, *DFPI,* 4:316–19, 471. For a complete explanation of Israel's neutrality and eventual transition to the West, see Bialer, *Between East and West.*

14. NSC 47, 16 May 1949, PSF, Subject File; ORE 68-49, 18 July 1949, PSF, Intelligence File, box 256; memorandum of conversation by Webb, 10 Nov. 1949, RG 59, lot 54 D 403, box 10. See also Humelsine to Acheson, 10 Nov. 1949, memorandum of conversation by Acheson, 19 Jan. 1950, RG 59, General Records of the Executive Secretariat, E394; Acheson to Truman, 19 Jan. 1950, PSF, Subject File, box 181.

15. Elath to Sharett, 12 Oct. 1949, *DFPI,* 4:536–37. See also minutes of meeting (Hebrew), 15 Dec. 1949, Keren to Eytan (Hebrew), 1 June 1950, RG 130.02, 2414/26; minutes of meeting (Hebrew), 31 Jan. 1950, USD to embassy in Washington (Hebrew), 15 May 1950, RG 130.20, 2479/8; USD to Eban (Hebrew), 15 May 1950, RG 130.20, 2460/5a.

16. Acheson to Keeley, 27 Jan., 25 Feb. 1949, Acheson to Childs, 29 Jan. 1949, Forrestal to Acheson, 10 Feb. 1949, Ethridge to Acheson, 19 Feb. 1949, Acheson to embassy in Baghdad, 16 Mar. 1949, Douglas to Acheson, 18 Mar. 1949, Acheson to Douglas, 18 Mar. 1949, Satterthwaite to Acheson, 24 Mar. 1949, Childs to Ibn Saud, 30 May 1949, Webb to legation in Amman, 31 May 1949, *FRUS, 1949,* 6:712–13, 756–57, 770–71, 843–44, 850, 863–64, 1078–79, 1204, 1579–81, 1600–1602; memorandum of conversation by Marshall, 27 Oct. 1948, RG 59, lot 53 D 444, box 12.

17. Satterthwaite to Acheson, 9 May 1949, RG 59, lot 54 D 403, box 9; Acheson to Webb, 26 May 1949, *FRUS, 1949,* 6:1057–58; Elath to Sharett, 28 May, 28 July 1949, Eban

to Sharett, 17 Aug. 1949, *DFPI,* 4:73, 261–63, 363–65; Egyptian aide-mémoires, 10 June, 25 July, 12 Aug. 1949, RG 59, lot 55 D 5, box 2.

18. Rusk to Acheson, 3 Aug. 1949, editorial note, Power to Ross, 4 Sept. 1949, memorandum of conversation by Margrave, 14 Nov. 1949, *FRUS, 1949,* 6:1277–80, 1283–84, 1342n, 1490–91; memorandum of conversation by Power, 2 Aug. 1949, RG 59, lot 54 D 403, box 9; Acheson to Truman, 1 Sept. 1949, WHCF-HST (Confidential); memorandum of conversation by Acheson, 1 Sept. 1949, RG 59, General Records of the Executive Secretariat, E394; Barber to Desvernine, 12 Sept. 1949, RG 59, lot 54 D 403, box 11.

19. McGhee to Acheson, 27 Jan. 1950, RG 59, lot 484, box 1. See also Patterson to Acheson, 17 Aug. 1949, memorandum of conversation by Margrave, 14 Nov. 1949, *FRUS, 1949,* 6:1322–23, 1490–91; memorandum of conversation by Mattison, 23 Jan. 1950, RG 59, lot 55 D 5, box 5; Keeley to Acheson, 6 Mar. 1950, *FRUS, 1950,* 5:778–81; Ogden to COS, 4 May 1950, Bolte to COS, 15 June 1950, Larkin to COS, 25 July 1950, RG 319, Army COS Files, 091 Egypt; Bolte to assistant COS, 14 June 1950, RG 319, Army COS Files, 091 Israel.

20. Memorandum of conversation by Acheson, 31 Jan. 1950, Acheson Papers, S/S File, memorandum of conversation folder; Acheson to McDonald, 17 Jan. 1950, *FRUS, 1950,* 5:696–97. See also memorandum of conversation by Elliott, 14 Oct. 1949, RG 59, lot 54 D 403, box 9; McGhee to Acheson, 27 Jan. 1950, RG 59, lot 484, box 1; USD to Sharett (Hebrew), 27 Jan. 1950, memorandum to Kollek (Hebrew), 17 Feb. 1950, RG 130.02, 2403/18.

21. Mitchell to Elliott, 8 Mar. 1950, RG 330, 6-2-47. See also memorandum of conversation by Elliott, 1 Feb. 1950, RG 59, lot 484, box 1; Eban to Kollek, 24 Mar. 1950, RG 130.20, 2467/7; Keren to USD, 28 Mar. 1950, RG 130.20, 2460/5a; Herzog to deputy chief (Hebrew), 14 Apr. 1950, RG 130.02, memorandum for the record by Irwin, 23 May 1950, RG 319, Army COS Files, 091 Israel.

22. Keren to USD, 14 Feb. 1950, USD to Keren (Hebrew), 2 Mar. 1950, RG 130.02, 2403/18; Arzi to Kollek et al., 1 Mar. 1950, RG 130.20, 2467/7; USD to Elath, 7 Apr. 1950, Elath to Sharett, 8 Apr. 1950, *DFPI,* 5:246, 248–50; memorandum of conversation by Hare, 9 Mar. 1950, *FRUS, 1950,* 5:789–92.

23. Hahn, "View," 516–18.

24. Eban to Kollek, 24 Mar. 1950, RG 130.20, 2467/7; Eban and Rafael to Sharett, 10 May 1950, *DFPI,* 5:321–22. See also Elath to Sharett, 31 Jan. 1950, Elath to USD, 26 Apr., 5 May 1950, Elath to Sharett, 11 May 1950, Sharett to Eban, 16 May 1950, *DFPI,* 5:88, 297–98, 315–16, 324, 330.

25. Battle to Acheson, 14 Apr. 1950, Acheson Papers, S/S File, memorandum of conversation folder; State Department report, 20 Apr. 1950, *FRUS, 1950,* 5:135–41. See also NSC 65, [28 Mar. 1950], *FRUS, 1950,* 5:131–35; memorandum for the president, 7 Apr. 1950, PSF, NSC File, box 220; memorandum of conversation by Acheson, 18, 24 Apr. 1950, memorandum to the file, 19 Apr. 1950, RG 59, General Records of the Executive Secretariat, E394, E396.3.

26. Text of Tripartite Declaration in a circular cable from Webb, 20 May 1950, *FRUS, 1950,* 5:167–68; Webb to Truman, 17 May 1950, WHCF-HST (Confidential). See also Satterthwaite to Jones, 27 Apr. 1949, RG 59, lot 54 D 403, box 9; Bradley to Johnson, 2 May 1950, RG 330, CD 337; NEA paper, 10 May 1950, RG 59, lot 484, box 2; Bevin to Attlee, 12 May 1950, PREM 8/1251; minutes of meeting, 17 May 1950, DEFE 4/31, COS(50)77; report by Admiral Conolly, 20 May 1950, RG 330, CD 9-4-29; Condit, *History,* 115–16.

27. "Defending the Near East," *New York Times*, 26 May 1950, p. 22.

28. Circular cable by Eytan, 26 May 1950, *DFPI*, 5:347–48. See also Keren to USD (Hebrew), 29 May 1950, RG 130.02, 2403/18; Goldmann to Browdy, 31 May 1950, Goldmann Papers, Z6/436; Stone to Scott, 2 June 1950, Goldmann Papers, Z6/372; Lipsky to Acheson, 2 June 1950, Stone to Keren, 2 June 1950, Palov to Keren, 22 June 1950, RG 93.08, 366/13; Herlitz and Kollek to Feinberg, 7 July 1950, Taft to Stone, 11 July 1950, RG 130.20, 2467/7.

29. Memorandum of conversation by Barrow, 17 June 1950, Progress Report on NSC 65/3, 7 Aug. 1950, *FRUS, 1950*, 5:932–33, 176–78. See also Harrison to Acheson, 7 May 1950, RG 59, 683.84A; Childs to Acheson, 25 May 1950, Keeley to Acheson, 19 June 1950, McGhee to Acheson, 20 Nov. 1950, *FRUS, 1950*, 5:933–34, 1048–49, 1178n.

30. Acheson to Keeley, 14 July 1950, *FRUS, 1950*, 5:1212; deputy chief to Shiloah (Hebrew), 29 Mar. 1951, RG 130.20, 2479/9; conclusions of meeting, [21 Feb. 1951], *FRUS, 1951*, 5:65. See also Webb to Keeley, 19 Sept. 1950, Berry to Acheson, 21 Sept. 1950, Acheson to Holmes, 22 Nov. 1950, and circular cable by Acheson, *FRUS, 1950*, 5:1012–13, 1015–17, 1220–21, 1223; memorandum of conversation by Stabler, 5 Mar. 1951, RG 59, lot 55 D 5, box 1.

31. Acheson to embassy in London, 24 June 1950, Acheson to embassy in Manila, 8 Aug. 1950, *FRUS, 1950*, 5:940, 967–68; Johnson to Acheson, 28 June 1950, RG 330, CD 9-4-29; USD policy survey (Hebrew), [1 Aug. 1950], RG 130.20, 2479/8; USD to embassy in Washington (Hebrew), 13 Aug. 1950, RG 130.20, 2467/7; State Department brief, 16 Oct. 1950, RG 330, CD 092 Egypt; Herzog to ambassador (Hebrew), 21 Nov. 1950, RG 93.08, 338/23; Burns to McGhee, 2 Feb. 1951, RG 330, CD 210.681 Syria; Marshall to Ben-Gurion, 12 June 1951, RG 93.08, 337/1.

32. State Department briefing book, n.d. [ca. 2 Dec. 1950], PSF, Subject, box 164. See also paper by Stabler, 24 Oct. 1950, RG 59, lot 55 D 5, box 6.

33. Paper by Stabler, 24 Oct. 1950, RG 59, lot 55 D 5, box 6; McGhee to Acheson, 27 Dec. 1950, RG 59, lot 64 D 563, box 30; steering group paper, 26 Dec. 1951, RG 59, lot 55 D 5, box 6. See also NE policy paper, 28 Dec. 1950, *FRUS, 1950*, 5:271–78; CIA, SE-1, 11 Jan. 1951, PSF, Intelligence, box 258.

34. CIA, NIE-26, 25 Apr. 1951, PSF, Intelligence File, box 253; position paper, 4 Sept. 1951, RG 59, lot 55 D 5, box 6; Hahn, *United States*, 109–28.

35. Jessup to Acheson, 25 July 1950, *FRUS, 1950*, 5:188–92; McGhee to Jessup, 19 Oct. 1950, paper by Stabler, 24 Oct. 1950, RG 59, lot 55 D 5, box 6; report by Bendor, 14 Mar. 1951, RG 130.20, 2565/7; minutes of meeting, [22 Dec. 1951], Rafael memorandum, 29 Jan. 1952, Eliashev to Sharett, 1 Feb. 1952, Levavi to Sharett, 25 Feb. 1952, Shek to Levavi, 30 Mar. 1952, Eytan circular cable, 23 Dec. 1952, *DFPI*, 7:15–21, 64–65, 68–71, 92–93, 139–41, 725.

36. Keren to Sharett (Hebrew), 28 July 1950, Israeli representative in Prague to Sharett (Hebrew), 23 Aug. 1950, RG 130.02, 2414/26; Sharett to Marshall, 23 Dec. 1950, *FRUS, 1950*, 5:1077–82; Eban to Sharett, 15 Jan. 1951, Ben-Gurion to Kollek, 17 Jan. 1951, Ben-Gurion Diary, 7 Feb. 1951, Kollek to Ben-Gurion, 21 Jan. 1951, Eban to Ben-Gurion, 25 Jan. 1951, Shalit to Aranne, 5 Feb. 1951, Bendor to USD, 5 Feb. 1951, Sharett to Yadin, 12 Feb. 1951, *DFPI*, 6:29–30, 42–44, 49–52, 62–65, 89–92, 92–93, 98–99; M. Brecher, *Israel*.

37. Circular by Sharett, 3 July 1950, Sharett to Eytan, 20 Sept. 1950, *DFPI*, 5:425, 550–51; minutes of meeting, 31 Jan. 1951, Keren to Bendor, 14 June 1951, minutes of meeting, 9 July 1951, Sharett to Elath, 3 Sept. 1951, *DFPI*, 6:73–76, 379–81, 450–52, 606–7; daily top

secret summary, 17 May 1951, Davis to Acheson, 11 Nov. 1951, *FRUS, 1951,* 5:247, 686; minutes of meeting, 23 May 1952, *DFPI,* 7:251–61.

38. Mcghee to Davis, 28 Sept. 1951, RG 59, lot 55 D 5, box 6; minutes of meeting, 15 Oct. 1951, *DFPI,* 6:708–10; Acheson to Truman, 12 Sept. 1951, PSF, Subject, box 176. See also memorandum by Morrison, 28 June 1951, CAB 131/11, DO(51)81; NEA paper, 6 July 1951, RG 59, lot 64 D 563, box 30; chiefs of staff committee paper, 25 July 1951, DEFE 4/45, JP(51)131 (annex); McGhee to Davis, 28 Sept. 1951, RG 59, lot 55 D 5, box 6; circular memorandum by Eytan, 13 Oct. 1951, *DFPI,* 6:694–96; U.S. aide-mémoire, 13 Oct. 1951, RG 130.02, 2445/10.

39. Memorandum by McClanahan, 12 Oct. 1951, RG 59, lot 55 D 5, box 6; memorandum of conversation by Battle, 16 Oct. 1951, Acheson Papers, box 66; circular cable by Acheson, 19 Oct. 1951, circular cables by Webb, 18 Nov. 1951, memorandum of conversation by Palmer, 19 Nov. 1951, *FRUS, 1951,* 5:234–35, 248–49, 1013–16; McGhee to Webb, n.d. [ca. 31 Oct. 1951], RG 59, lot 55 D 5, box 1.

40. Minutes of meeting, 15 Oct. 1951, *DFPI,* 6:708–10. See also Eytan circular memorandum, 14 Oct. 1951, Eban to Eytan, 15 Oct. 1951, Eban to Ben-Gurion, 15 Oct. 1951, Sharett to Eytan, 16 Oct. 1951, Eban to Ben-Gurion and Sharett, 10 Nov. 1951, *DFPI,* 6:701–2, 705–6, 706–7, 712–13, 779.

41. Comay to Eban, 5 Nov. 1951, *DFPI,* 6:757–64; Elath to Comay, 3 Sept. 1952, RG 130.02, 2445/12. See also Kollek to USD, 1 Nov. 1951, Israeli *note verbale,* 8 Dec. 1951, *DFPI,* 6:749, 857–58; Investigative Branch intelligence summary (Hebrew), Nov. [1951], RG 130.02, 2445/11.

42. Memorandum of conversation by Sharett, 19 Nov. 1951, *DFPI,* 6:808–19. See also minutes of meeting, 10 Nov. 1951, *DFPI,* 6:775–78; Davis to Acheson, 11 Nov. 1951, memorandum of conversation by Plitt, 19 Nov. 1951, memorandum of conversation by Webb, 30 Nov. 1951, *FRUS, 1951,* 5:247, 935–40, 948–50.

43. PPS paper, 21 May 1952, RG 218, JCS Geographic File 1951–53, box 11, CCS 381 EMMEA (11-19-47); unsigned memorandum, 18 June 1952, RG 59, lot 64 D 563, box 30. See also memorandum of conversation by Stabler, 8 May 1952, paper by Foster, 4 June 1952, RG 59, lot 64 D 563, box 30.

44. Yoffay to Bendor (Hebrew), 26 May 1952, RG 130.20, 2491/13. See also Webb to Davis, 26 Feb. 1952, RG 59, 641.84A; Eban to Sharett, 3 Apr. 1952, *DFPI,* 6:151–52; Matthews to Lovett, 28 May 1952, RG 330, CD 092 Middle East; memorandum of conversation by State Department, 18 June 1952, British memorandum, [18 June 1952], Jessup to Nitze, 9 June 1952, RG 59, lot 64 D 563, box 30; Acheson to Webb, 27 June 1952, *FRUS, 1952–1954,* 9:251–54.

45. State Department position paper, 1 Aug. 1952, RG 59, 641.80; memorandum of conversation by Evans, 6 Nov. 1952, Acheson Papers, box 67a. See also memorandum for the president, 24 Apr. 1952, PSF, Subject File: NSC Meetings; memorandum of conversation by Daspit, 13 Oct. 1952, RG 59, lot 64 D 563, box 30; U.S. aide-mémoire, 5 Nov. 1952, RG 59, 780.5.

46. NSC 47/5, 14 Mar. 1951, State Department paper, [17 Mar. 1951], *FRUS, 1951,* 5: 95–97, 599–600. See also memorandum of conversation by Acheson, 28 Aug. 1950, RG 59, General Records of the Executive Secretariat, E394; Bradley to Marshall, 13 Mar. 1951, memorandum to the president, 15 Mar. 1951, PSF, Subject File: NSC meetings, boxes 212, 220; Defense Department brief, 17 May 1951, RG 330, CD 092 Israel.

47. Eban, *Autobiography*, 160–61. See also Liverhant to Eban, 24 Aug. 1950, RG 130.02, 2414/26; Keren to USD, 5 Jan. 1951, RG 130.20, 2479/8; circular by Lipsky, 16 Jan. 1951, Goldmann Papers, Z6/511; Kollek to Ben-Gurion (Hebrew), 13 Mar. 1951, RG 130.20, 2467/3; Keren to USD (Hebrew), 1 Feb. 1951, Eban to USD (Hebrew), 8 Mar. 1951, Foreign Ministry paper (Hebrew), 3 June 1951, RG 130.20, 2479/8–9; Weizmann to Truman, 30 Apr. 1951, *DFPI*, 6:272–73; circular cable by Acheson, 26 May 1951, *FRUS, 1951*, 5:151–52; memorandum by Eban, 7 May 1951, RG 93.08, 337/4; Ben-Gurion to Truman, 31 May 1951, PSF, Subject File, box 181; Kenen, *Israel's Defense Line*, 70–86.

48. Cannon to Acheson, 12 Apr. 1951, RG 59, 683.84A; memorandum of conversation by Stabler, 28 Mar. 1951, Mattison quoted in Jones to McGhee, 10 May 1951, RG 59, lot 55 D 5, box 1. See also Steel to Foreign Office, 17 Mar. 1951, FO 371/91721; Stabler to Sparks, 13 Apr. 1951, memorandum by Ortiz, 9 Apr. 1951, RG 59, lot 55 D 5, box 1.

49. Berry to Acheson, 15 Mar. 1951, minutes of meeting, 2 May 1951, *FRUS, 1951*, 5:594–98, 655–56. See also minutes of meeting, 4 Apr. 1951, RG 59, lot 64 D 563, box 77; Acheson to Truman, 5 Apr. 1951, RG 59, lot 64 D 563, box 30; briefing memorandum to Harriman, 4 May 1951, Harriman Papers, box 294; Lincoln to Lovett, 21 Apr. 1951, RG 330, CD 091.3 Israel.

50. Memorandum of conversation by Feinberg, 4 Apr. 1951, RG 130.02, 2414/27. See also Keren to USD (Hebrew), 1 Feb. 1951, RG 130.20, 2479/8.

51. McGhee to Acheson, 17 Apr. 1951, Bonesteel to Acheson, 18 Apr. 1951, testimony by McGhee, 3 Aug. 1951, circular cable by Acheson, 23 Oct. 1951, Acheson to Truman, 21 Dec. 1951, *FRUS, 1951*, 5:642–46, 156–61, 238, 971–72; Jones to McGhee, 24 May 1951, RG 59, lot 55 D 5, box 1; Keren to USD, 8 Aug. 1951, *DFPI*, 6:530–31.

52. Memorandum of conversation by Barrow, 10 Aug. 1951, circular cable by Acheson, 26 May 1951, Villard to Nitze, 1 June 1951, *FRUS, 1951*, 5:828–29, 151–54.

53. Memorandum of conversation by Palmer, 19 Nov. 1951, Acheson to Truman, 21 Dec. 1951, *FRUS, 1951*, 5:1013–16, 971–72. See also Elsey to Murphy, 5 Feb. 1952, WHCF-HST (Confidential), State Department Correspondence File; memorandum of conversation by Evans, 7 Feb. 1952, RG 59, General Records of the Executive Secretariat, E394.2, box 1; Truman to Harriman, [8 Feb. 1952], Harriman Papers, box 342; memorandum of conversation by Eban (Hebrew), [31 Mar. 1952], RG 130.20, 2460/5.

54. Memorandum of conversation by Byroade, 8 Aug. 1952, *FRUS, 1952–1954*, 9:262–66; Sharett to Goitein, 17 Apr. 1952, Eban to Sharett, 22 Apr. 1952, Sharett to Eban, 24 Apr. 1952, Eban to USD, 28 July 1952, Goitein to Comay, 21 Aug. 1952, *DFPI*, 6:170–71, 174–75, 183, 394–95, 451; Davis to Byroade, 27 July 1952, Eban to Acheson, 12 Aug. 1952, Davis to Acheson, 18 Dec. 1952, *FRUS, 1952–1954*, 9:971, 979–82, 1080–81; memorandum of conversation by Sharett, 31 July 1952, RG 130.20, 2474/27.

55. Memorandum of conversation by Waller, 17 June 1952, *FRUS, 1952–1954*, 9:942–44. See also Eban to USD, 7 June 1952, Horowitz to Sharett, 9 June 1952, Eban to Sharett, 11 June 1952, Sharett to USD, 20 June 1952, Levin to USD, 10 Nov. 1952, *DFPI*, 6:289–91, 299, 327–28, 330, 619; memorandum of conversation by Herlitz (Hebrew), 19 June 1952, RG 130.02, 2420/10; memorandums of conversations by Waller, 18, 20 June 1952, Acheson to Truman, 30 June 1952, Davis to Acheson, 25, 27 July 1952, *FRUS, 1952–1954*, 9:945–50, 953–59, 968–71; Kollek to Niles, 3 July 1952, Niles Papers, box 31; Berger to Harriman, 26 Nov. 1952, Harriman Papers, box 342.

56. Sharett to Eban, 25 Jan. 1952, *DFPI*, 6:50. See also memorandum of conversa-

tion by Patrick, 10 Jan. 1952, Ruffner to secretary of defense, 25 Feb. 1952, RG 330, CD 091.3 Israel; memorandum of conversation by Bradley, 14 Mar. 1952, RG 319, Army COS Files, 091 Israel; Vandenberg to Lovett, 19 Mar. 1952, RG 218, JCS Geographic File 1951–53, box 49, CCS 092 Palestine; memorandum by Eban (Hebrew), 21 Mar. 1952, RG 130.02, 2422/8; memorandum of conversation by Eban (Hebrew), [31 Mar. 1952], RG 130.20, 2460/5; Tannenwald to Murphy, 6 Oct. 1952, Harriman Papers, box 342.

57. Harriman to Truman, n.d. [ca. 6 Oct. 1952], Harriman Papers, box 342. See also Ruffner to Lovett, 25 Feb. 1952, RG 330, CD 091.3 Israel; Eban to USD, 14 Mar. 1952, *DFPI,* 6:112–13; Bolling to COS, 18 Mar. 1952, RG 319, Army COS Files, 091 Israel.

58. Davis to Acheson, 11 Nov. 1952, *FRUS, 1952–1954,* 9:1050–51; USD to Eban, 14 Nov. 1952, Sharett to Eban, 5 Dec. 1952, Eban to USD, 10 Nov. 1952, *DFPI,* 6:627–28, 681, 617. See also memorandum for the record by Smith, 25 Sept. 1952, RG 330, CD 311.5; memorandum of conversation by Ohly, 19 Nov. 1952, Harriman Papers, box 342; Byroade to Matthews, 24 Dec. 1952, RG 59, lot 55 D 5, box 1.

59. Stabler to Byroade, 27 Aug. 1952, Byroade to Matthews, 24 Dec. 1952, RG 59, lot 55 D 5, box 1. See also Caffery to Acheson, 18 Sept. 1952, Acheson to Truman, 30 Sept., 3 Oct. 1952, PSF, Subject File; memorandum of conversation by Byroade, 24 Dec. 1952, Byroade to Matthews, 24 Dec. 1952, RG 59, lot 55 D 5, box 1; JCS to Lovett, 16 Dec. 1952, RG 330, CD 091.3 Egypt.

60. Sharett to Ben-Gurion (Hebrew), 21 Oct. 1952, RG 130.02, 2422/8; Sharett to Davis, 2 Jan. 1953, RG 130.02, 2403/18; Eban to Foreign Office, 15 Nov. 1952, *DFPI,* 7:637; Lipsky to Acheson, 30 Dec. 1952, Goldmann Papers, Z6/585. See also Goitein to USD, 13 Nov. 1952, RG 130.02, 2403/18; memorandum of conversation by Ortiz, 29 Dec. 1952, RG 59, lot 55 D 5, box 1.

61. Eban to Sharett, 29 Dec. 1952, *DFPI,* 7:734; memorandum of conversation by Kitchen, 31 Dec. 1952, RG 59, General Records of the Executive Secretariat, E394.2, box 1; memorandum of conversation by Acheson, 7 Jan. 1953, Acheson Papers, S/S File; Acheson to Caffery, 13 Jan. 1953, *FRUS, 1952–1954,* 9:1961–62.

62. Mattison to Merriam, 15 Mar. 1949, RG 59, lot 54 D 403, box 2; Maddocks to army COS, 8 Apr. 1949, RG 319, P&O 091 Israel. See also McGhee to Acheson with attachment, 15 Mar. 1949, NSC 47/2, 17 Oct. 1949, *FRUS, 1949,* 6:827–42, 1430–40; Merriam to Kennan, 18 Mar. 1949, Jessup to Kennan, 18 Apr. 1949, RG 59, lot 64 D 563, box 30; JCS 1684/28, 6 May 1949, RG 319, P&O 091 Israel; JCS Guidelines for military attachés, 17 Mar. 1950, JCS 2105/2, JCS to British COS, 31 May 1950, RG 218, CCS 337 (2-20-50), boxes 50, 99.

63. Intelligence memorandum, 28 Feb. 1950, NSC Records, CIA File, box 2; report of Cairo Conference, 16 Mar. 1950, *FRUS, 1950,* 5:2–8. See also CIA 5-49, 17 May 1949, CIA, SR-61, 24 July 1950, PSF, Subject, box 206; U.S.-U.K. statement, 14 Nov. 1949, conclusions of meeting, n.d. [29 Nov. 1949], *FRUS, 1949,* 6:64–66, 168–75; records of discussion, 14–15 Nov. 1949, FO 371/75056, E14770/1026/65.

64. Franks to Bowker, 19 July 1951, FO 371/91182; NSC 129/1, 24 Apr. 1952, PSF, Subject File. See also memorandum for the president, 13 Oct. 1950, PSF, Subject File; State Department policy paper, 6 Feb. 1951, *FRUS, 1951,* 5:570–77.

65. Conclusions of meeting, n.d. [29 Nov. 1949], *FRUS, 1949,* 6:168–75; NSC 129/1, 24 Apr. 1952, PSF, Subject File; Hoskins to Byroade, 25 July 1952, *FRUS, 1952–1954,* 9:256–62. See also memorandum for the president, 14 Feb. 1951, PSF, Subject File; NSC staff study, 18 Jan. 1952, RG 59, lot 64 D 563, box 30; Hoskins to McGhee, 7 Apr. 1952, *FRUS, 1952–1954,* 9:204–18.

Chapter 6

1. Memorandum by McClintock, 12 Jan. 1949, RG 59, lot 54 D 403, box 11; Rusk to Acheson, 28 Jan. 1949, RG 59, 501.BB PALESTINE; Sasson to Lourie, 12 Mar. 1949, RG 93.08, 366/32; Burdett to Acheson, 9 Apr. 1949, PSF, Subject File, box 181. For an overview of international and U.N. peacemaking in the aftermath of the 1948–49 war, see Caplan, *Futile Diplomacy*, vol. 3.

2. Ethridge to Acheson, 9 May 1949, RG 59, 501.BB PALESTINE; Avner to Sharett, 1 May 1949, Eytan to Sharett, 30 Apr. 1949, *DFPI*, 4:3–6; 2:613–16; Ethridge to Acheson, 4 May 1949, *FRUS, 1949*, 6:975–77. See also Ethridge to Acheson, 19, 28 Apr., 17 May 1949, *FRUS, 1949*, 6:923–24, 955–56, 1018–20; Halderman to Rusk, 29 Apr. 1949, RG 59, 501.BB PALESTINE.

3. Ethridge to Acheson, 20 May 1949, *FRUS, 1949*, 6:1036–38; CIA, ORE 68-49, 18 July 1949, PSF, Intelligence File, box 256. See also Ethridge to Acheson, 10, 12, 18 May 1949, *FRUS, 1949*, 6:992–94, 998–99, 1028–29; memorandum of conversation by Halderman, 23 May 1949, State Department memorandum, 30 June 1949, RG 59, lot 54 D 403, boxes 9, 11; Rabinovich, *Road*, 54–64.

4. Sharett to Shiloah and Sasson, 28 July 1949, *DFPI*, 4:258–61; McGhee to Acheson, 16 Aug. 1949, *FRUS, 1949*, 6:1315–16. See also Stabler to Acheson, 21 July 1949, RG 59, 501.BB PALESTINE; Porter to Acheson, 26, 28 July 1949, Acheson to Porter, 28 July 1949, *FRUS, 1949*, 6:1254–55, 1266, 1267; Shiloah to Sharett, 29 July 1949, Eytan to Shiloah, 9, 11 Aug. 1949, *DFPI*, 4:264–66, 307–9, 316–19.

5. Ethridge to Acheson, 20 Apr. 1949, *FRUS, 1949*, 6:925–27. See also McDonald to Acheson, 2 May 1949, *FRUS, 1949*, 6:966–67.

6. Memorandum of conversation by Acheson, 28 Mar. 1949, Acheson Papers, box 64; Truman to Abdallah, 28 Mar. 1949, *FRUS, 1949*, 6:878–79. See also Rusk to Acheson, 28 Jan. 1949, Satterthwaite to Acheson, 16 Mar. 1949, Rusk to Acheson, 28 Mar. 1949, RG 59, 501.BB Palestine; memorandum of conversation by Acheson, 26 Apr. 1949, *FRUS, 1949*, 6:944–47.

7. Ethridge to Acheson, 10 June 1949, memorandum by Webb, 7 June 1949, State Department to Truman, 10 June 1949, *FRUS, 1949*, 6:1112–14, 1092, 1110. See also Webb to Truman, 27 May 1949, PSF, Subject File, box 159; Eytan to Boisanger, 31 May 1949, *DFPI*, 4:79–80; CIA 6-49, 15 June 1949, PSF, Subject File, box 206; memorandum of conversation by Mattison, 21 June 1949, RG 59, lot 54 D 403, box 9.

8. Webb to Truman, 27 May 1949, PSF, Subject File, box 159; Truman to Ben-Gurion, 28 May 1949, memorandum by Webb, 10 June 1949, Acheson to Porter, 9 Aug. 1949, *FRUS, 1949*, 6:1072–74, 1109, 1291.

9. Eytan to Sharett, 30 June 1949, Weizmann to Truman, 24 June 1949, *DFPI*, 4:186–89, 168–72. See also McDonald to Acheson, 29 May 1949, Israeli aide-mémoire, 8 June 1949, Webb to Connelly, 23 June 1949, *FRUS, 1949*, 6:1074–75, 1102–6, 1166–67; Kenen to Zinder, 13 June 1949, RG 93.08, 366/32; Eban to Sharett, 17 June 1949, *DFPI*, 4:139–40; McGhee to Acheson, 14 July 1949, RG 59, lot 54 D 403, box 8; McDonald to Clifford, 11 June 1949, Elath to Clifford, 15 Aug. 1949, Clifford Papers, box 13.

10. Elath to Sharett, 19 Aug. 1949, *DFPI*, 4:375. See also Elath to Shiloah, 4 Aug. 1949, RG 93.08, 366/32; Ford to Acheson, 9 Aug. 1949, RG 59, 501.BB PALESTINE; Shiloah to Sharett (Hebrew), 9 Aug. 1949, Elath to Clifford, 15 Aug. 1949, *DFPI*, 4:303, 352–57; Ache-

son to Porter, 11 Aug. 1949, Truman to Weizmann, 13 Aug. 1949, circular cable by Acheson, 16 Aug. 1949, *FRUS, 1949*, 6:1301–2, 1305–8, 1316–18.

11. McDonald to Acheson, 20 June 1950, *FRUS, 1950*, 5:935–36. See also memorandum, n.d. [14 Nov. 1949], *FRUS, 1949*, 6:1488–90; memorandum of conversation by Stabler, 18 Oct. 1949, RG 59, 501.BB PALESTINE; Hare to Acheson, 6 Dec. 1949, RG 59, lot 54 D 403, box 11; memorandum by Halderman and Barco, 3 Jan. 1950, Palmer to Acheson, 28 Jan. 1950, circular cable by Acheson, 3 Apr. 1950, Palmer to Acheson, 19, 22 Apr. 1950, Palmer to Acheson, 24 Aug. 1950, *FRUS, 1950*, 5:661–65, 707–8, 835–36, 865–68, 978–80.

12. Palmer to Acheson, 28 June 1951, *FRUS, 1951*, 5:735–37. See also Fritzlan to Acheson, 29 Feb., 7 Mar. 1952, circular cable by Acheson, 4 Mar. 1952, Crocker to Acheson, 9 Mar. 1952, Minor to Acheson, 10 Mar. 1952, Cannon to Acheson, 11 Mar. 1952, *FRUS, 1952–1954*, 9:899–900, 905–8; minutes of meeting, 9 June 1951, Sharett to Rosenne, 30 June 1951, Sharett to Ben-Gurion, 23 Aug. 1951, *DFPI*, 6:368–69, 421, 566–69.

13. Acheson to Palmer, 27 July 1951, Palmer to Acheson, 12, 14, 17, 21, 24, 27 Sept., 4 Oct. 1951, Davis to Acheson, 20 Sept. 1951, Acheson to Davis, 26 Sept. 1951, *FRUS, 1951*, 5:799–801, 856–62, 864–69, 870–71, 873–80, 885–87; circular cables by Eytan, 5, 19 Oct. 1951, minutes of meeting, 19 Nov. 1951, *DFPI*, 6:684–85, 722, 808–19; Waldo to Jones, 29 Oct. 1951, RG 59, 684.84A.

14. Bruce to U.S. mission to U.N., 17 Dec. 1952, *FRUS, 1952–1954*, 9:1080. See also Eban to USD, 18 Sept., 10 Nov. 1952, Herlitz to Eban, 11 Dec. 1952, Eban to Sharett, 19 Dec. 1952, Bendor to Eban, 26 Dec. 1952, *DFPI*, 7:525–26, 617, 666–67, 717–21, 728–29.

15. Memorandum of conversation by McGhee, 8 Feb. 1950, *FRUS, 1950*, 5:730–34. See also memorandum of conversation by Eytan, 22 Jan. 1950, RG 130.02, 2403/18; Symmes to Acheson, 6 Mar. 1950, RG 59, 683.84A; memorandum of conversation by Clark, 1 Aug. 1950, *FRUS, 1950*, 5:1104; Rabinovich, *Road*, 65–110.

16. Truman to Abdallah, 22 Dec. 1949, WHCF-HST (Confidential), box 43. See also Abdallah to Truman, 5 Nov. 1949, Acheson to Truman, 29 Dec. 1949, WHCF-HST (Confidential), box 43; note on talk by Keren, 21 Dec. 1949, *DFPI*, 4:752–53; draft agreement, 28 Feb. 1950, *DFPI*, 5:146–53; Rabinovich, *Road*, 111–67.

17. Gibson to Acheson, 16 Feb. 1950, Drew to Acheson, 2 Mar. 1950, circular cable by Acheson, 8 Mar. 1950, Keeley to Acheson, 28 Mar. 1950, *FRUS, 1950*, 5:745–46, 773–74, 787, 822–25; Sharett to Eban, 5 Mar. 1950, *DFPI*, 5:174; Hare to Acheson, 7 Mar. 1950, RG 59, lot 54 D 403, box 11; memorandum of conversation by Acheson, 9 Mar. 1950, Acheson Papers, box 64b; Mattison to Acheson, 16 Mar. 1950, RG 59, lot 54 D 403, box 10.

18. Paper by Bevin, 20 Apr. 1950, CP(50)78, CAB 129; minutes of cabinet meeting, 25 Apr. 1950, CAB 128, CM25(50)2; minutes of meeting, 27 Apr. 1950, *DFPI*, 5:300–302; State Department paper, 28 Apr. 1950, RG 59, lot 54 D 403, box 11.

19. Memorandum of conversation by Stabler, 12 Aug. 1950, RG 59, lot 55 D 5, box 5. See also M. Sasson to E. Sasson, 1 May, 12 June 1950, *DFPI*, 5:305–7, 408–9; Acheson to McDonald, 6 June 1950, McDonald to Acheson, 9, 30 June 1950, Drew to Acheson, 27 June 1950, *FRUS, 1950*, 5:922–23, 925, 944–45.

20. Drew to Acheson, 5 Dec. 1950, *FRUS, 1950*, 5:1069–70. See also Ben-Gurion to Abdallah, 9 Jan. 1951, circular cable by Sharett, 24 July 1951, minutes of meeting, 1 Aug. 1951, *DFPI*, 6:16, 495, 511–13; note for the record, 2 Jan. 1952, Eytan to Eban, 27 Oct. 1952, *DFPI*, 7:9, 595–96.

21. Davis to Acheson, 23 Jan. 1952, Acheson to Davis, 15 Jan. 1952, *FRUS, 1952–1954*, 9:

884, 877–78. See also Davis to Acheson, 16 Jan. 1952, Drew to Acheson, 21 Jan. 1952, Davis to Acheson, 13 Feb. 1952, *FRUS, 1952–1954*, 9:878–79, 881–82, 896; editorial note, Israel-Jordan agreements, 13 May, 13 Nov., 29 Dec. 1952, *DFPI,* 7:67–68, 225, 625–26, 736–37.

22. Policy paper, "Egypt," 5 July 1950, RG 59, 611.74. See also Caffery to Acheson, 14 Nov. 1949, RG 59, 767N.83; Caffery to Acheson, 2, 4 Jan. 1950, *FRUS, 1950*, 5:658, 666–67; Sharett to Elath, 5 Jan. 1950, Eban to Elath, 14 Feb. 1950, Sharett to Kaplan, 19 Mar. 1950, *DFPI,* 5:13–14, 125–26, 190–91; Caffery to Acheson, 29 Jan. 1950, Acheson to McDonald, 3 Feb. 1950, Nelson to Berry, 24 Feb. 1950, *FRUS, 1950*, 5:284–87, 709, 721; memorandum of conversation by Stabler, 16 May 1950, RG 59, lot 55 D 5, box 5.

23. Memorandum of discussions, 19 Sept. 1950, FO 371/80383, JE 1055/55; memorandum of conversation by Acheson, 19 Oct. 1950, *FRUS, 1950*, 5:311–15. See also Acheson to Caffery, 11 Sept. 1950, Ford to Acheson, 9 Oct. 1950, *FRUS, 1950*, 5:999, 1027–28; memorandum of conversation by McClintock, 27 June 1951, memorandum of conversation by Kopper, 9 June 1952, RG 59, lot 55 D 5, box 1; memorandum of conversation by Goitein, 7 Mar. 1952, RG 130.20, 2460/5; Rabinovich, *Road*, 168–208.

24. Ben-Gurion quoted in editorial note, *DFPI,* 7:453–54. See also Sharett to Eban, 31 July 1952, Rafael to Sharett, 30 July 1952, Yafeh to Bendor, 4 Aug. 1952, Divon to Sharett, 23 Aug. 1952, *DFPI,* 7:401–2, 409–10, 455–56; Davis to Acheson, 1, 19, 22, 27 Aug. 1952, *FRUS, 1952–1954*, 9:976–77, 984–86, 988. For records on actual meetings in Paris, see *DFPI,* 7:469–70, 471–72, 484–85, 587. Regarding MAC, see *DFPI,* 7:464–65; *FRUS, 1952–1954*, 9:987, 989, 1013.

25. Sharett to Eban, 28 July 1952, *DFPI,* 7:396. See also Eban to Sharett, 31 July, 8 Aug. 1952, Sharett to Eban, 22 Aug., 2 Sept. 1952, Eban to USD, 20 Oct. 1952, *DFPI,* 7:402, 418, 454, 476, 580–81; Bruce to Caffery, 20 Aug. 1952, Caffery to Acheson, 26 Aug., 8, 23 Sept. 1952, Acheson to Davis, 28 Aug., 13 Sept. 1952, Davis to Acheson, 4, 12, 17 Sept. 1952, *FRUS, 1952–1954*, 9:984–85, 987–88, 990–91, 994–95, 1000–1001, 1007–8.

26. Eban to USD, 18 Nov. 1952, *DFPI,* 7:640–41. See also Caffery to Davis, 28 Oct. 1952, RG 59, lot 60 D 48, box 1; Eban to Sharett, 3 Nov. 1952, Divon to Shiloah, 15 Nov., 7 Dec. 1952, *DFPI,* 7:604–5, 638–39, 690; memorandum of conversation by Burns, 7 Nov. 1952, *FRUS, 1952–1954*, 9:1045–49.

27. Editorial note, *DFPI,* 6:179; Waldo to Kopper, 6 Apr. 1951, RG 59, 683.84A.

28. Divon to Eban, 29 Mar. 1951, *DFPI,* 6:193–94; memorandum of conversation by Waldo, 29 Mar. 1951, Waldo to Kopper, 6 Apr. 1951, RG 59, 683.84A.

29. Memorandum of conversation by Barrow, 30 Mar. 1951, RG 59, 683.84A. See also Cannon to Acheson, 20 Feb., 2 Mar. 1951, Webb to Cannon, 8 Mar. 1951, Acheson to Davis, 17 Mar. 1951, memorandum of conversation by Barrow, 30 Mar. 1951, RG 59, 683.84A; Bolling to chief of staff, 4 Apr. 1951, RG 319, Army COS Files, 091 Israel.

30. Eytan to Eban, 5 Apr. 1951, *DFPI,* 6:215–16. See also Avner to Eban, 1 Apr. 1951, USD to Eban, 2 Apr. 1951, *DFPI,* 6:206–7, 211–12; cable from Acheson, 6 Apr. 1951, RG 59, 683.84A.

31. Sharett to Ben-Gurion, 16 Apr. 1951, *DFPI,* 6:249–50. See also Eban to Sharett, 7, 13, 17 Apr. 1951, circular cable by Eytan, 9 Apr. 1951, Ben-Horin to Avner, 12 Apr. 1951, Sharett to Eban, 16, 24 Apr. 1951, Sharett to Ben-Gurion, 25 Apr. 1951, *DFPI,* 6:227–28, 234–35, 239–40, 243, 251–52, 255, 264–65.

32. Acheson to Davis, 8 Apr. 1951, RG 59, 683.84A. See also memorandums of conversations by Barrow, 6, 10 Apr. 1951, Acheson to Davis, 7 Apr. 1951, circular cables by

Acheson, 10, 17 Apr. 1951, Jones to Berry, 26 Apr. 1951, RG 59, 683.84A; Howard to Jones et al., 24 Apr. 1951, RG 59, lot 55 D 5, box 1.

33. Acheson to Cannon, 5 Apr. 1951, circular cable by Acheson, 7 Apr. 1951, RG 59, 683.84A. See also memorandum of conversation by Barrow, 9 Apr. 1951, Cannon to Acheson, 12, 15 Apr. 1951, RG 59, 683.84A.

34. Acheson to Cannon, 3, 6, 9 May 1951, Acheson to Davis, 4 May 1951, Davis to Acheson, 4, 5, 8 May 1951, Cannon to Acheson, 6, 7, 10 May 1951, memorandum of conversation by Stabler, 7 May 1951, RG 59, 683.84A; Eban to Sharett, 15 May 1951, *DFPI*, 6:310–11.

35. Circular cable by Eytan, 21 May 1951, *DFPI*, 6:335–36. See also Unger to Goldmann, 7 May 1951, Kirchwey to Truman, 17 May 1951, Goldmann Papers, Z6/511, Z6/552; cable from Acheson, 11 May 1951, Cannon to Acheson, 17 May 1951, RG 59, 683.84A; Eban to Sharett, 15, 16 May 1951, USD to Eban, 17 May 1951, *DFPI*, 6:311–16; Weizmann to Truman, 18 May 1951, WHCF-HST (Official), box 775; Herlitz to Levin, 8 June 1951, RG 130.20, 2479/9.

36. Truman to Acheson, 19 May 1951, RG 59, 683.84A. See also United Nations Security Council resolution, 18 May 1951, *FRUS, 1951*, 5:693–96; Sharett to Eban, 18 May 1951, *DFPI*, 6:321.

37. Cannon to Acheson, 17 May 1951, memorandum of conversation by Barrow, 21 May 1951, circular cable by Acheson, 29 May 1951, RG 59, 683.84A. See also Acheson to Crocker, 17 May 1951, Clark to Acheson, 27, 28 May 1951, RG 59, 683.84A.

38. Keren to Sharett, 18 May 1951, *DFPI*, 6:329–30. See also Riley-Sharett agreement, 3 June 1951, Sharett to Yadin, 11 June 1951, *DFPI*, 6:357, 369–71; Truman to Weizmann, n.d. [1 June 1951], WHCF-HST (Official), box 775; Davis to Acheson, 6 June 1951, Jones to Cannon, 8 June 1951, Acheson to Gifford, 9 June 1951, RG 59, 683.84A.

39. Circular cable by Acheson, 2 July 1951, *FRUS, 1951*, 5:727–28. See also Bruins to McGhee, 20 June 1951, Davis to Acheson, 3 July 1951, memorandums of conversations by Barrows, 3, 6 July 1951, RG 59, 683.84A; Cannon to Acheson, 5 July 1951, *FRUS, 1951*, 5:744–45.

40. Waller to Hart, 14 Nov. 1952, RG 59, 683.84A. See also circular cables by Acheson, 18 July, 19 Dec. 1951, Acheson to Davis, 6 July 1951, Davis to Acheson, 9, 14, 20 July 1951, Austin to Acheson, 14, 24, 29 Aug. 1951, Acheson to Austin, 25 Aug. 1951, Acheson to Cannon, 16 Oct. 1951, Clark to Acheson, 4 Dec. 1951, Moose to Acheson, 8 Dec. 1952, RG 59, 683.84A.

41. Goitein to Comay, 21 Aug. 1952, Goitein and Ben-Horin to USD, 26 Aug. 1952, *DFPI*, 7:451, 463. See also Cannon to Acheson, 9 Jan. 1952, Acheson to Davis, 14 Jan. 1952, *FRUS, 1952–1954*, 9:875–77; Tekoah to Comay, 21 Aug. 1952, *DFPI*, 7:450; memorandum of conversation by Maffitt, 29 Aug. 1951, RG 59, 683.84A.

Chapter 7

1. Notes on meeting, 20 Aug. 1948, Connelly Papers, box 1; General Assembly resolution, 11 Dec. 1948, quoted in memorandum by Hope, 11 May 1949, RG 59, lot 54 D 403, box 11. See also State Department paper, 27 Apr. 1949, RG 59, lot 441, box 3; Acheson to secretary of defense, 4 May 1949, RG 218, JCS Decimal File, CCS 400.354 (9-1-48), box 160; State Department paper, 19 May 1949, RG 59, lot 70 D 303, box 5.

2. Shertok to Comay, 22 July 1948, Shertok to Weizmann, 22 Aug. 1948, *DFPI*, 1:

374, 369–72. See also Morris, *Birth*; Teveth, "Palestine Arab Refugee Problem"; Childers, "Wordless Wish"; Masalha, *Expulsion*.

3. Sharett to Eban, 9–10 Feb. 1949, *DFPI*, 2:422–24; memorandum of conversation by McClintock, 29 Jan. 1949, *FRUS, 1949*, 6:708–9. See also MacDonald to Marshall, 3 Aug. 1948, RG 59, 501.BB PALESTINE; Knox to Acheson, 4 Feb. 1949, RG 59, 767N.00; Herlitz to Elath, 24 Feb. 1949, *DFPI*, 2:456–57; State Department position paper, 15 Mar. 1949, RG 59, lot 441, box 3.

4. State Department position papers, 15 Mar., 27 Apr. 1949, RG 59, lot 441, box 3. See also memorandum of conversation by Sanger, 10 Feb. 1949, RG 59, lot 441, box 4; Abdallah to Truman, 13 Apr. 1949, WHCF-HST (Confidential), box 43.

5. Stabler to Marshall, 21 Oct. 1948, RG 59, 501.BB PALESTINE; Mattison to Satterthwaite, 18 Feb. 1949, RG 59, lot 54 D 403, box 9. See also Marshall to Truman, 19 Aug. 1948, *FRUS, 1948*, 5:1324–26; Denfield to Forrestal, 1 Sept. 1948, Leahy to Forrestal, 22 Sept. 1948, RG 218, box 160, CCS 400.354 (9-1-48); Forrestal to Truman, 1 Oct. 1948, Truman to Forrestal, 4 Oct. 1948, Forrestal to Connally, 25 Jan. 1949, RG 330, CD 6-3-27; Griffis to Marshall, 20 Oct. 1948, RG 59, 501.BB PALESTINE; Royall to Forrestal, 9 Nov. 1948, RG 319, P&O 383.7; Lovett to Truman, 14 Jan. 1949, *FRUS, 1949*, 6:663–65.

6. Austin quoted in Acheson to McDonald, 3 Feb. 1949, *FRUS, 1949*, 6:722–23; Truman to Abdallah, 14 Apr. 1949, WHCF-HST (Confidential), box 43. See also Satterthwaite to Acheson, 7 Feb. 1949, RG 59, lot 54 D 403, box 9; Acheson to McDonald, 17 Feb., 1 Apr. 1949, McDonald to Acheson, 22 Feb. 1949, *FRUS, 1949*, 6:754–55, 761–64.

7. Keeley to Marshall, 6 Nov. 1948, RG 59, 501.BB PALESTINE. See also Hare to Marshall, 12 Aug. 1948, RG 59, lot 54 D 403, box 8; Marshall to Austin, 14 Aug. 1948, RG 59, 501.BB PALESTINE; CIA, addendum to ORE 38-48, 31 Aug. 1948, PSF, Intelligence, box 249.

8. State Department position paper, 15 Mar. 1949, RG 59, lot 441, box 3; Mattison to Satterthwaite, 9 May 1949, RG 59, lot 54 D 503, box 9.

9. State Department position paper, 15 Mar. 1949, RG 59, lot 441, box 3; Johnson to Acheson, 14 June 1949, RG 218, JCS Decimal File, CCS 400.354 (9-1-48), box 160; Ethridge to Rusk, 15 June 1949, RG 59, lot 441, box 3. See also Acheson to Johnson, 4 May 1949, RG 218, JCS Decimal File, CCS 400.354 (9-1-48), box 160; Lawson, "Truman Administration."

10. State Department position paper, 15 Mar. 1949, RG 59, lot 441, box 3. See also Kirk to Gross, 22 Feb. 1949, RG 59, 501.BB PALESTINE; Acheson to Truman, 15 Mar. 1949, WHCF-HST (Confidential), box 39.

11. Ethridge to Acheson and Truman, 28 Mar. 1949, *FRUS, 1949*, 6:876–78; Ethridge to Acheson, 9 Apr. 1949, PSF, Subject File, box 181. See also Lovett to Ethridge, 19 Jan. 1949, *FRUS, 1949*, 6:681–83; Patterson to Acheson, 6 Mar. 1949, RG 59, 501.BB PALESTINE; minutes of meeting, 24 Feb. 1949, Eytan to Sharett, 18 Mar. 1949, Eban to Sharett, 27 Apr. 1949, *DFPI*, 2:441–54, 512, 595; Burdett to Acheson, 9 Apr. 1949, PSF, Subject File, box 181.

12. Acheson to McDonald, 9 Mar. 1949, memorandum of conversation by Acheson, 5 Apr. 1949, Truman to Ethridge, 29 Apr. 1949, *FRUS, 1949*, 6:804–5, 890–94, 957. See also Rusk to Acheson, 23 Apr. 1949, RG 59, lot 54 D 403, box 9; memorandum of conversation by Acheson, 28 Apr. 1949, Acheson Papers, box 64.

13. Eban to Sharett, 29 Apr. 1949, Weizmann to Truman, 1 May 1949, *DFPI*, 2:604, 4:6–8. See also Herlitz to Sharett, 8 Apr. 1949, Eban to Eytan, 15 Apr. 1949, Elath to Sharett, 29 Apr. 1949, *DFPI*, 2:564–65, 574, 605–6; memorandum of conversation by Acheson, 25 Apr. 1949, RG 59, General Records of the Executive Secretariat, E394.

14. Memorandum of conversation by Hope, 5 Apr. 1949, RG 59, lot 441, box 3. See also memorandum of conversation by Hope, 25 Mar. 1949, Satterthwaite and McGhee to Rusk, 28 Apr. 1949, RG 59, lot 54 D 403, box 9; record of meeting, 13 Apr. 1949, State Department policy paper, 27 Apr. 1949, RG 59, lot 441, box 3; Rusk to Webb, 3 Mar. 1949, Burdett to Acheson, 19 Apr. 1949, *FRUS, 1949,* 6:788, 923–24; Acheson to Johnson, 4 May 1949, RG 218, JCS Decimal File, CCS 400.354 (9-1-48), box 160.

15. Circular cable by Acheson, 29 Apr. 1949, *FRUS, 1949,* 6:959–60. See also Middle East Committee paper, 26 Apr. 1949, CAB 134/501, ME(O) (49)10; memorandum by Hope, 11 May 1949, RG 59, lot 54 D 403, box 11; memorandum of conversation by Acheson, 12 May 1949, Acheson Papers, box 64; Acheson to Truman, 4, 9 May 1949, Andrews to Steelman, 10 May 1949, WHCF-HST (Confidential), box 43; memorandum by Webb, 26 May 1949, RG 59, lot 441, box 4.

16. Keeley to Acheson, 14 July 1949, *FRUS, 1949,* 6:1226–28. See also Stabler to Acheson, 1 May 1949, Keeley to Acheson, 2 May 1949, *FRUS, 1949,* 6:962–64, 965–66; memorandum of conversation by Muir, 24 May 1949, RG 59, lot 53 D 444, box 12; Acheson to Stabler, 16 May 1949, Stabler to Acheson, 21 May, 30 June, 1, 14 July 1949, RG 59, 501.BB PALESTINE.

17. Crocker to Acheson, 7 May 1949, RG 59, 501.BB Palestine. See also memorandum of conversation by Mattison, 17 May 1949, RG 59, lot 53 D 444, box 12; Patterson to Acheson, 24 May 1949, Pinkerton to Acheson, 1 July 1949, RG 59, 501.BB PALESTINE; memorandum of conversation by Mattison, 10 June 1949, RG 59, lot 53 D 444, box 12; Burdett to Acheson, 6 July 1949, *FRUS, 1949,* 6:1203–5.

18. Circular cable by Acheson, 29 June 1949, *FRUS, 1949,* 6:1214–15. See also Patterson to Acheson, 27 June 1949, Stabler to Acheson, 29 June, 20 July 1949, circular cable by Acheson, 9 July 1949, Keeley to Acheson, 18 July 1949, *FRUS, 1949,* 6:1188–89, 1186n, 1207n, 1214–15, 1233n.

19. Israeli aide-mémoire, n.d. [4 May 1949], RG 59, lot 441, box 3; Israeli aide-mémoire, 8 June 1949, *FRUS, 1949,* 6:1102–6. See also Sasson to Sharett, 8 May, 2 June 1949, Elath to Sharett, 12 May, 1 June 1949, statement by Sharett, 25 May 1949, Eban to Sharett, 1 June 1949, *DFPI,* 4:28–29, 42, 66–70, 87–90; memorandum of conversation by Webb, 31 May 1949, RG 59, lot 53 D 444, box 12.

20. Memorandum of conversation by Rusk, 25 June 1949, *FRUS, 1949,* 6:1177–78; memorandum of conversation by Webb, 10 June 1949, RG 59, 501.BB PALESTINE. See also minutes of cabinet meeting (Hebrew), 3 May 1949, Protocols-PGI; Comay to Eytan, 11 May 1949, RG 130.02, 2443/3; McDonald to McGhee, 24 May 1949, RG 59, 501.BB PALESTINE; Eytan to Sharett, 27 May 1949, *DFPI,* 4:70; Patterson to Acheson, 27 June 1949, *FRUS, 1949,* 6:1188–89; Gazit, "Ben-Gurion's 1949 Proposal."

21. Elath to Sharett, 27 May 1949, Eban to Sharett, 1 June 1949, Kollek to Sharett, 10 June 1949, *DFPI,* 4:71–72, 88, 115–17; Kollek to Eban, 6 June 1949, RG 130.02, 2443/3; McDonald to Clifford, 11 June 1949, Clifford Papers; Weizmann to Truman, 24 June 1949, *FRUS, 1949,* 6:1168–73.

22. Webb to Truman, 27 May 1949, *FRUS, 1949,* 6:1060–63; memorandum of conversation by Webb, 31 May 1949, RG 59, General Records of the Executive Secretariat, E394; memorandum by Webb, 9 June 1949, *FRUS, 1949,* 6:1109–10. See also Rusk to Ethridge, 24 May 1949, Ethridge to Acheson, 26 May 1949, memorandum by Webb, 31 May 1949, *FRUS, 1949,* 6:1051–53, 1058–59, 1074–75.

23. Webb to McDonald, 28 May 1949, *FRUS, 1949*, 6:1072–74; Rusk to Webb, 9 June 1949, State Department to Truman, 10 June 1949, *FRUS, 1949*, 6:1107; U.S. aide-mémoire, n.d. [24 June 1949], PSF, Subject File, box 184. See also Ethridge to Rusk, 15 June 1949, RG 59, lot 441, box 3; memorandum by Webb, 16 June 1949, RG 59, General Records of the Executive Secretariat, E394; Herlitz to Heyd, 11 July 1949 (Hebrew), *DFPI*, 4:217–18.

24. Eban to Eytan, 24 June 1949, Heyd to Herlitz, 1 July 1949, *DFPI*, 4:165–67, 194–96. See also editorial note, *DFPI*, 4:206.

25. Sharett to Eban, 6 July 1949, Eban to Sharett, 8, 27 July 1949, Lourie to Sharett, 12, 19 July 1949, *DFPI*, 4:207, 210–12, 218–19, 227, 257; Lourie to Eytan, 22 July 1949, RG 130.20, 2479/8; memorandum of conversation by Rusk, 28 July 1949, *FRUS, 1949*, 6:1261–64.

26. Acheson to McDonald, 16 Aug. 1949, *FRUS, 1949*, 6:1321. See also Ford to Acheson, 9 Aug. 1949, RG 59, 501.BB PALESTINE; memorandum of conversation by Wilkins, 9 Aug. 1949, RG 59, lot 54 D 403, box 9.

27. Shiloah to Sharett, 31 July, 5, 15 Aug. 1949, Sasson to Sharett, 25 Aug. 1949, Elath to Sharett, 9, 11, 18 Aug. 1949, *DFPI*, 4:267–69, 289, 300–301, 309–10, 320, 333–34, 343–47, 368–69, 393–95; Porter to Acheson, 3 Aug. 1949, Clifford Papers, box 14; Truman to Weizmann, 13 Aug. 1949, *FRUS, 1949*, 6:1305–8; memorandum by Hillenkoetter, 5 Aug. 1949, PSF, Intelligence File, box 249.

28. Truman to Weizmann, 13 Aug. 1949, *FRUS, 1949*, 6:1305–8; Shiloah to Sharett, 14 Aug. 1949, *DFPI*, 4:333–34. See also McGhee to Thorp, 15 Aug. 1949, *FRUS, 1949*, 6:1311–13.

29. Elath to Sharett, 2 Sept. 1949, *DFPI*, 4:424. See also memorandum of conversation by Hare, 25 Aug. 1949, *FRUS, 1949*, 6:1328–31.

30. McGhee to Acheson, 13 July 1949, RG 59, lot 441, box 4; memorandum by McGhee, 18 Aug. 1949, RG 59, 501.BB PALESTINE; McGhee to Acheson, 16 Aug. 1949, *FRUS, 1949*, 6:1315–16.

31. "Terms of Reference of the Economic Survey Mission," 1 Sept. 1949, *FRUS, 1949*, 6:1346–48. See also Acheson to Truman, 27 July 1949, PSF, General, box 117; memorandum of conversation by Kirk, 2 Aug. 1949, RG 59, 501.BB PALESTINE; Truman Diary, 2 Sept. 1949, PSF, Truman Diaries File, box 278; Clapp, "Approach."

32. Memorandum of conversation by Clark, 2 Sept. 1949, *FRUS, 1949*, 6:1350–54. See also Burdett to Acheson, 22 Aug. 1949, Fritzlan to Acheson, 22 Aug. 1949, Dorsz to Acheson, 24 Aug., 2, 3 Sept. 1949, Patterson to Acheson, 24 Aug. 1949, Tenney to Acheson, 9 Sept. 1949, McGhee to Clapp, 16 Sept. 1949, RG 59, 501.BB PALESTINE; circular cable by Acheson, 9 Sept. 1949, Clapp to McGhee, 1 Oct. 1949, *FRUS, 1949*, 6:1369n, 1415–17; McGhee to Clapp, 17 Oct. 1949, Clapp Papers, box 3.

33. Clapp to Acheson, 13 Oct. 1949, *FRUS, 1949*, 6:1425–26. See also Elath to Sharett, 1 Sept. 1949, Sasson to Sharett, 30 Sept. 1949, *DFPI*, 4:424, 517–20; memorandum of conversation by Waldo, 6 Sept. 1949, RG 59, 501.BB PALESTINE.

34. Editorial notes, memorandum of conversation by Root, 9 Nov. 1949, State Department to Truman, n.d. [late Nov. 1949], *FRUS, 1949*, 6:1472–76, 1476–81, 1505–6, 1548–51.

35. Memorandum of conversation by Root, 8 Nov. 1949, RG 59, 501.BB PALESTINE; Sandifer and Hare to Acheson, 22 Nov. 1949, Clapp Papers, box 3. See also Burdett to Acheson, 29 Oct. 1949, *FRUS, 1949*, 6:1456–59.

36. McGhee to Clapp, 16 Nov. 1949, RG 59, 501.BB PALESTINE; Acheson to Johnson, 23 Dec. 1949, *FRUS, 1949*, 6:1557–58; Hare to Acheson, 28 Dec. 1949, Clapp Papers,

box 3; Acheson to Truman, 30 Jan. 1950, Blandford to Acheson, 16 May 1950, editorial note, *FRUS, 1950,* 5:709–10, 892–93, 921.

37. Elath to Eytan, 18 Jan. 1950, *DFPI,* 5:39; Clapp to Knight, 19 June 1950, Clapp Papers, box 3. See also Lloyd to Murphy and Elsey, 19 Jan. 1950, Lloyd Papers, box 5; Murphy to Elsey, 16 Jan. 1950, Elsey Papers, box 60.

38. Palmer to Acheson, 9 May 1951, *FRUS, 1951,* 5:671–73. See also Palmer to Acheson, 9 Sept. 1950, *FRUS, 1950,* 5:992–93; Acheson to Palmer, 12 June 1951, Palmer to Acheson, 12, 14, 23 June, 18, 21 Sept. 1951, State Department position paper, 12 Oct. 1951, Webb to Palmer, 15 Nov. 1951, *FRUS, 1951,* 5:714–17, 728–30, 856–62, 864–69, 873–75, 892–903, 929.

39. Acheson to Truman, 1, 24 Nov. 1950, McCandless to Andrews, 5 Dec. 1950, Truman to Acheson, 6, 20 Dec. 1950, WHCF-HST (Confidential), box 43; memorandum of conversation by Smith, 19 Jan. 1951, Acheson Papers, box 66; minutes of meeting, 18 Feb. 1951, *DFPI,* 6:110–12; Acheson to Palmer, 19 June 1951, *FRUS, 1951,* 5:725; Acheson to Truman, 27 July 1951, RG 59, lot 53 D 444, box 7; Eban to USD, 5 May 1952, *DFPI,* 7:211–12; State Department paper, 4 Oct. 1952, *FRUS, 1952–1954,* 9:1017–26.

40. Truman to Locke, 14 Jan. 1952, PSF, Subject File, box 182. See also memorandum of conversation by Webb, 5 Nov. 1951, RG 59, General Records of the Executive Secretariat, E394, box 2; Locke to Truman, 26 Dec. 1951, 19 Feb., 7 May 1952, PSF, Subject File, box 182; Locke to Truman, 25 Apr. 1952, Harriman Papers, box 342.

41. Memorandum of conversation by Bruce, 1 Dec. 1952, RG 59, General Records of the Executive Secretariat, E394, box 2. See also Harriman to Acheson, 8 Apr. 1952, Neustadt to Murphy, 2 May 1952, Harriman Papers, box 342; Locke to Truman, 24 Sept. 1952, Locke Papers.

42. Memorandum of conversation by Funkhouser, 15 Nov. 1952, RG 59, 611.83. See also Bruce to Davis, 18 Nov. 1952, *FRUS, 1952–1954,* 9:1065–67.

43. Sharett to Eban, 21 Nov. 1952, *DFPI,* 7:651–52; Bruce to Davis, 25 Nov. 1952, *FRUS, 1952–1954,* 9:1069–71; memorandum of conversation by Plitt, 14 Nov. 1952, RG 59, lot 53 D 444, box 14. See also Sharett to Eban, 24 Nov. 1952, *DFPI,* 7:663–64; Moose to Acheson, 25 Nov. 1952, *FRUS, 1952–1954,* 9:1071–72.

44. Circular cable by Acheson, 8 May 1952, paper by Byroade, 25 July 1952, minutes of meeting, 28 Nov. 1952, *FRUS, 1952–1954,* 9:927–28, 256–62, 1072–76; Toner to Davis, 30 Apr. 1952, PSB Records, box 24.

Chapter 8

1. Benvenisti, *City,* 3–4. See also Slonim, *Jerusalem*; Cattan, *Question*; Said, "Projecting"; Lustick, "Fetish." Earlier studies include M. Brecher, *Decisions,* 10–53; Bovis, *Jerusalem Question*; M. Kaufman, *America's Jerusalem Policy*; Feintuch, *U.S. Policy*; Neff, "Jerusalem," 20–45.

2. Minutes of cabinet meeting (Hebrew), 23 Feb. 1949, Protocols-PGI, vol. 19; Sharett to Eban, 16 Jan. 1949, minutes of meeting, 22 Apr. 1949, *DFPI,* 2:377, 585–89; Rockwell to Mattison, 20 Apr. 1949, RG 59, lot 54 D 403, box 9; Stabler to Acheson, 8 June 1949, RG 59, 501.BB PALESTINE.

3. Ethridge to Acheson, 8 Feb. 1949, McDonald to Acheson, 14 Feb. 1949, *FRUS, 1949,* 6:735–38, 749–50n. See also minutes of meeting, 7 Apr. 1949, *DFPI,* 2:555–62; Burdett to Acheson, 9 Apr. 1949, PSF, Subject File, box 181; Golani, "Zionism."

4. Acheson to McDonald, 24 June 1949, *FRUS, 1949*, 6:1137, 1174–77. See also Webb to McDonald, 14 June 1949, *FRUS, 1949*, 6:1137.

5. Most discussions of Jerusalem's "holy places" referred to ten sites in the Jerusalem-Bethlehem area: the Church of the Holy Sepulchre, Deir al Sultan, the Garden of Gethsemane, the Sanctuary of the Ascension, the Basilica of the Nativity, the Milk Grotto, and Shepherds Field (Christian); the Western Wall and Rachel's Tomb (Jewish); and Haram esh-Sharif (Muslim). See, e.g., unsigned policy paper, 28 July 1952, RG 59, lot 57 D 298, box 1.

6. Rusk to Acheson, 28 Mar. 1949, RG 59, 501.BB PALESTINE. See also Burdett to Marshall, 13 Jan. 1949, *FRUS, 1949*, 6:661–63; Acheson to Burdett, 3 Mar. 1949, RG 59, 501.BB PALESTINE; memorandum by Satterthwaite, 22 Apr. 1949, RG 59, lot 54 D 403, box 9.

7. Acheson to embassy in Baghdad, 3 Mar. 1949, RG 59, 501.BB PALESTINE. See also Lovett to Burdett, 19 Jan. 1949, Lovett to Ethridge, 19 Jan. 1949, *FRUS, 1949*, 6:681–84.

8. Satterthwaite to Acheson, 9 Feb. 1949, *FRUS, 1949*, 6:739–41; memorandum of conversation by Acheson, 10 Feb. 1949, RG 59, lot 54 D 403, box 11; Acheson to McDonald, 10, 12 Feb. 1949, RG 59, 501.BB PALESTINE; Shertok to Elath, 11 Feb. 1949, *DFPI*, 2:426; minutes of cabinet meeting (Hebrew), 23 Feb. 1949, Protocols-PGI, vol. 19.

9. Memorandum of conversation by Acheson, 5 Apr. 1949, Burdett to Acheson, 9 Apr. 1949, *FRUS, 1949*, 6:890–94, 902–4. See also Rusk to Acheson, 23 Apr. 1949, RG 59, lot 54 D 403, box 9; Eban to Elath, 27 Apr. 1949, RG 130.02, 2443/3; Weizmann to Truman, 1 May 1949, WHCF-HST (Confidential), box 43.

10. Ethridge to Acheson, 13 Apr. 1949, *FRUS, 1949*, 6:911–16.

11. Palestine Conciliation Commission, "Draft Instrument," 1 Sept. 1949, *FRUS, 1949*, 6:1356. See also Halderman to Hare, 9 Sept. 1949, RG 59, lot 54 D 403, box 11.

12. Comay to Eytan, 11 May 1949, RG 130.02, 2443/3; Foreign Ministry paper (Hebrew), 16 Sept. 1949, RG 93.08, 366/32; McDonald to Acheson, 18 Oct. 1949, *FRUS, 1949*, 6:1444–45. See also Eban to Sharett, 13 Sept. 1949, *DFPI*, 4:462–63; Burdett to Acheson, 16 Sept. 1949, Ford to Acheson, 20 Sept. 1949, *FRUS, 1949*, 6:1390–92; Keren to Comay, 21 Sept. 1949, RG 130.02, 2443/3.

13. State Department position paper, 14 Sept. 1949, *FRUS, 1949*, 6:1383–87; Acheson to McDonald, 30 Sept. 1949, RG 59, 501.BB PALESTINE. See also Truman to Weizmann, 13 Aug. 1949, editorial note, *FRUS, 1949*, 6:1305–8, 1394; Eban to Sharett, 2 Aug. 1949, Keren to Comay, 21 Sept. 1949, RG 130.02, 2443/3; McGhee to Rusk, 21 Sept. 1949, RG 59, lot 54 D 403, box 10.

14. McDonald to Clifford, 30 Nov. 1949, Clifford Papers, box 13; Elath to Eytan, 24 Nov., 2 Dec. 1949, *DFPI*, 4:646, 674. See also intelligence report 192 A/4, 7 Dec. 1949, RG 130.02, 2443/5.

15. Acheson to Truman, 21 Nov. 1949, *FRUS, 1949*, 6:1498–99; memorandum of conversation by Acheson, 21 Nov. 1949, RG 59, General Records of the Executive Secretariat, E394.

16. Memorandum of conversation by Power, 12 Dec. 1949, RG 59, lot 54 D 403, box 9; Sharett to Evatt, 6 Nov. 1949, Levin to Comay, 25 Nov. 1949, RG 130.02, 2443/4.

17. Memorandum of conversation by Acheson, 6 Dec. 1949, *FRUS, 1949*, 6:1522–23; intelligence report 197 A/4, 8 Dec. 1949, RG 130.02, 2443/5.

18. "The Jerusalem Dilemma," *New York Times*, 21 Jan. 1950, p. 16; "The Jerusalem

Plan," *New York Times*, 6 Apr. 1950, p. 28. See also Feldblum, *American Catholic Press*, 71–90.

19. Sharett to Ben-Gurion, 10 Dec. 1949, *DFPI*, 4:694; McDonald to Acheson, 5 Dec. 1949, *FRUS, 1949*, 6:1521–22. See also Sharett to Eytan, 12 Dec. 1949, Eban to Eytan, 12 Dec. 1949, Eytan to Sharett, 13 Dec. 1949, *DFPI*, 4:702–3, 703–4, 709.

20. Memorandum of conversation by Stabler, 20 Sept. 1949, RG 59, lot 54 D 403, box 9. See also Sharett to Shiloah and Sasson, 9 Aug. 1949, Sharett to Eban, 15 Aug. 1949, *DFPI*, 4:304–7, 347–51; Hare to Rusk, 8 Sept. 1949, McDonald to Acheson, 11 Sept. 1949, *FRUS, 1949*, 6:1366, 1367; Bialer, "Road."

21. Hare to Acheson, 17 Dec. 1949, memorandum of conversation by Rockwell, 15 Dec. 1949, *FRUS, 1949*, 6:1547–48, 1543–44. See also Ben-Gurion Diary, 14 Dec. 1949, Sharett to Eytan, 14 Dec. 1949, Ben-Gurion to Sharett, 16 Dec. 1949, *DFPI*, 4:716–20, 722, 729–30; Acheson to McDonald, 20 Dec. 1949, *FRUS, 1949*, 6:1555.

22. State Department policy paper, "Israel," 6 Feb. 1951, memorandum of conversation by McGhee, 11 Jan. 1950, *FRUS, 1951*, 5:570–77, 682–84.

23. Acheson to McDonald, 4 Jan. 1950, *FRUS, 1950*, 5:667–68. See also Acheson to Ford, 1 Sept. 1950, *FRUS, 1950*, 5:991; memorandum by Lourie, 6 Feb. 1951, RG 93.08, 338/11; circular cable by Sharett, 10 Aug. 1951, *DFPI*, 6:540–41.

24. Circular telegram by Eytan, 5 May 1952, U.S. aide-mémoire, 9 July 1952, *DFPI*, 7: 209, 355. See also Bruce to Davis, 3 July 1952, Davis to Acheson, 6, 9 July 1952, *FRUS, 1952– 1954*, 9:960–61, 961–62; Eban to Bendor, 19 May 1952, *DFPI*, 7:229–30.

25. Rosenne to Eytan, 11 July 1952, RG 130.02, 2444/4; Eban to USD, [23] July 1952, *DFPI*, 7:392–93. See also memorandum of conversation by Waller, 23 July 1952, *FRUS, 1952–1954*, 9:965–68; Eban to USD, 7 Aug. 1952, *DFPI*, 7:417–18.

26. Davis to Acheson, 11 Aug. 1952, *FRUS, 1952–1954*, 9:978–79; Sharett to Eban, 10 Aug. 1952, Sharett to Eban, 24 Dec. 1952, *DFPI*, 7:421–22, 726.

27. Memorandum of conversation by Yeomans, 14 Dec. 1949, RG 59, lot 54 D 403, box 9; memorandum of conversation by Acheson, 20 Dec. 1949, RG 59, General Records of the Executive Secretariat, E394; Eban to Garreau, 30 Dec. 1949, *DFPI*, 4:773–74; progress report on NSC 27/3, 28 Feb. 1950, RG 319, P&O 091 Israel 1950 (section 1); Sayre to Truman, 4 Apr. 1950, *FRUS, 1950*, 5:837–39.

28. Acheson to Sayre, 14 Jan. 1950, *FRUS, 1950*, 5:690. See also Eytan to Eban, 22 Dec. 1949, *DFPI*, 4:755–56; memorandum of conversation by McGhee, 17 Jan. 1950, *FRUS, 1950*, 5:692–96; Elath to Sharett, 17 Jan. 1950, minutes of meeting, 23 Jan. 1950, Eban to Elath, 21 Feb. 1950, Eban to Lourie and Elath, 28 Mar. 1950, *DFPI*, 5:36–37, 47–48, 137, 201; memorandum of conversation by Rockwell, 19 Apr. 1950, Austin to Acheson, 14 June 1950, *FRUS, 1950*, 5:864–65, 931.

29. Memorandum of conversation by Maffitt, 13 June 1950, *FRUS, 1950*, 5:927–28; Eban to Sharett, 30 Aug. 1950, *DFPI*, 5:504–5; Berry to Acheson, 21 Sept. 1950, *FRUS, 1950*, 5:1015.

30. Memorandum of conversation by Rockwell, 26 July 1950, *FRUS, 1950*, 5:957–58. See also Progress Report on NSC 27/3, 15 July 1950, State Department policy paper, 10 Oct. 1950, *FRUS, 1950*, 5:953–54, 1029–32.

31. Eban to Eytan, 28 Dec. 1949, *DFPI*, 4:770–71; Weizmann to Truman, 3 Jan. 1950, *FRUS, 1950*, 5:658–61. See also McDonald to Clifford, 13 Dec. 1949, Clifford Papers, box 13; Rafael to Sharett, 29 Dec. 1949, *DFPI*, 4:763; memorandum by Crum, 2 Feb. 1950, PSF, Subject, box 181; Weizmann to Ewing, 2 Jan. 1950, RG 130.02, 2403/18.

32. Hahn, "Alignment," 678–84.

33. Memorandums of conversations by Clark, 1, 28 Aug. 1950, *FRUS, 1950,* 5:981–82, 1100–1106. See also memorandum of conversation by Stabler, 30 Aug. 1950, *FRUS, 1950,* 5: 982n; State Department policy statement, "Iraq," 9 Nov. 1950, RG 59, 611.87.

34. Austin to Acheson, 20 Dec. 1952, *FRUS, 1952–1954,* 9:1083–86. See also report of the Jerusalem Committee, 20 Aug. 1952, Comay to Eban, 17 Sept. 1952, Eytan to Eban, 5 Nov. 1952, Sharett to Eban, 24 Nov. 1952, *DFPI,* 7:447–49, 525, 608–9, 662; Davis to Acheson, 14 Nov. 1952, *FRUS, 1952–1954,* 9:1055–56.

35. State Department position paper, 4 Oct. 1952, Minor to Acheson, 19 Dec. 1952, *FRUS, 1952–1954,* 9:1025, 1083.

36. State Department policy paper, "Jerusalem," 12 Oct. 1951, *FRUS, 1951,* 5:903–5; memorandum of conversation by Bruce, 18 Dec. 1952, RG 59, General Records of the Executive Secretariat, E394, box 2. See also memorandum of conversation by McGhee, 4 Sept. 1951, editorial note, *FRUS, 1951,* 5:850, 905n; Bruce to Davis, 18 Nov. 1952, *FRUS, 1952–1954,* 9:1067.

Chapter 9

1. Gass to Bernstein, 30 July, 4 Aug. 1948, Bernstein to Gass, 31 July, 3 Aug. 1948, Eytan to Ladas, 16 Aug. 1948, RG 130.02, 2420/4; Mattison to Hare, 12 July 1949, *FRUS, 1949,* 6: 137–40; memorandum by Wilkins, 9 Nov. 1949, RG 59, lot 54 D 403, box 10.

2. Elath to Henderson, 16 June 1948, RG 130.02, 2420/4. See also Kirschner to Shertok, 13 Sept. 1948, Eliash to Comay, 23 June 1949, RG 130.02, 2420/4; Epstein to Ben-Gurion, 14 Oct. 1948, *DFPI,* 2:57.

3. Memorandum of conversation by Henderson, 28 May 1948, RG 59, lot 53 D 444, box 11; Hare to Satterthwaite, 26 Feb. 1949, RG 59, 767N.83; State Department policy paper, 5 May 1949, *FRUS, 1949,* 6:216–17; memorandum of conversation by Nelson, 12 Aug. 1949, RG 59, 501.BB PALESTINE.

4. Eytan to Eban, 11 Apr. 1949, *DFPI,* 2:569; Acheson to Gifford, 1 Aug. 1949, RG 59, 501.BB PALESTINE. See also Eban to Elath, 26 July 1949, Eban to Lie, 1 Sept. 1949, *DFPI,* 4:250–52, 421; Austin to Acheson, 26 July 1949, Ross to Acheson, 3 Sept. 1949, Patterson to Acheson, 10 Sept. 1949, *FRUS, 1949,* 6:1253–54, 1358, 1373–74; memorandum of conversation by McEnerney, 8 Sept. 1951, *FRUS, 1949,* 6:1367–69.

5. Eakens to Barrow, 19 Aug. 1949, *FRUS, 1949,* 6:143–45. See also Bromley to Clark, 20 June 1949, Patterson to Acheson, 26 Sept. 1949, RG 59, 501.BB PALESTINE; Acheson to Holmes, 20 July 1949, Douglas to Acheson, 15, 23 Aug. 1949, embassy in Baghdad to Acheson, 24 Aug. 1949, Webb to Patterson, 26 Sept. 1949, *FRUS, 1949,* 6:137–41, 142–49, 1373–74, 1404–5; record of meeting by Brinson, 12 June 1950, FO 371/82467.

6. Acheson to Holmes, 30 Dec. 1949, *FRUS, 1949,* 6:162–64; memorandums of conversations by Funkhouser, 31 Jan., 6 Feb., 25 Apr. 1950, *FRUS, 1950,* 5:21–23, 47–51.

7. State Department paper, 21 Apr. 1950, RG 59, 501.BB PALESTINE. See also NEA policy statement, "Iraq," 11 Sept. 1950, RG 59, 611.87; memorandum of conversation by Barrow, n.d. [Sept. 1952], *FRUS, 1952–1954,* 9:2336–38.

8. Memorandum of discussion, 19 Sept. 1950, *FRUS, 1950,* 5:301–2; Thayer to McGhee, 20 Oct. 1950, Thayer to Perry, 15 Feb. 1951, RG 59, lot 55 D 5, box 2; paper by Bevin, 27 Nov. 1950, CAB 129, CP(50)283, PRO; minutes of meeting, 30 Nov. 1950, CAB 128/18,

CM 79(50)4; memorandums of conversations by Stabler, 27 Apr., 19 June 1951, Caffery to Acheson, 4 May 1951, *FRUS, 1951,* 5:363–65, 368–70, 661.

9. McGhee to Acheson, 16 May 1951, RG 59, lot 55 D 5, box 1. See also memorandum by Wilkins, 9 Nov. 1949, RG 59, lot 54 D 403, box 10; U.S.-U.K. statement, 17 Nov. 1949, Webb to legation in Lebanon, 23 Nov. 1949, circular cable, 1 Dec. 1949, *FRUS, 1949,* 6:80– 81, 156–57; memorandum of conversation by Morrison, 3 Apr. 1951, FO 800/636, Eg/51/2; minutes of meeting, 5 Apr. 1951, CAB 128, CM 24(51)3; Acheson to Gifford, 23 May 1951, Acheson to Caffery, 12 June 1951, *FRUS, 1951,* 5:697–98, 712–14; Jones to White, 19 June 1951, RG 59, lot 55 D 5, box 1.

10. Caffery to Acheson, 5 Feb. 1950, *FRUS, 1950,* 5:722; Eytan to McDonald, 14 Feb. 1950, *DFPI,* 5:124–25; memorandum of conversation by Stabler, 12 Feb. 1951, memorandum by Ortiz, 30 Apr. 1951, RG 59, lot 55 D 5, box 1.

11. Eban to Sharett, 29 June 1951, *DFPI,* 6:419–20. See also Comay to Eytan, 22 June 1951, editorial note, Eban to Sharett, 1 July 1951, *DFPI,* 6:395–96, 404, 424–27; memorandum by Meroz, 10 July 1951, RG 130.02, 2419/8.

12. Davis to Acheson, 20 July 1951, *FRUS, 1951,* 5:787–88; Eban to Sharett, 1, 21 July 1951, *DFPI,* 6:424–27, 488–89. See also Sharett to Eban, 5 July 1951, circular cable by Eytan, 8 July 1951, Eytan to Eban, 13 July 1951, Lourie to Sharett, 17 July 1951, *DFPI,* 6:441–46, 460–62, 470.

13. Morrison to Franks, 7 July 1951, FO 371/90194, JE 1261/125. See also memorandum of conversation by Waldo, 10 July 1951, RG 59, lot 55 D 5, box 1; Franks to Morrison, 10 July 1951, FO 371/90194, JE 1261/129; Gifford to Acheson, 11 July 1951, *FRUS, 1951,* 5:763; minutes of meeting, 16 July 1951, CAB 128, CM52(51)2.

14. Acheson to Caffery, 16 July 1951, Caffery to Acheson, 17 July 1951, *FRUS, 1951,* 5:772, 776. See also Austin to Acheson, 18 July 1951, *FRUS, 1951,* 5:780.

15. Jones to McGhee, 17 July 1951, RG 59, lot 55 D 5, box 1; Acheson to Caffery, 7 July 1951, *FRUS, 1951,* 5:753. See also memorandum of conversation by McGhee, 15 June 1951, *FRUS, 1951,* 5:720–22.

16. Gross to Acheson, 20 July 1951, *FRUS, 1951,* 5:788–90. See also Austin to Acheson, 3 July 1951, Caffery to Acheson, 25 July 1951, *FRUS, 1951,* 5:743, 797; Jones to McGhee, 19 July 1951, RG 59, lot 55 D 5, box 1.

17. Acheson to Austin, 9 July 1951, *FRUS, 1951,* 5:756–57. See also Acheson to Caffery, 19, 24 July 1951, Austin to Acheson, 19 July 1951, *FRUS, 1951,* 5:781–82, 784–85, 796–97.

18. Keren to USD, 6 Aug. 1951, *DFPI,* 6:523–24. See also Austin to Acheson, 30 July 1951, Webb to Caffery, 31 Aug. 1951, *FRUS, 1951,* 5:807–8, 848; Ortiz and Stabler to Acheson, 8 Aug. 1951, Stabler to Jones, 13 Aug. 1951, Jones to McGhee, 30 Aug. 1951, RG 59, lot 55 D 5, box 1; Jebb to Morrison, 24 July 1951, FO 371/90196, JE 1261/181.

19. Eban to McGhee, 22 Aug. 1951, circular cable by Acheson, 23 Aug. 1951, Security Council resolution, 1 Sept. 1951, *FRUS, 1951,* 5:838–39, 840, 848–49; Eban to Sharett, 24 Aug. 1951, Rafael to Eytan, 31 Aug. 1951, *DFPI,* 6:570–71, 587–88; McGhee to Acheson, 28 Aug. 1951, RG 59, lot 55 D 5, box 1; minute by Garnett, 22 Aug. 1951, FO 371/90198, JE 1261/251.

20. Memorandum of conversation by Ludlow, 15 Aug. 1951, RG 59, lot 55 D 5, box 2. See also Jones to McGhee, 30 Aug. 1951, RG 59, lot 55 D 5, box 1; Caffery to Acheson, 11 Sept. 1951, *FRUS, 1951,* 5:855.

21. Acheson to Caffery, 8 Feb. 1952, *FRUS, 1952–1954,* 9:892–93; U.S. aide-mémoire,

n.d. [2 Sept. 1952], RG 59, lot 55 D 5, box 4. See also minutes of meeting, 14 Feb. 1952, *DFPI*, 6:80–83; Kopper to Bryan, 10 Mar. 1952, RG 59, lot 55 D 5, box 1.

22. Eban to Ben-Gurion, 15 Oct. 1951, *DFPI*, 6:706–7. See also Comay to Eban, 10 Jan. 1952, Eban to Eytan, 21 May 1952, USD to Eban, 26 Sept. 1952, *DFPI*, 7:26–27, 240–41, 545; Gross to Hickerson, 22 Jan. 1952, memorandum of conversation by Waller, 5 Jan. 1953, *FRUS, 1952–1954*, 9:883–84, 1088–93.

23. Memorandum of conversation by Acheson, 20 Oct. 1950, *FRUS, 1950*, 5:1033–35. See also Heyd to Herlitz, 1, 8 Feb. 1949, Heyd to Sharett, 16 Feb. 1949, *DFPI*, 2:413, 420; memorandum of conversation by Wilkins, 25 July 1949, RG 59, lot 54 D 403, box 9; memorandum of conversation by Acheson, 8 May 1951, *FRUS, 1951*, 5:667–70.

24. State Department policy paper, 6 Feb. 1951, *FRUS, 1951*, 5:570–77. See also progress report on NSC 47/2, 27 Feb. 1950, State Department report, 28 Apr. 1950, NE paper, 28 Dec. 1950, *FRUS, 1950*, 5:138–41, 763–66, 271–78; minute by Wardrop, 26 Oct. 1950, FO 371/82550.

25. Acheson to Truman, 21 Dec. 1951, *FRUS, 1951*, 5:971–72. See also McDonald to Acheson, 8 Aug. 1950, memorandum of conversation by Acheson, 20 Oct. 1950, *FRUS, 1950*, 5:966–67, 1033–35; Keren to USD, 24 Aug. 1950, *DFPI*, 5:493–97.

26. Sharett to Elath, 21 Oct. 1949, *DFPI*, 4:567. See also unsigned memorandum, 23 Nov. 1948, memorandum of conversation by Satterthwaite, 2 Dec. 1948, Mattison to Mulliken, 2 Feb. 1949, RG 59, lot 54 D 403, box 2; Acheson to Truman, n.d. [ca. Mar. 1949], PSF, Subject, box 159.

27. Hare to Acheson, 6 Dec. 1949, RG 59, lot 54 D 403, box 11; memorandum by MLP [probably Moshe Perlzweig], 27 Jan. 1950, Goldmann Papers, Z6/2006. See also memorandum of conversation by Stabler, 18 Oct. 1949, RG 59, 501.BB PALESTINE; minutes of Foreign Ministry meeting, 31 Oct. 1949, Goldmann Papers, Z6/242.

28. Progress report, 13 Sept. 1950, *FRUS, 1950*, 5:1005–6; memorandum of conversation by Barrow, 7 May 1951, memorandum of conversation by Jones, 2 Aug. 1951, *FRUS, 1951*, 5:663–67, 813–15.

29. Adenauer statement to Bundestag, 27 Sept. 1951, minutes of meeting by Sharett, 19 Nov. 1951, *DFPI*, 6:665–66, 808–19; memorandum of conversation by Webb, 8 Nov. 1951, RG 59, lot 53 D 444, box 14; memorandum of conversation by Acheson, 19 Nov. 1951, *FRUS, 1951*, 5:935–40; Sharett to Eban, 5 Sept. 1952, circular cable by information division, 8 Sept. 1952, *DFPI*, 7:498, 503–5; Acheson to Truman, 22 Apr. 1952, PSF, Subject File, box 181; memorandum of conversation by Byroade, 11 Mar. 1952, Acheson papers, box 67; Acheson to State Department, 25 May 1952, Acheson to Sharett, 3 June 1952, and Sharett to Acheson, 16 June 1952, *FRUS, 1952–1954*, 9:938–40.

30. Donnelly to Acheson, 16 Sept. 1952, *FRUS, 1952–1954*, 9:999–1000. See also Palmer to Acheson, 7 June 1951, Acheson to Palmer, 19 June 1951, *FRUS, 1951*, 5:704–6, 725; Cannon to Acheson, 3 Mar. 1952, Acheson to Cannon, 12 Mar. 1952, Donnelly to Acheson, 6 Sept. 1952, *FRUS, 1952–1954*, 9:901–10, 991; Sharett to Eban, 7 Sept. 1952, *DFPI*, 7:501.

31. Minutes of meeting, 22 Sept. 1952, *DFPI*, 7:533–38; Acheson to Donnelly, 6 Sept. 1952, circular cable by Acheson, 23 Sept. 1952, memorandum of conversation by Waller, 22 Sept. 1952, *FRUS, 1952–1954*, 9:992, 1002–3.

32. Caffery to Acheson, 12 Nov. 1952, Lobenstine to Acheson, 30 Sept. 1952, *FRUS, 1952–1954*, 9:1052–53, 1013–14. See also memorandum of conversation by Stabler, 15 Nov. 1952, Hart to Jernegan, 19 Nov. 1952, RG 59, lot 55 D 5, boxes 1, 5; memorandum of conversation by Funkhouser, 1 Apr. 1953, *FRUS, 1952–1954*, 9:1160–64.

Chapter 10

1. McDonald to Acheson, 5 Feb. 1949, RG 59, 711.67N; Franks to Bevin, 27 Apr. 1950, FO 371/82523; report by Herlitz (Hebrew), 7 June 1951, RG 130.20, 2467/3. See also Eytan to Keren (Hebrew), 19 June 1950, Herlitz to Keren (Hebrew), 23 June 1950, RG 130.20, 2479/8; Foreign Ministry paper (Hebrew), 3 June 1951, RG 130.20, 2479/9; Ben-Gurion to Truman, 31 May 1951, Truman to Ben-Gurion, 6 June 1951, RG 93.08, 337/1, 4; memorandum by Bendor (Hebrew), 19 July 1951, RG 130.20, 2467/4.

2. Minutes of meeting, 9 July 1951, *DFPI*, 6:450–52; memorandum of conversation by Sharett, 1 July 1952, RG 130.20, 2474/27. See also memorandum by Bartley Crum, 2 Feb. 1950, PSF, Subject, box 181; note of an interview, [30 Aug. 1950], RG 130.20, 2464/8.

3. Elath to McDonald, 16 Mar. 1949, RG 93.08, 373/23. See also McDonald to Clifford, 16, 24 Aug. 1948, 11 June 1949, Clifford Papers, box 13; Lourie to Eytan, 22 July 1949, Kollek to Keren (Hebrew), 30 June 1950, Keren to Kollek (Hebrew), 18 July 1950, Keren to USD (Hebrew), 23 May 1951, RG 130.20, 2479/8–9; Sharett to Niles, 18 Mar. 1951, RG 130.02, 2414/27; Kollek to Niles, 31 May 1951, Ben-Gurion to Harriman, 31 May 1951, Ben-Gurion Papers, Correspondence File; Jacobson to Cohn, 1, 15 Apr. 1952, Weizmann Papers, box 1; Eban to Sharett (Hebrew), 21 Apr. 1952, RG 130.20, 2460/5.

4. Eban to Sharett, 13 May 1952, RG 130.20, 2466/5. See also Epstein to Celler, n.d. [Jan. 1949], RG 93.08, 366/26; Epstein to Shertok, 2 Feb. 1949, RG 130.20, 2479/10; Herlitz to Sharett (Hebrew), 8 Oct. 1950, RG 130.02, 2414/26; Keren to USD, 5 Jan. 1951, RG 130.20, 2479/8.

5. Herlitz to Levin, 8 June 1951, RG 130.20, 2479/9. See also Hahn, "View," 525–27.

6. Humelsine to Acheson, 7 June 1949, RG 59, General Records of the Executive Secretariat, E394; memorandum by Sablalot, 15 May 1948, RG 330, CD 6-3-1; Humelsine to Acheson, 9 June 1949, RG 59, General Records of the Executive Secretariat, E394. See also paper by Kennan (PPS/36), 19 Aug. 1948, RG 59, lot 64 D 563, box 30; brief by naval attaché, 18 Apr. 1949, RG 330, CD 18-2-42.

7. Hare to Webb, 3 July 1950, *FRUS, 1950*, 5:947n. See also unsigned memorandum to Truman, 4 May 1950, PSF, Subject File, box 184; memorandum of conversation by Webb, 18 May 1950, memorandum of conversation by Acheson, 6 July 1950, RG 59, General Records of the Executive Secretariat, E394; memorandum of conversation by Acheson, 6 June 1950, Acheson Papers, box 65; memorandum of conversation by Lloyd, 18 Oct. 1950, Elsey Papers, box 60.

8. Eytan to Sharett, 13 June 1949, minutes of meeting, 9 July 1951, Keren to USD, 24 Aug. 1950, *DFPI*, 4:121–28, 6:450–52, 5:493–97. See also Heyd to Sharett (Hebrew), 15 Feb. 1949, circular cable by Sharett, 3 July 1951, *DFPI*, 2:430–31, 6:429–31; circular cable by Eytan (Hebrew), 20 Feb. 1950, USD to Elath (Hebrew), 21 Feb. 1950, RG 130.20, 2479/8.

9. NSC 47/2, 17 Oct. 1949, *FRUS, 1949*, 6:1430–40; USD policy survey (Hebrew), n.d. [ca. 1 Aug. 1950], RG 130.20, 2479/8.

10. Bloom to Truman, 3 Aug. 1948, Celler to Truman, 4 Aug. 1948, PSF, Subject File, box 184; Marshall to Truman, 23 Aug. 1948, RG 59, lot 54 D 403, box 8; McDonald to Truman, 18 Jan. 1949, Clifford Papers, box 14; Elath to Sharett, 24 Jan. 1949, *DFPI*, 2:395; Acheson to Truman, 27 Jan. 1949, WHCF-HST (Official), box 775.

11. Burdett to Acheson, 20 Apr. 1949, *FRUS, 1949*, 6:923n, 927–30. See also memorandum of conversation by Marshall, 17 Sept. 1948, memorandum of conversation by Webb, 2 Mar. 1949, RG 59, lot 53 D 444, box 12; Epstein to Lovett, 22 Dec. 1948, RG 93.08, 366/32;

Epstein to Sharett, 25 Feb. 1949, *DFPI,* 2:457; Rusk to Acheson, 23 Apr. 1949, RG 59, lot 54 D 403, box 9.

12. Elath to Sharett, 10 May 1949, *DFPI,* 4:38–39; Acheson to Ethridge, 12 May 1949, *FRUS, 1949,* 6:1004–5. See also Elath to Sharett, 4 May 1949, *DFPI,* 4:19–20.

13. Elath to Sharett, 25 Aug. 1949, *DFPI,* 4:396–97. See also Rockwell to Acheson, 10 Sept. 1949, *FRUS, 1949,* 6:1375; Elath to Sharett, 26 Aug. 1949, *DFPI,* 4:400.

14. CIA, SR-13, 27 Sept. 1949, PSF, Intelligence File, box 260; Ethridge to Truman, 11 Apr. 1949, *FRUS, 1949,* 6:905–6; minutes of undersecretary's meeting, UM M-234, 18 Aug. 1950, RG 59, General Records of the Executive Secretariat, E396.3; memorandum of conversation by McGhee, 13 Dec. 1950, RG 59, lot 55 D 5, box 5. See also CIA, CIA 9-48, 16 Sept. 1948, CIA, CIA 11-48, 17 Nov. 1948, PSF, Subject File, box 204.

15. Memorandum of conversation by Defense Department, 17 Dec. 1951, *FRUS, 1951,* 5:1071–72; CIA, SR-13, 27 Sept. 1949, PSF, Intelligence File, box 260. See also minutes of meeting, 23 Jan. 1952, RG 59, lot 64 D 563, box 77.

16. PPS memorandum, 24 July 1950, RG 59, lot 64 D 563, box 30; minutes of NSC meeting, 13 Oct. 1950, PSF, NSC File, box 220; State Department staff study, 5 Oct. 1950, RG 59, lot 54 D 403, box 8; memorandum by Stabler, 3 Jan. 1951, RG 59, lot 55 D 5, boxes 5, 1.

17. Memorandum of conversation by Stabler, 12 Aug. 1950, RG 59, lot 55 D 5, box 5. See also Lovett to Truman, 13 Jan. 1949, PSF, Subject File, box 170; State Department paper, "Jordan," 17 Apr. 1950, *FRUS, 1950,* 5:1094–99; State Department staff study, 5 Oct. 1950, RG 59, lot 54 D 403, box 8; Van Atten to Acheson, 5 Oct. 1951, RG 330, CD 091.3 (Russia).

18. CIA memorandum, 20 July 1951, PSF, Intelligence series; McGhee to Acheson, 20 July 1951, PPS Paper, 24 July 1951, Drew to Acheson, 31 July 1951, Drew to Acheson, 20 Sept. 1951, *FRUS, 1951,* 5:983–84, 985–89, 990–91, 994–96; Satloff, *From Abdullah to Hussein.*

19. Memorandum of conversation by Acheson, 4 Mar. 1949, RG 59, lot 53 D 444, box 12; memorandum of conversation by Clark, 1 Aug. 1950, *FRUS, 1950,* 5:1100–1106. See also Pinkerton to Lovett, 11 Jan. 1949, Acheson to Pinkerton, 11 Feb. 1949, *FRUS, 1949,* 6: 641–42; Acheson to embassy in Beirut, 5 Mar. 1949, RG 59, 711.90; Pinkerton to Acheson, 19, 24 Apr. 1950, RG 59, 611.83A.

20. Minor to Acheson, 6, 7 Nov. 1951, RG 59, 611.83A; Bruins to Acheson, 21 July 1951, RG 59, 611.83A4.

21. Memorandum of conversation by Plitt, 28 Oct. 1952, Acheson Papers, box 67a; Funkhouser to Hart, 24 Oct. 1952, RG 59, 611.83A. See also Lobenstine to Acheson, 23 Sept., 2 Oct. 1952, *FRUS, 1952–1954,* 9:1008–9, 1014–16.

22. Memorandum of conversation by Awalt, 12 Dec. 1949, RG 59, lot 57 D 298, box 6; draft policy statement, 18 May 1949, RG 59, 711.90F; Ibn Saud to Truman, 31 Mar. 1949, WHCF-HST (Confidential), box 41. See also Wooldridge to secretary of navy, 24 Feb. 1949, RG 330, CD 6-3-3; memorandum by NEA, 3 Oct. 1949, RG 59, lot 54 D 403, box 11; Hare to Rusk, 2 Dec. 1949, RG 59, 711.90F; Wilkins to Pirhalla, 21 July 1950, RG 59, lot 57 D 298, box 10.

23. Draft policy statement, 18 May 1949, RG 59, 711.90F; memorandum of conversation by Childs, 28 Sept. 1949, *FRUS, 1949,* 6:1613–15; memorandum of conversation by Awalt, 12 Dec. 1949, RG 59, lot 57 D 298, box 6. See also Hare to Lovett, 25 Aug. 1948, RG 59, lot 53 D 444, box 12.

24. Memorandum of conversation of meeting, n.d. [23 Mar. 1950], WHCF-HST (Confidential), box 41. See also Childs to Marshall, 9 Dec. 1948, RG 59, 711.90F; Acheson to Truman, 8 Aug. 1951, Truman to Graham, 11 Aug. 1951, Awalt to Jones, 9 July 1951, *FRUS, 1951*, 5:1059–62; Ibn Saud to Truman, 3 Mar. 1952, PSF, Subject File, box 170.

25. State Department policy paper, "Saudi Arabia," 5 Feb. 1951, *FRUS, 1951*, 5:1027–42. See also memorandum of conversation by McGhee, 7 Apr. 1950, McGhee Papers, box 1; Childs to Acheson, 1 May 1950, RG 59, 611.83A; Ibn Saud to Truman, 24 Aug. 1951, WHCF-HST (Confidential), box 42.

26. Memorandum of conversation by Plitt, 21 Oct. 1952, Acheson Papers, box 67A; Crocker to Acheson, 19 June 1950, RG 59, 611.87. See also State Department memorandum, 7 July 1950, PSF, Subject File, box 159; NEA policy statement, "Iraq," 11 Sept. 1950, Berry to Acheson, 16 Dec. 1952, RG 59, 611.87; paper on Iraq, 26 Dec. 1951, RG 59, lot 55 D 5, box 6; memorandum of conversation by Barrow, n.d. [Sept. 1952], *FRUS, 1952–1954*, 9:2336–38.

27. Memorandum by Stabler, 21 Feb. 1951, Stabler to Jones, 24 Sept. 1951, RG 59, lot 55 D 5, box 1. See also State Department policy statement, "Egypt," 5 July 1950, RG 59, 611.74; memorandum of conversation by Stabler, 17 July 1950, RG 59, lot 55 D 5, box 5.

28. Minutes of NSC meeting, 23 Apr. 1952, PSF, NSC series, box 220. See also State Department policy statement, "Egypt," 5 July 1950, RG 59, 611.74; draft intelligence brief, 22 Oct. 1951, steering group paper, 20 May 1952, RG 59, lot 55 D 5, boxes 4, 5; memorandum by McClintock, 1 Nov. 1952, RG 59, lot 60 D 48, box 1.

29. Memorandum by McClintock, 1 Nov. 1952, RG 59, lot 60 D 48, box 1; U.S.-U.K. "Joint Appreciation of the Egyptian Situation," 16 Sept. 1952, FO 371/96982, JE 1024/3; briefing paper for Acheson, 4 Nov. 1952, RG 59, lot 55 D 5, box 5; memorandum of conversation by Kitchen, 8 Dec. 1952, RG 59, General Records of the Executive Secretariat, E394.2, box 1; Gordon, *Nasser's Blessed Movement*.

30. Memorandum UM D-29, 19 Apr. 1949, Humelsine to Acheson, 25 Apr. 1949, RG 59, General Records of the Executive Secretariat, E394; memorandum of conversation by Acheson, 25 Apr. 1949, Acheson Papers, box 64; memorandum by Hillenkoetter, 27 Apr. 1950, PSF, Intelligence File, box 250; Hart to Gardiner, 30 July 1952, RG 59, lot 54 D 403, box 8.

31. McGhee to Burns, 11 Aug. 1950, RG 330, CD 210.3; Geren to Acheson, 28 May 1951, *FRUS, 1951*, 5:1076–78. See also memorandum of conversation by Barrow, 7 July 1949, RG 59, 711.90D; McGhee to Johnson, 1 Aug. 1949, Bolte to COS, 18 Aug. 1949, RG 319, Army COS Files, 091 Syria; Cannon to Acheson, 10 Feb. 1951, RG 59, 683.00.

32. Hart to Byroade, 13 Nov. 1952, RG 59, lot 54 D 403, box 10. See also Clark to Acheson, 18 Oct. 1951, *FRUS, 1951*, 5:1081–82; Sasson to Eliav [Hebrew], 3 July 1952, RG 130.20, 2460/5; memorandum of conversation by Funkhouser, 15 Nov. 1952, RG 59, 611.83.

33. Minor to Acheson, 19 Dec. 1952, *FRUS, 1952–1954*, 9:1082–83. See also memorandum of conversation by Acheson, 20 Aug. 1951, circular memorandum by Ortiz, 18 Oct. 1951, RG 59, lot 55 D 5, boxes 6, 1.

Chapter 11

1. Ambrose, *Eisenhower: Soldier and President*.
2. Immerman, *John Foster Dulles*.

3. Ibid., 46. See also Ambrose, *Eisenhower: The President*; Pach and Richardson, *Presidency*; Brands, *Cold Warriors*.

4. Bowie and Immerman, *Waging Peace*; Dockrill, *Eisenhower's New-Look National Security Policy*.

5. Eisenhower, *Mandate*, 249. See also Heiss, *Empire*; Petersen, "Anglo-American Rivalry"; Dimbleby and Reynolds, *Ocean*, 220.

6. Accounts critical of Eisenhower include McMahon, *Cold War*; Kolko, *Confronting*; Stookey, *America*; Saunders, *United States*. For sympathetic accounts, see Bowie and Immerman, *Waging Peace*, 213–21; Stivers, *America's Confrontation*; B. I. Kaufman, *Arab Middle East*.

7. NSC 155/1, 14 July 1953, *FRUS, 1952–1954*, 9:399–406. See also memorandum by Partridge, 26 Feb. 1953, RG 319, Army COS Files, 091 Egypt; paper by Joint Strategic Plans Group, 26 Feb. 1954, RG 218, JCS Geographic File 1954, box 11A, 381 EMMEA (11-19-47); NSC 5428, 23 July 1954, *FRUS, 1952–1954*, 9:525–36; Watson, *History*, 324–40.

8. Caraway to Radford, 20 Mar. 1956, RG 218, CJCS Radford, box 16, 091 Palestine; OCB quoted in memorandum to Nixon, 27 June 1956, WHO Files, OSANSA, Special Assistant Series, box 3. See also memorandum by Johnson, 8 Dec. 1955, JCS 1887/184, 11 May 1956, RG 218, JCS Geographic File 1954, boxes 11A, 12, 381 EMMEA (11-19-47).

9. Memorandum by Smith, 30 Sept. 1955, WHO Files, OSANSA, Special Assistant Series, box 1. See also memorandum by Gullion, 25 Feb. 1953, RG 59, lot 64 D 563, box 30; paper by Troxel, 4 Mar. 1954, RG 59, lot 57 D 298, box 5.

10. Memorandum by Gullion, 25 Feb. 1953, memorandum by Dulles, 1 June 1953, RG 59, lot 64 D 563, box 30. See also NSC 155/1, 14 July 1953, *FRUS, 1952–1954*, 9:399–406; paper by Troxel, 4 Mar. 1954, RG 59, lot 57 D 298, box 5; NSC 5428, 23 July 1954, *FRUS, 1952–1954*, 9:525–36.

11. Nizameddin, *Russia*, 20–22; Golan, *Soviet Policies*, 1–10; Behbehani, *Soviet Union*, 89–93.

12. NSC 5428, 23 July 1954, *FRUS, 1952–1954*, 9:525–36; memorandum to Nixon, 27 June 1956, WHO Files, OSANSA, Special Assistant Series, box 3. See also NSC 155/1, 14 July 1953, *FRUS, 1952–1954*, 9:399–406.

13. NSC 5428, 23 July 1954, *FRUS, 1952–1954*, 9:525–36; memorandum by Johnson, 8 Dec. 1955, RG 218, JCS Geographic File 1954, box 11A, 381 EMMEA (11-19-47); memorandum by Burdett, 31 Dec. 1955, RG 59, 684A.86; memorandum to Nixon, 27 June 1956, WHO Files, OSANSA, Special Assistant Series, box 3.

14. Armstrong to Dulles, 21 Dec. 1955, RG 59, 661.83. See also Hahn, *United States*, 191–93; State Department intelligence report, 12 Sept. 1955, RG 59, lot 66 D 70, box 64.

15. NEA draft paper, n.d. [Feb. 1953], RG 59, lot 57 D 298, box 1; memorandum by Dulles, 1 June 1953, RG 59, lot 64 D 563, box 30. See also NSC 155/1, 14 July 1953, NSC 5428, 23 July 1954, *FRUS, 1952–1954*, 9:399–406, 525–36.

16. Memorandum of conversation by Burdett, 4 May 1953, RG 59, 780.5; circular cable by Dulles, 30 July 1953, RG 59, 780.5. See also memorandum of conversation by Jernegan, 24 Apr. 1953, RG 59, 611.74; Fechteler to secretary of defense, 23 June 1953, RG 330, CD 091.1 (Middle East); Everest to Wilson, 11 Aug. 1953, RG 218, JCS Geographic File 1951–53, box 12, CCS EMMEA (11-19-47).

17. Minutes of meeting, 9 July 1953, *FRUS, 1952–1954*, 9:394–98; Phillips to Wilson, 14 Nov. 1953, RG 218, JCS Geographic File 1954, box 11A, CCS 381 EMMEA (11-19-47). See

also Berry to Dulles, 27 Feb., 22 Mar. 1953, RG 59, 780.5; minutes of NSC meeting, 1 June 1953, Whitman File: NSC Series, box 4; Wilson to Dulles, 24 Nov. 1953, RG 59, 780.5.

18. Persson, *Great Britain*, emphasizes the Anglo-U.S. origins of the pact. Anglo-Iraqi and Iraqi-Turkish origins are emphasized in Jasse, "Baghdad Pact," and Sanjian, "Formulation," respectively. Podeh, *Quest*, suggests that the pact originated in Iraqi-Egyptian rivalry for control of the Arab Middle East.

19. JSPC 883/78, 11 Aug. 1955, memorandum by Johnson, 8 Dec. 1955, RG 218, JCS Geographic File 1954, box 11A, 381 EMMEA (11-19-47). See also unsigned memorandum of conversation, 30 June 1955, RG 59, lot 66 D 70, box 65; JSPC 883/78, 11 Aug. 1955, RG 218, JCS Geographic File 1954, box 11A, 381 EMMEA (11-19-47).

20. JSPC 883/78, 11 Aug. 1955, RG 218, JCS Geographic File 1954, box 11A, 381 EMMEA (11-19-47). See also memorandums by Phillips, 31 Jan., 7 Feb. 1956, RG 218, JCS Geographic File 1954, box 12, 381 EMMEA (11-19-47).

21. Podeh, *Quest*, 125. See also minutes of meeting, 3 Sept. 1954, Whitman File: NSC Series, box 5; memorandum of conversation by Bergus, 3 Aug. 1955, RG 59, 684A.85322; Trevelyan to Eden, 3 Nov. 1955, PREM 11/859; Harkins to assistant chief of staff, 16 Dec. 1955, RG 319, Army COS Files, 091 Jordan.

22. Paper from chiefs of mission conference, 14 May 1954, NIE 30–54, 22 June 1954, NSC 5428, 23 July 1954, *FRUS, 1952–1954*, 9:510–12, 516–20, 525–36; Dulles to Lawson, 19 Jan. 1955, RG 59, 684A.86; Lawson to Dulles, 17 Feb. 1955, RG 59, 684A.86.

23. Memorandum by Radford, 12 Oct. 1955, RG 218, JCS Geographic File 1954, box 11A, 381 EMMEA (11-19-47); Radford to Wilson, 23 Mar. 1956, RG 218, JCS Geographic File 1954, box 12, 381 EMMEA (11-19-47). See also CJCS talking paper, 26 May 1955, RG 218, JCS Geographic File 1954, box 11A, 381 EMMEA (11-19-47); report by Cassady, 30 Nov. 1955, RG 218, JCS Geographic File 1954, box 12, 381 EMMEA (11-19-47); Struble to Radford, 20 Dec. 1955, RG 218, CJCS Radford, box 22, 092.2 Baghdad Pact; Radford to Wilson, 23 Dec. 1955, RG 218, JCS Geographic File 1954, box 12, 381 EMMEA (11-19-47).

24. Radford to Wilson, 30 Sept. 1955, RG 218, JCS Geographic File 1954, box 11A, 381 EMMEA (11-19-47); Troxel to Gay, 7 Dec. 1955, RG 59, lot 57 D 298, box 5; memorandum by Burdett, 31 Dec. 1955, RG 59, 684A.86; Dulles to Eisenhower, 28 Mar. 1956, Whitman File: Diary Series, box 13; State Department briefing paper SUEZ D-4/1, 10 Aug. 1956, RG 59, lot 62 D 11, box 1; State Department position paper, 18 Nov. 1956, RG 59, lot 66 D 487, box 76.

25. Stivers, "Eisenhower"; Persson, *Great Britain*; Stookey, *America*, 138; Ovendale, *Britain*; Rees, *Anglo-American Approaches*; Freiberger, *Dawn*, 83–106; Podeh, *Quest*; Ashton, *Eisenhower*.

26. NSC 5428, 23 July 1954, *FRUS, 1952–1954*, 9:525–36; Layton to Radford, 29 Mar. 1956, Whitman File: Administration Series, box 23. See also State Department position paper, 7 May 1953, *FRUS, 1952–1954*, 9:1215–18; OCB progress report on NSC 155/1, 29 July 1954, *FRUS, 1952–1954*, 9:537–39.

27. State Department paper, 7 May 1953, *FRUS, 1952–1954*, 9:1215–18; memorandum by Dulles, 1 June 1953, RG 59, lot 64 D 563, box 30; minutes of NSC meeting, 9 July 1953, Whitman File: NSC folder, box 4. See also memorandum by Gullion, 25 Feb. 1953, RG 59, lot 64 D 563, box 30; NSC 155/1, 14 July 1953, NSC 5428, 23 July 1954, *FRUS, 1952–1954*, 9: 399–406, 525–36.

28. Memorandum of conversation by Shiloah (Hebrew), 14 May 1953, RG 130.20,

2481/1. See also Eden to Churchill, 6 Mar. 1953, PREM 11/486; memorandum of conversation, 23 Mar. 1953, Dulles-Princeton Papers, Telephone Conversation Series, box 1; memorandum by Dulles, 1 June 1953, RG 59, lot 64 D 563, box 30; NSC 155/1, 14 July 1953, *FRUS, 1952–1954,* 9:399–406.

29. Aide-mémoire by Malik, 3 Apr. 1953, RG 59, lot 64 D 563, box 30; Green to Dulles, 13 May 1953, RG 59, 684A.86.

30. Unsigned policy paper, n.d. [ca. Nov. 1953], Whitman File: Administration Series. See also conclusions of conference, 14 May 1954, WHO Files, NSC Staff Papers, box 77.

31. Minutes of meeting (Hebrew), 30 Apr. 1953, RG 130.20, 2481/1; Sharett to Eytan (Hebrew), 11 Apr. 1953, RG 130.02, 2414/27. See also Sharett to Eban, 9 Mar. 1953, RG 130.02, 2450/1; address by Sharett (Hebrew), 7 Apr. 1953, RG 130.02, 2479/11; Ben-Gurion Diary (Hebrew), 30 Apr. 1953, Ben-Gurion Papers; policy paper, n.d. [ca. Nov. 1953], Whitman File: Administration Series; memorandum of conversation by Dulles, 21 Apr. 1954, Dulles Papers, White House Memoranda Series, box 1.

32. Israeli memorandums of conversations, 13, 14 May 1953, RG 130.20, 2474/4. See also Ben-Gurion Diary (Hebrew), 30 Apr. 1953, Ben-Gurion Papers; Eban to USD (Hebrew), 5, 6 May 1953, Eban to Sharett (Hebrew), 11 May 1953, RG 130.20, 2474/4; Dulles to State Department, 12 May 1953, *FRUS, 1952–1954,* 9:2065–69; Foreign Ministry paper (Hebrew), 18 May 1953, memorandum by Eliav (Hebrew), 1 June 1953, RG 130.20, 2481/1.

33. Conclusions of conference, 14 May 1954, WHO Files, NSC Staff Papers, box 77. See also memorandum by McGay, 9 Nov. 1953, RG 59, lot 57 D 298, box 2.

Chapter 12

1. Davis to Dulles, 2 Feb. 1953, *FRUS, 1952–1954,* 9:1112–13. See also Dulles to Davis, 22 Jan. 1953, Davis to Dulles, 22, 23, 27 Jan., 9 Feb. 1953, *FRUS, 1952–1954,* 9:1100–1102, 1106–7, 1123–25. For an Israeli revisionist overview of the situation on Israel's borders with Jordan and other Arab states, see Morris, *Israel's Border Wars.*

2. Bendor to Sharett (Hebrew), 29 Jan. 1953, RG 130.02, 2415/1; minutes of meeting (Hebrew), 2 Feb. 1953, RG 130.02, 2458/7; Davis to Dulles, 5 Feb. 1953, RG 59, 684A.85.

3. Green to Dulles, 5, 14 Feb. 1953, Tyler to Dulles, 8 Feb. 1953, RG 59, 684A.85.

4. Dulles to Lodge, 11 Feb. 1953, RG 59, 684A.86; Goitein to USD, 30 Jan. 1953, *DFPI,* 8:81. See also Partridge to COS, 12 Feb. 1953, RG 319, COS Files, 091 Israel; circular cable by Dulles, 12 Feb. 1953, *FRUS, 1952–1954,* 9:1131–33.

5. U.S. aide-mémoire, 16 Feb. 1953, RG 130.02, 2414/27; Davis to Dulles, 20 Feb. 1953, *FRUS, 1952–1954,* 9:1140–42. See also USD to Eban (Hebrew), 20 Feb. 1953, RG 130.02, 2309/12.

6. Tyler to Dulles, 24 Apr. 1953, RG 59, 684A.85; Smith to Russell, 27 May 1953, *FRUS, 1952–1954,* 9:1231–32. See also Eytan to Eban (Hebrew), 24 Apr. 1953, Ben-Gurion to Dulles, 24 May 1953, local commanders agreement, 8 June 1953, *DFPI,* 8:313, 411–12, 460–61; Russell to Dulles, 5 May 1953, RG 59, 684A.85; Ben-Gurion Diary (Hebrew), 14 May 1953, Ben-Gurion Papers; Dulles to Russell, 16 June 1953, *FRUS, 1952–1954,* 9:1241.

7. Sharett to Eban, 18 Oct. 1953, RG 130.02, 2377/1; Eban to Sharett (Hebrew), 20 Oct., 11, 26 Nov. 1953, RG 130.02, 2331/2–3, 2440/1; Rafael to Sharett (Hebrew), 23 Oct. 1953, RG 130.02, 2382/22.

8. Seelye to Dulles, 15 Oct. 1953, *FRUS, 1952–1954,* 9:1358–59; Russell to Dulles, 17 Oct.

1953, RG 59, 684A.85; Hacohen to Sharett, 16 Oct. 1953, *DFPI,* 8:759; Rokach, *Israel's Sacred Terrorism,* 14. See also Eban to Rafael (Hebrew), 15 Oct. 1953, RG 130.02, 2331/2; Debevoise to Craig, 16 Oct. 1953, WHCF-DDE (Confidential), box 49; Rafael to Eytan (Hebrew), 28 Nov. 1953, RG 130.02, 2381/11; Morris, "Israeli Press."

9. United Nations Security Council resolution, 24 Nov. 1953, *FRUS, 1952–1954,* 9:1436–37; memorandum of conversation by Waller, 20 Nov. 1953, RG 59, 683.84A. See also State Department press release, 18 Oct. 1953, *FRUS, 1952–1954,* 9:1367; Eban to Sharett (Hebrew), 21 Nov. 1953, RG 130.02, 2331/3.

10. Eban to Sharett, 11 Nov. 1953, *DFPI,* 8:847–49.

11. Memorandum of conversation by Shiloah, 23 Mar. 1954, RG 130.20, 2475/2; Byroade to Dulles, 7 Apr. 1954, RG 59, 684A.86; Dulles to Byroade, 10 Apr. 1954, RG 59, 684A.85. See also memorandum of conversation by Burns, 31 Mar. 1954, RG 59, 684A.85; memorandum of conversation by Dorsey, 1 Apr. 1954, RG 59, lot 57 D 298, box 11; Tyler to Dulles, 17 Apr. 1954, RG 59, 684A.86.

12. Dulles to State Department, 12–13 Apr. 1954, Aldrich to State Department, 21 Apr. 1954, circular cable by Smith, 28 Apr. 1954, *FRUS, 1952–1954,* 9:1513–14, 1529–30, 1532–36; Dulles to Byroade, 11 May 1954, RG 59, 684A.86.

13. Russell to Dulles, 3 Aug. 1954, RG 59, 684A.85. See also Mallory to Dulles, 24 May 1954, Aldrich to Dulles, 14 June 1954, U.S. aide-mémoire, 19 June 1954, Dulles to Russell, 22 June, 1 July 1954, Smith to Mallory, 13 July 1954, Russell to Dulles, 30 July 1954, RG 59, 684A.85.

14. Mallory to Dulles, 9, 28 Apr. 1955, Hoover to Mallory, 21 Apr. 1955, RG 59, 684A.85; Mallory to Dulles, 9 June, 25 Oct. 1955, RG 59, 684A.86; Lawson to Dulles, 17 Oct. 1955, RG 59, 674.84A; Dann, *King Hussein,* 19–38.

15. Memorandum of conversation, 13 May 1953, RG 130.20, 2481/1; Kahani to Kidron (Hebrew), 8 June 1953, RG 130.02, 2410/1; memorandum of conversation by Kollek (Hebrew), 23 Aug. 1953, circular cable by Eytan (Hebrew), 1 Mar. 1954, RG 130.02, 2409/2; Divon to Eytan (Hebrew), 12 Nov. 1953, *DFPI,* 8:859; Russell to Dulles, 30 Aug. 1954, *FRUS, 1952–1954,* 9:1635–36; Jernegan to Murphy, 27 Jan. 1955, RG 59, 601.84A11.

16. Circular cable by Eytan, 5 Oct. 1953, minutes of meeting (Hebrew), 18 Nov. 1953, *DFPI,* 8:718, 873–76; Russell to Dulles, 24 Aug. 1954, Lawson to Dulles, 3 Nov. 1954, RG 59, 674.84A.

17. Caffery to Dulles, 25 Apr. 1954, *FRUS, 1952–1954,* 9:1530–31; Dulles to Caffery, 5 Nov. 1954, Jones to Dulles, 20, 28 Jan., 5 Feb. 1955, Lawson to Dulles, 27 Jan., 4, 12 Feb. 1955, RG 59, 674.84A; Kane to assistant chief of staff, 14 Oct. 1954, RG 319, G-3 091 Israel; Dulles to Lawson, 14 Feb. 1955, Lawson to Dulles, 14 Feb. 1955, RG 59, 684A.86.

18. Lawson to Dulles, 1–5 Mar. 1955, Byroade to Dulles, 1 Mar. 1955, Cole to Dulles, 5–9 Mar. 1955, RG 59, 674.84A; memorandum of conversation by Allen, 14 Mar. 1955, RG 59, 684A.86.

19. Allen to Dulles, 9 Mar. 1955, RG 59, 674.84A. See also army attaché to Dulles, 1 Mar. 1955, Wadsworth to Dulles, 2, 11 Mar. 1955, Dulles to Lodge, 3, 10, 23 Mar. 1955, Dulles to Lawson, 9 Mar. 1955, RG 59, 674.84A; Glidden to Allen, 24 Mar. 1955, RG 59, 684A.86.

20. Israeli intelligence digest (Hebrew), Mar. 1955, RG 130.02, 2428/9. See also State Department paper, 15 Mar. 1955, RG 59, 611.84A; memorandum of conversation by Bergus, 25 Mar. 1955, RG 59, 674.84A; Harman to Shiloah, 25 Mar. 1955, memorandum of conversation by Hirschman, 19 May 1955, RG 130.20, 2480/7; progress report on NSC 5428, 7 Apr. 1955, White House Office: NSC Staff Files, OCB Files, box 78.

21. Lawson to Dulles, 1 Apr. 1955, Byroade to Dulles, 24 Mar., 6 Apr. 1955, RG 59, 674.84A. See also Lawson to Dulles, 25–29 Mar., 4–5 Apr. 1955, Byroade to Dulles, 26 Mar. 1955, RG 59, 674.84A; memorandum of conversation, 5 Apr. 1955, RG 130.20, 2480/7.

22. Byroade to Dulles, 24 Mar. 1955, circular cable by Dulles, 31 Mar. 1955, RG 59, 674.84A.

23. Dulles to Byroade, 6, 16 Apr. 1955, Byroade to Dulles, 8, 11–14, 19 Apr., 12 May 1955, Cole to Dulles, 11, 14 Apr. 1955, Lawson to Dulles, 22–23 Apr., 17 May 1955, memorandum of conversation by Bird, 26 Apr. 1955, RG 59, 674.84A.

24. Lodge to Dulles, 20 Apr. 1955, RG 59, 674.84A. See also Dulles to Lodge, 11, 19 Apr. 1955, Lawson to Dulles, 18, 22 Apr. 1955, RG 59, 674.84A.

25. Lawson to Dulles, 18–23 May 1955, RG 59, 684A.86; Byroade to Dulles, 19 May, 4, 8 June 1955, Dulles to Byroade, 1 July 1955, Dulles to Lawson, 20 May 1955, RG 59, 674.84A; Dorsey to Allen, 1 June 1955, RG 59, 674.84A3; memorandum of conversation by Dulles, 15 June 1955, unsigned memorandum of conversation, 16 June 1955, *FRUS, 1955–1957*, 14: 245–48.

26. Jenkins to Dulles, 6 June 1955, RG 59, 674.84A. See also Moose to Dulles, 6 June 1955, Gellman to Dulles, 6 June 1955, RG 59, 684A.86; memorandums of conversations by Jernegan, 16 June, 1 July 1955, RG 59, 674.84A.

27. Lawson to Dulles, 29 June 1955, RG 59, 674.84A. See also Lawson to Dulles, 12–13, 18 June, 5 July, 3, 11 Aug. 1955, Byroade to Dulles, 9–13 June, 4, 19 July, 22, 24 Aug. 1955, Dulles to Lawson, 10, 20 June 1955, Cole to Dulles, 8, 15–16, 21, 25 July, 1, 16 Aug. 1955, RG 59, 674.84A.

28. Lawson to Dulles, 31 Aug. 1955, RG 59, 674.84A. See also memorandum of conversation by Russell, 25 Aug. 1955, unsigned messages from embassy in Cairo, 26 Aug., 1 Sept. 1955, *FRUS, 1955–1957*, 14:397–99, 437–38; Byroade to Allen, 27 Aug. 1955, RG 59, 684A.86; Lawson to Dulles, 26 Aug.–1 Sept. 1955, Byroade to Dulles, 27, 31 Aug. 1955, RG 59, 674.84A.

29. Memorandum of conversation, 31 Aug. 1955, Dulles-Princeton Papers, Telephone Conversation Series, box 4; memorandum of conversation by Burdett, 31 Aug. 1955, Lawson to Dulles, 1 Sept. 1955, Byroade to Dulles, 1 Sept. 1955, RG 59, 674.84A.

30. Circular cable by Dulles, 30 Aug. 1955, Mallory to Dulles, 1, 4 Sept. 1955, RG 59, 684A.86; Moose to Dulles, 2 Sept. 1955, Byroade to Dulles, 4 Sept. 1955, RG 59, 674.84A; minutes of NSC meeting, 8 Sept. 1955, Whitman File: NSC Series, box 7.

31. Heath to Dulles, 13, 15 May 1955, Lawson to Dulles, 13, 14, 17, 19 May 1955, Cole to Dulles, 3 Aug. 1955, RG 59, 683A.84A.

32. Lawson to Dulles, 29 Sept., 3 Oct. 1955, Emmerson to Dulles, 29 Sept. 1955, Wilkins to Russell, 5 Oct. 1955, Dulles to Lawson, 6 Oct. 1955, RG 59, 683A.84A; memorandum of conversation by Boardman, 4 Oct. 1955, RG 59, 684A.86.

33. Reports on meetings (Hebrew), 15, 19 Jan. 1953, Eytan to Eban (Hebrew), 18 Mar. 1953, *DFPI*, 8:32–35, 41–45, 231–32; Davis to Dulles, 26, 27 Feb., 18 Mar. 1953, Dulles to Moose, 21 Mar. 1953, memorandum of conversation by Smith, 8 June 1953, Israeli aide-mémoire, 23 Dec. 1953, memorandum of conversation by Allen, 16 Mar. 1954, Moose to Dulles, 30 June 1954, RG 59, 683.84A.

34. Memorandum of conversation by Burdett, 6 July 1955, RG 59, 674.84A; memorandums of conversations by Burdett, 29 Aug., 22 Sept. 1955, RG 59, 683.84A.

35. White to Dulles, 21 Dec. 1955, RG 59, 683.84A. See also Moose to Dulles, 13, 15 Dec. 1955, Lawson to Dulles, 13 Dec. 1955, Allen to Murphy, 23 Dec. 1955, RG 59, 683.84A.

36. Dulles to Moose, 13 Dec. 1955, RG 59, 684A.86. See also White to Dulles, 12 Dec. 1955, RG 59, 683.84A; memorandum of conversation, 13 Dec. 1955, RG 59, 684A.86.

37. Moose to Dulles, 25 Jan. 1956, RG 59, 684A.86. See also Dulles to Lawson, 13 Dec. 1955, Allen to Murphy, 23 Dec. 1955, Lodge to Dulles, 24 Jan. 1956, RG 59, 683.84A; Moose to Dulles, 15, 20 Dec. 1955, RG 59, 684A.86.

38. These points echo Oren, *Origins.*

Chapter 13

1. M. Brecher, *Decisions,* 174–94.

2. Division of Research Report #45, 26 July 1949, RG 59, lot 70 D 303, box 5; memorandum of conversation by McGhee, 25 June 1951, Bruins to Acheson, 10 Aug. 1951, Drew to Acheson, 15 Aug. 1951, *FRUS, 1951,* 5:730–31, 829–31, 835–36; minutes of meeting, 14 Feb. 1952, USD to Eban, 29 July, 30 Nov. 1952, *DFPI,* 7:80–83, 399, 671; State Department paper, 4 Oct. 1952, Acheson to Davis, 9 Jan. 1953, *FRUS, 1952–1954,* 9:1017–26, 1094–95.

3. Dulles to Green, 9 June 1953, *FRUS, 1952–1954,* 9:1238–39. See also memorandum by Gardiner, 29 Apr. 1953, RG 59, lot 57 D 298, box 5; brief by Foreign Office, 12 May 1953, RG 130.20, 2481/1.

4. Jernegan to Dulles, 10 Aug. 1953, *FRUS, 1952–1954,* 9:1269–75.

5. Lynch to Dulles, 21 Sept. 1953, *FRUS, 1952–1954,* 9:1319–20; Bruins to Dulles, 17 Sept. 1953, RG 59, 684A.86. See also Jernegan to Dulles, 10 Aug. 1953, *FRUS, 1952–1954,* 9: 1269–75.

6. Dulles to Russell, 12 Sept. 1953, *FRUS, 1952–1954,* 9:1310–11; Russell to Dulles, 13, 25–28 Sept. 1953, memorandum by Worcester, 29 Sept. 1953, RG 59, 683.84A; Bennike to Sharett, 23 Sept. 1953, RG 130.02, 3688/7; Ben-Gurion Diary (Hebrew), 23 Sept. 1953, Ben-Gurion Papers; Tekoah to Sharett (Hebrew), 6 Oct. 1953, circular cable by Sharett (Hebrew), 23 Oct. 1953, *DFPI,* 8:720–21, 797–98; Shalit to USD (Hebrew), 14 Oct. 1953, RG 130.02, 2480/1.

7. Ben-Gurion to Eban (Hebrew), 18 Oct. 1953, Sharett to Eban (Hebrew), 18 Oct. 1953, *DFPI,* 8:766–68, 771–72; record of press conference, 20 Oct. 1953, Smith to Eisenhower, 21 Oct. 1953, United Nations Security Council resolution, 27 Oct. 1953, State Department press release, 28 Oct. 1953, circular cable by Dulles, 28 Oct. 1953, *FRUS, 1952–1954,* 9:1369–72, 1388–91, 1392–93; memorandum of conversation by Simmons, 27 Oct. 1953, RG 59, lot 57 D 298, box 12.

8. Memorandum of conversation by Byroade, 19 Dec. 1953, RG 59, 684A.85. See also memorandum of conversation by Hart, 28 Dec. 1953, RG 59, 684A.85322; United Nations Security Council resolution, 20 Jan. 1954, *FRUS, 1952–1954,* 9:1482; Jernegan to Byroade, 2 Jan. 1954, Byroade to Dulles, 7 Jan. 1954, Hart to Byroade, 29 Jan. 1954, RG 59, lot 57 D 298, box 11.

9. Lourie to Aldrich, 11 Oct. 1953, minutes of meeting, 21 Oct. 1953, *FRUS, 1952–1954,* 9:1345–48, 1373–77. The JVP was officially titled "The Unified Development of the Water Resources of the Jordan Valley Region."

10. Johnston to Eisenhower, 17 Nov. 1953, *FRUS, 1952–1954,* 9:1418–23. See also Lourie to Aldrich, 11 Oct. 1953, *FRUS, 1952–1954,* 9:1345–48.

11. Seelye to Dulles, 15 Oct. 1953, Dulles to Russell, 26 Oct. 1953, *FRUS, 1952–1954,* 9: 1358–59, 1387. See also Dulles to Johnston, 13 Oct. 1953, Caffery to Dulles, 17 Oct. 1953,

Moose to Dulles, 17 Oct. 1953, *FRUS, 1952–1954*, 9:1348–52, 1361–64; Lynch to Dulles, 11 Nov. 1953, RG 59, 684A.85.

12. For details of Johnston's meetings in Beirut, Amman, Cairo, Tel Aviv, and Damascus, see *FRUS, 1952–1954*, 9:1380–84, 1391–92, 1394–95, 1400–1402. See also Johnston to Eisenhower, 17 Nov. 1953, *FRUS, 1952–1954*, 9:1418–23; memorandum of conversation by Waller, 18 Mar. 1954, RG 59, lot 57 D 298, box 11; Dulles to Eisenhower, 7 May 1954, Whitman File: Dulles-Herter Series, box 2; State Department paper, 20 Dec. 1954, RG 59, 684A.85322.

13. Memorandum of conversation by Goodpaster, 17 Jan. 1955, Whitman File: Diary Series, box 3; Dulles to Johnston, 7 Feb. 1955, Dulles to embassy in Beirut, 8 Mar. 1955, RG 59, 684A.85322; memorandum of conversation by Allen, 21 Feb. 1955, RG 59, 684A.85; minutes of meeting, 1 Mar. 1955, RG 59, lot 57 D 298, box 5.

14. Ben-Gurion Diary (Hebrew), 26 June 1954, Ben-Gurion Papers; Lawson to Dulles, 17 Feb. 1955, RG 59, 684A.86. See also minutes of meetings, 27 Jan., 1 Feb. 1955, RG 59, 611.84A; minutes of meeting, 14 Mar. 1955, RG 59, lot 70 D 303, box 3; Allen to Dulles, 14 Mar. 1955, RG 59, 684A.85322.

15. Minutes of meetings, 15, 23 June 1955, Dulles to Johnston, 30 Aug. 1955, Johnston to Dulles, 31 Aug., 8 Oct. 1955, RG 59, 684A.85322; minutes of meeting, 27 June 1955, RG 59, 611.84A; Johnston to Sharett, 23 Aug. 1955, RG 59, lot 57 D 298, box 1; Green to Dulles, 18 Oct. 1955, RG 59, 684A.86; statement by Johnston, 25 Oct. 1955, RG 59, lot 70 D 246, box 1.

16. Memorandum of conversation by Gardiner, 16 Mar. 1956, RG 59, 684A.85322. See also Moose to Dulles, 28 Jan. 1956, Gallman to Dulles, 4 Feb. 1956, circular cable by Dulles, 9 Feb. 1956, RG 59, 684A.86; memorandum of conversation by Boardman, 7 Feb. 1956, Dulles to Lawson, 8 Feb. 1956, Hoover to Byroade, 10 Mar. 1956, RG 59, 684A.85322; Hart to Dulles, 3 Feb. 1956, Dulles to Mallory, 4 Feb. 1956, Byroade to Dulles, 18 Feb. 1956, RG 59, 683.84A.

17. Byroade to Dulles, 14 Mar. 1956, RG 59, 684A.85322. See also Dulles to Mallory, 4 Feb. 1956, RG 59, 683.84A; circular cables by Dulles, 23 Feb., 3 Apr. 1956, Byroade to Dulles, 27 Feb. 1956, Mallory to Dulles, 21 Mar. 1956, Dulles to embassy in Syria, 1 Mar. 1956, Barnes to Johnston, 8 Mar. 1956, Lawson to Dulles, 18 Mar. 1956, RG 59, 684A.85322; Moose to Dulles, 9 May 1956, RG 59, 684A.86.

18. Dulles, "Report on the Near East," 1 June 1953, *State Department Bulletin* 28:729 (15 June 1953): 831–35; Dulles to Johnston, 13 Oct. 1953, *FRUS, 1952–1954*, 9:1348–52. See also unsigned policy paper, n.d. [ca. Nov. 1953], Whitman File: Administration Series.

19. Dillon to Dulles, 15 Oct., 6 Nov. 1953, circular cable by Smith, 11 Dec. 1953, Lynch to Dulles, 31 Dec. 1953, *FRUS, 1952–1954*, 9:1360, 1405–6, 1458–59, 1468–69; statement by Rifai, 3 Nov. 1954, RG 59, lot 57 D 298, box 11; Sabini to Dulles, 5 May 1955, Russell to Hart, 6 May 1955, RG 59, 684A.85.

20. Memorandum of conversation by Waller, 8 Apr. 1953, *FRUS, 1952–1954*, 9:1164–70. See also circular cable by Dulles, 27 Feb. 1953, Davis to Dulles, 4 Mar. 1953, *FRUS, 1952–1954*, 9:1144–45, 1147; USD to Eban, 4 Mar. 1953, *DFPI*, 8:179–81; Israeli memorandum of conversation, 13 May 1953, RG 130.20, 2474/4.

21. Israeli memorandum of conversation, 13 May 1953, RG 130.20, 2474/4. See also Foreign Ministry paper (Hebrew), 18 May 1953, memorandum by Eliashev, 1 June 1953, RG 130.20, 2481/1; Eban to USD (Hebrew), 2 June 1953, RG 130.20, 2474/4.

22. Statement by Eytan, 10 July 1953, RG 130.02, 2444/1. See also circular cable by Eytan, 10 July 1953, USD to Eban (Hebrew), 12 July 1953, *DFPI*, 8:522–23, 526.

23. Dulles to Sharett, 5 Sept. 1953, RG 130.02, 2444/6; Sharett to Dulles, 27 July 1953, RG 130.02, 2444/6; Russell to Dulles, 7 Oct. 1953, *FRUS, 1952–1954*, 9:1339–40. See also Dulles to Russell, 24 July 1953, Russell to Dulles, 2 Sept. 1953, *FRUS, 1952–1954*, 9:1263–64, 1297–98; Sharett to Dulles, 27 July 1953, RG 130.02, 2444/6; Foreign Ministry statement, 29 July 1953, RG 130.02, 2443/10; Kollek to Goldmann, 16 Aug. 1953, Goldmann Papers, Z6/721.

24. Memorandum of conversation by Jernegan, 4 Aug. 1953, *FRUS, 1952–1954*, 9:1265–68; Eban to USD, 13–14 Aug. 1953, minutes of meeting, 12 Sept. 1953, *DFPI*, 8:648–56, 583–87; Eban to Sharett, 19 Aug. 1953, RG 93.01, 2209/6.

25. Dulles to Russell, 14 May, 16 June 1954, *FRUS, 1952–1954*, 9:1564–65; progress report on NSC 155/1, 30 July 1954, WHO Files, NSC Staff Papers, box 77; Russell to Dulles, 10 Aug. 1954, RG 59, 674A.84; Lawson to Dulles, 22 July 1955, *FRUS, 1955–1957*, 14:325–26n.

26. Intelligence digest (Hebrew), July–Aug. 1955, RG 130.02, 2428/9; Wilkins to Allen, 27 July 1955, Hoover to Lawson, 13 Sept. 1955, *FRUS, 1955–1957*, 14:325–26, 464; Lawson to Dulles, 21–22 Sept. 1955, RG 59, 611.84A; Hoover to Aldrich, 26 Sept. 1955, Murphy to Aldrich, 10 Oct. 1955, RG 59, 611.84A.

27. State Department position paper, 8 May 1953, *FRUS, 1952–1954*, 9:1219–21. See also brief by Foreign Office, 12 May 1953, RG 130.20, 2481/1.

28. Address by Bolton, 19 May 1953, *Congressional Record*, vol. 99, pt. 4, p. 5175. See also State Department position paper, 8 May 1953, U.N. resolution, 27 Nov. 1953, State Department paper, 10 Nov. 1954, *FRUS, 1952–1954*, 9:1219–21, 1441–42, 1685–91; UNRWA memorandum, 8 May 1953, Allen to Dulles, 19 June 1956, Wilcox to Dulles, 20 June 1956, RG 59, lot 70 D 303, boxes 4–5; memorandum by Troxel, n.d. [12 Aug. 1953], RG 59, lot 57 D 298, box 2.

29. State Department position paper, 8 May 1953, *FRUS, 1952–1954*, 9:1219–21. See also Cay to Hart, 22 Nov. 1954, RG 59, 320.511; Watson to Dulles, 2 May 1955, Dulles to Lodge, 6 May 1955, RG 59, 674.84A; Wilkins to Rountree, 7 Sept. 1956, RG 59, lot 70 D 303, box 4; Shadid, *United States.*

30. Memorandum by Troxel, 7 May 1953, RG 59, lot 57 D 298, box 3; unsigned policy paper, n.d. [ca. Nov. 1953], Whitman File: Administration Series.

31. Position paper, 5 Jan. 1953, RG 59, lot 57 D 298, box 3; Dulles to Davis, 28 Feb. 1953, Davis to Dulles, 5 Mar. 1953, position paper, 8 May 1953, *FRUS, 1952–1954*, 9:1146–47, 1149, 1219–21; minutes of meeting (Hebrew), 30 Apr. 1953, RG 130.20, 2481/1.

32. Circular cable by Dulles, 3 Apr. 1953, RG 59, lot 57 D 298, box 3; brief by Foreign Office, 12 May 1953, RG 130.20, 2481/1.

33. DeGolia to Gay, 16 Oct. 1953, RG 59, lot 57 D 298, box 1.

34. Unsigned memorandum, n.d. [ca. July 1953], RG 59, lot 70 D 298, box 1; Israeli aide-mémoire, 15 Nov. 1955, RG 59, 684A.86.

35. DeGolia to Gay, 16 Oct. 1953, RG 59, lot 57 D 298, box 1. See also Eddy to Davies, 16 Sept. 1953, RG 59, lot 57 D 298, box 1; memorandum of conversation by Gay, 10 Dec. 1953, RG 59, lot 57 D 298, box 5; progress report on NSC 155/1, 30 July 1954, WHO Files, NSC Staff Papers, box 77; Hart to Byroade, 17 Nov. 1954, RG 59, lot 57 D 298, box 3.

36. Shiloah to Divon (Hebrew), 9 Feb. 1953, Divon to Shiloah (Hebrew), 15 Feb. 1953,

RG 130.02, 2410/1; minutes of meeting (Hebrew), 27 Mar. 1953, RG 130.02, 2449/1; Elath to Sharett (Hebrew), 23 Sept. 1953, *DFPI*, 8:677–79; Elath to Eytan, 21 Jan. 1954, RG 130.02, 2419/1; Dulles to Caffery, 4 Oct. 1954, *FRUS, 1952–1954*, 9:1663–66.

37. Memorandum of conversation by Hart, 23 Dec. 1953, RG 59, 684A.85322. See also Eban to USD, 8 Apr. 1953, *DFPI*, 8:278–79; minutes of meeting, 13 May 1953, RG 130.20, 2474/4; Eban to USD (Hebrew), 11 Sept. 1953, RG 130.02, 2450/1; Wainhouse to Key, 26 Jan. 1954, RG 59, lot 57 D 298, box 11.

38. Dulles to Russell, 7 Aug. 1954, memorandum of conversation by Smith, 16 Aug. 1954, *FRUS, 1952–1954*, 9:1604–6, 1613–14; Hahn, *United States*, 169–70.

39. Kidron to president of Security Council, 19 Sept. 1956, RG 130.02, 2419/4. See also Dulles to Caffery, 4 Oct. 1954, *FRUS, 1952–1954*, 9:1663–66.

40. Caffery to Dulles, 7 Oct. 1954, Dulles to Caffery, 1 Dec. 1954, *FRUS, 1952–1954*, 9: 1666–67, 1702–3; memorandum of conversation by Hart, 10 Oct. 1954, RG 59, lot 57 D 298, box 5; minute by Shuckburgh, 13 Oct. 1954, FO 371/108585, JE 1261/133; paper by Eban, 1 Dec. 1954, RG 130.20, 2480/6; Dulles to Byroade, 28 July 1955, RG 59, 974.7301.

41. Glidden to Bergus, 29 Aug. 1956, RG 59, lot 59 D 582, box 5.

42. Statement by Sharett, 13 Sept. 1955, RG 130.02, 2419/5. See also Wilkins to Jernegan, 9 Sept. 1955, RG 59, 674.84A; Lawson to Dulles, 12 Aug., 14 Sept. 1955, RG 59, 974.7301.

Chapter 14

1. NSC 5428, 23 July 1954, *FRUS, 1952–1954*, 9:525–36. See also memorandum of conversation by Merchant, 5 Nov. 1954, British aide-mémoire, 5 Nov. 1954, U.S. aide-mémoire, 17 Nov. 1954, *FRUS, 1952–1954*, 9:1683–85.

2. Wadsworth to Dulles, 10 Dec. 1954, RG 59, 684A.86; Byroade to Dulles, 22 Nov. 1954, RG 59, 684A.86; Shuckburgh to Stevenson, 15 Feb. 1955, FO 371/102780, VR1076/22G. See also Caffery to Dulles, 11 Dec. 1954, Moose to Dulles, 13 Dec. 1954, Mallory to Dulles, 23 Dec. 1954, Meyer to Dulles, 10 Jan. 1955, Lawson to Dulles, 14 Feb. 1955, RG 59, 684A.86; NEA paper, 14 Jan. 1955, memorandum of conversation by Dulles, 14 Feb. 1955, *FRUS, 1955–1957*, 14:9–19, 53–54.

3. Memorandum of conversation by Hart, 27 Jan. 1955, memorandum of conversation by Dulles, 14 Feb. 1955, *FRUS, 1955–1957*, 14:28–32, 53–54; memorandum of conversation, 9 Feb. 1955, Dulles Papers, General Correspondence and Memoranda Series, box 1.

4. Murphy to Hoover, 23 May 1955, Dulles to Hoover, 6 June 1955, *FRUS, 1955–1957*, 14:199–205, 222–26.

5. Dulles to Hoover, 12 May 1955, *FRUS, 1955–1957*, 14:185–86; Murphy to Hoover with attachments, 23 May 1955, *FRUS, 1955–1957*, 14:199–205.

6. Byroade to Dulles, 21 Mar. 1955, RG 59, 684A.86; Byroade to Dulles, 20 May 1955, *FRUS, 1955–1957*, 14:192. See also Dulles to Hoover, 24 Feb. 1955, Byroade to Dulles, 4 Mar., 3, 5 Apr., 30 May 1955, Russell to Dulles, 9 Mar. 1955, RG 59, 684A.86; minutes of meeting, 3 Mar. 1955, Whitman File: NSC Series, box 6.

7. Lawson to Russell, 5 Mar., 14 May 1955, RG 59, 684A.86; Shimoni to Rafael (Hebrew), 28 Apr. 1955, RG 130.20, 2480/7. See also Lawson to Dulles, 7 Jan., 15, 17, 21 Feb., 5 May 1955, Dulles to Lawson, 9, 14 Feb., 14 Apr. 1955, memorandum of conversation by Bergus, 10 May 1955, Lawson to Russell, 14 May 1955, RG 59, 684A.86; Lawson to Dulles, 26 Mar. 1955, RG 59, 674.84A.

8. Hoover to Byroade, 19 Mar. 1955, RG 59, 684A.86; Dulles to Hoover, 6 June 1955, Dulles to Byroade, 9 July 1955, *FRUS, 1955–1957*, 14:222–26, 282–83.

9. Minutes of meeting, 14 July 1955, RG 59, 684A.86; Dulles to Eisenhower, 19 Aug. 1955, Whitman File: Dulles-Herter Series, box 4; circular cable by Dulles, 24 Aug. 1955, RG 59, 684A.86. See also Byroade to Dulles, 3, 11 July 1955, Russell to Dulles, 8 July 1955, RG 59, 674.84A; Dulles to Aldrich, 25 Aug. 1955, RG 59, 684A.86; Alpha statement, 19 Aug. 1955, Dulles to Eisenhower, 1 Sept. 1955, Whitman File: Dulles-Herter Series, box 4.

10. Memorandum of conversation by Bergus, 6 Sept. 1955, Wadsworth to Dulles, 28 Aug. 1955, RG 59, 684A.86. See also Lawson to Dulles, 25 Aug., 10 Sept. 1955, Gallman to Dulles, 24 Aug., 7 Sept. 1955, Geren to Dulles, 26 Aug., 20 Sept. 1955, Byroade to Dulles, 27 Aug., 11, 17 Sept. 1955, Moose to Dulles, 30 Aug. 1955, memorandum of conversation by Allen, 31 Aug. 1955, Heath to Dulles, 2–3 Sept. 1955, RG 59, 684A.86; circular cable by Sharett (Hebrew), 13 Sept. 1955, Rafael to Sharett (Hebrew), 30 Sept. 1955, RG 130.02, 2403/14.

11. Circular cable by Dulles, 30 Aug. 1955, RG 59, 684A.86; Dulles to Eisenhower, 1 Sept. 1955, Whitman File: Dulles-Herter Series, box 4; minutes of meeting, 20 Sept. 1955, *FRUS, 1955–1957*, 14:485–91.

12. Memorandum of conversation by Bergus, 11 Oct. 1955, *FRUS, 1955–1957*, 14:570–76. See also intelligence digest (Hebrew), July–Aug. 1955, RG 130.02, 2428/9; Byroade to Dulles, 10, 21 Sept. 1955, White to Dulles, 26–28 Oct. 1955, Moose to Dulles, 3 Dec. 1955, RG 59, 674.84A; unsigned memorandum to Dulles, 20 Oct. 1955, RG 59, 684A.86; Lawson to Dulles, 12 Nov. 1955, *FRUS, 1955–1957*, 14:739–40.

13. SNIE 30-3-55, 12 Oct. 1955, *FRUS, 1955–1957*, 14:577–86; unsigned memorandum of conversation, 1 Nov. 1955, Whitman File: Diary Series, box 9; Dulles to Hoover, 12 Nov. 1955, RG 59, 684A.86. See also Byroade to Dulles, 18 Oct. 1955, Heath to Allen, 29 Oct. 1955, Aldrich to Dulles, 11 Nov. 1955, Hoover to Byroade, 18 Nov. 1955, RG 59, 684A.86.

14. Memorandum of conversation by Bergus, 2 Dec. 1955, RG 59, 684A.86. See also Dulles to Eisenhower, 18 Nov. 1955, WHCF-DDE (Confidential), box 70; Byroade to Dulles, 9, 17, 27 Nov. 1955, Mallory to Dulles, 11 Nov., 1 Dec. 1955, Emmerson to Dulles, 18 Nov. 1955, Gallman to Dulles, 18 Nov. 1955, memorandum of conversation by Boardman, 21 Nov. 1955, RG 59, 684A.86; U.S. aide-mémoire, 21 Nov. 1955, RG 59, lot 66 D 70, box 65; Israeli aide-mémoire, 6 Dec. 1955, RG 130.02, 2414/28.

15. Hoover to Lodge, 22 Mar. 1956, RG 59, 684A.86. See also Layton to Radford, 12 Oct. 1955, RG 218, CJCS Radford, box 8, 091 Egypt; minutes of meeting, 3 Nov. 1955, Lawson to Dulles, 10 Jan. 1956, *FRUS, 1955–1957*, 14:696–700, 15:16–19; Totten to Joint Staff, 7 Nov. 1955, RG 218, JCS Geographic File 1954–56, box 12, 381 EMMEA (11-19-47); Dulles to Wilson, 6 Feb. 1956, RG 218, CJCS Radford, box 8, 091 Egypt; memorandum of conversation by Geren, 23 Feb. 1956, RG 59, 684A.85; Foreign Ministry paper (Hebrew), 22 Apr. 1956, RG 130.02, 2409/2.

16. Wilkins to Allen, 8 Feb. 1956, RG 59, lot 59 D 582, box 5; Powers to Radford, 27 Feb. 1956, memorandum by Intelligence Advisory Committee, 7 Mar. 1956, RG 218, CJCS Radford, box 16, 091 Palestine. See also Byroade to Dulles, 14 Mar. 1956, RG 59, 674.84A.

17. Memorandum by Lay, 17 Oct. 1955, *FRUS, 1955–1957*, 14:592–603. See also editorial note, *FRUS, 1955–1957*, 14:588.

18. Allen to Dulles, 15 Aug. 1955, memorandum by Lay, 17 Oct. 1955, minutes of meetings, 20, 27 Oct. 1955, *FRUS, 1955–1957*, 14:351–53, 592–603, 616–30, 661–68; minutes of meeting, 13 Oct. 1955, Whitman File, NSC Series, box 7.

19. Memorandums of conversations, 30–31 Jan. 1956, *FRUS, 1955–1957*, 15:101–12. See also Allen to Hoover, 20 Feb. 1956, RG 59, 684A.86.

20. JCS to CINCNELM, 27 Apr. 1956, RG 218, JCS Geographic File 1954–56, box 12, CCS 381 EMMEA (11-19-47). See also memorandum by Hedding, 23 Feb. 1956, unsigned memorandum, 9 Apr. 1956, RG 218, CJCS Radford, box 16, 091 Palestine; JCS to Wilson, n.d. [ca. 1 Mar. 1956], Radford to Wilson, 28 Mar. 1956, RG 218, JCS Geographic File 1954–56, box 27, CCS 092 Palestine (5-3-46); CNO to JCS, 3 Apr. 1956, Picher to Currie, 4 Apr. 1956, JCS 1887/174, 17 Apr. 1956, circular cables by JCS, 18–19 Apr. 1956, CNO to CINCNELM, 21 Apr. 1956, commander in chief, U.S. European Command, to army, 25 Apr. 1956, Radford to Wilson, 6 July 1956, RG 218, JCS Geographic File 1954–56, boxes 12–13, CCS 381 EMMEA (11-19-47).

21. Allen to Hoover, 20 Feb. 1956, Rountree to Hoover, 8 Mar. 1956, RG 59, 684A.86; memorandum of conversation, 16 May 1956, *FRUS, 1955–1957*, 15:642–43.

22. Caraway to Radford, 20 Mar. 1956, RG 218, CJCS Radford, box 16, 091 Palestine; JCS to CINCNELM, 27 Apr. 1956, RG 218, JCS Geographic File 1954–56, box 12, CCS 381 EMMEA (11-19-47). See also memorandum by Hedding, 7 Mar. 1956, Caraway to Radford, 20 Mar. 1956, RG 218, CJCS Radford, box 16, 091 Palestine.

23. Memorandum of conversation by Goodpaster, 2 Feb. 1956, Whitman File: Diary Series, box 12. See also Burke to Radford, 27 Feb., 4 Apr. 1956, RG 218, CJCS Radford, boxes 8, 16, 091 Egypt; Hedding to Allen, 2 Feb. 1956, CNO to CINCNELM, 2 Feb. 1956, Burke to Radford, 3 July 1956, RG 218, CJCS Radford, box 16, 091 Palestine.

24. Memorandum of conversation by MacArthur, 9 Apr. 1956, MacArthur to Dulles, 14 Apr. 1956, *FRUS, 1955–1957*, 15:496–98, 532–37; Hanes to MacArthur, 1 May 1956, Dulles Papers, White House Memoranda Series, box 4; memorandums by Radford, 25 May 1956, Radford to Wilson, 19 Sept. 1956, RG 218, CJCS Radford, box 16, 091 Palestine; memorandum of conversation by Dulles, 13 July 1956, Dulles to Eisenhower, 28 Sept. 1956, Dulles Papers, White House Memoranda Series, boxes 3–4; Gowen to Dulles, 14, 25 July 1956, RG 59, 684A.86.

25. Ben-Gurion to Eisenhower, 14 Feb. 1956, SNIE 30-56, 28 Feb. 1956, memorandum of conversation by Dulles, 25 Jan. 1956, *FRUS, 1955–1957*, 15:185–87, 248–54, 74–76. See also Sharett to Dulles, 16 Jan. 1956, Eisenhower to Ben-Gurion, 27 Feb. 1956, *FRUS, 1955–1957*, 15:26–27, 242; Lawson to Dulles, 29 Feb. 1956, RG 59, 684A.86.

26. Memorandum of conversation by Goodpaster, 6 Mar. 1956, Dulles to Hoover, 3, 6 May 1956, *FRUS, 1955–1957*, 15:307–8, 601–2, 615–19; Eisenhower Diary, 8 Mar. 1956, Whitman File: Diary Series, box 13; Byroade to Dulles, 23 May 1956, RG 59, 674.84A.

27. *Washington Post* quoted in Zucker, *U.S. Aid*, 117; Hoover to Dulles, 1 Mar. 1956, *FRUS, 1955–1957*, 15:260–61. See also Kenen, *Israel's Defense Line*, 123–30.

28. Memorandums of conversations by Russell, 2, 29 Mar. 1956, memorandum of conversation by Dulles, 26 Apr. 1956, *FRUS, 1955–1957*, 15:276–81, 427–29, 585. See also memorandum of conversation by Goodpaster, 28 Mar. 1956, Whitman File: Diary Series, box 13; Silver to Dulles, 27 Apr. 1956, Silver Papers, Correspondence 11-1 File.

29. Eisenhower to Ben-Gurion, 30 Apr. 1956, *FRUS, 1955–1957*, 15:589. See also Hoover to Dulles, 5 Mar. 1956, memorandum of conversation by Russell, 28 Mar. 1956, Lawson to Dulles, 5 Apr. 1956, Dulles to Merchant, 12 Apr., 18 July 1956, Dulles to Hoover, 3 May 1956, *FRUS, 1955–1957*, 15:292–94, 405–8, 473–76, 527–28, 601–2, 858–59.

30. Eisenhower Diary, 11 Jan. 1956, Whitman File: Diary Series, box 9. See also memo-

randum of conversation, 9 Nov. 1955, Whitman File: Dulles-Herter Series, box 5; memorandum of conversation by Dulles, 11 Jan. 1956, Dulles Papers, White House Memoranda Series, box 4. For details of Anderson's undercover travel, see memorandum of conversation, 10 Aug. 1965, RG 130.02/2, 4327/9.

31. Unsigned message to Anderson, 4 Feb. 1956, *FRUS, 1955–1957*, 15:138–40. See also memorandum of conversation by Lawson, 30 Dec. 1955, RG 59, 684A.86; Hahn, *United States*, 196.

32. Eisenhower Diary, 13 Mar. 1956, Whitman File: Diary Series, box 9. See also Ben-Gurion Diary (Hebrew), 15 Jan. 1956, Ben-Gurion Papers; Dulles to Anderson, 19 Jan. 1956, RG 59, 683.84A; aide-mémoire by Eban, 30 Jan. 1956, RG 130.20, 2480/9; memorandum of conversation by Hoover, 12 Mar. 1956, Dulles Papers, White House Memoranda Series, box 4; minutes of meeting, 13 Mar. 1956, Whitman File: Diary Series, box 9.

33. Dulles to Lodge, 2 Mar. 1956, Hoover to Dulles, 15 Mar. 1956, Eisenhower to Ben-Gurion, 9 Apr. 1956, Eisenhower to Nasser, 9 Apr. 1956, RG 59, 684A.86; memorandum of conversation by Goodpaster, 6 Mar. 1956, Whitman File: Diary Series, box 13.

34. Byroade to Dulles, 9 Apr. 1956, RG 59, 684A.86; Lawson to Dulles, 12 Apr. 1956, RG 59, 674.84A. See also Byroade to Dulles, 6 Apr. 1956, Lawson to Dulles, 12, 20 Apr. 1956, RG 59, 674.84A; Burdett to Wilkins, 6 Apr. 1956, RG 59, lot 59 D 582, box 5; Layton to Radford, 11 Apr. 1956, RG 218, CJCS Radford, box 16, 091 Palestine.

35. Lawson to Dulles, 14 Apr. 1956, RG 59, 674.84A. See also Wilkins to Rountree, 17 Apr. 1956, RG 59, lot 59 D 582, box 5; Byroade to Dulles, 24 Apr. 1956, RG 59, 611.74; Lawson to Dulles, 10 Apr. 1956, RG 59, 674.84A; Phipps to Layton, 27 Apr. 1956, RG 218, CJCS Radford, box 16, 091 Palestine; Lodge to Dulles, 7 May 1956, Ludlow to Wilcox, 12 June 1956, RG 59, 684A.86.

36. Paper by Matthews, 19 Apr. 1956, Walmsley to Dulles, 19 Apr. 1956, editorial note, *FRUS, 1955–1957*, 15:549–53, 555–56, 567–68; Bohlen to Dulles, 4 May 1956, Russell to Dulles, 5 June 1956, Dulles to Lodge, 12 May 1956, RG 59, 684A.86; memorandum of conversation, 12 May 1956, Dulles-Princeton Papers, Telephone Conversation Series, box 5.

37. Memorandum of conversation by Russell, 21 June 1956, Lawson to Dulles, 3 July 1956, *FRUS, 1955–1957*, 15:739–41, 767–69; Dulles to Lawson, 14 July 1956, Lawson to Dulles, 18 July 1956, RG 59, 684A.85; Sanger to Dulles, 23 July 1956, RG 59, 684A.85; Byroade to Dulles, 24 July 1956, RG 59, 684A.86.

38. Bar-On, *Gates*, 89; Caplan, *Futile Diplomacy*, 4:262–89.

Chapter 15

1. Hahn, *United States*, 211–39; Freiberger, *Dawn*, 159–209; Kyle, *Suez*, 135–290.

2. Memorandum of conversation by O'Connor, 6 Sept. 1956, Dulles Papers, box 7, Suez folder. See also Gallman to Dulles, 6 Sept. 1956, Sanger to Dulles, 13 Sept. 1956, Heath to Dulles, 14 Sept. 1956, RG 59, 974.7301; Hare to Dulles, 26 Sept. 1956, memorandum of conversation by Rountree, 9 Oct. 1956, *FRUS, 1955–1957*, 16:586–88, 668–70; memorandum of conversation by Bergus, 28 Sept. 1956, RG 59, 684A.85.

3. Editorial notes, Anderson to Dulles, 23, 24 Aug. 1956, memorandum of conversation by Wilkins, 1 Sept. 1956, *FRUS, 1955–1957*, 16:246–47, 273–75, 282–83, 296–97, 301–3, 347–49; Saud to Eisenhower, 24 Aug. 1956, State Department report, 6 Sept. 1956, Whitman File: International Series, box 42; memorandum of conversation by Rockwell, 27 Sept. 1956, RG 59, 974.7301.

4. Minutes of NSC meeting, 9 Aug. 1956, Whitman File, NSC Series, box 8; State Department briefing book, 11 Aug. 1956, RG 59, 974.7301; Russell to Dulles, 4 Aug. 1956, *FRUS, 1955–1957,* 16:136–38. See also memorandum of conversation by Goodpaster, 31 July 1956, Whitman File: Diary Series, box 16; SNIE 30-3-56, 31 July 1956, *FRUS, 1955–1957,* 16: 78–93; Murphy to Dulles, 30 July 1956, RG 59, 974.7301; minutes of NSC meeting, 9 Aug. 1956, Whitman File, NSC Series, box 8.

5. Foreign Ministry paper (Hebrew), 5 Aug. 1956, Eytan to Levin, 23 Aug. 1956, RG 130.02, 2409/5–7. See also Ben-Gurion Diary (Hebrew), 27 July 1956, Ben-Gurion Papers; minutes of meeting (Hebrew), 29 July 1956, Eban to Meir (Hebrew), 1 Aug. 1956, Israeli aide-mémoire, 12 Aug. 1956, USD to Eban (Hebrew), 13 Aug. 1956, General Intelligence Department paper (Hebrew), 14 Aug. 1956, Rosenne to Robinson, 2 Sept. 1956, RG 130.02, 2409/5–8; Teller to Goldmann, 1 Aug. 1956, Goldmann Papers, Z6/1105; memorandum of conversation by Blackiston, 9 Aug. 1956, RG 59, 974.7301.

6. Memorandum by Gazit (Hebrew), 27 July 1956, Foreign Ministry paper, 5 Aug. 1956, RG 130.02, 2409/5; minutes of NSC meeting, 9 Aug. 1956, Whitman File, NSC Series, box 8; Hamilton to Dulles, 5 Sept. 1956, Lawson to Dulles, 27 Sept. 1956, RG 59, 974.7301; Wilkins to Rountree, 12 Sept. 1956, RG 59, lot 59 D 582, box 5.

7. USD to Eban (Hebrew), 28 Sept. 1956, RG 130.20, 2480/10; memorandum of conversation by Wilkins, 28 Sept. 1956, RG 59, 974.7301. See also Eban to Dulles 4 Oct. 1956, memorandum of conversation by Rountree, 12 Oct. 1956, RG 59, 974.7301; Eban to Meir (Hebrew), 2 Oct. 1956, Rafael to Eban (Hebrew), 4 Oct. 1956, RG 130.02, 2409/9.

8. Memorandum of conversation by Blackiston, 10 Sept. 1956, MacArthur to Rountree, 20 Sept. 1956, RG 59, 974.7301. See also Sabini to Dulles, 17 Aug., 4 Sept. 1956, RG 59, 674.84A.

9. Dean to Dulles, 11 July 1956, memorandum of conversation by Blackiston, 30 July 1956, Rountree to Allen, 13 Aug. 1956, *FRUS, 1955–1957,* 15:809–11, 16:50–53, 197–98; memorandum of conversation by Blackiston, 9 Aug. 1956, RG 59, 974.7301; Shalmon to Foreign Ministry (Hebrew), 23 Aug. 1956, RG 130.20, 2480/11.

10. Memorandum by Dean, 14 Sept. 1956, memorandum by MacArthur, 15 Sept. 1956, Armstrong to Hoover, 21 Sept. 1956, Rountree to Lawson, 22 Sept. 1956, memorandum of conversation by Wilkins, 28 Sept. 1956, memorandum of conversation by Bergus, 23 Oct. 1956, *FRUS, 1955–1957,* 16:498–500, 504–5, 559–60, 562–63, 608–10, 768–69; Comay to Lurie, 22 Nov. 1957, RG 130.23, 3107/1.

11. Memorandum of conversation by Goodpaster, 28 July 1956, Whitman File: Diary Series, box 16; Murphy to Dulles, 30 July 1956, Radford to Wilson, 28 Aug. 1956, Armstrong to Hoover, 21 Sept. 1956, Hoover to Rountree, 6 Oct. 1956, *FRUS, 1955–1957,* 16: 42–45, 313–14, 559–60, 653–54; Collins to JCS, 2 Oct. 1956, RG 218, JCS Geographic File 1954–56, box 27, CCS 092 Palestine (5-3-46).

12. Collins to JCS, 26 Sept. 1956, RG 218, CJCS Radford, box 16, 091 Palestine. See also Wilkins to Rountree, 14 Sept. 1956, Mallory to Dulles, 18 Sept. 1956, memorandum of conversation by Blackiston, 26 Sept. 1956, RG 59, 684A.85; Collins to JCS, 21 Sept. 1956, RG 218, 381 EMMEA (11-19-47), s. 44; Hertzog to Meir (Hebrew), 25 Sept. 1956, RG 130.20, 2480/10.

13. Memorandum of conversation by Eliav (Hebrew), 18 Sept. 1956, RG 130.20, 2480/ 10; memorandum of conversation by Bergus, 28 Sept. 1956, RG 59, 684A.85. See also memorandum of conversation by O'Connor, 27 Sept. 1956, Dulles Papers, box 7, Suez

folder; minutes of meetings, 20, 27 Sept. 1956, Whitman File: NSC Series, box 8; Eban to Hertzog (Hebrew), 27 Sept. 1956, memorandum of conversation by Arad (Hebrew), 8 Oct. 1956, RG 130.20, 2480/10.

14. Collins to JCS, 21 Sept. 1956, RG 218, 381 EMMEA (11-19-47), s. 44; Collins to JCS, 24 Sept. 1956, RG 218, CJCS Radford, box 16, 091 Palestine; Gallman to Dulles, 27 Sept. 1956, RG 59, 684A.85.

15. Dulles to Mallory, 27 Sept. 1956, *FRUS, 1955–1957*, 13:52–53; Lawson to Dulles, 28 Sept. 1956, RG 59, 684A.85; memorandum of conversation by Ludlow, 7 Oct. 1956, RG 59, 974.7301; Nicholls to Lloyd, 18 Oct. 1956, Lloyd to Nicholls, 18 Oct. 1956, PREM 11/1454.

16. Ben-Gurion Diary (Hebrew), 1 Oct. 1956, Ben-Gurion Papers; Lawson to Dulles, 1 Oct. 1956, Dulles to Lawson, 4 Oct. 1956, RG 59, 684A.85. See also Dulles to Lawson, 29 Sept., 3 Oct. 1956, RG 59, 684A.85.

17. Ben-Gurion to Eisenhower, 20 Oct. 1956, Whitman File: International Series, box 42. See also USD to Eban, 9 Oct. 1956, Kidron to USD (Hebrew), 10 Oct. 1956, Ministry of Defense to Foreign Ministry, 10 Oct. 1956, RG 130.02, 2409/9; Duke to Foreign Office, 11 Oct. 1956, Foreign Office to Duke, 12, 14 Oct. 1956, PREM 11/1454; Collins to JCS, 12 Oct. 1956, RG 218, CJCS Radford, box 16, 091 Palestine; memorandum of conversation by Meroz (Hebrew), 17 Oct. 1956, memorandum of conversation by Arad (Hebrew), 19 Oct. 1956, RG 130.20, 2480/11.

18. Hoover to Lawson, 10 Oct. 1956, RG 59, 684A.85; minutes of NSC meeting, 12 Oct. 1956, Whitman File: NSC Series, box 8; memorandum of conversation by Dulles, 15 Oct. 1956, Dulles Papers, White House Memoranda Series, box 4; Dulles to Strong, 16 Oct. 1956, RG 59, 684A.86; policy paper, 17 Oct. 1956, RG 59, lot 59 D 582, box 5.

19. Memorandum of conversation by Dulles, 15 Oct. 1956, Dulles Papers, White House Memoranda Series, box 4; memorandum by Eisenhower, 15 Oct. 1956, Whitman File: Diary Series, box 18.

20. Gallman to Dulles, 11, 16, 17 Oct. 1956, RG 59, 684A.85; minutes of NSC meeting, 12 Oct. 1956, Whitman File: NSC Series, box 8; Collins to JCS, 21 Sept. 1956, RG 218, 381 EMMEA (11-19-47), s. 44; memorandum of telephone conversation, 12 Oct. 1956, Dulles-Princeton Papers, Telephone Conversation Series, box 11; editorial note, *FRUS, 1955–1957*, 16:775–76.

21. Circular cable by JCS, 17 Oct. 1956, RG 218, JCS Geographic File 1954–56, box 14, CCS 381 EMMEA (11-19-47); minutes of NSC meeting, 26 Oct. 1956, Whitman File: NSC Series, box 8. See also Dulles to Lodge, 17, 23 Oct. 1956, RG 59, 684A.85; Bergus to Wilkins, 25 Oct. 1956, RG 59, lot 59 D 582, box 5.

22. Minute by Lloyd, [16] Oct. 1956, FO 800/725. See also Ben-Gurion Diary (Hebrew), 3 Oct. 1956, Ben-Gurion Papers.

23. Ben-Gurion Diary (Hebrew), 22, 25 Oct. 1956, Ben-Gurion Papers. See also editorial note, *FRUS, 1955–1957*, 16:776–77. For a survey of the British and French approaches to Sèvres and a discussion of historians' discovery of the protocol during the 1980s, see Shlaim, "Protocol."

24. Ben-Gurion Diary (Hebrew), 22–25 Oct. 1956, Ben-Gurion Papers.

25. Minutes of meeting, 30 Aug. 1956, Whitman File, NSC Series, box 8; memorandum of discussion, 31 Aug. 1956, SNIE 30-4-56, 5 Sept. 1956, *FRUS, 1955–1957*, 16:342–44, 382–91; Collins to JCS, 6 Sept. 1956, RG 218, CJCS Radford, box 8, 091 Egypt; memorandum of conversation by Goodpaster, 27 Oct. 1956, Dulles Papers, White House Memo-

randa Series, box 4; Eisenhower to Ben-Gurion, 27, 28 Oct. 1956, Ben-Gurion Papers, Correspondence File; Dulles to Hare, 27 Oct. 1956, RG 59, 684A.86; Luce to CINCNELM, 28 Oct. 1956, RG 218, JCS Geographic File 1954–56, box 14, CCS 381 EMMEA (11-19-47).

26. Lawson to Dulles, 28 Oct. 1956, Dulles to Aldrich, 26 Oct. 1956, RG 59, 684A.86; Allen Dulles to Phleger, 11 May 1964, Allen Dulles Papers, box 71. See also Lawson to Dulles, 26 Oct. 1956, RG 59, 674.84A; Hitchcock to Intelligence Advisory Committee, 26 Oct. 1956, special report, 28 Oct. 1956, *FRUS, 1955–1957*, 16:787–88, 798–99.

27. Memorandum of conversation, 28 Oct. 1956, Whitman File: Diary Series, box 18. See also memorandums of telephone conversation, 28–29 Oct. 1956, Dulles-Princeton Papers, Telephone Conversation Series, box 5; memorandum of conversation by Beam, 28 Oct. 1956, RG 59, 684A.86; memorandum of conversation by O'Connor, 29 Oct. 1956, Dulles Papers, Subject Series, box 7; journal entry, 9 Nov. 1956, Randall Journals, box 3.

28. Circular cable by JCS, 26 Oct. 1956, RG 218, JCS Geographic File 1954–56, box 14, CCS 381 EMMEA (11-19-47); minutes of NSC meeting, 26 Oct. 1956, Whitman File: NSC Series, box 8; Eisenhower Diary entries, 26–28 Oct. 1956, Whitman File: Diary Series, box 8; editorial note, *FRUS, 1955–1957*, 16:794n; Lesch, *Syria*; Little, "Cold War."

29. Dulles to Dillon, 29 Oct. 1956, RG 59, 684A.86; memorandum of conversation, 29 Oct. 1956, Whitman File: Diary Series, box 18.

30. Memorandum of conversation by Wilkins, 29 Oct. 1956, Dulles to Dillon, 29 Oct. 1956, RG 59, 684A.86; record of meeting by Greene, 29 Oct. 1956, RG 59, 674.84A; memorandum of conversation by Goodpaster, 29 Oct. 1956, Whitman File: Diary Series, box 19.

31. Memorandum by Eisenhower, 1 Nov. 1956, Dulles Papers, White House Memoranda Series, box 4. See also Ben-Gurion to Eisenhower, 29 Oct. 1956, Ben-Gurion Papers, Correspondence File; Arad to USD (Hebrew), 16 Nov. 1956, RG 130.20, 2480/11.

32. Eisenhower to Hazlett, 2 Nov. 1956, in Griffith, *Ike's Letters*, 172–76. See also Zucker, *U.S. Aid*, 84–87, 114–22; Gallup, *Gallup Poll*, 1454–57.

33. Minutes of NSC meeting, 1 Nov. 1956, Whitman File: NSC Series, box 8. See also editorial notes, *FRUS, 1955–1957*, 16:881–82, 932–33; Hahn, *United States*, 229–32.

34. Memorandum for the record by Lodge, 3 Nov. 1956, editorial note, Lodge to Hoover, 5 Nov. 1956, *FRUS, 1955–1957*, 16:956–57, 960–64, 982–83; memorandums of conversations by Goodpaster, 3–4 Nov. 1956, Whitman File: Diary Series, box 19; Gallup, *Gallup Poll*, 1454–57.

35. Hare to Dulles, 4 Nov. 1956, RG 59, 684A.86. See also memorandum of conversation by Wilkins, 30 Oct. 1956, RG 59, 684A.86; Hare to Dulles, 31 Oct. 1956, RG 59, 641.74; Stewart to State Department, 8 Nov. 1956, RG 59, 974.7301; Hoover to Hare, 10 Nov. 1956, WHCF-DDE (Confidential), box 82.

36. Saud to Eisenhower, 30 Oct. 1956, Whitman File: International Series, box 42; memorandum of conversation by Rockwell, 3 Nov. 1956, *FRUS, 1955–1957*, 16:949–52. See also Heath to Dulles, 30 Oct.–13 Nov. 1956, Gallman to Dulles, 30 Oct.–10 Nov. 1956, Mallory to Dulles, 31 Oct., 3 Nov. 1956, Moose to Dulles, 30 Oct.–8 Nov. 1956, Carrigan to Dulles, 6 Nov. 1956, RG 59, 684A.86; U.S. air attaché in Baghdad to Chief of Staff, U.S. Air Force, 10 Nov. 1956, RG 218, JCS Geographic File 1954–56, box 14, CCS 381 EMMEA (11-19-47).

37. Memorandum of conversation by Rockwell, 3 Nov. 1956, *FRUS, 1955–1957*, 16:949–52; minutes of NSC meeting, 8 Nov. 1956, Whitman File: NSC Series, box 8. See also Eisenhower to Saud, 2 Nov. 1956, Hoover to Heath, 9 Nov. 1956, RG 59, 684A.86.

38. Dulles to Bohlen, 31 Oct. 1956, Bohlen to Dulles, 30 Oct. 1956, Dillon to Dulles, 1 Nov. 1956, Dulles to Hoover, 1 Nov. 1956, RG 59, 684A.86; report by Joint Middle East Planning Committee, 3 Nov. 1956, RG 218, CCS 381 EMMEA (11-19-47), sec. 47; Golan, *Soviet Policies*, 47–49.

39. Bulganin to Eisenhower, 5 Nov. 1956, RG 59, 684A.86; Bohlen to Dulles, 6 Nov. 1956, RG 59, 684A.86; memorandum of conversation by Goodpaster, 6 Nov. 1956, Whitman File: Diary Series, box 19. See also Lodge to Dulles, 7 Nov. 1956, WHCF-DDE (Confidential), box 72; Golan, *Soviet Policies*, 47–54.

40. Memorandum of conversation by Goodpaster, 5 Nov. 1956, Whitman File: Diary Series, box 19; CIA, SNIE 11-9-56, 6 Nov. 1956, *FRUS, 1955–1957*, 16:1018–20; memorandum of conversation by Goodpaster, 6 Nov. 1956, Whitman File: Diary Series, box 19; minutes of NSC meeting, 8 Nov. 1956, Whitman File: NSC Series, box 8. See also Moose to Dulles, 9 Nov. 1956, RG 59, 661.83.

41. Circular cable by JCS, 7 Nov. 1956, RG 218, JCS Geographic File 1954–56, box 14, CCS 381 EMMEA (11-19-47). See also Wentworth to Radford, 29 Oct. 1956, JCS to Eisenhower, 6 Nov. 1956, Radford to Goodpaster, 15 Nov. 1956, CJCS Radford, box 16, 091 Palestine; circular cable by Radford, 30 Oct. 1956, CNO to JCS, 4 Nov. 1956, CINCNELM to CNO, 11 Nov. 1956, RG 218, JCS Geographic File 1954–56, box 14, CCS 381 EMMEA (11-19-47); Condit, *History*, 186–89.

42. Hare to Dulles, 7 Nov. 1956, Seager to FitzGerald, 3 Dec. 1956, *FRUS, 1955–1957*, 16:1029–30, 1236–38; Lodge to Dulles, 7 Nov. 1956, WHCF-DDE (Confidential), box 82; Hoover to Hare, 18 Nov. 1956, Lodge to Dulles, 19 Nov. 1956, RG 59, 684A.86.

43. Ben-Gurion Diary (Hebrew), 7–8 Nov. 1956, Ben-Gurion Papers. See also Mallory to Dulles, 6 Nov. 1956, RG 59, 684A.86; Hare to Dulles, 6 Nov. 1956, Hoover to Hare, 6 Nov. 1956, *FRUS, 1955–1957*, 16:1027–28, 1032–33.

44. Joint Intelligence Staff brief, 29 Nov. 1956, RG 218, CJCS Radford, box 16, 091 Palestine. See also Burke to JCS, 13 Nov. 1956, memorandum by Rowden, 28 Nov. 1956, RG 218, JCS Geographic File 1954–56, box 14, CCS 381 EMMEA (11-19-47); Norstad to army, 24 Nov. 1956, RG 218, CJCS Radford, box 16, 091 Palestine; CIA, SNIE 11-10-56, 29 Nov. 1956, in U.S. Central Intelligence Agency, *CIA Cold War Records*, 147–52.

Chapter 16

1. Hahn, *United States*, 232–38.

2. Memorandum of conversation by Bergus, 19 Nov. 1956, RG 59, 684A.86; Ben-Gurion to Smith, 2 Jan. 1957, Ben-Gurion Papers, Correspondence File.

3. Memorandum of conversation by Bergus, 7 Nov. 1956, Lawson to Dulles, 31 Dec. 1956, 8 Jan. 1957, Dulles to Lawson, 5 Jan. 1957, Dulles to Eban, 8 Jan. 1957, RG 59, 674.84A; memorandum of conversation by Murphy, 13 Nov. 1956, RG 59, 684A.86; Collins to CJCS, 14 Nov. 1956, RG 218, CJCS Radford, box 16, 091 Palestine.

4. Eisenhower to Ben-Gurion, 7 Nov. 1956, Whitman File: International Series, box 29; Ben-Gurion to Eisenhower, 8 Nov. 1956, RG 130.23, 3088/6. See also memorandum of conversation by Wilkins, 1 Nov. 1956, Lawson to Dulles, 9 Nov. 1956, RG 59, 684A.86; Eban to Meir, 7 Nov. 1956, Ben-Gurion Papers, Correspondence File; memorandum of conversation by Bergus, 7 Nov. 1956, RG 59, 674.84A; Ben-Gurion Diary (Hebrew), 8 Nov. 1956, Ben-Gurion Papers; Foreign Ministry to Eban (Hebrew), 16 Nov. 1956, circular cable

by Eytan (Hebrew), 23 Nov. 1956, Arad to Hertzog (Hebrew), 30 Nov. 1956, RG 130.20, 2480/11.

5. Arad to USD (Hebrew), 16 Nov. 1956, RG 130.20, 2480/11. See also Engel et al. to Dulles, 3 Nov. 1956, RG 59, lot 62 D 11, box 6; resolutions, 27 Nov. 1956, Bernstein et al. to Eisenhower, 27 Nov. 1956, Goldmann Papers, Z6/1064; memorandum for the record by Hanes, 10 Dec. 1956, Dulles Papers, Special Assistant Series, box 11.

6. Memorandum by Arad (Hebrew), 6 Nov. 1956, Shiloah to Meir (Hebrew), 13 Nov. 1956, Eliav to Eban (Hebrew), 14 Nov. 1956, RG 130.20, 2480/11; memorandum of conversation by Bergus, 8 Nov. 1956, RG 59, lot 60 D 580, box 1; Herlitz to Foreign Ministry (Hebrew), 9 Nov. 1956, RG 130.23, 3107/1; Ben-Gurion Diary (Hebrew), 14, 24 Nov., 4 Dec. 1956, Ben-Gurion Papers.

7. Hoover to Lodge, 30 Nov. 1956, RG 59, 684A.86. See also circular cable by Eytan (Hebrew), 14 Nov. 1956, RG 130.02, 2414/28; memorandum of conversation by Gamon, 28 Nov. 1956, RG 59, 684A.86; Ben-Gurion Diary (Hebrew), 2 Dec. 1956, Ben-Gurion Papers; circular cable by Foreign Ministry (Hebrew), 3 Dec. 1956, RG 130.23, 3089/7; Wilkins to Rountree, 11, 26 Dec. 1956, Lawson to Dulles, 23 Dec. 1956, RG 59, lot 59 D 582, box 5; Lodge to Dulles, 11, 23 Jan. 1957, RG 59, 674.84A.

8. Memorandum of conversation by Bergus, 3 Dec. 1956, RG 59, 684A.86; Lawson to Dulles, 8 Jan. 1957, *FRUS, 1955–1957*, 17:12–14. See also memorandums of conversations by Bergus, 26 Nov., 28 Dec. 1956, RG 59, 684A.86; Lawson to Dulles, 31 Dec. 1956, 4 Jan. 1957, RG 59, 674.84A; memorandum of conversation by Gamon, 2 Jan. 1957, RG 59, lot 60 D 113, box 43.

9. Ben-Gurion Diary (Hebrew), 29 Dec. 1956, Ben-Gurion Papers; Lawson to Dulles, 22 Dec. 1956, RG 59, 674.84A; Ben-Gurion to Smith, 2 Jan. 1957, Ben-Gurion Papers, Correspondence File. See also memorandum of conversation by Yofay (Hebrew), 19 Nov. 1956, RG 130.20, 2480/11; Lawson to Dulles, 31 Dec. 1956, memorandum of conversation by Bergus, 22 Jan. 1957, RG 59, 674.84A.

10. Memorandum of conversation by Dulles, 31 Dec. 1956, Dulles to Lawson, 28 Dec. 1956, 5, 12 Jan. 1957, RG 59, 674.84A; Rountree to Dulles, 7 Jan. 1957, RG 59, lot 59 D 582, box 5; Rountree to Dulles, 16 Jan. 1957, RG 59, 974.7301; Rountree to Dulles, 17 Jan. 1957, RG 59, lot 69 D 488, box 2.

11. Lodge to Dulles, 29 Nov. 1956, RG 59, 684A.86. See also memorandum of conversation by Bergus, 7 Dec. 1956, RG 59, 684A.86.

12. Lodge to Dulles, 22 Feb. 1957, RG 59, 684A.86. See also editorial notes, *FRUS, 1955–1957*, 17:39, 78–79.

13. Memorandum of conversation by Stoltzfus, 7 Feb. 1957, *FRUS, 1955–1957*, 17:101–5. See also Ben-Gurion Diary (Hebrew), 7 Jan. 1957, Ben-Gurion Papers; Moose to Dulles, 16 Jan., 19 Feb. 1957, Lawson to Dulles, 25 Jan.–18 Feb. 1957, Hare to Dulles, 14 Feb. 1957, Israeli aide-mémoire, 15 Feb. 1957, RG 59, 674.84A; Ben-Gurion to Eisenhower, 8 Feb. 1957, Whitman File: International Series, box 29; memorandum of conversation by Newsom, 25 Feb. 1957, RG 59, 974.7301.

14. Lodge to Dulles, 5 Feb. 1957, RG 59, 674.84A. See also Lodge to Dulles, 23–25, 30 Jan., 5, 6 Feb. 1957, RG 59, 674.84A; Lodge to Wilcox, 24 Jan. 1957, RG 59, 684A.86; Lodge to Dulles, 24, 29 Jan. 1957, RG 59, 974.7301.

15. Memorandum of conversation, 12 Feb. 1957, *FRUS, 1955–1957*, 17:142–44; "Israel, Egypt, and the U.N.," *New York Times*, 11 Feb. 1957, p. 28; memorandum of conversation,

10 Feb. 1957, *FRUS, 1955–1957*, 17:120. See also Dulles to Lodge, 25, 29 Jan. 1957, memorandum of conversation by Hoffacker, 9 Feb. 1957, RG 59, 674.84A; Dulles to Lodge, 28 Jan. 1957, RG 59, 974.7301; Wilcox to Dulles, 7 Feb. 1957, RG 59, lot 59 D 582, box 5; Kenen, *Israel's Defense Line*, 133–37.

16. State Department aide-mémoire, 11 Feb. 1957, RG 59, 674.84A; memorandum of conversation by Wilkins, 15 Feb. 1957, RG 59, 674.84A. See also memorandum of conversation by Wilkins, 11 Feb. 1957, memorandums of conversations by Rountree, 16, 17 Feb. 1957, RG 59, 674.84A.

17. Memorandum of conversation, 13 Feb. 1957, *FRUS, 1955–1957*, 17:151. See also memorandum of conversation by Murphy, 11 Feb. 1957, RG 59, 611.84A; Eisenhower to Saud, 14 Feb. 1957, Whitman File: International Series, box 42; circular cable by Dulles, 14 Feb. 1957, RG 59, 674.84A; Ben-Gurion Diary (Hebrew), 16 Feb. 1957, Ben-Gurion Papers.

18. Memorandum of conversation by Dulles, 16 Feb. 1957, *FRUS, 1955–1957*, 17:178–80; memorandum of conversation by Adams, 18 Feb. 1957, RG 59, 674.84A. See also Yost to Dulles, 19 Feb. 1957, memorandum of conversation by Adams, 19 Feb. 1957, RG 59, 674.84A.

19. Address by Rogers, 11 Feb. 1957, address by Flood, 11 Feb. 1957, *Congressional Record*, vol. 103, pt. 2, pp. 1921, 1931; memorandum of conversation, 18 Feb. 1957, *FRUS, 1955–1957*, 17:196–97. See also Johnson to Dulles, 11 Feb. 1957, Whitman File: Dulles-Herter Series, box 6; addresses by Sikes, O'Hara, Addonizio, Roosevelt, Dingell, 11–21 Feb. 1957, *Congressional Record*, vol. 103, pt. 2, pp. 1914–15, 1919, 2029, 2445; voluminous correspondence from members of Congress, ca. 11 Feb. 1957, RG 59, 674.84A.

20. Notes on meeting by Johnson, n.d. [20 Feb. 1957], Johnson Papers, Senate Files, box 421; minutes of meeting, 20 Feb. 1957, Whitman File: Legislative Meetings Series, box 2.

21. Memorandums of conversations, 12, 22 Feb. 1957, *FRUS, 1955–1957*, 17:142–44, 239–40. See also record of phone call, 21 Feb. 1957, Whitman File: Diary Series, box 21; memorandum of conversation, 25 Feb. 1957, Johnson Papers, Senate Files, box 421; Lehman to Miller, 25 Feb. 1957, RG 130.23, 3088/8; proceedings of debate, 26 Feb. 1957, *Congressional Record*, vol. 103, pt. 2, pp. 2625–52.

22. Eisenhower to Macmillan, 23 Feb. 1957, RG 59, 974.7301; memorandum of conversation, 24 Feb. 1957, *FRUS, 1955–1957*, 17:253. See also Eisenhower to Ben-Gurion, 20 Feb. 1957, Whitman File: International Series, box 29; Ben-Gurion to Eisenhower, 22 Feb. 1957, Ben-Gurion Papers, Correspondence File; memorandum of conversation, 22 Feb. 1957, Dulles Papers, Special Assistant Series, box 11; memorandum of conversation, 22 Feb. 1957, Whitman File: Diary Series, box 21.

23. Memorandums of conversations, 24 Feb. 1957, *FRUS, 1955–1957*, 17:268–70, 280–83. See also memorandum of conversation by Rountree, 24 Feb. 1957, RG 59, 674.84A; memorandum of conversation by Gamon, 25 Feb. 1957, RG 59, lot 60 D 113, box 43; Dulles to Eisenhower, 26 Feb. 1957, *FRUS, 1955–1957*, 17:280–83.

24. Ben-Gurion Diary (Hebrew), 25 Feb. 1957, Ben-Gurion Papers; memorandum of conversation by Bergus, 25 Feb. 1957, Lodge to Dulles, 26 Feb. 1957, memorandum of conversation by Murphy, 1 Mar. 1957, Lawson to Dulles, 4–8 Mar. 1957, RG 59, 674.84A; Bernau to Dulles, 27 Feb. 1957, RG 59, 784A.00; memorandum for the record by Dulles, 28 Feb. 1957, Dulles Papers, Subject Series, box 7.

25. Memorandum of conversation, 28 Feb. 1957, *FRUS, 1955–1957*, 17:317–18. See also memorandum of conversation by Elbrick, 28 Feb. 1957, circular cable by Dulles, 28 Feb. 1957, memorandum of conversation by Wilkins, 1 Mar. 1957, RG 59, 674.84A; Hare to Dulles, 28 Feb. 1957, *FRUS, 1955–1957*, 17:322–23.

26. Ben-Gurion to Eisenhower, 13 Mar. 1957, Ben-Gurion Papers, Correspondence Series. See also memorandum of conversation by Goodpaster, 8 Mar. 1957, WHO Files, Office of Staff Secretary, International Series, box 8; memorandum of conversation by Rountree, 13 Mar. 1957, Dulles to Lodge, 19 Mar. 1957, RG 59, 674.84A; minutes of NSC meeting, 14 Mar. 1957, Whitman File: NSC Series, box 8.

27. Record of telephone conversation, 14 Mar. 1957, Whitman File: Diary Series, box 22; Eisenhower to Ben-Gurion, 13 Mar. 1957, Whitman File: International Series, box 29. See also Herter to Hare, 12, 13 Mar. 1957, Dulles to Lawson, 14 Mar. 1957, memorandum of conversation by Bergus, 18 Mar. 1957, RG 59, 674.84A; memorandum for the record by Herter, 14 Mar. 1957, Herter Papers, box 18; memorandum by Eisenhower, [21] Mar. 1957, Whitman File: Diary Series, box 22; Eisenhower to Mollet, 14 Mar. 1957, *FRUS, 1955–1957*, 17:418–19.

28. Memorandum by DePalma, 14 Mar. 1957, RG 59, lot 60 D 113, box 43. See also Hare to Dulles, 27 Mar. 1957, RG 59, 974.7301; Lodge to Dulles, 28 Mar. 1957, RG 59, 674.84A; Wilkins to Rountree, 29 Mar. 1957, Lawson to Dulles, 4 Apr. 1957, RG 59, 674.84A; NE briefing paper, 2 Apr. 1957, RG 59, lot 60 D 113, box 42.

29. Memorandum of conversation by Newsom, 25 Mar. 1957, RG 59, 974.7301. See also Wilkins to Rountree, 29 Mar. 1957, RG 59, 674.84A; minutes of NSC meeting, 29 Mar. 1957, Whitman File: NSC Series, box 8; Wadsworth to Dulles, 9 Apr. 1957, RG 59, 974.7301.

30. Memorandum of conversation by Bergus, 9 Mar. 1957, RG 59, lot 60 D 113, box 43; Metzger to Barbour, 18 Mar. 1957, minutes of meeting, 23 Mar. 1957, RG 59, lot 62 D 11, box 8; Dulles to Lawson, 14 Mar. 1957, memorandums of conversations by Bergus, 18, 29 Mar. 1957, Wilkins to Rountree, 29 Mar. 1957, RG 59, 674.84A.

31. Davidson to CNO, 17 Apr. 1957, RG 218, CJCS Radford, box 16, 091 Palestine. See also staff notes, 30 Mar. 1957, Whitman File: Diary Series, box 23; Hare to Dulles, 10 Apr. 1957, Hare to Dulles, 11 Apr. 1957, aide-mémoire from Nashashibi, 17 Apr. 1957, RG 59, 974.7301; Burke to Radford, 19 Apr. 1957, RG 218, CJCS Radford, box 16, 091 Palestine; memorandum for the record by Radford, 19 Apr. 1957, *FRUS, 1955–1957*, 17:557–58.

32. Memorandum of conversation by Bergus, 19 Apr. 1957, RG 59, 684A.86. See also briefing paper, n.d. [ca. 1 Apr. 1957], RG 218, JCS Geographic File 1957, box 4, CCS 381 EMMEA (11-19-47); Lawson to Dulles, 4 Apr. 1957, RG 59, 674.84A; Rountree to Dulles, 27 Apr. 1957, RG 59, lot 59 D 582, box 5; Lawson to Dulles, 10 May 1957, RG 59, 611.84A.

33. Lodge to Dulles, 19 Nov. 1956, Dulles to Hoover, 14 Dec. 1956, RG 59, 684A.86; memorandum of conversation, 26 Dec. 1956, Dulles-Princeton Papers, Telephone Conversation Series, box 5; memorandum of conversation by Dulles, 31 Dec. 1956, RG 59, 674.84A; Hare to Dulles, 10 Jan. 1957, RG 59, 674.00; Rountree to Dulles, 17 Jan. 1957, RG 59, lot 69 D 488, box 2; State Department paper, n.d. [ca. 25 Jan. 1957], WHCF-DDE (Confidential), box 73.

34. Minutes of NSC meeting, 7 Feb. 1957, Whitman File: NSC Series, box 8. See also State Department paper, n.d. [ca. 25 Jan. 1957], WHCF-DDE (Confidential), box 73; circular cable by Dulles, 13 Feb. 1957, Dulles to Hare, 29–30 Mar., 2, 8 Apr. 1957, RG 59, 974.7301; memorandum of conversation, 23 Feb. 1957, Whitman File: Diary Series, box 21;

State Department paper, 8 Mar. 1957, RG 59, lot 60 D 113, box 43; Hare to Dulles, 15 Feb. 1957, RG 59, 684A.86.

35. Minutes of meeting, 24 Jan. 1957, Whitman File: NSC series, box 8; Dulles to Lodge, 6 Feb. 1957, Rountree to Herter, 8 Mar. 1957, RG 59, 974.7301; memorandum of conversation by Murphy, 11 Feb. 1957, RG 59, 611.84A; Israeli aide-mémoire, 15 Feb. 1957, memorandum of conversation by Rountree, 24 Feb. 1957, RG 59, 674.84A.

36. Memorandum of conversation by Raymond, 4 Apr. 1957, RG 59, lot 69 D 488, box 2. See also Herter to Lawson, 9 Mar. 1957, RG 59, Lawson to Dulles, 4–5 Apr. 1957, Wilkins to Rountree, 16 Apr. 1957, RG 59, 674.84A; Dulles to Nasser, 19 Mar. 1957, Dulles-Princeton Papers, Selected Correspondence Series, box 123; Lawson to Dulles, 29 Mar. 1957, Dulles to Hare, 4 Apr. 1957, RG 59, 974.7301.

37. Memorandum of conversation by Elbrick, 18 Mar. 1957, RG 59, 674.84A; memorandum by Eisenhower, [21] Mar. 1957, Whitman File: Diary Series, box 22; minutes of meetings, 23 Mar., 3 Apr. 1957, RG 59, lot 62 D 11, box 8; Dulles to Lodge, 17 Apr. 1957, circular cable by Dulles, 26 Apr. 1957, Dulles to embassy in London, 11 May 1957, RG 59, 974.7301; memorandum of conversation by Goodpaster, 18 Apr. 1957, Whitman File: Diary Series, box 23; Eisenhower to Macmillan, 28 Apr. 1957, *FRUS, 1955–1957*, 17:574–75.

Chapter 17

1. Eisenhower to Dulles, 12 Dec. 1956, Whitman File: Dulles-Herter Series, box 6; memorandum of conversation by Goodpaster, 15 Dec. 1956, Whitman File: Diary Series, box 19. See also memorandum by Eisenhower, 8 Nov. 1956, Whitman File: Diary Series, box 19; NEA to Eisenhower, 21 Nov. 1956, RG 59, lot 66 D 487, box 76; memorandum of conversation by Dulles, 9 Dec. 1956, Dulles Papers, General Correspondence Series, box 1.

2. Eisenhower to Hazlett, 2 Nov. 1956, 5 Apr. 1957, in Griffith, *Ike's Letters*, 172–76, 179–80; Macmillan, *Riding*, 240. See also Bartlett, *"Special Relationship"*, 89–90.

3. Soviet statement quoted in Behbehani, *Soviet Union*, 153. See also NSC staff study on NSC 5801, 16 Jan. 1958, RG 273.

4. Paper by Dulles, 3 Feb. 1957, Dulles Papers, Subject Series, box 5. See also memorandum of conversation by Wilkins, 6 Feb. 1957, Whitman File: International Series, box 34; Baxter to Rountree, 16 May 1957, RG 59, lot 59 D 582, box 4.

5. Minutes of meeting, 1 Jan. 1957, Whitman File: Legislative Meetings Series, box 2; memorandum of conversation by Persons, 29 Jan. 1957, Whitman File: Diary Series, box 21. See also editorial note, *FRUS, 1955–1957*, 17:7–8.

6. Address by Ellender, 27 Feb. 1957, address by Morse, 2 Mar. 1957, *Congressional Record*, vol. 103, pt. 3, pp. 2689–93, 2940–48.

7. Proceedings of debate, 25 Feb. 1957, *Congressional Record*, vol. 103, pt. 2, pp. 2517–44; "A Soviet Counter-Blast," *New York Times*, 14 Feb. 1957, p. 26; Dulles to Eisenhower, 4 Mar. 1957, Whitman File: Dulles-Herter Series, box 6; Eisenhower to Richards, 9 Mar. 1957, WHCF-DDE (Official), box 594; Dulles to Richards, 9 Mar. 1957, RG 59, 120.1580.

8. Staff Notes #62, 9 Jan. 1957, special staff note, 1 Apr. 1957, Whitman File: Diary Series, boxes 21–22; Heath to Dulles, 8 Feb. 1957, RG 59, 683A.86; Mallory to Dulles, 16 Mar. 1957, RG 59, 120.1580; Rountree to Dulles, 4, 16, 17 Apr. 1957, RG 59, lot 57 D 616, box 14.

9. Reinhardt to Herter, 27 May 1960, *FRUS, 1958–1960*, 13:582–86. See also Hare to Dulles, 10 Jan. 1957, editorial note, *FRUS, 1955–1957*, 17:16–19, 565–66; Hare to Dulles, 15 Feb. 1957, RG 59, 684A.86; Rountree to Herter, 11 Apr. 1957, RG 59, lot 59 D 582, box 5.

10. Ben-Gurion Diary (Hebrew), 8 Apr. 1957, Ben-Gurion Papers. See also Lawson to Dulles, 8 Jan. 1957, RG 59, 974.7301; circular cable by Eytan (Hebrew), 6 Jan. 1957, RG 130.23, 3088/3; circular cable by Foreign Ministry (Hebrew), 20 Jan. 1957, RG 130.23, 3089/7; Wilkins to Rountree, 16 Apr. 1957, RG 59, 674.84A; Foreign Ministry paper (Hebrew), n.d. [Apr. 1957], RG 130.02/2, 4330/8.

11. Memorandum of conversation, 1 May 1957, Herter Papers, Telephone Conversation Series, box 10. See also Dulles to Richards, 18 Apr. 1957, Richards to Dulles, 4 May 1957, *FRUS, 1955–1957,* 17:552–53, 597–601; Israeli memorandum of conversation, 3 May 1957, RG 130.02/2, 4330/8; Ben-Gurion Diary (Hebrew), 3, 17–18 May 1957, Ben-Gurion Papers; Rountree to Dulles, 8 May 1957, memorandum by Richards, 25 May 1957, RG 59, lot 57 D 616, boxes 14, 16.

12. Radford to Wilson, 13 June 1957, JCS 1837/363, 13 June 1957, RG 218, JCS Geographic File 1957, box 5, CCS 381 EMMEA (11-19-47).

13. Radford to Wilson, 13 June 1957, JCS 1887/424, 20 Dec. 1957, RG 218, JCS Geographic File 1957, boxes 5, 7, CCS 381 EMMEA (11-19-47).

14. Joint Staff paper, 22 July 1957, RG 218, JCS Geographic File 1957, box 6, CCS 381 EMMEA (11-19-47); Radford briefing memorandum, 23 July 1957, RG 218, CJCS Radford, box 16, 091 Palestine.

15. JCS 1887/462, 17 June 1958, RG 218, JCS Geographic File 1958, box 144, CCS EMMEA (11-19-47). See also memorandum by JCS, 21 Feb. 1958, JCS 1887/461, 27 June 1958, Twining to secretary of defense, 27 June 1958, RG 218, JCS Geographic File 1958, box 144, CCS EMMEA (11-19-47); Twining to secretary of defense, 28 Mar. 1958, JCS Decimal File, box 92, CCS 381 (8-23-57); army COS to JCS, 14 Apr. 1958, JCS Decimal File, box 84, CCS 360 (12-9-42).

16. State Department position paper, n.d. [ca. 25 Jan. 1957], WHCF-DDE (Confidential), box 73. See also Chapin to Dulles, 22 Nov. 1956, RG 59, 684A.86.

17. Memorandum of conversation by Dulles, 5 Feb. 1957, Dulles Papers, General Correspondence and Memoranda Series, box 1; JCS to Wilson, 29 Nov. 1956, RG 218, JCS Geographic File 1954–56, box 14, CCS 381 EMMEA (11-19-47). See also State Department position paper, 18 Nov. 1956, RG 59, lot 66 D 487, box 76; Collins to Radford, 23 Nov. 1956, RG 218 CJCS Radford, 092.2 Baghdad Pact, box 22.

18. Elishar to West Europe Department (Hebrew), 21 Feb. 1957, RG 130.23, 3110/38. See also memorandum by Eliav (Hebrew), 18 Dec. 1956, memorandum by Cohn (Hebrew), n.d. [Jan. 1957], RG 130.23, 3110/38; Moose to Dulles, 16 Jan. 1957, RG 59, 684A.86; State Department paper, n.d. [ca. 25 Jan. 1957], WHCF-DDE (Confidential), box 73; comments on proceedings of conference, 26 Feb. 1957, Whitman File: International Series, box 42.

19. State Department position paper, 18 Nov. 1956; statement by Dulles, 16 Nov. 1956, RG 59, lot 66 D 487, box 76; Rountree to Dulles, 5 Dec. 1956, RG 59, 611.84A. See also memorandum of conversation, 24 Dec. 1956, Dulles-Princeton Papers, General Correspondence File, box 1; JCS 1887/374, 8 July 1957, RG 218, JCS Geographic File 1957, box 6, CCS 381 EMMEA (11-19-47); Rountree to Dulles, 19 Nov. 1957, RG 59, lot 59 D 582, box 5; minutes of meeting, 6 Feb. 1958, Whitman File: NSC Series, box 9.

20. Record of meeting, 27 July 1958, PREM 11/2400. See also minutes of meeting, 31 July 1958, Whitman File: NSC Series, box 10; Twining to McElroy, 15 Jan. 1959, RG 218, JCS Central File, box 118, CCS 9070 Baghdad Pact; State Department briefing book, 14 Mar. 1959, McElroy to Eisenhower, 1 Sept. 1959, WHCF-DDE (Confidential), box 78.

21. JCS 1887/340, 1 Feb. 1957, Twining to Rafiq, 4 Mar. 1957, Radford to Wilson, 11 June 1957, RG 218, JCS Geographic File 1957, box 4, CCS 381 EMMEA (11-19-47); Rountree to Dillon, 31 Mar. 1958, Rountree to Dulles, 16 Apr., 9 June 1958, memorandum of conversation by Rockwell, 22 Apr. 1958, RG 59, lot 61 D 20, box 1; Dulles to embassy in Beirut, 5 June 1958, RG 59, lot 59 D 600, box 2.

22. Eisenhower to Saud, 12 Sept. 1957, *FRUS, 1955–1957*, 17:734–36. See also Chairman's Staff Group to Radford, 11 Feb. 1957, RG 218, CJCS Radford, box 13, 091 Radford; comments on proceedings of Arab conference, 26 Feb. 1957, Whitman File: International Series, box 42; Hare to Dulles, 28 Feb. 1957, RG 59, 684A.86; Bergus to Rockwell, 9 Sept. 1957, RG 59, lot 59 D 582, box 5; Golan, *Soviet Policies*, 52–54.

23. Memorandum of conversation by Bergus, 6 Aug. 1957, Rountree to Dulles, 23 Aug. 1957, *FRUS, 1955–1957*, 17:701–6, 712–13; memorandum of conversation by Bergus, 12 Sept. 1957, memorandum of conversation by Rountree, 12 Oct. 1957, RG 59, 684A.86; CIA, "The Arab-Israeli Arms Problem," 30 Sept. 1958, CIA Records, ORIS; Rountree to Herter, 20 Oct. 1958, RG 59, lot 60 D 580, box 1.

24. Memorandum of conversation by Bergus, 6 Aug. 1957, memorandum of conversation by Brown, 31 Oct. 1957, *FRUS, 1955–1957*, 17:701–6, 784. See also Rockwell to Rountree, 12 Sept. 1957, RG 59, lot 59 D 582, box 5; memorandum of conversation by Rountree, 12 Oct. 1957, RG 59, 684A.86; memorandum of conversation by Hamilton, 26 Nov. 1958, RG 59, lot 61 D 12, box 2.

25. Eisenhower to Hazlett, 2 Nov. 1956, Whitman File: Diary Series, box 20; circular cable by Hoover, 21 Nov. 1956, RG 59, lot 66 D 487, box 76. See also memorandum of conversation by Goodpaster, 2 Nov. 1956, Whitman File: Diary Series, box 19; position paper by Dulles, 3 Feb. 1957, Dulles Papers, Subject Series, box 5; Dulles to Eisenhower, 5 Feb. 1957, Whitman File: Dulles-Herter Series, box 6.

26. Memorandum of conversation, 10 Dec. 1956, *FRUS, 1955–1957*, 16:1284–87. See also Lodge to Dulles, 23 Nov., 10 Dec. 1956, Moose to Dulles, 20 Nov., 7 Dec. 1956, Dulles to Lodge, 8 Dec. 1956, Wadsworth to Dulles, 15 Dec. 1956, RG 59, 684A.86; Hare to Dulles, 16 Dec. 1956, *FRUS, 1955–1957*, 16:1314–21; memorandum of conversation by Dulles, 31 Dec. 1956, RG 59, 674.84A.

27. Memorandum of conversation by Rockwell, 9 Dec. 1957, RG 59, 684A.86; memorandum of conversation by Newsom, 5 Dec. 1957, RG 59, 684A.86. See also extract of Arab memorandum, 18 Jan. 1957, Dulles Papers, Subject Series, box 11; State Department position paper, n.d. [ca. 25 Jan. 1957], WHCF-DDE (Confidential), box 73; Wilkins to Berry, 4 June 1957, RG 59, lot 59 D 582, box 5; memorandum of conversation by Rockwell, 17 Oct. 1957, RG 59, 611.84A; Hood to Foreign Office, 11 Dec. 1957, FO 371/128117.

28. Memorandum of conversation by Bergus, 29 Nov. 1957, RG 59, 684A.86. See also minutes of seminar, 11 July 1957, memorandum of conversation by Bergus, 21 Nov. 1957, RG 59, 684A.86; memorandum of conversation by Bergus, 6 Aug. 1957, *FRUS, 1955–1957*, 17:701–6.

29. Memorandum of conversation by Looram, 9 May 1957, RG 59, 974.7301; memorandum of conversation by Elbrick, 12 Nov. 1957, Whitman File: Dulles-Herter Series, box 7. See also Staff Notes #103, 26 Apr. 1957, Whitman File: Diary Series, box 23; memorandum of conversation by Dorman, 18 Dec. 1957, RG 59, 684A.86.

30. Memorandum of conversation by Wilkins, 6 Feb. 1957, Whitman File: International Series, box 34; agreed minutes of meeting, 23 Mar. 1957, RG 59, lot 62 D 11,

box 8. See also Sprague to Rountree, 2 Apr. 1957, RG 59, 674.84A; Lodge to Dulles, 5 June 1957, Dulles to Lodge, 13 June 1957, *FRUS, 1955–1957*, 17:633–34, 642; Dulles to Zellerbach, 13 June 1957, RG 59, lot 59 D 582, box 5.

31. Taylor to Wilson, 4 Dec. 1957, *FRUS, 1955–1957*, 17:837–38. See also CINCNELM to CNO, 7 Nov. 1957, RG 218, JCS Geographic File 1957, box 7, CCS EMMEA (11-19-47); memorandum of discussion, 13 Dec. 1957, *FRUS, 1955–1957*, 17:852–56.

32. Minutes of NSC meeting, 22 Jan. 1958, Whitman File: NSC Series, box 9.

33. NSC 5801, 24 Jan. 1958, RG 273. See also NSC Staff Study on NSC 5801, 16 Jan. 1958, RG 273.

34. Caccia to Lloyd, 7 Nov. 1957, FO 371/128116. See also memorandums of conversations by Dorman, 22, 25 Oct. 1957, *FRUS, 1955–1957*, 17:766–70, 774–75; Lloyd to Foreign Office, 23 Oct. 1957, FO 371/128116; State Department talking paper, 23 Nov. 1957, Lodge to Dulles, 20 Dec. 1957, RG 59, lot 59 D 582, box 5; memorandum of conversation by Dulles, 2 Jan. 1958, RG 59, 684A.80.

35. Minutes of meeting, 16 Oct. 1958, Whitman File: NSC Series, box 10; memorandum by Meyer, 10 July 1959, RG 59, lot 61 D 43, box 2. See also Eban to Dulles, 26 June 1958, RG 130.23, 3089/9; memorandum of conversation by Parker, 2 June 1958, RG 59, lot 61 D 20, box 2; minutes of meeting, 21 Aug. 1958, Whitman File: NSC Series, box 10; NSC 5820/1, 4 Nov. 1958, RG 273; progress report by OCB, 3 Feb. 1960, WHO Files, OSANSA, OCB Series, box 4.

36. Weir to O'Regan, 23 Nov. 1960, FO 371/150854. See also Weir to Rothnie, 15 July 1960, FO 371/150854; unsigned memorandum of conversation, 26 Nov. 1960, RG 130.23, 3294/1.

Chapter 18

1. Mallory to Dulles, 3 Apr. 1957, RG 59, 120.1580; Collins to assistant to secretary of defense, 15 Apr. 1957, RG 218, CJCS Radford, box 16, 091 Palestine; Parker, "United States," 107–13; Dann, *King Hussein*, 55–77.

2. Collins to assistant to secretary of defense, 15 Apr. 1957, RG 218, CJCS Radford, box 16, 091 Palestine. See also Dulles to Moose, 29 Mar. 1957, Mallory to Dulles, 22 Apr. 1957, Dulles to Lawson, 23 Apr. 1957, RG 59, 684A.85; memorandum of conversation by Waggoner, 28 Mar. 1957, RG 59, 683.84A; Mallory to Dulles, 3 May 1957, RG 59, 684A.86.

3. Circular cable by JCS, 25 Apr. 1957, RG 218, JCS Geographic File 1957, box 5, CCS 381 EMMEA (11-19-47). See also memorandum by Decker, 18 Feb. 1957, JMEPC 300/12, 19 Feb. 1957, RG 218, CJCS Radford, box 16, 091 Palestine; Drain to Dulles, 24 Apr. 1957, Dulles Papers, Special Assistant Chronological Series, box 11; circular cable by JCS, 25 Apr. 1957, CINCNELM to commander in chief, U.S. Atlantic Fleet, 26 Apr. 1957, memorandum by army COS, 7 May 1957, RG 218, JCS Geographic File 1957, box 5, CCS 381 EMMEA (11-19-47).

4. Herter to embassy in London, 1 May 1957, RG 59, 974.7301; Hare to Herter, 2 May 1957, Herter to Dulles, 3 May 1957, Dulles to Herter, 3 May 1957, editorial note, memorandum of conversation by Tyler, 6 May 1957, *FRUS, 1955–1957*, 17:586–87, 587–90, 595–96, 596–97, 601–3.

5. Lawson to Dulles, 25 Apr. 1957, RG 59, 684A.85; Rountree to Dulles, 27 Apr. 1957, RG 59, lot 59 D 582, box 5. See also Lawson to Dulles, 23 Apr. 1957, Dulles to Lawson, 23 May 1957, Dulles to Mallory, 29 May 1957, RG 59, 684A.85.

6. Mallory to Dulles, 24 July 1957, Dulles to Mallory, 24 July, 6, 19, 22, 28 Aug. 1957, memorandum of conversation by Parker, 26 July 1957, RG 59, 684A.85.

7. Rountree to Dulles, 30 Aug. 1957, RG 59, lot 59 D 582, box 5; Dulles to Lodge, 30 Aug. 1957, Dulles to Lawson, 30 Aug., 10 Sept. 1957, Dulles to Lodge, 5 Sept. 1957, RG 59, 684A.85; memorandums of conversations by Bergus, 12 Sept., 29 Nov. 1957, RG 59, 684A.86; Dulles to Ben-Gurion, 23 Oct. 1957, Ben-Gurion Papers, Correspondence Series.

8. Ben-Gurion Diary (Hebrew), 24 Oct. 1957, Ben-Gurion Papers; memorandum of conversation by Gamon, 30 Oct. 1957, RG 59, lot 60 D 113, box 43. See also memorandums of conversations by Bergus, 12 Sept., 29 Nov. 1957, RG 59, 684A.86; Dulles to Mallory, 4 Nov. 1957, Dulles to Lodge, 18 Nov. 1957, 7 Jan. 1958, RG 59, 684A.85; Israeli aide-mémoire, 18 Dec. 1957, RG 59, lot 60 D 113, box 43.

9. Rockwell to Rountree, 5 Oct. 1957, RG 59, lot 59 D 582, box 5; Dulles to Mallory, 23 Oct. 1957, Rockwell to Rountree, 30 June 1959, RG 59, 684A.85; Herter to Dulles, 22 Dec. 1957, Herter Papers, box 9; Franklin to Dulles, 4 June 1958, Dulles to Wright, 12 June 1958, RG 59, 684A.86.

10. Meir to Dulles, 7 Nov. 1958, RG 130.02/2, 4321/12. See also Dulles to Hare, 30 Oct. 1958, Dulles to Lawson, 31 Oct., 28 Nov. 1958, RG 59, 684A.85; memorandum of conversation by Brewer, 30 Oct. 1958, RG 59, 684A.86B; Ben-Gurion Diary (Hebrew), 6 Nov. 1958, Ben-Gurion Papers.

11. Morris to Rothnie, 29 Jan. 1960, FO 371/151195.

12. Minutes of meeting, 18 July 1957, Whitman File: NSC Series, box 9; Hare to Dulles, 26 Nov. 1957, RG 59, 611.74; memorandum of conversation by Stabler, 14 Jan. 1958, RG 59, 674.84A. See also minutes of NSC meeting, 24 May 1957, Whitman File: NSC Series, box 8; memorandum of conversation by Rountree, 12 Oct. 1957, RG 59, lot 60 D 580, box 1.

13. Memorandum of conversation by Bergus, 27 Feb. 1958, *FRUS, 1958–1960,* 13:20–27. See also memorandum of conversation by Ludlow, 13 Feb. 1958, RG 59, 684A.85; Dulles to Lawson, 19 Feb. 1958, memorandum of conversation by Parker, 10 Mar. 1958, RG 59, 684A.86; memorandum of conversation by Bergus, 9 May 1958, RG 59, lot 61 D 12, box 2; Kerr, *Arab Cold War,* 10–25.

14. Collins to CJCS, 8 Feb. 1957, RG 218, CJCS Radford, box 16, 091 Palestine; memorandum of conversation by Waggoner, 1 Apr. 1957, Dulles to Lodge, 30 Apr., 16 May 1957, Lodge to Dulles, 1, 16 May 1957, Dulles to Moose, 22 May 1957, RG 59, 683.84A.

15. Minutes of meeting, 18 July 1957, Whitman File: NSC Series, box 8; memorandum of conversation by Parker, 23 July 1957, RG 59, 683.84A. See also circular cable by Dulles, 9 July 1957, memorandum of conversation by Wilkins, 10 July 1957, RG 59, 683.84A; memorandum of conversation by Bergus, 12 Sept. 1957, RG 59, 684A.86.

16. Memorandum of conversation by Lawson, 14 Dec. 1958, *FRUS, 1958–1960,* 13:131–36. See also memorandum of conversation by Eagleton, 20 Feb. 1958, circular cable by Dulles, 1 Apr. 1958, Lawson to Dulles, 8 Apr. 1958, RG 59, 684A.86; Rockwell to Rountree, 5 Dec. 1958, Herter to Lawson, 11 Dec. 1958, Hare to Dulles, 13 Dec. 1958, RG 59, 684A.86B; Meyer to Hart, 18 Dec. 1958, RG 59, lot 60 D 580, box 1.

17. Rockwell to Rountree, 27 Jan. 1959, RG 59, lot 61 D 43, box 2; memorandum of conversation by Wilcox, 29 Jan. 1959, RG 59, 684A.86B; Reid to Herter, 2 Feb., 18 Feb. 1960, RG 59, 684A.86; memorandum of conversation by Hamilton, 1 Feb. 1960, Dillon to Lodge, 25 Feb. 1960, *FRUS, 1958–1960,* 13:261, 272–73.

18. Gendzier, *Notes*; Petran, *Struggle*; State Department paper, 12 May 1958, intelligence paper, 14 May 1958, RG 59, lot 59 D 600, box 1.

19. Minutes of meetings, 27, 29 May, 3 June 1958, Whitman File: NSC Series, box 10.

20. Twining to secretary of defense, 8 Jan. 1958, RG 218, JCS Geographic File 1958, box 143, CCS EMMEA (11-19-47); memorandum of conversation by Bergus, 27 Mar. 1958, RG 59, 684A.86; memorandum by Wentworth, 7 Apr. 1958, RG 218, JCS Decimal File, box 92, CCS 381 (8-23-57); McClintock to Dulles, 13 May 1958, intelligence paper, 14 May 1958, memorandum of conversation by Thompson, 20 May 1958, RG 59, lot 59 D 600, box 1.

21. Minutes of meeting, 29 May 1958, Whitman File: NSC Series, box 10; State Department paper, 10 June 1958, memorandum of conversation by Sisco, 13 June 1958, RG 59, lot 59 D 600, box 2; Dulles to embassy in Beirut, 11 June 1958, Whitman File: International Series, box 34.

22. Burke to CINCNELM, 17 June 1958, RG 218, JCS Geographic File 1958, box 155, CCS 381 Lebanon; memorandum of conversation by Bernau, 20 June 1958, *FRUS, 1958–1960*, 11:163–64; memorandum of conversation by Bergus, 30 June 1958, RG 59, 611.84A; "Lebanon: Mideastern Austria," *New York Times*, 9 July 1958, p. 26. See also memorandum of conversation by Hanes, 15 June 1958, memorandum of conversation by Parker, 2 July 1958, RG 59, lot 59 D 600, box 2; memorandum of conversation by Rountree, 1 July 1958, Whitman File: Diary Series, box 35.

23. Dulles to embassy in Beirut, 18 June 1958, Whitman File: International Series, box 34; CINCNELM to commander, Middle East Forces, 4 July 1958, RG 59, lot 59 D 600, box 2; memorandum of conversation by Bergus, 30 June 1958, RG 59, 611.84A. See also Barnes to JCS, 23 June 1958, RG 218, JCS Geographic File 1958, box 155, CCS 381 Lebanon; Dulles to Lodge, 26 June 1958, circular cables by Herter, 4 July 1958, RG 59, lot 59 D 600, boxes 2–3; minutes of meeting, 3 July 1958, Whitman File: NSC Series, box 10.

24. Memorandum of conversation by Goodpaster, 14 July 1958, *FRUS, 1958–1960*, 11: 211–15; memorandum of conversation, 16 July 1958, Whitman File: Diary Series, box 34. See also military attaché to army, 14 July 1958, Dulles to McClintock, 15 July 1958, circular cable by Dulles, 15 July 1958, Murphy to Dulles, 17–19, 22, 30 July 1958, Chamoun to Eisenhower, 21 July 1958, RG 59, lot 59 D 600, boxes 3–4.

25. Memorandum of conversation by Goodpaster, 15 July 1958, Eisenhower to Humphrey, 22 July 1958, Whitman File: Diary Series, box 35. See also memorandum of conversation by Goodpaster, 14 July 1958, *FRUS, 1958–1960*, 11:211–15; record of meeting, 27 July 1958, PREM 11/2400; Jackson to Dulles, 7 Aug. 1958, Jackson Papers, box 63; Gallup, *Gallup Poll*, 1560–61.

26. Minutes of meeting, 31 July 1958, Whitman File: NSC Series, box 10. See also memorandum for the record by Stimpson, 4 Aug. 1958, Herter Papers, Memorandum Series, box 18; Little, "His Finest Hour?"

27. Memorandum of conversation by Goodpaster, 16 July 1958, Whitman File: Diary Series, box 35. See also Allen Dulles briefing notes, 14 July 1958, WHO Files, Office of Staff Secretary, International Series, box 10; CNO to commander, U.S. Sixth Fleet, 17 July 1958, RG 218, JCS Decimal File, box 92, CCS 381 (8-23-57).

28. Record of conversation, 14 July 1958, PREM 11/2387; Thompson to Dulles, 19 July 1958, Whitman File: International Series, box 36; memorandum of conversation, 15 July 1958, Whitman File: Diary Series, box 34. See also memorandum of conversation, 14 July 1958, Whitman File: Diary Series, box 34; Allen Dulles briefing notes, 14 July 1958, WHO Files, Office of Staff Secretary, International Series, box 10.

29. Thompson to Dulles, 16 July 1958, RG 59, lot 59 D 600, box 4; Thompson to Dulles, 19 July 1958, Whitman File: International Series, box 36. See also Whisenand to Twining, 16 July 1958, memorandum by Joint Staff, 22 July 1958, RG 218, JCS Decimal File, box 92, CCS 381 (8-23-57); Phillips to CJCS, 18 July 1958, RG 218 CJCS Twining, box 9, 091 Middle East; intelligence synopsis, 23 July 1958, Whitman File: International Series, box 35; Leverton to CNO, 19 July 1958, Twining statement, 24 July 1958, RG 218, JCS Geographic File 1958, box 155, CCS 381 Lebanon.

30. Ben-Gurion Diary (Hebrew), 17 July 1958, Ben-Gurion Papers. See also Foreign Office to Salt, 17 July 1958, Foreign Office to Caccia, 17 July 1958, Macmillan to Ben-Gurion, 17 July 1958, Ben-Gurion to Macmillan, 17 July 1958, Rundall to Lloyd, 21 July 1958, PREM 11/2377; memorandum of conversation, 18 July 1958, Herter Papers, Telephone Conversation Series, box 11.

31. Burrows to Lloyd, 21 July 1958, PREM 11/2377; Ben-Gurion Diary (Hebrew), 18 July 1958, Ben-Gurion Papers; memorandum of conversation, 18 July 1958, Herter Papers, Telephone Conversation Series, box 11. See also minutes of meeting, 22 July 1958, Whitman File: Diary Series, box 35; Oren, "Test," 66–83.

32. Ben-Gurion Diary (Hebrew), 18 July 1958, Ben-Gurion Papers. See also memorandum of conversation by Reinhardt, 19 July 1958, *FRUS, 1958–1960*, 11:340–43.

33. Memorandum of conversation, 16 July 1958, Herter Papers, Telephone Conversation Series, box 11. See also JCS to CINCSPECOMME, 16 July 1958, CNO to commander, U.S. Sixth Fleet, 17 July 1958, CNO to CINCSPECOMME, 18 July 1958, RG 218, JCS Decimal File, box 92, CCS 381 (8-23-57); memorandum of conversation by Goodpaster, 20 July 1958, Whitman File: Diary Series, box 35; Lodoen to Twining, 23 July 1956, RG 218, CJCS Twining, box 9, 091 Middle East.

34. Macmillan to Eisenhower, 22 July 1958, *FRUS, 1958–1960*, 11:366–67; Foreign Office to Caccia, 22 July 1958, PREM 11/2377.

35. Memorandum of conversation by McKinnon, 23 July 1958, *FRUS, 1958–1960*, 11:374–76; record of meeting, 27 July 1958, PREM 11/2388. See also Eisenhower to Macmillan, 24 July 1958, PREM 11/2377; JCS to CINCSPECOMME, 24 July 1958, CNO to CINCSPECOMME, 25 July 1958, RG 218, JCS Decimal File, box 92, CCS 381 (8-23-57).

36. JCS to CINCSPECOMME, 24 July 1958, RG 218, JCS Decimal File, box 92, CCS 381 (8-23-57); Ben-Gurion Diary (Hebrew), 24 July 1958, Ben-Gurion Papers; Eisenhower to Ben-Gurion, 25 July 1958, RG 130.23, 3294/3. See also Rundall to Lloyd, 19 July 1958, PREM 11/2377; Ben-Gurion Diary (Hebrew), 17–26 July 1958, Ben-Gurion Papers; Ben-Gurion to Eisenhower, 24 July 1958, Dulles to Eisenhower, 27 July 1958, Whitman File: International Series, box 36.

37. Rundall to Lloyd, 2 Aug. 1958, PREM 11/2377. See also Ben-Gurion Diary (Hebrew), 1–2 Aug. 1958, Ben-Gurion Papers; CNO to CINCSPECOMME, 3 Aug. 1958, RG 218, JCS Decimal File, box 93, CCS 381 (8-23-57); Rundall to Lloyd, 3 Aug. 1958, Hood to Lloyd, 3 Aug. 1958, PREM 11/2377.

38. Memorandum of conversation by Rockwell, 3 Aug. 1958, *FRUS, 1958–1960*, 11:426–27; Rundall to Lloyd, 4 Aug. 1958, PREM 11/2377; Ben-Gurion Diary (Hebrew), 4 Aug. 1958, Ben-Gurion Papers.

39. Ben-Gurion Diary (Hebrew), 10 Aug. 1958, Ben-Gurion Papers; Eban quoted in *FRUS, 1958–1960*, 11:427n. See also JCS to CINCSPECOMME, 5 Aug. 1958, RG 218, JCS Geographic File 1958, box 155, CCS 381 Lebanon; Hood to Lloyd, 5–6 Aug. 1958,

PREM 11/2377; minutes of meeting, 7 Aug. 1958, Whitman File: NSC Series, box 10; JCS to CINCSPECOMME, 21 Aug. 1958, RG 218, JCS Decimal File, box 93, CCS 381 (8-23-57); Ben-Gurion Diary (Hebrew), 26 Aug. 1958, Ben-Gurion Papers.

40. Memorandum of conversation by Bergus, 12 Aug. 1958, memorandum of conversation by Freers, 12 Aug. 1958, *FRUS, 1958–1960*, 11:455–61, 461–67. See also Rundall to Lloyd, 29 Aug. 1958, FO 371/134313.

41. Memorandum of conversation by Reinhardt, 8 Aug. 1958, *FRUS, 1958–1960*, 11: 444–45. See also Middleton to Lloyd, 4 Aug. 1958, Hood to Lloyd, 8 Aug. 1958, FO 371/ 134313; minute by Hadow, 14 Aug. 1958, Rundall to Hadow, 12 Sept. 1958, FO 371/134313.

42. Macmillan, *Riding*, 534. See also memorandums of conversations, 14, 23 Aug. 1958, Herter Papers, Telephone Conversation Series, box 11; memorandum of conversation by Lakeland, 15 Oct. 1958, RG 59, lot 61 D 20, box 1; Morris to Hadow, 10 Dec. 1958, Caccia to Lloyd, 18 Dec. 1958, FO 371/134313.

Chapter 19

1. Staats to OCB, 29 Apr. 1957, WHO Files, NSC Staff Papers, box 79; Wilcox to Herter, 10 May 1957, RG 59, lot 60 D 113, box 44.

2. Wilcox and Rountree to Dulles, 2 July 1957, RG 59, lot 60 D 113, box 44. See also Wilcox to Rountree, 11 Mar. 1957, Wilcox to Herter, 10 May, 12 Dec. 1957, Wilcox to Dulles, 2 Oct. 1957, RG 59, lot 60 D 113, boxes 43–44; Gustin to Staats, 30 Apr. 1957, WHO Files, NSC Staff Papers, box 79; Rountree to Dulles, 25 May 1957, RG 59, lot 59 D 582, box 5; memorandum of conversation by Palmer, 25 Aug. 1959, *FRUS, 1958–1960*, 13:190–93.

3. Lawson to Dulles, 12 May 1957, RG 59, 674.84A; memorandum of conversation by Wilcox, 25, 31 May, 6 June 1957, Wilcox and Rountree to Dulles, 2 July 1957, RG 59, lot 60 D 113, box 44; addresses by Javits, 5, 24 June, 9 July 1957, *Congressional Record*, vol. 106, pt. 6, pp. 8362–63, pt. 8, 10093–94, 11067–69.

4. Wilcox and Rountree to Dulles, 2 July 1957, Villard to Herter, 6 Aug. 1957, RG 59, lot 60 D 113, box 44.

5. Rountree to Dulles, 14 June 1957, RG 59, lot 59 D 582, box 5; memorandum of conversation by Bergus, 6 Aug. 1957, RG 59, 611.80; Villard to Dulles, 30 Sept. 1957, Howe to Herter, 8 Aug. 1957, *FRUS, 1955–1957*, 17:706–8, 741–43; Liebesny to Parker, 10 Dec. 1957, RG 59, lot 61 D 20, box 2.

6. Villard to Herter, 24 Dec. 1957, RG 59, lot 60 D 113, box 44. See also Villard to Dulles, 21 Nov. 1957, Herter to Dulles, 16 Dec. 1957, *FRUS, 1955–1957*, 17:807–16, 857–59; Rountree to Dulles, 6 Dec. 1957, RG 59, lot 59 D 582, box 5; Villard to Herter, 28 Apr. 1958, Dillon to Herter, 4 Nov. 1958, *FRUS, 1958–1960*, 13:51–54, 108–14.

7. McClintock to Herter, 29 Jan. 1958, Herter to McClintock, 13 Feb. 1958, Herter Papers, box 20. See also Villard to Herter, 6 Mar. 1958, RG 59, lot 61 D 12, box 2.

8. Herter to embassy in London, 28 Nov. 1958, *FRUS, 1958–1960*, 13:120–22. See also Rountree to Herter, 5 Aug. 1958, RG 59, lot 61 D 12, box 2; memorandum by Herter, 1 Dec. 1958, Herter Papers, box 11.

9. Memorandum of conversation by Newsom, 21 Nov. 1958, Gore and McGee to Eisenhower, 19 Nov. 1959, *FRUS, 1958–1960*, 13:114–16, 226–28. See also memorandum of conversation by Ludlow, 1 Dec. 1958, *FRUS, 1958–1960*, 13:122–24; Meyer to McClintock, 24 July 1959, RG 59, lot 61 D 43, box 1; Hare to Herter, 17 Dec. 1959, RG 59, 611.86B.

10. Herter to Lodge, 12 Mar. 1959, Hammarskjöld to Dillon, 4 June 1959, *FRUS, 1958–1960*, 13:154–56, 180–81. See also memorandum of conversation by Walmsley, 23 Apr. 1959, *FRUS, 1958–1960*, 13:170–71.

11. Memorandum of conversation by Atherton, 4 Nov. 1959, RG 59, lot 61 D 20, box 1; Lodge to Dulles, 5 Nov. 1959, memorandums of conversations by Brewer, 10, 24 Nov. 1959, Herter to Lodge, 25 Nov. 1959, Davis to Wilcox, 25 Apr. 1960, memorandum of conversation by Palmer, 5 Oct. 1960, *FRUS, 1958–1960*, 13:215–18, 231–33, 237–38, 376–79, 311–12.

12. Memorandum of conversation by Ludlow, 15 Mar. 1960, *FRUS, 1958–1960*, 13:300–302; Ben-Gurion Diary (Hebrew), 6 Dec. 1959, Ben-Gurion Papers; memorandum of conversation by Meyer, 10 Mar. 1960, *FRUS, 1958–1960*, 13:291–92. See also Ben-Gurion Diary (Hebrew), 3, 22 Nov. 1959, Ben-Gurion Papers; Reid to Herter, 2 Dec. 1959, *FRUS, 1958–1960*, 13:239–40; Eban to Eliav, 14 Dec. 1959, RG 130.23, 3089/10; State Department paper, 5 Mar. 1960, WHCF-DDE (Confidential), box 79.

13. Foreign Ministry paper (Hebrew), 11 Jan. 1960, RG 130.23, 3294/3. See also Eliav to Comay (Hebrew), 7 Nov. 1958, RG 130.23, 3089/10; memorandum of conversation by Wahl, 7 Dec. 1959, *FRUS, 1958–1960*, 13:244–46; Foreign Ministry paper (Hebrew), 10 Jan. 1960, RG 130.23, 3294/3.

14. Memorandum of conversation by Funseth, 7 June 1960, *FRUS, 1958–1960*, 13:330–33. See also Cargo to Wilcox, 25 May 1960, Herter to Warren, 13 Aug. 1960, *FRUS, 1958–1960*, 13:322–27, 361–63; Herter to Eisenhower, 10 June 1960, Whitman File: Dulles-Herter Series, box 10.

15. Memorandum of conversation by State Department, 22 Sept. 1960, Whitman File: International Series, box 34; memorandum of conversation by Jones, 26 Sept. 1960, *FRUS, 1958–1960*, 13:600–607. See also circular cables by Herter, 22 June, 9 Sept., 1 Oct. 1960, *FRUS, 1958–1960*, 13:338–40, 368, 375–76; Gazit to Raphael (Hebrew), 16 Sept. 1960, RG 130.23, 3294/13; memorandum of conversation by John Eisenhower, 22 Sept. 1960, Whitman File: International Series, box 34.

16. Villard to Dulles, 8 Oct. 1957, *FRUS, 1955–1957*, 17:749–51; memorandum of conversation by Bergus, 10 Mar. 1958, Herter to Hare, 8 May 1959, Hare to Herter, 4 Dec. 1959, RG 59, 684A.85322; Johnston to Herter, 9 Apr. 1959, *FRUS, 1958–1960*, 13:158–61; Rockwell to Rountree, 25 May 1959, RG 59, lot 61 D 43, box 1.

17. Franklin to Dulles, 19–20 Nov., 4 Dec. 1957, Dulles to Franklin, 14 Nov. 1957, memorandums of conversations by Bergus, 3, 27 Mar. 1958, RG 59, 684A.85322; Berry to Herter, 10 Feb. 1958, Ludlow to Bergus, 19 Mar. 1958, RG 59, 684A.8531.

18. Ben-Gurion Diary (Hebrew), 7 Mar. 1958, Ben-Gurion Papers; Rountree to Dulles, 27 Feb. 1958, Cutler to Eisenhower, 28 Mar. 1958, *FRUS, 1958–1960*, 13:20–23, 34–36; Rountree to Herter, 5 Apr. 1958, U.S. aide-mémoire, 1 Aug. 1958, RG 59, 684A.85322; memorandum of conversation by Bergus, 30 June 1958, RG 59, 611.84A.

19. McClintock to Herter, 12 Jan. 1960, RG 59, 684A.85322. See also memorandums of conversations by Hamilton, 27 Jan., 9 Mar., 22 Apr., 22 July 1959, Dillon to Reid, 24 July 1959, Hare to Herter, 4 Dec. 1959, Mills to Herter, 10 Dec. 1959, RG 59, 684A.85322; Israeli aide-mémoire, 17 July 1959, RG 59, lot 61 D 43, box 2; State Department position paper, 6 Mar. 1960, WHCF-DDE (Confidential), box 79.

20. Memorandum of conversation by Atherton, 8 Dec. 1959, RG 59, 684A.85322. See also Rountree to Dillon, 19 Feb. 1959, Meyer to Reid, 28 Sept. 1959, RG 59, lot 61 D 43, boxes 1–2; U.S. aide-mémoire, 7 May 1959, memorandum of conversation by Wahl, 28 Oct. 1959,

Mills to Dillon, 15 Dec. 1959, Dillon to Mills, 18 Dec. 1959, Herter to McClintock, 20 Jan. 1960, RG 59, 684A.85322; Meyer to Hart, 14 Oct. 1959, RG 59, 611.84A.

21. Hart to Dillon, 17 Nov. 1959, Herter to Reid, 20 Nov. 1959, Dillon to Reid, 9 Jan. 1960, RG 59, 684A.85322; Meyer to Hart, 1 Dec. 1959, RG 59, lot 61 D 43, box 2; minutes of meetings (Hebrew), 28–29 Dec. 1959, RG 130.23, 3088/7; progress report by OCB, 3 Feb. 1960, WHO Files, OSANSA, OCB Series, box 4; Ben-Gurion Diary (Hebrew), 4 Mar. 1960, Ben-Gurion Papers; State Department position paper, 6 Mar. 1960, WHCF-DDE (Confidential), box 79.

22. Statement by Arab envoys, 24 May 1957, *FRUS, 1955–1957,* 17:625–26; Rountree to Dulles, 25 May 1957, RG 59, lot 59 D 582, box 5. See also Eisenhower to Saud, 11, 16 May 1957, Whitman File: International Series, box 42; Wilcox to Dulles, 16 May 1957, RG 59, lot 69 D 488, box 2; Rountree to Herter, 7 June 1957, RG 59, 974.7301; Arneson to Dulles, 17 July 1957, RG 59, 684A.86.

23. Rountree to Dulles, 24 June 1957, *FRUS, 1955–1957,* 17:656–59. See also Wilkins to Meeker, 3 June 1957, Wilkins to Rountree, 27 June 1957, RG 59, 974.7301; Saudi Arabian aide-mémoire, 25 June 1957, Whitman File: International Series, box 42.

24. Eisenhower to Dulles, 27 June 1957, Whitman File: Dulles-Herter Series, box 7; U.S. aide-mémoire, n.d. [12 July 1957], Whitman File: International Series, box 42; minutes of meeting, 19 July 1957, Whitman File: NSC Series, box 8. See also memorandum of conversation, 27 June 1957, Dulles Papers, Telephone Conversation Series; Eisenhower to Saud, 10 July 1957, Whitman File, Dulles-Herter Series, box 7; Wadsworth to Dulles, 14 July 1957, RG 59, 684A.86; Eisenhower to Saud, 12 Sept. 1957, Whitman File: International Series, box 42; memorandum of conversation by Brewer, 29 Nov. 1957, RG 59, 684A.86.

25. Memorandum of conversation by Bergus, 13 June 1957, *FRUS, 1955–1957,* 17:642–45; Eban quoted in Rountree to Herter, 7 June 1957, RG 59, 974.7301. See also memorandum of conversation by Sherwood, 9 May 1957, air attaché Cairo to air force chief of staff, 16 May 1957, RG 59, lot 69 D 488, box 2; Rountree to Dulles, 21 May 1957, RG 59, lot 59 D 582, box 5; Gallman to Dulles, 28 May 1957, RG 59, 684A.86; Israeli aide-mémoire, 29 May 1957, RG 59, 974.7301.

26. Lawson to Dulles, 8 Apr. 1958, *FRUS, 1958–1960,* 13:39–41. See also minutes of meeting, 14 June 1957, Whitman File: NSC Series, box 8; NSC Staff Study on NSC 5801, 16 Jan. 1958, RG 273; Ben-Gurion Diary (Hebrew), 28 Mar. 1958, Ben-Gurion Papers; Lawson to Dulles, 18 June 1958, RG 59, 611.84A.

27. Dulles to Lawson, 18 May 1957, RG 59, 974.7301. See also Dulles to Cannon, 21 May 1957, RG 59, 974.7301; Rountree to Dulles, 25 May 1957, RG 59, lot 59 D 582, box 5; Ben-Gurion Diary (Hebrew), 22 July 1957, Ben-Gurion Papers; Lawson to Dulles, 29 Jan. 1958, RG 59, 674.84A6; Meir to Hammarskjöld, 6 Jan., 28 Oct. 1958, RG 130.02/2, 4321/13.

28. Meyer to Reid, 28 Sept. 1959, RG 59, lot 61 D 43, box 2. See also Rockwell to Rountree, 10 June 1959, Meyer to Jones, 14 July 1959, Jones to Herter, 14 Sept. 1959, Meyer to Hart, 16 Nov. 1959, RG 59, lot 61 D 43, box 2; State Department briefing book, 4 Mar. 1960, WHCF-DDE (Confidential), box 79.

29. Rountree to Herter, 29 Apr. 1959, *FRUS, 1958–1960,* 13:530–34. See also Dillon to Herter, 17 July 1959, memorandum of conversation by Herter, 11 Dec. 1959, *FRUS, 1958–1960,* 13:541–42, 567–68.

30. Jones to Meyer, 5 Oct. 1959, RG 59, lot 61 D 43, box 2; memorandum of conversation by Wahl, 7 Dec. 1959, *FRUS, 1958–1960,* 13:245. See also Meyer to Jones, 9 Sept. 1959, RG 59, lot 61 D 43, box 2; Meir to Hammarskjöld, 16 Nov. 1959, RG 130.02/2, 4321/13.

31. Memorandum of conversation by Jones, 16 Dec. 1959, RG 59, 684A.86B; Foreign Ministry paper (Hebrew), 11 Jan. 1960, RG 130.23, 3294/3; Dillon to Reid, 27 Feb. 1960, *FRUS, 1958–1960*, 13:274–75. See also Meyer to Jones, 11 Dec. 1959, RG 59, lot 61 D 43, box 2; memorandum of conversation by Wahl, 29 Dec. 1959, RG 59, 684A.86B; memorandum of conversation by Hart, 7 Oct. 1960, WHO Files, Office of Staff Secretary, box 9.

32. Rountree to Herter, 11 July 1958, RG 59, 611.84; memorandum of conversation by Hamilton, 11 June 1959, RG 59, 611.84A; memorandum of conversation by Hamilton, 9 Mar. 1959, *FRUS, 1958–1960*, 13:151–52. See also memorandum of conversation by Bergus, 30 June 1958, RG 59, 611.84A; circular by Herter, 20 Feb. 1959, *FRUS, 1958–1960*, 13: 147–49.

33. Dulles to Eisenhower, 5 Mar. 1957, Whitman File, Dulles-Herter Series, box 7. See also Ben-Gurion Diary (Hebrew), 25 Feb. 1958, Ben-Gurion Papers; Rountree to Dulles, 27 Feb. 1958, memorandums of conversations by Bergus, 21–22 Apr. 1958, *FRUS, 1958– 1960*, 13:20–23, 44–46, 49–51; memorandum for the record by Herter, 22 Apr. 1958, Eisenhower Library, Herter Papers, box 11.

34. Memorandum by Meyer, n.d. [ca. Mar. 1959], RG 59, lot 61 D 43, box 2.

35. Harman to Avner (Hebrew), 10 Feb. 1960, RG 130.23, 3294/3. See also address by Javits, 5 June 1957, *Congressional Record*, vol. 103, pt. 6, pp. 8362–63; memorandum of conversation by Bergus, 6 Aug. 1957, RG 59, 611.80; Macomber to Javits, 9 Jan. 1959, RG 59, lot 61 D 43, box 1; Dillon to Fulbright, 2 May 1960, *FRUS, 1958–1960*, 13:315–18.

36. Circular cable by Herter, 22 Apr. 1960, *FRUS, 1958–1960*, 13:310; memorandum of conversation, 2 May 1960, Whitman File: Diary Series, box 50; Russell to Twining, 6 May 1960, RG 218, CJCS Twining, box 9, 091 Middle East; memorandum of conversation, 28 Apr. 1960, Dillon to Fulbright, 2 May 1960, Reid to Herter, 19 May 1960, *FRUS, 1958– 1960*, 13:313–18, 321; Kenen, *Israel's Defense Line*, 148–53.

37. Memorandum of conversation by Rountree, 12 Oct. 1957, RG 59, lot 60 D 580, box 1. See also NSC staff study on NSC 5801, 16 Jan. 1958, RG 273.

38. Minutes of NSC meeting, 22 Jan. 1958, Whitman File: NSC Series, box 9; Rockwell to Rountree, 19 Feb., 9 Mar. 1959, State Department briefing book, 17 Mar. 1959, RG 59, lot 61 D 43, boxes 1–2; Anschuetz to Dulles, 1 Mar. 1959, Hare to Dulles, 9 Apr. 1959, RG 59, 611.84A.

Chapter 20

1. Minutes of meeting, May 1953, RG 130.20, 2474/4; memorandum by Dulles, 1 June 1953, RG 59, lot 64 D 563, box 30; memorandum of conversation by Goitein, 6 Mar. 1953, RG 130.20, 2460/6; Avner to Bender, 9 Sept. 1953, RG 130.20, 2475/2. See also memorandums of conversations by Goitein, 11, 27 Feb. 1953, RG 130.20, 2479/10; Eban memorandum, 8 Oct. 1953, RG 130.20, 2460/6; record of conference, 14 May 1954, WHO Files, NSC Staff Papers, OCB Series, box 77.

2. Eban memorandum, 8 Oct. 1953, RG 130.20, 2460/6; Ben-Gurion Diary (Hebrew), 2, 11 July 1954, Ben-Gurion Papers. See also Ben-Gurion Diary (Hebrew), 28 Mar. 1953, Ben-Gurion Papers; Silver to Adams, 24 May 1955, Silver Papers, Correspondence 6-1 File; Eban, *Autobiography*, 172–75.

3. Tivnan, *The Lobby*, 37–50; Goldberg, *Foreign Policy*, 15–17.

4. Gallup, *Gallup Poll*, 1454–57, 1464, 1484–85; Gilboa, *American Public Opinion*, 32–

33. For accounts emphasizing the closeness of U.S.-Israeli relations in the late 1950s, see Little, *American Orientalism*, 93–95; Little, "Making"; Safran, *Israel*, 353–80; Alteras, *Eisenhower*.

5. Sharett to Dulles, 12 Apr. 1955, RG 59, 601A.86; Jernegan to Dulles, 13 Apr. 1955, RG 59, 601.84A11; Lawson to Dulles, 17 Nov. 1955, RG 59, 684A.86. See also memorandum of conversation by Goitein, 25 Feb. 1953, RG 130.20, 2460/6; notes by Eytan, 17 June 1954, RG 130.20, 2480/4.

6. Circular telegram by Dulles, 24 Aug. 1955, RG 59, 684A.86; memorandum of conversation by Brown, 31 Oct. 1957, RG 59, 611.84A; Shiloah to Eban (Hebrew), 10 Feb. 1958, RG 130.23, 3088/6; Dulles to Eisenhower, 5 Mar. 1958, Whitman File: Dulles-Herter, box 7; memorandum of conversation by Rockwell, 3 Aug. 1958, *FRUS, 1958–1960*, 13:82–83; Eban to Meir (Hebrew), 11 Oct. 1958, summary of discussion (Hebrew), 1 Dec. 1958, Eliav to Eban (Hebrew), 6 Apr. 1959, Eban to Eliav (Hebrew), 28 Apr. 1959, RG 130.23, 3088/6–7.

7. Memorandum of conversation by Jones, 16 Dec. 1959, RG 59, 684A.86B; Avnon to Herzog (Hebrew), 27 July 1959, RG 130.23, 3089/10; State Department position paper, 5 Mar. 1960, WHCF-DDE (Confidential), box 79. See also Eliav to Herzog (Hebrew), 6 Apr. 1959, Herzog to USD (Hebrew), 16 Dec. 1959, RG 130.23, 3089/10; memorandum of conversation by Jones, 12 Aug. 1959, RG 59, 601.84A11; Meyer to Jones, 9 Sept. 1959, RG 59, 611.84A; Foreign Ministry paper (Hebrew), 10 Jan. 1960, RG 130.23, 3294/3.

8. Eban to Dulles, 31 Jan. 1956, RG 130.20, 2480/9; Rountree to Dulles, 8 June 1956, RG 59, 611.84A. See also memorandum of conversation by Grant, 10 Apr. 1953, RG 330, CD 092 Israel; memorandum of conversation by Elliott, 15 Nov. 1953, RG 59, lot 57 D 298, box 12; Kohn to Eban, 7 Mar. 1956, RG 130.20, 2480/10.

9. Memorandum of conversation, 10 Mar. 1960, WHO Files, Office of Staff Secretary, International Series, box 8. See also JCS 1887/347, 14 Mar. 1957, RG 218, JCS Geographic File 1957, box 4, CCS EMMEA (11-19-47); Gazit to Ben-Gurion (Hebrew), 11 Sept. 1957, RG 130.23, 3089/8; memorandum of conversation by Bergus, 30 June 1958, RG 59, lot 60 D 580, box 1; Avner to Eban (Hebrew), 21 Dec. 1958, RG 130.23, 3088/6; Foreign Ministry paper (Hebrew), 10 Jan. 1960, RG 130.23, 3294/3; Herter to Ben-Gurion, 4 Aug. 1960, RG 130.23, 3294/3.

10. Reinhardt to Herter, 24 Dec. 1960, Merchant to Reid, 31 Dec. 1960, *FRUS, 1958–1960*, 13:609–11, 399–400. See also minutes of NSC meeting, 8 Dec. 1960, Herter to Reid, 9 Dec. 1960, *FRUS, 1958–1960*, 13:391–92, 393–94; memorandums of conversations by Goodpaster, [19 Dec. 1960], 12 Jan. 1961, circular cable by Herter, 22 Dec. 1960, WHO Files, Office of the Staff Secretary, International Series, box 8.

11. Minutes of NSC meeting, 1 Nov. 1956, *FRUS, 1955–1957*, 16:907; Ben-Gurion to Smith, 2 Jan. 1957, Ben-Gurion Papers, Correspondence File. See also Eisenhower to Ben-Gurion, 7 Nov. 1956, Whitman File: International Series, box 29; Ben-Gurion to Eisenhower, 8 Feb. 1957, Ben-Gurion Papers, Correspondence File; memorandum of conversation by Bergus, 2 Apr. 1957, *FRUS, 1955–1957*, 17:504–9.

12. Memorandum of conversation by Goodpaster, 24 July 1958, Whitman File: Diary Series, box 35; minutes of NSC meeting, 21 Aug. 1958, *FRUS, 1958–1960*, 12:154–56.

13. NSC 5820/1, 4 Nov. 1958, RG 273. See also minutes of NSC meeting, 16 Oct. 1958, Whitman File: NSC Series, box 10.

14. Avner to Hertzog (Hebrew), 12 Aug. 1958, Hertzog to Avner (Hebrew), 21 Aug. 1958, RG 130.23, 3088/6.

15. Rockwell to Rountree, 9 June 1959, RG 59, lot 61 D 43, box 2; memorandum of conversation by Hamilton, 11 June 1959, RG 59, 611.84A. See also memorandum of conversation by Hamilton, 7 May 1959, RG 59, 611.84A; memorandum by Meyer, 10 July 1959, Meyer to Jones, 9 Sept. 1959, RG 59, lot 61 D 43, box 2.

16. Lawson to Dulles, 29 Feb. 1956, RG 59, 684A.86; Lawson to Dulles, 20 Apr. 1956, RG 59, 674.84A; Bergus to Lawson, 16 Mar. 1957, RG 59, lot 59 D 582, box 4. See also Mart, "Tough Guys."

17. Hahn, *United States*, 155–210; Gerges, *Superpowers*; Wahab Sayed-Ahmed, *Nasser*.

18. Minutes of meeting, 15 Nov. 1956, Whitman File, NSC Series, box 8; Hoover to Hare, 11 Dec. 1956, RG 59, 684A.86; Eisenhower to Dulles, 12 Dec. 1956, Dulles to Hare, 20 Dec. 1956, Whitman File: Dulles-Herter Series, box 6.

19. "Conference on Suez," *New York Times*, 30 July 1956, p. 20. See also Gilboa, *American Public Opinion*, 27–33; Gallup, *Gallup Poll*, 1464.

20. Office of Naval Intelligence paper, 6 Feb. 1957, RG 218, JCS Geographic File 1957, box 7, CCS 092 Egypt (7-28-56); Hare to Dulles, 2 July 1957, *FRUS, 1955–1957*, 17:677–79. See also Dulles to Hare, 25 Feb. 1957, RG 59, 974.7301; State Department memorandum, 8 Mar. 1957, RG 59, lot 60 D 113, box 43; memorandum of conversation, 21 May 1957, Whitman File: Dulles-Herter Series, box 6; Rountree to Dulles, 8 Oct. 1957, RG 59, 611.74.

21. State Department paper, 20 Nov. 1956, RG 59, 684A.86; Little, "Cold War"; Lesch, *Syria*; Saunders, *United States*.

22. Moose to Dulles, 19 May 1957, RG 59, 683.84A. See also circular cable by JCS, 13 Apr. 1957, RG 218, JCS Geographic File 1957, box 4, CCS 381 EMMEA (11-19-47); minutes of meeting, 16 May 1957, Whitman File: NSC Series, box 8; Collins to CJCS, 17 June 1957, RG 218, CJCS Radford, box 16, 091 Palestine; memorandum of conversation, 14 Aug. 1957, Herter Papers, Telephone Conversation Series, box 10; Little, "Cold War," 69–75.

23. Memorandum of conversation by John Eisenhower, 21 Aug. 1957, Whitman File: International Series, box 43; memorandum of conversation by Goodpaster, 7 Sept. 1957, Whitman File: International Series, box 43. See also circular by JCS, 21 Aug. 1957, RG 218, JCS Geographic File 1957, box 6, CCS 381 EMMEA (11-19-47); circular by CJCS, 23 Aug. 1957, RG 218, JCS Decimal File, 381 (8-23-57), box 41.

24. Memorandum of conversation by Goodpaster, 7 Sept. 1957, Whitman File: International Series, box 43; memorandum of conversation by Dulles, 28 Oct. 1957, Dulles Papers, General Correspondence and Memoranda Series, box 1. See also memorandums for the record by Goodpaster, 26, 28 Aug. 1957, Whitman File: International Series, box 43; Dulles to embassy in Jidda, 27 Aug. 1957, RG 59, 683.00.

25. Memorandum for the record by Goodpaster, 26 Aug. 1957, memorandum of conversation by Goodpaster, 7 Sept. 1957, Eisenhower to Saud, 12 Sept. 1957, Whitman File: International Series, boxes 42–43. See also Dulles to Eisenhower, 20 Aug. 1957, Whitman File: Dulles-Herter Series, box 7; memorandum of conversation by Eliav (Hebrew), 17 Sept. 1957, RG 130.23, 3089/8; circular cable by Twining, 27 Sept. 1957, RG 218, JCS Geographic File 1957, box 6, CCS 381 EMMEA (11-19-47); Bergus to Baxter, 4 Oct. 1957, RG 59, lot 59 D 582, box 4.

26. Memorandum of conversation by Macomber, 6 Oct. 1957, Dulles Papers, General Correspondence and Memoranda Series, box 1. See also memorandum of conversation by Stearns, 6 Sept. 1957, RG 59, 674.85; Wilcox and Rountree to Dulles, 4 Oct. 1957, RG 59, lot 60 D 113, box 43; Rockwell to Rountree, 15 Oct. 1957, RG 59, 674.83.

27. Minutes of meeting, 6 Feb. 1958, Whitman File: NSC Series, box 9. See also Moose to Dulles, 16 Jan. 1957, RG 59, 684A.86; Yost to Dulles, 15, 24 Jan. 1958, RG 59, 674.83; unsigned paper, n.d. [ca. early 1960], Whitman File: Dulles-Herter Series, box 10.

28. Dulles to Herter, 29 Jan. 1958, *FRUS, 1958–1960*, 13:412–13; Dulles to embassy in Baghdad, 8 Feb. 1958, RG 59, 674.83. See also Herter to Eisenhower, 30 Jan. 1958, Whitman File: International Series, box 42; Dulles to Eisenhower, 8 Feb. 1958, Whitman File: Dulles-Herter Series, box 7.

29. Circular cable by Herter, 15 Feb. 1958, *FRUS, 1958–1960*, 13:425–26. See also circular cable by Dulles, 21 Jan. 1958, circular cable by Herter, 25 Jan. 1958, Herter to Dulles, 25 Jan. 1958, RG 59, 674.83; minutes of meeting, 6 Feb. 1958, Whitman File: NSC Series, box 9; Hare to Dulles, 10 Feb. 1958, Dulles to embassy in Baghdad, *FRUS, 1958–1960*, 13: 422–25, 430–32.

30. Eisenhower to Dulles, 13 Nov. 1957, Whitman File: Dulles-Herter Series, box 7; memorandum of conversation by Rockwell, 9 Dec. 1957, RG 59, 611.74. See also Hart to Dulles, 30 Oct. 1957, RG 59, 611.74; Lodge to Dulles, 7 Nov. 1957, memorandum of conversation by Shaw, 2 Dec. 1957, RG 59, 611.74; State Department paper, 2 July 1958, RG 59, lot 59 D 600, box 2; Dulles to Eisenhower, 25 July 1958, *FRUS, 1958–1960*, 13:464–65.

31. Memorandum of conversation by Dorman, 3 Mar. 1958, Murphy to Hare, 8 Aug. 1958, *FRUS, 1958–1960*, 13:432–34, 469; memorandum of conversation by Corrigan, 11 Aug. 1958, Whitman File: International Series, box 49. See also Reid to Dulles, 28 Feb. 1958, RG 59, 684A.86; memorandum of conversation by Brewer, 4 Sept., 8 Oct. 1958, Dulles to Hare, 29 Sept. 1958, Hare to Dulles, 7 Nov. 1958, RG 59, 611.86B.

32. Minutes of meeting, 15 Jan. 1959, Whitman File: NSC Series, box 11. See also Hare to Dulles, 15 Dec. 1958, *FRUS, 1958–1960*, 13:505–9; briefing book, 14 Mar. 1959, WHCF-DDE (Confidential), box 78; Meyer to Hart, 22 Oct. 1959, RG 59, lot 61 D 43, box 2; Henderson to Hare, 12 Dec. 1959, RG 59, 684A.85322.

33. Memorandum of conversation by John Eisenhower, 23 Dec. 1958, *FRUS, 1958–1960*, 13:509–11; Rockwell to Rountree, 31 Mar. 1959, RG 59, lot 61 D 43, box 2. See also Rountree to Kamel, 9 Mar. 1959, Hare to Herter, 13 Sept. 1959, *FRUS, 1958–1960*, 13:152–54, 547–49.

34. Eliav to Arnon (Hebrew), 21 May 1958, circular by Meir (Hebrew), 18 Dec. 1958, RG 130.23, 3089/9–10; Ben-Gurion Diary (Hebrew), 7 Dec. 1958, Ben-Gurion Papers. See also Eliav to minister in Washington (Hebrew), 3 Jan. 1958, Eliav to Meroz (Hebrew), 20 Apr. 1958, Arnon to Mahav (Hebrew), 12 May 1958, paper by Eliav (Hebrew), 29 Dec. 1958, RG 130.23, 3089/8–10.

35. Reinhardt to Herter, 5 July 1960, *FRUS, 1958–1960*, 13:587–89. See also Herter to Reid, 7 Nov. 1959, Herter to Hare, 7, 9 Nov. 1959, Herter to Lodge, 22 July 1960, RG 59, 684A.86B; Weir to Rothnie, 13 June 1960, FO 371/150918; Dillon to Eisenhower, 25 Aug. 1960, Whitman File: Dulles-Herter Series, box 11.

36. Eisenhower to Dillon, 25 Aug. 1960, Whitman File: Dulles-Herter Series, box 11; memorandum of conversation by Hagerty, 20 Sept. 1960, Jones to Reinhardt, 11 Oct. 1960, *FRUS, 1958–1960*, 13:369–72, 607–9. See also Jones to Reinhardt, 6 Sept. 1960, memorandum of conversation by Brewer, 14 Sept. 1960, *FRUS, 1958–1960*, 13:596–98, 598–600.

37. Arnon to USD (Hebrew), 16 Sept. 1960, memorandum by Cohen (Hebrew), 2 Oct. 1960, Arnon to Harman (Hebrew), 6 Oct. 1960, report by Gazit (Hebrew), 12 Oct. 1960, RG 130.23, 3294/19; memorandum of conversation by Hagerty, 20 Sept. 1960, Whitman File: Diary Series, box 52.

38. Memorandum of conversation by Jones, 26 Sept. 1960, Whitman File: Diary Series, box 53. See also Reinhardt to Herter, 24 Dec. 1960, *FRUS, 1958–1960*, 13:609–11.

39. Memorandum by Meyer, 27 June 1959, RG 59, lot 61 D 43, box 1. See also Dulles to Eisenhower, 5 Feb. 1957, Whitman File: Dulles-Herter Series, box 6; Heath to Dulles, 8 Feb. 1957, RG 59, 683A.86; Heath to Rountree, 6 Mar. 1957, Waggoner to Rockwell, 29 July 1957, RG 59, lot 59 D 582, box 5; memorandum of conversation by Waggoner, 8 Nov. 1957, RG 59, 674.84A; Dillon to Eisenhower, 21 Sept. 1960, Whitman File: Diary Series, box 53.

40. Memorandum by Eisenhower, 31 Jan. 1957, Whitman File: Dulles-Herter Series, box 6. See also memorandum of conversation by Goodpaster, 30 Jan. 1957, Whitman File: Diary Series, box 21; Eisenhower to Saud, 14, 28 Feb. 1957, Whitman File: International Series, box 42.

41. Levin to Meir (Hebrew), 18 Jan. 1957, RG 130.23, 3089/7. See also Fellman to Eban, 21 Jan. 1957, Voron to Eban (Hebrew), 30 Jan. 1957, RG 130.23, 3089/7.

42. Minutes of meeting, 12 Mar. 1957, CAB 128, CC 17(57)7; JCS 1887/347, 14 Mar. 1957, circular cable by JCS, 13 Apr. 1957, RG 218, JCS Geographic File 1957, box 4, CCS 381 EMMEA (11-19-47); Eisenhower to Chamoun, 25 Apr. 1957, Whitman File: International Series, box 32; Dann, *King Hussein*; Satloff, *From Abdullah to Hussein*.

43. Unsigned paper, n.d. [ca. 1 Apr. 1957], RG 218, JCS Geographic File 1957, box 4, CCS 381 EMMEA (11-19-47); Hamilton to Dulles, 30 Apr. 1957, RG 59, 684A.85; minutes of meeting, 16 May 1957, Whitman File: NSC Series, box 8; State Department briefing paper, 24 June 1957, RG 59, lot 61 D 20, box 1; Bergus to Rockwell, 30 Sept. 1957, RG 59, lot 59 D 582, box 5.

44. Memorandum of conversation by Rountree, 27 July 1958, Dulles to Hare, 28 Oct. 1958, memorandum of conversation by Hamilton, 26 Nov. 1958, *FRUS, 1958–1960*, 13:74–77, 497–98, 116–17; Rountree to Dulles, 31 Oct. 1958, Dulles to Ben-Gurion, 31 Oct. 1958, RG 59, 684A.85.

45. Memorandum of conversation, 25 Mar. 1959, Whitman File: Dulles-Herter Series, box 39; memorandum by Meyer, 6 July 1959, RG 59, lot 61 D 43, box 1. See also State Department briefing paper, 11 Mar. 1959, RG 59, lot 61 D 43, box 2; Herter to Eisenhower, 21 Mar. 1959, White House Office: Office of Staff Secretary, box 9; Meyer to Barrows, 21 July 1959, RG 59, lot 61 D 43, box 1.

46. Memorandum of conversation by Brewer, 30 Apr. 1959, *FRUS, 1958–1960*, 13:534–40; Herter to Mills, 10 Sept. 1960, WHO Files, Office of Staff Secretary, box 9; Dillon to Eisenhower, 6 Oct. 1960, memorandum of conversation by Hart, 7 Oct. 1960, Reinhardt to Herter, 3 Nov. 1960, WHO Files, Office of Staff Secretary, International Series, boxes 4, 9.

47. Memorandum of conversation by Fritzlan, 11 Oct. 1954, *FRUS, 1952–1954*, 9:2389–90; NIE 36.2-56, 17 July 1956, *FRUS, 1955–1957*, 12:997–1010; memorandum of conversation by Rountree, 5 Feb. 1957, Whitman File: Dulles-Herter Series, box 6; memorandum of conversation by Berry, 6 Feb. 1957, RG 59, lot 61 D 20, box 1; JCS 1887/347, 14 Mar. 1957, RG 218, JCS Geographic File 1957, box 4, CCS 381 EMMEA (11-19-47); Herter to embassy in Amman, 13 Feb. 1958, *FRUS, 1958–1960*, 11:274–75.

48. Jackling to Foreign Office, 13 Sept. 1958, Wright to Foreign Office, 4–5 Nov. 1958, Trevelyan to Foreign Office, 20 Dec. 1958, FO 371/133086; Cohen to Hertzog (Hebrew), 12 Sept. 1958, Eliav to Meroz (Hebrew), 14 Sept. 1958, RG 130.23, 3089/13; Rountree to Murphy, 16 Oct. 1958, Rockwell to Rountree, 26 Nov. 1958, RG 59, lot 61 D 20, box 1; min-

utes of meeting, 23 Dec. 1958, Whitman File: NSC Series, box 10; Thacher, "Reflections"; Axelgard, "U.S. Support."

49. Memorandum by Lakeland, 15 Jan. 1959, RG 59, lot 61 D 43, box 1; memorandum of conversation by Dulles, 19 Jan. 1959, RG 59, 611.74. See also minutes of meeting, 18 Dec. 1958, Whitman File: NSC Series, box 10; Rountree to Dulles, 17 Jan. 1959, RG 59, 611.84A; State Department briefing book, 14 Mar. 1959, WHCF (Confidential), box 78; minutes of meetings, 17, 23, 30 Apr., 13, 17 May 1959, Whitman File: NSC Series, box 11.

50. Minutes of meeting, 5 Mar. 1959, Whitman File: NSC Series, box 11; Hare to Herter, 17 Dec. 1959, *FRUS, 1958–1960,* 13:569–71; memorandum for the record, 4 Jan. 1960, with NSC 5820/1, memorandum for the record, 13 Jan. 1960, with NSC 6011, RG 273; NSC staff paper, 2 June 1960, WHO Files, OSANSA, NSC Series, box 13.

51. Eliav to Eban (Hebrew), 21 Sept. 1959, RG 130.23, 3088/7. See also Ben-Gurion Diary (Hebrew), 2 Jan. 1960, Ben-Gurion Papers.

BIBLIOGRAPHY

Unpublished Primary Sources

UNITED STATES

Abilene, Kansas
Dwight D. Eisenhower Library
  John Foster Dulles Papers
    Chronological Series
    General Correspondence and Memoranda Series
    Special Assistant Series
    Subject Series
    Telephone Conversations Series
    White House Memoranda Series
  Dwight D. Eisenhower Papers (White House Central File)
    Confidential File
    General File
    Official File
  Dwight D. Eisenhower Papers (Ann Whitman File)
    Administration Series
    Cabinet Series
    Diary Series
    Dulles-Herter Series
    International Meetings Series
    International Series
    Legislative Meetings Series
    Name Series
    National Security Council Series
    Ann Whitman Diary Series
  Gordon Gray Papers
  Alfred M. Gruenther Papers
  John W. Hanes Jr. Papers
  Christian A. Herter Papers
    Chronological Series
    Memoranda-Correspondence Series
    Telephone Conversations Series

C. D. Jackson Papers
Thomas P. Pike Papers
Clarence Randall Journals
Walter Bedell Smith Papers
White House Office Files
  NSC Staff Papers
  Office of the Special Assistant for National Security Affairs
  Office of the Staff Secretary

Austin, Texas
Lyndon B. Johnson Library
  Lyndon B. Johnson Papers

Cleveland, Ohio
The Temple
  Rabbi Abba Hillel Silver Papers

Hyde Park, New York
Franklin D. Roosevelt Library
  Henry Morgenthau Jr. Diary
  Franklin D. Roosevelt Papers (Official File)
  Franklin D. Roosevelt Papers (President's Personal File)
  Franklin D. Roosevelt Papers (President's Secretary's File)
    Diplomatic Correspondence File
    Safe File
    Subject File
  Samuel Rosenman Papers

Independence, Missouri
Harry S. Truman Library
  Dean G. Acheson Papers
  Eben A. Ayers Papers
  Gordon R. Clapp Papers
  Clark M. Clifford Papers
  Matthew J. Connelly Papers
  Robert L. Dennison Papers
  George M. Elsey Papers
  Harry N. Howard Papers
  Edward Jacobson Papers
  David Lloyd Papers
  Edwin A. Locke Papers
  George C. McGhee Papers
  National Security Council Papers
  Naval Aide to the President Office Files
  David K. Niles Papers

Psychological Strategy Board Papers
John W. Snyder Papers
Stephen J. Spingarn Papers
Harry S. Truman Papers (President's Secretary's File)
    Appointments File
    Chronological Name File
    Diaries File
    General File
    Historical File
    Intelligence File
    Political File
    Subject File
    Trip File
    White House File
Harry S. Truman Papers (White House Central File)
    Confidential File
    General File
    Official File
    President's Personal File
Chaim Weizmann Papers
Sidney R. Yates Papers

New Haven, Connecticut
Yale University
    Dean G. Acheson Papers
    Chester Bowles Papers
    Ogden Reid Papers

Princeton, New Jersey
Princeton University
    Allen W. Dulles Papers
    John Foster Dulles Papers

Washington, D.C.
Library of Congress
    Benjamin V. Cohen Papers
    Averell Harriman Papers
National Archives
    General Records of the Department of State (RG 59)
    Records of the Army Staff, Operations Division (RG 165)
    Records of the Army Staff, Plans and Operations Division (RG 319)
    Records of the Central Intelligence Agency (RG 263)
    Records of the Joint Chiefs of Staff (RG 218)
    Records of the National Security Council (RG 273)
    Records of the Office of the Secretary of Defense (RG 330)

GREAT BRITAIN

London
Public Record Office
  Political Correspondence of the Foreign Office (FO 371)
  Records of Cabinet Committees, General Series (CAB 134)
  Records of Commonwealth and International Conferences (CAB 133)
  Records of the Cabinet Office (CAB 128, 129)
  Records of the Foreign Secretary's Office (FO 800)
  Records of the Prime Minister's Office (PREM 8, 11)

ISRAEL

Jerusalem
Central Zionist Archives
  Nachum Goldmann Papers
  Jewish Agency for Palestine—American Section Papers
Israel State Archive
  Protocols of the Cabinet
  Protocols of the Provisional Government of Israel
  Records of the Foreign Minister and Director-General of the Foreign Ministry (RG 130.02)
  Records of the Foreign Ministry, Central Registry, Political Files (RG 130.23)
  Records of the Israeli Embassy in Washington (RG 93.08)
  Records of the Prime Minister (RG 43)
  Records of the U.S. Division, Foreign Ministry (RG 130.20)

Sde Boqer
David Ben-Gurion Library
  David Ben-Gurion Papers
    Correspondence Files
    Diary
    General Chronological Documents
    Oral History Interviews
    Protocols

Tel Aviv
Histadrut Archive
  Records of the International Division, Histadrut

Published Primary Sources

OFFICIAL DOCUMENTS

Israel. State Archive. *Documents on the Foreign Policy of Israel.* Vol. 1, *15 May–30 September 1948.* Jerusalem: Government Printer, 1981.

————. *Documents on the Foreign Policy of Israel.* Vol. 2, *October 1948–April 1949.* Jerusalem: Government Printer, 1984.

————. *Documents on the Foreign Policy of Israel.* Vol. 3, *Armistice Negotiations, 1949.* Jerusalem: Government Printer, 1983.

————. *Documents on the Foreign Policy of Israel.* Vol. 4, *May–December 1949.* Jerusalem: Government Printer, 1986.

————. *Documents on the Foreign Policy of Israel.* Vol. 5, *1950.* Jerusalem: Government Printer, 1988.

————. *Documents on the Foreign Policy of Israel.* Vol. 6, *1951.* Jerusalem: Government Printer, 1991.

————. *Documents on the Foreign Policy of Israel.* Vol. 7, *1952.* Jerusalem: Government Printer, 1992.

————. *Documents on the Foreign Policy of Israel.* Vol. 8, *1953.* Jerusalem: Government Printer, 1995.

————. *Documents on the Foreign Policy of Israel.* Vol. 14, *1960.* Jerusalem: Government Printer, 1997.

U.S. Central Intelligence Agency. *CIA Cold War Records: Selected Estimates on the Soviet Union, 1950–1959.* Washington, D.C.: Central Intelligence Agency, 1993.

U.S. Congress. *Congressional Record.* Washington, D.C.: U.S. Government Printing Office, 1948–60.

U.S. Department of State. *Bulletin* 28:729 (15 June 1953).

————. *Foreign Relations of the United States, 1946.* Vol. 7, *The Near East and Africa.* Washington, D.C.: U.S. Government Printing Office, 1969.

————. *Foreign Relations of the United States, 1947.* Vol. 5, *The Near East and Africa.* Washington, D.C.: U.S. Government Printing Office, 1971.

————. *Foreign Relations of the United States, 1948.* Vol. 5, *The Near East, South Asia, and Africa.* Washington, D.C.: U.S. Government Printing Office, 1975.

————. *Foreign Relations of the United States, 1949.* Vol. 6, *The Near East, South Asia, and Africa.* Washington, D.C.: U.S. Government Printing Office, 1977.

————. *Foreign Relations of the United States, 1950.* Vol. 5, *The Near East, South Asia, and Africa.* Washington, D.C.: U.S. Government Printing Office, 1978.

————. *Foreign Relations of the United States, 1951.* Vol. 5, *The Near East and Africa.* Washington, D.C.: U.S. Government Printing Office, 1982.

————. *Foreign Relations of the United States, 1952–1954.* Vol. 9, *The Near and Middle East.* Washington, D.C.: U.S. Government Printing Office, 1986.

————. *Foreign Relations of the United States, 1955–1957.* Vol. 12, *Near East: Multilateral Relations; Iran; Iraq.* Washington, D.C.: U.S. Government Printing Office, 1992.

————. *Foreign Relations of the United States, 1955–1957.* Vol. 13, *Near East: Jordan-Yemen.* Washington, D.C.: U.S. Government Printing Office, 1989.

————. *Foreign Relations of the United States, 1955–1957.* Vol. 14, *Arab-Israeli Dispute, 1955.* Washington, D.C.: U.S. Government Printing Office, 1989.

————. *Foreign Relations of the United States, 1955–1957.* Vol. 15, *Arab-Israeli Dispute, January 1–July 26, 1956.* Washington, D.C.: U.S. Government Printing Office, 1989.

————. *Foreign Relations of the United States, 1955–1957.* Vol. 16, *Suez Crisis: July 26–December 31, 1956.* Washington, D.C.: U.S. Government Printing Office, 1990.

————. *Foreign Relations of the United States, 1955–1957.* Vol. 17, *Arab-Israeli Dispute, 1957.* Washington, D.C.: U.S. Government Printing Office, 1990.

———. *Foreign Relations of the United States, 1958–1960*. Vol. 11, *Lebanon and Jordan*. Washington, D.C.: U.S. Government Printing Office, 1992.

———. *Foreign Relations of the United States, 1958–1960*. Vol. 12, *Near East Region; Iraq; Iran; Arabian Peninsula*. Washington, D.C.: U.S. Government Printing Office, 1993.

———. *Foreign Relations of the United States, 1958–1960*. Vol. 13, *Arab-Israeli Dispute; United Arab Republic; North Africa*. Washington, D.C.: U.S. Government Printing Office, 1992.

UNOFFICIAL SOURCES

Frontline Diplomacy: The U.S. Foreign Affairs Oral History Collection. Arlington, Va.: Association for Diplomatic Studies and Training, 2000 [CD-ROM].

Gallup, George H. *The Gallup Poll: Public Opinion, 1935–1971*. New York: Random House, 1972.

Griffith, Robert, ed. *Ike's Letters to a Friend, 1941–1958*. Lawrence: University Press of Kansas, 1984.

Hurewitz, J. C., ed. *The Middle East and North Africa in World Politics: A Documentary Record*. 3 vols. New Haven: Yale University Press, 1975.

New York Times, 1945–60.

Rabinovich, Itamar, and Jehuda Reinharz. *Israel in the Middle East: Documents and Readings on Security, Politics, and Foreign Relations, 1948–Present*. New York: Oxford University Press, 1984.

Toye, Patricia, and Angela Seay, eds. *Israel: Boundary Disputes with Arab Neighbours, 1948–1964*. 10 vols. [London]: Archives International Group, 1995.

MEMOIRS

Acheson, Dean. *Present at the Creation: My Years in the State Department*. New York: Norton, 1969.

Clapp, Gordon R. "An Approach to Economic Development: A Summary of the Reports of the United Nations Economic Survey Mission for the Middle East." *International Conciliation* 460 (April 1950): 203–17.

Clifford, Clark M. "Recognizing Israel." *American Heritage* 28:3 (April 1977): 4–11.

Clifford, Clark M., with Richard Holbrooke. *Counsel to the President: A Memoir*. New York: Random House, 1991.

Eban, Abba. *An Autobiography*. New York: Random House, 1977.

Eisenhower, Dwight D. *Mandate for Change, 1953–1956: The White House Years*. Garden City, N.Y.: Doubleday, 1963.

———. *Waging Peace, 1956–1961: The White House Years*. Garden City, N.Y.: Doubleday, 1965.

Eytan, Walter, *The First Ten Years: A Diplomatic History of Israel*. New York: Simon and Schuster, 1958.

Kennan, George. *Memoirs*. Boston: Little, Brown, 1972.

Kollek, Teddy. *For Jerusalem: A Life*. New York: Random House, 1978.

Macmillan, Harold. *Riding the Storm, 1956–1959*. New York: Harper and Row, 1971.

McDonald, James G. *My Mission in Israel, 1948–1951*. New York: Simon and Schuster, 1951.

McGhee, George. *Envoy to the Middle World: Adventures in Diplomacy.* New York: Harper and Row, 1983.

Meir, Golda. *My Life.* New York: Dell, 1975.

Peres, Shimon. *David's Sling.* London: Weidenfeld and Nicolson, 1970.

Rafael, Gideon. *Destination Peace: Three Decades of Israeli Foreign Policy: A Personal Memoir.* New York: Stein and Day, 1981.

Truman, Harry S. *Memoirs.* Garden City, N.Y.: Doubleday, 1955–56.

Weizmann, Chaim. *Trial and Error: The Autobiography of Chaim Weizmann.* Westport, Conn.: Greenwood, 1949, 1972.

Secondary Sources

Alin, Erika G. *The United States and the 1958 Lebanon Crisis: American Intervention in the Middle East.* Lanham, Md.: University Press of America, 1994.

Allen, Harry C. *Conflict and Concord: The Anglo-American Relationship since 1783.* New York: St. Martin's, 1959.

Alteras, Isaac. *Eisenhower and Israel: U.S.-Israeli Relations, 1953–1960.* Gainesville: University Press of Florida, 1993.

Alterman, Jon B. *Egypt and American Foreign Assistance, 1952–1956: Hopes Dashed.* New York: Palgrave, 2002.

Ambrose, Stephen E. *Eisenhower: Soldier and President.* New York: Simon and Schuster, 1990.

———. *Eisenhower: The President.* New York: Simon and Schuster, 1984.

Amirahmadi, Hooshang. "The United States and the Middle East: A Search for New Perspective." In *The United States and the Middle East: A Search for New Perspective*, ed. Hooshang Amirahmadi, 3–31. Albany: State University of New York Press, 1993.

Anderson, Benedict. *Imagined Communities: Reflections on the Origins and Spread of Nationalism.* Rev. ed. London: Verso, 1991.

Anderson, Terry H. *The United States, Great Britain, and the Cold War, 1944–1947.* Columbia: University of Missouri Press, 1981.

Ariel, Yaakov. *On Behalf of Israel: American Fundamentalist Attitudes toward Jews, Judaism, and Zionism, 1865–1945.* Brooklyn, N.Y.: Carlson, 1991.

Aronson, Geoffrey. *From Sideshow to Center Stage: U.S. Policy toward Egypt, 1945–1956.* Boulder, Colo.: Lynne Riener, 1986.

Ashton, Nigel John. *Eisenhower, Macmillan, and the Problem of Nasser.* New York: St. Martin's, 1996.

Axelgard, Frederick W. "U.S. Support for the British Position in Pre-Revolutionary Iraq." In *The Iraqi Revolution of 1958: The Old Social Classes Revisited*, ed. Robert A. Fernea and William Roger Louis, 77–94. London: Tauris, 1991.

Bain, Kenneth Ray. *The March to Zion: United States Policy and the Founding of Israel.* College Station: Texas A&M University Press, 1979.

Ball, George W., and Douglas B. Ball. *The Passionate Attachment: America's Involvement with Israel, 1947 to the Present.* New York: Norton, 1992.

Baram, Phillip J. *The Department of State in the Middle East, 1919–1945.* Philadelphia: University of Pennsylvania Press, 1978.

Barnet, Richard J. *Intervention and Revolution: America's Confrontation with Insurgent Movements around the World.* Rev. ed. New York: Meridian, 1980.

Bar-On, Mordechai. *The Gates of Gaza: Israel's Road to Suez and Back, 1955–1957.* New York: St. Martin's, 1994.

Bar-Siman-Tov, Yaacov. *Israel, the Superpowers, and the War in the Middle East.* New York: Praeger, 1987.

Bartlett, C. J. *"The Special Relationship": A Political History of Anglo-American Relations since 1945.* London: Longman, 1992.

Bar-Zohar, Michael. *Ben-Gurion: A Biography.* Trans. Peretz Kidron. New York: Delacorte, 1978.

Baylis, John. *Anglo-American Defence Relations, 1919–1980: The Special Relationship.* New York: St. Martin's, 1981.

———. *The Diplomacy of Pragmatism: Britain and the Formation of NATO, 1942–1949.* Kent, Ohio: Kent State University Press, 1993.

Behbehani, Hashim S. H. *The Soviet Union and Arab Nationalism, 1917–1966.* London: Routledge, 1986.

Bendersky, Joseph W. *The "Jewish Threat": Anti-Semitic Politics of the U.S. Army.* New York: Basic Books, 2000.

Benson, Michael T. *Harry S. Truman and the Founding of Israel.* Westport, Conn.: Praeger, 1997.

Benvenisti, Meron. *City of Stone: The Hidden History of Jerusalem.* Berkeley: University of California Press, 1996.

Ben-Yehuda, Nachman. *The Masada Myth: Collective Memory and Mythmaking in Israel.* Madison: University of Wisconsin Press, 1995.

Ben-Zvi, Abraham. *The United States and Israel: The Limits of the Special Relationship.* New York: Columbia University Press, 1993.

Berkowitz, Michael. *Western Jewry and the Zionist Project, 1914–1933.* Cambridge: Cambridge University Press, 1997.

Berman, Aaron. *Nazism, the Jews, and American Zionism, 1933–1948.* Detroit: Wayne State University Press, 1990.

Best, Richard A., Jr. *"Cooperation with Like-Minded Peoples": British Influences on American Security Policy, 1945–1949.* Westport, Conn.: Greenwood, 1986.

Bialer, Uri. *Between East and West: Israel's Foreign Policy Orientation, 1953–1956.* New York: Cambridge University Press, 1990.

———. *Oil and the Arab-Israeli Conflict, 1948–1963.* New York: St. Martin's, 1999.

———. "The Road to the Capital: The Establishment of Jerusalem as the Official Seat of the Israeli Government in 1949." *Studies in Zionism* 5:2 (Autumn 1984): 273–96.

Botti, Timothy J. *The Long Wait: The Forging of the Anglo-American Nuclear Alliance, 1945–1958.* Westport, Conn.: Greenwood, 1987.

Bovis, H. Eugene. *The Jerusalem Question, 1917–1968.* Stanford, Calif.: Hoover Institution Press, 1971.

Bowie, Robert R., and Richard H. Immerman. *Waging Peace: How Eisenhower Shaped an Enduring Cold War Strategy.* New York: Oxford University Press, 1998.

Boyer, Paul. *When Time Shall Be No More: Prophecy Belief in Modern American Culture.* Cambridge: Belknap Press of Harvard University Press, 1992.

Brands, H. W. *Cold Warriors: Eisenhower's Generation and American Foreign Policy.* New York: Columbia University Press, 1988.

———. *Inside the Cold War: Loy Henderson and the Rise of American Empire, 1918–1961.* New York: Oxford University Press, 1991.

———. *Into the Labyrinth: The United States and the Middle East, 1945–1993.* New York: McGraw-Hill, 1993.

Brecher, Frank W. *Reluctant Ally: United States Foreign Policy toward the Jews from Wilson to Reagan.* New York: Greenwood, 1991.

Brecher, Michael. *Decisions in Israel's Foreign Policy.* London: Oxford University Press, 1974.

———. *The Foreign Policy System in Israel: Setting, Images, Process.* London: Oxford University Press, 1972.

———. *Israel, the Korean War, and China: Images, Decisions, and Consequences.* Jerusalem: Hebrew University Press, 1974.

Brown, L. Carl. "The Middle East: Patterns of Change, 1947–1987." *Middle East Journal* 41:1 (Winter 1987): 26–39.

Brown, Michael. *The Israeli-American Connection: Its Roots in the Yishuv, 1914–1945.* Detroit: Wayne State University Press, 1996.

Bryson, Thomas A. *Seeds of Mideast Crisis: The United States Diplomatic Role in the Middle East during World War II.* Jeffersonville, N.C.: McFarland, 1981.

Caplan, Neil. *Futile Diplomacy.* Vol. 2, *Arab-Zionist Negotiations and the End of the Mandate.* London: Cass, 1986.

———. *Futile Diplomacy.* Vol. 3, *The United Nations, the Great Powers, and Middle East Peacemaking, 1948–1954.* London: Cass, 1997.

———. *Futile Diplomacy.* Vol. 4, *Operation Alpha and the Failure of Anglo-American Coercive Diplomacy in the Arab-Israeli Conflict, 1954–1956.* London: Cass, 1997.

———. *Palestine Jewry and the Arab Question, 1917–1925.* London: Cass, 1978.

Cattan, Henry. *The Question of Jerusalem.* London: Third World Centre, 1980.

Chace, James. *Acheson: The Secretary of State Who Created the American World.* New York: Simon and Schuster, 1998.

Childers, Erskine. "The Wordless Wish: From Citizens to Refugees." In *The Transformation of Palestine: Essays on the Origins and Development of the Arab-Israeli Conflict,* ed. Ibrahim Abu-Lughod, 165–202. Evanston, Ill.: Northwestern University Press, 1971.

Christison, Kathleen. *Perceptions of Palestine: Their Influences on U.S. Middle East Policy.* Berkeley: University of California Press, 1999.

Citino, Nathan J. *From Arab Nationalism to OPEC: Eisenhower, King Saud, and the Making of U.S.-Saudi Relations.* Bloomington: Indiana University Press, 2002.

Clark, Ian. *Nuclear Diplomacy and the Special Relationship: Britain's Deterrent and America, 1957–1962.* Oxford: Clarendon, 1992.

Cockburn, Andrew, and Leslie Cockburn. *Dangerous Liaison: The Inside Story of the U.S.-Israeli Covert Relationship.* New York: HarperCollins, 1991.

Cohen, Michael J. *Churchill and the Jews.* London: Cass, 1985.

———. *Fighting World War Three from the Middle East: Allied Contingency Plans, 1945–1954.* London: Cass, 1997.

———. *Palestine and the Great Powers, 1945–1948.* Princeton: Princeton University Press, 1982.

———. *Palestine, Retreat from the Mandate: The Making of British Policy, 1930–1945.* London: Elek, 1978.

———. *Palestine to Israel: From Mandate to Independence.* London: Cass, 1988.

———. *Truman and Israel.* Berkeley: University of California Press, 1990.

Cohen, Mitchell. *Zion and State: Nation, Class, and the Shaping of Modern Israel.* New York: Blackwell, 1987.

Cohen, Naomi W. *The Year after the Riots: American Responses to the Palestine Crisis of 1929–1930.* Detroit: Wayne State University Press, 1988.

Condit, Kenneth W. *History of the Joint Chiefs of Staff.* Vol. 2, *The Joint Chiefs of Staff and National Policy, 1947–1949.* Wilmington, Del.: Glazier, 1979.

Dann, Uriel. *King Hussein and the Challenge of Arab Radicalism: Jordan, 1955–1967.* New York: Oxford University Press, 1989.

DeConde, Alexander. *Ethnicity, Race, and American Foreign Policy: A History.* Boston: Northeastern University Press, 1992.

Devereux, David R. *The Formulation of British Defense Policy towards the Middle East, 1948–1956.* New York: St. Martin's, 1990.

Dimbleby, David, and David Reynolds. *An Ocean Apart: The Relationship between Britain and America in the Twentieth Century.* New York: Vintage, 1989.

Dobson, Alan P. *Anglo-American Relations in the Twentieth Century.* London: Routledge, 1995.

Dockrill, Saki. *Eisenhower's New-Look National Security Policy, 1953–1961.* New York: St. Martin's, 1996.

Donovan, Robert J. *Conflict and Crisis: The Presidency of Harry S. Truman, 1945–1948.* New York: Norton, 1977.

Doran, Michael. *Pan-Arabism before Nasser: Egyptian Power Politics and the Palestine Question.* New York: Oxford University Press, 1999.

Eisenberg, Laura Zittrain. *My Enemy's Enemy: Lebanon in the Early Zionist Imagination.* Detroit: Wayne State University Press, 1994.

Eppel, Michael. "The Decline of British Influence and the Ruling Elite in Iraq." In *Demise of the British Empire in the Middle East: Britain's Responses to Nationalist Movements, 1943–55,* ed. Michael J. Cohen and Martin Kolinsky, 185–97. London: Cass, 1998.

Evensen, Bruce J. "A Story of 'Ineptness': The Truman Administration's Struggle to Shape Conventional Wisdom on Palestine at the Beginning of the Cold War." *Diplomatic History* 15:3 (Summer 1991): 339–59.

———. *Truman, Palestine, and the Press: Shaping Conventional Wisdom at the Beginning of the Cold War.* New York: Greenwood, 1992.

Evron, Boas. *Jewish State or Israeli Nation?* Bloomington: Indiana University Press, 1995.

Farouk-Sluglett, Marion, and Peter Sluglett. "The Historiography of Modern Iraq." *American Historical Review* 96:5 (December 1991): 1408–21.

Feiler, Gil. *From Boycott to Economic Cooperation: The Political Economy of the Arab Boycott of Israel.* London: Cass, 1998.

Feintuch, Yossi. *U.S. Policy on Jerusalem.* New York: Greenwood, 1987.

Feldblum, Esther Yolles. *The American Catholic Press and the Jewish State, 1917–1959.* New York: Ktav, 1977.

Ferrell, Robert H. *Harry S. Truman: A Life.* Columbia: University of Missouri Press, 1994.

Flapan, Simha. *The Birth of Israel: Myths and Realities.* New York: Pantheon, 1987.

Foot, Rosemary J. "Anglo-American Relations in the Korean Crisis: The British Effort to Avert an Expanded War, December 1950–January 1951." *Diplomatic History* 10:1 (Winter 1986): 43–57.

Foyle, Douglas C. *Counting the Public In: Presidents, Public Opinion, and Foreign Policy.* New York: Columbia University Press, 1999.

Fraser, T. G. *The U.S.A. and the Middle East since World War 2.* New York: St. Martin's, 1989.

Freiberger, Steven Z. *Dawn over Suez: The Rise of American Power in the Middle East, 1953–1957.* Chicago: Dee, 1992.

Friedman, Isaiah. *Palestine: A Twice-Promised Land?* Vol. 1, *The British, the Arabs, and Zionism, 1915–1920.* New Brunswick, N.J.: Transaction, 2000.

Fry, Michael G., and Miles Hochstein. "The Forgotten Middle Eastern Crisis of 1957: Gaza and Sharm al-Sheikh." *International History Review* 15:1 (February 1993): 46–83.

Gal, Allon. *David Ben-Gurion and the American Alignment for a Jewish State.* Bloomington: Indiana University Press, 1991.

———. "Zionist Foreign Policy and Ben-Gurion's Visit to the United States in 1939." *Studies in Zionism* 7:1 (Spring 1986): 37–50.

Ganin, Zvi. *Truman, American Jewry, and Israel, 1945–1948.* New York: Holmes and Meier, 1979.

Gazit, Mordechai. "Ben-Gurion's 1949 Proposal to Incorporate the Gaza Strip with Israel." *Studies in Zionism* 8:2 (Autumn 1987): 223–43.

Geertz, Clifford. *The Interpretation of Cultures: Selected Essays.* New York: Basic Books, 1973.

Gelber, Yoav, "Jewish-Arab Talks during the War of Independence." *Journal of Israeli History* 15:3 (Autumn 1994): 283–312.

Gellner, Ernest. *Nations and Nationalism.* Oxford: Blackwell, 1983.

Gendzier, Irene L. *Notes from the Minefield: United States Intervention in Lebanon and the Middle East, 1945–1958.* New York: Columbia University Press, 1997.

Gerges, Fawaz A. *The Superpowers and the Middle East: Regional and International Politics, 1955–1967.* Boulder, Colo.: Westview, 1994.

Gerner, Deborah J. "Missed Opportunities and Roads Not Taken: The Eisenhower Administration and the Palestinians." In *U.S. Policy in Palestine from Wilson to Clinton,* ed. Michael W. Suleiman, 81–112. Normal, Ill.: Association of Arab-American University Graduates, 1995.

———. *One Land, Two Peoples: The Conflict over Palestine.* Boulder, Colo.: Westview, 1991.

Gilboa, Eytan. *American Public Opinion toward Israel and the Arab-Israeli Conflict.* Lexington, Mass.: Heath, 1987.

Ginat, Rami. *The Soviet Union and the Middle East.* London: Cass, 1993.

Golan, Galia. *Soviet Policies in the Middle East: From World War II to Gorbachev.* Cambridge: Cambridge University Press, 1990.

Golani, Motti. "Zionism without Zion: The Jerusalem Question, 1947–1949." *Studies in Zionism* 16:1 (Spring 1995): 39–52.

Goldberg, David Howard. *Foreign Policy and Ethnic Interest Groups: American and Canadian Jews Lobby for Israel.* New York: Greenwood, 1990.

Gordon, Joel. *Nasser's Blessed Movement: Egypt's Free Officers and the July Revolution.* New York: Oxford University Press, 1992.

Gowing, Margaret. *Independence and Deterrence: Britain and Atomic Energy, 1939–1952.* New York: St. Martin's Press, 1974.

Green, Stephen. *Taking Sides: America's Secret Relations with a Militant Israel.* New York: Morrow, 1984.

Greenfeld, Liah. *Nationalism: Five Roads to Modernity.* Cambridge: Harvard University Press, 1992.

Grose, Peter. *Israel in the Mind of America.* New York: Knopf, 1983.

———. "The President versus the Diplomats." In *The End of the Palestine Mandate,* ed. William Roger Louis and Robert Stookey, 32–60. Austin: University of Texas Press, 1986.

Hahn, Peter L. "Alignment by Coincidence: Israel, the United States, and the Partition of Jerusalem, 1949–1953." *International History Review* 21:3 (September 1999): 665–89.

———. *The United States, Great Britain, and Egypt, 1945–1956: Strategy and Diplomacy in the Early Cold War.* Chapel Hill: University of North Carolina Press, 1991.

———. "The View from Jerusalem: Revelations about U.S. Diplomacy from the Archives of Israel." *Diplomatic History* 22:4 (Fall 1998): 509–32.

Halpern, Ben. *The Idea of a Jewish State.* 2d ed. Cambridge: Harvard University Press, 1969.

Hamby, Alonzo. *Man of the People: A Life of Harry S. Truman.* New York: Oxford University Press, 1995.

Harbutt, Fraser J. *The Iron Curtain: Churchill, America, and the Origins of the Cold War.* New York: Oxford University Press, 1986.

Hathaway, Robert M. *Ambiguous Partnership: Britain and America, 1944–1947.* New York: Columbia University Press, 1981.

Heiss, Mary Ann. *Empire and Nationhood: The United States, Great Britain, and Iranian Oil, 1950–1954.* New York: Columbia University Press, 1997.

Heller, Joseph. *The Birth of Israel, 1945–1949: Ben-Gurion and His Critics.* Gainesville: University Press of Florida, 2000.

Hersh, Seymour M. *The Samson Option: Israel's Nuclear Arsenal and American Foreign Policy.* New York: Random House, 1991.

Hogan, Michael J. *The Marshall Plan: America, Britain, and the Reconstruction of Western Europe, 1947–1952.* New York: Cambridge University Press, 1987.

Holland, Matthew F. *America and Egypt: From Roosevelt to Eisenhower.* Westport, Conn.: Praeger, 1996.

Hourani, Albert. *Arabic Thought in the Liberal Age, 1798–1939.* London: Oxford University Press, 1970.

———. *A History of the Arab Peoples.* Cambridge: Belknap Press of Harvard University Press, 1991.

Hunt, Michael H. *Ideology and U.S. Foreign Policy.* New Haven: Yale University Press, 1987.

Hussein, Asaf. *The United States and Israel: Politics of a Special Relationship.* Islamabad, Pakistan: Quaid-I-Azam University, 1991.

Ilan, Amitzur. *Bernadotte in Palestine, 1948: A Study in Contemporary Humanitarian Knight Errantry.* London: Macmillan, 1989.

———. *The Origin of the Arab-Israeli Arms Race: Arms, Embargo, Military Power, and Decision in the 1948 Palestine War.* New York: New York University Press, 1996.

Immerman, Richard H. *John Foster Dulles: Piety, Pragmatism, and Power in U.S. Foreign Policy.* Wilmington, Del.: Scholarly Resources, 1999.

Jansen, Michael E. *The United States and the Palestinian People*. Beirut: Institute for Palestine Studies, 1970.

Jasse, Richard L. "The Baghdad Pact: Cold War or Colonialism?" *Middle Eastern Studies* 27:1 (January 1991): 140–56.

Jones, Martin. *Failure in Palestine: British and United States Policy after the Second World War*. London: Mansell, 1986.

Kaplan, Robert D. *The Arabists: Romance of an American Elite*. New York: Free Press, 1993.

Karsh, Efraim. *Fabricating Israeli History: The "New Historians."* London: Cass, 1997.

Kaufman, Burton I. *The Arab Middle East and the United States: Inter-Arab Rivalry and Superpower Diplomacy*. New York: Twayne, 1996.

Kaufman, Menahem. *An Ambiguous Partnership: Non-Zionists and Zionists in America, 1939–1948*. Trans. Ira Robinson. Jerusalem: Magnes, 1991.

———. *America's Jerusalem Policy, 1947–1948*. Jerusalem: Institute of Contemporary Jewry, 1982.

Kenen, I. L. *Israel's Defense Line: Her Friends and Foes in Washington*. Buffalo, N.Y.: Prometheus, 1981.

Kerr, Malcolm. *The Arab Cold War: Gamal Abd al-Nasir and His Rivals*. 3d ed. London: Oxford University Press, 1971.

Kimmerling, Baruch, and Joel S. Migdal. *Palestinians: The Making of a People*. New York: Free Press, 1993.

Khalidi, Rashid. "Arab Nationalism: Historical Problems in the Literature." *American Historical Review* 96:5 (December 1991): 1363–73.

———. *Palestinian Identity: The Construction of Modern National Consciousness*. New York: Columbia University Press, 1997.

———. "United States Policy and the Palestine Problem: Historical Dimensions and the Creation of an 'Alternative Narrative.'" In *History, the White House, and the Kremlin: Statesmen as Historians*, ed. Michael G. Fry, 20–37. London: Pinter, 1991.

Khalidi, Walid. "The Arab Perspective." In *The End of the Palestine Mandate*, ed. William Roger Louis and Robert Stookey, 104–36. Austin: University of Texas Press, 1986.

Khashan, Hilel. *Arabs at the Crossroads: Political Identity and Nationalism*. Gainesville: University Press of Florida, 2000.

Khoury, Philip S. "Continuity and Change in Syrian Political Life: The Nineteenth and Twentieth Centuries." *American Historical Review* 96:5 (December 1991): 1374–95.

Klieman, Aaron S. *Israel and the World after Forty Years*. Washington, D.C.: Pergamon-Brassey's, 1990.

Kochavi, Arieh J. "Anglo-American Discord: Jewish Refugees and the United Nations Relief and Rehabilitation Administration Policy, 1945–1947." *Diplomatic History* 14:4 (Fall 1990): 529–51.

———. *Post-Holocaust Politics: Britain, the United States, and Jewish Refugees, 1945–1948*. Chapel Hill: University of North Carolina Press, 2001.

Kolinsky, Martin. *Law, Order, and Riots in Mandatory Palestine, 1928–1935*. London: St. Martin's, 1993.

Kolko, Gabriel. *Confronting the Third World: United States Foreign Policy, 1945–1980*. New York: Pantheon, 1988.

Kolsky, Thomas A. *Jews against Zionism: The American Council for Judaism, 1942–1948*. Philadelphia: Temple University Press, 1990.

Kostiner, Joseph. *The Making of Saudi Arabia, 1916–1936: From Chieftaincy to Monarchical State.* New York: Oxford University Press, 1993.

Kuniholm, Bruce R. *The Origins of the Cold War in the Near East: Great Power Conflict and Diplomacy in Iran, Turkey, and Greece.* Princeton: Princeton University Press, 1980.

Kyle, Keith. *Suez.* New York: St. Martin's, 1991.

Lawson, Fred H. "The Truman Administration and the Palestinians." In *U.S. Policy in Palestine from Wilson to Clinton*, ed. Michael W. Suleiman, 59–80. Normal, Ill.: Association of Arab-American University Graduates, 1995.

Leffler, Melvyn P. *A Preponderance of Power: National Security, the Truman Administration, and the Cold War.* Stanford, Calif.: Stanford University Press, 1992.

Lenczowski, George. *American Presidents and the Middle East.* Durham, N.C.: Duke University Press, 1990.

Lesch, David W. *Syria and the United States: Eisenhower's Cold War in the Middle East.* Boulder, Colo.: Westview, 1992.

———, ed. *The Middle East and the United States: A Historical and Political Reassessment.* 2d ed. Boulder, Colo.: Westview, 1999.

Levey, Zach. *Israel and the Western Powers, 1952–1960.* Chapel Hill: University of North Carolina Press, 1997.

Little, Douglas. *American Orientalism: The United States and the Middle East since 1945.* Chapel Hill: University of North Carolina Press, 2002.

———. "Cold War and Covert Action: The United States and Syria, 1945–1958." *Middle East Journal* 44:1 (Winter 1990): 51–75.

———. "His Finest Hour? Eisenhower, Lebanon, and the 1958 Middle East Crisis." In *Empire and Revolution: The United States and the Third World since 1945*, ed. Peter L. Hahn and Mary Ann Heiss, 17–47. Columbus: Ohio State University Press, 2001.

———. "The Making of a Special Relationship: The United States and Israel, 1957–1968." *International Journal of Middle East Studies* 25:4 (November 1993): 563–85.

Louis, William Roger. *The British Empire in the Middle East: Arab Nationalism, the United States, and Postwar Imperialism.* London: Oxford University Press, 1984.

———. "British Imperialism and the End of the Palestine Mandate." In *The End of the Palestine Mandate*, ed. Wm. Roger Louis and Robert W. Stookey, 1–31. Austin: University of Texas Press, 1986.

———. *Imperialism at Bay: The United States and the Decolonization of the British Empire, 1941–1945.* London: Oxford University Press, 1984.

Louis, William Roger, and Hedley Bull, eds. *The "Special Relationship": Anglo-American Relations since 1945.* Oxford: Clarendon, 1986.

Louis, William Roger, and Roger Owen, eds. *Suez, 1956: The Crisis and Its Consequences.* New York: Oxford University Press, 1989.

Luard, Evan. *A History of the United Nations.* Vol. 1, *The Years of Western Domination, 1945–1955.* New York: St. Martin's, 1982.

Lucas, W. Scott. *Divided We Stand: Britain, the U.S., and the Suez Crisis.* London: Hodden and Stoughton, 1991.

———. "The U.S. and Arab Nationalism in the Early Cold War." In *The United States and Decolonization: Power and Freedom*, ed. David Ryan and Victor Pungong, 140–67. New York: St. Martin's, 2000.

Lustick, Ian S. "The Fetish of Jerusalem: A Hegemonic Analysis." In *Israel in Comparative Perspective: Challenging the Conventional Wisdom*, ed. Michael N. Barnett, 143–72. Albany: State University of New York Press, 1996.

Maddy-Weitzman, Bruce. *The Crystallization of the Arab State System, 1945–1954*. Syracuse, N.Y.: Syracuse University Press, 1993.

Mansour, Camille. *Beyond Alliance: Israel in U.S. Foreign Policy*. Trans. James A. Cohen. New York: Columbia University Press, 1994.

Marr, Phebe. *The Modern History of Iraq*. Boulder, Colo.: Westview, 1985.

Marsot, Afaf Lufti Al-Sayyid. "Survey of Egyptian Works of History." *American Historical Review* 96:5 (December 1991): 1422–34.

Mart, Michelle. "Tough Guys and American Cold War Policy: Images of Israel, 1948–1960." *Diplomatic History* 20:3 (Summer 1996): 357–80.

Masalha, Nur. *Expulsion of the Palestinians: The Concept of "Transfer" in Zionist Political Thought, 1882–1948*. Washington, D.C.: Institute for Palestine Studies, 1992.

Mattar, Philip. *The Mufti of Jerusalem: Al-Hajj Amin al-Husayni and the Palestinian National Movement*. New York: Columbia University Press, 1988.

McCarthy, Justin. *The Population of Palestine: Population History and Statistics of the Late Ottoman Period and the Mandate*. New York: Columbia University Press, 1990.

McCullough, David. *Truman*. New York: Simon and Schuster, 1992.

McIntyre, W. David. *British Decolonization, 1946–1997*. New York: St. Martin's, 1998.

McMahon, Robert J. *The Cold War on the Periphery: The United States, India, and Pakistan*. New York: Columbia University Press, 1994.

———. "Eisenhower and Third World Nationalism: A Critique of the Revisionists." *Political Science Quarterly* 101:3 (Fall 1986): 453–73.

Medoff, Rafael. *Militant Zionism in America: The Rise and Impact of the Jabotinsky Movement in the United States, 1926–1948*. Tuscaloosa: University of Alabama Press, 2002.

Melisson, Jan. *The Struggle for Nuclear Partnership: Britain, the United States, and the Making of an Ambiguous Alliance, 1952–1959*. Groningen, the Netherlands: Styx, 1993.

Meyer, Gail E. *Egypt and the United States: The Formative Years*. Rutherford, N.J.: Farleigh Dickinson University Press, 1980.

Miscamble, Wilson D. *George F. Kennan and the Making of American Foreign Policy, 1947–1950*. Princeton: Princeton University Press, 1992.

Morris, Benny. *The Birth of the Palestinian Refugee Problem, 1947–1949*. New York: Cambridge University Press, 1987.

———. "The Israeli Press and the Qibya Operation, 1953." *Journal of Palestine Studies* 25:4 (Summer 1996): 40–52.

———. *Israel's Border Wars, 1949–1956: Arab Infiltration, Israeli Retaliation, and the Countdown to the Suez War*. Oxford: Clarendon, 1993.

———. *1948 and After: Israel and the Palestinians*. Oxford: Clarendon, 1990.

———. *Righteous Victims: A History of the Zionist-Arab Conflict, 1881–1999*. New York: Knopf, 1999.

Nachmani, Amikan. *Great Power Discord in Palestine: The Anglo-American Committee of Inquiry into the Problems of European Jewry and Palestine, 1945–1946*. London: Cass, 1987.

Nadelmann, Ethan. "Setting the Stage: American Policy toward the Middle East, 1961–1966." *International Journal of Middle East Studies* 14:4 (November 1982): 435–57.

Neff, Donald. *Fallen Pillars: U.S. Policy towards Palestine and Israel since 1945*. Washington, D.C.: Institute for Palestine Studies, 1995.

———. "Jerusalem in U.S. Policy." *Journal of Palestine Studies* 23:1 (Autumn 1993): 20–45.

Nicholas, H. G. *Britain and the U.S.A.*. Baltimore: Johns Hopkins Press, 1963.

Nizameddin, Talal. *Russia and the Middle East: Towards a New Foreign Policy*. New York: St. Martin's, 1999.

Obenzinger, Hilton. *American Palestine: Melville, Twain, and the Holy Land Mania*. Princeton: Princeton University Press, 1999.

Offner, Arnold A. *Another Such Victory: President Truman and the Cold War, 1945–1953*. Stanford, Calif.: Stanford University Press, 2002.

Organski, A. F. K. *The $36 Billion Bargain: Strategy and Politics in U.S. Assistance to Israel*. New York: Columbia University Press, 1990.

Oren, Michael B. "Canada, the Great Powers, and the Middle Eastern Arms Race, 1950–1956." *International History Review* 12:2 (March 1990): 280–300.

———. *Origins of the Second Arab-Israel War: Egypt, Israel, and the Great Powers, 1952–1956*. London: Cass, 1992.

———. "The Test of Suez: Israel and the Middle East Crisis of 1958." *Studies in Zionism* 12:1 (Spring 1991): 55–83.

Ovendale, Ritchie. *Britain, the U.S., and the Transfer of Power in the Middle East, 1945–1962*. New York: Leicester University Press, 1996.

———. *The English-Speaking Alliance: Britain, the United States, the Dominions, and the Cold War, 1945–1951*. London: Allen and Unwin, 1985.

Pach, Chester J., and Elmo Richardson. *The Presidency of Dwight D. Eisenhower*. Lawrence: University Press of Kansas, 1991.

Painter, David S. *Oil and the American Century: The Political Economy of U.S. Foreign Oil Policy, 1941–1954*. Baltimore: John Hopkins University Press, 1986.

Pappé, Ilan. *Britain and the Arab-Israeli Conflict, 1948–1951*. New York: St. Martin's, 1988.

———. "British Rule in Jordan, 1943–55." In *Demise of the British Empire in the Middle East: Britain's Responses to Nationalist Movements, 1943–55*, ed. Michael J. Cohen and Martin Kolinsky, 198–219. London: Cass, 1998.

———. *The Making of the Arab-Israeli Conflict, 1947–1951*. London: Tauris, 1991.

———. "Moshe Sharett, David Ben-Gurion, and the 'Palestine Option,' 1948–1956." *Studies in Zionism* 7:1 (Spring 1986): 77–96.

Parker, Richard B. "The United States and King Hussein." In *The United States and the Middle East: A Historical and Political Reassessment*, 2d ed., ed. David W. Lesch, 100–113. Boulder, Colo.: Westview, 1999.

Pelling, Henry. *Britain and the Marshall Plan*. New York: St. Martin's, 1988.

Penkower, Monty Noam. *The Emergence of Zionist Thought*. New York: Associated Faculty Press, 1986.

Persson, Magnus. *Great Britain, the United States, and the Security of the Middle East: The Formation of the Baghdad Pact*. Lund, Sweden: Lund University Press, 1998.

Peters, F. E. *Jerusalem: The Holy City in the Eyes of Chroniclers, Visitors, Pilgrims, and Prophets from the Days of Abraham to the Beginnings of Modern Times*. Princeton: Princeton University Press, 1985.

Peters, Joan. *From Time Immemorial: The Origins of the Arab-Jewish Conflict over Palestine*. New York: Harper and Row, 1984.

Petersen, Tore Tingvold. "Anglo-American Rivalry in the Middle East: The Struggle for the Buraimi Oasis, 1952–1957." *International History Review* 14:1 (February 1992): 71–91.

———. *The Middle East between the Great Powers: Anglo-American Conflict and Co-operation, 1952–1957*. New York: St. Martin's, 2000.

Peterson, J. E. "The Arabian Peninsula in Modern Times: A Historiographical Survey." *American Historical Review* 96:5 (December 1991): 1435–49.

Petran, Tabitha. *The Struggle over Lebanon*. New York: Monthly Review Press, 1987.

Podeh, Elie. *The Quest for Hegemony in the Arab World: The Struggle over the Baghdad Pact*. Leiden, the Netherlands: Brill, 1995.

Podet, Allen H. "Anti-Zionism in a Key United States Diplomat: Loy Henderson at the End of World War II." *American Jewish Archives* 30:2 (November 1978): 155–87.

Quandt, William B. *Peace Process: American Diplomacy and the Arab-Israeli Conflict since 1967*. Washington, D.C.: Brookings Institution, 1993.

Rabinovich, Itamar. *The Road Not Taken: Early Arab-Israeli Negotiations*. New York: Oxford University Press, 1991.

Raphael, Marc Lee. *Abba Hillel Silver: A Profile in American Judaism*. New York: Holmes and Meier, 1989.

Raviv, Dan, and Yossi Melman. *Friends in Deed: Inside the U.S.-Israel Alliance*. New York: Hyperion, 1994.

Rees, G. Wyn. *Anglo-American Approaches to Alliance Security, 1955–1960*. New York: St. Martin's, 1996.

Reich, Bernard. *Quest for Peace: United States–Israel Relations and the Arab-Israeli Conflict*. New Brunswick, N.J.: Transaction, 1977.

———. "Themes in the History of the State of Israel." *American Historical Review* 96:5 (December 1991): 1466–78.

———. *The United States and Israel: Influence in the Special Relationship*. New York: Praeger, 1984.

Reinharz, Jehuda. *Chaim Weizmann: The Making of a Zionist Leader*. New York: Oxford University Press, 1985.

Reynolds, David. *The Creation of the Anglo-American Alliance, 1937–1941: A Study in Competitive Cooperation*. Chapel Hill: University of North Carolina Press, 1982.

Rokach, Livia. *Israel's Sacred Terrorism: A Study Based on Moshe Sharett's Personal Diary and Other Documents*. 3d ed. Belmont, Mass.: Association of Arab-American University Graduates, 1986.

Rose, Norman. *Chaim Weizmann: A Biography*. New York: Viking, 1986.

Roshwald, Aviel. *Estranged Bedfellows: Britain and France in the Middle East during the Second World War*. New York: Oxford University Press, 1990.

Rothwell, Victor. *Britain and the Cold War, 1941–1947*. London: Cape, 1982.

Rotter, Andrew J. "Saidism without Said: *Orientalism* and U.S. Diplomatic History." *American Historical Review* 105:4 (October 2000): 1205–16.

Rubenberg, Cheryl A. *Israel and the American National Interest: A Critical Examination*. Urbana: University of Illinois Press, 1986.

Sachar, Howard M. *A History of Israel: From the Rise of Zionism to Our Time*. New York: Knopf, 1988.

Safran, Nadav. *Israel: The Embattled Ally*. Cambridge: Belknap Press of Harvard University Press, 1978.

Said, Edward W. *Culture and Imperialism.* New York: Knopf, 1993.

———. *Orientalism.* New York: Vintage, 1988.

———. "Projecting Jerusalem." *Journal of Palestine Studies* 25:1 (Autumn 1995): 5–14.

———. *The Question of Palestine.* New York: Vintage, 1979.

Said, Edward W., and Christopher Hitchens, eds. *Blaming the Victims: Spurious Scholarship and the Palestinian Question.* London: Verso, 1988.

Sanjian, Ara. "The Formulation of the Baghdad Pact." *Middle Eastern Studies* 33:2 (April 1997): 226–66.

Satloff, Robert B. *From Abdullah to Hussein: Jordan in Transition.* New York: Oxford University Press, 1994.

Saunders, Bonnie F. *The United States and Arab Nationalism: The Syrian Case, 1953–1960.* Westport, Conn.: Praeger, 1996.

Sayigh, Yezid, and Avi Shlaim, eds. *The Cold War and the Middle East.* Oxford: Clarendon, 1997.

Schnapper, Dominique. *Community of Citizens: On the Modern Idea of Nationality.* Trans. Daniel Bell. New Brunswick, N.J.: Transaction, 1998.

Schoenbaum, David. *The United States and the State of Israel.* New York: Oxford University Press, 1993.

Schulze, Kirsten E. *Israel's Covert Diplomacy in Lebanon.* New York: St. Martin's, 1998.

Schulzinger, Robert D. "The Impact of Suez on United States Middle East Policy." In *The Suez-Sinai Crisis, 1956: Retrospective and Reappraisal,* ed. Selwyn Ilan Troen and Moshe Shemesh, 251–65. London: Cass, 1990.

Seale, Patrick. *The Struggle for Syria: A Study of Postwar Arab Politics, 1945–1958.* London: Tauris, 1965.

Segre, Dan V. *A Crisis of Identity: Israel and Zionism.* Oxford: Oxford University Press, 1980.

Sha'ban, Fuad. *Islam and the Arabs in Early American Thought: The Roots of Orientalism in America.* Durham, N.C.: Acorn, 1991.

Shadid, Mohammed K. *The United States and the Palestinians.* London: Croom Helm, 1981.

Shamir, Ronen. *The Colonies of Law: Colonialism, Zionism, and Law in Early Mandate Palestine.* Cambridge: Cambridge University Press, 2000.

Shapira, Anita. *Land and Power: The Zionist Resort to Force, 1881–1948.* Trans. William Templer. New York: Oxford University Press, 1992.

Shapiro, Edward S. *A Time for Healing: American Jewry since World War II.* Baltimore: Johns Hopkins University Press, 1992.

Sheffer, Gabriel. *Moshe Sharett: Biography of a Political Moderate.* Oxford: Clarendon, 1996.

Shemesh, Moshe. *The Palestinian Entity, 1959–1974: Arab Politics and the PLO.* 2d ed. London: Cass, 1996.

Shepherd, Naomi. *Ploughing Sand: British Rule in Palestine, 1917–1948.* New Brunswick, N.J.: Rutgers University Press, 2000.

Shlaim, Avi. *Collusion across the Jordan: King Abdullah, the Zionist Movement, and the Partition of Palestine.* New York: Columbia University Press, 1988.

———. "Conflicting Approaches to Israel's Relations with the Arabs: Ben-Gurion and Sharett, 1953–1956." *Middle East Journal* 37:2 (Spring 1983): 180–201.

———. "The Debate about 1948." *International Journal of Middle East Studies* 27:3 (August 1995): 287–304.

———. *The Iron Wall: Israel and the Arab World.* New York: Norton, 2000.

———. "The Protocol of Sèvres, 1956: Anatomy of a War Plot." *International Affairs* 73:3 (July 1997): 509–30.

Shpiro, David H. *From Philanthropy to Activism: The Political Transformation of American Zionism in the Holocaust Years, 1933–1945.* New York: Pergamon, 1994.

Silberstein, Laurence J., ed. *New Perspectives on Israeli Historiography: The Early Years of the State.* New York: New York University Press, 1991.

———. *The Postzionism Debates: Knowledge and Power in Israeli Culture.* New York: Routledge, 1999.

Silverfarb, Daniel. *The Twilight of British Ascendancy in the Middle East: A Case Study of Iraq, 1941–1950.* New York: St. Martin's, 1994.

Singh, Anita Inder. *The Limits of British Influence: South Asia and the Anglo-American Relationship, 1947–1956.* New York: St. Martin's, 1993.

Slonim, Shlomo. *Jerusalem in America's Foreign Policy, 1947–1997.* The Hague: Kluwer Law International, 1998.

———. "Origins of the 1950 Tripartite Declaration on the Middle East." *Middle Eastern Studies* 23:2 (April 1987): 135–49.

Smith, Anthony D. *The Ethnic Origins of Nations.* New York: Blackwell, 1986.

Smith, Charles D. *Palestine and the Arab-Israeli Conflict.* 2d ed. New York: St. Martin's 1992.

Snetsinger, John. *Truman, the Jewish Vote, and the Creation of Israel.* Stanford, Calif.: Hoover Institution Press, 1974.

Sofer, Sasson. *Zionism and the Foundations of Israeli Diplomacy.* Trans. Dorothea Shefet-Vanson. Cambridge: Cambridge University Press, 1998.

Spiegel, Steven L. *The Other Arab-Israeli Conflict: Making America's Middle East Policy from Truman to Reagan.* Chicago: University of Chicago Press, 1985.

Stanger, Cary David. "A Haunting Legacy: The Assassination of Count Bernadotte." *Middle East Journal* 42:2 (Spring 1988): 260–72.

Stein, Kenneth W. "A Historiographical Review of Literature on the Origins of the Arab-Israeli Conflict." *American Historical Review* 96:5 (December 1991): 1450–65.

Sternhell, Zeev. *The Founding Myths of Israel: Nationalism, Socialism, and the Making of the Jewish State.* Trans. David Maisel. Princeton: Princeton University Press, 1998.

Stivers, William. *America's Confrontation with Revolutionary Change in the Middle East, 1948–1983.* New York: St. Martin's, 1986.

———. "Eisenhower and the Middle East." In *Reevaluating Eisenhower: American Foreign Policy in the 1950s,* ed. Richard A. Melanson and David Mayers, 192–219. Urbana: University of Illinois Press, 1987.

Stokesbury, James L. *A Short History of World War I.* New York: Morrow, 1981.

Stookey, Robert. *America and the Arab States: An Uneasy Encounter.* New York: Wiley, 1975.

Suleiman, Michael W. *The Arabs in the Mind of America.* Brattleboro, Vt.: Amana, 1988.

———. "Palestine and the Palestinians in the Mind of America." In *U.S. Policy in Palestine from Wilson to Clinton,* ed. Michael W. Suleiman, 9–26. Normal, Ill.: Association of Arab-American University Graduates, 1995.

Takeyh, Ray. *The Origins of the Eisenhower Doctrine: The U.S., Britain, and Nasser's Egypt, 1953-1957*. New York: St. Martin's, 2000.

Tal, David. "Israel's Road to the 1956 War." *International Journal of Middle East Studies* 28:1 (February 1996): 59-81.

Taylor, Alan R. *The Superpowers and the Middle East*. Syracuse, N.Y.: Syracuse University Press, 1991.

Terry, Janice J. *Mistaken Identity: Arab Stereotypes in Popular Writing*. Washington, D.C.: Arab-American Affairs Council, 1987.

Tessler, Mark. *A History of the Israeli-Palestinian Conflict*. Bloomington: Indiana University Press, 1994.

Teveth, Shabtai. "Charging Israel with Original Sin." *Commentary* 88:3 (September 1989): 24-33.

———. "The Palestine Arab Refugee Problem and Its Origins." *Middle East Studies* 26:2 (April 1990): 214-49.

Thacher, Nicolas G. "Reflections on U.S. Foreign Policy toward Iraq in the 1950s." In *The Iraqi Revolution of 1958: The Old Social Classes Revisited*, ed. Robert A. Fernea and William Roger Louis, 62-77. London: Tauris, 1991.

Thorne, Christopher. *Allies of a Kind: The United States, Britain, and the War against Japan*. New York: Oxford University Press, 1981.

Tillman, Seth P. *The United States in the Middle East: Interests and Obstacles*. Bloomington: Indiana University Press, 1982.

Tivnan, Edward. *The Lobby: Jewish Political Power and American Foreign Policy*. New York: Simon and Schuster, 1987.

Troen, S. Ilan. "The Discovery of America in the Israeli University: Historical, Cultural, and Methodological Perspectives." *Journal of American History* 81:1 (June 1994): 164-82.

Tschirgi, Dan. *The Politics of Indecision: Origins and Implications of American Involvement with the Palestine Problem*. New York: Praeger, 1983.

Urquhart, Brian. *Ralph Bunche: A Life*. New York: Norton, 1993.

Vitalis, Robert. *When Capitalists Collide: Business Conflict and the End of Empire in Egypt*. Berkeley: University of California Press, 1995.

Vogel, Lester I. *To See a Promised Land: Americans and the Holy Land in the Nineteenth Century*. University Park: Pennsylvania State University Press, 1993.

Wahab Sayed-Ahmad, Muhammed Abdel. *Nasser and American Foreign Policy, 1952-1956*. London: Laam, 1989.

Walzer, Michael. "History and National Liberation." *Journal of Israeli History: Politics, Society, Culture* 20:2-3 (Summer–Autumn 2001): 1-8.

Warner, Geoffrey. "The Anglo-American Special Relationship." *Diplomatic History* 13:4 (Fall 1989): 479-99.

Watson, Robert J. *History of the Joint Chiefs of Staff*. Vol. 5, *The Joint Chiefs of Staff and National Policy, 1953-1954*. Washington, D.C.: Joint Chiefs of Staff Historical Division, 1986.

Watt, D. Cameron. *Succeeding John Bull: America in Britain's Place, 1900-1975*. Cambridge: Cambridge University Press, 1984.

Wilson, Evan M. *Decision on Palestine: How the U.S. Came to Recognize Israel*. Stanford, Calif.: Hoover Institution Press, 1979.

Woods, Randall Bennett. *A Changing of the Guard: Anglo-American Relations, 1941–1946.* Chapel Hill: University of North Carolina Press, 1990.

Yergin, Daniel. *The Prize: The Epic Quest for Oil, Money, and Power.* New York: Simon and Schuster, 1991.

Zerubavel, Yael. *Recovered Roots: Collective Memory and the Making of an Israeli National Tradition.* Chicago: University of Chicago Press, 1995.

Zucker, Bat-Ami. *U.S. Aid to Israel and Its Reflection in the* New York Times *and the* Washington Post, *1948–1973.* Lewiston, N.Y.: Mellen, 1991.

Zweig, Ronald. *Britain and Palestine during the Second World War.* London: Boydell, 1985.

———. "Restitution and the Problem of Jewish Displaced Persons in Anglo-American Relations, 1944–1948." *American Jewish History* 78:1 (September 1988): 54–78.

INDEX

Abdallah Ibn-Hussein (emir, king of Jordan), 30; rise to power, 9–10, 13; policy in Palestine, 17, 34; and peace process, 88–91; assassination of, 91, 97, 127, 138, 142, 172; and Palestinian refugees, 101, 108; and Jerusalem, 120; and United States, 138

Abdul Ilah (prince of Iraq), 18, 34, 228, 273

Acheson, Dean G., 282–84; and Israel, 61, 70–71, 72–73, 133–37; relationship with Truman, 67–68; policy in Middle East, 70, 77–82; and peace process, 87, 89, 92–93, 95–97; and Palestinian refugees, 102, 103, 105; and Jerusalem, 112–22; and oil issues, 123–25, 131–32; and Suez Canal, 125–29, 131–32; and minor Arab-Israeli disputes, 129–32; and Arab states, 138, 140, 142–43

Adenauer, Konrad, 130

Alling, Paul H., 30

Alphand, Hervé, 231

Alpha peace plan, 182–86, 191–93, 230–32, 234, 249

Altalena, 70

American Council for Judaism, 16

American Israel Public Affairs Committee, 262

American Jewish Committee, 48, 211

American Jewish Labor Council, 48

American League for a Free Palestine, 24

American Zionist Committee for Public Affairs, 262

American Zionist Council, 79, 82, 96

American Zionist Emergency Council, 15–16, 57, 130

Ammoun, Fouad, 139

Anderson, Benedict, 12

Anderson, Robert, 190–93, 195–96

Anglo-American Committee of Inquiry, 33–35, 42

Arab Blood Society, 24

Arab Higher Committee, 49

Arabian-American Oil Company, 16–17, 22, 30, 36, 46

Arab-Israeli disputes: borders, 1, 55–56, 87–89, 158–69, 216–20; Jerusalem, 1, 55, 90, 112–22, 170, 174–76, 181, 248, 257, 259; Jordan Valley waters, 1, 170–74, 181, 248, 252–54, 259; Palestinian refugees, 1, 55, 99–111, 170, 176–78, 181, 248–52, 259; Suez Canal, 1, 123–29, 131–32, 163–64, 178–81, 194–96, 216, 218–20, 248, 255–56, 259; trade and boycotts, 1, 123–29, 131–32, 159, 170, 178–79, 181, 257–59; immigrants to Israel, 53, 123, 129, 131–32, 258–59; German reparations to Israel, 93, 123, 130–32; Huleh crisis, 93–98, 125, 126, 127, 135, 170; Jews in Arab states, 123, 129–30, 131–32; Gulf of Aqaba blockade, 126, 178, 180–81, 214, 216–20, 248, 252–55, 259; nuclear arms, 264. *See also* Alpha peace plan

Arab-Israeli War (1948–49), 1; origins, 44–49; early phases, 51–52; October phase, 56–57; late phases, 59–63; legacy of, 137, 158

Arab-Israeli War (1967), 207

Arab League, 4, 14–15, 37, 46, 49, 75, 89, 90, 92–93, 96, 120, 131, 174, 178–79, 270

Arab Legion, 52, 61, 138, 161, 162, 198, 272

Arab Revolt (1936–39), 13

Arab states: and intra-Arab relations, 4, 29–30, 52, 69, 75, 77–78, 83, 90, 97, 153, 174, 199–200, 235–37, 239, 273; and nationalism, 4, 10–15, 24, 69, 83, 127–28, 137–38, 140–42, 149–50, 162, 195–96, 205, 223, 225, 240, 242, 273; reaction to Bernadotte plan, 55–56; and 1948–49 war, 62; and Palestinian refugees, 99–100, 110–11, 177–78; and peace process, 155. *See also* Soviet Union: relations with Arab states; United States foreign relations—Arab states

Arab Youth Movement, 24

Arad, Shimshon, 239